W9-CLG-163

COLLECTED WORKS OF ERASMUS

VOLUME 14

Phillips

THE CORRESPONDENCE OF
ERASMUS

LETTERS 1926 TO 2081

1528

translated by Charles Fantazzi

annotated by James M. Estes

University of Toronto Press

Toronto / Buffalo / London

The research and publication costs of the
Collected Works of Erasmus are supported by
University of Toronto Press.

© University of Toronto Press 2011
Toronto / Buffalo / London
Printed in Canada

ISBN 978-1-4426-4044-3

Printed on acid-free paper

Library and Archives Canada Cataloguing in Publication

Erasmus, Desiderius, d. 1536
[Works]
Collected works of Erasmus.

Each vol. has special t.p. ; general title from half title page.
Translation of: Opus epistolarum Des. Erasmi Roterodami.
Includes bibliographies and indexes.

Partial Contents: v. 14. The correspondence of Erasmus, letters 1926–2081,
1528 / translated by Charles Fantazzi ; annotated by James M. Estes.
ISBN: 0-8020-2831-4 (set). – ISBN: 978-1-4426-4044-3 (v. 14)

1. Erasmus, Desiderius, d. 1536 – Collected works. I. Title

PA8500.1974   199'.492   C740-06326-x rev

University of Toronto Press acknowledges the financial assistance to its
publishing program of the Canada Council and the Ontario Arts Council.

University of Toronto Press acknowledges the financial support for its
publishing activities of the Government of Canada through the Book Publishing
Industry Development Program (BPIDP).

Collected Works of Erasmus

The aim of the Collected Works of Erasmus
is to make available an accurate, readable English text
of Erasmus' correspondence and his
other principal writings. The edition is planned
and directed by an Editorial Board, an Executive Committee,
and an Advisory Committee.

EDITORIAL BOARD

William Barker, University of King's College
Alexander Dalzell, University of Toronto
James M. Estes, University of Toronto
Charles Fantazzi, East Carolina University
James K. Farge, Pontifical Institute of Mediaeval Studies
John N. Grant, University of Toronto
Paul F. Grendler, University of Toronto
Brad Inwood, University of Toronto
James K. McConica, Pontifical Institute of Mediaeval Studies, *Chairman*
John H. Munro, University of Toronto
John O'Malley, Georgetown University
Mechtilde O'Mara, University of Toronto
Hilmar M. Pabel, Simon Fraser University
Jane E. Phillips, University of Kentucky
Erika Rummel, University of Toronto
Robert D. Sider, Dickinson College
James D. Tracy, University of Minnesota
Mark Vessey, University of British Columbia

EXECUTIVE COMMITTEE

Alexander Dalzell, University of Toronto
James M. Estes, University of Toronto
Charles Fantazzi, East Carolina University
Lynn Fisher, University of Toronto Press
Paul F. Grendler, University of Toronto
James K. McConica, Pontifical Institute of Mediaeval Studies

John O'Malley, Georgetown University
Mechtilde O'Mara, University of Toronto
Jane E. Phillips, University of Kentucky
Erika Rummel, University of Toronto
R.M. Schoeffel, University of Toronto Press, *Chairman*
Robert D. Sider, Dickinson College
James D. Tracy, University of Minnesota
John Yates, University of Toronto Press

ADVISORY COMMITTEE

Jan Bloemendal, Conseil international ASD
H.J. de Jonge, Rijksuniversiteit te Leiden
Anthony Grafton, Princeton University
Ian W.F. Maclean, Oxford University
Jean-Claude Margolin, Centre d'études supérieures de la
Renaissance de Tours
Clarence H. Miller, Saint Louis University
John Rowlands, The British Museum
John Tedeschi, University of Wisconsin
J. Trapman, Conseil international ASD
Timothy J. Wengert, The Lutheran Theological Seminary
at Philadelphia

Contents

Illustrations

Preface

This volume contains the surviving correspondence of Erasmus for the year 1528. As in virtually all the years since the onset of 'the sorry business of Luther,' the predominant theme of the letters of 1528 is that of controversy between Erasmus and a variety of critics and opponents. The most important of these controversies focused on the question of whether or not Erasmus was a good Catholic. But the first two to occupy an important place in the year's correspondence had more to do with whether or not Erasmus was a decent human being.

The new year was scarcely a month old when the five-year-old feud with Heinrich Eppendorf was suddenly and unexpectedly reignited. In 1523 Erasmus had accused Eppendorf, until then a friend and member of his circle, of having engineered the breach between him and Ulrich von Hutten.[1] After Eppendorf had departed from Basel and settled in Strasbourg, Erasmus persuaded himself that Eppendorf was behind a number of strongly worded attacks on him that were published in that city.[2] Among those whom Erasmus informed of his suspicions was Eppendorf's patron, Duke George of Saxony, who responded by making it clear that Eppendorf no longer enjoyed his good opinion or support.[3] Feeling himself grievously injured by these developments, Eppendorf journeyed to Basel, where he complained bitterly to the city council and to Erasmus' friends and threatened legal action. Beatus Rhenanus and Bonifacius Amerbach, who were friendly to both parties, undertook the mediation of an out-of-court settlement that Erasmus and Eppendorf signed on 3 February.[4] In return for Eppendorf's promise not to publish anything against him, Erasmus undertook to write to Duke

* * * * *

1 Erasmus' account of the early stage of the feud is in Ep 1437:10–113.
2 Epp 1459, 1466, 1485, 1496, 1543, 1804, 1901
3 See Ep 1448:30–7.
4 Epp 1933–4, 1936–7

George retracting the charges against Eppendorf, to signal the return of good relations by dedicating a book to him, and to pay an indemnity in the form of sums to be distributed to the poor. The truce, however, was destined not to last. Erasmus immediately provided the required letter to Duke George as well as the promised letter of dedication,[5] though the latter was not yet attached to a published work. Within days, however, Eppendorf advanced new demands that were not part of the settlement,[6] and he subsequently boasted widely about his glorious 'triumph' over Erasmus.[7] Erasmus' immediate reaction was a long letter to Willibald Pirckheimer in which he once again summarized the conflict in detail and defended his own behaviour in it.[8] At the same time, he refused Eppendorf's repeated demands for the production of the promised work dedicated to him, excusing himself on the ground that he was too busy with other things. So the feud between the two persisted, with a hostile exchange of pamphlets in 1530,[9] until the spring of 1531, when Julius Pflug, a humanist jurist and churchman in the service of Duke George, succeeded in persuading them both to maintain silence.[10]

Far more significant than this prolonged contest between an internationally renowned humanist scholar and a provincial German of little consequence was the uproar that followed the publication in March 1528 of the satirical dialogue *Ciceronianus*.[11] The dialogue was Erasmus' long-planned response to Italian critics (and their northern allies) who refused to use much of the vocabulary of Christian discourse – for example, words like *trinitas* and *evangelium* – because it was not found in the works of Cicero, and who mocked as barbaric the eclectic Latin style that Erasmus deemed necessary if Latin was to remain a living language capable of expressing Christian ideas adequately. Erasmus expected the Italian Ciceronians to be offended by his mockery of them, but he was taken completely by surprise at the hostile response in France to an ironic jest in which one of the characters in the dialogue declares the greatest of the French humanists, Guillaume Budé, to be inferior as a Ciceronian to the Paris publisher and bookseller Josse Bade.

* * * * *

5 Epp 1940, 1941
6 Ep 1950
7 Epp 1991:26–35, 1997:1–3
8 Ep 1992. Erasmus did not publish the letter, but he subsequently expanded its contents into the *Admonitio adversus mendacium* of 1530.
9 Eppendorf's response to the *Admonitio* (see preceding note) was his *Iusta querela* (Haguenau: J. Setzer 1531).
10 Epp 2450, 2451
11 Epp 1948, 2021

Although a number of Erasmus' friends in France – Louis de Berquin, Germain de Brie, and Gervasius Wain – remained sympathetic, many of Budé's admirers, interpreting the jest as a statement of Erasmus' real opinion, concluded indignantly that it was evidence of hostility to the French in general and of petty envy of Budé in particular. Erasmus was compelled to spend a good deal of time and effort trying to mend fences. He composed a rejoinder to the French critics in the form of a letter to Brie that he included in a volume of *Selectae epistolae*,[12] copies of which were quickly dispatched to French recipients in September. At the same time, he wrote to Budé,[13] with whom relations had never been easy, but Budé was not mollified and never again wrote to Erasmus, not even after the latter had altered the offending passage in the second edition of the *Ciceronianus* (1529). As if this were not enough, a number of Erasmus' friends, including Juan Luis Vives,[14] took offence at his careless exclusion of them from the list of those honoured in the dialogue with praise of their accomplishments as Latin stylists and had to be appeased by the addition of complimentary references to them in the second edition.

More important still than this epidemic of injured ego and national pride among the literary elite was the continuing effort of Erasmus' conservative Catholic critics to convict him of heresy. To those willing to be persuaded of it, Erasmus had long since made clear his opposition to Luther and his followers, first in *De libero arbitrio* (1524) and then, more decisively, in parts 1 and 2 of *Hyperaspistes* (1526/7). Erasmus' friends and supporters in the ranks of Catholic princes, prelates, and scholars were delighted. But his conservative critics remained unmoved, and their campaign against him continued uninterrupted. The geographical focus of the opposition, however, had now shifted. While Erasmus still regarded Louvain, the original focal point of conservative hostility to him, as an unfriendly place, he reported in August 1528 that it had become 'more lenient.'[15] If that seemed to be the case, it was primarily because his two principal antagonists there, Nicolaas Baechem (Egmondanus) and Vincentius Theoderici, had both died in 1526 and Frans Titelmans would not emerge clearly as their successor until 1529. Meanwhile, Spain and France had become the most active centres of anti-Erasmian sentiment and action. The machinations of his adversaries in both places are an almost constant theme in the

* * * * *

12 Ep 2046
13 Ep 2047
14 Epp 2040, 2061
15 Ep 2033:33

correspondence, even when only mentioned in passing in letters devoted to other topics.

In Spain, the 1520s and early 1530s were in fact the period of Erasmus' greatest influence.[16] The circulation of his works in Latin had won him support and acclaim among humanist scholars, while Spanish translations of the *Enchiridion* and some of the *Colloquies* had been warmly received in pious lay circles. Erasmus also had friends in high places. At the imperial court, which was then resident in Spain, the emperor himself and his grand chancellor, Mercurino Gattinara, were more than well disposed. His supporters among Spanish prelates included Alonso de Fonseca, archbishop of Toledo and primate of Spain, as well as Alonso Manrique de Lara, archbishop of Seville and inquisitor-general. On the other hand, the scholastic theologians who were influential members of Spain's religious orders took umbrage at Erasmus' works, particularly the *Enchiridion*, and submitted to the Inquisition twenty articles accusing him of heresy. The conference of theologians that met at Valladolid in the summer of 1527 to examine these charges was prorogued by the inquisitor-general after only a few weeks, well before it had completed its work or rendered a decision.[17] This was a victory of sorts for Erasmus: he had not been formally exonerated of the charges against him, but he had not been found guilty of them either. In the following autumn Erasmus, ignoring the unwelcome advice of his Spanish friends to leave well enough alone and not respond to the charges brought against him, wrote his *Apologia adversus monachos quosdam Hispanos*.[18] The work was quickly printed by Froben but withheld from publication pending the formal approval of the dedicatee, the inquisitor-general Manrique de Lara. For reasons unknown, no such approval reached Erasmus, but in March 1528 he decided to publish the book anyway,[19] with a new preface in which he alleged as his reason for doing so the danger of an unauthorized version by 'someone in Cologne' who had procured 'by cunning' a copy of the Froben edition.[20] In their reaction to the apology, Erasmus' friends in Spain expressed their continued friendship and support but were unable to disguise their fear that 'its outspokenness against judges of such high rank' would strengthen the opposition.[21] Their fears were well founded. By the

* * * * *

16 See Epp 1431:31–56, 1432:13–14, 1455:24, 1742.
17 Ep 1814
18 Ep 1879
19 Epp 1980:22–8, 1985:21–2
20 Ep 1967:43–50
21 Ep 2004:29–30; cf Ep 2003.

Francis I with his children and advisers listening to Antoine Macault read to them
French School
Musée Condé, Chantilly

mid-1530s, the conservative theologians had gained the upper hand, and one prominent Erasmian after another found himself in trouble with the Inquisition and was forced to recant.

While 'the Spanish melodrama' had thus come to an interim conclusion seemingly favourable to Erasmus, the 'disorderly tumults' of the conservative theologians in France continued unabated.[22] Since 1523 the leader of the opposition to Erasmus in France had been Noël Béda, syndic (presiding officer) of the faculty of theology at the University of Paris. Undeterred by the hostility of King Francis I, who was opposed to any general condemnation of Erasmus, Béda devoted his best efforts to a relentless campaign aimed at proving that Erasmus and the kind of scholarship he practised were the real origin of the Lutheran heresy. Erasmus' forthright and unyielding defence of his orthodoxy and learning, both in an exchange of letters with Béda that ended in November 1527 and in three *apologiae* replying to Béda's *Annotationes* against Erasmus and Lefèvre d'Etaples (1526–7), left the adamant syndic unmoved. On 16 December 1527 the faculty, which had already condemned Erasmus' *Colloquies* in May of the previous year, condemned 112 propositions drawn largely from the *Paraphrases* on the New Testament and from Erasmus' books against Béda. Then, on 23 June 1528, the entire university endorsed the faculty's condemnation of the *Colloquies*. News of these actions reached Erasmus fairly quickly but, as late as August, Gervasius Wain in Paris had still not been able to procure for him a copy of the faculty's censure of the previous December.[23] In the end, Erasmus would wait until Béda published the censures in 1531 before responding to them in 1532. Meanwhile, in 1528, he resisted the urging of French friends that he should confront the Paris faculty openly, arguing that he had already written enough on the subject and that he was too busy with other things.[24] He did, however, publish in the *Selectae epistolae* a long letter to his friend John Longland, bishop of Lincoln, in which he added to his defence of the *Colloquies* against conservative critics in England indignant and sarcastic references to the condemnation of the *Colloquies* and other works at Paris.[25] Only when Béda published his *Adversus clandestinos Lutheranos* in 1529 did Erasmus once again address himself directly to Béda and the Paris theologians in his *Responsio ad notulas Bedaicas*.

* * * * *

22 On the recent history, through to the end of 1527, of Erasmus' relations with Béda and the Paris faculty of theology, see Ep 1902.
23 Ep 2027:33–5
24 Epp 2048:35–50, 2053:2–5
25 Ep 2037

Intimately bound up with Erasmus' conflict with the Paris faculty of theology was the fate of his young friend Louis de Berquin, the humanist scholar whose ardent and often indiscreet enthusiasm for Erasmus, as well as his lively interest in the works of Luther and other reformers, had attracted the hostile attention of the Paris faculty of theology and the Parlement of Paris. In 1523 and again in 1526, Berquin was tried and found guilty of heresy. In the first instance, Berquin had formally abjured his errors, which meant that his second conviction was for relapse into heresy, a crime that made him liable to the death penalty. The direct intervention of the king prevented the imposition of the penalty, but it did not invalidate the sentence, which Berquin decided to appeal. This led to his fatal third trial, which got under way in March 1528. Informed by Gervasius Wain of the danger confronting Berquin,[26] Erasmus wrote to him, expressing his concern and urging caution.[27] But Berquin, heartened by the knowledge that the case was being heard by a panel of jurists appointed by the king rather than by the judges who had found him guilty in 1526, proceeded defiantly with his appeal.[28] In what proved to be his final letter to Berquin, Erasmus reproved him gently for the needless 'provocations' that had inflamed the opposition to them both and expressed his fear that Berquin's confidence in victory was unwarranted.[29] In the end, Erasmus' fear proved more prescient than Berquin's confidence: on 16 April 1529 Berquin was found guilty of relapse into heresy and on the following day he was executed.[30]

Meanwhile, Alberto Pio, prince of Carpi, the most formidable of the Italian critics of Erasmus' learning and religion (rather than his style), had shown up in Paris. Like Béda and the other critics in the ranks of 'monks and theologians,' Pio could see no difference between Erasmus and Luther but, unlike them, he was a prodigy of humanist learning who could not be accused of hostility to 'good letters' or ridiculed for his ignorance of Latin and Greek. He was, moreover, a well-connected aristocrat, a distinguished diplomat, and a man highly regarded in the loftiest circles of church and state in Italy. Rightly fearing the hostile criticism of so influential a man in so important a place, Erasmus had long been worried by well-founded rumours that Pio and his friend Girolamo Aleandro were busily denouncing him at the papal curia as the source of Luther's errors. In October

* * * * *

26 Ep 2027:1–16
27 Ep 2048
28 Ep 2066:18–33
29 Ep 2077
30 Erasmus' account of what he had learned of the execution is found in Ep 2188.

1525 Erasmus wrote to Pio, objecting that the accusation was completely unjustified.[31] By May 1526 Pio had composed a response to the letter and by the following September Erasmus had received a manuscript copy of it from him. Erasmus soon began work on a reply but, following the sack of Rome in May 1527, was unsure of Pio's whereabouts. So in April 1528 Erasmus wrote directly to Pope Clement VII, noting the circulation among papal officials of Pio's untitled 'pamphlet' and decrying as unjust the accusations in it.[32] By the beginning of the following September, Erasmus had heard that Pio had taken refuge in France,[33] and a few weeks later Louis de Berquin informed him that Pio was indeed in Paris, circulating manuscript copies of his work against Erasmus and planning to publish it.[34] In the hope of forestalling a public controversy with Pio, Erasmus wrote to him on 23 December, urging him not to publish his 'little book' before first reading the response to it that Erasmus was going to send to him and considering that a 'personal colloquy' would be preferable to an open battle.[35] But it was too late: Pio's *Responsio accurata et paraenetica* was published by Josse Bade at Paris in the first week of January 1529, and in March Froben published Erasmus' *Responsio ad epistolam Alberti Pii*. The public controversy thus inaugurated would continue until 1532, with Pio's own final contribution to it being published after his death in 1531.[36]

In the midst of these battles with his detractors, Erasmus could still boast, with considerable justification, that he had on his side 'all the most important and most upright men' of 'almost every region – England, Brabant, Spain, Germany, France, Hungary, [and] Poland.'[37] In December 1527, Emperor Charles V had sent a most gratifying letter of encouragement and support from Spain,[38] and, as already noted above, friendly letters continued to pour in from prominent Spanish prelates. The imperial good will applied to Brabant as well, where the regent, Margaret of Austria, was so eager for Erasmus to return that she made the further payment of his imperial pension conditional on his doing so.[39] In addition to that, there was the

* * * * *

31 Ep 1634
32 Ep 1987
33 Ep 2042:19
34 Ep 2066:64–70
35 Ep 2080
36 For a detailed history of the controversy and the translated texts of Erasmus' contributions to it, see CWE 84.
37 Ep 2049:43–8
38 Ep 1920
39 Ep 1871

enduring friendship and support of Conradus Goclenius and others at the Collegium Trilingue in Louvain.[40] As for France, Erasmus knew at least that King Francis I, who had once invited him to France,[41] and his sister, Margaret of Angoulême (since 1527 queen of Navarre), were well disposed towards him, even if the Parlement and the Paris theologians were not. Henry VIII had invited Erasmus to settle in England,[42] where the long-standing friendship and patronage of William Warham, the archbishop of Canterbury,[43] and other prelates, as well as that of Sir Thomas More,[44] continued undiminished. In Germany, Erasmus still enjoyed the important, if often bad-tempered, support of Duke George of Saxony,[45] and had also received testimonies of good will from prominent imperial bishops like Hermann von Wied in Cologne and Christoph von Stadion in Augsburg.[46] Meanwhile, the contact with prominent Poles that had developed since 1525 out of Erasmus' friendship with Jan (II) Łaski had produced an invitation from King Sigismund I to come to Poland.[47] And finally, Archduke Ferdinand of Austria, who since 1526 was also king of Bohemia and Hungary, had invited Erasmus to settle in Vienna.[48]

Some, at least, of these flattering offers had been made in the full knowledge of Erasmus' increasingly untenable position in Basel, where the Zwinglian branch of the evangelical movement was rapidly gaining ground under the leadership of Erasmus' former friend Johannes Oecolampadius and would triumph in the winter and spring of 1529. Erasmus was willing to live in a confessionally divided city with a tolerant atmosphere but not in one that officially proscribed belief in the Real Presence and other doctrines that were clearly taught by the church and that even the Lutherans accepted. His letters of 1528 are liberally sprinkled not only with derogatory comments about 'evangelical' troublemakers in general and those in Basel in particular but also with expressions of his determination to move elsewhere rather than live under a regime dominated by them. But where to go? As always, Erasmus was unwilling to become a courtier and a partisan of any of the warring monarchs of Europe. For that reason

* * * * *

40 Ep 1994A
41 Ep 1375
42 Ep 1878
43 Ep 1965
44 Ep 1959
45 Ep 1929
46 Epp 1995, 2029
47 Ep 1952
48 Epp 2000, 2005

alone, all the countries whose monarchs had invited him would have been ruled out,[49] even if there had not been other reasons for staying away. But there were in fact many other reasons: the hostile faculty of theology and Parlement in Paris; unhappy memories of enmity at Louvain; the length and difficulty of the journey to England and the danger of becoming entangled in the controversy over the royal divorce; the intimidating unfamiliarity of Vienna and Cracow; and the general reluctance of an elderly and often infirm man to endure a radical change of scene. In the end, Erasmus would move to the university town of Freiburg im Breisgau, which was Catholic, quiet, safe, and close enough to Basel for efficient communication with the Froben press. In the meantime, he declined all the royal invitations to resettle. Sigismund of Poland had extended his invitation in the certain knowledge that it would be refused, so Erasmus only had to thank him for the gift of 100 ducats that had accompanied it.[50] Henry VIII and Ferdinand of Austria, on the other hand, received diplomatic letters citing Erasmus' health as the chief reason for rejecting their flattering offers.[51]

As one would expect, a fair number of the letters of 1528 deal with purely personal matters rather than with the great issues of the day. Of these, perhaps the most important are the ten letters that constitute the year's contribution to the extensive correspondence between Erasmus and the Antwerp banker Erasmus Schets.[52] Although Schets was no scholar and wrote awkward Latin, he was utterly devoted to Erasmus and his welfare. Since 1525, he had managed Erasmus' financial affairs in the Netherlands and England, to such good effect that Erasmus now had an income from various annuities and pensions that was both reliable and adequate to his needs, even though his unwillingness to return to Brabant had cost him his imperial pension.

As was ever the case with Erasmus, he did not allow public controversies or private cares to detract him seriously from scholarship. The list of new works that actually made it into print in 1528 was, by Erasmus' stan-

*****

49 In the west, the bitter dynastic conflict between Charles V and Francis I, which had begun in 1521 and had been interrupted only briefly by the Treaty of Madrid in 1526, would not come to an interim conclusion until the Peace of Cambrai in August 1529. Only with difficulty did Henry VIII manage to avoid direct involvement in this conflict. Meanwhile, to the east, Charles V's brother, Ferdinand of Austria, was at war with his rival for the kingship of Hungary, John Zápolyai, who was an ally of Sigismund of Poland.
50 Ep 2034
51 Epp 1998, 2005–6
52 Epp 1931, 1993, 1999, 2001, 2014, 2015, 2024, 2039, 2057, 2072

dards, rather short. Besides the *Ciceronianus*, there were only *De recta pro-nuntiatione*, the exposition of Psalm 85, and a new, enlarged edition of the *Adagia*.[53] On the other hand, it was a year filled with hard, exhausting labour on two long planned but slowly realized projects that would be completed in 1529. One was the ten-volume Froben edition of Augustine that had been under way, with many interruptions, since 1517. Juan Luis Vives' edition of the *City of God* had been published separately in 1522, but the balance of the Augustinian corpus would appear only in the *Augustini opera omnia* of 1529. The other project, under way since 1525, was a new edition of Seneca to re-place the defective one that had appeared under Erasmus' name in 1515. Simultaneously dealing with the burden of two such large projects was ex-hausting. In late October Erasmus complained: 'The Augustine is almost killing me, and added to that is the Seneca, an insuperable task.'[54] By this time, the printing of the volumes of Augustine had been well under way for more than a year. Copies of it were in circulation by the following sum-mer.[55] Meanwhile, the search for good manuscripts of Seneca had continued until the beginning of September, by which time the new edition had gone to press. Copies were in circulation by the following February.[56]

Of the 158 letters in this volume, 104 were written by Erasmus and 53 were addressed to him. One other (Ep 1936), written by Heinrich Eppendorf to Huldrych Zwingli, was included by Allen because of its direct bearing on Erasmus' difficult relations with Eppendorf at the time. These surviving let-ters include nearly four dozen references to letters that are no longer extant. Since several of these references are to an unspecified number of letters, no exact total of letters known to have been written can be determined, but 225 would be a good conservative estimate. More than half of the surviv-ing letters, 85, were published by Erasmus himself. Of these, 70 appeared in the *Opus epistolarum* of 1529, 4 in the *Selectae epistolae* of 1528, and 1 in the *Epistolae floridae* of 1531. Another 6 were dedicatory prefaces for works

* * * * *

53 For the *Ciceronianus*, see n11 above. For the other works, see Epp 1949, 2019, and 2022–3.
54 Ep 2070:9–10
55 For the progress of the edition of Augustine up to 1522, when Vives' edition of *De civitate Dei* was published, see Ep 1309 introduction. For the subsequent history of the project, which got under way again in 1524 (Ep 1473 n5), see Allen Ep 2157 introduction.
56 On the first edition, the defects of which Erasmus blamed on others, see Epp 325, 1341A:449–63. On the search for manuscripts and the progress of the sec-ond edition, work on which began in 1525 (Ep 1656), see Epp 2026, 2040, 2056, 2061, Allen Ep 2091 introduction.

or editions by Erasmus, 3 were inserts or addenda in one of his works, and one was a dedicatory letter for the work of someone else. Of the remaining 73 letters, one was published by its recipient and the rest were published by a variety of scholars in the period from Erasmus' death to 1928. Twenty of them were first published by Allen. To allow the reader to discover the sequence in which the letters became known, the introduction to each letter cites the place where it was first published and identifies the manuscript source if one exists.

Except for Ep 1948, which was translated by Betty I. Knott for inclusion in CWE 28, and Ep 1949, which was translated by Maurice Pope for inclusion in CWE 26, all the letters in this volume were translated by Charles Fantazzi. Allen's text and, with one exception, his ordering of the letters has been followed. The letter to Maarten Davidts to which Allen assigned the date 'c May 1522?' and published as Ep 1280 in his volume 5 has been redated to 1528 and is included here as Ep 1997A.

All of Erasmus' correspondents and all of the contemporaries of Erasmus who are mentioned in the letters are referred to by the version of their name that is used in CEBR. Wherever biographical information is supplied in the notes without the citation of a source, the reader is tacitly referred to the appropriate article in CEBR and to the literature there cited. The index to this volume contains references to the persons, places, and works mentioned in the volume, following the plan for the correspondence series in CWE. When that series of volumes is completed, the reader will also be supplied with an index of topics, as well as of classical, scriptural, and patristic references.

As with all the other volumes in this series, P.S. Allen's exemplary Latin edition of Erasmus' correspondence was the basis for the translation and the annotation of the text. Although Allen's notes seldom needed to be corrected, they frequently needed to be updated or expanded, and I owe a debt of gratitude to the colleagues who helped me do so. The great majority of the classical, patristic, and humanist references that were not identified by Allen were supplied by the translator, Charles Fantazzi, as were a number of notes explaining difficult matters of language. James K. Farge gave me the benefit of his matchless knowledge of the operations of the Paris faculty of theology and the Parlement of Paris. Moreover, both he and Alexander Dalzell read the entire manuscript with meticulous care and made many suggestions that led to significant improvements in both the translation and the annotations. Mark Crane, Elaine Fantham, Erika Rummel, A.H. van der Laan, Timothy J. Wengert, and Piotr Wróbel all responded generously and helpfully to my requests for information on specific matters of language, classical lore, history, or bibliography. The notes on coinage and the appendix on the coinages and monetary policies of Henry VIII were supplied by John H. Munro. The copyeditor, Mary Baldwin, did her work with a meticulous attention to detail that contributed significantly to the accuracy and clarity of the final text. The book was typeset by Lynn Browne and Philippa Matheson.

Of the libraries used in the preparation of this volume, two were of special importance: that of the Centre for Reformation and Renaissance Studies at Victoria College in the University of Toronto, and that of the Pontifical Institute of Mediaeval Studies on the campus of St Michael's College in the University of Toronto. To Kimberly Yates, Assistant to the Director of the CRRS (2002–8), and to William Edwards, reference librarian at PIMS, I am indebted for their cheerful insistence that someone working on the Toronto Erasmus edition is entitled to special treatment.

JME

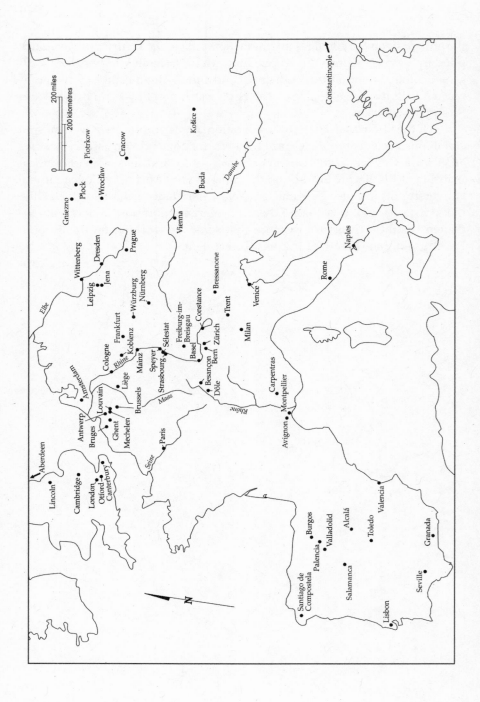

THE CORRESPONDENCE OF ERASMUS

LETTERS 1926 TO 2081

1926 / To Hermann von Neuenahr   Basel, 3 January 1528

This letter was first published in the *Opus epistolarum*, which is the source of the
date. Allen's text was based on the autograph, which in 1928 belonged to the
Basel industrialist and manuscript collector Karl Geigy-Hagenbach (d 1949). In
1961 the autograph was purchased at auction by the Rotterdam City Library,
where it bears the shelf mark 94 D 4.

A friend of Erasmus since meeting him in Cologne in 1515, Hermann, count
of Neuenahr (Ep 442), was a Greek and Hebrew scholar of some distinction and an enthusiastic supporter of the humanist cause. In January 1524 he
had become provost and archdeacon of the Cologne cathedral chapter and, by
virtue of that office, was chancellor of the University of Cologne. He was also
a close collaborator of Archbishop Hermann von Wied (Ep 1976).

Greetings. As terrible as was my fear that Spain might swallow you up,[1] so
keen is my joy that you have returned to us, not only safe and sound but
even in more prosperous health. This is what I have been told, although the
incident at Calais, if it actually happened, is a great annoyance.[2]

Your little book,[3] which I read carefully, has been returned to you,   5
I presume, together with my letter. You had already started out on your
journey, but your servant said that he would overtake you. I have no doubt
that you learned of the tragic fuss created by the pseudomonks in Spain,[4]
concerning which I am eager to know any further details that you may have.
You can write of them freely via the present messenger. I sent him with   10
specific instructions to go to Antwerp[5] and return here immediately.

* * * * *

1926
1 Over the years, a number of Erasmus' friends and patrons had died in Spain
  or on the road to it: Philip the Handsome (1506), the brothers François (1502)
  and Jérôme de Busleyden (1517), Jean Le Sauvage (1518), Pedro Ruiz de la
  Mota (1522), and Jean Glapion (1522). The nature of the business that took
  Neuenahr to Spain is not known.
2 The incident in question has not been identified.
3 Probably the edition of Faustus of Riez for which Erasmus wrote a preface in
  June. See Ep 2002.
4 A reference to the conference of Spanish theologians (27 June–13 August 1527),
  called to consider the charges of heresy made against Erasmus by the four
  religious orders of Spain. The conference ended without reaching a decision
  one way or the other. See Epp 1742, 1786 n5, 1791, 1814. Many of the letters of
  the spring and summer of 1527 reflect Erasmus' preoccupation with the attacks
  on him in Spain. The same is true of a number of letters in this volume; see
  especially Epp 1967, 2003–4.
5 Carrying with him a letter to Erasmus Schets that is answered by Ep 1931

Not to invoke a bad omen, but the way things are starting out here presages some dire tempest.[6] And I do not see where I may find refuge. Both the king and the archbishop invite me to England in very friendly letters.[7] But I don't see any suitable place for me there. This spring perhaps I will come visit you.[8]

If perchance you leave Cologne, make sure that my messenger finds a letter from you there. He will not be staying very long in Brabant. Word has it that King Ferdinand has issued a decree, which I shall not say is unjust but is certainly severe.[9] People suspect that Fabri was behind it.[10] In any case, I wish that all will turn out for the best for the excellent prince. But it is more a wish than a hope. Farewell, my distinguished friend. I am terribly distressed that Sobius lost both his eyes.[11]

3 January 1528, at Basel

Erasmus, most devoted servant of his Highness, in my own hand

* * * * *

6 Cf Epp 1929:21–3, 1967:6. The 'tempest' that Erasmus feared was the victory of the Zwinglian Reformation in Basel, which would take place in January–February 1529 (Ep 2000 n4). Cf n8 below.

7 Henry VIII's letter is Ep 1878. Erasmus replied to Archbishop Warham on 30 November 1527 and 4 January 1528 (ie on the same day as this letter) see Ep 1965:1–3.

8 Because of his dismay at the rapid progress of the Reformation in Basel (cf n6 above), Erasmus' letters of this period contain frequent expression of his growing desire to leave the city: Epp 1861 n2, 1889:30–2, 1931:36–8, 1939:13–14, 1943:44–5, 1955:12–13, 1971:14, 1972:11, 1977:29–30, 2006:5–6, 2029:99–100, 2038:1.

9 An apparent reference to the persecution of the Anabaptists in the Austrian Hapsburg territories at this time. See Epp 1977:50–2, 1983:10–32; and cf Ep 1924:25–6. The years 1525 through 1529 were the period of the most rapid expansion of Anabaptism in Switzerland, South and Central Germany, and the Austrian lands. In the period 1527–33, the authorities reacted to this with the bloodiest period of persecution in the history of Anabaptism in that area: 679 executions in all, 352 in 1528–9 alone. The persecution was fiercest in Bavaria and Austria. See Claus-Peter Clasen *Anabaptism, A Social History, 1525–1618* (Ithaca and London 1972) chapter 11, 'Persecution.' On Ferdinand of Austria, the emperor's brother, see Ep 1935 n5.

10 Johannes Fabri (Ep 386), Erasmus' friend and frequent correspondent, was a patron of learning and an advocate of Catholic reform, but a wholehearted opponent of the Lutheran Reformation and, when it appeared, of the Radical Reformation. In 1523, he was appointed to the court of Ferdinand of Austria, where he strongly supported Ferdinand's hostility to heresy in all its forms, and in 1530 he became archbishop of Vienna. On Erasmus' anxiety about Fabri's appetite for harsh measures, see Epp 1397:16–21, 1398:5–7, 1690.

11 Jacobus Sobius (Ep 1775), who was in failing health and died shortly after this letter was written

1927 / To Maximilian (II) of Burgundy   Basel, 4 January 1528

First published in the *Opus epistolarum*, this letter was written to replace Ep 1859, which had not reached the addressee (see Epp 1859, 1898). Maximilian of Burgundy (1514–58) was the son and heir of Adolph of Burgundy (d 1540), prince of Veere (lines 2–3), whose mother, Anna van Borssele (c 1471–1518), had been an early patron of Erasmus (see Epp 80, 88, 128, 129, 145, 146). Young Maximilian was to be the dedicatee of Erasmus' *De recta pronuntiatione* (Ep 1949).

ERASMUS OF ROTTERDAM TO MAXIMILIAN OF BURGUNDY,
GREETING

My dear Maximilian, I began to know and to love your illustrious father, the prince of Veere, while he was still a toddling infant nurtured at his nurse's breast. For even then there shone out in him a nobility of charac- 5
ter and a peaceful nature, without trace of violence. And he in turn gave unmistakable signs of fondness for me. This mutual affection grew ever stronger with the years. That what I say is not mere fantasy is proved, I think, by the letter I wrote to him when he was a boy,[1] which for so many years now has been widely read; I do not doubt that you have read it at- 10
tentively, and not only read it, but drawn from it some incentive for study and pious living. It gave me all the more pleasure to learn in a letter from that good man Jan Becker,[2] your childhood teacher, that you are so enthusiastic for the study of literature and for my own literary efforts that you seem to succeed no less to your father's feelings of good will towards me 15
than to his princely inheritance. On this account I congratulate the excellent prince, yourself, and humane learning, which has won the hearts of men of distinction and will shed lustre on your noble line, as it also will draw splendour from the celebrity of your ancestors. Now it will be permitted us to hope for that happy state of affairs that Plato often wishes 20
for, when the sons of princes will be taught philosophy before the exercise of power.[3] I pray that Christ, all good and all powerful, will pre-

* * * * *

1927
1 *Epistola exhortatoria ad capessendam virtutem ad generosissimum puerum Adolphum, principem Veriensem*, which was the first piece in the *Lucubratiunculae* of 1503 and was included (under the titles *Exhortatio ad virtutem* and *Oratio de virtute amplectenda*) in later editions of the same collection. Although in the form of a letter, Erasmus never published it in any of his collections of correspondence. Ep 93 consists of Allen's extracts from the work, chosen because they refer directly to Adolph.
2 Ep 1984
3 *Republic* 6.502

serve this natural excellence of yours intact and will carry it to ever greater successes.

I had written to you several months ago,[4] but unfortunately the letter was lost through the treachery of someone or other. I hear that you are very displeased at this loss.[5] To add to this misfortune my original draft here has disappeared.[6] So, in the midst of my occupations I have written this at the spur of the moment, putting together from memory the content of the previous letter, with the promise to send you a more detailed letter shortly if you will accept this as a token payment. Make sure that the pleasures of courtly life do not undermine your love of study and moral rectitude.[7]

Farewell. At Basel, 4 January, 1528

1928 / From Johannes Cochlaeus   Aschaffenburg, 8 January 1528

The manuscript of this letter, autograph throughout, was in the ill-fated Burscher Collection at Leipzig (Ep 1254 introduction). It was published as Ep 80 in Förstemann/Günther. It is the second of the surviving letters (Ep 1863 being the first) in the correspondence between Erasmus and Johannes Cochlaeus (d 1552), the learned humanist and vitriolic opponent of the Reformation. Since 1526 Cochlaeus had been a prebendary at St Victor in Mainz and, as this letter shows, was now about to become chaplain to Duke George of Saxony. Erasmus' reply is Ep 1974.

Aschaffenburg, 8 January, 1528
Greetings. Scarcely two days ago, most esteemed Erasmus, I sent a special envoy to you from Mainz with a letter from George, duke of Saxony.[1] I did not add one of my own, fearing that perhaps you would not answer my previous letter[2] when you learned that I was not at home. I sent you another letter by another courier whom I had dispatched to Bern.[3] Now I have set out

* * * * *

4 See Ep 1859.
5 Ep 1898:10–16
6 The draft (Ep 1859) was found again in time to be published in the *Opus epistolarum*, immediately before this letter.
7 It was anticipated that Maximilian would soon enter the household of the cardinal of Liège. See Epp 1898:21–3, 1949:27–8, 1984:23–4.

1928
1 In reply to Ep 1869
2 Not extant
3 Shortly before his departure from Mainz, Cochlaeus sent his own messenger to the city council of Bern, warning them against going over to the Zwinglian

on a journey to the illustrious Duke George of Saxony, who wishes to retain my services in the place of our friend Emser, who died on 8 of November.[4] He intends to bestow on me those priestly offices which he had formerly conferred upon Emser. For my part, my dear Erasmus, I should prefer to remain at home with my aged mother; yet I dare not oppose the wish and invitation of this great prince, which I consider sacrosanct. I am going, therefore, accompanied by a single horseman, whom he has sent to me.

It is with great difficulty, however, that I obtain permission to leave here; the prince, my most revered and illustrious lord of Mainz,[5] is reluctant to see me go. Yesterday he said to me with a deep sigh that an inevitable uprising of the Anabaptists is imminent;[6] he is astonished that none of us takes up his pen against them. I answered that up to now that sect has appeared so absurd that I thought it was not necessary to write anything against them. 'But,' he said, 'we see that they are gaining power and growing in numbers.' Someone wrote to him that there are over eighteen thousand Anabaptists in Germany today.[7] I therefore ask and entreat you, my dear Erasmus, in the name of God and the holy church, to write some brief tract against this terrible sect, and, immediately upon my return, I shall translate it from Latin into German.[8] I shall ask the same thing of the most revered bishop of Rochester.[9] Do not deny us this service, I beg you, in this time of great crisis

* * * * *

camp. When the council went ahead with its reformation anyway, Cochlaeus published, in the early summer of 1528, a pamphlet denouncing the city's 'supposed reformation.' See Ep 1988.

4 Hieronymus Emser, humanist and theologian, was Duke George's secretary and chaplain from 1505 until his death in November 1527. Always a great admirer of Erasmus but a vehement opponent of Luther, Emser was particularly gratified by *De servo arbitrio* and even more so by the *Hyperaspistes*, which he translated into German.

5 Albert of Brandenburg, cardinal-archbishop-elector of Mainz (Ep 661).

6 Here and in lines 21–2, 33 below, Cochlaeus refers to them as 'the rebaptized' (*rebaptizati*), though the Greek loanword *Anabaptistae* was by now frequently used. Cf Ep 1369 introduction.

7 Claus-Peter Clasen *Anabaptism, A Social History, 1525–1618* (Ithaca and London 1972) chapter 2, 'Advance and Numerical Strength,' estimates that for the whole period from 1525 through 1618, Anabaptism in the huge area of Switzerland, South and Central Germany, and Austria attracted only about 30,000 persons, with 1525–8 being the period of most rapid growth. (Clasen's study deliberately excludes North Germany and the Netherlands, where Anabaptism attracted much larger numbers in the 1530s and after.)

8 Erasmus ignored this request.

9 John Fisher (1469–1535), who had written extensively against the continental Reformers. Just days before writing this letter, Cochlaeus had published a

Cardinal Albert of Brandenburg as St Jerome
Lucas Cranach the Elder, 1526
The John and Mable Ringling Museum of Art, Sarasota, Florida

for our country and of great peril to souls. You will not only be performing a
service most pleasing to God but to many princes. I think this work, which
I hope you could complete in three days, is far more important than all
others.   30

I am very dissatisfied at the cunning tactics of the jurists consulted by
the illustrious duke and prince elector palatine of the Rhine[10] in passing
judgment on eighteen Anabaptists whom he has had confined in the prison
of Alzey for a long time now.[11] Several times they were arraigned to suffer the supreme penalty, but the perverse cleverness of the jurists always   35
created difficulties, sometimes through judicial procedures because of the
collusion of the judge, as it is reported. And in the meantime the people are
scandalized that they cannot be killed legitimately, and the sect continues
to increase. Help us, I beseech you, and may fortune smile on you, peerless
glory of our age.   40

Yours from the bottom of my heart, Johannes Cochlaeus

I hear that there are five principal articles sworn to by the Anabaptists:
1/ Never to enter a walled house of God
2/ Never to hear mass in the form in which it is currently celebrated
3/ That everything shall be in common – wives, virgins, worldly goods, etc   45
4/ Not to obey any secular power, but God alone
5/ Force all people into their sect or kill them if they refuse

To the renowned master, Erasmus of Rotterdam, most eloquent theologian. Basel

1929 / To Duke George of Saxony   Basel, 16 January 1528

This letter was first published in the *Opus epistolarum*. Since writing Ep 1924
to Duke George, Erasmus had received a number of letters from Saxony via

* * * * *

German translation (*Funff Vorredde*) of the prefaces to the five books of Fisher's
long treatise *De veritate corporis et sanguinis Christi in eucharistia* (Cologne 1527),
written in refutation of the treatise *De genuina verborum Dei: 'Hoc est corpus meum' etc expositione liber* (Basel 1525), in which the Basel reformer Johannes Oecolampadius had attacked both the Catholic and Lutheran doctrines
of the Real Presence. See Martin Spahn *Johannes Cochläus: Ein Lebensbild aus
der Zeit der Kirchenspaltung* (Berlin 1898; repr Nieuwkoop 1964) 349 no 50;
Richard Rex *The Theology of John Fisher* (Cambridge 1991) 136–7. Cf Ep 1930
introduction.
10 Ludwig v (ruled 1508–44)
11 Alzey was twenty-five miles south of Mainz in the Palatinate (not, as Allen
states, in Hessen).

Mainz (Ep 1928:2–3). None of them has survived. One, from Simon Pistoris (Epp 1934:41–2, 1940:2–3), was answered on 5 February with Ep 1943.

ERASMUS OF ROTTERDAM TO DUKE GEORGE OF SAXONY

Most serene Prince, I am happy that the second volume of the *Hyperaspistes* reached you together with my letter;[1] I am happier still that it did not displease your illustrious Highness. I would not be wearied by my labour or the indignities I must abide if I saw that some special fruit derived   5
from them. For me Christ is sufficient in compensation for all life's vicissitudes. I received Luther's letter addressed to your illustrious Highness and your answer to him translated into Latin.[2] Likewise Emser's response to Luther translated into Latin.[3] I received no letter to which I did not respond. But not all letters that are sent reach their destination,   10
something which I experience often, not without serious personal inconvenience.[4]

The person who delivered this letter had a letter of your Highness to H. Eppendorf addressed to Basel,[5] although for some time now he has been at Strasbourg and in the interim has never set foot again in Basel; I am quite   15
astonished that you were unaware of this.

* * * * *

1929
1 Ep 1869; for *Hyperaspistes* 2 see Ep 1853.
2 Allen speculated that this was perhaps a belated reference to letters of Luther and Duke George written in December 1525 and sent to Erasmus in Latin translation in April 1526. See Epp 1693:17–23, 1743:66–7.
3 The reference is to Emser's *Bekentnis das er den Tittel auff Luthers sendbrief an den König zu Engelland gemacht . . . hatt* of 1527. It was a reply to Luther's *Antwort auf des Königs zu England Lästerschrift Titel* of the same year, which had been written in response to Henry VIII's recent *Literarum quibus . . . Henricus octavus respondit ad quandam epistolam M. Lutheri* (December 1526). This in turn was King Henry's contemptuous response to an open letter from Luther apologizing for the harshness of his denunciation of the king in 1522 (see Ep 1773 n7). Henry's letter, which Luther suspected had been written by Erasmus, was published in Dresden at the beginning of 1527, with a title indicating that in his letter Luther had offered 'to recant' (*palinodiam cantare*; cf Ep 2013 n6). Luther wrote *Antwort* to dispel any notion that he had offered a recantation of his faith rather than an apology for his rude language. In response to Luther's statement that he did not know who was responsible for the offending title, Emser wrote his *Bekentnis* in affirmation that it had been he. For further details, see the introduction to Luther's *Antwort* in WA 23 17–26.
4 For a recent example of this see Ep 1922.
5 Cf Epp 1934:39–41, 223, and 529–30, 1940:1–2, 1943:6–7, 1992:113–14, 201–2, and 228–9.

I am grieved that Emser has been taken from us[6] but rejoice that he has passed on to a happier life. I wrote to you a few days ago but only briefly.[7] The St Augustine edition, in addition to other things, weighs me down. Now it will appear in its entirety with all due magnificence.[8]   20

New tragedies arise each day; I know not what the outcome will be.[9] One may pray for the best; I do not see what else is left to us in this general upheaval. I wish your illustrious Highness the best of health and pledge to you my complete service and devotion.

Given at Basel, 16 January, 1528   25

1930 / From Willibald Pirckheimer   [Nürnberg, 19 January 1528]

This letter was first published by Allen from the autograph rough draft in the Stadtbibliothek Nürnberg (MS PP 325). It has since been published as Ep 1149 in WPB, with the same date as that assigned by Allen. The draft is clearly incomplete. Immediately below the last line and to the left Allen found two columns of jottings, which may have been a list of further topics to be discussed in the letter:

	our school		Augustine
	in great debt to him		Glareanus
	the stone		Kleberger
	Alber		Dürer
5	Ferdinand	10	I am anxious

Since comments on Augustine, Glareanus, Kleberger are found in Ep 1977, and since this draft clearly responds to Ep 1893, Allen concluded that this was probably the beginning of Pirckheimer's intermediate letter and identified it as that of 19 January 1528 (Ep 1977:67).

On Pirckheimer (1470–1530), Nürnberg patrician, accomplished humanist, and frequent correspondent of Erasmus, see Ep 1880. Having initially given his support to Luther and his reformation, which was officially adopted in Nürnberg in 1525, Pirckheimer subsequently realigned himself with Rome and wrote against Johannes Oecolampadius' Zwinglian views of the Eucharist – a subject originally broached in Ep 1893 and referred to again here. Cf Ep 1928 n9.

* * * * *

6 On 8 November 1527; see Ep 1928:8–9.
7 Ep 1924
8 Ep 2157 (May 1529) is the preface to the completed Froben edition of Augustine.
9 Cf Epp 1926:12–13, 1967:6.

Greetings. That I write to you less often,[1] most eminent Erasmus, is not due to my laziness. But you know how few people one can trust in these times, when letters are either not delivered or suppressed or even opened to pry into men's secrets. Hence it is that I and all good men must be very discreet in what we write in a letter and to whom we entrust it: so true is it that everything is full of snares and wicked men.

For the rest I am most pleased that you accepted my apology for introducing your name in the Oecolampadius affair.[2] However, my dear Erasmus, I never meant to offend you in any way by mentioning your name, since you have never deserved ill of me and I have the greatest affection for you among all mortals not only, as I have written before, because of your prodigious learning but also because I have always found your writings to be seasoned with great wisdom, a quality discernible in few people today and lacking in most.[3] Who can doubt that if the evangelical movement had been seasoned with wisdom instead of stupidity, not only would all that turmoil and bloodshed have ceased but everything would have turned out more auspiciously as well. But thus has God willed it, who permitted ancient errors to manifest themselves under the disguise of his gospel so that new ones which arise every day could be rightly censured. And what more would we deserve than divine punishment when we all know what is right but so few of us practise what we teach others? Therefore, my dear Erasmus, I did not wish to sully your name with any reproach but rather, since the opportunity offered itself, mentioned your name out of respect for you. But if I had thought that this would displease you, I would have refrained altogether from mentioning you; nevertheless I think that I did not blacken your name.

The reason for my writing to you will become clearer perhaps with the passage of time, since it is no longer safe to write much on the subject. But, as you learned from me earlier,[4] I was under such pressure that if I had not written, and written in such a way that I would not seem to be in collusion with Oecolampadius, I would neither have survived nor escaped a great calamity. I was compelled to defend the truth to the best of my ability while not being untrue to myself, although I knew that as a man worn

* * * * *

1930
1 See Ep 1893:9.
2 For the origins of this affair, see Ep 1880, where the apology in question is in lines 24–40. Erasmus' response to it is in the opening paragraph of Ep 1893.
3 Ep 1880:35–7
4 Cf Ep 1880:4–6.

out by legal proceedings and public affairs I was not equal to such a great
challenge. Wherefore if I could have been silent, I would have preferred to   35
remain silent rather than betray my want of eloquence. But so God willed
and necessity constrained me.

But it is good, my dear Erasmus, to feel that you have been mollified.
Nor do I esteem it a fault that you trust so few people, since this age reveals
so many people for what they are. I [am eager] . . .   40

1931 / From Erasmus Schets   Antwerp, 24 January 1528

This letter was first published by Allen on the basis of the autograph in the
University Library at Basel (Scheti epistolae 13). For the date of its delivery,
see Ep 1955 introduction.

Since 1525, the Antwerp merchant and banker Erasmus Schets (Ep 1541)
had taken over from Pieter Gillis (Ep 184) the management of Erasmus' financial affairs in the Netherlands and England; see Ep 1671 n6. More than
seventy letters from their correspondence, which lasted until Erasmus' death,
are extant.

Greeting. All that I desired to hear out of my deep affection for you, O most
learned of men and dearest of friends, I have learned by the present messenger, who safely brought your letter to me,[1] together with others destined
for England.[2] In order to respond to your letter I shall see to it immediately and with all speed that these letters be delivered to their respective   5
addressees with no less security than if they were delivered personally.

I was pleased to learn that you knew about the disposition of those
fifty crowns that I gave orders a year ago to be consigned in your name to
Froben at the Frankfurt fair, since Luis de Castro received them from the
bishop of London in England and changed them for me there.[3] Likewise in   10

* * * * *

1931
1 Ie the letter, now lost, to which this is the answer; cf Ep 1926 n5.
2 One of these was Erasmus' letter to Archbishop Warham of 4 January; see Ep
   1965:3.
3 On this transaction see also Epp 1781:1–3, 1866:15–16. Luis de Castro had succeeded his brother Alvaro as Schets' agent in London for the collection and
   remittance of Erasmus' English revenues; cf Ep 1764:4–6. On Cuthbert Tunstall, the bishop of London, see Ep 1726 introduction. On the fifty crowns, see
   also Epp 1781 n2 and 1866 n7; and 'The Coinages and Monetary Policies of
   Henry VIII' 442–7 below for the introduction of the crown with the single rose,
   in August 1526 and the new, higher valued crown of the double rose, issued

Erasmus Schets
Unknown artist, 1530
Bibliothèque Royale Albert I, Brussels

that dubious matter of the cups,[4] it was, as you write, probably a question of fortune or chance in the College of the Lily rather than of the contrivance of someone trying to give less and take more.

About that sum of ninety nobles, which the brewer Pieter Weldanck received some time ago from the Archbishop of Canterbury,[5] I wrote to England a few days ago to Luis de Castro, asking that he seek him out and find out what had become of the money. He acknowledges that he had received it and had arranged through friends that it be paid to you. Luis passed over the matter, taking him at his word, and did not pursue it any further, nor did he write back. So it happens that many good men are duped because of their trustfulness. Nonetheless, I wrote again more forcefully than before. But what of it? Things will probably turn out as you say. What tricks will Birckmann come up with this time?[6] I came to know that this Pieter fellow was Birckmann's other half in England. Nor would it surprise me if this Pieter should have given this money in good faith to Birckmann to be looked after for you but he, entirely unscrupulous, has so far concealed the matter.[7] At this very moment I shall write to Luis instructing him to collect the necessary information for getting to the bottom of this matter and communicate it to me as soon as possible.

I shall also tell the same Luis about the ninety angels that will be owed to you for the coming feast of the Purification.[8] I think you have written

* * * * *

in November 1526. This appendix is based on extensive new research, and it challenges the views of several renowned monetary historians whose works were cited in earlier CWE volumes. This appendix therefore supersedes notes in previous volumes of CWE concerning the coinages of Henry VIII.

4 On these and other personal belongings that Erasmus had left behind at the College of the Lily in Louvain, see Ep 1355:20–43.

5 On the ninety nobles from Warham sent to Erasmus through Pieter Weldanck, see Ep 1866:4–5 with n3.

6 Franz Birckmann, the Antwerp bookseller and printer's agent with shops and connections in Germany, France, and England as well as the Netherlands. He was much involved in the distribution of Froben's publications and played a role in the transfer of Erasmus' pension from England. Erasmus distrusted him, apparently with good reason, and complained frequently that Birckmann had cheated him of sums owed him. See Epp 258:14n, 265:4–6, 283:184–96, 1362:1–8, 1388:27–8 with n23, 1507, 1560:16–19, 1804:294–6, 1816:24–6.

7 For more on Erasmus' distrust of Birckmann and Weldanck, see Epp 1955:9, 1993:12–15, 2040:34–7.

8 2 February. The reference is evidently to the sum of money given to Quirinus in April 1527; see Ep 1993:30–1, 47–9. Allen (30n) states that it was worth £30 sterling. That was the value of 90 gold angel-nobles up to Henry VIII's first de-

to your English patrons[9] that your pensions there be paid to the same Luis
under my name for your use. If they would do this, all this confusion could
be avoided.

Your wish is that I keep the money paid to you in my name for your   35
future use. Very well, I shall carry out whatever you command. You cannot
imagine what joy it gave me to know that there was some hope that you
would be returning to our midst.[10] What a happy day that will be to so
many of your friends.

There is nothing new here worthy of reporting. There is still no end   40
in sight of those terrible disturbances, which threaten to get worse. The emperor wishes that the terms agreed to at the Madrid meeting with the French
king, while he was a prisoner, should be observed. The French king, violating his oath and abandoning the children given as hostages, refuses; in
the meantime, Mars laughs at the harm done to ordinary Christian people.[11]   45

* * * * *

basement, of the gold coinage, on 22 August 1526, which raised the value of the
gold angel-noble by 10 percent: from 6s 8d (80d) to 7s 4d (88d). On 5 November 1526, Henry VIII's second debasement, of both the gold and silver coinages,
raised the value of the gold angel-noble by a further 2.27 percent – for an overall increase of 12.5 percent – to 7s 6d (90d). For these two debasements, see the
Appendix 440–50 with Tables 1–3, 457–76 below. Thus, if this sum had been
given in actual gold angel-nobles, its value would have increased by 12.50 percent to £33 15s 0d sterling. But in Ep 2001:10–11 (24 June 1528) Erasmus Schets
refers to 'nobles of the kind of which three are equal to one pound sterling,
and not of those struck in gold' (quorum tres conficiunt unam libram sterlingorum,
et non in spetie auri excussi). Evidently, therefore, these 90 'nobles' were not the
actual gold coins but instead a convenient money-of-account – each worth a
third of a pound sterling (in silver values) – and one that was not affected
by Henry VIII's debasements of August and November 1526. If this transaction is expressed in terms of this unchanged money-of-account, rather than in
terms of the actual gold angel-nobles, then 90 such accounting 'nobles' would
have still been worth £30 sterling. See also Epp 1993 n9, 2001:5–22 with nn2–4.
To earn this sum, a master mason at Cambridge would have had to work for
1,200 days (at 6d per day), or 5.71 years (at 210 days per year).

9 Warham, Baron Mountjoy, and John Longland, bishop of Lincoln. But Bishop
Tunstall too occasionally made presents; see Ep 2072.
10 See Ep 1926 n8.
11 At the battle of Pavia (24 February 1525), which was an annihilating defeat for
the French at the hands of Charles V's Spanish and German troops, Francis I
was taken prisoner and sent to Madrid. By the Treaty of Madrid (14 January
1526), Francis was granted his freedom in return for the renunciation of all his
claims to Italy and Burgundy as well as his suzerainty over Flanders and Ar-
tois. Leaving two of his sons behind in Madrid as hostages, Francis returned
to France and in May, after having declared the Treaty of Madrid null and

Preparations for war proceed on both sides. In these days there is no room for peace or for pity. May God, the author of peace, deign in his mercy to reverse all this, and to you, dearest friend, may he grant a happy existence.

Farewell from Antwerp, 24 January 1528

Yours sincerely, Erasmus Schets   50

To the most learned man and consummate interpreter of the Sacred Scriptures, Erasmus of Rotterdam. At Basel

1932 / From Jan van der Cruyce

College of the Lily, Louvain, 28 January [1528]

The autograph of this letter, which was first published as Ep 12 in Enthoven, is in the Rehdiger Collection in the University Library at Wrocław (ms Rehd 254.56). The year-date is confirmed by the reference in a letter (25 March 1528) of Pieter de Corte to Frans van Cranevelt to a no-longer-extant letter of Erasmus written in answer to this one (details in Allen's introduction). It is also clear that Ep 1955 was written after receipt of the news concerning Richard Pace contained in this letter (lines 156–62).

Jan van der Cruyce (d before 22 August 1533) was a native of Bergen (now Bergues on the French side of the border between Belgium and France). After studying in Louvain at the College of the Lily, he was appointed professor of logic at the Lily in 1520. In 1522 he went to England on Erasmus' recommendation to become a private tutor to the children of William Blount, Baron Mountjoy. This letter is Cruyce's account of the reasons for his return to Louvain in the autumn of 1527.

TO ERASMUS OF ROTTERDAM, FATHER OF ALL LEARNING,
JAN VAN DER CRUYCE OF BERGEN GIVES GREETING

The reason, great patron of the world of letters, that I have not yet responded to your most kind letter,[1] which was delivered to me I know not how long ago, but in England at any rate, is that during all the time that I was there I   5

* * * * *

void, entered into the anti-imperial League of Cognac with the papacy, Milan, and Venice. The renewed war in Italy led to, among other things, the sack of Rome by the emperor's mutinous troops in May 1527. Peace was temporarily restored with the so-called Ladies' Peace concluded at Cambrai in August 1529.

1932
1 Not extant

had no opportunity or facility to engage a messenger worthy of trust. You know how the Muses of Mountjoy love country life: I don't think I was ever farther from London, during the five years of my continuous sojourn in England, than one hundred miles at one time and sixty at another and never closer than Bedwell,[2] where there are still writings of yours, most learned Erasmus, that shall never perish. It is to these in great part that I owe my flourishing health, except for barely one or two days, and the ability to consume the hours of tedium of such prolonged solitude; if I were to deny this – I can sum up my shamefulness in a single word – I should be accounted an ingrate. All the same, if I may presume on your knowledge,[3] Bedwell is not so close to London that one who is responsible for the upbringing of his children can casually make visits to London whenever the spirit moves him.

On one occasion I chanced to happen upon your friend Lievin,[4] but so unexpectedly that I had neither the time nor the opportunity to write anything worth reading in the midst of those immense and weighty occupations that the tottering state of Christendom has laid upon you. I urgently requested the man to seek pardon from you for this culpable silence, if you consider it to be such. If he fulfilled this embassy, I may hope that you will be more favourably disposed to this greeting from your friend Cruyce, one that is late, to be sure, but that could not have been sent sooner or at a more proper time. You yourself are not unaware that it is often not safe, not to say inadvisable, to write about matters pertaining to England in England. And regarding the status quo here, although it cannot very well be kept secret, since there are so many who wish to gratify Erasmus with the latest news, it nevertheless seemed to be my duty not to keep silent about the role I have to play in the drama that has recently begun. One might wonder at first why I should have assumed this role, but, when you hear by what intermediate stages I came to play this part, you will see that it has been imposed upon me against my will rather than freely accepted.

To begin at the beginning, a certain weariness with my position in England, a position that was more one of outward show than of real substance,[5]

* * * * *

2 A manor in Hertfordshire, east of Hatfield and about twenty miles north of London, belonging to Sir William Say, father-in-law of Baron Mountjoy, who inherited the manor on Say's death in December 1529
3 Erasmus had visited Bedwell in the company of Baron Mountjoy in 1499; see Ep 103 introduction.
4 Lieven Algoet, Erasmus' servant-pupil, who often carried letters for him (see Ep 1091 introduction). He was in England April–July 1524 and again in January 1525: see Ep 1430 n7, and Allen Ep 1537:2n.
5 Ie remunerative. The phrase, Greek in the text, means roughly 'for daily bread.'

began to creep over me, as it seemed to provide little hope for sustaining
my meagre fortunes (which are more in need of some present deity) – a situation that confirmed in reality what you said would happen when I set out.
For Mountjoy, whom you describe in your letter to your friend Bombasius 40
as more blessed in intelligence than in possessions,[6] is of the opinion that
whether it falls to one's lot to have a loyal servant or one who is useless and
slothful, he thinks that person should not be recommended or thrust upon
anyone else: he believes that he himself has as much need of personal advantage as the prince and, further, that it ill befits the integrity of a Mount- 45
joy to weigh down someone else with a useless burden that he has rejected.
Although many disapprove of the great man's opinion in this matter, I think
it worthy of a wise person. I would wish, however, that it be joined with
a generosity that could arm his friends against the envy of fortune, which
could carry Mountjoy off, since he is both mortal and, as is the common fate 50
of the ruling class, subject to varied and sudden changes of fortune.[7] But as
far as I am concerned, I would rather belong to Mountjoy than to Alexander,[8] if by the power of some magic wand it were possible to be a liege of
Mountjoy forever in this life and he were always to have a place at the table of the gods. And this would not be difficult for this man if he wished 55
to make use of the authority he enjoys. The reason for his not doing so, I
think, lies in a philosophical preference for Diogenes over Aristippus.[9] I answered him on several occasions that there were more Aristippuses around
than Diogenes, and I added in a very Erasmian manner that it is not the part
of a wise man to fight against his age. But these were words to the deaf;[10] 60
yet I took it less ill since this has been the experience of many others whose
exhortation should have carried more weight.

Nonetheless, it was not this established practice of Mountjoy but rather
the smoke that was beginning to rise that was the principal reason for my
leaving England. If it had ended up as a fire, there was fear that every- 65
thing I had acquired, both in England, which was very little, and in our
own land, which was more stable and somewhat more substantial, would
all go up in flames. Ships were kept in port, dire rumours were in circulation

* * * * *

6 See Ep 334:60–6 (to Domenico Grimani, not Paolo Bombace).
7 Mountjoy was chamberlain to Queen Catherine, to whom he remained openly
   loyal throughout her trial (1529) and beyond. See n11 below.
8 Presumably Alexander the Great
9 Diogenes the Cynic was indifferent to material possessions, while Aristippus
   of Cyrene was addicted to a worldly and luxurious mode of life.
10 *Adagia* I iv 87

about the divorce of Jupiter and Juno,[11] the nobility seemed more depressed,
there were continual rumours of war:[12] would that they were mere rumours!   70
Amidst these storms there was only one sacred anchor that could be hoped
for,[13] Mountjoy himself, who promised that he would take care of me and
my possessions as he would his own. The memory of the war with France,
however, which did not allow even the hero himself to escape, convinced
me that I could find no refuge in that quarter[14] if another tumult carried him   75
away and he were to follow in the train of the prince and if, God forbid!
English weapons were sent against us.[15]

* * * * *

11 Ie the divorce of Henry VIII and Catherine of Aragon. By early 1527 King
   Henry had made up his mind to divorce Queen Catherine in order to marry
   Anne Boleyn. Because Catherine was the widow of Henry's brother Arthur,
   it had taken a papal dispensation from Julius II to remove the impediment of
   the Levitical prohibition of marriage to the widow of one's brother (Lev 18:16,
   20:21). The first step toward dissolving the marriage was taken in May, when
   Cardinal Wolsey convened a gathering of canon lawyers to examine the question. But the issue quickly became more theological than canonical, centering
   on whether the Levitical prohibition of marriage to the widow of one's brother
   was a matter of divine law (and thus beyond the pope's power to dispense)
   and also of what one was to make of Deut 25:5–10, which seemed to command
   the marriage of a man to his brother's childless widow. The controversy, which
   dragged on until 1533, involved theologians, lawyers, and diplomats all over
   Europe. Nearly all of Erasmus' friends and patrons in England, most notably
   John Fisher, supported the queen. Thomas More, on the other hand, maintained a scrupulous silence, and Cardinal Wolsey, who supported the king,
   paid with his life for his failure to produce papal consent to the divorce. On
   Henry and Catherine as 'Jupiter and Juno,' cf Epp 2040:45 with n18, 2061:84–5.
12 The insubstantial peace between Charles V and Francis I that followed the
   French defeat at Pavia in 1525 and the conclusion of the Treaty of Madrid in
   1526 had begun to break down almost immediately (see Ep 1931 n11). Since
   then, England had been having a difficult time remaining aloof from the
   League of Cognac (the papacy, Venice, Milan, Florence, and France), which
   was aimed openly at depriving Charles V of his gains in Italy and France.
13 'Sacred anchor,' one's last remaining defence; see *Adagia* I i 24.
14 Ie with Mountjoy, who had been deeply involved in the war of 1513–14 (Ep
   334:60–3)
15 Presumably against the Netherlands as part of a campaign against Charles
   V. At this point, relations between Henry VIII and Charles V were extremely
   tense, and there was a possibility of Henry allying himself with Francis I of
   France against Charles. In January, the English had delivered a declaration of
   war to Charles in Spain, though in the end nothing came of it. See Ep 1993 n2.
   In the Netherlands, meanwhile, Karl van Egmond, duke of Gelderland, with
   Francis I as his ally, spent much of 1528 in rebellion against the Hapsburg
   government of Charles V. See Ep 1998 n7.

As I was fluctuating between hope and fear, Pieter de Corte oppor-
tunely addressed a letter to me.[16] Since the end of November he has been
the sole director and administrator of the College of the Lily without the   80
help of any assistants. He invited me in his usual gracious manner to stay
with him and share his pleasant, if not luxurious, lodgings. After comparing
Mountjoy's Milesian feasts,[17] with the dangers I feared they entailed, with
Corte's Spartan fare, free from the vicissitudes of fortune, I asked leave of
Mountjoy both to resume the studies that I had interrupted for five years   85
and to safeguard my life and possessions. I obtained my request after much
pleading on the condition that whenever I pleased I would find my daily ra-
tions undiminished at Mountjoy's estate if I were to return to England with
the prospect of a richer offer. I made straight for Louvain, where for the last
three months I have been living most agreeably with Corte.   90

His fervent dedication to the study of good letters, both Greek and
Latin, is not unknown to you, my dear Erasmus, nor will the world long be
ignorant of it. The *Christian Priest*, which he is now working on, will be, if I
am any judge, an amply persuasive testimony of his ability both in elegance
of style and religious knowledge.[18] At the present moment he has become a   95
new champion of Greek learning in instituting the study of Greek for the
young men enrolled in his college which I hope will have success.[19] If the
directors of the other colleges follow him in this initiative as best they can,[20]
who does not see that the door is open for the introduction into the schools
of the study of Aristotle in Greek?   100

It is not that he has departed rashly from the usual curriculum; his program has the backing and encouragement of numerous people. Many men of
good judgment perceived that philosophy was doomed unless it could recommend itself to men of learning in real fact rather than through trickery.
As a result they have gradually forsaken those contentious sophistries: these 105
have given way, at least at the College of the Lily, to Rodolphus Agricola
and writers of like integrity,[21] without infringing on the privileged position

* * * * *

16 On de Corte see Ep 1347 n66.
17 *Adagia* I iv 8
18 There is no record of this or any other work by Corte having been published.
19 Corte's course in the Lily would have been in addition to the one taught by
   Rutgerus Rescius (Epp 546, 1758 n10), professor of Greek in the Collegium
   Trilingue.
20 The three other arts colleges were the Pig, the Falcon, and the Castle.
21 On Agricola (1444–85), the celebrated Frisian humanist and pioneer of the
   'new learning' in northern Europe, see Ep 23:58n.

of Aristotle. And so that the students will continue in the study of philosophy, these same arbiters have ruled that Greek literature, which is usually
learned outside the college without counting towards a degree,[22] be taught,   110
and it is being brought forth by not a few from the shadows of private study
to be used as a sweetener for the bitterness of philosophy.

Beleaguered by arguments of this kind arising from various quarters,
since he was president of a college pre-eminent among all others for its pursuit of humane studies, Corte revealed his predicament to me on my return.   115
He explained that he would like to comply with the wishes of his advisers
but was deterred by the revolutionary character of the enterprise, which was
certain to arouse secret, if not open hostility. Nevertheless, choosing to cede
to necessity rather than at great cost to alienate friends who were looking
towards the common good, he entreated me by right of the close friendship   120
that had long existed between us to lend whatever help I could to a friend
who was the victim of coercion. He asked that I oblige the College of the
Lily, help the youth, assist the educational program (which in the view of
many was in danger) in its general pedagogical responsibilities, and comply
with the demands of his supporters, who would surpass him in whatever   125
bold innovations he would be alleged to have attempted.

I hesitated for some time, partly because this venture would require
another Hercules, partly because I feared men's opinions, which in the current state of affairs proclaim that such teaching is the first step towards
Lutheranism or some worse heresy, things that I find completely abhorrent.   130
To put it briefly, Corte, or rather the leading men of the university pleading
in his stead with very persuasive arguments, won out in the end. I agreed
that Greek would be taught under my auspices – may the gods make it
prosper. It was begun at the beginning of January of this year. My plan
is first to pass rapidly through the grammar and then to go back over and   135
analyse every phrase with the same exactness and care used with Latin.
This has been scheduled for two o'clock in the afternoon, at which time
de Neve used to explicate Cicero.[23] I will strive with all my strength to
fulfil this function, with untiring efforts, if I can testify to others that my
labours receive your approbation. I shall take care with all assiduity not to   140
provoke anyone if my initiative, as it well deserves, should attract some
favour.

* * * * *

22 In this period, those wanting to learn Greek normally had to do so by engaging
   private tutors.
23 On Jan de Neve see Epp 298, 1347.

This is a rather haphazard account, my dear Erasmus, of the changes
your friend Cruyce has introduced at Louvain at the instigation of his
friends. I will know that this spontaneous act of homage met with your   145
approval if in the future I shall be numbered among those to whom you do
not deny the favour of your correspondence.

All await your *Augustine* with incredible expectation,[24] to be followed,
I implore you, my dear Erasmus, with no great interval of time, by the *Ra-*
tio concionandi, if you wish that there be many workers for the gospel har-   150
vest.[25] For it is of such great importance to many people that, according to
Erasmus' precept, the preacher be evangelical that they prefer to remain
silent rather than speak without benefit of the teaching of one who for several years now has promised us this work and whose eloquent *Lingua* has
renewed this hope.[26]   155

From England nothing worth reporting arrives here. Concerning the
controversy between the bishop of Rochester and Pace over the Septuagint
translation,[27] printed on glossy paper but printed nonetheless,[28] I do not

* * * * *

24 The ten-volume Froben Augustine was published in 1529 (Ep 2157)
25 For a long time now, Erasmus had been claiming to be writing a work on
   the theory of preaching (see Epp 1321 n1, 1332:41, 1341A:1334–38, 1660 n10,
   1804:147–50 1851:34–7, 1881:55–8, 1907:35–6), but it would not be completed
   and published until 1535 as the *Ecclesiastes sive de ratione concionandi*. Cf Epp
   2016:27–9, 2029 introduction, 2033:49–51, 2065:75–6.
26 See Ep 1593.
27 Cruyce's date (August 1527) for this dispute between John Fisher, bishop of
   Rochester, and Richard Pace (Ep 1955 introduction) placed it soon after the
   outbreak of the controversy over the royal divorce. This led Allen to surmise
   that the dispute might have been part of that controversy and that it possibly
   centred on the meaning of the Old Testament texts (Lev 20:21 and Deut 25:5–
   10) that were being cited for and against the legitimacy of Henry VIII's marriage to Catherine of Aragon. We now know, however, that Fisher and Pace
   were engaged in a purely theological dispute unrelated to contemporary political events. In his *Praefatio in Ecclesiasten recognitum ad Hebraicam veritatem*
   (London: Pynson n d [c July/August 1527]), Pace argued that the Septuagint
   version of the Old Testament was a purely human artifact, devoid of divine
   inspiration. In his reply to the *Praefatio*, which survives in an unpublished
   manuscript, Fisher made the case for divine inspiration, thus upholding the
   authority of those passages (not including the ones listed above) in which the
   Septuagint text diverged from the Hebrew (Massoretic) text. See Richard Rex
   The Theology of John Fisher (Cambridge 1991) 148–61.
28 The meaning of this reference to glossy paper is not clear. Rex (as in preceding
   note) 149 omits these words from his translation of this sentence and thus
   offers no explanation of them.

doubt that you have known of it for some time since it took place last
August, when I was still on very familiar terms with Pace. I was living to-   160
gether with him at the time in the convent of Syon,[29] where he had gone as
a result of an illness.

Corte, a devoted follower of yours and your works if ever there was
one, who offers himself and all that he has for Erasmus to dispose of at his
will, asked me to give you his greetings. He also entreats you to maintain   165
your association with his College of the Lily, which has already given you
a good name, with that same dedication that you reserve for those who are
devoted to you.

Pardon, in the name of the Muses, most generous Erasmus, the pro-
lixity and gauche loquaciousness of this letter, which proceeded from a de-   170
sire to greet you, a desire which, while it knows not how to be still, expresses itself worse in speech. Remember that there is at Louvain a man
named Cruyce who puts all that he has at the disposition of Erasmus. For
the holy labours with which you do not cease to adorn the church, the spouse
of Christ, may the good and almighty Christ, who promised to be present   175
with his assistance to his followers until the end of time,[30] long preserve
you free from harm.

At Louvain, the College of the Lily, 5 February.

To the father of all learning, Erasmus of Rotterdam, at Basel

1933 / To Bonifacius Amerbach   [Basel, c 1 February 1528]

This letter is the first of a series (1933–4, 1936–7, 1940–1, 1943, 1950, 1991–2)
dealing with the latest episode in the rancorous feud between Erasmus and
Heinrich Eppendorf that was to last until 1531. For details see the introduction
to Ep 1934.

The manuscript, autograph except for the address in a secretary's hand, is Basel MS AN III 15 2. It was first published in the *Epistolae familiares*, then by Allen,
and then as Ep 1233 in AK. Allen assigned an approximate date, adopted by AK
as well, between the arrival of Eppendorf in Basel on about 30 January (see Ep
1934 introduction) and the conference on 2 February that preceded Ep 1937.

On Amerbach, who was now teaching at the University of Basel and would
in 1530 assume the chair of Roman law, see Ep 408.

* * * * *

29 The Bridgettine house of Syon at Islesworth, which was a twin foundation with
   the Carthusian house down the river at Shene. Both were closely associated
   with reform circles. Cf Ep 314:12n.
30 Matt 28:20

Greetings. The nobleman Eppendorf is here,[1] uttering dire threats and threatening court action. Rhenanus[2] thinks it wise that we should meet tomorrow at Baer's[3] house to consult together, to see if we cannot settle this matter verbally among ourselves without any fuss.[4] I would like you to be present, if you can do so conveniently, for I have neither the experience nor 5 the time for litigation. Farewell. Think about it overnight.

To the most learned doctor in both laws Bonifacius Amerbach

1934 / To Johannes von Botzheim   Basel, 1 February 1528

The only source for this letter is *Pirckheimeri Opera* 292, where the text is corrupt. Corrected versions are found in LB III-2 *Appendix epistolarum* 346 and C. Saxius *De Henrico Eppendorpio commentarius* (Leipzig 1745) 12–13. For the appended statements of Eppendorf and Erasmus, there are three contemporary sources: Erasmus' *Admonitio adversus mendacium* (Basel: Froben 1530) fol A 3 verso, Eppendorf's *Iusta querela* (Haguenau: J. Setzer 1531) fol A 6, and Erasmus' *Opera omnia* (Basel: Froben 1540) IX 1383–4.

Two references to Botzheim in the third person (lines 273, 336) seem to cast doubt on the address of the letter. On the other hand, the qualities of the person addressed fit no one as well as Botzheim: versed in law (lines 184–5), so devoted a friend that he can be asked to come in a hurry (line 496), and living in the opposite direction from Burgundy and Holland (lines 493–5). Allen speculated that the references in question were either lapses on Erasmus' part in the heat of composition or else information inserted in the copy of the letter that was sent to Pirckheimer.

Heinrich Eppendorf (Ep 1122 n5), a Saxon with a dubious claim to noble status, had already taken a BA at Leipzig when he visited Erasmus at Louvain

* * * * *

1933
1 On Eppendorf's bogus claim to noble status, which Erasmus initially took to be genuine, see Epp 1122 n5, 1283:16–18, 1371:1, 1437:86–90, 1551:27–9. Here, as in Epp 1901:6 and 1934:381, the term *eques* (nobleman or knight) is used with heavy-handed irony.
2 Beatus Rhenanus (Ep 327), humanist, editor, and historian, was one of Erasmus' closest friends. Resident in Basel from 1511, he had by 1527 settled permanently in his native Sélestat but was currently on a visit to Basel.
3 Ludwig Baer (Epp 488 introduction, 1571 n6, 1674 n17, and 1780 introduction) was professor of theology at Basel and provost of the collegiate church of St Peter's in the same city. Erasmus relied on Baer for theological advice, most notably during the composition of *De libero arbitrio* (Epp 1419–23).
4 The conference (Ep 1992:304–12) actually took place in Erasmus' house: see CWE 78 381 (*Admonitio adversus mendacium*).

Bonifacius Amerbach
Hans Holbein the Younger, c 1525
Kupferstichkabinett, Kunstmuseum Basel

in 1520. Two years later, after studying at Freiburg at the expense of Duke George of Saxony, he appeared in Basel and attached himself to Erasmus (Ep 1284 n4). But when the quarrel between Erasmus and Ulrich von Hutten broke out the following year (Epp 1331 n24, 1341A:1024–1191) Eppendorf sided with Hutten, and Erasmus became convinced that Eppendorf had engineered the breach with Hutten. Erasmus' account of the early stages of the ensuing feud is found in Ep 1437. In 1523, Eppendorf moved to Strasbourg, where he won fame as a translator of the classics into German. But Erasmus saw Eppendorf's hand behind a number of attacks on him that originated from Strasbourg (Epp 1477B, 1485, 1496:120–31, 1543, 1804:180–3, 1901:6–7). Among those to whom he complained was Eppendorf's patron, George of Saxony (Ep 1448 introduction), who eventually wrote to Eppendorf (Ep 1929:13–14) admonishing him to cease annoying Erasmus. Frustrated by this and having managed to obtain a copy of Erasmus' letter to the duke, Eppendorf remonstrated three times by letter (Ep 1940:20–1 and n9). Getting no satisfaction by that route, he decided early in 1528 to go to Basel to demand compensation for his injuries and was prepared to take legal action to get it. The chronology that follows is that compiled by Allen on the basis of the contemporary record in Erasmus' correspondence, especially this letter and Ep 1992.

Eppendorf arrived in Basel no later than 30 January, going first to Beatus Rhenanus (Ep 1933 n2) to pour out his complaints against Erasmus (lines 7–12). The next day he went to the burgomaster and then paid a visit to Erasmus (lines 22–8). During the interview, Beatus and other friends arrived and in due course Eppendorf departed, promising to send his terms of settlement the next day (lines 173–8, 501–26.) They arrived as promised, and on 1 February Erasmus sent a copy of them to Botzheim (lines 495–6).

Erasmus was initially determined to take his chances in court, but Beatus Rhenanus persuaded him to accept arbitration by himself and Bonifacius Amerbach (lines 51–2), who were friendly to both sides, and Eppendorf generously agreed to be bound by the decision of two of Erasmus' closest friends. Erasmus then sent Ep 1933 to Amerbach inviting him to the meeting that was to be held the next day in the home of Ludwig Baer (Ep 1933 n3). The meeting took place on 2 February, but in Erasmus' own house (Ep 1933 n4). Although Erasmus refused to admit that he had written the letter to Duke George, he readily accepted the decision of the arbitrators that was announced on the following day (Epp 1937, 1992:304–6) and was generous to Eppendorf. Erasmus was to write to Duke George affirming Eppendorf's good character and to dedicate a book to him. He was also to pay the sum of twenty florins to be donated to the poor under the supervision of the arbitrators. In return, Eppendorf promised not to publish a book that he had written against Erasmus. Apart from the settlement of the dispute without litigation, that is all that Erasmus received. On the next day, 4 February, Erasmus invited everyone to dinner and gave the departing Eppendorf the required letter to Duke George (Ep 1940) and the letter of dedication, which was, however, not yet attached to any particular book (Ep 1992:312–23, 403–16).

The truce was not destined to last. Eppendorf not only advanced new demands that were not part of the settlement (Ep 1950) but also boasted widely about his glorious 'triumph' over Erasmus (Epp 1991, 1997). Erasmus' immediate reaction was to write a long letter, which he left unpublished, to Willibald Pirckheimer, once again summarizing the conflict in detail and defending his own behaviour in it (Ep 1992). Moreover, now convinced of Eppendorf's ill will, Erasmus refused Eppendorf's repeated demands for the production of the promised work dedicated to him, excusing himself on the ground that he was too busy with work on the editions of Augustine and Seneca then in preparation. See AK Epp 1285 (Eppendorf to Amerbach, August/September 1528), 1294 (Amerbach to Eppendorf, 1 October 1528), and 1321 (Eppendorf to Amerbach, 12 January 1529). Erasmus was not too busy, however, to insert into the September 1528 edition of the *Adagia* a scornful passage about German Junkers that was aimed directly at Eppendorf (see n35 below), as was the colloquy Ἱππεὺς ἄνιππος, *sive Ementita nobilitas* 'The Knight Without a Horse, or Faked Nobility' that he composed for addition to the new edition of the *Colloquies* published in March 1529 (CWE 40 880–90).

Towards the end of 1530, Erasmus published his own account of the quarrel, the *Admonitio adversus mendacium*, and in February 1531 Eppendorf replied with his *Iusta querela*. At this point, Julius Pflug, the distinguished humanist churchman and jurist in the service of Duke George, intervened to mediate a truce that finally brought an end to the controversy, which had done credit to neither man (Epp 2450, 2451).

Erasmus' great friend and confidant since 1520, Johann von Botzheim (Epp 1285, 1341A), was a doctor of canon law and a patron of artists and scholars. A canon at Constance from 1512, he had now, following the triumph of the Reformation at that city in 1527, moved with the cathedral chapter to Überlingen, where he died in 1535.

ERASMUS TO HIS FRIEND BOTZHEIM, GREETING

How I wish you were here to defend your friend Erasmus, who must face a new obstacle. Up to now I have exercised the gladiatorial profession,[1]

* * * * *

1934
1 Erasmus often described himself as engaged in gladiatorial combat with his opponents; see Epp 1815 n19, 1969:52, 1987:16, 2045:361, and cf Ep 1943 n4.

joining battle with the likes of Béda and Cousturier;[2] now, if the gods so
will it, I become a litigator and from Hercules I go over to the side of Mer-   5
cury.[3] Heinrich Eppendorf has arrived here, changed from a Thraso into a
Phormio, or I should say, a combination of the two.[4] Scarcely had he entered
the city than everyone knew that he was going to bring me to trial. He ran
into Beatus and vented his spleen upon him. He said that because of a letter of mine the friendly relations that he had enjoyed with Duke George   10
had turned into bitter hostility,[5] and that he had been deprived of a sizeable
fortune worth at least three thousand florins.[6] He was referring, I think, to
a marriage. Beatus, being a man too good to believe that such monstrous
things can take place among men and a lover of peace and well disposed
towards both parties besides, persuaded him to discuss the matter first with   15
me and then make his decisions. That is the way rulers act. Eppendorf did
not altogether rule out the colloquy, but said that he would not come to my
house, even though I was in such bad health that I had not set foot outside
my house for five months.[7] Meanwhile, in the public square, in the inns,

* * * * *

2 Ep 1943 n6 (Béda) and n7 (Cousturier)
3 While Hercules was known for his prowess in battle, Mercury, particularly in
   his Greek guise as Hermes, was known as a god of cunning, eloquence, and
   persuasion and as the patron of orators.
4 Thraso is the braggart soldier in Terence's play *The Eunuch*, while the scheming
   parasite Phormio is the protagonist of the play of that name.
5 See Ep 1893:44–8.
6 If these 3,000 unspecified florins were Florentine gold coins (or close imitations), this 'sizeable fortune' would have been worth £1,000 groot Flemish, or
   £6,825 tournois, or about £700 sterling. If, however, they were Rhenish florins
   (Four Imperial Electors) – with 18.50 rather than 24 carats fineness and lower
   weight – then this sum would have been worth £737 10s 0d groot Flemish (at
   59d groot per florin), or £487 10s 0d or £500 sterling (at 39 or 40d per florin),
   or £4,500 tournois (at £1 10s 0d per florin). But if Erasmus had instead meant
   the now common Flemish Hapsburg florin money-of-account, worth 40d groot
   Flemish (so that six florins equalled one pound groot), as he frequently does in
   his correspondence, then this sum would have been worth only half as much:
   £500 groot Flemish. If Erasmus had meant gold coins, he probably would have
   used the term *florenorum aureorum* (or *in auro*). See CWE 1 314, 316–18; CWE 12
   650 Table 3D. Note that this florin money-of-account, rivalling or even sur-
   passing the Flemish pound groot in common use, also became the primary
   Dutch money-of-account (known popularly as the guilder); with 20 stuivers
   per florin. The stuiver, worth 2d groot, thus served as the 'shilling' in this
   money-of-account. See the Appendix Table 3, 476 below.
7 On Erasmus' poor health at this time, see Epp 1893:29–30 and 49–51, 1921:5–7,
   1939:13–14, 1965:4, 1989 n4.

and in the streets he blared out publicly and privately with great histrionics   20
what indignities he had suffered at the hands of Erasmus.

That was towards evening. On the next day he went to see the burgomaster,[8] as I have heard, signifying that he wished to bring legal action
against me. The reply was given that the town council was too busy and that
he should put it off for a few days. On the next day after lunch he came   25
to the colloquy, having put on a studied look of anger quite remarkable to
behold. You would have said that he was some Mezentius from the tragic
stage.[9] He read me a letter written to George, Duke of Saxony, in a hand
unknown to me, in which there was concocted a story about how he had
conducted himself in Freiburg, then in Basel, and finally in Strasbourg,[10] in   30
which there was hardly anything besides those exploits he usually boasts
about. I wish you had been there to see the expression on the face of this·ac-
tor, whom you know too well, playing his part without a mask. I marvel that
he could restrain himself from laughter; I at any rate could not, even though
I was ill and it was an unpleasant situation. When he expostulated concern-   35
ing various points in the letter that it was an unseemly crime to damage the
reputation of a simple, innocent person, I responded that I did not recognize this letter and that it was not my right either to defend or condemn
something which I did not know if I had written or not. I suggested that he
produce the letter that the duke had written to him,[11] which would be clear   40
proof that I had not written such things. Simon Pistoris, the duke's chancellor, had written me a summary of its contents.[12] Now that I had denied
authorship of the letter, what was left to him but to prove that it was mine
or to hold his peace? Nonetheless he kept on reading. Finally, when he asserted that it had my signature with the symbol of the god Terminus,[13] I   45
ordered him to produce it. I knew that he could not do so. And he has never
brought it forth as evidence since that time, although that paragon of truth-
fulness had asserted so many times that he was in possession of it. I have
answered, nevertheless, in a cursory way to some points, but as though to
things pertaining to someone else.   50

* * * * *

8 Adelberg Meyer; see Epp 1585 n5, 1744 n9.
9 Mezentius, legendary Etruscan king, who in Virgil's *Aeneid* 7–10 appears as a
   bloodthirsty and impious tyrant who is killed by Aeneas
10 Cf lines 73–4, 464–5 below, and the similar description in Ep 1940:4–10. Erasmus here and at lines 221–4 below firmly repudiates his authorship of the
   letter, but in Ep 1940 betrays some uncertainty.
11 See Ep 1929 n5, and cf lines 224–5 below.
12 See Ep 1929 introduction.
13 On the image of the god Terminus found on Erasmus' signet ring, see Ep 2018.

Beatus intervened in our dispute, urging us to forget our quarrels and try to effect a reconciliation. I declared that I was ready to do so. In the meantime Eppendorf kept on protesting noisily that his previously unsullied reputation had been defiled. I answered that he had attacked me more seriously, doing so three times in more than hostile letters containing threats 55 so terrible as to bring sudden death on a sickly and scared old man,[14] as we know has often happened. And I strongly suspect that he wrote such things with the intention of either extorting money from me or killing me. In one of them this model of innocence called me a wicked scoundrel worthy of the gallows. He answered that he was not serious in his intention. 'Other- 60 wise,' he said, 'do you think I would have put it off so long?' Isn't that a fine defence? With this excuse any thief could defend himself: 'I stole, but not intentionally.' Then he claimed that he had been harmed first. To which I retorted that I was the first to be harmed, because he had incited Hutten against me and had had his book published.[15] Not satisfied with this, 65 he made use of the mad fury of a certain Otto against me.[16] When he denied this, as I knew he would, I admitted it was not easy to prove, but insisted that it was inferred from so much evidence that I considered it proven fact. I cited Heresbach as a witness,[17] I cited Karl Harst:[18] they said that it was he who had corrected the proofs of Hutten's book;[19] similarly, when 70 Otto's book[20] was being printed, he was constantly in the publishing house of Schott, the printer.[21]

He was particularly infuriated that in the letter he was called the champion of the most wicked church.[22] I answered that he was celebrated under this title in books published by Otto and Lonicerus.[23] Otto in fact filled 75

* * * * *

14 Cf lines 110–11, 192–3 below; and see Ep 1940 n9.
15 The *Expostulatio*; see Ep 1356 n9.
16 Otto Brunfels; see Epp 1405–6.
17 Konrad Heresbach, whom Erasmus had visited at Freiburg in March 1523; see Ep 1316 introduction.
18 Erasmus' former famulus (Ep 1215)
19 The *Expostulatio cum Erasmo Roterodamo*; see Ep 1341A:1020–5 with n283.
20 *Pro Vlricho Hutteno ... Responsio*; see Ep 1405.
21 See Ep 1429 n1. He published both Hutten's *Expostulatio* and Brunfels' *Responsio*.
22 Ie in the letter that Erasmus denied having written: cf lines 28 (with n10) above, and 221–4 below; for its purported attribution to Eppendorf of Lutheran sympathies, see lines 409–12 below.
23 Johannes Lonicerus (Lonitzer), d 1569, an Augustinian friar from Saxony who, after going over to the Reformation, lived first in Freiburg (1521–2) and then in Strasbourg (1523–7), where he worked for a number of publishers. In 1527

several pages with eulogies of him and Lonicerus often calls him, in capital letters, the 'Leader of Germany.'[24] Thereupon he denied with great impudence that he knew he was named in Otto's books. Concerning Lonicerus he became menacing, implying that I was inventing it. For this truth-speaking man is of the opinion that a lie is a crime worthy of capital punishment. I 80 said that the book had been published in Strasbourg and was for sale all over the place in case he doubted my word. Otto also added in his book that he was doing this without the knowledge of Eppendorf.[25] What is more stupid than this ruse? This is betrayal, not accusation. But for kings any pretext is sufficient.[26]   85

He laid to my charge a letter that Hummelberg sent here, supposed to have been written by Melanchthon.[27] I had sent it to Hedio,[28] in whom I had complete trust at the time. He, it appears, divulged it to Capito, and Capito to Eppendorf.[29] For Thraso N.[30] I had put H.E. Eppendorf had understood these letters to mean that there was someone else whose first and last name 90 began with these same letters and said that he had written about this matter to Melanchthon, who wrote back confirming that this was the case. At that point I could not help laughing, knowing that the truth was otherwise. For I can produce an autograph letter of Philippus in which he affirms that he never wrote to Eppendorf and never received a letter from him.[31] Ep- 95 pendorf added that he had a letter from Willibald, written in his hand, in

* * * * *

he became the first professor of Greek at the newly founded University of Marburg.
24 This reference has not been traced.
25 See Ep 1406:249–51.
26 Cf lines 465–8 below.
27 Cf Ep 1496:126–32. The letter in question was one from Melanchthon to Hummelberg, dated by MBW at 'the second half of December 1523.' In it Melanchthon writes: 'What do I hear? Is Philophoebus [Eppendorf] still alive? I would have thought that by now he had been hanged. I have known him for more than twelve years. I have never seen anyone more vain, worthless, or foolish than he' (MBW T 2 Ep 300:1–3 = CR 1 649, where the date is 'beginning of 1524'). For the background of Melanchthon's poor opinion of Eppendorf, see *Supplementa Melanchthoniana: Werke Philipp Melanchthons die im Corpus Reformatorum vermisst werden* ed Otto Clemen 6/1 (Leipzig 1926; repr Frankfurt 1968) 232–3. On Hummelberg see Ep 1454 n1.
28 Ep 1477B introduction
29 See Ep 1496:120–31. On Capito, see Epp 1368, 1374, and 1437 n48.
30 'N' (short for 'nomen' or 'name') was commonly used, as 'X' is today, to conceal the identity of the person referred to.
31 Cf Ep 1991:67–70.

which he was exhorted to take up his pen against Erasmus and defend his name. This buffoon simulated passionate intensity in look and intonation, not without a gnashing of teeth. I answered that Willibald had made known to me in a recent letter in his own hand that he had written to Eppendorf to put an end to his madness,[32] and that the letter was available if he wished to see it.

He charged that in the letter to the duke it was written that he assumed the role of a nobleman. (At this he called upon me to witness whether he had ever played the part of a nobleman, although in the past he boasted to me about his nobility.) I remained silent, wondering why he said this. He repeated the same words. I answered with an exclamation, not a word, as if it did not concern me. Then, with a marvellous straight face he said, 'And perhaps what really disturbs the prince is that I conceal my nobility.' In this regard, in his last note – in which he declared war for the third time[33] – he wrote in his own hand, *Henricius ab Epphendorpio, eques.*[34] His coat of arms hangs in front of inns, with helmet and vizier, and a sword runs diametrically through the middle of the shield. And he does not designate his place of origin in the ordinary way, as a man from Rome says that he is a Roman, but he adds a preposition, as if he were lord of the place. Ancient writers used this form of expression to mean some office or function, as the imperial chamberlain is called *a cubiculo Caesaris*, that is, in charge of the emperor's bedchamber. So a bishop was said to be 'of' Hippo because he presided over that city. Nowadays great princes take their names in the same way from a place, not because they were born there but because they have dominion over it. No doubt that is why he is Heinrich von Eppendorf, perhaps after a beer tavern run by his ancestors.[35]

How many times during the last six years has he filled my ears with the mention of his father's castle, recounting an interminable tale about a certain monk, who was a very skilful archer, to whom his father had given

* * * * *

32 Possibly in the missing part of Ep 1930
33 See n14 above.
34 Heinrich von Eppendorf, Knight
35 On the ancestral tavern, cf lines 392–3 below. On the 'von,' cf the passage added to the *Adagia* (I ix 44) in the edition of 1528, with Eppendorf clearly in mind (CWE 32 205): 'Suppose [a nobleman] ... is born in a village – let us say his name is Ornithoplutus [Fowl-riches = *Hahn-reich*] and his village is called Isocômus [Equal- or Even-village = *Eben-dorf*] – he never signs himself an Isocomian; any plebeian could do that. He is Ornithoplutus *von* Isocômum.' See also n40 below.

hospitality in his castle. Furthermore, when he said that he did not care how the prince felt towards him, to which I said, 'Then what are you afraid of?' he responded with a very serious look that he was afraid the prince might seize his father's castle. I have no doubt that he must have made these same indiscreet remarks to you, for I know he has done so with many others. At   130
Constance, when the bishop asked Beatus whether Eppendorf was a nobleman, and Beatus answered equivocally, Eppendorf kept silent and accepted the place of honour at table.[36]

He followed us on this journey on a pathetic-looking horse. But he said that at Rheinfelden he would get a horse on loan from the nobility there.[37]   135
Nothing came of this; obviously the nobility were elsewhere. He played the same trick at Schaffhausen and again at Constance; as the thief knows the thief, according to the proverb, and the wolf knows the wolf,[38] so the nobleman knows the nobleman. By some bad strokes of fortune those whom he wished to see were never there. He took offence that in my *Spongia* I called   140
him the faithful Achates of Hutten;[39] but he was not offended that in that same work I had called him a nobleman, for at the time I had the suspicion he was not altogether a commoner. Why did he not admit that he was not a nobleman? Besides, he has servants, of whom two are Germans who always address him as a Junker.[40] What more can I say? He seems to do everything pos-   145
sible to be regarded as a nobleman. He was fully aware that I knew this, but he was not embarrassed by this kind of language. He added that he attached such importance to his family, however humble it might be, that he would not allow any prince to cast aspersion on their reputation with impunity.

* * * * *

36 This would have taken place in September 1522, during the visit to Constance on which Eppendorf accompanied Erasmus; see Ep 1342:369–71. The bishop there was Hugo von Hohenlandenberg (d 1535).
37 Rheinfelden is on the Rhine in the Swiss canton of Aargau, about 9.5 miles east of Basel.
38 *Adagia* II iii 63
39 LB X 1636C; Ulrich von Hutten *Opera quae reperiri potuerunt omnia* ed Eduard Böcking (Leipzig 1859–6; repr Aalen 1963) 2 333 §50. Achates was the devoted companion of Aeneas.
40 Cf the same passage in the *Adagia* referred to in n35 above (CWE 32 204–5): 'And this [resort to 'trickery and crime' to improve one's finances] is a special plague ... in our modern Germany, especially among those who pride themselves on a title of nobility; although there are some who boast a fictitious nobility so that they can do this with the greater impunity, who suborn men to call them Junkers, pride themselves on their ancestral castles ... and add at the end of their letters the magic EQU [abbreviation for *eques* = knight].'

Hugo von Hohenlandenberg
Meister vom Bodensee, 1502
Staatliche Kunsthalle Karlsruhe

You would laugh all the more at this braggadoccio if you had read   150
what Egranus said of his family,[41] what Emser wrote,[42] and what even the
common people now know. After several complaints of this sort his speech
turned to the hostility of the duke towards him and the attack made on
his inviolable reputation, the loss of which he considered such a grave offence that he said he would not pardon the emperor himself for such an   155
affront and that he would sooner lose his life than suffer injury to his
name. I answered that when I was still living with Froben[43] he told me
he was in disfavour with the duke. When I asked him the reason he answered, 'He would like me to be a lowly schoolmaster.' He said, 'I cannot.' I asked him why he feared the duke if he asked nothing of him. 'I   160
fear,' he said, 'for my father's castle, that he might seize it, and for my
brothers.' He did not say that this was not done, but later he said that the
duke had been reconciled to him and that action was being taken for him
to be recalled to his native country with great advantage to him. Thereupon I said, 'If the duke was angry because you did not answer to his ex-   165
pectations, how was he reconciled later when at times you lived more dis-
solutely than before? Besides, there was no need of Erasmus to provoke
the prince's anger against you when you had Hieronymus Emser, a mortal foe, at the court of the duke.' But at the mention of Emser's name he
began to make loud mutterings as if he wished to tear the man to pieces.   170
He had heard, I think, that Emser was dead,[44] so it was safe to act like a
wild beast. Again his friends who were present interrupted this unending
series of complaints, inviting him to forgiveness and reconciliation. He did
not reject this altogether, provided there were certain conditions. He was
asked to present them. He answered solemn-faced that he was too emotion-   175
ally upset at the moment; he would inform us of the conditions on the next
day[45] through Beatus. The terms were delivered on the next day, written in
his own hand, a copy of which I send to you.[46] I answered in my hand, a
copy of which I also send to you.[47] We discussed ways of finding a com-
promise. We agreed on two exemplary men of this city, no less friendly to   180

* * * * *

41 What Egranus (Ep 1377 introduction) said on this subject is unknown.
42 Ep 1551:27–31
43 Erasmus had lived in Froben's house for ten months in 1521–2; see Epp 1289
   n14, 1341A:1790–1, 1528:61–2.
44 Emser died on 8 November 1527.
45 1 February
46 See lines 501–26 below.
47 See lines 527–49 below.

him than to me: Beatus Rhenanus and Bonifacius Amerbach, professor of
Roman law.

That is the plot of the play up to now; what will follow I know not. I
wish you were here so that I could benefit from the advice of one learned
in jurisprudence. I am deliberating whether it is better to accept Eppen-   185
dorf's terms and purchase my tranquillity from a frivolous idler who was
born for nothing else but such things or whether I should submit to a lawsuit. I chose the latter. I was acquainted with the empty talk of this braggart and knew that he was more concerned with his purse than his reputation, that is, it was more a matter of famine than defamation no matter   190
how militant a look he put on and despite the flood of pompous language.
He had promised as much in his last missive, in which he declared war,
saying, 'There will be a replay of the Hutten tragedy.'[48] This time he was
not lying, contrary to his custom. It is exactly the same tragedy. You know
yourself with what amazing tricks and stratagems the prey was captured   195
on that occasion after Hutten, having recourse to the sacred anchor,[49] from
a brigand turned into an impostor. But, so that you will recognize the ar-
chitect of each plot, see how he conceals his lust for plunder. He gave as
a pretext the injury done to his reputation, an inestimable loss, to be sure,
especially in the case of such a man, who never had a good reputation to   200
begin with, since there is nothing so immoral as his life and so far is it from
being hidden that he even boasts about it. Then he asks that a book be dedicated to his glorious name, then a letter to the duke, as if the duke did
not know this scoundrel's character after being so deceived by him. Then,
to top it all, this saintly man looks after the needs of the poor in Freiburg,   205
where he lived such a pious existence that he has never returned there, and
also at Basel, where he is much better known than he thinks. To come to
their aid this man of mercy demands three hundred florins.[50] He does not
wish to be in charge of dispensing this sum lest some suspicion or stigma
might attach to his unblemished reputation. But since in Strasbourg there is   210
a great crowd of poor people whom he knows and loves, in whose number, I believe, Heinrich Eppendorf himself figures in the front lines, he
asks for two hundred ducats to bring with him and dispense at his discretion. He does not explain, however, this fastidious individual, what kind
of ducats he demands, (de camera, largos, in gold, in silver, or Hungarian   215

* * * * *

48 See n14 above.
49 *Adagia* I i 24; cf Ep 1932 n13.
50 In lines 513–19 below, Eppendorf specifies one hundred ducats each for Freiburg and Basel.

ducats).[51] Perhaps he will accept crowns for ducats, provided they are the right weight. This was his craftiness, to put in the last place that which was the heart of the whole manoeuvre and disguise the shameful business under the laudable name of charity. For who does not know that the care of the poor was always close to his heart? 220

After my denying authorship of the letter that he produced, since I was sure he could not prove that it was mine – and I do not think I wrote it[52] – what would he have done if I took him to court? That it was not written by me is made clear from the duke's letter to him,[53] which he did not wish to bring forward under any circumstances, but which he would undoubtedly 225 have done if it contributed to his cause. And if he had proved it, I had a more terrible counter-accusation ready, that he had declared war in the most intimidating terms he could find. I would have said that it was a crime of homicide to strike such terror into an old man in poor health and timid nature and finally so broken and exhausted by his labours, especially since I 230 was fully aware of the valour of the duke and the might of his soldiers. And we have heard of more than a few who suffered sudden death in this way. What is the difference whether you die by the sword or die of fright? And it is probable that he wrote these terrifying pages so that either I should die or – which, I think, in his kind-heartedness he preferred – that by sending him 235

* * * * *

51 Cf lines 518–20 below. The ducats in question may have been Hungarian gold ducats, imitations of Venetian ducats (as in Ep 1958:2). Struck from 1328 at the same fineness as the Venetian ducat (nominally 24 carats), they had a slightly inferior weight: 3.54 grams rather than 3.56 grams. If these were the latter gold ducats (equal in value to gold Florentine florins), then this sum would have been worth about £46 13s 4d sterling, or £66 13s 4d groot Flemish, or £455 tournois. Erasmus' suggestion here that Eppendorf accept English crowns in place of ducats (pro ducatis coronatos) 'provided that they are of the right weight' would not have been advantageous to him unless these were ducats of inferior weight, for the English rose crown (from November 1526) contained only 3.404 grams fine gold, while Venetian ducats (if full weight) contained 3.559 grams fine gold. See CWE 12 646–50 Table 3; Peter Spufford Money and its Use in Medieval Europe (Cambridge and New York 1988) 322 Table 6; Michael North and John H. Munro 'Money and Coinage: Central and Eastern Europe, Western Europe' in Europe 1450 to 1789: Encyclopedia of the Early Modern World ed Jonathan Dewald et al (New York 2004) IV 173–84. See also the Appendix 440–50 with Tables 2, 467 and 3, 476 below, which provide a slight correction to CWE 12 646 Table 3A for the pure gold content of the new double-rose crown (see Ep 1931 n3).
52 Cf lines 28–30 above.
53 Cf lines 40–1 above.

a sum of money I would appease his generous heart. I could have produced many letters from many men worthy of trust in which he is depicted in his true colours.

But this alternative[54] displeased Beatus to begin with, then Bonifacius and Baer, who were of the opinion that peace had to be made under any conditions with this long-winded, false, and do-nothing playboy. They were convinced that he would certainly fill this part of the country with stories and rumours to the effect that Erasmus was brought before the town council of Basel. Then there would be a good number of people who would have it in for me because of my war with the Lutherans; and now the times are such that any clown can injure your reputation with impunity. They have astonishing licence even in Germany, and young men equally impecunious would not be lacking to lend their aid in this kind of business.

I recognized the truth of these and similar considerations; but, most of all, I was concerned with my tranquillity. I was supporting five printing presses on my shoulders, sometimes seven. I was putting my new books, *De pronuntiatione* and *Ciceronianus*,[55] through the press, works that treat of minute matters, making for even more difficulty. And at this time of year, just before the market days,[56] the printing shops are a pandemonium. He could not have chosen a better moment for himself or a worse one for me, for these two books, *De pronuntiatione* and *Ciceronianus*, had already begun to be printed – of slight subject matter, as I said, but for that reason all the more difficult. Need I say more? I was unequal to the task, even if no further troubles had been added. Then I thought of the commotion being stirred up by the monks in Spain[57] and by the theologians in Paris,[58] although the Spanish affair ended happily, and I hope the rumpus in Paris will have an even happier ending. Then I felt sorry for my friends, for whom that windbag was stirring up trouble. They would have to be running back and forth to the emperor, a lawyer and patron would have to be procured, supporters solicited. Add to this the repugnance it would engender in one who has the greatest aversion for such trivial matters. Even if I had the time and the inclination to engage in litigation, the greater part of my case rested on suspicions so numerous that for me they constituted certainty, but so slim in themselves that they would not win the attention of a judge. So far is he from admitting that he instigated Hutten to take up his pen against me that

240

245

250

255

260

265

270

* * * * *

54 Ie a lawsuit
55 See Epp 1948–9.
56 Ie the spring book fair at Frankfurt
57 See Epp 1791, 1877.
58 See Epp 1721–3.

he boasts that he did all in his power to keep him from harming me. And yet, when we were at Constance, at which time he feigned the greatest respect towards me, he blurted out certain things to my host from which it was clear that he entertained no friendly feelings in my regard.[59] He did the same here in Basel when he paid me daily visits to court my favour. I did not so much ignore as despise this show of flattery.   275

When Hutten arrived here I declined a meeting with him, through the intermediacy of Eppendorf, unless it concerned something serious.[60] Eppendorf told me repeatedly that he had delivered this message faithfully and that Hutten had graciously accepted my excuses. I learned from Heresbach[61] 280 and in a letter from Hutten that the truth was quite otherwise.[62]

When Hutten continued to stay on here, uttering dire threats against me to his close associates, Eppendorf, concealing all of this, pretended that he was on peaceful terms with me. If some remark escaped my lips, he reported it to him, distorting its meaning, as in the following example. When 285 I asked why Hutten had written a scathing pamphlet against the count palatine, which he would even have published if he had been able to find a printer mad enough to do so, he said, 'Because he tortured one of his most faithful servants, an innocent young man who was caught red-handed in an act of armed assault and robbery against three abbots under the prince's ju- 290 risdiction.'[63] 'But,' he added, 'he did it at the order of his master.' At this I said, laughing, 'Would this excuse have freed my servants from blame if, when they were caught committing a theft, they said that whatever they did they did at my command?' He only smiled in response but immediately reported the story to Hutten, who was infuriated that I had compared that 295 noble act of brigandry to an everyday theft. I found many incidents of this type, and could have discovered many more except that no one could be less curious than I about such trivia.

Finally Hutten withdrew from here out of fear.[64] In his frequent visits to him Eppendorf would tell him one thing and me another. I often 300

* * * * *

59 This happened during the visit to Botzheim at Constance (n36 above); see Ep 1437:20–5.
60 See Ep 1331 n24.
61 See n17 above.
62 None of Hutten's letters to Erasmus during their controversy in 1522–3 have survived. Of Erasmus' letters to Hutten, only Ep 1356 survives. For traces of the lost letters, see the following three paragraphs and Ep 1356 introduction.
63 On this incident see Ep 1341A:1071–2. The 'scathing pamphlet' was never published.
64 For Mulhouse (line 302 below), on 18 January 1523. See Ep 1331 n24.

suspected this and later confirmed my suspicions. I had written by chance
through another intermediary to Hutten while he was in Mulhouse, without Eppendorf's knowledge. He answered in these words, 'Where did you
get this tiresome story about my being confined to my bedroom, since no
mention of this has ever been made at my house? Even if you had reported   305
this to Eppendorf, he would have had a ready answer, that you need not
take the trouble to mention this to me since I often spend two or three hours
conversing with my friends in the marketplace, never mind not being able
to leave my bedroom.' Yet Eppendorf had told me that because of illness
Hutten could not leave his bedroom. Often he had told me that Hutten was   310
not offended that I did not invite him to see me. But afterwards I learned
from Heresbach and others that this was not the case. Another time in answer to a letter of mine Hutten wrote, 'What you continue to affirm, Eppendorf strongly denies.' Therefore when Eppendorf came to see me in his
usual way, as if it were a friendly visit, I said, 'But didn't I give you this   315
message to be delivered to Hutten?' He said yes. 'Didn't you say that this
was his answer?' He said yes. Then I brought out the letter; I asked him to
read it, which he did. On various occasions he put other words into Hutten's
mouth. The poor fellow was at a loss but he was not embarrassed. I laughed.
He pretended that he had advocated the suppression of the pamphlet that   320
Hutten had written,[65] but I do not doubt that Hutten wrote it at his instigation. He exaggerated the matter with my friends so that they would try
to avert this catastrophe through the payment of money.[66] He himself made
it known that he was willing to expend fifty florins to prevent the publication of this book,[67] obviously to elicit the generosity of my friends. Froben,   325
terrified, offered fifty. I suspected it before Froben confirmed it to me. Eppendorf told me there was someone in Basel who was offering fifty florins
so that the book would not see the light of day, waiting to see what offer I
would make. I gave no answer save that I was previously unaware that I had
such friends in Basel. They thought that after the offer of Froben was known   330
the money was a sure thing. When Hutten's servant departed he said in the
presence of Beatus, as if he were concerned about me: 'Would that this book
did not appear. I would give fifty florins of my own, yes, of my own, I say.'
The truth is that at that time Hutten and Eppendorf did not have half that
sum between them.   335

* * * * *

65 The *Expostulatio*; see n19 above.
66 On this see Ep 1437:45–54.
67 On the value of the florin see n6 above; on the value of the crown, see n51
   above.

Shortly afterwards Johann von Botzheim, who he[68] knew was very devoted to me, frightened by this vicious rumour, hastened here from Constance.[69] I perceived that this was the purpose of his visit as soon as we had
the opportunity to speak in private, for Eppendorf, the director of the show,
was always around, as if acting as a spy. I asked him if this was the reason   340
for his visit: he said yes. 'There was no mention of money, I hope.' He admitted that it had been mentioned. 'How much are they asking?' I said. 'A
modest sum, he said, 'seventy florins.' One day in a conversation with Eppendorf when I recounted to him how Hutten had thrown away in disgust
a letter from Abbot Volz in which there was a gold crown, he answered that   345
such a gift was unworthy of Hutten. 'And what if he had sent fifty florins?'
I said. He expressed his approval.[70] By such tricks he gave notice of my
obligations.

Finally, to inspire more terror in me, he showed me the written book,[71]
which he said he had not opened before showing it to me. I asked him to   350
read from it. He read the beginning. I laughed, saying there was nothing
particularly shocking about it, although I knew he was expecting a different reaction. He hoped that I would be terrified. Then he said, 'But there are
other things in what follows' – and he had just said that he had not looked
at the book! Liars are seldom consistent. They had both entered into a life   355
and death friendship, and each of them had great debts and not a penny to
their name. Hutten was also burdened with various indictments; Eppendorf
was the object of many suspicions. These problems constituted an additional
factor in dealing with such friends. I had warned my friends not to give
them a single penny. For the book had already passed through many hands,   360
and after the money had been paid out they would laugh at us. The reason
for their being so angry with me was that the booty had slipped through
their fingers. Such are the conjectures that have occurred to me, and there
were many more that I cannot rehearse. I am not going to mention the slanderous rumours that they blurt out to others. At this point if anyone reads   365
Hutten's letters to me delivered by Eppendorf,[72] they breathe nothing but
rapacity.

* * * * *

68 Eppendorf
69 Cf Ep 1437:48–9.
70 Paul Volz (1480–1554), Benedictine abbot and member of the literary society at
   Sélestat. The second edition of the *Enchiridion militis christiani* (1518) was dedicated to him (Ep 858). On the value of crowns and florins see nn51 and 6 above.
71 The *Expostulatio*
72 On these letters and that mentioned in the following sentence, see n62 above.

When Eppendorf finally realized that he was more and more laden
with suspicion – for his duplicity was apparent to many – he rushed off
to Zürich to see Hutten, and he brought back a letter that most carefully   370
demonstrated that the book would never have appeared if he had listened
to Eppendorf's advice. He thought I was so devoid of intelligence that I
could not track down these manoeuvres. Isn't such an elaborate apology
equal to an accusation? He withdrew to Strasbourg, but not before he had
testified to me that he was a nobleman. Hutten's book was not delivered to   375
the press until he had arrived there, and those who came here from Strasbourg affirmed that he corrected the proofs. When he saw that my *Spongia*
appeared at that very moment[73] and that he had not drawn in anything with
his net, he suborned Otto,[74] and, lest any suspicion fall on him, he instructed
him to say that the book was published without Eppendorf's knowledge.[75]   380
He saw to it that his title of nobleman be given great publicity,[76] and for this
purpose he took advantage of the good character of Lonicerus, who regretted his action later. He was undertaking these things because in Germany
nothing is denied noblemen, and they are feared by many people, to such
an extent that creditors think they are being harshly treated if noblemen do   385
not ask for a very large sum of money, that is, if they the creditors are not
grandly plundered under the pretence of a loan.

In addition, I have letters from many people who paint him in his true
colours, which to preserve his honour I have never divulged even to my
closest friends. Petrus Mosellanus reproves me because I make Eppendorf   390
out to be a nobleman in the *Spongia*, when it is a known fact that he is of plebeian origin.[77] Emser wrote that his uncle or his father was a beer merchant
in the village from which he takes his name,[78] and that his mother did not
enjoy a favourable reputation; his sisters were cut from the same cloth and
he himself was very unpopular with the duke. What is more, many people   395
say that his sister is the mistress of a certain cardinal. They say that he too
is involved in a love affair with the owner of the inn where he is staying,
which accounts for his extra expenses. And there are those who suspect that
he knows how to make use of his hands if he chances upon something that
is not guarded. Whether these things are true or false does not concern me.   400

* * * * *

73 September 1523; see Ep 1378.
74 Brunfels; see line 66 with n16 above.
75 See Ep 1406:241–9 and lines 82–3 above.
76 Cf Ep 1933 n1.
77 See Ep 1437:86–90. On Mosellanus, see Ep 1305.
78 Cf line 121–2 above.

What makes me wonder, and many others with me, is that he has been living an idle life now for eight years,[79] without ever visiting his native land
or the duke, to whom he owes much gratitude, although the trip is not very
long. He blamed this on me, alleging that because of my letters he ran the
risk of having his head cut off by the duke if he returned to his country. The   405
duke must have conceived this hatred for other reasons, for not even in the
letters that Eppendorf read aloud to me was there anything that was written of the death penalty. He must have a very bad opinion of the prince if,
simple and innocent man that he is, he fears such great peril from him. He
was annoyed that I had accused him of Lutheranism, although even today   410
he professes himself a defender of Hutten, who is the chief protector of the
Lutheran church. Nor did he deny it while Hutten was alive, boastfully recounting to us the perils he faced to accompany him in his flight hither and
yon. I for one never suspected him of having given any thought to evangelical beliefs: he has other interests. He is offended by the charge of falsity   415
while in a singular encounter he uttered so many shameless lies and was
not ashamed to reiterate them in the presence of people who had heard him
say the very opposite to me. Such is his utter lack of shame.

I have a letter written in his hand to Otto,[80] nobleman of the duke
of Saxony, in which he boasts that he, Eppendorf, paid Hutten's debts and   420
for that reason ran the risk of being thrown into jail. The sum exceeded
one hundred fifty florins[81] – as if he ever paid a cent or promised that he
would ever pay a cent for Hutten. Of course he will pay a debt incurred
by another when he himself cannot pay the debts he has contracted himself!
In that same letter he says that he has devoted all his efforts and all his   425

* * * * *

79 Cf Ep 1991:55, where Erasmus puts it at seven years.
80 Otto von Pack (c 1480–1537) was a trusted councillor in the service of Duke
George of Saxony from at least 1519. He was also a crook who embezzled
money by using forged documents. In January 1528, fearing seemingly inevitable detection of his crimes, he launched the famous 'Pack Affair' by giving Landgrave Philip of Hessen forged documentary evidence of a supposed
alliance of King Ferdinand, Duke George, and several other Catholic princes
and prince-bishops, aimed at destroying Lutheranism in their territories and
conquering Hessen and Electoral Saxony. Alarmed, and eager for gain at the
expense of his Catholic neighbours, Philip of Hessen urged Saxony to join
him in preparations for a pre-emptive strike. But the Saxon government, with
Luther and Melanchthon urging caution, restrained the landgrave, and the
whole enterprise collapsed when Duke George exposed Pack's evidence as
fraudulent. It was still too early for Erasmus to know anything about these
matters.
81 On the value of the one hundred fifty florins, see n6 above.

energies to the present day to one goal, that he may contribute service and
distinction to his prince and his country. What could be more impudent than
this deceitfulness? And he does not hesitate to write similar things to our
wise prince. This Otto must be a very saintly man that Eppendorf should
entrust both his life and his fame to him in this same letter.   430

He shows himself quite clever in introducing into his play the most
upright men of this city, Beatus, Bonifacius, and Ludwig Baer, to whom,
as he knows, my reputation is dearer than it is to me. They are such honest men that they could not believe men of such extreme malice existed. I
finally began to realize this myself, although I had contended with such im-   435
postors before, with whom I have been engaged in a fateful conflict since
childhood.[82] Before I knew what lying or trickery was, I hated this pestilen-
tial race through some secret instinct, and they in turn have been my most
bitter enemies.[83] I never gave him any reason to be prejudiced against me.
I was his steadfast adviser. On many occasions in the past I recommended   440
him to the duke[84] and to the leading men at Louvain. Once at my recommendation he received fifty florins; Petrus Mosellanus wrote a draft for that
amount.[85] He forced himself upon my company, and almost every day at
two o'clock after lunch he left off his games of cards to converse with me.

* * * * *

82 Cf the *Compendium vitae* (CWE 4 409:154–7 / Ep 1437:387–90): 'His character
   was straightforward, and his dislike of falsehood such that even as a child
   he hated other boys who told lies, and in old age even the sight of such
   people affected him physically.' The phrase 'his dislike of falsehood ... physically' comes almost verbatim from the *Spongia* (1523) against Hutten (CWE 78
   124).
83 Ie Hutten and all those whom Erasmus perceived to have allied themselves
   with him in his attack on Erasmus: not only Eppendorf, but Otto Brunfels, Hermannus Buschius, Wolfgang Capito, and Caspar Hedio. See CWE 10
   xiv–xv.
84 Cf Epp 1122:12–13, 1125:57, 1283:16–19, 1325:5–9.
85 In Ep 1437:13–15, Erasmus puts the duke's gift at 100 florins. For florins (type
   unspecified), see n6 above. A 'draft' is a bill of exchange (*cambium*), the single
   most important financial innovation in later medieval Europe, of uniquely Italian origin. See Raymond de Roover *L'evolution de la lettre de change, XIVe–XVIIIe
   siècles* (Paris SEVPEN 1953); John Munro 'Bullionism and the Bill of Exchange
   in England, 1272–1663: A Study in Monetary Management and Popular Prejudice' in *The Dawn of Modern Banking* ed Fredi Chiappelli, Center for Medieval
   and Renaissance Studies, University of California (New Haven and London
   1979) 169–239; Markus A. Denzel 'The European Bill of Exchange: Its Development from the Middle Ages to 1914' in *Cashless Payments and Transactions
   from the Antiquity to 1914* ed Sushil Chaudhuri and Markus A. Denzel, Beiträge
   zur Wirtschafts-und Sozialgeschichte 114 (Stuttgart 2008) 153–94.

He brought with him whomever he wished, including someone dressed in 445
a leather coat, whom he presented to me as a nobleman, although I subsequently found out he was the cook of some rich man in the country, and
shortly after that he fled from the inn, stealing a couple of horses.[86] That is
the kind of conversationalist he brought to my house: someone who didn't
even know Latin. But it was poverty, not hatred, that motivated him. Add 450
to that unreliability and a stupidity equal to his malice.

I shall give you an example. He had pleaded with me a long time ago
to recommend him to the duke. I wrote some preposterous praise of him
on a piece of paper: that he was a remarkably serious young man, never
drank, had nothing to do with cards or dice, no association with whores; 455
was never seen in the market place or in the inn, but was either in the church
praying or in the library studying; there was only one thing to be feared,
that in his excessive study habits he might injure his health. Jokingly I sent
a servant to him with this piece of paper to see if he was pleased with the
recommendation, thinking he would be amused at the irony. He approved 460
of it in all seriousness except the part about the danger to his health. From
this you may judge the man's intelligence.

Listen to this equally funny story. In the course of that boastful conversation, after reading the section of the letter which mentioned that he was
saddled with many debts,[87] twisting his head towards me he said, 'Well, 465
do you think it is dishonourable to be in debt? Then the greatest kings and
princes are dishonourable.' What could such an impostor say more true to
form? Fine, Eppendorf has something in common with emperors and kings.
I think the day will come when following the example of kings he will declare war against those who rouse his anger, confiscate their property, and 470
drive them into exile. And he is terribly pleased with this bon mot, since
it's always on his lips in the presence of other people as well. But let him
ask some good men whether it is honourable for a young man with little or
no substance, and no noble blood, to squander so much money shamelessly
and not pay the slightest attention to what people are saying who wonder 475
where such a sum of money spent on pleasures comes from while he does
nothing to pay off his debts. If you were to sum up all of this, what good
omen could be made of it? No shame, a lying tongue, the sweetness of a
life of leisure, extravagance in luxury and lust, a contempt for the unvoiced
judgments of good men and the murmurs of the crowd, intimate association 480
with the worst types, so many years living away from his native country,

* * * * *

86 This is possibly a reference to the 'Hannoverian' of Ep 1371.
87 Cf nn10 and 22 above.

extreme looseness of morals, insufferable conceit, questionable servants constantly dashing about hither and thither, so much prodigality without any apparent source of income – who would not be regarded with suspicion in a city of good morals with a record like that? But he chooses those cities that favour the greatest licence. That is why he liked Basel, but Strasbourg even more. Let him live that way in Nürnberg or in his native city and he will hear what he does not want to hear. There are countless arguments of this kind, but where shall we find judges who have the time to listen to them patiently? For that matter I don't think he will ever appear before judges, but in the meantime he will deliver harangues in the square and in the inn, just as he does now, for he is everywhere, and nothing shames him.

I could have written more, but I am not too certain about this courier. He arrived from Burgundy; he looks like a Dutch vagrant. But he assures me that he is willing to set out in your direction. I gave him some money and this letter. If it reaches you, hasten here as soon as you can. I am afraid the authority of the arbitrators will have little effect. In any case, I am in danger. Farewell.

Given at Basel on the vigil of the Purification, in the year of Our Lord, 1528

CONDITIONS UNDER WHICH I ACCEPT RECONCILIATION
He exposed me to ridicule not only before the prince, who, one might say, holds the right of life and death over me, but also before many private individuals. Because of him my reputation is at stake, for which reparation must be made. This can hardly be done by one or two letters but will require the dedication of a book,[88] in which in his skilful manner he will so present the matter that his own disgraceful conduct will be apparent and he will leave no grounds for suspicion against me in the mind of the reader. I do not solicit dedications of any other sort. Let him write to the prince or to the court, where I know his letter has been circulated, and restore again the expectations men once had of me,[89] but let me read the letter first, lest through his insinuations and ambiguities I may be more disgraced than redeemed.

For having attempted to cause the ruin of an innocent man in this way, and for having fabricated the story about me that I was forced to leave Freiburg for instigating a tumult, although the city knows otherwise and all its citizens can testify to the upright life I led there, for the harm done to my innocence of life, he is to donate one hundred ducats to the poor of

* * * * *

88 See Ep 1941.
89 Cf Ep 1992:188–9.

that city. He shall do the same in this glorious city and donate two hundred ducats for the people of Strasbourg,[90] which I shall take personally there and distribute to the needy at my discretion. All of this for the assault upon candour and innocence.   520

As for the injury done to my reputation, even if it is too great to be calculated, in consideration of past services received,[91] and motivated by Christian piety, I gladly grant pardon, if he accepts the previous conditions. But if Erasmus refuses, let him know that I would rather put my life in danger than my reputation.   525

THE RESPONSE OF ERASMUS OF ROTTERDAM
I do not recognize the letter from which he quotes.[92] I neither think that I wrote such things nor do I find a copy among my papers.[93] And the letter of the duke,[94] if he will produce it, will testify that I did not write such things. I merely advised the duke that he recall that man from a life of leisure to a respectable occupation, or at least that he prevail upon him to leave me in peace.[95] Concerning the dedication of a book,[96] if I see that he has become more kindly disposed towards me, I shall not object to it, and would do it more in the name of friendship.   535

How angry the prince is with him I know not, and I have no certain knowledge about the reasons for his anger. Eppendorf had a mortal enemy at court in the person of Emser.[97] If through my complaints the prince has become more unfavourable to him,[98] I shall not consider it an inconvenience to alleviate this situation with a polite letter,[99] to the extent that one can intervene with princes of such eminence.   540

As for almsgiving, I shall see to that when God shall so inspire me. It is no concern of mine what kind of life he led here or in Freiburg. The more holy a life he lived the happier I am. Concerning the gold ducats he demands of me, it is best to remain silent, lest it seem that he has filed suit   545

* * * * *

90 Cf lines 205–14 above, where Erasmus gives the figures as three hundred florins for Freiburg and Basel together and two hundred ducats for Strasbourg.
91 Doubtless a reference to the support offered in 1522; see Ep 1437:10–15.
92 Cf nn10 and 22 above.
93 Cf Ep 1940:11–13.
94 See Ep 1929 n5.
95 Cf Ep 1940:16–18.
96 See Ep 1941.
97 Cf lines 392–5 above.
98 Cf Ep 1923.
99 Ep 1940

for this reason. If he behaves in a friendly manner and ceases to stir up the people against me, I shall not allow myself to be outdone in civility. I can be of much greater profit to him by my friendly offices than by giving him two hundred gold ducats.

1935 / From Johann Hornburg   Buda, 2 February 1528

> On Hornburg, secretary to the bishop of Trent, see the introduction for Ep 1779, the only other surviving letter from him to Erasmus. The manuscript of this letter, which was first published as Ep 81 in Förstemann/Günther, was in the Burscher Collection at Leipzig (Ep 1254 introduction)

Greetings. You may well reproach me for grave discourtesy and negligence since it is a year, if I am not mistaken, since my most reverend lord of Trent wrote to you[1] and I sent you my crude scribblings,[2] to which you so graciously responded. But in the meantime I have long been silent and have not written back to you, as I should have, a man *sans pareil*, the greatest man in the world of letters for many a century. So perhaps you will wonder why Hornburg recalls himself once again to your memory. Learn therefore, most revered Erasmus, of the various reasons for my hesitation.

At the time your letter to me arrived together with another to my most reverend lord,[3] I had gone away to my native city in Eastern Franconia,[4] where I remained for almost four months. When I returned to Trent some time later I received your letter but was not able to respond both because of the long distance and for lack of messengers. Finally, when my most reverend lord had returned to his royal Majesty in Hungary,[5] the tumults of

* * * * *

1935
1 The letter from Bishop Bernhard von Cles (Ep 1357) mentioned here is not extant, but he wrote again soon afterwards (Ep 1973).
2 Ep 1779
3 Neither letter is extant; cf lines 3–4 above and 61 below.
4 On the meaning and significance of this designation, see Ep 1779 introduction.
5 King Ferdinand. Brother of Emperor Charles v, Ferdinand of Hapsburg (1503–64) ruled independently as archduke of Austria and was currently imperial viceroy during the emperor's prolonged absence (1521–30) from the Empire. In 1526, following the death in battle of his brother-in-law, Louis II of Bohemia and Hungary, Ferdinand was elected as Louis' successor in both kingdoms. He was, however, unable to establish his control in Hungary because his rival for the kingship, John (János) Zápolyai (1487–1540), had the support of the Turks. The twin pillars of Ferdinand's policy were first, defence of his hereditary lands and of the Empire against the Turks (who would reach the gates

war and the pressures of my responsibilities presented no small hindrance   15
to my desire to write. Yet I would not have omitted to write to that revered
deity, my Erasmus, if I had had a courier at my disposal, so that you would
not forget this devoted admirer of you and your writings. Just as I have
always considered myself fortunate to have lived in these times, in which
you, chief luminary of the world of letters, have propagated true learning,   20
so now it causes me profound sorrow to see you receive such ill recompense
for your services in the cause of learning, not only to our country of Germany but to the whole world. Those who have received most benefit from
you bring accusations against a tried and true soldier so that you are never
free of their wrangling and calumnies. And we, who up to now, while you   25
were able to pursue your studies in peace, reaped the abundant fruits of
your labours, now suffer a great loss.

But that is what this corrupt age of ours brings with it – and what evil
does it not bring? Look at all the classes of society and you will find nothing
but ruin and total moral degeneracy. Most pernicious of all, however, is the   30
dissension within the church. There are many, no doubt, who, inspired by a
zeal for good, strive to plant the Christian faith. But Satan always sprinkles
his seed in together with their efforts so that they seem not so much to
plant the seed of faith as to choke it. We have seen this happen for quite
a few years now in many unorthodox beliefs, in which those who at the   35
beginning were firmly united are now in wide disagreement. And yet all
of them formerly were said to possess the Spirit of God, and not only are
they themselves convinced of this but so is the multitude as well. Even now,
whoever teaches a certain doctrine wishes that it be received as if it came
from the Spirit of God. But of all those disputing among themselves, whom   40
are we to believe? They have taught that the word of God is sufficiently clear
of itself, that there is no need of human commentary. But now they attempt
to settle the dispute with new commentaries, and so after our miserable
attempt to escape the perils of Charybdis they hurl us against Scylla.[6] But
would that they did not obscure the light more than it was obscured in   45
the past! Therefore let no one expect to live a good life in the midst of
such confusion. In such a state of uncertainty, waiting to see the end of
these dissensions, what could we do but wander about in various directions.
May God forgive those who have an interest in sympathizing with them!

* * * * *

of Vienna in 1529), and second, opposition to the spread of heresy in the Empire. Cf lines 30–48 below. On Erasmus' relations with King Ferdinand, see
Ep 2000 n2.
6 *Adagia* I v 4

John Zápolyai
Erhard Schön
Thomas Fisher Rare Book Library, University of Toronto

You foresaw all of this. I remember reading in your writings many years   50
ago that you were afraid that this conflagration would spread so widely that
it could not be extinguished without a great universal catastrophe. Would
that our leaders had followed the salutary advice you gave on various occasions in this matter! Certainly, as experience has proved so far, many evils
would not have occurred. But perhaps it is God's plan to overturn every-   55
thing at once and start anew. Therefore, as we plummet towards destruction
we must implore him for his mercy. You, my dear Erasmus, must console
yourself in your old age; dismiss the vanities of men, and be certain that if
the world persecutes you, great will be your glory with God in heaven.[7] I
am allowing myself more familiarity with you than is fitting, but you may   60
attribute it to the confidence you inspired in me in your letter.

I would write more fully about events here if I did not fear that I might
bore you. Our most serene King Ferdinand is still engaged in pursuing the
enemy, who continue to occupy some hidden retreats within the boundaries
of Hungary.[8] We are leading a life that is too courtly, which is to say, mis-   65
erable: Hungary has devoured many outstanding men. My most reverend
lord is well; he takes great delight in your works. Whatever free time he can
find he spends in reading them. He is now weighed down with an enormous number of duties, for his royal Majesty has imposed on him the burden of the grand chancellorship. Caspar Ursinus Velius is his official histo-   70
rian.[9] The Turks are threatening to renew the war against this kingdom next
spring much more fiercely than this past spring. May God avert it. The emperor Charles is making great preparations for war against Italy to recover
the territories seized from the Duchy of Milan by the French and the Vene-
tians.[10] The pope has made an alliance with the emperor, but there are great   75
doubts about his trustworthiness.[11] All is filled with Mars, who threatens

* * * * *

7 Cf Matt 5:11–12.
8 Ferdinand was exploiting recent victories over his rival for the kingship of
   Hungary, John Zápolyai, who fled to Poland in March 1528 and soon allied
   himself with the advancing Turks.
9 See Ep 1917:15–18.
10 In the summer of 1527 the forces of Francis I had overrun Lombardy, captured
   Genoa, and invaded the Kingdom of Naples. But the tide turned in the emperor's favour in the summer of 1528 and the French retreated rapidly. By the
   summer of 1529 they had been expelled from Italy and peace was concluded
   at Cambrai in August. Cf Ep 1931 n11.
11 Pope Clement VII, who was vacillatory by nature as well as preoccupied with
   the welfare of his native Florence, the papal states, and Italy in general, had
   changed sides so many times in the Hapsburg-Valois struggle for control of

the world with destruction. These are the things we wretched men busy ourselves with while you theologians dispute the articles of faith. A tiny portion of our lives redounds to the glory of God. May he have mercy on us, else he cannot be far from venting his terrible anger upon us. If I can 80 be of service to you in any way at court, you have only to give the command, for I sincerely wish to show some token of my devotion towards you. Farewell.

Buda, 2 February, in the year 1528

Yours, ever at your service, Johann Hornburg, secretary of the most 85 reverend bishop of Trent

To the most renowned and learned Master Erasmus of Rotterdam, revered teacher

1936 / Heinrich Eppendorf to Huldrych Zwingli   3 February 1528

This letter was clearly written in the morning, before the arbitration described in the following letter. See Ep 1934 introduction. The autograph of the letter is in the Staatsarchiv at Zürich (E II 339 173). It was first published in Johann Kaspar Hess *Lebensbeschreibung M. Ulrich Zwinglis* (Zürich 1811) II (= the 'litteraraisch-historischer Anhang' by Leonard Usteri) 603.

Greetings. I had intended to go to Bern to hear how you and the brethren were comparing the Scriptures,[1] but under the pressure of various duties,

* * * * *

Italy that his reliability as an ally was open to question, particularly by the Hapsburgs. Most recently he had joined with Francis I in the League of Cognac (1526) against Charles V, only to abandon it in favour of a truce with the emperor in March 1527 and then rejoin it in April (Pastor 9 371–84). A month later the sack of Rome made Clement the virtual prisoner of the emperor, with no choice but to seek an accommodation with him. By October 1528, relations between pope and emperor had improved sufficiently that Clement, who had fled Rome at the end of 1527, could return to it (cf Ep 1987 n1). Full reconciliation would come in the form of the Treaty of Barcelona in June 1529 (cf Ep 2038 n11).

1936
1 The reference is to the Bern Disputation (6–26 January 1528), which had been called by the government of Bern and was attended by representatives (both theologians and laymen) of a number of Swiss and German cities, including Zürich and Strasbourg. The result was a victory for Zwingli's doctrinal position, which the city council of Bern enacted into law in its *Religionsmandat* of 7 February. For more details, see Ep 1988 n1.

after the feast, as they say,[2] I landed in Basel, inquiring of others what I had
expected to hear in person. However, I do not doubt that Christ was there
to further his own purposes, however loud the opposition of those who give   5
their favour to the Antichrist.

I am here now to force the great Erasmus to recant. For by heaping up
so many falsehoods against me in secret and without my knowledge he has
traduced me before our prince, George of Saxony, so that not only my reputation is at stake but all my fortunes and my life itself. I hope that I shall con-   10
duct the case in such a way that the old man will repent of his malice. If you
have any works of Hutten, I ask that you send them to us or at least let me
know in the space of four days. I shall not linger long here, taking care that
the deceased receive the honour that is due him.[3] In the meantime keep well.

From Basel, 3 February 1528   15
Heinrich Eppendorf
To the excellent Master Huldrych Zwingli of Zürich, his dear friend etc

1937 / From Beatus Rhenanus and Bonifacius Amerbach

3 February 1531

The original manuscript of this letter, in the hand of Bonifacius Amerbach, is
in the Bibliothèque municipale in Nantes (MS 674 fol 15). The letter was first
published in Erasmus' *Admonitio adversus mendacium* (Freiburg 1530) fol A 5,
and then in the other two sources for the documents appended to Ep 1934. On
the content of the letter, see Ep 1934 introduction.

Since you have both agreed to give us the right of peacefully settling the
dispute between you, we have decided that, to avoid trouble and to further
Christian concord, Master Erasmus shall fulfil the first two articles, as he has
agreed in writing. In place of the third he will not object to give, in the same
spirit, approximately twenty florins in aid of the poor to be distributed at   5
our discretion.[1]

* * * * *

2 An allusion to the adage 'You have come too late for the feast,' ie you have
  missed an important piece of business; *Adagia* I ix 52, II ix 52
3 A puzzling passage, the meaning of which seems to be that Eppendorf considered Hutten's reputation as well as his own to be at stake in the arbitration
  with Erasmus, which he expected to be concluded quickly.

1937
1 The type of florin, whether a gold coin or a money-of-account, is not specified. Possibly these are Imperial (Rhenish) gold florins. For other references

And we are of the opinion that these actions can be taken without prejudice to either side; in such a way that with all offences, grievances, and suspicions on both sides laid to rest, you may engage anew in a contest of benevolence, forgetting all of the past, as if nothing had ever been said or done.   10

Master Heinrich Eppendorf will suppress whatever he has written; and to each party we give the freedom either to exchange some symbol of benevolence or be satisfied with mutual good will.

Done at Basel on the day after the feast of the Purification, in the year 1528   15

Beatus Rhenanus and Bonifacius Amerbach

1938 / To George of Austria   Basel [c 3 February 1528]

First published in the *Opus epistolarum*, the letter is clearly contemporary with Ep 1939.

George of Austria (1504–57) was a bastard son of Emperor Maximilian I who grew up at the court of Margaret of Austria in the Netherlands and was educated there with the future Charles v and Ferdinand I. In the autumn of 1525, after studies at Alcalá, he was elected bishop of Bressanone (Brixen) but spent much time at the courts of his Hapsburg relatives. In 1539 he became bishop of Valencia and then, in 1544, prince-bishop of Liège, where he resided until his death. Although he probably never met Erasmus, George took an interest in his writings, and this letter is Erasmus' polite refusal of an invitation to reside in Bressanone and enjoy George's patronage there.

ERASMUS OF ROTTERDAM TO GEORGE, BISHOP OF BRESSANONE, GREETING

The letter from Jerome Viromandus, as learned as it was gracious, most illustrious Prince George, gave me no ordinary or simple pleasure.[1] This was because, first of all, I understood that an office of responsibility was entrusted to a man of your exceptional talent, born for great things, not so   5 much through the favour as through the wisdom of Emperor Charles and King Ferdinand, so that you might display, exercise, and show forth the excellent endowments of your nature and character. If it is true, according to

* * * * *

to unspecified florins see Epp 1934:12 and 442, 1993:51, 1994A:78–9, 2000:25–6, 2014:38–9, 2015:1–2, 2024:10–11 and 18–19, 2033:20, 2036:5, and 2053:19.

1938
1 See Ep 1939.

the Greek proverb, that the exercise of office is what proves a man's worth,[2]   10
as the courage of a good leader is evident in war and the skill of a good
helmsman in a storm, then I can have no doubt that this lofty, upright, and
pious mind of yours is destined for greater accomplishments by the decree
of God, who governs the affairs of men by his eternal wisdom. But divine
providence wished this to be only the first step, the apprenticeship or the   15
aedileship, as I might put it, of your career. When you have given conspicuous proof of your abilities you will quickly be elevated to the praetorship
and then to the consulship, that is, to the pinnacle of power, not only by the
judgment of kings but by the unanimous votes of everyone.[3]

In the meantime, most esteemed Bishop, I should like to congratulate   20
your Eminence and even more the royal authority itself, which has been
granted such an excellent helmsman in the midst of so many storms and
in the general turbulence of the times, who not only by his authority but
also by his skill, wisdom, prudence, and good judgment will be able to calm
the chaotic disturbances of our days. It is also a cause for personal rejoic-   25
ing; I am grateful to you that you are so kindly disposed towards my humble writings that you lend me your sincere support and openly defend me
against my detractors, whose licence in these times knows no limit, and finally, that you go so far as to offer me to share in your good fortunes if ever
I should wish to take up my abode in your province. In this I acknowledge   30
and admire greatly the extraordinary kindness and enthusiastic favour of
your father, Emperor Maximilian, towards those who cherish piety and the
study of good letters, in whose number you seem so kind as to include me.
As for myself, I acknowledge no other merit, if I can claim any at all, than
my steadfast determination and untiring efforts.   35

But although I am sometimes gratified and deem myself fortunate to be
invited by the most kind and honorific letters of so many princes, kings, and
prelates to accept circumstances by no means to be disdained,[4] I must also
sometimes deplore my lot, which bears some resemblance to that suffered by
Tantalus in the underworld, as the instructive tales of the poets tell us.[5] They   40
say that, as he was tormented by hunger and thirst, a stream of drinkable

* * * * *

2 *Adagia* i x 76
3 Roman politicians generally followed a *cursus honorum* 'path of honours' that
  moved through four ranks, starting with 'quaestor' and proceeding through
  'aedile' and 'praetor' to 'consul.'
4 Most recently to France (Ep 1805:174–6), to Poland (Ep 1652:116–32), to England (Epp 1697:103–5, 1816:27–45), and to Leipzig (Ep 1683:1–3). Cf Epp 2029:
  100–2, 2037 n40, 2054:5–11.
5 *Adagia* ii vi 14

water that lay beneath him reached his lips and fruit dangled before his
mouth, but in such a way that despite his pitiful longing he could not enjoy either the food or the drink. What is in question is not so much my age,
although it too is becoming burdensome, but my health, more fragile than   45
glass, although up to now, because of my well-ordered life, it survives the
great exertions involved in my studies, which a robust young man could
hardly have sustained. If this were not so, my mind would not shrink from
leaving this city: I have enjoyed its hospitality for many years, not disagree-
ably, to be sure, but I wish those who gave themselves up to new beliefs   50
had been fewer.

For that reason I do not entirely refuse what you in your great kindness
offer to me. I shall consider what the situation itself counsels. For it is not just
any climate whatsoever, or any wine or diet, that is suitable for this frail little
body. Otherwise I should wish to spend whatever life is left to me under the   55
protection of such a genial prince, even at my own expense, and all the more
willingly since I hear that Bernhard, bishop of Trent,[6] whose extraordinary
devotion to me has manifested itself on more than one occasion, lives not
far away. In the meantime, I am no less grateful, illustrious Prince, than if I
had accepted the gift of your kindness, since I enjoy your generous favour.   60
I pray God Almighty that it be his will that the ecclesiastical career that you
have begun may continue to be blessed with prosperity and good fortune.
Given at Basel

1939 / To Hieronymus Viromandus   Basel, 3 February 1528

Very little is known about Hieronymus Viromandus, who was probably from
Vermand (near Saint-Quentin). After studies at the Collegium Trilingue (lines
5–6), he was in 1525 secretary to Sir Richard Wingfield, English ambassador to
Spain. He was now secretary to George of Austria and had evidently written
the letter (answered by Ep 1938) in which George invited Erasmus to reside
in Bressanone.

This letter was first published in the *Opus epistolarum*.

ERASMUS OF ROTTERDAM TO HIERONYMUS VIROMANDUS,
GREETING
Your letter, my dearest Viromandus, gave me very great pleasure, since it
contained nothing that was not joyful and cheering. I was delighted from
the first by the very fact that you declare yourself a student of Jérôme de   5

* * * * *

6 Bernhard von Cles (Ep 1357). For Erasmus' most recent relations with him,
see Ep 1935:2–3, 66–8.

Busleyden. In addition I took special pleasure in the elegance, clarity, and refinement of your letter, but much more in the friendly sentiments that emanated from it. Most delightful of all was the news that an excellent young man, in whom the favour and generosity of the emperor Maximilian towards the world of learning lives on, so to speak, has been appointed to the diocese of Bressanone, especially since his sentiments towards me are such as you describe. Would that such a patron existed somewhere in the near vicinity! For I have long been thinking of leaving here,[1] although my state of health not only persuades me but almost compels me to stay. Up to now I was in very good favour with both sides in the city; now I feel I am malodorous to the more revolutionary among the citizen body. But first of all I am terrified by the length of the journey and secondly by the mountainous region, whose quality of wines is unknown to me. These harsh, rustic wines are very unsuitable to my constitution because of the kidney stone; I drink Burgundy wine, only the light reds. I wrote to your reverend prelate but somewhat tardily.[2] So many tasks and so many tragic events have intervened that I have almost lost my mind.[3] I wish you the best of health.

Given at Basel on the eve of the Purification. In the year 1528

1940 / To Duke George of Saxony   [4 February] 1528

This is the letter that Erasmus was required to write to Duke George as part of the mediated settlement with Heinrich Eppendorf. See Ep 1934 introduction.

The original manuscript, in a secretary's hand but signed by Erasmus, is in the Staatsarchiv Dresden (Loc 10300 fol 27). The letter was first published as Ep 11 in Horawitz I.

Greetings, most serene Prince. I do not know what your Highness has written to Heinrich Eppendorf;[1] I know only from a letter of Simon Pistoris that you wrote to him.[2] But a few days after receiving your letter he came to Basel,[3] very much disturbed and threatening to bring me to trial, brandishing a

* * * * *

1939
1 See Ep 1926 n8.
2 Ep 1938
3 See Ep 1926 n6.

1940
1 See Ep 1929:13–14 and n5.
2 Pistoris' letter is not extant; probably of the same date as the letter from Duke George that was answered by Ep 1929.
3 C 30 January; see Ep 1934 introduction.

certain letter that he suspected I had written to your illustrious Highness,[4]   5
in which it was alleged that he was forced to move from Freiburg to Basel
partly because of the tumult he had stirred up there and partly because of
debts he had amassed;[5] and that when he had similarly distinguished himself in Basel he moved from here to Strasbourg and there displayed himself
as a leader and champion of the impious Lutheran cause.[6]   10

.I had no knowledge whatsoever of this letter written in a hand unknown to me, nor do I find it among my papers, nor do I think it originated from me. I am not aware whether your serene Highness is angry
with Heinrich Eppendorf, and if you are, it is not clear to me for what reasons you should be so. I should certainly have wished that he were in your   15
good graces by his merits. I know that I wrote to your Highness asking that
you would divert this young man of exceptional talents from a life of indo-.
lence and luxury to some honourable occupation.[7] I wrote in a similar vein
to Hieronymus Emser, at the time of the last fair,[8] when Heinrich Eppendorf was threatening hostile action by letter for the third time,[9] adding that   20
I did not wish in any way that your illustrious Highness would inflict any
harm on him but that at one and the same time you would both look after
his interests and provide a respite from him for me and my studies. I often
wrote letters to your illustrious Highness and to the officials at your court,
especially Emser and Pistoris, but I cannot recall everything I wrote.   25

But if through any of my writings and complaints you have become
more unfriendly to him, I should wish that you renew your former favour
and benevolence towards this beneficiary of your kindness. This is especially
fitting since we have reaffirmed the friendship between us, laying aside all
resentments and suspicions, as it behoves Christians to do, and shall here-   30
after rival one another once again in manifestations of good will. This was
brought about by mutual friends, learned and virtuous men, who thought it
would be to the advantage of us both, especially to me since, worn out by old
age and poor health and the immense fatigues of my studies and untrained in

* * * * *

4 See Ep 1934:10–11, 73–4, 464–5.
5 Allen (7n) cites a protocol of the University of Freiburg, dated 13 May 1522, indicating that at the instance of his creditors a citation had been issued against
  'the noble Heinrich von Eppendorf in Basel.'
6 Cf Ep 1934:73–5, 410–12.
7 C April 1524. See Epp 1122, 1313, 1893:44–8. Many of Erasmus' letters on this
  subject were intercepted and long delayed; see Ep 1448 introduction.
8 In September 1527, at the same time as Ep 1869. Cf Ep 1923:1–3.
9 Eppendorf's letter is not extant, but see Ep 1934:55, 110, 192. Traces of its two
  predecessors are found in Epp 1377:2–5, 1449:67–72.

the language of litigation, I am not at all prepared to engage in a lawsuit. Ru- 35
mours are often ill-founded and suspicions not infrequently are in error. But
if Heinrich Eppendorf will fulfil the expectations of your most serene Highness, he will render himself dear to me on two counts: because I shall have acquired a friend instead of an enemy and because he will gain the approval of
the prince to whom I have recommended him more than once in my letters.[10] 40
To the latest letter of your eminent Highness,[11] brief but full of affection, I
responded some time ago,[12] entrusting it to a young man conspicuous for his
good qualities. I wish for your most serene Highness unending happiness.

Given at Basel in the year of our Lord 1528

To your eminent Highness, your most devoted servant Erasmus of Rot- 45
terdam. Signed by my own hand

To the most illustrious Prince George, duke of Saxony, landgrave of
Thuringia and margrave of Meissen

1941 / To Heinrich Eppendorf   [Basel, circa 5 February 1528]

This is the dedicatory letter that Erasmus undertook to write as part of his
settlement with Eppendorf. It was preserved in Eppendorf's *Iusta querela* (see
Ep 1934 introduction), fol A8. According to Eppendorf's own account in that
work (cited in Allen's introduction), Erasmus refused to produce it until Eppendorf had complied with his demand for an affirmation of a more friendly
disposition (cf Ep 1934:533–5).

ERASMUS OF ROTTERDAM TO HEINRICH EPPENDORF, GREETING
The rich send to the rich horses, tapestries, precious stones, and gold, mute
and impermanent gifts, which cannot make better or more worthy of honour
the one to whom they are sent, while they make poorer the one from whom
they originate. Among those who are joined by a common love of literature 5
it is fitting that different kinds of gifts should be exchanged, which do not
take away from the giver and bring both profit and honour to the recipient. Therefore I send this little book dedicated to your name, a memento of
the literary association that once existed between us, which I strongly wish
will endure forever. And let us not allow evil tongues to destroy our friend- 10
ship, which was brought about under the auspices of the Muses, despite the
efforts of some people to set us against each other.

* * * * *

10 See Ep 1934 n84.
11 The duke's letter of early January; see Ep 1928:2–3.
12 In Ep 1929. Duke George had not yet responded to Ep 1924; see Ep 1951:4–5.

But I shall not detain you any further, so that you may be free to hear what my little book has to say.

1942 / To Duke George of Saxony   Basel, 5 February 1528

The manuscript, in Erasmus' own hand (except for the address), is in the University Library at Leiden (Papenbroeck 2). In his introduction, Allen gives the evidence for concluding that, until sometime after 1706, the manuscript was part of the Deventer Letter-book. The letter was first published in the *Opus epistolarum*. It is striking that, except perhaps in lines 10–11, Erasmus makes no reference to Ep 1940, which he had written the previous evening as part of the settlement with Eppendorf.

SINCERE GREETINGS, MOST SERENE PRINCE
I neither had the time to write (and your Highness perhaps even less time to read a prolix letter) nor did I have anything important to write about. But since I ran into Frans van der Dilft,[1] a young man born of a family that was not only renowned and wealthy but also of upright morals, whose un- 5 feigned and noble character I have been able to observe from daily contacts, I decided to send at least my greeting to your illustrious Highness through him. If you will deign to grant him an audience, you will be able to learn from him all that pertains to my affairs, which he knows better than I. He is a man of the highest trustworthiness and reliability. I have learned at my 10 own expense how unsafe it is to commit everything to a letter. May the Lord preserve happy and prosperous your illustrious Lordship, to whom I offer myself entirely.
    Given at Basel on the Nones of February, 1528
    The servant of your eminent Lordship, Erasmus of Rotterdam. In my 15 own hand
    To the most illustrious Prince, Duke George of Saxony, landgrave of Thuringia and margrave of Meissen

* * * * *

1942
1 Dilft (Ep 1663), member of a wealthy Antwerp family who later had a successful political career in imperial service, was now at the end of a second period of residence with Erasmus in Basel. At this point, Dilft embarked on a leisurely journey through Germany, visiting many of Erasmus' friends and patrons on the way and eventually arriving in the Netherlands (Epp 1942–5, 1972, 1977, 1979, 1981–2, 1991, 1994A).

1943 / To Simon Pistoris   Basel, 5 February 1528

The autograph of this letter, which was first published as Ep 8 in Horawitz
II is in the Staatsbibliothek zu Berlin (Preussische Kulturbesitz MS Boruss Fol
201.14). On Simon Pistoris (1489–1562), chancellor to Duke George of Saxony
and a trusted supporter of Erasmus, see Ep 1125 n6. For the letter to which
this is a response, see Ep 1929 introduction.

Cordial greetings. After the incredible fuss that Heinrich Eppendorf stirred
up here, the matter has been settled between us through the mediation of
good men under conditions that you will be able to ascertain from Frans van
der Dilft, the bearer of this, a young man of noble station in his own country
and perfect honesty.[1] Whether you will think these conditions fair I do not   5
know; as for myself, I think I have bought my peace at a small price. The
letter from the duke[2] had sent him into a frenzy. I foresaw that this would
be the case, although I understood from your letter that it was written in
a polite manner. Nevertheless, I am most grateful to you, my dear Pistoris,
for your solicitude.   10
      I wished to reread your letter but I could not lay my hands on it. If I
remember, you seem to betray in it a less than high regard for my writings.
You say that many things can be found in them contrary to the dogmas of
the ancient writers, but you excuse me with the pretext that I do not have the
obstinacy of a Montanus[3] or a Luther. I'll pass over the obstinacy. I should   15
like you to point out to me which beliefs of mine are contrary to the primitive beliefs of the orthodox writers of the church. For I have not yet been
able to discover them, although there are many things in my writings that
are at variance with the foolish opinions and depraved morals of men. We
see that the world is heading in a fatal spiral towards a profound change.   20
For the present we have experienced the results obtained by the articles
and protests of theologians and the violent behaviour of some. This pestilence demands another remedy, believe me. At the beginning of this evil
my sage advice was not heeded; as it progressed my repeated admonitions

* * * * *

1943
1 Ep 1942 n1
2 See Ep 1929:12–13.
3 Montanus, founder (in the second century) of the apocalyptic and ascetic movement known as Montanism, which won the adherence of the African church
   Father Tertullian

were not heeded. Now I hear that certain people are planning even more 25
brutal measures, and I fear that the situation may get worse. Only by the
mutual agreement of rulers and the abolition or correction of certain things
can this tempest be quelled. I see no other remedy.

I do not write this in favour of those who bring destruction upon themselves – that is what many of them desire for me – but in favour of princes 30
and the state. And I fear that I shall be called too veracious a prophet when
it is too late. If peace cannot be negotiated immediately between rulers, then
at least a truce can be declared for a few years. In the meantime through a
common strategy some remedy could be found. You see, my dear Pistoris,
how much hatred I have fomented for myself in all of Germany, although 35
previously I enjoyed great popularity there. I alienated the learned, of whom
a great number favour the new beliefs. And yet I was not unaware that certain stupid theologians allied with unprincipled monks would set upon me
with a gladiator's spirit.[4] I never had any disagreements with holy monks or
sincere theologians, but rather was in perfect accord with them. Now neither 40
can the emperor, despite his wholehearted support of my cause, defend me
from the mad fury of the monks in Spain,[5] nor can the king of France himself,
though he sincerely wishes me well, save me from the frenzies of men like
Béda[6] and Cousturier.[7] I see that I must leave Germany, as hatreds mount

* * * * *

4 Just as Erasmus frequently described himself as a gladiator doing battle with
  his enemies (see Ep 1934 n1), so he also described those enemies as attacking
  him 'with a gladiator's spirit,' ie with the intention either to kill or get killed;
  see Adagia I iii 76, and Epp 2046:374, 2053:2.
5 See Ep 1926 n4.
6 Noël Béda (Ep 1571) was the arch-conservative syndic (presiding officer) of
  the faculty of theology at Paris and Erasmus' most relentless critic in France.
  Convinced of the unorthodoxy of the views of Erasmus, Lefèvre d'Etaples,
  and other humanist scholars, Béda from 1519 took every opportunity in the
  deliberations of the theological faculty to attack them as secret supporters of
  Luther. Starting in April 1525 (Ep 1571), he and Erasmus engaged in an extensive and increasingly hostile correspondence that lasted until November 1527
  (Epp 1579, 1581, 1596, 1609–10, 1620, 1642, 1679, 1685, 1906). Meanwhile, in
  1526, Béda published his Annotationes against Erasmus and Lefèvre (Ep 1642
  n5). In 1526–7, Erasmus replied not only with a series of published works,
  culminating in the Supputatio errorum in censuris Bedae, but also with appeals
  to the faculty of theology, King Francis I, and the Parlement of Paris to silence Béda (Epp 1902, 1905, 2033 nn14–16). Béda, however, continued his campaign against Erasmus with the full support of the theological faculty, and the
  controversy continued unabated through 1528 and into 1529.
7 Pierre Cousturier (known in Latin as Sutor), a French Carthusian who was the
  ally of Noël Béda in his opposition to the views and methods of the humanists.

and sects multiply.[8] But if I had even a fraction of the spirit you seem to   45
suspect I have, I would not put up with this. I still do not regret my actions.

But I have dwelt on this too long. Do not cease, on your part, to commend me to the most serene Prince.

Farewell. Given at Basel 5 February 1528

I ask that the young man whom I send to you be made aware that I   50
have recommended him to you most warmly.

To the distinguished Master Simon Pistoris, chancellor of the most illustrious duke of Saxony

1944 / To Philippus Melanchthon   Basel, 5 February 1528

Of the several extant manuscripts of this letter (= MBW Ep 654) the best, first
published by Allen, is MS Lat 10357.19 in the Camerarius collection of the Bayerische Staatsbibliothek Munich. It is the copy of the letter that Melanchthon
himself made and sent to Joachim Camerarius soon after receiving the original. Subsequently, Melanchthon also supplied Camerarius with a copy in
which he had softened the harsh comment on Luther in lines 3–5 by eliminating Luther's name and putting everything into the passive voice. This was
the basis for the first printed version of the letter, the one found in volume
2 of Camerarius' edition of the letters of Helius Eobanus Hessus, *Libellus al-
ter epistolas complectens Eobani* (Leipzig 1557). The Camerarius version can be
seen in *Supplementa Melanchthoniana: Werke Philipp Melanchthons die im Corpus
Reformatorum vermisst werden* 6/1 ed Otto Clemen et al (Leipzig 1926; repr
Frankfurt 1968) 414 no 640. The text reproduced in CR 2 844 from yet another
sixteenth-century printed edition is misdated at 1535. For further information,
see Allen's introduction.

The letter is an olive branch extended by Erasmus to Melanchthon after
the bad feelings caused by the recently published *Hyperaspistes* 2 (Ep 1853).
Melanchthon's reply is Ep 1981.

* * * * *

At the beginning of 1525 he published an attack on all new translations of the
Bible, including that of Erasmus (*De tralatione Bibliae*), to which Erasmus responded a few months later with *Apologia adversus Petrum Sutorem*. This was
the beginning of a controversy that would last several years and involve additional publications on both sides. Erasmus regarded Cousturier as one of
his most malevolent and incompetent critics, given to opinions so extreme as
to place him outside the bounds of acceptable academic debate. See Epp 1571
n10, 1591, 1614, 1658 n7, 1687:2.

8 See Ep 1926 n8.

Greetings. Certain Articles have arrived here;[1] but some that were included in the table of contents were missing from the book.[2] I wonder how this happened. Would that Luther had been equally zealous in avoiding occasions to create disorder and in promoting good morals as he was vehement in the defence of dogmas! As for myself, since I see there is no remedy in these 5 disturbances, I support the cause of good letters, and yet I have a foreboding of their doom. In this sphere you have greater influence, being younger and more learned and more fortunate; and yet I too have achieved some results.

The bearer of this letter is a young man of unblemished character, 10 born of a family highly respected in his region, strongly devoted to all men of learning, but especially to you; you would make him exceedingly happy if you would deign to grant him an audience. His name is Frans van der Dilft,[3] a man who has lived with me in my household and has earned my high regard and approval. He is a person of unimpeachable integrity. 15 Farewell.

Given at Basel, 5 February 1528

Erasmus of Rotterdam wrote this in his own hand.

To the most learned and accomplished Philippus Melanchthon

1945 / To Joachim Camerarius   Basel, [c 5 February] 1528

The manuscript, autograph throughout, is in the Camerarius collection of the Bayerische Staatsbibliothek Munich (MS Lat 10357.18). The letter, clearly contemporary with Epp 1942–4, was first printed in Camerarius' edition of the letters of Eobanus (Ep 1944 introduction). On Camerarius, see Ep 1501 introduction.

* * * * *

1944

1 Melanchthon was a member of the commission appointed by Elector John of Saxony in 1527 to conduct a visitation of all the parishes in his lands. For the guidance of the visitors in examining the doctrine of the pastors, Melanchthon wrote *Articuli de quibus egerunt per visitatores in regione Saxoniae* (CR 26 7–27), which in August 1527 were published without his knowledge by Nicholas Schirlentz at Wittenberg and became the subject of theological controversy (see Ep 1981 n9). Erasmus' interest would doubtless have been aroused by the Basel reprint of the *Articuli* issued by Froben sometime in the autumn of 1527.

2 The list of topics on the verso of the title page of the *Articuli* (CR 26 7–8) was not a table of contents at all but rather a list of twenty subjects on which the pastors were to be examined.

3 Ep 1942 n1

Autograph letter from Erasmus to Joachim Camerarius
Camerarius Collection, MS Lat 10357.18
Bayerische Staatsbibliothek München

I do not complain about your silence,[1] as long as your long-standing good will towards me continues. I greatly desire to know how literary studies are faring there. I heard they are not doing too well.[2] No matter how much conflicts of opinion rage, we are of one mind in our common desire to enhance the study of good letters. Our efforts at Louvain are progressing very well, 5 despite the murmurings of monks and theologians.[3]

The bearer of this letter, Frans van der Dilft,[4] is a young man of rare talent and unblemished integrity, who has undertaken this journey for no other reason than to meet the scholars of Germany in person. Let him see for himself that Joachim is exactly as I described him. Farewell. 10

Given at Basel in the year 1528

To the most learned Master Joachim, professor of Greek literature at Nürnberg

1946 / From Justin Gobler   Koblenz, 5 February 1528

First published as Ep 59 in Enthoven, the autograph of this letter is in the Rehdiger Collection at the University Library in Wrocław (MS Rehd 254.76).

After taking a degree in law, Justin Gobler (c 1502–67), of St Goar on the Rhine near Boppard, had settled in Koblenz (in the archbishopric of Trier), where he continued his legal studies under the patronage of the archbishops Richard von Greiffenklau (d 1531) and Johann von Metzenhausen (d 1540). Starting in the 1530s, he wrote works on history and law while in the service of a number of city councils, princes, and bishops (further details in Allen's introduction). In 1559 he retired to Frankfurt to devote himself to his studies and writing. The letter was written in response to a request for a manuscript wanted for inclusion in Beatus Rhenanus' second edition of Tertullian (Basel: Froben, March 1528).

CORDIAL GREETINGS, MOST LEARNED ERASMUS
You seem to have made the same urgent request by letter of Doctor George

* * * * *

1945
1 Perhaps since Ep 1501 in 1524
2 See Epp 1901:21–3, 2006:19–20, 2008:39–40.
3 Probably a reference to the Collegium Trilingue. Ep 1932, with its gratifying account of developments at the College of the Lily, would not have reached him yet.
4 Ep 1942 n1

and the Carthusian monk[1] that Carinus made to the chancellor,[2] both of
you earnestly pleading that Tertullian's little work *De spectaculis* be sent
there to Froben to be printed. It is believed that after the death of Doctor   5
Fabricius,[3] a good man of cherished memory, the book passed into the hands
of his wife. Since it was I who married her, I had a visit, after the death of
George, from Furster[4] and the prior concerning this matter. They were both
eager to support your cause and that of good letters generally. Although
I would have gladly been of service to them in any circumstances, not to   10
speak of such a just request, I regretted very much that I was not able to
help them. I searched my library from top to bottom, wishing to give proof
of my friendship and devotion first of all to you, the most learned man in
the world of letters, then also to my very good friend Carinus and to the
printer, Froben. But I must confess that for the present I have not set eyes   15
on it or been able to find it. My wife says that it may have been taken to
Spain with other books and disappeared there, for after the death of her
husband various books were carried off hither and thither by those from
whom he was accustomed to borrow them. Torresani[5] had borrowed for

* * * * *

1946
1 The identity of 'Doctor George' is uncertain. Allen speculated that Erasmus,
  informed that the desired manuscript was in Carthusian hands, might have
  addressed his appeal for it to Gregor Reisch (Ep 308 introduction), who had
  been visitor of the Carthusian province of the Rhine but who, unbeknownst
  to Erasmus, had died in 1525. The Carthusian monk is evidently the prior
  referred to in line 8 below.
2 Ludovicus Carinus (see Ep 1799 introduction), who had been living in Koblenz
  as a private tutor, had evidently returned to Basel with his pupil, Valentin
  Furster (line 8 below). For reasons that are not clear, Carinus and Erasmus
  would soon have a bitter falling-out (Epp 2048:54–6, 2063). The chancellor of
  Richard von Greiffenklau, archbishop of Trier, was Ludwig Furster (d 1528/9),
  not the 'Henricus Duntginus' tentatively identified by Allen.
3 A native of Koblenz, Ulricus Fabricius (Ulrich Windemacher, 1489–1526), studied at Erfurt and became a humanist scholar in the service of Richard von
  Greiffenklau, devoting much time and effort to the search for ancient manuscripts during embassies to Spain and Italy. His only published work is the
  Processus iudiciarius (Basel c 1542), which includes in the prefatory material
  a biography of him that is presumably by Gobler, who edited the volume.
  Fabricius' extensive correspondence has apparently been lost.
4 Valentin; see Ep 1798 introduction.
5 The reference is to either Gianfrancesco Torresani of Asola (Ep 1349 introduction) or his father Andrea (Ep 212 6n), who were now running the Aldine
  press in Venice.

a time Fortunatianus, Victorinus and the author of *De curatione boum* to- 20
gether with other anonymous books,[6] but I see no mention of Tertullian
written in the inventory. Therefore I cannot imagine in whose hands the
book of this great theologian has fallen, where it is exiled, or where it is
lurking. If I should happen upon a copy of it in some way, it will be delivered to you, Erasmus, as quickly as possible, as I swear by the Muses. Far 25
from wishing to seek any personal gain in this matter, I would procure it
at my own expense to oblige you. It grieves me that I am prevented from
demonstrating my good will to you when such an opportunity presents itself, which would be a source of great pride for me, and I am sorry to see
you disappointed in your expectations. 30

But there are among other things two ancient manuscripts belonging
to someone else; one of them contains Dionysius the Areopagite, the other
Polycrates, both of them written in a beautiful Greek hand.[7] If you should
like to compare them with your own copies or if you think them worthy of
commentary or of an edition by Froben, I shall have no objections to sending 35
them to you; indeed I shall discharge my obligations to their rightful owners.

I have written to the official at Trier, Doctor Matthias,[8] once a very
close friend of Fabricius, to ask that if he should learn something about the
Tertullian he would communicate it to us. I wish and desire earnestly to
oblige you in this matter. Farewell, and may you live on for many years for 40
your Germany.

At Koblenz, on the feast of Agatha the Virgin, in the year 1528

* * * * *

6 The works of Chirius Fortunatianus, a late Roman author (fl 450), were published by the Aldine firm in 1523; his manual of rhetoric in question-and-
   answer form became popular in schools in the early modern period. Marius
   Victorinus (born around AD 300) wrote two books of commentary on Cicero's
   De inventione that were published by the Aldine firm in 1522. Neither in the
   case of Fortunatianus nor in that of Victorinus was any acknowledgment made
   of the loan of the manuscript. *De curatione boum* is unidentified. No such work
   was published by the Aldine press.
7 Four philosophical treatises were attributed to the Christian Platonist author
   (fl c 500) who took the name of the convert of Paul mentioned in Acts 17:34:
   *On the Divine Names; On the Celestial Hierarchy; On the Ecclesiastical Hierar-
   chy;* and *Mystical Theology.* He is now usually known as Pseudo-Dionysius
   the Areopagite. The Polycrates referred to here was probably the early Christian bishop, Polycrates of Ephesus (c 130–96), who is remembered chiefly for
   a letter to Pope Victor on the appropriate date for the celebration of Easter
   (Eusebius *Ecclesiastical History* 5.24).
8 Matthias von Saarburg (d 1539), who had recently become the 'official' of the
   archbishop of Trier, ie the presiding judge of the archiepiscopal court

Justin Gobler, citizen of Koblenz
To Erasmus of Rotterdam, at Basel, the most learned of all men by far

1947 / From Theoderich Zobel   Mainz, 9 February 1528

Theoderich (Dietrich) Zobel von Giebelstadt (d 1531) was (from 1506) vicar-
general of the archbishop of Mainz and (from 1518) scholaster of the cathedral chapter, a post that involved the supervision of teaching at the cathedral
school (see line 13). Particularly influential as an adviser to Archbishop Albert of Brandenburg, he was a patron and defender of humanists who practised moderation in response to the challenge of Lutheranism. Erasmus, who
may have been personally acquainted with Zobel (Ep 880 introduction), paid
him a flattering compliment in his dedicatory letter for Johann Schöffer's
new edition of Livy in 1519 (Ep 919). This letter was written in connection
with the early preparations for the Froben Livy, which appeared in March
1531.
    First published in Förstemann/Günther, the autograph of the letter, written
hastily in a difficult hand, was in the Burscher Collection at Leipzig (Ep 1254
introduction). Allen had difficulty deciphering the year-date, which could be
read as either 1528 or 1528/9. He opted for the former as being more consistent with German practice and more suited to the description of Hieronymus
Froben as the 'surviving heir,' an epithet most likely to be used of someone
whose father had died recently (26 October 1527). On the other hand, as Allen
also observes, the later date (February 1529) would place the letter closer to
the completion of the Froben Livy.

GREETINGS, O MOST CULTURED AND LEARNED OF MEN
AND TRUE THEOLOGIAN
I aspire after nothing more than to comply with the wishes of a man of such
stature, who has rendered such great service to Christian letters. For that
reason, I shall see immediately to the accomplishment of the small favour   5
you ask of me, to deliver into the hands of the surviving heir, Hieronymus Froben, the copy of Livy that you say is in the recesses of our library.
And since Hieronymus himself will be coming to the next fair, I shall grant
him his wish, since with you as his author and editor he cannot but produce excellent offspring. In the meantime be of good health and may Christ,   10
greatest and best, preserve you as long as possible for his religion.
    From Mainz, 9 February 1528
    Theoderich Zobel, master of the cathedral school
    To the most learned Master Erasmus of Rotterdam at Basel, great cham-
pion of sacred letters, patron worthy of every act of homage and respect   15

1948 / To Johann von Vlatten   Basel, 14 February 1528

This is the preface to the first edition of the *Dialogus cui titulus Ciceronianus, sive de optimo genere dicendi* (Basel: Froben, March 1528), which was published with *De recta pronuntiatione* (see Ep 1949). A revised version, with a new letter to Vlatten (Ep 2088) added, was published in October 1529.

For several years, Erasmus' relations with the Italian humanists had been getting increasingly acrimonious. They delighted in finding errors in his editions and translations of classical and patristic authors, criticized his Latin style, and impugned his orthodoxy (Epp 1341A:527–66, 1479, 1482, 1660 n9). He, in turn, found ludicrously narrow the refusal of some of the Italians to use much of the vocabulary of Christian discourse because it had not been used by Cicero (substituting *coelestis philosophia* for *evangelium*, for example), and he was quick to see this as the cover for a pagan spirit (Ep 1717 n2). The immediate target of the *Ciceronianus* was, however, a northerner, Christophe de Longueil (1488–1522). In 1519 Longueil, a native of Brabant who had been converted to Ciceronianism during studies in Italy, voiced criticisms of Erasmus' eclectic Latin style (Ep 914) to which Erasmus' wrote a carefully measured response (Ep 935). Later, the posthumous publication of Longueil's works in 1524 (see Ep 2059 n7) confirmed Erasmus' conviction that the young man had been a promising scholar spoiled by Ciceronianism. It also led to renewed Italian criticism of Erasmus as a Dutch barbarian unworthy among the northerners to be compared with the elegant Longueil (Epp 1675, 1701, 1706, 1713). It seems that by 1526 Erasmus had decided to respond (Ep 1720:50–6), and the topic was much on his mind in 1527 (Epp 1805:69–98, 1875:164–82, 1885:133–76). At the cost of some effort (Ep 1934:251–3) the work was completed and then published in the spring of 1528.

Erasmus expected the Italians to be furious, but he was surprised and dismayed by the uproar in France caused by a heavily ironic jest about Guillaume Budé being inferior as a Ciceronian to the publisher and bookseller Josse Bade (Epp 2021, 2027, 2038, 2050, 2056, 2066, 2077, 2088, 2105, 2119). The observation about the relative merits of Budé and Bade was made by the character Nosoponus, whom Erasmus had made the voice of Longueil and the Italian Ciceronians (Bulephorus being the personification of his own views). But the French equated Nosoponus with Erasmus and were outraged. Erasmus was obliged to explain himself at considerable length (Epp 2044, 2046, 2047, 2048) and to modify the offending passage in the second edition. He also found it necessary to apologize to some old friends, like Juan Luis Vives, whom he had thoughtlessly omitted from the list of those honoured with a favourable mention in the dialogue (Epp 2008, 2040, 2056) and to repair that oversight in the second edition. In Germany, Joachim Camerarius and Julius Pflug, both admirers of Erasmus, waxed indignant over the *Ciceronianus* but avoided public comment until after Erasmus' death. Melanchthon, who did not share the indignation of Camerarius and Pflug, privately belittled the *Ciceronianus* as little more than an act of posthumous revenge against Longueil. See MBW Epp 693, 696, 714, 2018, 2051.

For a more detailed discussion of the background, content, and reception of the *Ciceronianus*, see Betty I. Knott's introduction to her translation of the dialogue in CWE 28 324–34. The translation of the dedicatory letter to Vlatten used here is that made by Dr Knott and originally published in CWE 28 337–8. The annotation has been redone, incorporating the information supplied by Dr Knott in her notes.

Johann von Vlatten (Ep 1390) was an old friend and correspondent who in 1524 had become councillor to the duke of Cleves.

DESIDERIUS ERASMUS OF ROTTERDAM TO THE HONOURABLE
JOHANN VON VLATTEN, GREETING

My honourable friend, to prosper the state by wise and honest counsel is a noble task, and one especially appropriate to kingship. Homer for this reason calls the person in his poem who wielded supreme authority *boule-* 5 *phorus* 'giver of counsel.'[1] Men of this kind do the highest service to cities and countries at all times, and especially in our own age when some fated upheaval has thrown everything into total confusion – the Christian faith, kingdoms and republics, and the world of scholarship and letters. Everything is in such turmoil that the Greek proverb 'counsel is sacred'[2] is truer 10 than it ever was.

So it may seem irresponsible, criminal even, to claim your attention when you are engaged in this noble activity, which you perform with such honesty, alertness, and ability. But Horace rightly, I think, told his friend, 'Amidst your schemes and planning find frivolity a place,'[3] so here is a little 15 book from Erasmus to distract you with its nonsense from your gloomy and important preoccupations – though, to quote Horace again, 'this kind of nonsense has serious consequences.'[4] Far from having nothing to do with matters of public concern, it is particularly relevant to you as director of education in Aachen.[5] 20

* * * * *

1948
1 A frequent epithet of princes and leaders in the *Iliad*
2 *Adagia* II i 47
3 Horace *Odes* 4.12.27
4 Horace *Ars poetica* 451
5 Since 1517, Vlatten had been scholaster of the chapter of St Mary's in Aachen.

Good letters, which had begun to flourish and make some healthy growth, are now, as a result of general indifference combined with low moral standards, everywhere on the verge of extinction; and, as if this were not enough, there have been in existence for some time now persons who are trying to foist upon us what is more or less a new sect – 'Ciceroni- 25 ans' is the name they have taken, and they reject with intolerable arrogance any literary work that does not reproduce Cicero's stylistic characteristics. They keep the young from reading other writers and restrict them to the meticulous imitation of Cicero as their only model, yet no one reproduces Cicero's manner less effectively than these very persons who make 30 such ostentatious claims for themselves by brandishing this insubstantial title.

But what a disaster it would be for scholarship if it were accepted that no one but Cicero was to be read or imitated! There is, however, a suspicion of something else afoot under cover of this name, and that is to make us 35 pagans instead of Christians – though I believe our prime object is to ensure that good letters proclaim the glory of Christ our Lord and God, with all the richness, brilliance, and magnificence that Cicero displayed in speaking of things pagan. Moreover, I observe that a number of young men returning to us from Italy, especially from Rome, have been considerably infected by 40 these attitudes.

So it seemed to me that I would be doing something to serve religion and to aid the studies of our young people if I contributed some small work to the subject – not to dissuade young persons who are learning to write and speak from imitating Cicero (what could be stupider than that?), but 45 to show how we can genuinely represent Cicero and combine his supreme powers of expression with the faith of Christ.

This is the work I am now sending you. I have written it in dialogue form so that it will hold the reader's attention better and make more of an impression on the attitudes of students. Farewell. 50
Basel, 14 February 1528

1949 / To Maximilian (II) of Burgundy   Basel, [c February] 1528

This is the preface to *De recta Latini Graecique sermonis pronuntiatione dialogus* (Basel: Froben, March 1528). Second and third editions of the dialogue, without any change in this preface, appeared from the same press in October 1529 and March 1530. In all three cases, it was accompanied by the *Ciceronianus*. For an introduction to *De recta pronuntiatione*, which is a much livelier and broadly conceived work than its title indicates, see Maurice Pope's preface to his translation of the work in CWE 26 348–62. The translation of the letter used here is that made by Professor Pope (ibidem 365), whose annotations have been adapted to fit the present context.

On Maximilian of Burgundy, see Ep 1927 introduction. The presentation copy of this dialogue was delivered to the thirteen-year old Maximilian in Louvain on 15 March 1528 (Ep 1984).

DESIDERIUS ERASMUS OF ROTTERDAM TO THE MOST NOBLE YOUTH
MAXIMILIAN OF BURGUNDY, GREETING

Your eagerness to have a letter from me, dearest Maximilian, was most welcome testimony to your affection for me, and it was in no grudging spirit that I tried to satisfy your wishes in this matter. Although I was not just 5
busy, but swamped with work, I sent you a letter in my own hand, [1] reckoning that this would give it added value in your eyes. But when it was not delivered, and you were more upset than you would have been if you had lost one of your most cherished possessions, [2] your distress, to be honest, was deeply gratifying; for here was unmistakable proof that you were succeed- 10
ing, as by right of inheritance, to that remarkable attachment to me which was felt by your distinguished grandmother, Anna, and your most honoured father, Adolph, prince of Veere, whose friendship remained steady and undiminished from his earliest years. [3] But in the hope that a gracious act on my part may ease the pain caused by the treachery of others, I am 15
sending you, not a letter, but a book, *De recta pronuntiatione*; for in Greek and Latin alike the pronunciation that we use today has been to a large extent debased.

I decided to dedicate this work to you, not only because it seemed to suit your age and interests, but also because I have drawn a good propor- 20
tion of the examples from the vernacular speech of the Dutch, Brabanters, and French, with all of which I knew you to be familiar. Since the material is not in itself particularly entertaining, involving as it does some fine argument on points of detail, I have tried to dress it up in more alluring and attractive garb by treating it in the form of a dialogue, varying the 25
argument from time to time with passages to relieve or overcome the tedium of reading. Although I hear that you are being called from Louvain to the life of the palace, [4] the news has not deterred me from making the

* * * * *

1949
1 Ep 1859
2 Sentiments conveyed in Ep 1898
3 On Anna van Borssele and Adolph of Burgundy see Ep 1927.
4 See Ep 1927 n7.

dedication as I planned, since there is a place for study in a palace too, especially in the palace of a cardinal. For you must never abandon, either 30 in court or in the field, that love of sacred things you imbibed long ago with your lessons from Jan of Borsele, dean of Veere,[5] a man of great learning and of a most devout and upright character. If you take this advice, my dear Maximilian, then you will follow our most respected emperor in the distinction of your career as you recall him by your name, you will add 35 glory and lustre to the famous line of your ancestors, and finally you will do no inconsiderable service to the imperial court and to your country as a whole.

If this book pleases you, please be kind enough to share it with Maximilian van Ysselstein,[6] a young man of exceptional talent, and with the rest of 40 your companions, with whom you have entered on the most glorious contest of all, not of birth or wealth or rank, but of learning and honour. Farewell.

Basel, in the year of our Lord 1528

1950 / To [Bonifacius Amerbach]   [Basel, February 1928]

The manuscript (MS AN III 15 3 in the University Library at Basel) is a memorandum in Erasmus' hand enumerating, evidently for the arbitrators in his dispute with Eppendorf, new demands from the latter in excess of what had been agreed to in the settlement of 3 February. For the first six items on the list, cf Ep 1992:370–84. Like the editors of the *Epistolae familiares*, where the letter was first published as Ep 27, Allen viewed the text as a letter to Amerbach. The editors of AK, however, did not include it in their edition. Allen assigned the approximate date on the basis of the reference to the departure of the booksellers for the Frankfurt book fair (line 24).

The Latin original is sprinkled with verbs in the third person singular with no indication in the text itself of the identity of the 'he' or the 'it' in question. The names or words in brackets in items 1 and 2 supply the missing information.

* * * * *

5 Jan Becker (Ep 1984)
6 Maximiliaan van Egmond, lord of Ysselstein (d 1548). In 1519, while Maximiliaan was a student in Louvain, Erasmus took a personal interest in him, recommending Conradus Goclenius as his tutor (Ep 1018). Two years later, Erasmus reported that the young man visited him from time to time and was admirably proficient in Greek (Ep 1192:92–4). By the time of this letter, Maximiliaan had already served three years at the court of Erard de la Marck, prince-bishop of Liège, and had recently joined the court of Charles v in Spain (Ep 1984:17–21). In later years he had a distinguished career as a soldier and statesman in the service of the Hapsburgs in the Netherlands.

It is an established fact that Erasmus has more than complied with the terms
required by the arbitration.

1/ First of all, [Eppendorf] prescribed that [Erasmus] write [a letter] to the
Duke:[1] this exceeded the terms of the agreement.

2/ [Eppendorf] prescribed what should be included in [the letter]: this also
exceeded the terms of the agreement.

3/ He required on the evening before that the letter be ready on the next
morning:[2] this also exceeded the terms of the agreement.

4/ That after it was read by him it should be sealed in his presence:[3] this
also exceeded the terms of the agreement.

5/ That the letter be given to him to be delivered: this likewise.

6/ He demanded a preface[4] for the book before the book was written: this
likewise.

7/ Erasmus did not promise a dedication save in the name of friendship,
and on condition that he felt that Eppendorf had sincerely become his friend.
Whether Eppendorf fulfilled this obligation I have no knowledge. At any
rate he himself admits in a letter[5] that he had blabbed about many thousands of ducats. And the letter he makes so much of contains the insulting
charge of perfidy.

8/ Disregarding all of this, it is clear that this was not possible,[6] even if a
date had been stipulated; to which all who know me can testify.

9/ I can promise him nothing before the next book fair. The only thing I
have is the book on Chrysostom, in Greek,[7] which is not suitable for him,
and I promised it a year and a half ago to a Carthusian monk to whom I
feel great obligation.[8] Nonetheless I shall dedicate it to him if he wishes,
although I am not obliged to do so.

10/ Conclusion: He asks for what is not possible and is not owed to him according to the agreement. If in the meantime he engages in hostile intrigue,
he will be violating the obligations of the agreement.

* * * * *

1950
1 See Ep 1940.
2 On 5 February; see Ep 1992:410–12.
3 Cf Ep 1992:416–18.
4 See Ep 1941 and cf Ep 1992:413–14.
5 Not extant. Cf Epp 1991:30–1; 1992:168–71, 275–6, 436–8.
6 Ie the production of a book in such a hurry. Cf items 9 and 10.
7 Quite possibly the *Aliquot opuscula divi Chrysostomi Graeca* published in 1529
  with a dedicatory letter to Karel Uutenhove (Ep 2093). But see the following
  note.
8 Perhaps Levinus Ammonius, who had encouraged Erasmus to publish something of Chrysostom in the original Greek; see Ep 1463:159–61.

They are numbering the days before departure for the book fair.[9] But the book should have been ready by now if it were to be printed.   30

1951 / From Simon Pistoris   Dresden, 18 February 1528

The autograph of this letter, first published as Ep 83 in Förstemann/Günther, was in the Burscher Collection at Leipzig (Ep 1254 introduction). On Simon Pistoris, see Ep 1943.

S. T.[1]

Cordial greetings. In a recent letter written in response to the letter addressed to Emser I indicated to you that our prince would not write back. The reason for this was the hasty departure of the courier.[2] Therefore he is now sending a reply to certain parts of your letter, which on re-reading he   5
found somewhat disturbing.[3] And this formal response, I can assure you, is entirely his. For in the case of the letters sent to you in his name up until now, he supplied only the subject matter, but the style is of another. This answer, however, he formulated from his own head, composed and addressed in his own hand, and there is nothing here of anyone else except that it was   10
copied out by a scribe. For the rest I am extremely happy that you have accepted my apologies and have rid yourself of any suspicions. And you will be all the more convinced of my innocence from what I have related to you in the previously mentioned letter. Merely see to it that you treat these matters with the same secrecy as that in which they were written.   15

And since I am of that hope, I send you with this a copy of the letter Eppendorf sent here, which I opened in Otto's absence.[4] You will readily

* * * * *

9 The customary time of departure was early March; see Allen's introductions to Epp 795 and 1667, and Ep 1083:45–6.

1951
1 Abbreviation for *salvo titulo* 'saving your title,' a formulaic apology for the omission of an honorific heading. Cf Ep 1521.
2 The letter to Emser, Ep 1923, which Erasmus had written before he learned of Emser's death, was probably delivered in Dresden on 4 February (see the introduction there). In his 'recent' reply, which is not extant, Pistoris informed Erasmus that the duke would not reply to Ep 1924 because the courier who had delivered it had already departed (cf Ep 1924:3–4).
3 In his reply, which is not extant, Duke George took umbrage at the criticisms in Ep 1924 of the use by princes of violence against heretics by princes. Erasmus responded with Ep 1983.
4 The reference is to Otto von Pack; see Ep 1934 n80. On the letter in question, from Eppendorf to Pack, see Allen Ep 2086:67–9.

perceive from it the close friendship that exists between us. He wrote a letter of practically the same import to the prince, but in the vernacular tongue, otherwise I should have sent it. I do not think Otto was responsible for what you told Emser had been indicated to you about a confidante.[5]

And now it is clear to you that Eppendorf cannot accomplish his purpose by circulating that letter. I am still not convinced that he has received a copy of it. I shall make every effort to make him understand that his intention to expose you to scorn is severely displeasing to the prince. I think this will have much more effect than if the prince should deliver him a stern written reprimand.

As for Ceratinus I could not be more surprised, for I cannot recall ever having mentioned anything to him about the letter you wrote to the prince.[6]

At the request of the prince, I am sending a little book written in German concerning communion under one species, to Carlowitz[7] which he is to translate into Latin for your perusal.[8] The prince is most anxious to have

* * * * *

5 Ie that 'someone in the confidence' of Duke George had given Eppendorf a copy of the letter from Erasmus to the duke to which the latter's reply was Ep 1448. See Ep 1923:3–5.

6 Jacobus Ceratinus (Ep 622:34n) had not remained long in the professorship of Greek at Leipzig that he received on Erasmus' recommendation. Erasmus suspected, incorrectly, that this was because Ceratinus had developed Lutheran sympathies and, as indicated here, apparently said as much to Duke George in a letter. Cf Epp 1561 n3, 1564–8, 1611:5–8 with n2, 1717:77–81, 1899 n25.

7 Christoph von Carlowitz (or Carlewitz, Karlewitz, 1507–78) was a Saxon noble who studied under Petrus Mosellanus at Leipzig. He was probably the student of Mosellanus who visited Erasmus in Basel in 1524, carrying letters from Melanchthon and Camerarius (Epp 1501–2) and returning with Erasmus' answers (Epp 1523–4). In the autumn of 1527, after a brief sojourn studying with Conradus Goclenius (Ep 1994A) in Louvain, he returned to Basel (Epp 1899:97–104, 1912:11–15), where he became a member of Erasmus' household. Erasmus' admiration for the young man's learning and character was expressed not only in his letters (Epp 1923–4) but also in the *Ciceronianus* (CWE 28 427). By the time this letter from Pistoris had arrived, Carlowitz had gone off to the Franche-Comté to study at Dôle (Ep 1983:59–61). In March 1529 he took leave of Erasmus, who warmly recommended him for employment to both King Ferdinand and Duke George of Saxony (Epp 2121–3, 2130, 2141, 2166). By August of that year Carlowitz had entered the service of Duke George, to whose council he was appointed in the following year. Consistently Erasmian in his views, he became a moderate Protestant who worked for religious conciliation in Saxony and in the Empire. He enjoyed his greatest influence under Duke and Elector Maurice of Saxony (1541–53).

8 The work in question was a tract by Duke George himself in defence of the Catholic practice of communion in one kind against Luther's demand for communion in both kinds. The Dresden manuscript has been published in *Akten*

your frank opinion of it.[9] Then I shall inform you who the author of the book is. Few people know from what workshop it originates. Take good care of your health and, as you promised, write me a longer letter.   35

Dresden, 28 February, in the year of our redemption 1528

Your most devoted Simon Pistoris, chancellor of the duke

To the irreproachable theologian, standard-bearer of literary studies, Erasmus of Rotterdam, at Basel

To be opened only by him   40

1952 / From Sigismund I   Piotrków, 19 February 1528

This is King Sigismund's reply to Ep 1819. The surviving manuscript is a rough draft in a secretary's hand, with corrections and additions in other hands. It was in the private library of Count Maurice Zamoyski in Warsaw, who allowed Allen to examine it in July 1922. The Zamoyski family library is now in the Polish National Library in Warsaw, where the manuscript bears the shelfmark MS BN BOZ 2053 vol 7 fol 123. The letter was first published in the *Opus epistolarum*, where the text, with heading and dates added, was based on the letter actually received. Erasmus' response is Ep 2034.

SIGISMUND, BY THE GRACE OF GOD KING OF POLAND, GRAND DUKE OF LITHUANIA, RUSSIA, PRUSSIA, LORD AND LEGITIMATE HEIR TO THE THRONE OF MAZOVIA, ETC

Most learned Erasmus, your letter, written on the first of June,[1] was delivered to us, from which we could easily discern that you are truly the   5

* * * * *

und Briefe zur Kirchenpolitik Herzog Georgs von Sachsen ed Felician Gess 2 vols (Leipzig 1905–17; repr Cologne 1985) II 818–36: The printed version, the 'little book' referred to here, had just been published at Dresden (12 February, Wolfgang Stöckel): *Widder Luthers trostunng ann die Christen zu Hall ... szo viel die entpfahung des hochwirdigen Sacraments belangt ... MDXXVIII.* Carlowitz's Latin translation was published at Besançon in October: *Responsio ... adversus consolationem Lutheri in gratiam illustriss. Princ. Georgii Sax. Sucis etc e germanico in Latinum traducta per Christophorum a Carlewitz.* See Gess II 818 n2.

9 No record of Erasmus' opinion of the work survives.

1952

1 Ep 1819 is dated 15 May 1527. The discrepancy could be merely a secretary's error; alternatively, Erasmus might have left a blank so that the bearer of the letter, Jan Łaski (Ep 1954), could fill in the date if there were a delay in transit.

person you are said to be, namely, in addition to your great learning and wisdom, a man of the highest integrity, profoundly committed to civic tranquillity and Christian concord. Although we never doubted this, your letter has greatly confirmed this opinion we had of you. We clearly recognize in it the mark of a true Christian soul and have no doubt that you remain steadfast in all circumstances whether you are dealing with trivial or serious matters.

In the first place we express our special thanks for your eloquent words of praise, which we fear may not be so befitting to us as you wish to affirm. It is true that it is of great concern to us to help the Christian community in its degenerate condition to the best of our abilities and to preserve our kingdom tranquil, as far as possible, uncontaminated by the worse than Lutheran contagion which is now tearing Germany apart. Yet if our efforts have had some success up to now we attribute it to God rather than claim or seek any praise for ourselves. On the contrary, we implore the Lord's mercy with more fervent prayers that just as he has preserved us and our kingdom intact and unharmed up to now, so he will continue to do for the future as long as this will be pleasing to his will. Without that all our efforts will be in vain unless he prosper our undertakings.

Nevertheless, this homage of yours cannot but be most gratifying to us. We have always entertained a very high regard for you, but moved by this act of kindness on your part, we should be more pleased to oblige you in some way since by your letter you have rendered us more commendable among all men. Naturally we would be able to bestow our favours upon you more abundantly if you could be persuaded to betake yourself here. But since we have learned from your devoted followers that other princes, who sought with great petitions and inducements to attract you to their lands,[2] have been unsuccessful in their attempts, we fear that we too will undertake this initiative in vain. In order, however, that you may have some proof of our benevolence and appreciation, we send you a gift of one hundred gold ducats,[3] which we hope you will be pleased to accept for the present. Later on you will receive from us a more bounteous manifestation of our good will and favour towards you.

Given in our city of Piotrków, 19 February in the year of our Lord 1528, the twenty-second year of our reign

* * * * *

2 See Ep 1938 n4.
3 Cf Ep 1953:18–19. Ep 1958:2 shows that, like Tomicki's (Ep 1953 n2), they were Hungarian ducats; on their value see Ep 1934 n51.

1953 / From Piotr Tomicki   Piotrków, 19 February 1528

This letter answers Erasmus' letter of self-introduction, Ep 1919. The manuscript is a rough draft in secretarial hand in the Zamoyski collection at the Polish National Library (see Ep 1952 introduction): MS BN BOZ 2053, vol 9 fol 52. For some reason, the letter was not included in the *Opus epistolarum* along with Epp 1952, 2034, and 2035. It eventually appeared with the *De pueritate tabernaculi* (Basel: Froben and Episcopius, c February 1536).

On Tomicki (1464–1535), bishop of Cracow, vice-chancellor to King Sigismund I, and patron of humanist learning, see Ep 1919.

TO THE MOST RENOWNED AND LEARNED DESIDERIUS ERASMUS
OF ROTTERDAM, HIS MOST DEAR FRIEND

It is quite some time now that you have been known and endeared to me both through your erudite writings and also through what the physician Antonin has told me of you.[1] But now of your own accord you have 5 welcomed me into your friendship by your letter, which has strengthened my feelings of devotion towards you, since through no merits of my own but moved only by your generosity, you took the pains in the midst of your unparalleled labours and long vigils beyond compare to write me a letter that was no less elegant than friendly. Thus it is diffi- 10 cult for me to say how much I owe to you, and how much I value this friendship. Receive, therefore, most learned Erasmus, this brief response from one burdened with many duties but sincerely devoted to you, who will never cede to anyone in his attachment to you and in his admiration for your great learning and who would consider it his good fortune 15 to be able to oblige you in any way. May you on your part continue to show signs of your good will towards me as you have done and be pleased to accept this small gift, which I send to you as a pledge and token of our mutual affection.[2] I am reluctant to write about the ill health of your friend Antonin;[3] I would prefer that you learn of it from oth- 20 ers. May you enjoy the best of health, most learned sir, and be blessed by fortune.

* * * * *

1953
1 Jan Antonin (Ep 1602) had become Erasmus' friend during a visit to Basel in 1524 and was now personal physician to King Sigismund and bishop Tomicki.
2 Sixty Hungarian ducats; see Epp 1997:7–8, 2035:30–1, and cf Ep 1952 n3.
3 On Antonin's illness, see Ep 2011:10–22.

Given at the General Assembly of Piotrków[4]
20 February, in the year of our Lord 1528

1954 / From Jan (II) Łaski   Piotrków, 20 February 1528

This is Łaski's response to Ep 1915; Erasmus reply to Łaski is Ep 2033. The letter was first published in *Lasciana, Nebst den Ältesten Evangelischen Synodalpro-
tokollen Polens, 1555–1561* ed Hermann Dalton (Berlin 1898; repr Nieuwkoop
1973) Ep 16. The manuscript, a copy in the hand of a professional scribe, was
part of a folio volume in the Imperial Library at St Petersburg. Following the
Treaty of Riga between the Soviet Union and Poland (1921), the manuscript
volume was returned to the Polish Republic and placed in the National Library at Warsaw, where it was destroyed by German bombardment in World
War II.

On Jan (II) Łaski (1499–1560), Polish nobleman, canon of Cracow, provost of
Gniezno, royal secretary, central figure of Polish Erasmianism, and (eventually) Calvinist reformer, see Epp 1593 n18, 1821 introduction.

COPY OF A LETTER OF THE REVEREND PROVOST OF GNIEZNO
The wisdom, if such there is, that you attribute to me, dearest Erasmus,
is rather yours than mine. For I have merely followed your advice: those
whom I can neither persuade nor command to do my will I either avoid
or, if matters cannot be settled without them, I show them civility rather   5
than provoke them. And this policy has already proved successful a number of times. Would that we could continue in the future to achieve success by this method, so that if we cannot make good use of these depraved
minds we can at least make some use of them on occasion to further our
own goals.   10
There is hardly anyone here who does not think very highly of you,
so much influence did your letter to the prince have.[1] The prince himself is
most devoted to you, save that now he is harassed by continued warfare,

* * * * *

4 The Polish diet, which developed in the fifteenth century out of the royal
  council, consisted of two chambers: the Sejm, the lower chamber made up of
  regional deputies; and the Senate, the upper chamber, whose members were
  appointed by the monarch from among the highest state officers. This diet at
  Piotrków had been in session since 25 November 1527 (Ep 1958 n7).

1954
1 Ep 1819 to Sigismund I

especially with the Scythians;[2] as a general rule, however, he will not initiate hostilities unless there is grave provocation. He has just answered your 15
letter, not in the most elegant of styles perhaps, but in a friendly spirit. He
included one hundred gold ducats,[3] which our friend Justus from Cracow
will deliver to you together with the letter.[4] The chief persons responsible
for this action were the chancellor Krzysztof and the bishop of Płock.[5] Even
if their intervention was not at all necessary to accomplish this, since the 20
prince ordered this to be sent to you of his own will, I preferred that the
matter be handled by these two men as if it were done on their initiative so
that it would have greater authority in the eyes of other observers. Nothing
could have been more pleasing to the archbishop than the Ambrose edition.[6]
He wishes that I convey his apologies for not writing to you. The truth is 25
that he is so occupied with cares and responsibilities that he has no time to
eat except at night. For we are holding our diet at the present time and he
is compelled to preside over the Senate until nightfall as long as this meeting lasts.[7] It should adjourn within the next few days. He will write to you
when he has the time and will add some token of his good will towards 30
you.[8]

As for myself I am not certain whether I shall go to Spain or elsewhere. This matter has been put off until the return of our queen,[9] who is
now absent but will return any day now. And I must admit that my brother
Hieronim's absence has lingered on up to the present. I do not know where 35
he is or when I may expect him to return.[10] I fear something may happen
to him in his wanderings, which would greatly upset us. Here, wherever
you turn, everything seems to point more towards war rather than peace.
Germany has been divided into several parts and something seems to be

* * * * *

2 Poland was at this time engaged in border warfare with the Tatars of the
Crimean Khanate.
3 See Ep 1952 n3.
4 Ep 1952. On Justus Decius see Ep 1958.
5 Krzysztof Szydłowiecki (Epp 1593, 1918, 2032) and Andrzej Krzycki (Epp 1629,
2030)
6 Jan (I) Łaski, archbishop of Gniezno, uncle of Jan (II). Erasmus had dedicated
his edition of Ambrose to him. See Ep 1855.
7 Cf Ep 1953 n4.
8 The archbishop, who distrusted Erasmus' attitude towards Luther and thought
of him as pro-Hapsburg, never did this. This expression of gratitude at second
hand may be a fiction contrived by Jan (II).
9 Bona Sforza (1494–1557), daughter of Giangaleazzo Sforza, duke of Milan
10 Hieronim (Ep 1341A:1218–69) was in Constantinople negotiating with the
sultan.

brewing there. Hungary is so torn apart that they say the Turks have either 40
already invaded it or will soon invade it with a huge army. We undertook
a virtually unending war against the Scythians. At home we are enjoying
perfect peace. May the good and gracious God will that it be unending. Let
us take diligent care that Luther and his faction do not gain ground here or,
from the opposite viewpoint, that those to whom we owe all present evils 45
should come to power. I would wish that they have as much influence elsewhere as they now have here. And yet from what you have written me I understand that even in Spain the mad fury of other factions is being brought
under control. Yet I am afraid that they will be more moved to anger than
chastened unless the severity of princes be brought to bear. 50

I am most grateful to you, my dear Erasmus, for communicating to me
news about others and of yourself, which gives me great pleasure. I cannot
cease to wonder at the zeal for calumny that possesses these people. I am
not surprised at Béda showing himself true to form:[11] I know the man's
character and his stupidity.[12] Such a great theologian is afraid that he will 55
have to lose his income rather than his reputation if he should admit his
ignorance of some point or that he learned it from you. I feel grief certainly
at the death of Froben.[13] I fear that his son will not be such a careful printer
as his father, for in the book you sent me there are a great many errors,[14]
which is proof that he devoted less care to the printing. Your book on the art 60
of preaching[15] is eagerly awaited by all, as is the Augustine.[16] I responded
to Beatus, Glareanus and Amerbach as best I could.[17] I received everything
that you sent through Severinus but I did not see Severinus himself nor do
I think that he came here.[18] I shall write to you again shortly if I can, either

* * * * *

11 On Béda, see Ep 1943 n6.
12 See Ep 1902 introduction.
13 See Ep 1900.
14 Hieronymus Froben (1501–63) had published the *Apologia adversus monachos
quosdam Hispanos* (Ep 1879), which at the end had one and one-half pages of
errata.
15 See Ep 1932 n25.
16 The ten-volume edition of Augustine would be published in 1529; see Ep 2157.
17 Dalton (see introduction) Ep 17 to Beatus Rhenanus, dated 20 February 1528,
which answered BRE Ep 265 of 15 December 1527; Dalton Ep 18 to Henricus
Glareanus, dated 20 February 1528; Dalton Ep 15 to Bonifacius Amerbach,
dated 20 February 1527 (= AK Ep 1242), which answered AK Ep 1220 of c 9
December 1527.
18 The messenger Severinus Olpeius departed from Basel in September 1527
laden with letters from Erasmus to Łaski and others (Epp 1915 n17, 1916:10–
11). None of the letters he carried has survived.

through Justus[19] or a close acquaintance of the bishop of Płock who is to set   65
out to see you in a few days to bear you letters.[20] Farewell, most excellent
Erasmus, and grant me your friendship, as you have done in the past.

    Piotrków, 20 February 1528
    Yours sincerely, Jan Łaski
    Written in my own hand   70

1955 / To Richard Pace   Basel, 20 February 1528

> In 1525, while on duty as English ambassador in Venice, Erasmus' old friend
> Pace (Ep 211:53n) had been taken seriously ill, possibly with syphilis (Epp 1594
> n16, 1595 n4, 1624 n3). The resulting physical and mental deterioration led to
> his being placed in custodial care. Having received from Jan van der Cruyce
> news of Pace that seemed to indicate that he was well again (Ep 1932:156–
> 62), Erasmus wrote this letter, first published the the *Opus epistolarum*, in the
> attempt to resume relations with him.

ERASMUS OF ROTTERDAM TO RICHARD PACE, GREETING
I can scarcely contain my joy, most distinguished sir, in hearing that you
have returned from that turbulent sea of business affairs to your own sweet
country and to the Muses, sweeter still than your country. I congratulate you
that to your previous studies you have also added the study of Hebrew. I   5
shall not detain you with further discourse for the moment. I have sent my
friend Quirinus,[1] who has served me with more devotion than any man, to
England to perform certain missions, the two most important being: first,
to put an end finally to the embezzlements of that criminal impostor,[2] and
second, since the archbishop of Canterbury and his royal Majesty have both   10
invited me to England in very cordial letters,[3] to investigate together with

* * * * *

19 See n4 above.
20 Andrzej Zebrzydowski; see Epp 1826 introduction, 1958 n1, 2030–1.

1955
 1 Quirinus Talesius (Ep 1966), who had been dispatched to England via the
   Low Countries. By mid-March he was at Louvain and by the beginning of
   April in Antwerp. He reached England later that month and brought back
   Epp 1990 and 1993 (see Epp 1959–60, 1964, 1984:1–2, 2001:2–3). By 1 June he
   had returned to Basel (Ep 1998:32–8).
 2 Probably Pieter Weldanck (Ep 1931:14–22), but possibly Franz Birckmann (ibidem lines 23–7)
 3 See Ep 1926 n7.

my friends whether that can conveniently be arranged. For I shall probably have to move from here, whether I wish to or not.[4] You will be able to
learn more about both of these matters from the account of this young man,
whom I commend to you, my dear Pace, not as a servant but as a dearly   15
beloved son, in the event that he may have need of your services. I wish
you continuing good fortune.

Given at Basel, 20 February 1528

1956 / To Felix   Basel, 21 February 1528

This letter was first published in the *Opus epistolarum*, where the index indicates that the Felix to whom it was addressed was from Dôle in Burgundy.
The identity of the addressee is unclear. Allen speculated that he might have
been the doctor of laws referred to in Epp 1533:12–15 and 1610:40–44, and that
all three references might possibly be to Petrus Phoenix (a name that Erasmus
could easily have confused with 'Felix'), professor of law at the University of
Dôle.

ERASMUS OF ROTTERDAM TO FELIX, DOCTOR OF LAWS, GREETING
I was most grateful for your speaking in my defence, most celebrated Doctor, and on that account I avow my great debt to your kindness, but I greatly
wonder where this petulance (or should I say pestilence?) of evil tongues
comes from. I always thought the Burgundians were serious and honourable   5
men. Where did this weed-infected crop of garrulous men come from? I suspect it is the pseudo-evangelicals, who can be found everywhere, who are
sowing such rumours there also.

Here are the facts of the matter.[1] I was in poor health, as is often the
case; furthermore, I was tired from the journey and suffering from the stone.   10
The weakness of this frail body recoiled from the eating of fish, whereas
my spirit wished to avoid any offence to my neighbour. With this meaning
in mind I said several times in jest among friends that my stomach was
Lutheran but my spirit was Christian. From a man in such a state of health
as I was, neither God nor the laws of pontiffs require the eating of fish. And   15
besides, I have a dispensation from the pope that allows me to eat meat on

* * * * *

4 See Ep 1926 n8.

1956
1 Erasmus' visit to Besançon in April 1524, first mentioned in Ep 1440:4–6, is
described in some detail in Ep 1610, with further details in Ep 1679 (see n4).

any day whatsoever without exception.[2] Even if I did not have it, I still have
a more legitimate reason for eating meat than I could wish. Nevertheless,
since I was suffering from a violent fever, I abstained from fish and wine,
but did not partake of meat in order not to offend anyone. That was the   20
Christian spirit I spoke of. So great was the pain in my stomach that it had to
be relieved by frequent vomiting. This was my Lutheran stomach, as I said
jokingly. And so, sick as I was, I mounted my horse and I took to my bed
here for a month.[3] This, and this only, was my contribution to the slanderous
talk of stupid men.   25

Here is the story about the womb of the Blessed Virgin.[4] I was din-
ing with the proctor of the archdeacon.[5] After the meal the host's servant
recited a long prayer of thanksgiving; it could have passed for a short
mass. First a 'Kyrie eleison,' then a 'De profundis,' then a 'Pater noster'
repeated several times: why not? Finally he seemed to have finished and   30
we answered 'Amen!' When he was silent for a while, thinking that was
the end of it, I turned to the guests and was about to thank the host
when the servant unexpectedly added 'And blessed is the womb of the
Virgin Mary.' Embarrassed and wishing to point out that the thanksgiving had been long enough without that finale, I said playfully 'That's all   35
we needed, the blessed womb.' I did not mean this in any way as disre-
spectful to the Virgin but rather to make it clear that that act of thanksgiving was a hodgepodge of heterogeneous elements. My fervent devotion to the Virgin is proved by the two prayers I published some time ago,
the Paean and the Supplication.[6] Likewise the new mass that I published,   40
which had the approval of the archbishop of Besançon.[7] And these are the
proofs they bring forward to make me a Lutheran. This rumour has even
reached Paris, as Béda indicated to me in a letter.[8] I have not the least
doubt that this originated with the pseudo-evangelicals. There is nothing

* * * * *

2 See Epp 1079 n1 and 1542.
3 See Ep 1452 n22.
4 For a similar account of this incident see Ep 1679:100–15.
5 The archdeacon was Ferry de Carondelet (Epp 1350 n6 and 1749 introduction).
   Allen identified the proctor as Antoine Bercin (c 1490–1538), who was indeed
   a canon of Besançon but master of the school rather than proctor (see Epp
   1610:57 with n18 and 2138 introduction). The archdeacon's proctor was also
   named Antoine, but his surname is unknown (see Ep 1610:59–60 with n20). It
   would appear that Allen here confused one Antoine with the other.
6 See Ep 93:133n.
7 Antoine de Vergy (Ep 1679 n25); see Epp 1391 and 1573.
8 See Ep 1642:73–9.

they do not plot against me because I am unwilling to join them in their 45
madness.

I learned of the service you performed for me from the noble and
learned young man, Christoph von Carlowitz.[9] If he had returned here I
would have written in more detail through him. I have entrusted this brief
note, written on the spur of the moment, to messengers who happened to 50
show up. I have given you an accurate description of what happened. I have
wished that you be informed of it so that you will be better equipped to
refute these gossips. I wish you the best of health, distinguished sir.

Given at Basel, 21 February 1528

1957 / To ?   Basel, 27 February 1528

> First published in the *Opus epistolarum*, this letter is addressed to someone who
> had protected Erasmus against an enemy and thus helped restore the quiet
> necessary for his studies. Allen speculated that it might have been Otto von
> Pack (Ep 1934 n80) who, as a trusted official of Duke George of Saxony, might
> have played a role in the settlement of the controversy with Eppendorf; see
> Ep 1934 introduction. The friend in line 6 could then be Simon Pistoris, who
> mentions Pack in Ep 1951:17. By the time he prepared the letter for publication,
> Erasmus would have known of Pack's disgrace in the 'Pack affair' (Ep 1934
> n80) and might have thought it prudent to omit his name.

ERASMUS OF ROTTERDAM TO A CERTAIN GENTLEMAN, GREETING
Just as nature has created no poison for which there is not a remedy, so God
always interposes someone to the designs of the wicked to prevent them
from immediately accomplishing all their desires. For there are many persons of such a nature that you would say they were made for nothing else 5
but to do harm to the good. From a letter of a friend of mine I have learned
how devotedly and prudently you defended my cause. Even if you were to
perform this friendly office for me alone, I would be the most ungrateful of
men if I did not cherish and proclaim this kindness that you have afforded
me. But since this act of benevolence has profited not only me but humane 10
studies and the public peace, I laud your piety also. And would that the occasion arise some day when I might reciprocate in some way the meritorious
service you have done me.

Given at Basel, 27 February 1528

* * * * *

9 Ep 1951 n7. By this time, Carlowitz was studying in Dôle (Ep 1983:59–61).

1958 / From Justus Decius   Cracow, 28 February 1528

First published as Ep 84 in Förstemann/Günther, the manuscript was in the
Burscher Collection at Leipzig (Ep 1254 introduction). A tear down the right-
hand edge had removed the end of seven lines of text and two of the address,
but all but one of the gaps were successfully restored by Förstemann/Günther.
Erasmus' reply is Ep 2031. On Justus Ludovicus Decius, secretary to King
Sigismund I of Poland and patron of humanist scholars, see Ep 1341A n210.

Greetings. I send you by this noble young man, Zebrzydowski,[1] by order of
my king one hundred Hungarian gold ducats,[2] which I hope he will deliver
in good order. When you have received them, please let it be known to the
bishop of Cracow,[3] lest I seem to have been negligent in my duty.

The fact that you have not written to me for several years I have will- 5
ingly accepted as due to your more important occupations.[4] I wished to write
to you myself, but our friend Antonin always took it upon himself to do so.
Since he is suffering from such a long and grave illness he has deprived me
of this opportunity to send you my greetings more often.[5] I shall not continue to take up your valuable time since I am confident that we remain on 10
the best of terms. I shall never regret my course of action.

I send you in addition forty gold ducats to be given to Glareanus,[6]
which Jan Łaski gave me at the last assembly of the realm, to be delivered to
him.[7] I beg you to undertake this mission, for I do not know the man. You

* * * * *

1958
1 Andrzej Zebrzydowski (Ep 1826). This was the beginning of a stay of several
  months in Erasmus' household (Epp 2030, 2031, 2033, 2035, 2036). In September 1528, the young man departed for Paris (Epp 2052, 2078). After a brief
  return visit to Basel in the spring of 1529, he went off to Venice and Padua
  (Epp 2161, 2173). After that, there is no trace of further contact with Erasmus.
  Back in Poland in 1530, he embarked on an ecclesiastical career that eventually made him bishop of Cracow and chancellor of the University of Cracow.
  The inscription on his tomb declares that he was 'a student and disciple of the
  great Erasmus of Rotterdam.'
2 See Ep 1952 n3.
3 Piotr Tomicki (Epp 1919, 1953)
4 The only extant letter up to this point is Ep 1393.
5 On Antonin see Ep 1953 n1.
6 See Ep 2033:3–4.
7 According to Allen, who cites volume 10 (Posnan 1899) of the *Acta Tomiciana*
  (*Epistole, legationes, responsa, actiones, res geste serenissimi principis Sigismundi ...
  primi ... per Stanislaum Gorski ... collecte ...*), the diet, which had been meeting
  at Piotrków since 25 November 1527, had just broken up.

have news of our court and of other affairs from other sources. Farewell, 15
remember your friend Justus.

At Cracow, 28 February 1528

Yours, Justus Decius, secretary

To the illustrious Erasmus of Rotterdam, consummate theologian ...
and friend   20

1959 / To Thomas More   Basel, 29 February 1528

This letter was first published in the *Opus epistolarum*.

ERASMUS OF ROTTERDAM TO THOMAS MORE, GREETING
Amidst the many troubles that beset me on all sides, the most gracious letter from his Highness the king, in which he invites me to England with
promises worthy of such a generous prince, brought me much consolation.[1]
He reminds me of what I wrote a long time ago, that I had chosen to make 5
England the home of my old age. But now, my dear More, things have come
to such a pass that I must look around for a place of burial, where I may
have peace at least in death, since, as I see, this will not be my lot while
I am alive. All predict that great revolutions are imminent. The heresy of
the Anabaptists is ready to explode. It is far more widespread than anyone 10
would believe. You will learn of my calamities from my friend Quirinus,
who bears you this, a young man of proven loyalty.[2] I thought I should send
him ahead to England, since he knows my entire situation, so that through
him I could explore with my friends what is possible or expedient to do. I
would have liked to express my gratitude to the king for his generosity, but 15
since I had no time, exhausted by many labours, I preferred not to write to
the prince rather than write a letter without due care.[3] If you agree, you will
be able to represent my feelings, how I am neither unaware nor unmindful
of his extraordinary kindness, which he never ceases to offer me despite my
complete unworthiness. I pray that you and your dear ones are in excellent 20
health.

Given at Basel, 29 February 1528

* * * * *

1959
1 Ep 1878
2 See Epp 1955 n1, 1966.
3 Erasmus was understandably hesitant to take so decisive a step as to leave
   the protection of Emperor Charles v to join one of his rivals who might soon
   become an enemy. Not until June would he respond directly to the king's
   invitation by refusing it (Ep 1998).

1960 / To Catherine of Aragon   Basel, 1 March 1528

This letter was first published in the *Opus epistolarum*. Queen Catherine had taken no notice of the dedication to her of the *Institutio christiani matrimonii* (Ep 1727), causing Erasmus to speculate that it had displeased her (Ep 1804:313–15). Ep 1816 brought reassurance of her good opinion from Baron Mountjoy, but only this polite reminder elicited a gift from her (Ep 2040:50).

ERASMUS OF ROTTERDAM TO CATHERINE, QUEEN OF ENGLAND

Joy and peace from our Lord Jesus Christ, illustrious Queen, more blessed in your piety than in your sharing of an immense kingdom. It is a supreme good fortune among men to have been born of most noble and most powerful kings, to be joined in marriage to a king at the height of his prosperity; 5 but these things are as nothing when compared to the outstanding qualities of your soul. The former blessings have fallen to the lot not only of many but even sometimes of the wicked. The latter is a very rare example, that a woman born and brought up amidst the pleasures of the court, where fortune lavished such bounty upon her as would corrupt even the best moral 10 upbringing, should place all her hope, all her solace in sacred prayers and readings. These constitute a truly distinguished lineage; this is the diadem that renders you glorious before the angels of God. Would that this example of the queen might be followed at least by widows, who, forgetful of the Pauline precept,[1] spend their lives in luxury, like living corpses! Why do I 15 mention widows? Would that young unmarried women would imitate it, renouncing the pomp and pleasures of the world and dedicating themselves to Christ, their spouse. You owe both of these blessings to him who is the font and author of all honours and who in his ineffable goodness brings it about that things that seem evil to us because they are troublesome to nature 20 are, according to the teaching of Paul, turned into good for those who love God and in his words are called saints.[2] Indeed sometimes he even changes defects of the soul, which are truly evil, by some divine art into either a safeguard or a motive for piety.

Whoever truly loves God has secured the anchor of all his hope not in 25 the sterile sands of transitory things but on the solid rock that stands firm against the waves of worldly events. This is Jesus Christ, the spouse of pious souls, so shared by all that no spouse belongs so exclusively and un-

* * * * *

1960
1 Cf 1 Tim 5–6.
2 Rom 8:28

failing to his bride as he is exclusively present to each one. Whoever has
thrown himself upon his breast with full confidence and has transferred   30
all his anxieties to him alone who he knows has care of him, is at peace
in the midst of life's tumults and enjoys all delights, delights compared
to which all the sweetness the world has to offer is mere bilge water, as
the famous writer said.[3] Therefore the soul that has entrusted itself to this
spouse gives thanks no less in adversity than in prosperity. And yet if we   35
should wish to speak the truth, what is adversity but that which stands in
our way as we hasten on to eternal happiness? What is prosperity but that
which leads to it? Christ is our spouse and Lord and physician: spouse, because for love of us, led to death, he bound us to him and himself to us
in an eternal covenant; Lord, because at the price of his blood he saved   40
us from the tyranny of Satan; physician because he is our Saviour, and he
alone effectively heals men's ills, driving out death, restoring life. Often
he is more propitious to us when he sends bitter remedies than when he
smears the cup with sweetness. He knows what is useful for us and he neither ceases nor sleeps in caring for his own. We often consider the most   45
adverse fortune to be prosperity and interpret fortunate circumstances as
adversity. It is ours to obey, it is the spouse who decides. All prosperity is
from him: if it does not proceed from him it cannot be called prosperity.
From him also adversity comes to the pious; this he changes into a remedy or into a gain for piety. Through prosperity he comforts our weak-   50
ness so that we may bear up with it; through adversity he tests and crowns
our faith. Prosperity is more soothing to human feelings, but often adversity is more salubrious and even more profitable. There is no access to
heavenly glory except through the cross. There is a common path for all,
whether we be kings, as the poet said, or needy peasants.[4] Each one must   55
bear his cross.

I write these things, illustrious Queen, that you may call yourself more
happy in possessing things that are far more precious and cannot be taken
away from you against your will. It is necessary that virtue be known to
itself. Since virtue is a gratuitous gift of God, how will one preserve what   60
he has received or how will he give thanks to the divine goodness if he
does not know what he has received? The spouse in the Song of Songs
threatens his betrothed if she does not know herself.[5] A soul that attributes
to itself that which it does not possess does not know itself; it does not

* * * * *

3 Plautus *Curculio* 99
4 Horace *Odes* 2.14.11
5 In the Vulgate text of the Song of Songs (*Cantica canticorum*) 1:7

know itself if it ascribes to its own powers what should have been credited   65
to the liberality of the spouse. It does not know itself if it thinks itself
happy in these external goods rather than in those hidden gifts of the Holy
Spirit; if it is more grievously distressed by the deprivation of material possessions than by the loss of heavenly treasures. But where will my pen
carry me? I had resolved to congratulate you and I become your adviser,   70
although I know that in your active pursuit of piety and your untiring exertions in the reading of the sacred books there is no need of incentives or
admonitions.

   If the book I dedicated to your Majesty's name deserved the attention
of your eyes and ears, I shall esteem that this was a successful undertaking.   75
But if there is anything that gives offence, I shall have no difficulty in correcting it in the next edition. May the Lord Jesus, font of all happiness, make
your soul serene with unending and unadulterated joy, illustrious Queen
and singular exemplar of piety.

   Given at Basel, 7 March 1528   80

1961 / To Juan de Valdés   Basel, 1 March 1528

Juan de Valdés (c 1509/10–1541) was the younger brother of Alfonso de Valdés
(Ep 1807). Born into a family of Jewish *converso* origins, Juan was deeply influenced by the heterodox religious views of the *alumbrados* before studying
at Alcalá (c 1525–30), where he encountered members of the Erasmian élite
including Juan de Vergara (Ep 1277). While still a student in Alcalá, he published his *Diálogo de doctrina cristiana* (1529), in which the ideas of the *alumbrados* were cloaked in Erasmian language. Charged by the Inquisition with expressing heretical views in the *Diálogo*, Valdés moved to Rome (1531), where
he served as an imperial agent at the papal court. In 1535 he settled in Naples,
where he held a variety of administrative posts. He soon became the focal
point of a group of socially prominent people whose religious ideas helped
launch the Italian Reformation. The works written in this period, which included biblical commentaries and translations as well as a treatise on the Castil-
ian language, circulated in manuscript during his lifetime but were published
posthumously by his followers. Although there is no evidence that he was directly influenced by the Protestant reformers and although he never broke
with the Catholic church, his personal views, which included belief in justification by faith and the rejection of works as a means of salvation, were close
to those of Luther and Calvin.

   This letter, first published in the *Opus epistolarum*, is the first of three that
Erasmus sent to Valdés in Alcalá; the other two are Epp 2127 and 2251.

ERASMUS OF ROTTERDAM TO JUAN VALDÉS, GREETING
Most distinguished young man, your brother Alfonso de Valdés has rendered me and continues to render me so many good services that I must
have affection for whatever pertains to him in any way. I am told that you
so resemble him both in physical appearance and mental agility that you   5
might seem to be not two twins but a single person.[1] Thus I think it most
equitable to have equal affection for you both. I hear that you have dedicated yourself to liberal studies so that you may adorn your character, which
was born to virtue, with all kinds of distinction. Of what use is it to encourage you in this since you of your own accord have launched yourself upon   10
this most beautiful of careers? It is more fitting to congratulate and applaud
you. Be assured that I have closer associations to no one more than to your
brother and to you as much as to him.
    At Basel, 1 March 1528

1962 / To Lazare de Baïf   Basel, 1 March 1528

> First published in the *Opus epistolarum*, this is the first of two surviving let-
> ters of Erasmus to Baïf, the other being Ep 2447. With the publication of his
> *De re vestiaria* (Basel: J. Bebel, March 1526), Baïf (c 1496–1547) had achieved
> second rank among French scholars after Guillaume Budé. Erasmus greatly
> admired Baïf's classical learning, particularly his knowledge of Greek, hap-
> pily correcting the texts of *Adagia* I x 100 and III iv 52 in response to Baïf's
> friendly criticisms (see Ep 1479:6–21, especially n6) and praising his treatise
> on ancient dress in the *Ciceronianus* (CWE 28 421). Baïf was currently in the ser-
> vice of Jean de Guise, cardinal of Lorraine and bishop of Metz. In 1529, Francis
> I made him resident ambassador in Venice. In 1534 he became a magistrate in
> the Parlement of Paris.

ERASMUS OF ROTTERDAM TO LAZARE DE BAÏF, GREETING
To heap immoderate praise on those they hold dear is so customary among
men of learning, my dear Baïf, that to refuse it is to acknowledge it. So I
have decided from now on to tolerate anything of this kind in silence. But I

* * * * *

1961
1 On the basis of this passage, Allen declared Juan and Alfonso de Valdés to be
  twins, but this is unlikely. In his second letter to Juan, Erasmus describes the
  brothers as *tam gemellos*, ie 'so much like twins' or 'so twin-like' as to seem to
  be one person (Allen Ep 2127:11).

was gratified by your sincerity, which Herman of Friesland depicted to me 5
in his letter some time ago.[1] Since you refuse what I ask of you, I refuse in
turn what you ask of me, to be received into the crowd of those who emulate
my studies. On the contrary Baïf will hold the first place among my friends
of the first rank. I have played my part of the play in our times, now I make
way with equanimity to those more fortunate. 10

The disorderly tumults of the theologians give me great cause to wonder. I wrote about this to the Parlement of Paris and to the most sacred
Faculty.[2] They accuse me of saying that Christ condemns vows, which is no
wonder, since Béda has included so many transparent lies in one little book.[3]
If you prefer that your book *De vasculis culinariis* be published there, since 15
you are there yourself and 'the master's face is better than his back,'[4] I approve. But if they dally, we will have it printed here, provided you send a
copy that you have examined.[5]

Concerning the vases, I welcome the good will of the most reverend
cardinal.[6] But his administrator will forget and accuse the goldworkers of 20
not having kept their word. In such matters the servants of princes certainly
make haste slowly. I haven't seen a trace of the vases. I shall write to you
when I receive them.[7]

Michael Bentinus, after losing his wife, his wife's mother, one of his
guests, and on top of that a young child, after spending a few days in the 25
deserted house, was carried off by the same pestilence.[8] He was followed

* * * * *

1962
1 Haio Herman (Epp 903:14n, 1131). The letter from him answered by Ep 1479
 is not extant.
2 Epp 1905, 1902
3 The *Annotationes* against Lefèvre d'Etaples and Erasmus; see Ep 1943 n6.
4 *Adagia* I ii 19
5 After being revised by Erasmus, it was published by Froben at Basel in 1531
 with the second edition of *De re vestiaria*.
6 Jean de Guise (see introduction)
7 In 1527 Erasmus had dedicated his edition of St John Chrysostom's commentary on Galatians to the cardinal. It seems that he had been led to expect a reward in the form of gold vases (Ep 2009:19–23), though in the end he appears
 to have received money instead (Ep 2027:17–20).
8 Bentinus (cf Ep 1433 n2) was a Fleming who had worked in Basel (1520–3) as
 a corrector of Latin texts for Froben's press and in that capacity had earned
 Erasmus' displeasure by introducing errors into the text of the *Adagia* (Ep
 1437:174–81). After a sojourn in his native land, where he preached the 'new
 gospel' of the reformers, he returned to Basel in 1524, took a wife, worked for
 the presses of Curio and Cratander, established relations with Guillaume Farel

immediately by the one who had succeeded him as proofreader.[9] Johannes
Froben has also left us, to my irremediable grief.[10] As for his wife, she has
already married another.[11] I congratulate you on having a patron who is no
less generous than he is powerful. I am happy that he has become the com-   30
mon patron of us both.[12] I leave it to you to advise me if there is anything
in which I can oblige him. Farewell.

At Basel, 1 March 1528

1963 / From Henri de Bottis   Bourg-en-Bresse, 6 March 1528

This is Bottis' reply to Ep 1921. LB printed only the second paragraph and the
signature (with Bottis' name inserted). The complete text was first published as
Ep 60 in Enthoven, using the autograph in the Rehdiger Collection at Wrocław.
On Henri de Bottis (d 1544), who had taken his MA at the Collège de Montaigu
in Paris and was now the official of the diocese of Bourg-en-Bresse, see Ep 1921.

TO THE INCOMPARABLE ERASMUS OF ROTTERDAM,
HENRI DE BOTTIS GIVES WARM GREETINGS
I was happy to receive your letter, my dear sir, but not without some embarrassment, for I was sorry that in the midst of so many occupations
you wasted some time in writing back to me. Since this took away from   5
the public good, I think it was time not well employed. In the meantime the Augustine edition is lying there at Froben's press in mutilated
condition waiting to be healed by your poultices and perhaps complaining of having been deserted.[1] In the meantime I fear that the enemies
of good letters have become more brazen.[2] Therefore in the future take   10

* * * * *

(Ep 1341A n305), Johannes Oecolampadius (Ep 2000 n4), and the Strasbourg
reformers, and contemplated preaching the new faith in France (Epp 1514:18–
25, 1548:8–13). The plague claimed him and his family in November 1527.
9 Unidentified. Allen's suggestion that it might have been Gregorius Caselius
of Strasbourg is rejected as unconvincing by Peter Bietenholz in CEBR I 277.
10 Ep 1900
11 Johann Herwagen (Ep 2033 n24)
12 On Erasmus' relations with the cardinal of Lorraine, whose aid he had sought
in his dispute with the Paris faculty of theology, see Epp 1424 n4, 1841, 1911.

1963
1 Published in 1529 with Ep 2157 as its introduction
2 The literal translation here would be 'have raised their crests'; cf Adagia I viii
69.

thought, I pray you, for the public good rather than for us, and do not
be afraid that your memory will ever fade from our heart if you are slow
in writing back, since you speak to us every day in your many published
books. Add to this the fact that at the priory of Brou, the most precious
and elaborate in all of Christendom, which the illustrious Margaret, the   15
great-aunt of the emperor, is having constructed there,[3] is a skilled sculptor, Dutch by birth.[4] Every time he shows us your image reproduced from
life[5] – and he does so frequently – I seem almost to see you, and I cannot help renewing and increasing my affection for you and my memory
of you.   20

The hysteria in Spain has not yet reached us. I have the firm belief that
it has been mitigated by your Apology,[6] which was much milder than your
Jerome-like diatribe against the Spanish Vigilantius.[7] When I first read the
name Béda in your letter there rose up immediately the memory of the College of Montaigu, and I shuddered with fear that the master, lavish with   25
his blows, might strike me again with his ferule.[8] I once thought he was a
good man until, offended at that harmless little pleasantry, 'at Paris a beet
savours of wisdom,'[9] he burst forth into such a tirade of abuse that he could
not have exposed more clearly his feigned sanctity and the poison lurking

* * * * *

3 The Augustinian priory at Brou, close to Bourg-en-Bresse, was established
   on the site of a tenth-century Benedictine house by Margaret of Austria (Ep
   1380) in memory of her husband, Philibert of Savoy (d 1504). The splendidly
   decorated priory church, a masterpiece of flamboyant gothic style, was under
   construction from 1513 to 1532. Now deconsecrated, it is a museum.
4 Undoubtedly Konrad Meit (d 1551), who was a German from Worms rather
   than a Dutchman. By 1512, he had entered the service of Margaret of Austria
   as a sculptor. He spent the years 1526–31 working at Brou before returning to
   the Netherlands.
5 Probably the Metsys medal; see page 242.
6 The *Apologia adversus monachos quosdam Hispanos*; see Epp 1877, 1879, 1888,
   1967.
7 A reference to Erasmus' fierce denunciation of Diego López Zúñiga in the
   Apologia ad Stunicae conclusiones (1524), which Bottis compares to Jerome's
   polemic against the Gaulish priest Vigilantius in his *Contra Vigilantium* (AD
   406).
8 An allusion to Horace's stern schoolmaster, Orbilius, who became proverbial;
   Epistles 2.1.7. On Béda, see Ep 1943 n6. On the Collège de Montaigu, which
   Erasmus had attended briefly and unhappily, see Ep 43 introduction.
9 *Beta Luteciae sapit*. A pun on Béda's name (*beta* 'beet') inserted into the 1522
   edition of the *Familiarum colloquiorum formulae*. See CWE 39 12:1–2, and cf Mar-
   tial 13.13: 'Oh, how often will the cook ask for wine and pepper to give flavour
   to the insipid beet, the luncheon of artisans.'

beneath his hump.[10] Against this man and others like him as well as the tur-   30
bulent Luther may our Lord Jesus Christ grant you a strong and invincible
soul or at least, if it be his will, free you from these violent disputes. I wish
that you thrive as long as possible in him.

Farewell, my revered sir.

From Bourg-en-Bresse, 6 March 1528   35

Your humble servant, the official of Bourg

To the incomparable Desiderius Erasmus of Rotterdam, at Basel

1964 / From Johann von Vlatten   Speyer, 8 March 1528

First published as Ep 85 in Förstemann/Günther, the autograph was in the
Burscher Collection at Leipzig (Ep 1254 introduction). This is Vlatten's letter
of thanks for the dedication to him of the *Ciceronianus* (Ep 1948).

Greetings. I see again how much I owe to your generosity, beloved Erasmus, since in your elegant and immortal dialogue on the best manner of
speaking you deigned to make immortal mention of my name, which will
now live on into posterity, although in your sincere affection for me you
had most duteously accomplished this very thing in your dedication of the   5
Tusculan Disputations.[1] Hence it is that I debate within myself in what ways
I can somehow respond to Erasmus' great kindnesses to me. If I try to express my gratitude I find myself singing the same old song, but if I consider repaying you in proportion to my resources I shall rightly be accused
of rustic behaviour in wishing to return a cheap little gift for something   10
immortal. In the meantime, that you may be perfectly assured that I have
no desire to be branded by anyone with the charge of ingratitude, I put at
your disposition, my dear Erasmus, myself, my home, all my furnishings
and those of my family; I offer them to you as my Maecenas and the Maecenas of all men of letters, not with high-sounding words but with sincere   15
heart. If you love me, put Vlatten to the test to see if he would ever abandon
Erasmus in any way, as long as there is life in these limbs,[2] from whatever

* * * * *

10 *sub gibbo illo suo.* There is no other evidence to justify the inference that Béda
was hump-backed or deformed in any other way. The reference may rather be
to the habitually stooped posture of a scholar.

1964
1 See Ep 1390.
2 Virgil *Aeneid* 4.336

fortunes Christ has bestowed upon him. I send you this goblet as a token of
our friendship,[3] and so that you may know that one day I shall try to show
my gratitude, which if not equal to your merits will at least be an indication   20
of my feelings towards you. Quirinus,[4] truly a distinguished young man,
has recognized that you are a dear friend of mine and that it was Erasmus
who recommended him to me.

    Farewell.

    At Speyer, Reminiscere Sunday, 1528   25

    Johann von Vlatten, Erasmian to the core

    To the eminent scholar Erasmus of Rotterdam, respected and revered
friend

1965 / From William Warham   Knole, 8 March [1528]

> The manuscript, in a secretary's hand but signed by Warham, is in the Royal
> Archives at Brussels (Arch Jésuit Flandro-Belg 1529). It was first published by
> Allen, who assigned the year-date from the invitation to England (see Epp
> 1878, 1998). On Warham (d 1532), archbishop of Canterbury and Erasmus'
> loyal patron, see Ep 188. For more recent communication between the two,
> see Ep 1861.

Best greetings, most learned Erasmus. From your two letters, received
almost simultaneously, one in your own hand dated the feast of St Andrew, and the other in another's hand written on 4 January,[1] I learned that
because of your frail health and present occupations you cannot move to
England. Both his illustrious royal Majesty and I fervently wished to see   5
you here so that we could rescue and deliver you from the tumults and perils to which you are exposed and provide you a safe haven to pursue your
studies in peace and quiet. You write that you greatly appreciate the incomparable good will of our excellent prince towards you, which I think you
should continue to seek and cultivate by every good office. For, learned as   10
he is himself, he especially honours and extols men of learning. But since

* * * * *

3 The inventory of Erasmus' possessions done in 1534 lists a silver cup given to
  him by Vlatten. Bonifacius Amerbach, to whom it was bequeathed, gave it to
  Glareanus in memory of Erasmus. See Sieber 7 with n10.
4 Quirinius Talesius; see Ep 1966.

1965
1 Neither letter is extant. The one dated on the feast of St Andrew (30 November)
  answered the letter mentioned in Ep 1926:14.

you see that it is not expedient for you to move from where you are for the reasons expressed in your letter, I shall intercede with his royal Highness, as soon as I can conveniently do so, that he be willing graciously to accept your apologies and continue to keep you in the favour of his protection.   15

For the rest, if I did not see that all those who write against you promote, enhance, and consolidate your glory, I would be most grieved at your fate, seeing that you are set upon by evil beasts for something for which no thanks or rewards would be adequate to repay you. But I consider it a great advantage that you have the opportunity to conduct your defence while you   20 are still alive. In that way you derive from those beasts who would most wish to harm you more advantage and profit to ensure the immortality of your name and rescue it from the vagaries of chance than you do from all the friends everywhere who approve and extol your writings with the praise they deserve.   25

Therefore, 'Yield not to woes but ever onward go,'[2] and so crush the calumnies of these present monsters that future monsters will not dare raise their serpent's heads, thrust out their tongues and make their hissing sounds.

I give you an account of the pension that is owed you. Pieter Weldanck, who took it upon himself with a solemn pledge of assurance that he would   30 disburse the money to Pieter Gillis, has not lived up to my trust and expectations, and he adduces certain impediments that I do not find very credible that prevented him, so he claims, from fulfilling his obligations.[3] Well, for that neglect he will never again prevail upon me to put any faith in him or entrust him with my affairs or those of my friends. Therefore, some   35 time ago I gave to my revered confrère Tunstall, lord bishop of London, forty English pounds, which he undertook to have delivered to Antwerp to Pieter Gillis on good conditions and with the minimum of expenditure, as he reported to me by letter.[4]

* * * * *

2 Cf Virgil *Aeneid* 6.95.
3 Cf Ep 1931:14–20.
4 On Cuthbert Tunstall see Ep 1726 introduction. The transfer mentioned here may have taken place in the same year as that letter, 1526. The sum of £40 English sterling (*quadraginta libras nostrates*) was then worth 160 English rose crowns (at 5s each) or 106.67 angel-nobles (at 7s 6d each), which in turn were worth £320 tournois and £50 13s 4d gros Flemish. To earn such a sum, a master mason or carpenter in Cambridge, paid 6d per day (12–14 hours), would have had to work for 1,600 days, or 7.62 years (210 days per year). An Antwerp master mason, better paid than his Cambridge counterpart, at 10d groot Flemish per day (annual mean of summer and winter wages), would have had to work for 1,216 days (5.79 years) to earn the equivalent sum in Flemish pounds groot. A Cambridge master mason would have had to work for 1,600

I would have sent another twenty but decided to see first how these   40
forty would get to you. As soon as you write that you have received them, I
shall give the other twenty to the aforementioned Tunstall or, if you prefer,
to the Spaniard, Luis de Castro,[5] in whom you have great confidence. You
can be certain that I would rather that I myself be short of money than you.
Living here among friends I have various means of support, whereas living   45
among strangers you probably have few resources at your disposal. Since I
see that in all probability the perils of travel will become ever greater and
that the pursuit of your studies and activities will require more and more expenditures, we shall take greater pains than usual to make sure that money
is forwarded to you more safely and more carefully, and also in greater   50
quantity, and as far as my own personal support is concerned, nothing will
be lacking to you as long as I live; perhaps I can be of benefit to you even
after my death, as is my fervent wish. But if I shall not have the opportunity
of seeing you before I die, I beg you, since God in his goodness and mercy
will hearken to you, a man of learning and piety, that you recommend me   55
to his divine majesty in your pious prayers, just as I in turn will sincerely
recommend you to the Lord our God.

From my home in Knole,[6] 8 March, William of Canterbury

To my most beloved brother in Christ Master Erasmus of Rotterdam,
most learned by far of all men   60

1966 / To Quirinus Talesius   Basel, 12 March 1528

This letter was first published in the *Opus epistolarum*.

The son of a clothmaker of Haarlem, Quirijn Dirckszoon van Lipsen (1505–
73) was better known by the nickname Talesius (from a Greek adjective
for 'wool-spinning') because of his father's trade. After studies in Cologne
and Louvain, he became Erasmus' famulus in succession to Lieven Algoet.
This may have occurred as early as 1524, though Talesius is not mentioned
in Erasmus' correspondence until Ep 1890. Much praised by his master,
he remained in Erasmus' service until 1531, functioning as secretary, ac-
countant, and most trusted of messengers. In 1531 his father recalled him
to Holland, where he became pensionary of his hometown, married, and

* * * * *

days (7.62 years) to earn £40 sterling. See the Appendix Tables 2 and 3, 464–76
below; and CWE 12 695–6 Table 16.
5 See Ep 1931 n3.
6 A manor near Sevenoaks, Kent, and about three miles from Otford, where
Warham had built the archiepiscopal palace

then returned to the family cloth trade. Between 1543 and 1570 he was elected burgomaster of Haarlem a total of ten times. He remained a Catholic, and when in 1573 Haarlem was occupied by the forces of William of Orange, Talesius, together with his wife and daughter, were lynched by enraged citizens in reprisal for some executions that had been staged by the Spaniards.

At this time he was en route to England on Erasmus' behalf; see Ep 1955 n1.

ERASMUS OF ROTTERDAM TO QUIRINUS TALESIUS, GREETING

I have seen to it that you find this letter at the house of Marcus Laurinus[1] on your return from England. I have no doubt that you acquitted yourself there with that loyalty, zeal, and attention that has been characteristic of you, my dearest Quirinus, and that you lived up to the trust I have placed 5 in you. It is disgraceful to deceive one's master, but more disgraceful still to deceive a trusting friend. You know that with me nothing was ever concealed or hidden away from you, not even those things which others with many sets of keys keep from the eyes not only of their servants but even of their children. 10

It is not difficult to imagine why you lingered longer in England. I know how lax my friend Mountjoy is in all his dealings,[2] not solely in these kinds of affairs, and how loath that illustrious prince of the church is to dismiss his clients.[3] One cannot do battle with the gods. But try to make up for that delay now unless some new occurrence should detain you in 15 Flanders. For a long time now my studies and my house, which rely upon you, long for your presence. Do not, however, hasten your journey to such an extent that you do not give my fond and attentive greetings to my friend of long standing, Antonius Clava,[4] the very amicable Willem de Waele,[5] and my staunch patron, Jacob de Praet. The latter, I think, you would have met in 20

* * * * *

1966
1 In Bruges. For recent correspondence between Erasmus and his longtime friend, Marcus Laurinus, dean of St Donatian's Bruges (Ep 651), see Epp 1848, 1871.
2 Cf Ep 1816:11–13.
3 Possibly a reference to Cardinal Wolsey
4 Citizen and alderman of Ghent and a patron of letters, Clava (d 1529) had been a friend and correspondent of Erasmus since c 1503.
5 Waele (d 1540), whom Erasmus had met in 1514, was another of Erasmus' circle of friends in Ghent, where he became a member of the city council (1515) and then keeper of the archives of Flanders (1518).

England.[6] I have written to fewer people, partly because none of my affairs
are hidden from you, partly because I was certain that you would take the
place of any letter, however gossipy, with my friends. In the meantime, stay
away from Holland as you would from the Sirens' shore.[7] It is difficult to
renounce the lotus once you have tasted of it.[8]   25

Concerning the pension from Courtrai, do a thorough investigation of
the whole matter and whatever procedure time and opportunity afford you,
act upon it.[9] I leave the entire matter to your fidelity and prudence. Make
sure you do not take with you on your journey any money or rings except
for what is strictly necessary. To make your return to us more safe, deposit   30
your own money also, if you have any, with those whom I have indicated,
unless perchance you do not trust me as well. I am no banker; you will
receive back from me the entire sum intact, not depleted in any way, with
my usual faithfulness, which you have often experienced. Farewell.

Given at Basel, 12 March 1528   35

1967 / To Alonso Manrique de Lara   Basel, 14 March 1528

On the addressee, who was archbishop of Seville, inquisitor-general, and a
supporter of Erasmus, see Ep 1846.

This is the second preface to Erasmus' *Apologia adversus monachos quosdam
Hispanos* (the first was Ep 1879) as finally published by Froben in 1528 and
again, in a revised edition, in 1529. The work had been written in the autumn of 1527 as Erasmus' response to the charges of heresy made against him
at the conference of theologians in Valladolid during the preceding summer.
The printing was finished by mid-October, but Erasmus undertook not to publish the work until it had been approved by Manrique, to whom he sent an
advance copy. See Epp 1877, 1879, 1888. The formal approval was evidently
never given, so when Erasmus finally decided to let the book go out, he had
to make the excuses for doing so recorded in the opening paragraphs of this
letter and in Ep 1980.

* * * * *

6 The reference is to Louis (not Jacob) of Flanders, heer van Praet (Ep 1191), a
  member of Charles v's privy council. Louis had been Charles v's ambassador
  in England in the period 1522–5, but there is no evidence that Talesius had
  met him there.
7 As Allen suggests, this was probably an expression of Erasmus' fear that family
  connections would draw Talesius back to his native land, as they eventually did.
8 Cf *Adagia* II vii 62: *Lotum gustavit* 'He has tasted the lotus.'
9 On the current state of this source of income, see Epp 1993, 1999.

TO THE MOST REVEREND FATHER AND LORD IN CHRIST
ALONSO MANRIQUE, ARCHBISHOP OF SEVILLE AND CHIEF
INVESTIGATOR IN MATTERS OF THE FAITH IN SPAIN,
ERASMUS OF ROTTERDAM GIVES GREETINGS

'Pylos there is before Pylos,' as the joke in ancient comedy has it,[1] but the new tragedy[2] that is burning at white heat in these times suggests another saying: There is an apology before an apology, and there is no end or limit of apologies.

When this apologetic book was about to see the light of day, most honourable Bishop, I saw immediately that there would be need of a triple apology for the apology itself, one to appease your Highness, another to satisfy my learned friends, and a third to placate my enemies. It certainly would not be at all fitting to give offence to a bishop who, in addition to his illustrious lineage and the dignity of his high office, is pre-eminent in every virtue, nor would it be prudent to alienate the feelings of one on whose approval will depend not only my entire case but also the wishes of so many pious and learned men, who seem to be more concerned about this matter than I am myself. But I see that I need not be excessively preoccupied about this, since I am engaged in a just cause presided over by a sovereign judge, who is no less equitable and sagacious than he is supreme. Nothing makes you more worthy of this title of supreme than that you surpass by your goodness your prerogatives of nobility, dignity, and authority.

As promised, I had resolved to suppress the book, even if it entailed a financial loss, if I thought that this would have been more agreeable to your Excellency.[3] Indeed it was with the greatest reluctance that I had recourse to the collaboration of printers here, but I thought that there would be need of many copies for those who were charged with the duties of investigating this affair. I was aware too of how seldom packages sent to such far-off regions reach their destination. In addition, my copyists had more than enough to do, as always, and your letters arrived too late to have copies

* * * * *

1967
1 *Adagia* II viii 45, where Erasmus, quoting Plutarch, says that this was a proverb used in Messene 'when of two things one is selected as more highly valued and more distinguished ...' There were three ancient cities named Pylos, but the one associated with Nestor (king of Pylos in Homer's *Iliad*) was the most renowned.
2 Cf Epp 1926:12–13, 1929:21–3.
3 Cf Ep 1888:3–5.

made.[4] I was compelled for these reasons to seek the help of printers, whose techniques produce two thousand copies more quickly than the efforts of my copyists can produce two. Froben guaranteed that he would deliver ten copies to me and put the rest aside so that they would not fall into anyone's 35 hands without the express wish of your Excellency. If you were to order that they should not be published, he would suffer no loss, but all losses would be absorbed by me, who considered any expense to be of less importance than the loss of your favour.

The terms of the agreement were observed in good faith until the un- 40 expected death of Froben threw the whole family into such confusion that all cares were directed elsewhere and little precaution was taken in this matter.[5] Someone in Cologne succeeded by cunning in procuring a copy of the Froben edition and was making arrangements to have it printed. Such people are eager for gain, and they vie with one another far more passion- 45 ately than potter against potter.[6] At this point, I was faced with the decision, not whether the book should be suppressed or not, but rather whether I preferred to issue a very faulty edition or one that was more correct. Constrained on both sides, I chose the lesser of two evils, allowing it to appear in a revised version. If your Excellency approves of this action, I shall be 50 happy; if not, you will pardon me in your kindness and vent your wrath rather on necessity. I am so confident that this will be the case that I am afraid, knowing your readiness to forgive, that you may already be angry with me for having dwelt so long on a matter of such little importance.

Therefore it remains for me to appease my friends, who often berate 55 me both in person and by letter for wasting good hours in responding to everyone's petty criticisms. There are some people who are born with the instinct to spread slander; then again there are many so eager for fame that they even envy Erostratus his reputation.[7] Who is so dull-witted that he cannot find something in another person's work that he can turn into a pre- 60 text for calumny? There is no quicker or shorter road to fame. There is yet another class of people who use all their wiles and energy to create trouble

* * * * *

4 Among these were Epp 1904, 1907–8, 1913, 1920, as well as the letter from Alonso Ruiz de Virués answered by Ep 1968 and two letters from Diego Gracián, Ep 1913 and another dated 9 January 1528 (see Ep 1970:4)
5 Froben died in October 1527; see Ep 1900.
6 *Adagia* I ii 25
7 He burned the temple of Diana at Ephesus to establish for himself eternal fame.

for me and distract me from my studies. To reply to such people is to nour-
ish their malice and return a good deed for an evil one. They bring forward
a shameless calumny and win notoriety as their prize. This was the sum   65
total of their ambitions. Thus my friends conclude that this whole race of
rabble-rousers is to be completely ignored. No learned man deigns to read
their insipid nonsense, and certainly posterity will ignore it.

To these remonstrations of my friends I have little to respond except
to say that it was worthwhile to respond to some of my detractors. I did   70
not respond to all of them; to some I maintained silence. To none did I not
respond with a gentle touch, as they say, convinced that none of these disputes would survive into posterity.[8] I do not know if this will be so, but
certainly that is my wish. I deeply regret that I deemed certain people worthy of a response. The pamphlet you speak of certainly contained nothing   75
that merited a response.[9] I would not even have deigned to read it except
that the present situation in your country is such that these trifles would be
a source of trouble not only for universities and learned men but also for
the leading princes of the church and even for the sovereign power of the
imperial majesty, and would bring great tumult to all of Spain and pose a   80
stumbling block for the weak.

I come now to the matter of placating those with whom I am at odds,
for they will perhaps claim that their reputation has been damaged by this
publication. I shall first ask them that in their wisdom they should consider
that, had it been in my power, no one was more interested in having this   85
work suppressed than I. Second, since the nature of the case is such that it
would be an act of impiety for me not to refute the charges, and since the accusation reveals the ignorance, falsity, and malice of the accuser and cannot
be refuted without doing harm to his reputation, there can be no imputa-
tion of guilt against the one who defends his innocence, but rather the entire 90
burden of guilt lies with him who initiated the proceedings. If someone accused another of theft and dragged him back into court after he had been acquitted by the verdict of the judges, suing for damages because through the
argument for the defence he was considered a calumniator, what would he
hear from the judge? Simply this: 'Why did you bring a false charge against 95
him?' Who will give audience to someone seeking compensation from some-

* * * * *

8 Cf *Adagia* I iv 27: *Molli brachio, levi brachio*, 'by which we signify work not taken
   seriously' (CWE 31 339).
9 Evidently a pamphlet listing the passages in Erasmus' works that the monks
   objected to

one against whom he shot an arrow that rebounded from the other man's shield and put out his eye? Whatever wrong is involved here is to be ascribed not to the one who repelled the arrow but to the one who shot it. If there had been some probability of impiety, Christian moderation would   100 have dictated that it should be subjected to discussion and the duty of pronouncing a verdict be reserved exclusively to the judges. But now, although there are so many calumnies in circulation, still they never stop making their claims, never cease their revilings, unless perhaps it is not to be accounted as slanderous to say: 'Erasmus impugns the divinity, the dignity, and the   105 glory of Christ. Erasmus undermines the authority of Sacred Scripture.'

When I demonstrate the falsity of these and many other statements, I do not cast their accusations back at them but merely call it an impudent calumny. I could not use a milder term to describe it. And yet I do not mention names, although the ringleaders of this tumult are known to   110 me in each case. I wish that I could have defended my innocence without damaging any other person's reputation, not because any polite treatment is owed to such unprincipled individuals, who have disregarded the opinions of learned and good men, scorned the authority of leading prelates, defied even the imperial majesty, and as a consequence have thrown Spain,   115 a country that formerly enjoyed the greatest tranquillity, into confusion by their disorderly uprisings, but rather because I see that people everywhere are more disposed to hate monks than is reasonable or expedient for the Christian religion. The only thing I have left to say is to beseech the reader not to judge everyone by the morals of a few and to attribute these distur-   120 bances to ignorance or false persuasion rather than to perversity, and I exhort those people themselves in the name of Christ to pursue Christ's work with Christian integrity.

They will say, 'We have committed nothing to print against you' – as if those articles were not disseminated everywhere, or as if it is not a   125 much more serious offence to attack a person with the spoken word than in printed books. A printed book encounters its judges and gives the person under attack opportunity of responding, if he wishes, while it takes away from the aggressor the possibility of denial. But they have more power than a book since, dispersed in all the regions of the world, they never stop wag-   130 ging their tongues in concert against their neighbour, among women, craftsmen, courtiers, soldiers; at banquets, in private conversations, in the sacred confessional, in carriages and on board ship, in public lectures, in sacred sermons, in the marketplace, in schools, courts, and monasteries – and no more shamelessly anywhere than among the ignorant (their biggest audi-   135 ence), and they spread their calumnies in Spanish, French, Polish, Hungarian, German. Since they do not understand these things, it is very easy to deceive them, and my detractors say, 'With them Erasmus has no tongue: we are equipped with a great many tongues and have a great advantage over such a person. If we band together and stand firm with shameless effron- 140 tery, we will be sure to win and we will impale Erasmus with our tongues.' O what holy thoughts, worthy of Dominic and Francis! Here even those who advertise themselves with the title of Observance,[10] who crawled into their shells at first when Luther began his lawless rampaging, now play leading roles. Again and again I beg good and pious monks not to think that any 145 of this pertains to them. Would that the unscrupulous behaviour of these people permitted me to spare even the wicked who, just as they do not spare themselves, so they do more harm to their order than the most deadly enemy.

What example can I give now of the kind of thing they utter with those sacred tongues from those sacrosanct breasts? One of them in a crowded as- 150 sembly said that there were some heretical things in the books of Erasmus.[11] As he stepped down from the pulpit, he was accosted by a certain learned man who was a pensionary in that city.[12] He was asked to produce a hereti- cal passage. He answered that he had never read any books of Erasmus, that he had tried to read a work called the *Moria* but because of the abstruse 155 style he was afraid that Erasmus might have fallen into some heresy.[13] An- other person, in an effort to stir up the crowd, said that I had corrected the Magnificat. Asked at table what the correction was, he blurted out what- ever came to his mind,[14] namely, that I had translated 'to Abraham and to his seeds.' When the book was brought forth, it was proved to be a bla- 160 tant lie.[15] Another singularly unlearned learned doctor said in a sermon in my presence that those who corrected the Magnificat were guilty of a sin against the Holy Spirit, as were those who said that the preacher did not

* * * * *

10 The Observants (or Observantines) were those members of the Franciscan Or- der who claimed to 'observe' exactly the Rule of St Francis, in contrast to the Conventuals, whom they regarded as too worldly and lax. In 1517 the Obser- vants were formally separated from the Conventuals and declared to be the true order of St Francis.
11 The Franciscan Nicolas Bureau, suffragan bishop of Tournai; see Ep 1144 n12.
12 Frans van Cranevelt, then pensionary of the city of Bruges: cf Epp 1581:436 with n54, and 2045:161–75.
13 Epp 1581 and 2045:173 also identify the book in question as the *Moria* (ie the *Praise of Folly*), but in other accounts of the incident, Erasmus says that it was the *Paraphrases*; see Epp 1144:51, 1192:43, 1212:20–1.
14 Cf *Adagia* I v 73: *Quicquid in linguam venerit*. The identity of this accuser is unknown; see the earlier account of his groundless charge in Ep 948:99–107.
15 Cf Luke 1:55, where Erasmus translated correctly in the singular, 'to his seed' (LB VI 228B).

understand his subject, since the subjects of sermons are taken from Sacred
Scripture.[16] I had said at table once that a certain member of the same order   16
had misinterpreted the words of Peter, which he had taken for his theme.
What I said was the absolute truth. Another loudly proclaimed that in the
Lord's Prayer in the Gospel of Luke I had translated *peccata* [sins] instead of
debita [debts], although this is the church's reading of that evangelist both
in Greek and in Latin.[17]   17

What shall I say of the man who criticized me in a crowded lecture hall
for entertaining irreligious ideas about a life of chastity,[18] but afterwards in a
private conversation admitted that until then he had believed that a declamation was a church sermon and that celibacy was a virginal and angelic life.[19]

What about the person who exultantly declared that I had erroneously   17
written that Jerome did not lead a life of perpetual virginity, since he writes
to Eustochium: 'For we not only extol virginity but we preserve it,' when
for anyone who knows Latin *servare* in that context means 'to show how one
can preserve it.' And even if the meaning of the Latin was not clear, the
context itself and the tone of the language indicate it.[20]   18

I am embarrassed to mention the story about the person who, commenting on the passage in the *Enchiridion* where I praised the *germanam theologiam*

* * * * *

16 Sebastian Craeys (d 1523), Carmelite of Antwerp; see Epp 948:114–39 and
2045:46–59.
17 In all his editions of the New Testament, Erasmus agreed with the Vulgate in
the use of *peccata* to translate Luke 11:4 and Matt 6:12. In the *Annotationes* of
February 1527, he added notes on Matt 6:12 and Luke 11:4 in which he noted
that neither Luke nor St Augustine makes any distinction between *debita* and
peccata; see Ann Reeve's facsimile edition of *Erasmus' Annotations on the New
Testament: The Gospels* (London 1986) 35, 189. Erasmus' accuser in this case may
have been the preacher referred to in Epp 541:92–8 and 948:108–113.
18 An apparent reference to the Louvain theologian Jan Briart of Ath (Ep 670),
who in 1519 had publicly denounced Erasmus' *Encomium matrimonii* as an impious challenge to the ideal of celibacy; see Ep 946 introduction. Erasmus
responded with the *Apologia pro declamatione matrimonii* (CWE 71 86–95).
19 Briart had failed to understand that the *Encomium* was a *declamatio* and that
declamationes were exercises whose purpose was 'to treat the argument from
both sides, as for and against a tyrannicide, for and against an abductor,' or for
and against celibacy. Erasmus also alleges that Briart, with his poor knowledge
of Latin, had understood *coelibatus* to mean *vitam coelestem*, ie a heavenly way
of life, rather than simply the state of being unmarried. Cf CWE 71 91–3.
20 See Jerome Ep 22.23. This story is told in more detail and with greater clarity in
Epp 1858:531–55, 2045:192–203. At Ep 2045:192 Erasmus' accuser is identified
as a Dominican. As suggested in Ep 1858 n56, he might have been Erasmus'
old Louvain adversary Vincentius Theoderici.

of the apostles, which had subjugated the arrogance of philosophers and the sceptres of kings under the yoke of Christ, publicly proclaimed that I said there was no theology anywhere but in Germany, which was the greatest   185 supporter of heretics. But even children know that the word *germanus* means 'true' or 'genuine,' and the word is used in that sense also in Paul, if that person had not read the classical authors.[21]

Similar to this is the case of a great defender of the faith, as he thought of himself, who did not hesitate to accuse me before audiences of distin-   190 guished persons of saying to a Carthusian that it was better to eat meat than to suffer a slight headache, when I was reproving him for allowing his neighbour to put his life at stake because of a man-made law.[22]

But I shall cease burdening your Excellency with these trivia, although they are not meant for you but for my adversaries. It is such things, and   195 countless others more ignorant and stupid than these, that are spread abroad publicly before high-ranking men. What kind of rubbish should we imagine them whispering in secret? And yet these things reach the ears of sensible men – for we are not all fools or blockheads – and they pass them on to the crowd. And so it comes about that even without my uttering a word my ad-   200 versaries win for themselves the derision or the hatred of many. Whenever they are induced by the authority of princes to restrain from these excesses, they say, 'We must obey God rather than men.'[23] This saying was perfectly appropriate for the apostles, who after imprisonment and floggings gladly endured for the name of Jesus, were ordered by the impious Jews to ab-   205 stain from talking about what they had been commanded by Christ himself to preach throughout the whole world. But, when Christian and religious rulers restrain them from scurrilous abuse, from lying, from slander, from seditious outcries, how inappropriate is that saying, 'We must obey God rather than men'!   210

* * * * *

21 The passage in question is in the letter to Paul Volz that served as the preface to the 1518 edition of the *Enchiridion*: Ep 858:116–18 / CWE 66 10. On this incident, cf Epp 1858:471–87, 1985:10–15, 2045:228–33. For the use of the word by St Paul, see Phil 4:3 (Vulgate).
22 Cf *De esu carnium* LB IX 1205E. The accuser failed to understand that in the expression *in capitis venire discrimen* 'to put his life at stake' Erasmus' used the word *caput* 'head' as a figure of speech (synecdoche) for one's entire life, particularly when it is threatened (as in the English expression 'capital punishment'); he mistakenly thought that Erasmus was arguing that 'a slight headache (*levem capitis dolorem*) was a sufficient reason to ignore regulations of fasting and abstinence. This incident is recounted in somewhat more detail in Ep 1985:17–20.
23 Acts 5:29. Cf Epp 858:632, 1902:97, 1903:21, 1909:50.

What is your purpose, my excellent friends? Is it by these methods that you think the church of Christ should be supported? Do you attempt to restore the authority of your orders by these stratagems? An authority that was never harmed by me, not even to the extent that any of you was deprived of an egg or a piece of cheese through my doing.[24] You cannot inflict more grave harm on it than you are now doing, believe me. I am not issuing threats against you. Consider what kind of world this is, reflect on what sentiments people have towards you. I shall not mention what I am capable of with the pen, or if I were to ally myself with those factions that are plotting the destruction of your orders. Perhaps I can gain permission from princes to plead my case in French or in Spanish, which would only be just. But there is no danger that this will ever happen: you have in me a Jonah who would rather be thrown to the waves than be saved at risk of the common peril.[25] Plead your case yourselves with wisdom. If you do this, Christ will be present. If you persecute impious beliefs, no impious belief ever won my favour or ever will: in this you have me as your fellow soldier. If you are eager to repair and restore the authority of your orders, return to those virtues which procured so much authority and favour for your predecessors; and in this you will have Erasmus' applause. Let your defence be in Christ, whose glory must be served in all things. Through him you will conquer, if you fight under his auspices, and then you will truly gain a glorious victory, if you conquer for him. But if you turn your eyes away from Christ and place your hopes of victory in dishonesty, slander, cunning, outcries, whisperings, human favours, conspiratorial alliances, your plans will go astray and you will end up as the Jews did when they tried to obliterate the name of Christ and reinstate their former tyranny.

The gospel did not come down to earth from heaven to serve men's passions but to be a light to all men's ignorance, salt for their insipidity, an undeviating rule by which all actions of all men could be regulated. Let us stand firm on the solid rock so that through the rock we may conquer for the rock. Among men some are called powerful, others weak. In the presence of divine power we are all equally worms and gnats. No one is so powerful but that he can be pulverized if he should strike against this stone; no one is so weak but that he will be victorious if he will stand firm upon this rock.

* * * * *

24 Erasmus liked to refer contemptuously to his adversaries in the mendicant orders, whose members were required to beg for alms, as *tyrologi* ('cheese collectors' or 'cheese connoisseurs'), a word of his invention that punned on *theologi*.
25 Jon 1:12

I urge you to do this, my brothers. Indeed I should gladly give this advice to all Christians, so that they may bear in mind that this almost unheard of catastrophe of our time is the hand of the Almighty calling us to repentance. What evil is not present to us? War, pestilence, famine? We have seen terrible things, and unless God looks after us we shall see things more terrible still. In the clash of opinions when was there ever greater ferocity, greater stubbornness? The Ninevites, terrified by the threats of the prophet, turned to repentance and obtained mercy from the Lord.[26] Pharaoh himself, tormented by frogs, locusts, dogflies and other calamities, cried to the Lord and found solace.[27] We have been afflicted with so many plagues for so many years, but I do not see anyone who thinks of changing his life for the better; everyone is eager to pluck some personal advantage from the public woe. One casts blame upon the other, everyone flatters himself. But if acknowledging together the hand of the Lord that has been extended against us, we would turn, each of us, to a reformed way of life with sincere hearts, the wrath of the judge would be turned to mercy and he would unite the minds of princes, would remove from us the armed locusts who spare nothing, sacred or profane, would drive away the frogs of sects, and the God of patience and consolation would grant us, according to Paul's prayer,[28] to live in harmony with one another in accordance with Jesus Christ, so that with one mind and with one voice we may honour the God and Father of our Lord, Jesus Christ, not torn apart but joined together and made whole in the same understanding and the same feeling.

At the present moment the Lord has confused the tongues of the earth, since we have erected a gigantic tower into the sky and thus we speak diverse things because each talks about matters pertaining to him.[29] Let us all conceive Christ in our minds and let us all speak Christ with one mouth. Each one should remind himself of this, whether he be supreme pontiff or monarch or monk or prophet, for God has confined everything under the power of sin so that he may have mercy on all things,[30] and all of us are in need of the glory of God.[31] This evil is from the Lord; it is from him that we must seek a remedy. Why therefore do we not abandon the construction of Babel and instead dig wells so that we may find veins of tears by which the enkindled wrath of the Godhead may be extinguished? While

* * * * *

26 Jon 3:10
27 Exod 8:1–32
28 Rom 15:5–6
29 Cf Gen 11:1–9.
30 Rom 11:32; cf Gal 3:22.
31 Rom 3:23

this duty pertains to all in common, it is especially incumbent on the monks, 280
with whom the church once took refuge whenever the wrath of God pressed
hard upon it. It was they who by fasts, vigils, self-mortification, and prayers
did not cease to call upon the mercy of the Lord until serenity returned. This
is my advice, which, with Christ as my witness, I judge to be most salutary.
If I had any better advice, I would gladly impart it.   285

But, most distinguished Bishop, almost forgetting to whom I am speaking, I have lingered too long on things that pertain to others. Therefore, I
shall make an end of it, praying that Christ will bestow upon your illustrious
Highness every blessing and good fortune.

At Basel, 14 March 1528   290

1968 / To Alonso Ruiz de Virués   [Basel, c 15 March 1528]

This undated letter was first published in the *Opus epistolarum*. Clearly contemporary with Ep 1969, it answers one dated 13 December 1527 (see line 72)
that is not extant. Allen surmised that it arrived with the budget of letters that
included Ep 1920. In line 71, Ep 1969 is mentioned as already having been
written, which would seem to indicate that it should precede this letter. Allen,
however, preserved the order found in the *Opus epistolarum*, reasoning that it
probably reflected the sequence of composition and that line 71 was thus to be
regarded as a postscript.

On Virués, a Spanish Benedictine monk at Burgos who was sympathetic to
Erasmus' scholarship, see Ep 1684. Ep 2067:2–3 may refer to answers to this
letter and the three that follow.

ERASMUS OF ROTTERDAM TO ALONSO RUIZ DE VIRUÉS, GREETING
If it were for my sake that you undertook such strenuous tasks and exposed
yourself to such hatred, honourable brother in the Lord, I should have every
reason to have great esteem for you, unless I were so incredibly stupid that
I could not understand or so ungrateful that I could not acknowledge your   5
extraordinary devotion to me. Now, since you both do and suffer all of this
not so much for my sake as for the sake of piety and truth, I esteem you all
the more, my dearest Virués, and confess that I am much more obliged to
you, since my feelings in this matter are such that I prefer piety to win out
rather than Erasmus. If the victory will go to Christ, I shall consider myself 10
the victor, since that side will have won to which I am wholly committed.
Therefore I thank you on two counts, both for myself, in that you do me such
a friendly service, and for piety, whose cause you champion with diligence
and skill. And furthermore, I take new courage from your judgment of me,
the accuracy of which I cannot call into question because of your exceptional 15

honesty and learning. Would that the modesty of your order might be imitated by the other orders, who seem to believe that they can defend the Christian religion and the dignity of their reputation by means of shameless detraction, scurrilous abuse, and seditious turmoil – as if there were not someone dwelling in heaven who derides and sneers at these intrigues of mortal men.

My response to the articles was ready six months ago and I sent some copies to my friends.[1] You kindly advise me that I can overcome my enemies with moderation, but it seemed to me that I exercised admirable control over my pen, first of all by not mentioning anyone by name, and then by never resorting to abusive language, unless perhaps it is not abusive when they accuse me by name of impugning the divinity, dignity, and glory of Christ, and it is abusive when I call that insolent calumny. Monsters of this sort did not merit any kind of politeness. Any concessions I made were partly to the feelings of my friends, partly to Christian moderation. And yet there will be some to whom this apology will seem too mordant. They think so much respect is due to them. I refrain from mentioning names, although I am not unaware that some find it desirable to become known in whatever way they can. But in the meantime they rage with impunity against my name in public lectures, in which they utter such imbecilities that they are laughed at even by adolescents.[2] I warned one or two of them by letter;[3] they piously swear that they never made mention of my name except with respect.

In many regions Franciscans who call themselves Observants[4] are so involved in this business that it is quite evident that it is an organized plot. Nevertheless, they accomplish nothing except to make themselves more hated day by day by good and sensible men. This causes me no little sorrow since I always supported their integrity. They think their tactics are marvellously clever. They clandestinely remove my books from libraries. Even the books I gave them as gifts they criticize in secret and often disparage in public lectures. But they put nothing in writing, knowing that I also have a pen. In the present circumstances I have no way of avenging myself upon them. If I press the attack they deny that they said anything of the sort or

* * * * *

1968

1 The articles presented by the Spanish religious orders to the Inquisition in 1527 as charges against Erasmus: see Ep 1791 introduction. Erasmus' response was the *Apologia ad monachos* (Epp 1879, 1967).
2 Examples of this are recounted in Ep 1967.
3 In Ep 1823 to Frans Titelmans, for example
4 See Ep 1967 n10.

swear that they said something else. What can you do with them? Finally, if someone cannot justify himself, he is transferred to some other place where he can say even more atrocious things; and yet I never offended any of them 50
in my life. Of the many evils that Luther introduced into Germany, he had at least one good effect, which was to bring this breed of men more under control.

You write that Spain is free of sects and lives under the rule of the Roman pontiff. This gives me great pleasure, all the more so since I know 55
what misery it is to be torn apart by so many conflicting opinions. If the pope and those subject to him could live under Christ as you live under the pope, I should augur the same happiness to all of you. As things are, those who truly hold dear the glory of Christ see many things that make them weep. What else can they do? 60

I did not know previously that the *Enchiridion* had been translated by the archdeacon of Alcor.[5] There is not a thing to be changed in it. He conveys the same meaning as I although he uses other words. He admits that they will be worried that they may be found out to be telling lies about me if I begin speaking in Spanish. This is what I call pure spite.[6] I wish the same 65
thing could be done for my *Mercy of the Lord*, the four commentaries on the Psalms, the *Christian Matrimony*, and the *Paraphrases*, which do not treat contentious issues.[7] The *Declamation in Praise of Marriage* I wrote only to amuse myself, as an example of the deliberative style of oration.[8] Certain things I wrote only for the learned, which I should not wish to be translated. But I 70
have written these things to the archdeacon himself.[9]

This was written in response to your letter of 13 December.

* * * * *

5 Alonso Fernández de Madrid; see Ep 1969.
6 Cf Ep 1969:40–4.
7 A Spanish translation of *De immensa Dei misericordia* (Ep 1474), published c December 1527, was already in circulation; see Bataillon I 304–6, and 542n. At this point, Erasmus had published commentaries on the first four Psalms (Epp 327, 1304:504–5, 1427, 1535): see ASD V -2, CWE 63. In 1531 an anonymous translator, probably Alonso Fernández, published Spanish versions of those on Psalms 1 and 4; see Bataillon I 308–9. There were no sixteenth-century translations of either the *Institutio christiani matrimonii* (Ep 1727) or of the Paraphrases (either collectively or singly); see Bataillon I 304.
8 Much published as an independent declamation, *Encomium matrimonii* (Epp 604:12n, 1341A:652–4) was also included in *De conscribendis epistolis* (1522) as an example of an *epistola suasoria*; see CWE 25 129–45.
9 In Ep 1969

1969 / To Alonso Fernández de Madrid   Basel, 15 March 1528

First published in the *Opus epistolarum*, this is Erasmus' reply to Ep 1904.

Fernández, (Ep 1904 introduction), archdeacon of Alcor in the diocese of Palencia, was renowned for his intellectual gifts and for his preaching. His translation of Erasmus' *Enchiridion* was completed by the beginning of 1525. The first edition, no copies of which survive, was published before September 1526, at which time a second edition was published at Alcalá. The most important translation of any work of Erasmus to be published in Spain, it enjoyed enormous success (Bataillon I 205–42), but it was also the work principally responsible for the implacable hostility of the Spanish theologians (see Ep 1814:129–44).

ERASMUS OF ROTTERDAM TO THE ARCHDEACON OF ALCOR,
GREETING

I am not surprised, distinguished sir, that letters which are sent from so far away do not reach their destination, since those that are sent from nearby are often intercepted. I received no letter from you except the one written   5
from Palencia on 27 November – at least as far as I can recall.[1] I received one or two copies of your letters written to others, from which it was abundantly clear how much zeal you have for Christian piety and how sincerely devoted you are to me. This I had already learned from several letters from my friends. I admire in you your zeal for piety and I am most grateful to you,   10
as is only just, for your singular good will towards me. If you do this of your own good judgment, as I have no doubt you do, there is good hope that you will always remain faithful to your resolve. I learned from letters of many people that my *Enchiridion* speaks a very elegant Spanish. It is only now that I have learned by whose efforts it was produced. I am particularly gratified   15
that a man of your stature deemed this little work worthy of his efforts. If only it be of such utility as both of us desire! I would not care about envy, which usually accompanies good things. But if what your letter and those of my friends proclaim is true, not only am I not sorry but I rejoice and am grateful to you; not for the celebrity of my name, of which you write that   20
you are the staunch defender, but for the advancement of piety (I would prefer to be the most unknown of men than to have a reputation tempered by the ferment of envy, and without speaking of envy I have had more than

* * * * *

1969
1 Erasmus' memory of the date of Ep 1904 (13 November 1527) is slightly off.

enough experience of what a burden glory is, if this is indeed glory and not
merely celebrity).   25

But since this work has been successful, I should wish, according to
the Greek proverb which says that turtle-meat should be eaten or not eaten,[2]
that other works of mine should learn to speak Spanish as long as they are
an inducement to piety. Of this type are my books, *On the Mercy of the Lord*,
On Christian Matrimony, the *Paraphrases*, the commentaries on four Psalms,   30
and anything else of this nature, which when adapted by the proper translator can be conducive to an improvement of morals.[3] In this the skill of the
translator is of a great importance. I have written certain works for the pro-
motion of studies, some for correcting the opinion of the masses, and many I
have published only for the learned. I knew nothing about you except what   35
I have just mentioned. But a rumour was circulating both in writing and
by word of mouth that the *Colloquies* and *Lingua* and I know not what other
works were being printed there in Spain.[4] Although they contain nothing
that is impious, as I believe, everything has a time and a place.

What you say very wisely in a letter to a friend[5] is the absolute truth,   40
that certain persons who have placed their hopes of victory in slanderous
talk do not wish Erasmus to speak in the vulgar tongue lest the foolishness
of those who are eloquent in secret and in the company of the unlearned
be exposed.[6] That is the reason for their mutterings. Therefore we were
in agreement in principle even though I did not know the author of the   45
translation until now. And if I had known him, I would have never doubted
his sincerity.

In France a certain good man, learned and of noble rank, attempted
the same thing, unless I am mistaken, with exactly the same motivations,

* * * * *

2 *Adagia* I x 60: *Oportet testudinis carnes aut edere aut non edere* 'When you're offered turtle-meat, either eat or do not eat.' This, Erasmus explains, is 'directed
   against those who, having taken up some piece of business, go through with
   it slowly, neither finishing nor giving it up ... They say ... that turtle-meat
   eaten in moderate quantities causes griping of the bowels, which is relieved
   by larger amounts ... It amounts to a way of saying: Make up your mind.
   Either go to war or don't go to war; either study or don't study.'
3 Cf Ep 1968:65–8.
4 On Spanish translations of selected colloquies by Virués and Luis Mexía, see
   Ep 1873 introduction. The earliest documented translations of the *Lingua* date
   from 1531; see CWE 29 253–4 and ASD IV-1 226. See also Ep 1593 introduction.
5 Allen speculates that this may have been Vives, with whom Virués was now
   in correspondence: see Ep 1847:65–6, 81–2, 114–15.
6 Cf Ep 1968:61–4.

but it went badly both for him and for me.[7] Twice he risked losing his head, 50
and he would have perished, thanks to the clemency of the monks, unless
the king had come to his rescue.[8] I am still in the gladiatorial arena with the
theologians,[9] or rather, with the followers of Béda. For Béda is as much trouble as three thousand monks.[10] Nowhere are these wicked bands of monks
not to be found; yet nowhere have they had the power that they have exer- 55
cised in Spain.[11] For that reason you cannot claim to enjoy perfect happiness,
although you are fortunate enough in other respects.

Concerning your kind advice about the *Exomologesis*,[12] I take it upon
myself to finish it at the earliest possible opportunity, although it has been
finished by me so many times both before and after that little book ap- 60
peared. People do not consider what I undertook to discuss in that book,
nor for whom, at what time, and in what region it was written. What good
will an appendix do if it is not read or if it is read for the purpose of
defamation? I don't know what the situation is there; here that little book
has healed more people than the writings of others who consider themselves 65
advocates of confession. Nevertheless, I shall follow your advice.[13] May the
Lord protect you in all your undertakings, my illustrious friend.

Given at Basel, 15 March 1528

1970 / To Diego Gracián de Alderete   Basel, 15 March 1528

First published in the *Opus Epistolarum*, this is Erasmus' reply to Ep 1913. In
that letter, Gracián had sought to console Erasmus in his difficulties with his
Spanish critics, but Erasmus here takes no note of that. On Gracián, see Ep
1913 introduction.

* * * * *

7 Louis de Berquin (Ep 2027 n1), who had got himself into serious trouble with
  the Paris theologians as (among other things) the suspected translator into
  French of a number of Erasmus' works, including the *Encomium matrimonii*
  and the *Inquisitio de fide* : Cf Epp 2027, 2048, 2066. He was executed as a heretic
  in 1529; see Ep 2188.
8 See Ep 1722 introduction.
9 See Ep 1934 n1.
10 On Béda, see Ep 1943 n6.
11 See Ep 1926 n4.
12 See Ep 1904:26–9, where Fernández recommends the addition of a concluding
   section with a little more emphasis on auricular confession.
13 Erasmus did not in fact do so, though he had dealt with the question at length
   in the *Apologia adversus monachos* (Ep 1879); see LB IX 1062–4 and cf Ep 1904
   n4.

ERASMUS OF ROTTERDAM TO GRACIÁN THE SPANIARD

I received two of your letters at the same time, gracious Gracián, but they were very brief and of practically the same import. One bore the date 1 December and the other 9 January. Concerning the two previous ones I have to inform you that they have not yet been delivered to me; I suppose they will arrive eventually.[1]

I have long been aware of the renown of the illustrious Don Juan Manuel, a man endowed with extraordinary wisdom, who through his merits has come to enjoy great favour and influence at the imperial court.[2] I gladly welcome the favour and sympathy he extends to me. If there is anything in which you think I can gratify him, do not hesitate to suggest it to me. You will find me ready and willing.

Since you wish to know my age, I think I am now marking the year when Cicero died.[3] I would be in fairly good health if I hadn't had to contend with the stone for so many years.[4] I live by the day, prepared to leave my post when the supreme commander gives the order. Give fond and respectful greetings to your master. Farewell.

At Basel, 15 March 1528

1971 / To Juan Maldonado   Basel, 15 March 1528

First published in the *Opus epistolarum*, this is Erasmus' response to Ep 1908. On Maldonado, a diocesan administrator in Burgos and, at this stage of his life, an avid Erasmian, see Epp 1742, 1805, and 1839:10–15, 48–62.

ERASMUS OF ROTTERDAM TO JUAN MALDONADO, GREETING

Be assured that your lengthy letter, written in the month of September 1526,

* * * * *

1970
1 None of the letters mentioned is extant.
2 The Spanish grandee, Don Juan Manuel, lord of Belmonte (d 1543), a supporter of Hapsburg interests in Spain ever since the death of Queen Isabella in 1504, had served as the ambassador of Charles v in Rome (1520–22) and was now, as a member of the councils of state and finance in Spain, the principal opponent of the imperial chancellor, Gattinara. Gracián, who was Juan Manuel's secretary from 1527 to 1529, assisted him in his recreational reading of Latin works of edification, including Erasmus' version of the New Testament.
3 Another indication of the perpetual difficulty of determining Erasmus' exact age. Cicero was sixty-three when he died. If Erasmus had been born in 1466, which is the earliest possible date, he would now be in his sixty-second year.
4 See Epp 1376 n4, 1408 n2, 1729 n11.

in which you weave the history of events in your country,[1] was delivered
to me and gave me great pleasure on several counts. I returned a copious
answer.[2] But I understand that your complaint about undelivered letters is a   5
common one with many. I would have sent you another copy if it were not
too late, and perhaps you have already received the original. I shall send
one, however, if you request it.

You paint the picture of a seasoned veteran.[3] I wish there were fewer
like him! These days there is no place that does not abound with this type   10
of men. What astonishes me is that there in Spain they are given much more
licence than was ever permitted elsewhere. As for me, I shall pursue the
cause of piety with sincere heart until my last breath; Christ will see to the
outcome of it. I am preparing my bags to depart from here.[4]

I can reciprocate the affection of Diego Osorio,[5] but I do not see in what   15
other way I can repay him. He is most worthy not only of my affection but
of universal esteem, since to his noble lineage he has joined zeal for literature and piety and has added the most beautiful of colophons, contempt for
glory.

You have my autograph letter, very brief when one considers our warm   20
regard for one another but quite lengthy given my present occupations.
Farewell.

* * * * *

1971
1 Ep 1742
2 Ep 1805
3 Here, as in Ep 1908, identified by Allen as the Dominican Pedro de Vitoria,
   brother of the illustrious Francisco de Vitoria, also a Dominican, who studied at Paris and in 1526 assumed the *prima* chair in theology at Salamanca
   (Ep 1836 nn9, 14). On the basis of the contents of a letter from Juan Luis
   Vives (Ep 1836), Erasmus believed that Francisco was one of his defenders
   but that Pedro, by contrast, was hostile and had contributed to the campaign
   against him in Spain that led to the inquiry into his orthodoxy by the assembly of theologians at Valladolid in the summer of 1527. It was on this assumption that, in a letter to Francisco, Erasmus asked him to exercise a moder-
   ating influence on his brother (Ep 1909:46–64). James Farge has established,
   however, that Francisco was far less devoted to Erasmus than the latter believed, that indeed he found him to be at fault on most of the issues examined at Valladolid and, consequently, that it is highly possible that it was he
   rather than his brother who was the fierce Dominican critic referred to by Juan
   Maldonado in Ep 1908. See Epp 1836:23–36 with nn8, 10, and 12, 1908:23–40
   with n8.
4 Ie to leave Basel; see Ep 1926 n8.
5 A response to the greetings from Osorio communicated by Maldonado in Ep
   1908:71–2, 82.

Given at Basel, 15 March 1528

Give my sincere greetings to your congenial friend Osorio.

1972 / To Frans van der Dilft   Basel, 18 March 1528

This letter was first published in the *Opus epistolarum*. In February Dilft had departed Basel on a trip into Germany, carrying letters from Erasmus to friends
there (see Ep 1942 n1). The messages in this letter for Pieter Gillis and Erasmus
Schets (lines 9 and 16) seem to indicate that it was directed to Antwerp.

ERASMUS OF ROTTERDAM TO FRANS VAN DER DILFT, GREETING

If your odyssean voyage went well, in which 'You saw the towns and learned
the ways of many men,'[1] I wish to send you my hearty congratulations. I
am waiting to hear the full account from Hieronymus Froben, to whom you
may safely confide all matters. I am resolved to try everything with Birck-   5
mann before entering upon the last act of the tragedy.[2] If you have the opportunity, use your rhetoric to persuade the man to vie with me in good
services rather than in misdeeds. You know the topics and the manner of
treating them. Give my warm greeting to Pieter Gillis.[3] I have nothing to
write to him, especially since you can take the place of many letters. When   10
my servant Quirinus Talesius returns I shall set out on my journey.[4] You
may expect a guest, but not a troublesome one. I wish every happiness for
your mother, brothers and sisters. Let me know how your own health is
faring.

Given at Basel, 18 March 1528   15

Give my regards to Erasmus Schets and give him a copy of my book
On Pronunciation in my name.[5] I have nothing about which to write him.

1973 / To Nicolas Wary   Basel, 19 March 1528

This letter was first published in the *Opus Epistolarum*. On Nicolas Wary (d
1529), since 1526 president of the Collegium Trilingue, see Ep 1481 n17.

* * * * *

1972
1 Homer *Odyssey* 1.3
2 See Ep 1931:22–3 with n6.
3 Ep 184
4 See Ep 1926 n8. On Talesius see Ep 1966.
5 Ep 1949. On Schets see Ep 1931.

ERASMUS OF ROTTERDAM TO NICHOLAS WARY OF MARVILLE,
GREETING

You said you had nothing to write, but on the contrary it is a great deal, and
it gives me great pleasure to learn that everything is proceeding there in a
most favourable and propitious fashion and that with general approval you   5
are vigorously defending the cause of good letters. Concerning the dispute,
there are no accusations or suspicions apart from what I concluded from
your letter.[1] I am afraid that sometimes your liberty of speech, which I see
is something inborn in you, may provide some pretext for offence to those
who lack only the occasion for doing harm, as the proverb goes.[2] I hear that   10
Johannes Campester is possessed of this same candour.[3] Here I am more
diffident, since I know from personal experience how many woes my simplicity of spirit and frankness of speech have occasioned. But I am glad that
this anxiety of mine is ill founded.

As for these evangelicals that you mention, I dislike them for many   15
reasons, but especially because on account of them good letters languish
everywhere, lie stagnant, are neglected, and die out; but without them what
is man's life?[4] They love provisions for the journey and a wife, everything
else they consider worthless. I recommend that these impostors be kept far
away from your community. We have heard enough about the gospel, the   20
gospel, the gospel; what we are lacking are the morals of the gospel. How
silent the monks are there I do not know. In Spain they are more than sufficiently vocal.[5] And there is no lack elsewhere of those who blabber away,
especially certain barefoot monks.[6] I don't know what instigates them, but
they all fetch trouble for themselves on their own beast.[7]   25

Farewell. Given at Basel, 19 March 1528

Give my greetings to Merbecanus, Rescius and Campen, and to Goclenius too in case I do not have time to write.[8]

* * * * *

1973
1 Not extant
2 *Adagia* II i 68
3 Erasmus means Jan van Campen (Campensis), who held the chair of Hebrew
  at the Trilingue (1520–31). In line 27 below, Erasmus gets the name right.
4 Seneca Ep 82.3
5 See Ep 1791 introduction.
6 See Epp 1967:129–46, 1968:38–40.
7 *Adagia* I i 50
8 On Jan Stercke of Meerbeke (Merbecanus), first president (until 1526) of
  the Collegium Trilingue, cf Ep 1322. For recent correspondence involving

1974 / To Johannes Cochlaeus   Basel, 19 March 1528

First published in the *Opus Epistolarum*, this is Erasmus' reply to Ep 1928.

ERASMUS OF ROTTERDAM TO JOANNES COCHLAEUS, GREETING
For your earnest diligence in attending to the Tertullian and Livy,[1] I commend your devotion and alacrity of spirit, even though I had already received a definite answer about both of them. I judge from your response to
my request how much promptness you would employ if it ever happened   5
that I had need of your services. Emser always showed himself a true friend
to me. When you succeed to his post, I am confident that I will have in you
alone both Emser and Cochlaeus. Do not cease to stimulate the favour of
the illustrious prince in my regard.[2] As he is a man of great kindness, so
he is also a man of no ordinary discernment. Since at times I make a plea   10
for moderation, I have sometimes given him the impression of not being a
strong enough Antilutheran. But he would feel otherwise if he knew thoroughly the reason for my position. And perhaps the end result will teach
him that I defended the cause of Christ with sincere heart, at least with such
wisdom as I have.   15
     If you write anything to me from there, take every precaution to whom
you entrust the letter. Whatever is written to me is intercepted by these evangelical scoundrels. Some of them even pretend that they are going directly
to Basel to Erasmus and spontaneously offer to perform this duty. Once they
have received the letters, that's the last you see of them. Consequently, if I   20
have anything serious to communicate I usually send a servant or someone
well known to me and pay him for this service. Give my warm greetings to
Simon Pistoris, a pious man and sincere friend.[3] Farewell, my brother and
dear friend in the Lord.
     Given at Basel, 19 March 1528   25

          * * * * *

Rutgerus Rescius, since 1518 professor of Greek at the Trilingue, see Epp
1768:65–76, 1806A:1–18. For Campen see n3 above. For Conradus Goclenius
see Ep 1994A.

1974
1 Allen speculates that Erasmus was perhaps already working on his edition of
  1531, the preface to which (Allen Ep 2435:49–50) mentions a fragment received
  from Mainz, Cochlaeus' location before his move to Saxony.
2 On Hieronymus Emser, Cochlaeus' predecessor as secretary and chaplain to
  Duke George of Saxony, see Ep 1928 n4.
3 Ep 1943

1975 / To Johann von Vlatten   Basel, 19 March 1528

First published in the *Opus Epistolarum*. Although this letter deals with the same
subject matter Ep 1964, it does not appear to be a reply to it.

ERASMUS OF ROTTERDAM TO JOHANN VON VLATTEN, GREETING

I dedicated the *Ciceronianus* rather than *On Pronunciation* to you for a purpose;[1] I think you will approve. That it was not printed separately was the
fault of the printer; but it is of no importance. I think these books will frequently be reprinted by others; and then this can be corrected. I am exceed-   5
ingly happy that you are pleased with this study of mine. But what is this,
I pray, that you threaten that from this time on you will no longer be rich
only in promises?[2] Since I possess all of you by right of friendship, by that
token I consider all your possessions mine. My dear Vlatten, I prefer your
affection to any gold or precious stones; wherefore there is no reason for   10
you to be preoccupied by this care.

I shall send the book if I can do so conveniently. If not, it will be
very easy for you to procure a copy anywhere since it will be readily available. Be sure to commend me to your distinguished and cultivated friends
who, through you, are my friends as well. I pray that you may enjoy every   15
happiness and prosperity.

Given at Basel, 19 March 1528

1976 / To Hermann von Wied   Basel, 19 March 1528

Hermann von Wied (1477–1552) was elected archbishop-elector of Cologne
in 1515. His principal adviser was Erasmus' old friend Count Hermann von
Neuenahr (Ep 1926), who in 1520 informed Erasmus of the elector's admiration and urged him to visit Cologne (Ep 1078:72–6). This letter, written at the
urging of Neuenahr (lines 3–6), was first published in the *Opus epistolarum*.
Archbishop Hermann's reply, Ep 1995, was followed in 1529 by an invitation
to Erasmus, conveyed by Neuenahr (Ep 2137), to settle in Cologne. Erasmus
subsequently resolved to dedicate his edition of Origen to the elector, but did
not live to write the dedicatory letter (see Allen Ep 3128). The archbishop-
elector's interest in Catholic reform, already evident when the present letter

* * * * *

1975
1 See Ep 1948; *De pronuntiatione* was dedicated to Maximilian of Burgundy (Ep
   1949).
2 Ovid *Ars amatoria* 1.444

was written, eventually turned into a failed attempt to introduce a decidedly evangelical reform into his episcopal territory (1541–6), an effort that led to his excommunication by the pope (1546) and his resignation under imperial pressure (1547).

ERASMUS OF ROTTERDAM TO HERMANN VON WIED, GREETING

In addition to many other considerations that urged me to do so, most illustrious Prince, the words of the distinguished gentleman Count Hermann von Neuenahr repeatedly encouraged me, since I could not meet and speak to you in person, to address you in writing to acknowledge your lavish support of my studies or, I should say, of learning in general. But as I contemplated this, a sense of shame held me back, my occupations intervened,[1] and the splendour and majesty of your high position deterred me. Now that I have been given some respite from my occupations I have cast off both shame and deference by focusing on your exceptional generosity, which I have not experienced myself but have learned about from the declarations of many men whose opinion is not to be taken lightly. Even if you were to bestow this kindness on me for good reason, I would be most ungrateful if I did not acknowledge the benevolence of such a great prelate. But since you give your favour to one whom you have never seen and who did nothing to deserve it, I conclude that your Highness does not grant favour to Erasmus but to higher learning and to the Christian religion. I may be seen as one who has exerted some effort, with what success I do not know, but certainly unstinting, to restore and promote the first and to bring calm and stability to the second. For good letters have flourished through all the regions of the world with greater success than was expected, and many who had previously been estranged from sacred studies have been seized with love for them. Need I say more? The enterprise was going well except that certain seditious and unscrupulous people, suddenly attempting to give us a whole new world, almost succeeded through their dissident opinions and contentious beliefs in dislocating the framework of public life and in undermining the concord of the church. And in the midst of this turmoil the fruits and recompense of so many long vigils and toils sustained over the years were all but lost.

* * * * *

1976
1 For Erasmus' most recent works, see Epp 1948, 1949, and 1967. He was also hard at work on his editions of Seneca (see Ep 2056 n1) and Augustine (see Allen's introduction to Ep 2157).

But personal disadvantages would be less distressing if they were counterbalanced by public gain, especially by giving glory to Christ, who should be the single goal of all our actions. For nothing in human affairs can be truly happy and prosperous except that which Christ works in us so that, with human passions quelled, our will becomes subject to his will. There were already more than enough of these evils, even if the implacable wrath of monarchs had not yet supervened. Although they have already brought so many disasters into the world, nevertheless they grow more violent every day, threatening to throw everything into total confusion unless some *deus ex machina* suddenly appear and put an unexpected end to this tumultuous tragedy. In the meantime, in the midst of this raging tempest, as the situation becomes more and more desperate with nothing left but prayer, we cling to the remnants of the ship, hoping that Christ will provide some haven to those who have long been at the mercy of the waves.[2] I do not abandon all hope, if only the Lord, in whose hands the hearts of kings rest,[3] would deign to incline the minds of princes to think that it is more glorious to conquer their wrath than the enemy, much safer to consolidate their rule through benevolence than by force, and that to extend the boundaries of their realm clemency has more importance than the reputation of strength. Peace cannot be established when everything is in turmoil; truces can be made, at least for a few years. In the meantime it would be possible to make deliberations in peace to resolve the situation. In the present circumstances I fear that we would have what is called a Cadmean victory, one that is no less grievous to the victor than to the vanquished.[4]

But here, as I said, I have no weapon but prayers.[5] I have repeatedly exhorted the emperor to a love of peace,[6] but in his last letter he responds in this way: 'There is no reason for anyone to doubt that we have acted vigorously to the best of our ability thus far to promote peace in public affairs. What we are doing now and what we will do in the future we prefer to exemplify in deeds.'[7] These words do not quite smack of peace. Although war brings with it an immense train of evils, those evils make us wretched rather than impious. More serious is the calamity brought about by the conflict of

* * * * *

2 Cf Acts 27:44.
3 Cf Prov 21:1.
4 *Adagia* II viii 34
5 See lines 42–3 above.
6 See Epp 1255:121–8, 1873:25–31. See also the *Institutio principis christiani* CWE 27 203–88 passim.
7 Ep 1920:28–31

opinions, which rob us of our most precious possession, a sound mind. Here
the obstinacy of the contending factions is worse than that of warring monarchs, and it comes about by some strange fate that no one does more harm 65
to either cause than those who think they are its strongest defenders. Some
pull the cord of contention so forcefully that, as the proverb says, it breaks
from being stretched too far,[8] and both sides fall backwards.

One must not inquire into everything, much less pronounce on everything. It is enough to treat of those things that properly pertain to the gospel 70
teachings. The world has its laws, the schools have their exercises, but nothing should be passed on to the people except that which is absolutely certain
and necessary for the practice of the faith and conducive to pious living.
Certain people, to give an example, have made the rules of confession too
strict,[9] while others do away with them altogether, although there is a mean 75
between these two extremes. Likewise some have carried the mass to such
a point that it is more a source of profit for ignorant and vulgar priests and
a safe refuge for men of evil life; others in turn abolish it altogether. But
here too there was room for moderation, which would insure that we have
a more uncontaminated and sacred mass rather than none at all. Similarly 80
some in their immoderate and superstitious cult of the saints almost eclipse
the worship of Christ; on the opposite side others condemn all veneration
of the saints as impious. Some strive to overturn completely the institution
of monasticism; others on the contrary attribute too much to human constitutions, ceremonies, titles, and forms of dress. In these and other matters, it 85
would be possible, by a prudent sense of moderation, to have a better and
more certain comprehension of the dogmas of faith; confession would be
more sincere and less ridden with anxiety;[10] the mass would be more sacred
and worthy of reverence, and we would have fewer but better priests and
monks. 90

Although this tempest of the world gives me great torment, some hope
nevertheless remains with me that divine providence will turn these disturbances to a good end. To this the wise moderation of prelates will contribute
greatly by so restraining seditious impiety that there will always be provision for true piety, that is, the weeds will be pulled out without eradicating 95
the wheat.[11] This would be easier to accomplish if, laying aside private interests, we would all look to the one goal, that is, the glory of Christ. At

* * * * *

8 *Adagia* I v 67
9 Cf Ep 1901:80–1 with n15.
10 Cf Ep 1211:145–7 with n22. See also the *Apologia adversus monachos* LB IX 1063F.
11 Cf Matt 13:29–30.

present many pursue their own interests, and as a result there is neither public nor private prosperity. We all lay the blame on each other, although this universal calamity is the hand of God inviting all men to reform their 100 lives. If we all take refuge in him, he will easily turn this tempest in human affairs into peaceful serenity.

But this is more than enough on this subject to your Highness, since you have a much broader view of such matters than I. Your moderate prudence and your prudent moderation are known to me not only through what 105 men say of you but also in very fact. If I were to deny being pleased that a man of your distinction deems my little books worthy of your eyes and ears, I should be plainly lying. Yet together with this pleasure I feel a certain embarrassment, since I am aware that in these works that we have improvised to stimulate the interests of the young there is nothing that can appeal to 110 men of your calibre. It is my fervent wish that I be granted sufficient years and talent to produce something that deserves to be read by such a distinguished prelate and under the name of such a distinguished prelate.[12] In the meantime I wished to attest in this letter to your Highness that your benevolence in my regard is known to me and greatly appreciated. For my part, 115 as far as it lies in me, I shall make every effort not to seem unworthy of it. May the Lord long preserve your Highness free of harm.

Given at Basel, 19 March 1528

1977 / To Willibald Pirckheimer   Basel, 20 March 1528

This is Erasmus' reply to Ep 1930. It was first published in the *Opus epistolarum*, using a rough draft rather than a copy of the letter actually sent. Allen's text is based on the autograph, which in 1908, when Allen examined it, was in the possession of M. Raoul Warocqué of Mariemont in Hainault, Belgium. On the long history of the autograph before M. Warocqué acquired it, and on the differences between the autograph and text in the *Opus epistolarum*, see Allen's introduction. When he died in 1917, M. Warocqué willed all his private collections to the Belgian nation. The manuscript is now part of the Réserve Précieuse des trésors rassemblés par Raoul Warocqué in the Musée royal de Mariemont in Morlanwelz, Belgium (Aut 568/1). The text of this letter in WPB (Ep 1155) is also that of the Warocqué autograph.

* * * * *

12 Erasmus later proposed to dedicate his edition of Origen to Archbishop Hermann, but he died before the project was finished. The edition was completed by Beatus Rhenanus, who wrote the letter of dedication to Hermann. See Allen I 52 and Ep 3128 introduction.

Cordial greetings, my illustrious friend. I imagine Frans van der Dilft has been with you and that you found him to be as I described him.[1] After his departure your letter was delivered to me,[2] a lively and profuse letter, which banished from me all the sadness that I had derived from the earlier letter,[3] which had been interrupted by an attack of palsy.[4]

Concerning the fidelity of my friends, even after that complaint of mine,[5] my experience is such that I have fixed my sacred anchor[6] and my non-sacred anchor in Christ, who alone neither wishes to deceive nor is able to do so. It is amazing how human beings sometimes feign and pretend. And if there are some who love you sincerely, it is shocking how temporary this is and how at the slightest pretext it changes into hatred – then what a tenacious memory of offences, what profound oblivion of services rendered! There are those who could not be of help to us even if they wished, but there is no one who is incapable of harming us; there are those who while they are indiscreetly eager to help us do us the greatest harm. These are the kind of friends I have to deal with. I am sorry to say that this is a common affliction for both of us; I would bear it more moderately if this misfortune were mine alone.

You advise wisely and as a friend that I should be tolerant of men's morals unless I prefer to retreat into solitude. I can easily pardon human failings in my friends; but the pernicious betrayals of those to whom I have been immensely generous I cannot swallow without revulsion. God forbid that I should harbour such suspicions about you, but I know certain people who were born for no other purpose than to destroy the friendships that exist among good men. I take in good part what you write about the Oecolampadius affair,[7] provided that you approve of my maintaining silence concerning it. I had begun to write about

* * * * *

1977
1 On Dilft see Ep 1942 n1.
2 Ep 1930
3 Ep 1880
4 Pirckheimer's malady was gout. In 1522 he published his satirical *Apologia seu podagrae laus,* and in the following year resigned from the Nürnberg city council because of his condition.
5 Ie the denunciation of Eppendorf and other false friends in Ep 1934, a copy of which had gone to Pirckheimer
6 Cf *Adagia* I i 24.
7 Pirckheimer had recently published two books against Oecolampadius: see Epp 1880:1–2, 1893:57–8, 1930:7–8.

it,[8] but I realized immediately it would only have the effect of stirring up
trouble here, where things are festering too much already.[9] Already now I
am thinking of fleeing, but I don't know where [10]   30

In Spain the seven orders of monks have stirred up so much tumult
over the new book of Lee that neither the authority of the emperor nor that
of the archbishop can control them.[11] In Paris certain theologians under the
leadership of Béda are plotting extreme measures;[12] I held them back somewhat by writing a letter to the Parlement.[13] At Louvain the ringleader of   35
this butchery is my deadly enemy, as he is of all good men.[14] Both the king
and the archbishop of Canterbury kindly invite me to England; but there
are various things that keep me from going to that island.[15]

But what is the use of this deliberation when my health does not permit any setting out on a journey, when I can scarcely keep myself alive – if   40
you can call this life rather than just breathing one's last? Whether Philippus
helped Luther reply to my *Diatribe* is of no importance to me.[16] They have
reprinted the Articles here.[17] Luther seems to be more than a little flattering to his prince.[18] Wherever Lutheranism reigns, there literary studies are
annihilated. And yet this type of men thrive on literature. They seek two   45
things, money and a wife. Everything else the gospel furnishes them, that
is, the possibility to live just as they wish.

* * * * *

8 See Ep 1893:83–4.
9 See Ep 2000 n4.
10 See Ep 1926 n8.
11 On the tumult in Spain, see Ep 1926 n4. On the number of the religious orders
  involved, see Ep 1893:38 with n13. On Alonso de Fonseca who, as archbishop
  of Toledo, was primate of Spain, see Ep 1748. On Edward Lee, see Ep 1994A
  n13, and on Erasmus' conviction that Lee was behind the hostility to him in
  Spain, cf Epp 1774 n19, 1814 n39.
12 See Epp 1902 introduction, 1943 n6.
13 It was not either of Erasmus' letters to the Parlement (Epp 1721, 1905) but only
  that to King Francis I (Ep 1722) that held 'held them back somewhat.' See the
  introduction to that letter.
14 Nicolas Coppin, vice-chancellor of the university; see Epp 1549 n5, 1585 n11.
15 See Ep 1926:14 with n7. Erasmus was particularly unwilling to become involved in Henry's divorce from Queen Catharine.
16 Erasmus persistently attributed to Philippus Melanchthon a share in the writing of Luther's *De servo arbitrio*, his answer to Erasmus' *De libero arbitrio* δια-
  τριβή. See CWE 76 103 n44, 107 n64 and CWE 77 443 n447.
17 The Saxon Visitation Articles; see Ep 1944 n1.
18 Elector John of Saxony (Ep 1670)

The affairs of King Ferdinand are proceeding very well in Hungary,[19] and will continue to do so if only the Turks leave him in peace.[20] Ursinus Velius has already written a book about his exploits.[21] He[22] terrorizes the Anabaptists especially with threats of punishment since they are said to seek the overthrow of all legitimate rule.[23]

My stone has turned to limestone. I discharge a great quantity of it daily but the pain is bearable. I guess my malady comes from wine and sugar, which I think poisoners mix with lime.

I wish that instead of that water, which you say sustains you in existence,[24] your drink would be an ambrosial juice that would render you immortal so that you could serve your country as long as possible.

I am greatly distressed at the fate of Dürer.[25] I think you have read the passage where I make mention of him.[26] The whole work is now finished.[27] Perhaps you will say that it is too condensed. I admit it, but I had no other opportunity, and I think this book, such as it is, will have great currency. Kleberger left here quite some time ago and I don't know what he is doing. He visited me twice but did not say goodbye to me when he left.[28] Glareanus

* * * * *

19 See Ep 1935 n5.
20 The Turks did not leave him in peace. In May 1529 Suleiman I launched a new invasion of Hungary, capturing Buda in September and then laying siege to Vienna in September–October.
21 *De bello pannonico*, unpublished until the eighteenth century; see Ep 1917 n5.
22 King Ferdinand, not Velius
23 The persecution of Anabaptists in Austria in the years 1527–9 was both brutal and effective. By 1530 Anabaptism had virtually disappeared except in the province of the Tirol, where it persisted into the 1550s. See Claus-Peter Clasen, *Anabaptism: A Social History, 1525–1618* (Ithaca and London 1972), 22–4.
24 This must have been in the portion of Ep 1930 that does not survive.
25 Dürer was gravely ill and would die on 6 April 1528.
26 A reference to the complimentary passage on Dürer in the *De recta pronuntiatione* (CWE 26 398–9). But see also Ep 1558:41–57.
27 Ep 1949
28 Johann Kleberger (d 1546), a native Nürnberger whose commercial pursuits had taken him to Bern and Lyon. He was currently courting Pirckheimer's widowed daughter Felicitas. Pirckheimer agreed to the marriage on the condition that Kleberger live permanently in Nürnberg. Kleberger's subsequent departure from Nürnberg for Lyon shortly before the death of Felicitas (May 1530) caused a bitter breach in relations with his father-in-law. Kleberger amassed a fortune as a banker in Lyon, where his philanthropy won him the epithet *le bon allemand*. He remained on good terms with Erasmus, who in 1532 wrote him a courteous letter (Ep 2731) in which he recalled the two visits mentioned here.

is the only one here now who has numerous students.[29] He has no fixed   65
income; he is now forced to live from day to day.

So much in answer to your letter of 19 February. I think Dilft has
visited you. I would like to know what you think of the young man.

I send you a copy of the last letter the emperor sent me.[30] From the
Apology, which is now being published, you will become partly familiar   70
with the melodrama in Spain.[31] If the Lutherans had refrained from demol-
ishing the Eucharist, abolishing the mass, and removing images and had
begun by recalling their own followers to a purity of life, we might have
hoped for a happier outcome. Now Luther is quiet, Melanchthon is smooth-
ing things over; but too late have the Phrygians become wise, as the saying 75
goes.[32]

A few days ago Oecolampadius, wishing to mortify his flesh for Lent,
took a wife, a very lovely young woman.[33] Farewell, my distinguished
friend.

Given at Basel, 20 March 1528   80
Your friend Erasmus of Rotterdam, writing ex tempore
To the illustrious Willibald Pirckheimer, councillor to his imperial
Majesty. At Nürnberg

1978 / To Haio Herman   Basel, 20 March 1528

On Haio Herman (Hermannus Phrysius) of Emden in Friesland (1498/1500–
1539/40), see Epp 903:14n, 1131, and 1479. In December 1525, after several
years of study in Italy, he returned to Friesland with a doctorate in civil and
canon law. In July 1528 he was appointed a member of the council of Friesland,
and thereafter his political and administrative duties increasingly interfered

* * * * *

29 Henricus Glareanus (1488–1563), whom Erasmus considered the most eminent
    of the Swiss humanists, ran a private residential school (*bursa*) in Basel in the
    years 1522–9. In 1529 he moved to Freiburg, where he ran another school and
    became a professor of poetry at the university.
30 Ep 1920
31 See Ep 1967.
32 *Adagia* I i 28
33 Oecolampadius (Ep 2000 n4) married Wibrandis Rosenblatt (1504–64), a widow
    with two sons. The wedding appears to have taken place on 15 March 1528.
    Erasmus' sarcasm is repeated in Epp 1979:10–11 and 2054:29–32. After Oeco-
    lampadius' death, Wibrandis married Wolfgang Capito (1532). After Capito's
    death she married Martin Bucer (1542), whom she accompanied to England in
    1550.

Johannes Oecolampadius and Wibrandis Rosenblatt
Attributed to Hans Holbein the Younger
Kuratorium Carl J. Burckhardt, Vinsel, Switzerland
Reproduced with the permission of Mrs C.J. Burckhardt-de Reynold

with the realization of his ambitions as a scholar. He and Erasmus seem to have lost contact with one another in the interval since Ep 1479 (31 August 1524), for only now does Erasmus congratulate him on his return from Italy and his marriage. Erasmus would write to him again in October of this year (Ep 2056), enclosing letters of introduction to Erard de la Marck and Jean (II) de Carondelet (Epp 2054–5). In 1532, Haio became a member of the council of Utrecht, by which time contact between him and Erasmus had ceased, Ep 2261 (31 January 1530) being Erasmus' last letter to him. Their friendship may have been damaged by Erasmus' failure to mention Haio in the first edition of the *Ciceronianus* (see Ep 2108, where Erasmus indicates that Haio's name had been added to the second edition). But Erasmus' later conclusion (Ep 2587) that Haio had conceived a mortal hatred of him over that omission was probably not justified.

The letter was first published in the *Opus Epistolarum*.

ERASMUS OF ROTTERDAM TO HERMAN OF FRIESLAND, GREETING

I congratulate you on your return from Italy in good health and also on your happy marriage,[1] praying that you may enjoy both of these blessings for the rest of your days. To my dialogues *On Pronunciation* and the *Ciceronianus* I have added an oration of Rodolphus Agricola which he delivered, as it 5 seems, in Milan.[2] There is nothing that comes from that man that does not emanate some sort of divinity. Therefore I should not wish that anything of his be lost. You have an obligation, my dear Hermann, to your country and to your ancestry to take an interest in this matter.[3] Therefore, I ask you that you apply yourself vigorously to it. This gift is appropriate to no one more 10 than to you. Someone has written a profuse commentary to the work *On Rhetorical Invention*, a young man, as it appears, and not without learning or style. But there are many incidental comments, some of them rather tedious and childishly petulant.[4] I should prefer learned and pertinent notes. If I

* * * * *

1978
1 To Anna Occo, the daughter of Pompeius Occo (see n6 below). The date of the marriage is unknown.
2 The two dialogues were published together; see Epp 1948, 1949. On Agricola, see Ep 23:58n. The oration, *Rodolphi Agricolae Phrisii in laudem Matthiae Richili*, is on pages 448–62 of the first Froben edition (March 1528).
3 Agricola was his kinsman.
4 Agricola's *De inventione dialectica* was first published at Louvain in 1515 (cf Ep 336:1–10). In the preface to his edition (Cologne: H. Fuchs 1527) Johannes Matthaeus Phrissemius (d 1532) included much abuse of Petrus Hispanus (Ep 447:105n), who is compared unfavourably with Agricola. See Allen's note.

had not been weighed down with so many burdens, I would not be averse   15
to taking this upon myself; I have such regard for Rodolphus' memory.[5] If
you undertake this task, you will render your own name more illustrious.
This fame will bring you some advantage.

Give my fond regards to your father-in-law, Pompeius Occo.[6] I wish
you the best of health.   20

Given at Basel, 20 March 1528

1979 / To Adrianus a Rivulo   Basel, 21 March 1528

On the little-known Adrianus, a Fleming who had lived in Erasmus' household in 1524, see Ep 1584 n3. This letter, the only one to or from Rivulo still
extant, was first published in the *Opus epistolarum*.

ERASMUS OF ROTTERDAM TO ADRIANUS A RIVULO
My letters have grown silent but not my affection. Our exchange of letters
may have been interrupted, but not my memory of you. I have learned even
more fully of your loyal devotion towards me from what Frans van der Dilft
tells me.[1] I took great pleasure in his company, but his obligations have   5
separated him from me and also, I fear, from the Muses. You will hear from
him all that goes on here, so I can be more brief. If your affairs are going
favourably, I have reason to rejoice greatly. Surely your candour of spirit
merits a most prosperous fortune.

Oecolampadius has recently taken a wife, a quite attractive young   10
woman.[2] He wishes to mortify the flesh, I imagine. Some call the Lutheran
business a tragedy; to me it seems more of a comedy, for all the commotions
end in marriage.

If you have some good news, send it with my servant Quirinus Talesius.[3] Farewell.   15

At Basel, 21 March 1528

* * * * *

5 Cf Epp 184:18–19, 311:27–9, 606:19–21, 633:8–9.
6 Occo (cf Ep 485:28n), a Frisian merchant and banker in Amsterdam, was the
  nephew of Agricola's physician and friend, Adolph Occo, from whom he inherited Agricola's papers. Among these were the autograph manuscript of Agricola's *De inventione dialectica* as well as Agricola's annotated copy of the Treviso
  Seneca, which Erasmus was to use for his own edition of Seneca (Ep 2056).

1979
1 Ep 1942 n1.
2 See Ep 1977:78–9, with n33.
3 Ep 1966. For his movements at this time, see Ep 1955 n1.

1980 / To Alonso Manrique de Lara   Basel, 21 March 1528

First published in the *Opus epistolarum*, this letter announces the publication
of the *Apologia adversus quosdam monachos Hispanos*, which was dedicated to
inquisitor-general Manrique (Ep 1967). The manuscript, written in a secretary's hand but signed and addressed by Erasmus, is in the Real Academia de
la Historia, Madrid (MS Est 18 gr 1.5 fol 5).

Cordial greetings, most reverend prelate. The Lord is my witness that I was
more concerned lest the outrageous behaviour of the monks stir up disturbances in your country than I was for my own cause. For these dissensions
within the church cause me such torment that death seems almost more
preferable than life. If they were truly concerned with the glory of Christ 5
and the interests of piety, they would not disturb the public peace in this
way. But I fear that many of them have been carried off course by their
thirst for glory and the demands of the gullet and the belly.[1] It grieves them
that they have less importance than they were used to or than they would
wish; it grieves them that they are not allowed to do whatever they please; it 10
grieves them that many whose simplicity had once been a source of gain for
them have come to their senses. They should have rejoiced more in the gains
made by piety and in the glory of Christ. In this alone those who profess to
be dead to the world should place all their glory and wealth and authority
and pleasure. I give thanks to the Lord, who has deigned to calm their re- 15
bellious tumults through your authority. Nor am I unaware of how much I
owe to the consummate theologian, Luis Coronel.[2] Christ, who brings these
things about through you, will repay you with a reward which can never be
taken away from you. As for me, I shall patiently bear whatever the Lord
sends, be it joyful or sad, and to my last breath I shall try to the best of my 20
abilities to promote good letters and piety.

My *Apology* has burst into print. I strongly wished that it would not be
printed, not only because I suspected that your Highness preferred this but
also because it was in my interest that this matter should not become more
widespread. Its publication would only further irritate my enemies, who 25
were already sufficiently enraged, and would cause considerable hostility

* * * * *

1980
1 Erasmus was much given to charging that monks were, 'under the pretext of
  religion,' serving the cause of 'their own bellies.' See, for example, Ep 1166:15–
  16 with n3, and cf Epp 1805:233–4 with n53, 1985:20–1, 1986:7–8.
2 Manrique's secretary; see Epp 1274, 1791 n6.

among many. But I beg your pardon for this misfortune in the first preface,[3] which I placed before the other.

May the Lord preserve your Highness in good health, most reverend prelate, and may he deign through you and those like you to restore the peace and tranquillity of the church.   30

Given at Basel, 21 March 1528

Erasmus, the faithful servant of your Highness. Written in my own hand

I have also sent a copy of this letter with someone else.[4]   35

To the most reverend Lord and illustrious Prince Alonso Manrique, archbishop of Seville, etc

1981 / From Philippus Melanchthon   Jena, 23 March 1528

This letter (= MBW Ep 664) is Melanchthon's response to Ep 1944. The earliest source is a manuscript copy in the hand of Daniel Stiebar (Ep 2069), found on pages 668–9 of a copy of the *Epistolae ad diversos* that is now in the Cambridge University Library. The earliest printed version is Joachim Camerarius *Liber continens continua serie epistolas Philippi Melanchthonis ... ad Ioach. Camerar ...* (Leipzig: Voegelin 1569) 89. Stiebar's text, evidently a copy of the letter received in Basel, preserves an outspoken phrase about Luther (lines 24–5) that was toned down in the text published by Camerarius. All printed versions before Allen's, including CR 1 946–7, were based on the Camerarius text. For further details concerning both the manuscript and printed sources, see Allen's introduction and MBW T 3 287.

From August 1527 until early April 1528, Melanchthon spent most of his time in Jena, his headquarters as a leading participant in the visitation of the churches in Thuringia. While there he received and read *Hyperaspistes* 2 (Ep 1853), which is the principal subject of this letter. His opinion of the work, not indicated here, is frankly expressed in a letter to Justus Jonas of c 2 October 1527 (MBW T 3 Ep 599:19–26): 'On my return to Thuringia, I received the second volume of Erasmus' *Hyperaspistes*. And you thought that he, like a deserter, would not return to the battle! Indeed, he has returned, armed with tricks ... For he most cunningly subverts all of Luther's objections. But no one among the common people can understand this work. For it is confused and prolix, nor is it easy to understand clearly the author's opinion from his long and labyrinthine argument.'

* * * * *

3 In Ep 1967, which in the *Apologia* as published precedes Ep 1879
4 Probably with the letters of 14–15 March (Epp 1967–71).

PHILIPPUS MELANCHTHON TO ERASMUS OF ROTTERDAM
Although your letters on other occasions have given me much pleasure, your
last letter was much more pleasant than any previous one. For although for
some time I had doubts about your feelings towards me,[1] since in the first
Hyperaspistes there are signs of some feelings of annoyance,[2] this letter, writ- 5
ten in such a friendly and respectful manner, has removed this uneasiness
from me. I recognized very clearly in it your continued good will towards
me. And so I owe a great debt of gratitude to Dilft for bringing me this testimony of your benevolent feelings and friendship and for giving me this
most welcome opportunity to write to you.[3]   10

It would take a long time to enumerate all the reasons for the silence
that I have maintained up to now. But I beg you to assume any other reason
but a change in my feelings towards you. I bear in mind how much I owe
to you personally beyond all others and I am happy to proclaim it. And
since we cannot but hold dearest those persons whose talents and works we 15
admire, the excellent gifts of your intellect attract me strongly to you even
if I were to offer resistance to them. Since this is the case, you need not fear
that I shall ever be drawn by an excessive enthusiasm for anyone to exhibit
hostility towards you.

I thought it my duty to write these things to you. If they receive your 20
approval, you will readily exonerate me from those suspicions that were
interspersed in parts of the first *Hyperaspistes*. In the later one I have noticed
that you are more indulgent towards me.[4] Although I am not in the habit of
concealing my sentiments in this controversy, nevertheless I was never so
devoted to Luther that I should approve his harshness in disputation.[5] So 25
far is it from my mind that I would be willing to help and, so to speak, pour

* * * * *

1981
1 For an earlier episode of tensions between Erasmus and Melanchthon, see Epp
  1313:60–1 with n3 and 1466:21–4.
2 See CWE 76 101, 112–13, 205.
3 Frans van der Dilft (Ep 1942 n1) had delivered Ep 1944.
4 CWE 77 583, 640
5 In Allen's text, the main clause reads: 'tamen nunquam ita amavi Lutherum ut
  probarem eius in disputando *acerbitatem*.' The Camerarius text (as given in CR
  1 946) reads: 'tamen nunquam ita amavi Lutherum, ut *veluti instruxerim* eius
  in disputando *vehementiam*.' In classical and Renaissance rhetoric, *vehementia* is
  a technical term for fervency or forcefulness of expression. So in English the
  Camerarius version would be: 'I was never so devoted to Luther that *I should
  have given him, as it were, lessons in forcefulness of style* in disputation.'

oil on the fire.[6] And Luther himself is the best witness in support of this
statement. If only such a terrible conflict had never been joined between you!
Luther did not show you the respect you deserve and you in turn produced
an incredibly distorted picture of him. I consider him to be a better man than   30
he appears to be to one who judges him from the violence of his writings.
The zeal of each of you would be of much greater benefit to the church if it
were applied to the healing of these dissensions. May Christ bring it about
that this contention between you will cease! You should be the arbiters not
of dissension but of the most noble pursuits.   35

I see that you are angry with Nesen also.[7] Of him I wish that you
believe me when I say that he was your most devoted follower until his
last breath. He never spoke of you except in the most honorific terms. Nor
would I hesitate to affirm under oath that he demonstrated singular loyalty
in his devotion to you. It would not be appropriate to your wisdom and   40
your humanity to conceive lightly a different opinion of a deceased friend.
And he was taken from us by such a manner of death that even if he had
sinned in some part of his life it would be fitting to forget it and not burden
his poor shade any further.

As for your continued support of literary studies, I pray that Christ   45
will show his favour to your efforts. If this present age is ungrateful for
your outstanding merits, I hope that the judgment of posterity will be more
favourable. Like a common solider fighting under your standard, I also defend as best I can these vulnerable studies that stand aghast before the tumult of the times.   50

I hope that my exposition of the *Articuli*, of which you write,[8] did not
displease you. Here it encounters great criticism because it is more moderate
than some would like.[9] But nothing will ever be more important to me than

* * * * *

6 *Adagia* I ii 9
7 In both parts of the *Hyperaspistes* Erasmus has harsh things to say about Wilhelm Nesen, whom he calls Wilheyl; see CWE 76 100 nn23–4, CWE 77 640 n1290.
 In 1523, Nesen (1493–1524) had bitterly disappointed his former friend and
 patron Erasmus by going to Wittenberg to join the reformers, only to die the
 following year in a boating accident. Cf Ep 1523:216–17.
8 See Ep 1944 n1.
9 The *Articuli* appeared in the midst of a dispute between Melanchthon and
 Johannes Agricola, pastor and preacher in Eisleben, over the Lutheran distinction between law and gospel. Agricola objected to the content of the *Articuli*, arguing that in them Melanchthon, with his emphasis on teaching the
 law as well as the gospel, on respect for human traditions that were not in

the public peace, in the service of which I have exhorted to moderation those
who teach in the churches, and this I do at the order of my prince.[10]

With every good wish. From Jena, 23 March

1982 / From Philippus Melanchthon   Jena, 23 March [1528]

The only source for this letter (= MBW Ep 665), first published by Allen, is
a manuscript copy by Daniel Stiebar on page 668 of his copy of the *Epistolae ad diversos*, immediately preceding the manuscript of Ep 1981 (see the
introduction of that letter). Evidently written on the same day as Ep 1981,
which was carried by Frans van der Dilft (Ep 1942 n1), this letter was entrusted to Johann Reiffenstein, the youngest son of Wilhelm Curio Reiffenstein, a steward in the service of Count Botho von Stolberg (in the Harz
mountains). As a student in Louvain (circa 1520–2), Johann had known
Conradus Goclenius (Ep 1994A) and had met Erasmus. From 1523 he was
one of the students boarding with Melanchthon in Wittenberg. In the summer of 1528 he died, apparently of heart failure, while on a hunt in the
Taunus.

Greetings. Dilft has clearly surpassed your commendation of him; he is possessed of such charm and such good nature. Therefore I am very grateful
to you for allowing me to make the acquaintance of such a fine young man
or, as I prefer to interpret it, initiate a friendship with him. It was very sad
for me that we could not spend more than three days together.

I now in turn commend to you this letter-carrier, who I think is known
to you from long acquaintance. He was with you at one time in Louvain,
where the reputation of your name had attracted him. He lived there for a
long time as a close friend of Goclenius. His loyalty is known and proven to
me through the various vicissitudes of my fortune. I therefore ask of you,

* * * * *

conflict with the gospel, and on moderation in preaching against the teachings
of the old church, had yielded too much to Rome. Luther intervened to settle this dispute, and in so doing expressed his agreement with Melanchthon
(see Wengert chapters 3 and 4). The *Articuli*, much expanded, revised with
Luther's help, and translated into German, became the official Saxon Visitation Articles, published in March 1528 with an important preface by Luther:
Unterricht der Visitatoren an die Pfarrherrn im Kurfürstentum zu Sachsen (WA 26
195–240 / English translation in LW 40 269–320). See also Ep 2013:25–7.

10 Elector John of Saxony (Ep 1670)

since he is most eager to see you, that you grant him an interview. You can
confide whatever you wish to him without risk.

Every best wish. From Jena, 23 March

1983 / To Duke George of Saxony   Basel, 24 March 1528

This letter was first published in the *Opus epistolarum*. The surviving manuscript is an autograph rough draft in the Royal Library at Copenhagen (GKS
95 Fol, fol 197).

TO DUKE GEORGE OF SAXONY, GREETING

Your singular kindness, illustrious Prince, has given me the confidence to
write spontaneously and without premeditation to your Highness. I see that
your Highness was somewhat offended by the letter that I wrote on 30
December 1527,[1] a letter written with all sincerity of intention but, as it ap-   5
pears, with less circumspection than was befitting in addressing such a great
prince. And yet I have written similar letters on more than one occasion to
the emperor and to Ferdinand,[2] who, knowing my sincerity of spirit, take my
frankness in good part. I enclose the last letter I received from the emperor.[3]

Far be it from me to accuse the emperor or Ferdinand of cruelty;[4] I   10
owe them everything, and it is by their favour that I resist the attacks of
certain enemies, who for a long time now have been plotting my ruin by
means of extraordinary stratagems. In wishing to remedy this pestilence by
diplomacy and methods that avoid bloodshed rather than that thousands of
men be killed, I am in agreement with Augustine, Jerome, and, in a word,   15
all those stalwart defenders of the Christian faith. I am not acting in the interests of heretics but of princes and orthodox believers. We see how widely
this contagion has spread. If we are to resort only to the sword, many good
and pious men will be engulfed in this tempest, and the outcome of wars is
never certain. If I were to give in to my human feelings, that is, if I were to   20
wish as much evil upon the Lutherans as they do upon me, I would exhort

* * * * *

1983
1 Ep 1924, in which Erasmus criticized the use of violence against heretics
2 Ep 1935 n5
3 Ep 1920
4 In Ep 1924:25–6 Erasmus had described the emperor and his brother as seemingly inclined towards 'severity' (*severitas*), not 'cruelty' (*saevitia*), the word
  used here.

Duke George of Saxony
Lucas Cranach the Elder
Anhaltische Landesbücherei Dessau
Wissenschaftliche Bibliothek und Sondersammlungen

princes to violence with all my energies. But Christian charity and regard
for human nature suggest a different course. We must not always consider
what the impiety of heretics deserves but what is expedient for Christendom. At any rate, it is our duty always to plead for better counsels, but   25
that is not to say that princes cannot exercise their rights. Augustine intervened many times against the massacre of the Donatists, who were more
than heretics. And yet that pestilence was confined to Africa. In this case,
therefore, there is no need that anyone rebut the accusation of cruelty against
Caesar and Ferdinand, since in that same letter I admit that the outrageous   30
conduct of heretics is a provocation to cruelty.[5] He who incites to cruelty
certainly deserves cruelty himself.

I made no reference to the cruelty of the wars; and yet, if it were possible, I should wish that Christian concord could unite the minds of rulers,
and I have frequently exhorted the emperor to this. If this is not possible, I   35
shall not cease to pray that the emperor and Ferdinand might prevail with
the least possible shedding of human blood. I hope the outcome will be
happier than the beginnings seem to promise.

If your illustrious Highness knew what disturbances the monks have
stirred up in Spain despite the efforts of intervention by the emperor, the   40
archbishops of Toledo and Seville together with all the leading citizenry,[6]
and what certain disciples of Béda are plotting in Paris,[7] you would not
wonder that I find fault with certain monks and theologians. I do not accuse
everyone. Certainly the rash unscrupulousness of many of them has been an
obstacle to the tranquillity of the church. If bishops together with priests, in-   45
deed if all of us would turn sincerely to the Lord, seeing that behind all this
is the hand of God, he would take away his wrath from us and in his mercy
would give a happy ending to these disorders. It is the wish of a pious man
to prefer to heal those who have been led astray rather than kill them, and
to fear that the severity of princes may bring a graver harm than the mal-   50
ady is not the wish of one who favours heresies but one who has fears for
princes and the state. This is a recapitulation of my sentiments, which I pray
that your illustrious Highness will take in good part. If you would deign
to reread my letter, perhaps you will see more clearly what I meant. I have
recommended Christoph von Carlowitz to your Highness,[8] with the best   55
of hopes but not without some apprehension, since I have had cause to be

* * * * *

5 Ep 1924:26–8
6 See Ep 1926 n4, and of the references there, see especially Ep 1791.
7 See Ep 1943 nn6–7.
8 See Epp 1924:43–50, 1951 n7.

ashamed of such recommendations. Nevertheless I shall diligently instruct
and stimulate the young man to fulfil your expectations and live up to my
testimonies. I am led to believe by many proofs that he will do this. He has
withdrawn to Dôle, partly because of the warring factions and partly to learn   60
French. I shall see to it, nonetheless, that he receives what you sent him.[9] I
send a copy of the most recent letter that I have received from the emperor.[10]

All this was done in haste and on the spur of the moment because
the bearer of this packet of letters was getting ready to leave. I wish your
illustrious Majesty the very best of health.   65

Given at Basel 24, March 1528

1984 / From Jan Becker   Louvain, 25 March 1528

First published as Ep 61 in Enthoven, the autograph of this letter is in the
Rehdiger collection of the University Library at Wrocław (MS Rehd 254.35).

Jan Becker of Borsele in Zeeland (d after April 1536) became a close friend
of Erasmus during their time together in Louvain in 1502–3. On Becker and
his correspondence with Erasmus, of which this is the last surviving letter, see
the introductions to Epp 1321 and 1787. Becker was now employed as tutor
to Maximilian II of Burgundy (Epp 1859, 1927), the dedicatee of the *De recte
pronuntiatione* (Ep 1949). On Maximilian and Erasmus' earlier correspondence
with him, see Epp 1859, 1927.

Cordial greetings. Just before 15 March, your servant Quirinus delivered
to me your most awaited letter.[1] He also brought to our Maximilian the
excellent and learned work *On the Pronunciation of Greek and Latin*, which
you recently published, inscribed with a dedication to him by name and
with a most gracious prefatory letter testifying to your great affection for   5
him. You could not have presented anything more pleasing or acceptable
than this gift and homage either to the young man or to his father,[2] who is
greatly attached to you. He is still leaping for joy and kissing the book and
congratulates himself effusively that not only did you honour him with so

* * * * *

9 Duke George's tract on communion in one kind; see Ep 1951:30–33.
10 See n3 above.

1984
1 On Quirinus Talesius, see Ep 1966. The letter is not extant but, as Allen surmised, it was probably contemporary with Ep 1949.
2 Adolph of Burgundy (Epp 93, 266)

many letters written in your own hand but also dedicated a book to him 10
with a most complimentary preface, which you usually accord only to very
important personages or to those with whom you have very close ties of
friendship. Therefore there was no need to invite him to share the book
with some colleagues.[3] On the contrary, he should be cautioned not to share
it with so many lest it disappear somewhere, for there is no one to whom he 15
does not try to show it or even thrust it upon them unreasonably. You mentioned Maximiliaan of Ysselstein among his colleagues. I recognize your
long-standing affection for him. But he is no longer here; for more than
three years now, unless I am mistaken, he has been employed by the cardinal of Liège and recently, just before winter set in he transferred to Spain, 20
that is, to the imperial court.[4]

    We have both remained here in suspense for some time now, I waiting
to return to my priestly duties after completing the task of teaching, and he
(as I wrote) awaiting an appointment to the retinue of a cardinal.[5] But now
our master has changed this plan and intends to leave us here, as he has 25
indicated, even for the coming year. I think the reason is these tumults of
war. When these will come to an end is anyone's guess.[6] I will recommend
your servant Quirinus to the lord of Beveren in the highest terms possible,[7]
which will be easy to do since he has been so commended by you. I am now
hurrying off to Zeeland to show your book and your letter to my master, 30
for of all those that he has received hitherto Maximilian has sent copies to
his father.[8]

    The young man who has agreed to take this letter to you is a Frisian.
Since he is setting out from here to Burgundy, he wished to have the
opportunity of greeting you. For that reason he snatched this letter from 35
me such as it is although I was very occupied and making ready to set out
on a journey. He is certainly a good-natured young man, who has been with
me for a long time, most devoted to me and I no less to him.

* * * * *

3 See Ep 1949:39–41
4 Cf Ep 1949 n6.
5 Becker's priestly duties were as dean of the chapter of Zanddijk at Veere (Ep
  849:7n). Maximilian had been expecting to enter the service of the cardinal of
  Liège. See Ep 1898:21–3.
6 The second war between Francis I and Charles V, which had seen the sack of
  Rome by the emperor's troops in 1527, was still in progress and would not
  end until the Peace of Cambrai in 1529.
7 Adolph of Burgundy (see n2 above) was lord of Beveren in Flanders.
8 Cf lines 9–10 above. The only letter known to have reached Maximilian is Ep
  1927.

Farewell and continue your efforts to advance sacred and humane studies as you have been doing untiringly for so many years. I pray for your utmost success, and since here on earth men are supremely ungrateful, I pray that you will have your just reward in heaven. 40

At Louvain, 25 March 1528

Your most devoted and loyal friend Jan of Borsele

To the eminent theologian Erasmus of Rotterdam, most revered teacher. At Basel 45

1985 / To Henri de Bottis   Basel, 29 March 1528

First published in the *Opus epistolarum*, this is Erasmus' reply to Ep 1963.

ERASMUS OF ROTTERDAM TO HENRI DE BOTTIS, GREETING

If this is wasting time,[1] then please God that it be in passing many pleasant hours conversing with sincere friends. These days more than half of my time is devoted to reading and writing letters, which are many and prolix and often unpleasant.[2] 5

I wonder where that sculptor came upon a likeness of me, unless perhaps he has the one that Quinten cast in bronze in Antwerp.[3] Dürer did a portrait of me,[4] but it bears no resemblance to the sculpture.

The Spanish monks are so powerful by reason of their audacity that they are feared even by the emperor, whom they wish to be the ruler of the 10 world, but in the learned world they make no gains except to arouse ridicule and hatred. The leader of this rebellion, a member of this race of bare-footed and cord-bearing souls, condemned me particularly for having in my *Enchiridion* praised the *germanam theologiam* of the apostles, which subjected the sceptres of kings and the arrogance of theologians to the yoke of Christ. 15 He interpreted it to mean that the true theology existed only in Germany![5] Recently another monk accused me before the archbishop of Toledo for not approving those monks – I think it was the Carthusians – who in denying the eating of meat expose their neighbour to mortal danger, interpreting the

* * * * *

1985

1 See Ep 1963:4–5.

2 For other references to the volume of letters written and received, see Epp 1745:11–12, 1804:69–71, 1992:69–70, 2051:28–9, 2062:5–6, 2070:10.

3 See Ep 1963:17–20.

4 See CWE 8 28.

5 On this incident and the meaning of *germanam*, see Ep 1967:181–8.

phrase *capitis periculum* as 'a slight headache.'[6] These potbellies know neither   20
Greek nor Latin and they want to be judges of my writings![7] The *Apology*
has already appeared.[8] Béda,[9] with some of his followers, behaves wildly
in the same stupid manner, ignoring everything I have said in response to
him.[10] I wrote recently concerning this matter to the Parlement and to the sacred faculty of theology.[11] If this is not a fatal insanity, I don't know what is.   25
But the tumult of Luther, the monks, and the theologians is the least of my
evils; secret intrigues torment me far more. Since, however, all this is done
according to the divine plan, I have resolved to accept it with resignation.

Farewell. Basel, 29 March 1528

1986 / To Petrus Decimarius   Basel, 29 March 1528

Unable to find any information about Petrus Decimarius, the addressee of this
letter and Ep 2050, Allen speculated that the name might be fictitious. He speculated further, without quite convincing himself, that the real addressee might
have been Alfonso de Valdés (Ep 1807). But on the basis of the *Matricule de
Montpellier* 49, Peter Bietenholz has established that Decimarius was a native
of the Gironde who on 29 September 1526 matriculated at the University of
Montpellier (CEBR I 379). He was presumably still there when Erasmus wrote
this letter, evidently in reply to one from Decimarius that is now lost. The
greetings to Decimarius from Glareanus and Amerbach in Ep 2050:21 indicate
strongly that he had at some point visited Basel and become acquainted with
the circle of Erasmus' friends. Moreover, the greetings in the second paragraph of this letter as well as those in the final paragraph of Ep 2050 suggest
strongly that Decimarius was part of a group of medical scholars in Montpellier who had wished to be recommended to Erasmus. No further details of
Decimarius' life are known.

The letter was first published in the *Opus epistolarum*.

ERASMUS OF ROTTERDAM TO PETRUS DECIMARIUS
How long this fragile body will bear up with these labours only he knows
in whose power all mortal things lie. Those who spread the rumour that

* * * * *

6 Cf Ep 1967:189–93. The archbishop of Toledo was Alonso de Fonseca (Ep 1748).
7 On monks as potbellies, see Ep 1980 n1.
8 See Ep 1967.
9 Ep 1943 n6
10 See Ep 1906.
11 Epp 1905 (to the Parlement of Paris) and 1902 (to the faculty of theology)

my strength is exhausted, as you write, treat me a little more mercifully
than those who have me carried out for burial twice a year.[1] By the grace of 5
Christ, my health is now a little more stable than it was in previous years.
The potbellies[2] and evil shepherds earn nothing but hatred and ridicule,
and I am constantly astounded at human stupidity. Since the hand of God,
exasperated by the vices of men, has sent this tempest upon us, we cast
blame upon one another and, like dogs, we bite the stone that is thrown to 10
us,[3] without regard for who threw it. It is the Lord who calls us to a reform
of our life; we do not heed his warning but flatter ourselves with frivolous
excuses.

Give my kind greetings to William Carmel[4] and Stephen Florimundus.[5]
With the potbellies we must not engage in debate. The best way to take 15
vengeance upon them is through our moderation and good deeds.

I shall send you two books that have just been published, *On Pronunciation* and *On the Ciceronian Style*,[6] if my emissary will agree to undertake

* * * * *

1986
1 Cf Epp 1518:1–13 and 24–7, 1780:3n, 1921:5–6, 2033:45–7.
2 See Ep 1980 n1.
3 *Adagia* I x 34
4 'Guilhelmus Carmelus' is the name by which Erasmus at this point knew Guillaume Carvel (documented 1523–32). Carvel was a beneficed clergyman of the
diocese of Coutances who matriculated at the University of Montpellier in December 1525, eventually concluding his studies with a medical doctorate (*Matricule de Montpellier* 48). In 1528–9 he was prosecuted for heresy, along with
his friend Etienne Des Gouttes (see following note), but was eventually found
not guilty. In Ep 2050:10 Erasmus mentions that Carvel had written to him
from Lyon. There is no trace of Carvel's whereabouts following the completion
of his doctorate.
5 'Stephanus Florimundus' is the name by which Erasmus knew Etienne Des
Gouttes (documented 1518–29), member of a merchant family from Saint-
Symphorien-sur-Coise, fifty kilometres south-east of Lyon. He matriculated
in the medical school at Montpellier on 27 October 1518, using the name
Stephanus Florimundus (*Matricule de Montpellier* 35). In May 1528, Des Gouttes,
his friend Carvel, and one other student were arrested on suspicion of heresy.
Although Lutheran books were found among his possessions, the charges
against Des Gouttes and his friends were dismissed in September 1529. It
is probable that, like most of the other members of his family, Des Gouttes
subsequently embraced Calvinism. A family chronicle indicates that he became physician to Margaret of Angoulême, queen of Navarre, and died at
Nantes.
6 See Epp 1949 and 1948.

this task for me. I shall be glad to add two quatrains to the *Copia* or any similar book. That would not be so suitable to the *Proverbs*.[7] Farewell.   20

At Basel, 29 March 1528

1987 / To Clement VII   Basel, 3 April 1528

This letter was first published in the *Opus epistolarum* The manuscript is an autograph rough draft in the Royal Library at Copenhagen (MS GKS 95 Fol, fol 180).

Here Erasmus addresses to the pope a carefully worded complaint that his two most adamant Italian critics, Girolamo Aleandro (Ep 1553 n9) and Alberto Pio, prince of Carpi (Ep 1634), refused to take seriously his decisive break with Luther and were continuing to insist that his views were essentially identical to those of the German heresiarch. For the history of Erasmus' conviction that Aleandro and Pio were colluding against him, see Epp 1634, 1717:5–7 and 38–48, 1804:274–83. Unlike Noël Béda and most of the others who had made the same argument, Aleandro and Pio were accomplished humanists who could not be despised and belittled for either ignorance of 'good letters' or hostility towards them. They were, moreover, greatly influential at the papal court. To be accused by them of complicity in the Lutheran heresy was therefore not only wounding but also particularly dangerous, and Erasmus' resistance was correspondingly dogged. Several months after addressing this letter to the pope, Erasmus learned from Louis de Berquin (Ep 2066:64–9) that Pio, having fled Italy in the wake of the sack of Rome (see n1), was living in Paris and circulating there manuscripts of a book against Erasmus that he was planning to publish (see n2). In his reply to Berquin, Erasmus announced his intention to respond to Pio by letter (Ep 2077:54), and indeed he did so on the very same day, 23 December (Ep 2080).

ERASMUS OF ROTTERDAM TO CLEMENT VII

I shall pass over for the sake of brevity the deep sorrow I feel at the catastrophe in Rome, which could not but have been most grievous to every devout man.[1] Most blessed Father, I not only suspect but have also discovered

* * * * *

7 No such quatrains have been found in any edition of the *Copia* or the *Proverbia* (*Adagia*).

1987
1 The sack of Rome by the emperor's mutinous troops in May 1527. During the sack, the pope took refuge in the Castel Sant' Angelo, where he remained a

with virtual certainty – partly from words of your Holiness that certain 5
emissaries have reported, partly from two pamphlets, one sent to me by Alberto, prince of Carpi,[2] another that circulated among your domestic staff
with no title but by its style clearly indicating its author, Girolamo Aleandro,[3] archbishop of Brindisi – that some individuals have attempted to accuse me to your Holiness of having secretly favoured the Lutheran affair or 10
at least of having afforded it opportunities.

To answer the first charge, concerning my relations with Luther, I think
this is sufficiently confuted by his having written against me with a virulence that he has not shown against anyone else;[4] then again there are my
two books of the *Hyperaspistes*, in which I answer him in such a way that 15
no one could suspect collusion, since it is an outright gladiatorial combat.[5]
There is much less suspicion among people here, who know from experience how deeply those who belong to various factions hate me and how
many tribulations I suffer from their treacheries. I would wish that my state
of conscience was as clearly proven to your Holiness as I am confident I shall 20
prove it to be in the eyes of Christ. I wish only one thing, that this victory
go to Christ and to piety and to Christendom, not to the private ambitions
of this or that party. But we often see in the course of events that in such
chaos everyone steers the victory to his own advantage. I hope that your
Holiness, in your wisdom and sanctity, will employ all vigilance to prevent 25
this from happening.

It would take a long time to respond to the other accusation. I did
not respond to either pamphlet since I saw clearly that it was impossible to
defend myself without doing harm to others. At the same time I was afraid
that this matter would rekindle flames that had begun to subside. If I had 30
given occasion to this calamity, the Lutherans would lay this to my charge

* * * * *

virtual prisoner for several months. On 6 December 1527 he took flight, with a
few of his cardinals, to Orvieto, thus re-establishing a degree of independence.
By the beginning of October 1528, relations with the emperor had improved
to the point that Clement was able to return to Rome. See Pastor 9 388–423
and 466–7, 10 1–31.

2 Alberto Pio's *Responsio accurata et paraenetica* of May 1526, written in response
to Ep 1634 but not published until 1529. See Epp 1634 introduction, 2042 n9,
and 2066 n19. Erasmus had already made oblique reference to it in the *Ciceronianus*, indicating that Pio's work had been 'shaped by another's hand,' ie by
Aleandro; CWE 29 420.

3 The *Racha*; see Ep 1717 n18.

4 Principally in the *De servo arbitrio* of 1525

5 See Epp 1667, 1853 and CWE 76–7.

as they do everything else. But this suspicion is not bandied about except among certain monks and priests who are no less hostile to good letters than they are to factions. And in fact there is no person of good sense who does not see that this tempest is willed by fate, sent upon the earth because of the crimes of the people. And I am convinced that there will be no end to it unless we all in concert seek refuge in the mercy of the Lord. He who inflicted the wound will heal it. Let each man first amend his own life and let Christian charity gird itself to heal our neighbour. And may this quality not be lacking in severity if the wickedness of certain people requires severity. But if in this matter your Holiness relaxes the reins on those who, believe my word, do not serve your interests or those of Christ but look to their own personal ambitions – may my prophecy be in vain! – I fear that this badly treated cancer will break out elsewhere with greater menace to public tranquillity. Your purity of heart is known to everyone, but those who are evil never do greater harm than when they abuse the goodness of others for their own evil ends. Moreover, just as the wickedness of some inspires great fear in us, so your piety gives us high hopes of restoring religion as does your exceptional wisdom of warding off or restraining human passions.

I have candidly opened my heart to your Holiness as in the presence of Christ's vicar and of Christ himself, who I hope will be propitious to me in the last judgment in the measure that I conceal nothing from him. Until now I had no courier by whom I could send this. I hear now that your Holiness is closer to us.[6] I pray that Christ be with you in all that pertains to the public tranquillity of his church. If you wish to give me a command, you have a lamb ready for sacrifice, if your authority shall command it.

Given at Basel, 3 April 1528

1988 / To Johannes Cochlaeus   Basel, 3 April 1528

This letter is the 'Extract from a letter sent from Basel on 3 April' that Johannes Cochlaeus (Epp 1863, 1928, 1974) printed in German at the end of his pamphlet denouncing the decision of the city fathers in Bern to adhere to the Reformation: *An die Herren, Schultheis und Rat zu Bern, widder yhre vermainte Reformation* (Dresden: W. Stöckel 1528). There is nothing in the pamphlet itself to connect the extract with Erasmus, but in his *Johannes Cochläus: Ein Lebensbild aus der Zeit der Kirchenspaltung* (Berlin 1898; repr Nieuwkoop 1964) 140–1, 144–5, Martin Spahn unequivocally attributed the authorship of it to Erasmus. Thirty

* * * * *

6 An apparent reference to reports that Clement was in Nice; see Ep 2030 n7.

years later, however, when Allen inquired of Spahn concerning his grounds
for the attribution, Spahn could not remember what they were. For his part,
Allen notes that the letter reports events in Bern with the kind of detailed gossip that Erasmus communicated in Epp 1258 (about events in Wittenberg in
1521–2) and 2698 (the *Tragoedia Basiliensis* of August 1532). As Allen rightly
observes, however, 'this is scarcely enough to be convincing.' The most that
can be said with certainty is that the letter includes information about events
in Bern that Erasmus in Basel was well situated to receive, that an original by
Erasmus would have been in Latin, and that he would have been reluctant to
be identified publicly as the author of a letter so undiplomatic in its rejection
of the reformation in Bern.

The business at Bern went like this. When the disputation was over, the
prize of victory was awarded to the Zwinglians,[1] and it was decided that

* * * * *

1988
1 Bern was politically, economically, and militarily the most powerful city/can-
  ton in the Swiss Confederation. In 1527, after several years of tension between advocates and opponents of an evangelical reformation, the advocates
  gained control of the city government. Determined to achieve an orderly reformation with public support, the city council in mid-November decided to
  hold a public religious debate that would establish an agreed basis for enacting reforms and sent out invitations to all the cantons of the Confederation and their allies, to a number of South German cities, to the Catholic
  bishops concerned, and to all the beneficed clergy in its territory. The theses to be debated were a summary of the essential points of Zwinglian theology, and the council decreed that the standard of judgment was to be the
  pure text of the Bible without reference to later interpretation by the Fathers
  or anyone else. The ensuing 'Bern disputation' lasted for three weeks (6–26
  January 1528). The roster of those attending was a who's-who of the Swiss
  and South German Reformations: Huldrych Zwingli and Heinrich Bullinger
  from Zürich, Johannes Oecolampadius from Basel, Martin Bucer and Wolfgang Capito from Strasbourg, Berchtold Haller from Bern, and more besides. Because the Catholic bishops, in their refusal to concede the authority of a city council or of the Bible alone, stayed away, the Catholic side
  was weakly represented but was nonetheless given every opportunity to argue its case. The Lutherans were even more seriously outnumbered and out-
  gunned. In the end, the overwhelming majority of those present joined in
  declaring the theses that had been debated to be scriptural and thus acceptable as the basis for reform, and the Bernese clergy were ordered to teach
  nothing that contradicted them. Bern's adherence to the Zwinglian Reformation ended the political isolation in the Confederation that Zürich had
  suffered in consequence of its reform and contributed much to the victory in 1529 of the hitherto stalled reform movements in both Basel and

within seven days all the altars in all the churches and cloisters should be smashed and overturned. The mass has been forbidden to everyone and entirely abolished and the images have been smashed.[2] There are, however, some in Bern's territory who do not wish to obey or hearken to this un-Christian decision and command.[3] The eight cantons have met now for the third time in Lucerne, but it is not known what was finally decided.[4] Of the towns in Bern's territory, no fewer than six have made the decision, and confirmed it with an oath, that they will not depart by a finger's breadth from the order of the Christian church.[5] It is also reported that the citizens of Schaffhausen have with repentance changed their minds, altered their course, and abandoned their error.[6]

Claudius Meyer and one other man whose name I have forgotten, two of the leading citizens of the city of Bern and the chief dancing masters of the sect, have abruptly fallen down and died.[7] When the daughter of Claudius,

* * * * *

Schaffhausen (cf n6 below). On the Bern disputation and its aftermath, see Potter 253–66.

2 Shortly after the conclusion of the disputation, the council issued a *Reformationsmandat* (7 February) that (among other things) banned the celebration of mass and ordered all images that had not already fallen victim to iconoclasm to be removed from the churches; see Locher 279–80.

3 There were, in fact, two rebellions against the *Reformationsmandat* in Bern's subject territory (the Oberland), but they had been crushed by the end of 1528; see Locher 280–1.

4 It is not clear what meeting is referred to here or precisely which eight cantons were involved. Five of the cantons (Lucerne, Uri, Schwyz, Unterwalden, Zug) were the focus of Catholic resistance to the Reformation in the Confederation. Two of these, Uri and Unterwalden, together with the Valais, are known to have offered aid to the towns in the Bernese Oberland that rebelled against the *Reformationsmandat* in 1528. See Potter 264.

5 Potter 264, lists five towns that reintroduced the mass, expelled reformist clergy, and disobeyed orders from government officials.

6 In 1525 Schaffhausen, which was politically and geographically isolated and fearful of hostile action by Catholic neighbours in Switzerland and across the border in Germany, called a halt to the progress of the Reformation in the city and banished the two principal reformers, Sebastian Hofmeister and Sebastian Meyer. In 1528 the city sent no official delegation to the disputation in Bern, although it allowed its clergymen to participate. In the autumn of the following year, however, secure in the support of Zürich and Bern, the city fathers voted unanimously to adhere to the Reformation and in 1530 issued an appropriate *Reformationsmandat*. See Locher 376–8.

7 Claudius May (Mey, Meyer, d between 11 October 1527 and 3 April 1528), belonged to a distinguished family in Bern and had, as a member of the great council, been a leading advocate of the Reformation.

a nun of the Dominican order, heard of her father's death, she is reported to
have said: 'Thanks be to God our Lord that he has delivered me from this
father, who so often tried to induce me to leave the order so that he could
call me back into this wicked world.'[8]   20

They also say that two crowns appeared in the sky over Bern and a
bloody rod in between them. As to what it means, some say one thing and
some say another.

1989 / To Gianfrancesco Torresani   Basel, 19 April 1528

The autograph is Vatican MS Reg Lat 2023 fol 158. It was first published in P.
de Nolhac *Erasme en Italie* 2nd ed (Paris 1898).

Gianfrancesco Torresani of Venice (d after 1557) was the elder son of Andrea Torresani (Ep 212:6n), who was father-in-law and business partner of the
famed Venetian printer Aldo Manuzio (Ep 207). Both father and son were frequently called Asulanus, after Andrea's birthplace, Asola, and Erasmus invariably addressed the son as Franciscus Asulanus (see line 18 in this letter).
After the death of Aldo in 1515, Gianfrancesco helped his father run the Aldine press and, like his father, was notoriously tactless in dealing with scholarly authors (Epp 1349, 1592, 1623, 1746). Erasmus maintained civil relations
with Gianfrancesco but, as this letter shows, was little inclined to do him any
favours.

Cordial greetings. Overwhelmed with innumerable cares, I was greatly
cheered by your kind and friendly letter.[1] You have filled me with great
concern about how I may respond with reciprocal courtesy. As far as concerns young men, I should inform you that I have never been more averse
to any way of life than to assume the education of adolescents,[2] although   5
in Bologna my evil genius almost got me into this trap.[3] At the present

* * * * *

8 May's only known daughter was named Clara. In December 1525 she had
married Nikolaus von Wattenwyl, a Bern patrician and former priest whose
progress to the top of the Catholic hierarchy of Switzerland had ended with
his adherence to Zwingli and the Reformation. There is no evidence that she
had objected to leaving the convent or marrying Wattenwyl.

1989
1 Not extant
2 On Erasmus' attitude towards teaching, which had not been as uniformly negative as he indicates here, cf Epp 737, 1018, 1208.
3 In 1506–7, as tutor to the sons of Henry VII's physician, Giovanni Battista
Boerio; see Ep 194:33–6.

moment neither my occupations nor my precarious health allow me any respite,[4] nor does the present state of affairs, which everywhere is headed for the gravest tumult, encourage me to become involved. Otherwise I would most gladly respond to your excellent friend from Treviso[5] with mutual cor-   10 diality and would comply with your request. Glareanus is here, a man of wide learning, more suitable for this task and a very good friend of mine.[6] I have not yet received the book you sent me as a gift,[7] but the bearer of this letter promises that it will arrive.

I wish you and your family the best of health and ask that you give   15 them my greetings. I shall write in more detail when I have more time.

Basel, 19 April 1528

To the most distinguished gentleman Francesco Asulano, in Venice

1990 / From Zacharias Deiotarus   London, 20 April 1528

The writer, Zacharias Deiotarus of Friesland (d 1533), was a former servant-pupil of Erasmus who by 1521 had entered the service of William Warham, archbishop of Canterbury (Ep 1205). Though few of the letters exchanged between him and Erasmus survive (apart from this one there are only Epp 1491, 2237, and 2496), he was a faithful correspondent and was invariably helpful to Erasmus' famuli when they visited England.

First published as Ep 32 in Enthoven, the manuscript of this letter is in the Rehdiger Collection of the University Library at Wrocław (MS Rehd 254.59).

I was happy to afford hospitality to your servant Quirinus and aided him as I could in delivering your letters.[1] I was able to do both of these services with little inconvenience. I regret very much that I could not show my gratitude towards you, my lord and master, to whom I am obliged in so many ways and to whom I desire and am in duty bound to show kindness in my   5 turn.

* * * * *

4 Since about Easter (12 April), Erasmus had been suffering from a new attack of his old malady, the stone; see Epp 1998:34–6, 2006:6–9, 2013:1–2, 2021:143–4, 2022:55–6. For his graphic description of an earlier attach in 1526, see Ep 1729:17–23.
5 Unidentified
6 See Ep 1977:64–6.
7 Possibly the Aldine edition of Aulus Cornelius Celsus, which had been published in March.

1990
1 On Quirinus Talesius see Epp 1955 n1, 1966.

Albrecht Dürer
Self-portrait at the age of twenty-two, 1493
Louvre, Paris

I don't know whether Birckmann has disrupted the friendship between you and Polidoro;[2] I cannot bear witness to that. After the printing of Polidoro's books there were no more transactions between them. If there is anything going on between them, they make sure that I know nothing of it. Neither of them trusts the other,[3] as I hear; in fact, neither one of them trusts anyone. In consequence hardly anyone trusts either of them, one because of his untrustworthiness and the other because of his reputation for avarice and inconstancy.[4] I do not feel any obligations to Polidoro that you should thank him for my sake. I should wish that your recommendation be placed with someone else than with him, who has done and will do nothing except give empty promises. If he ever did anything for me, I merited it by my services. In that respect he is as indebted to me as I to him. Farewell, excellent lord and patron.

London, 20 April 1528
Your Worship's servant Zacharias Deiotarus
To Master Erasmus of Rotterdam, my revered lord
At Basel

1991 / To Willibald Pirckheimer   Basel, 24 April 1528

This letter (= Ep 1165 in WPB) was first published in *Pirckheimeri Opera*. On Pirckheimer, see Epp 1880, 1930, 1977.

Cordial greetings. Your letters were delivered to me, one after the other, and they gave me great solace.[1] What use is it to mourn the death of Dürer, since we are all mortal? The epitaph I prepared for him is contained in my book.[2]

* * * * *

2 Polidoro Virgilio (Epp 531:456n, 1175 introduction), eminent Italian humanist and historiographer to Henry VIII, had been displeased with Froben's edition of two of his works, a circumstance that appears to have caused some strain in the friendship between him and Erasmus (Ep 1702) but no lasting damage to it (Ep 1796:1–4). The implication here is that some tale borne by Franz Birckmann (Ep 1931 n6) might have been at the root of the strain.
3 For Polidoro's estimate of Birckmann see Ep 1666:26–9, 35–47.
4 As Allen points out, this is not the image of Polidoro that emerges from Ep 1666.

1991
1 Not extant. The first one doubtless included the news of Dürer's death on 6 April.
2 This is probably a reference to the flattering portrait of Dürer in *De pronuntiatione*, which Froben had published in March. See CWE 26 398–9.

A rumour has been brought here which greatly exhilarated the spir- 5
its of learned men, especially Bonifacius Amerbach,[3] that the *Pandects* are
being printed there at the expense and with the authority of the city council.[4] They have wished that the Greek version of Justinian might also be
printed.[5]

I think Dilft has told you about the charge brought against me. I acted 10
in compliance with the advice of Beatus Rhenanus and Ludwig Baer.[6] All
the same I knew he[7] would not do anything. By this time I know the man's
tricks. But he has always taken advantage of Rhenanus' good disposition
for this kind of drama. We avoided confusion at any cost, preferring an unjust peace to a just war.[8] Nothing was omitted; it was submitted to arbitra- 15
tion.[9] Two witnesses were called. The arbitrators exacted our guarantee under oath to accept the agreement. The agreement was read aloud. We both
gave our assent. We both signed it in our own hand. Then we drank from
the same cup, broke bread between us and shook hands. I prognosticated
that our friendship would last forever. He nodded and approved. A friendly 20
meal was provided for all. In departing he asked for a letter to the duke.[10]

* * * * *

3 Ep 1933
4 The Pandects, also called the Digest, was a collection in fifty books of excerpts from the writings and opinions of eminent lawyers. Compiled in the
sixth century at the order of Emperor Justinian, it was the most important part
of the *Corpus juris civilis*, the great codification of Roman law. At the strong
urging of Pirckheimer, the city of Nürnberg sponsored the publication of the
Digestorum seu Pandectarum libri quinquaginta edited by Gregorius Haloander
(Nürnberg: Johann Petreius, April 1529). See Guido Kisch 'Die Förderung der
Corpus iuris-Ausgabe Haloanders durch den Nürnberger Rat,' in his *Gestalten
und Probleme aus Humanismus und Jurisprudenz: Neue Studien und Texte* (Berlin
1969) 213–36.
5 The four books of the Institutes, which constitute the first part of the *Corpus
juris civilis*, were a general introduction to the study of Roman law compiled
at the direction of Emperor Justinian. The first edition of the *Institutiones iuris
civilis in Graecam linguam per Theophilum Antecessorem olim traductae, ac fusis-
sime planissimeque explicatae*, prepared by Viglius Zuichemus, was published
by Froben at Basel in March 1534.
6 Erasmus is assuming that Frans van der Dilft, who was currently making a
leisurely journey through Germany (Ep 1942 n1), had visited Pirckheimer in
Nürnberg (Ep 1977:1–2, 67–8) and told him about the latest episode in the feud
with Heinrich Eppendorf (Ep 1934 introduction).
7 Heinrich Eppendorf
8 Cicero *Ad familiares* 6.6.5
9 See Ep 1937.
10 See Ep 1940.

I consented to this, although it was not part of the agreement, to avoid giving him some pretext. He asked for the preface of the book that was to be dedicated to him. Absurd and silly as it was, I did this at the instigation of Bonifacius.[11]

What were the consequences? Soon afterwards, it is said, he sent one of his own servants just before the market days to spread the atrocious rumour that Erasmus was condemned at Basel in very severe terms to write a book and a letter against himself, and then to pay a fine.[12] And here before his departure he boasted that he had impelled Erasmus to submit to conditions to which he himself would not stoop for three thousand ducats.

It is incredible how much this rumour gladdened the hearts of the pseudo-evangelicals. What scenes of triumph! What exaltation over nothing! I expected this would happen, but I could not persuade Beatus or Baer what a schemer he was. And I was busier than ever, especially with my new books.[13] What is this German frivolity?[14] All the evangelicals were exultant that Erasmus' authority had been buried and gone to hell;[15] my friends feared for me. And these stories about Hutten, Otto,[16] and this dispute are being spread by a certain evangelist from Strasbourg,[17] who pretends to be my greatest friend and thinks I don't know about this. I am forced to turn a blind eye to it. I have always restrained princes from violence,[18] and in this pursuit I have incited the wrath of some of them. In future I shall neither restrain nor incite them but leave them to their own devices. I see no end to all of this except violence, and it is pitiful that it will affect many. But these things I leave to Christ.

I am sending to you his demands, my answer, and the decision of the arbitrators,[19] so that you may learn of the whole affair and communicate this information to your friends. I promise to inscribe his name on one of my books now that he is my friend, in the name of friendship. There is no prescribed time and I do not always have time to write books; and there are many persons to whom I owe this duty in return for their services. I promise a polite letter to the duke within the limits that one must observe

* * * * *

11 See Ep 1941.
12 It was in response to this rumour that Erasmus soon wrote Ep 1992.
13 See Ep 1934:251–3.
14 Cf Epp 1864:55–8, 1887:17–22.
15 Literally 'gone to the crows,' written in Greek. See *Adagia* II i 96.
16 Brunfels (Ep 1405)
17 Wolfgang Capito. Cf Epp 1437:106–8, 1477B:72–81, 1485, 1496:120–32.
18 Cf Epp 1976:93–6, 1983:10–31.
19 Ep 1934:501–26, Ep 1934:527–49, and Ep 1937

in relations with a prince of his rank. Perhaps he has bad feelings towards Eppendorf for reasons unknown to me. There must be some reason why he has been living here for seven years with nothing to do without ever paying 55 a visit to his native country.[20] The arbitration says explicitly 'to avoid trouble' and 'without disgrace to either party.' And it prescribes that 'offences and grievances on both sides be abolished.' It says that I must fulfil the first two articles 'as I have agreed in writing.'[21] You see the written document that Eppendorf read and approved. I have no objection to the almsgiving, 60 for the decision of the judges agrees with my own; no fixed time is prescribed and I voluntarily contribute more than is stipulated. Perhaps he will deny that he has spread these rumours. But if he did, what could be more detestable than this treachery?

He said in my presence that you had written to him: 'Defend your 65 reputation, take up your pen against Erasmus.'[22] I knew that this was not the case. He said that Melanchthon had answered his letter saying that what he[23] wrote was written concerning someone else. But Melanchthon affirmed that neither had he written anything to Eppendorf nor Eppendorf to him.[24] 70

I should wish, my dear Willibald, that a copy of these documents be circulated among your friends and that you solicit their advice, especially Hermann von Neuenahr[25] and Johann von Vlatten,[26] a man of boundless good will. I pray for your continued health. My own health is delicate but for the moment able to withstand immense labours. The Augustine is being 75 printed by four presses, the *Adages* by two, not to mention other things.[27] Keep me informed about the *Pandects*.[28]

At Basel, 24 April 1528

I have not reread it. Please pardon me. You recognize your friend.

To the illustrious Willibald Pirckheimer, councillor to his imperial 80 Majesty.

* * * * *

20 Cf Ep 1934:401–3.
21 Ep 1937:2–4, 7–9
22 Cf Ep 1934:96–8.
23 Melanchthon
24 Cf Ep 1934:86–95.
25 See Ep 1926.
26 See Epp 1390, 1948.
27 The ten-volume Froben edition of Augustine was published in the summer of 1529 (Ep 2157). The revised version of the *Adagia* appeared in September 1528 (Epp 2022–3). Erasmus was also at work on a revised edition of Seneca, which was published in March 1529 (Ep 2091).
28 See lines 5–8 above.

1992 / To Willibald Pirckheimer   Basel, 1 May 1528

Like Ep 1991, to which it is closely related, this letter (= Ep 1169 in WPB)
was first published in the *Pirckheimeri Opera*. Written after receiving Pirckheimer's report (lines 3–6) that the rumour of Eppendorf's 'triumph' over
Erasmus (Ep 1991:26–34) had spread all over Germany, it was intended to
supply Pirckheimer with ammunition for a response to the 'blabbermouths'
who had spread the rumour (cf lines 452–3). Although Erasmus never published the letter itself, he expanded its contents into the *Admonitio adversus
mendacium*, published at Freiburg in 1530.

THE LETTER OF ERASMUS TO PIRCKHEIMER AGAINST FALSE
RUMOURS

Who, I beseech you, are these evil-tongued people who, as you write, have
spread the rumour throughout all of Germany that I was treated in an atrocious manner by Heinrich Eppendorf and that I returned into his favour 5
under humiliating conditions? Even if it were partially true, how is it that
those who parade themselves as evangelicals, who preach nothing but peace
and pardon, are elated, exult, and rejoice? Let them pretend that I injured
Eppendorf or that I was injured by him or that we both did harm to one
another, or let them pretend that there were never any offences committed 10
and that our friendship was destroyed by human suspicions and the de-
nunciations of slanderers – is it just that they should jeer at me? or should
they not rather congratulate both of us for reaching an agreement? Where is
that evangelical spirit that is always dripping from their lips and depicted
in their letters? Where is that Christian charity that does not rejoice in any 15
man's misfortune? But they applaud the victory of Eppendorf. There were
those who gave applause to the temerity of Hutten – not undeservedly, if
his audacity had met with success. He professed to be a champion of gospel
truth, although no one more than he stood in the way of their gospel. What
do they have to do with Eppendorf? Do they think him to be Hutten's suc- 20
cessor? Whether he was or not I cannot say, but I do not think he makes
this claim. And if he did proclaim it, what has that to do with evangelical
truth? But to rejoice without reason at other people's woes is a bestial form
of malice very far removed from the spirit of the gospel.

Now I shall reveal how their gratification has been in vain. I will 25
not rehearse the reasons for our differences, lest I seem to forget my
promise to consign to oblivion our past offences and suspicions.[1] I shall

* * * * *

1992
1 Ep 1937:7–10

merely say this, that not even Eppendorf himself will deny my good ser- vices to him.[2] There is not one instance of less than friendly feelings in my actions in his regard, whereas he manifested his hostile feelings to- 30 wards me in innumerable ways, so that he had as much reason to thank me as I had to remonstrate with him, if I had the desire or the time to enter into dispute. But, as Paul said: 'The Lord's servant must not be contentious.'[3] And if piety did not forbid it,[4] I have learned by experi- ence how peace of mind can be regained by long-suffering. But I shall 35 not recall my good deeds towards him. I shall describe how I offended him.

I had written on more than one occasion to Duke George that he should call a young man endowed in other respects with good natural gifts from the life of indolence and luxury that he had led for so many years and di- 40 rect him to some honourable occupation.[5] And in addition I often exhorted him[6] to this both by word and, when I was away, by letter. If he had fol- lowed this advice, perhaps by now instead of the insubstantial and tri- fling distinctions he enjoys among his irresponsible companions, not with- out frequent delusions, he would be enjoying true and solid glory among 45 leading men and in the world of learning. And I promised him my aid in this endeavour. I heard reports and murmurs daily: 'Why is he hang- ing around here for so many years and never goes back to see his fam- ily?' 'What is he up to?' 'Where does he get the money to pay all these ex- penses?' 'What is the origin of his noble insignia?' 'Where does he have his 50 castle?' 'Why has he left it?' 'What has he in common with Hutten, who because of his notorious misdeeds had no safe refuge?' 'Who will pay the debts that he accumulates everywhere?' These and other things, which I do not care to mention at the moment, were being spread abroad by men of good sense, even by those who seemed to be his loyal friends. And in the 55 meantime he never ceased attacking my works, often sending very threat- ening letters here. I appealed to the duke's wisdom to take thought for his safety and my tranquillity. This was for my own good, certainly, but more especially for his good. What could be more friendly than this inten- tion? Would not a brother write the same thing for his brother or a father 60 for his son?

* * * * *

2 Cf Ep 1934:523
3 2 Tim 2:24
4 Ie contention
5 See Ep 1940:16–18.
6 Eppendorf

Since I knew this had been done, I did not deny it. But I refuse to acknowledge the letter he produced, since I knew nothing of it.[7] It was written
in a barbaric hand, without consul or date, as they say.[8] It had no signature,
no seal. It could be that someone forged it; it could be that someone added   65
what he wished. What could have been more stupid than that I should acknowledge such a letter, which he claimed was written several years ago?
Unless perhaps people think that I constantly have in mind everything I
have ever written, when, without counting books in progress, I sometimes
write forty letters a day,[9] of which I hardly reread any. In any case the sub-   70
stance of the letter was that the duke attract the young man to some honourable position in which, putting aside the pursuit of pleasure, he could
put his talents to good use.[10] This was what prompted Eppendorf's complaint. Suppose I put it a little bluntly; still the purpose was that he be recalled from his idleness and a life that exposed him to much gossip to a   75
comfortable and dignified existence. On my side I had many other causes
for grievance, which I prefer to suppress rather than supply material for
revoking our agreement. I was far from being an implacable foe. To admit
something of which you are doubtful is the height of stupidity. To show
favour to one who threatens you in this way is the height of folly.   80

Even if he produced a letter that bore some resemblance to my handwriting, unless I was certain that it had been written by me, it would have
been foolish to acknowledge immediately something that could do you
harm. There are some people practised in reproducing another person's
hand with such likeness that not even the one who is being traduced can de-   85
tect it. Alexander, the archbishop of St Andrew's, son of James, former king
of Scotland,[11] and brother of the now reigning king,[12] did this once for fun.
He showed me a book just issued from the presses that I was certain I had

* * * * *

7 See Ep 1934:28–41.
8 Erasmus is alluding to the Roman custom of dating documents by giving the
   names of the two consuls for that year.
9 Cf Ep 1985 n2.
10 Cf lines 37–41 above.
11 Alexander Stewart (c 1493–1513) was the illegitimate son of James IV of Scotland (1473–1513). In 1504, still a minor, he was made bishop of St Andrews.
   He was Erasmus' pupil in Italy in 1508–9. Erasmus, who greatly admired the
   young man's intellect, character, and piety, grieved for him after his early
   death and that of his father at the battle of Flodden (*Adagia* II v 1) and cherished the ring that the young archbishop had given him when they parted (Ep
   604:4n).
12 James V (1512–42)

King James IV of Scotland
In the collection of A Stirling of Keir

never read. He had made many annotations in the margins. 'I recognize,' I
said, 'the shape of the letters, but I never read or possessed this book.' He   90
answered: 'You read it once, but it has escaped your memory; otherwise how
can you explain your handwriting?' In the end he laughingly confessed his
trick.[13]

And what of that poor devil who was hanged, drawn, and quartered
in Strasbourg, a man not unknown to Eppendorf; how many calamities he   95
caused by forging the handwriting of scores of people![14] Did not enemies
of St Jerome try to defame him by falsifying a letter that they claimed was
written by him?[15] This is an old game with those who are up to no good. I do
not say this to imply that Eppendorf did such a thing, but rather that it could
have been done by someone else. Therefore, since I did not acknowledge the   100
letter as my own and he could not furnish any proof to convince me, there
was nothing left for him to do but to make a formal complaint against me.
But I had more cause to complain about him, who on that pretext not only
made gross demands of me but also threatened court action and the tribunal.

Furthermore, let us suppose that all the things that he read out had   105
been written by me; I did not deny that I had written them but I said that I
did not recognize them, and if I said that the letter he showed me was not
written by me I would not have been lying. For it was not my hand. At this
point someone will object: 'Bad faith.' No, it is good faith when one who
deserves to be deceived is deceived for a good end. In this way the doctor   110
deceives his patient. So did Christ sometimes deceive the Jews, because they
merited it; so he deceived the apostles, because it was necessary. But all
of this discussion is superfluous. Certainly the prince's letter in which he
ordered Heinrich Eppendorf to cease harassing me made it clear that I had
not written such things as were contained in the letter Heinrich brought   115
forward.[16] What I can honestly confess without any offence to him is that
except for the friendship which should be common to all Christians there
is no reason why I should wish to see or hear Heinrich Eppendorf. For that

* * * * *

13 This same incident is also recounted in Ep Allen 2874:148–56.
14 Johann Jakob Schutz of Ensisheim in Alsace (d 28 November 1524), who in
   1523 settled in Sélestat (Schlettstadt). Annoyed by the firm opposition of the
   burgomeister to the introduction of Lutheranism, Schutz forged a number of
   letters indicating that the burgomeister had invited the Hapsburg governor in
   Ensisheim to send Austrian troops to stamp out Lutheranism in Sélestat, thus
   causing alarm in both Sélestat and Strasbourg. Betrayed by fellow conspirators, Schutz was decapitated and quartered in Strasbourg.
15 See Erasmus' *Life of Jerome* CWE 61 45 with n127.
16 See Ep 1929 n5.

interior and sacred kind of friendship which is brought about by a similarity
of interests never existed between the two of us, and if it did exist I would   120
renounce it without hesitation. It is not because I desire to prevent anyone
from giving him the importance he demands for himself but because, for
an old man who leads an entirely different kind of life, the affection of
one so young can be of neither honour nor profit. The principal aim of the
agreement was that he would not create trouble or injure me by calumny,   125
which even a clown can do.

'But,' they say, 'he prescribed conditions and you accepted them.' I
accepted the conditions, I admit. But I did not acknowledge my guilt. I was
superior to him in my love of peace, not inferior in my defence. But does
the Gospel not counsel us to settle disputes with an adversary before we   130
go to trial?[17] One who accepts conditions is not automatically inferior. For
good men often prefer to concede the case to a dishonest litigant rather than
resort to a legal trial, and not infrequently they pay out money to a lowly
calumniator, buying back their peace with money. Tranquillity is a precious
thing. He who has bought it with money has not paid dearly. What about the   135
traveller who sometimes has to accept conditions from pirates, thieves, and
assassins and gives thanks? Similarly I would buy back tranquillity from
a pimp, a knave, a drunkard, a madman, even a Turk. Sometimes we buy
peace from a bothersome dog by throwing him a bone even if he is only
barking while we are conversing and cannot bite.   140

I do not wish it to appear that I am saying these things against Eppendorf but rather against those who spread such calumnies and, in their desire
to hurt me, dishonour their darling. Lastly, if he had extorted a large sum of
money from me, no wise person who was acquainted with both of us would
suspect other than that I had bought back a very valuable thing at a cheaper   145
price. Now that I was overburdened by so many diverse labours, peace of
mind, which I have always held dear and cherished, was more necessary to
me than ever before. To this day I have never called anyone into court, nor
have I been summoned to appear in court. I have so little time that I can
barely sustain my life in these labours that I endure for the general advance-   150
ment of studies. And the case would have to be conducted in German,[18] and
no doubt through lawyers. What friend could I have had the courage to burden with such a task? Add to this the fact that in the ulcerated condition of
human affairs there is no creature so vile, so abject, so worthless that is not

* * * * *

17 Matt 5:25
18 Which Erasmus persisted in claiming not to understand; see Ep 1313 n16 and
   lines 286–7 below.

capable of bringing charges against any good man. Therefore I chose the al- 155
ternative that was more suitable for us and our friends and more worthy of
a Christian.

I could have said these things even if I had accepted conditions that
were painful for me. But what is there about just conditions that they have to
be circulated by messengers and couriers? I cannot bring myself to believe 160
that Eppendorf is a man of so little faith that after shaking hands, after
pledging completely to forget all offences and suspicions, after entering into
a contest of performing deeds of kindness and good will, after sharing in
common the sacred cup of friendship, after being a guest at my table, he
has done all these things to disgrace me. I cannot imagine either that he is so 165
foolish as to think that such conditions should be bandied about, from which
men of good sense would readily form an unfavourable opinion of a man
who makes public the dedication of a book that does not exist. The story that
Eppendorf has spread that he had forced me to accept conditions to which
he would not descend for many thousands of ducats was, in my opinion, 170
invented before the signing of the agreement. And yet many people who
knew the man more intimately received the news with laughter. Therefore
I cannot convince myself that this is the work of Eppendorf, unless I first
persuade myself that he is a man of exceptional treachery, no less stupid
than malicious. May I not harbour such feelings about him unless he induces 175
my belief – which, please God, he will not do!

In those, therefore, who spread these rumours I find lacking not only
a Christian mentality but also any vestige of common sense, since in doing
this they sully his name more than mine. Our pact of friendship requires
that I defend his reputation as well as my own. What will sensible men say 180
when in the very first article they read these words: 'at the court of the
prince who is deemed to have the right of life and death over me.'[19] Has
he committed something punishable by death? Not even the letter that he
brought forth contained anything like that. What will those people think
who know that his life, free from crime certainly, we will admit, was one 185
of leisure and pleasure, which not even he conceals. And now he asks that
I see to it in my writings that no averse suspicion arise concerning him.

In the second article he asks that through my letter he may be restored
again to the expectations the prince formerly had of him.[20] What will the
sharp wits say of that? How am I to know what the prince expects of him, 190
except from what I learned from him, that the prince had supported his

* * * * *

19 Ep 1934:502–3
20 Ep 1934:509–11

studies so that when he had perfected himself in the study of law he might either teach at Leipzig or fulfil some other function. But in fact it is clear that the prince was angry with him even when I recommended him in my letter, and the prince was a little annoyed with me as well because I had spoken so highly of one who led that kind of life.[21] Nor is it in my power, no matter how much I would wish, to restore him again into the prince's good graces unless he furnishes what the prince expected of him. It is easy to infer what he expects. If he should provide this, I shall not be lacking in my duty. But how can he ask that I restore him into his former favour with the prince when he has stirred up this commotion against me in opposition to the letter of the prince? For the prince forbade him to cause me any trouble, while he, as if the prince had ordered it, has set this tragedy in motion.

Concerning the third article, what will shrewd observers suspect? He asks to be the distributor of the two hundred ducats;[22] and since this condition is placed last, they will suspect that this was the chief motive of the whole affair. It is well known that he lives sumptuously and has not a few debts, and his income is no secret. What was the purpose of supplying this occasion for suspicion to many, especially since, as I have said, I often hear people asking where Eppendorf gets the money that he squanders?[23] Certain others perhaps will not read without a sneer of disdain that part in which a man living such a licentious life is so concerned with his reputation that he would rather imperil his life than allow it to be defiled; or where he so often proclaims his guilelessness and innocence. If they truly favour Eppendorf, I see a lack of prudence in spreading the news of this abroad. If they do not favour him, I see a lack of Christian charity. To harm someone who does not deserve it is malice; to harm someone you are eager to benefit is a rare stupidity.

There is another reason for my considering those who boast about his demands to be lacking in prudence, as if it were unusual for people to make unfair demands in order to obtain what is fair, or as if it is not permitted to ask anything at all from anyone at all. It does not matter what he demanded but rather what I accepted and what the arbitrators prescribed, for a great part of the arbitrators' decision depends on my response. First of all, I do not acknowledge the letter as mine.[24] From that point on he has no claim to

* * * * *

21 In 1520–2; see Ep 1940 n10.
22 See Ep 1934:212–16 with n51, 518–20.
23 Lines 47–55 above
24 See Ep 1934:27–47, 528.

file suit; it is I who should complain that he brings charges against me when the duke himself wrote to him that I had not written the kind of things he accused me of, but only what I do not deny to have written.[25] But if because of the diffusion of my letter he has a bad reputation at court, let him impute that to the duke or to the nobleman Otto,[26] with whom, as their exchange of letters testifies, he had very close relations. It was through his doing, I am told, that my letter[27] passed through the hands of many people. They make sure that no one remains ignorant of this. He has more reason to be indignant with them than with me, who sent a sealed letter to one person.

As for the book, in what manner do I promise it?[28] It is not in order to admit guilt but rather to offer something in the name of friendship, provided that it is evident to me that he has laid aside his hostility and assumed an air of friendship. I can have no guarantee of this change of heart by words, nor can I be sure that it will be done on a specific day, since the Sacred Scriptures, which approve reconciliation, warn us not to consider ourselves safe from a reconciled friend.[29] The arbitration refers to the book in no other terms than those that I accepted. It cites my written reply. And what is more, there is no fixed time for the dedication of the book, for I do not always have the time and there are some to whom I have owed this obligation for many years; besides, not every subject is fitting for Eppendorf.

Concerning reconciliation with the prince, what is it that I promise?[30] 'If the prince has become more alienated from him because of my letter.' His spreading it abroad that there was the risk that the prince might cut off his head if he returned to his country, if we are to presume that was not made up, certainly owed nothing to my letter. I did not teach the prince anything new. He was not unaware of Eppendorf's manner of life. I merely showed the way in which he could improve the young man's character. I promised nothing but 'a politely written letter.' Not content with this, I added, 'As far as one can treat with such great princes.' For if I had praised Eppendorf to the skies, the prince, aware of things which perhaps not even I know, would think that I was making fun of him. Concerning the almsgiving, I promised nothing in my written reply.

* * * * *

25 See Ep 1929 n5.
26 Pack; see Ep 1934 n8o.
27 See Ep 1940:16–25.
28 Ep 1934:533–5
29 Ecclus 6:7–12
30 Ep 1934:538–41

There you have the demands and the responses; now consider the arbitration.[31] An accord was reached with the arbiters to which he made no stipulation, nor could he make any. In the arbitration the arbiters are spoken of in the preface as 'those to whom the right is given of settling a dispute in a friendly manner.' What they prescribe is mentioned in the preface. For me they have no prescriptions but 'to avoid trouble and to promote Christian concord.' They define the first two articles in exactly the same way as I accepted them in my written response. The text exists, which may be used to refute me if I am lying. What do they prescribe concerning the third article? 'In the same spirit,' they say 'he will not object.' What do they mean by 'in the same spirit'? Obviously 'to avoid trouble.' Not content with this they add 'without defamation of either party.' Do these words not indicate clearly enough to men of good sense what was the purpose of this agreement? What reason therefore do they have for boasting that Erasmus was treated severely?

And where are those terrible conditions to which Heinrich Eppendorf would not have condescended for many thousands of ducats? What of the fact that no time was fixed for the donation of money and that this could be remitted by the arbitrators? Besides, what need was there to grant me a remission when I of my own accord sometimes donate more money in a few days than what was there prescribed? And Eppendorf could have obtained a larger sum from me with a few politely spoken words. Again, when they prescribe the forgetting of offences, grievances, and suspicions on both sides, do they not make us equals in the case? And what is all this talk with reference to the gospel? Is it that I pardoned offences against me freely? This should merit praise as an act of piety. Is it that I chose to settle the matter through arbitrators rather than, extremely busy as I was, ignorant of the language, and inexperienced in judicial proceedings, choose to litigate with a man who has nothing to do and is a clever speaker? This was dictated by prudence.

But whatever the case, if they favour Eppendorf because he defends the cause of Hutten, it would be better for the sake of their well-deserving friend to keep silent about it. There were not lacking those who suspected, indeed there are not lacking those who maintain, that it was by the work of Heinrich Eppendorf that these rumours were spread and bruited about: if indeed it can be established that a servant of his was suddenly dispatched to Saxony with a letter. If this is true, what

* * * * *

31 Ep 1937

Punic perfidy,[32] I ask you, what Cecropian malice[33] can be compared with this? I had done him good services; I shall not make a formal reproach although I have grave reasons for complaint. I accepted the conditions for the sake of peace and concord. I never had need of Eppendorf's friendship nor have any wish, as I said, to see him or hear him except that I was motivated by the love of humane studies and Christian concord.[34]

The affair was conducted in the presence of two honourable witnesses,[35] Ludwig Baer and Henricus Glareanus.[36] The arbitrators exacted a solemn promise of compliance with their decision. We both promised. The arbitration was read aloud from the written document. It was approved by both parties, first orally and then by the affixing of our signatures. In sign of friendship we both broke bread that was offered to us and drank from the same goblet, which Duke George had sent as a gift.[37] Once again I pledged everlasting friendship; Eppendorf affirmed the same. We gave our right hand in friendship again. On the next day[38] I invited everyone to supper. I omitted nothing that a man who has forgotten all offences would do. You would say that such religious scruples were observed as might be used when a man is slain. After supper Eppendorf suddenly demanded the letter to the duke by the next morning. Although the arbitrators in their writ had given me the liberty to write to the duke or to the court without any prescribed time, nevertheless, since he insisted, I deferred to him beyond my obligations,[39] lest the feeling of good will be dissipated before it had sufficiently congealed. He demanded the preface[40] also. That was not only unfair but also absurd, since the book was not yet written. Reluctantly, but at the encouragement and petition of the arbitrators, I gave in also on this point. I inserted into the letter a passage to suit his wishes,[41] although it was not part of the agreement that I should write something at his dictation. He

* * * * *

32 The perfidy of the Carthaginians was proverbial. See *Adagia* I viii 28.
33 In both *Pirckheimeri Opera* and in Allen, the Latin text reads *Cecropum malitia*, which is a mistake for *Cercopum malitia*, or 'Cercopian malice.' On the villainous Cercopes, see *Adagia* II vii 35.
34 Cf lines 116–18 above.
35 On 3 February, in Erasmus' house (Ep 1933 n4)
36 On Baer see Ep 1933 n3; on Glareanus, Ep 1977 n29.
37 See Ep 1691:29–30.
38 4 February
39 By writing Ep 1940
40 Ep 1941
41 Possibly Ep 1940:36–40

demanded something else too, which the arbitrators did not dare propose   32
to me,[42] but I shall not mention it for the moment lest they also make this
public, to his disgrace.

After all this was done, if Eppendorf had seen to it that this false story
be spread all over Germany, what could be more wicked or more perfidious,
if you look at the plain facts, or what could be more stupid, if you regard   33
the judgment of thoughtful men? What will men of good sense think when
they hear talk about a dedication to a book that does not exist? Do people
think that the duke is so stupid that he does not understand that with this
letter I had bought back my tranquillity from a man with time on his hands?
Such extraordinary treachery, such great malice, such great stupidity I did   33
not attribute to Eppendorf even when I was angry at him, and I should
certainly not do so now after entering into this agreement with him. But the
more I absolve him from responsibility, the more I blame those by whose
guile these things are accomplished. He thought he suffered personal injury.
I never did any damage to their reputation unless harming another consists   34
in my not wishing to profess opinions of which I am not convinced. Even
concerning the past I am fairer to Eppendorf, because I infer from many
proofs that what he did was done at the instigation of others. And I am
not ignorant of their stratagems, although they think they fool everyone.
These same individuals instigated poor Hutten to take up his pen against   34
me. The same ones influenced Otto.[43] In this way, they say, we will diminish
Erasmus' authority. Oh what evangelical principles! Pretend that Erasmus'
authority, which even now is nonexistent or very slight, will be obliterated
everywhere – will you suddenly become gods? How much more rightly
you would strengthen your authority, not by defaming others with your   35
calumnies, but by a way of life worthy of the gospel, which the world has
long looked for in you.

Nothing will be accomplished by these machinations, and if you can
deceive the foolish for a while, one day your trickery will be laid bare and
the truth will burst forth. The Turks do not do more harm to the work   35
of the gospel than these seditious men by their corrupt and unevangelical
morals. Through them not only is the freedom of the gospel not restored

* * * * *

42 Perhaps, as Allen suggests, the ten florins for his journey, of which Erasmus
    learned only after Eppendorf's departure. See the *Admonitio adversus men-*
    dacium CWE 78 391 where, however, Erasmus reports that it was the request
    for the preface (lines 320–1 above) that the arbitrators had not dared to put
    before him.
43 Brunfels (Ep 1405)

but servitude is redoubled. For by whom has this harsh servitude been introduced if not by intractable men who refuse to obey those who give them
good advice? From whom does tyranny originate if not from citizens who   360
do not comply with the most equitable laws? If Luther has any sanity, and if
there are others to whom this matter is of some concern, they should hate no
one more than these rabble-rousers and utterly lawless men whom neither
bishops nor princes nor magistrates nor any republic can endure.

But this boasting has been succeeded by another rumour. They boasted   365
that Heinrich Eppendorf by word and by letter accused me of perfidy for
not producing the book I promised. Others may concern themselves with
what he said or did; not a word of it has reached me. What could one concoct
against him that would be more unworthy of an upright man? The agree-
ment was concluded just before the fair;[44] right after Easter[45] there was talk   370
of this perfidy – as if one could write books as easily as you wipe the mucus
from your nose. But suppose a year had passed. Perhaps he could politely
ask for the book. How could he charge me with perfidy, since no fixed date
was set? And if a date was to be set fairly and justly, the decision would
have been at the discretion of the arbitrators. But let us suppose it was pre-   375
scribed; would one be immediately guilty of perfidy if he did not produce
the book before the prescribed date? In that way one who does not produce
the money for his creditor before the prescribed date will be accused of perfidy, or one who does not return a loan before the designated time. Likewise with the blacksmith or the tailor who does not finish his work before   380
the promised date. Thus everything will be full of perfidy. If in civil contracts a saving clause is admitted – 'if it was not possible,' 'if it could not be
done conveniently' – how much more should it have been valid in this matter, which is regulated by the laws of friendship? Again, supposing that a
day was prescribed, it was not a simple promise, but two conditions were   385
added: 'In the name of friendship' and 'If I was assured that he had sincerely
become my friend.'[46]

Even if the rumours that he often vilifies my name in public gather-
ings, recites to his hosts some libellous book or other written against me,
and writes letters no less hostile than the previous ones are not to be be-   390
lieved, what sign has he given me that I can be sure he is my sincere friend?
Through whom has he sent me a friendly greeting? To whom has he spoken
kindly of me? And yet nothing is more common than these friendly offices,

* * * * *

44 On 3 February; see Ep 1937 and cf Ep 1950 n9.
45 12 April 1528
46 Ep 1934:533–5

nor could they be taken as proof of a person's good will towards you. If he does not show this by clear proofs, the book is not even owed to him. It was 395 not ruled by the arbitrators that he should require this book of me as a soldier exacts a stipulated sum of money from peasants and will burn down their barns if they don't pay up immediately, but as testimony of a friendship that has been mended and is being joined together to counter men's slanders. This should have been sought after by good services rather than 400 demanded with insulting talk.

You see that there is nothing in which my fidelity is lacking, since I provided much more than what was prescribed in the agreement.[47] First he demanded, not in a friendly or polite manner, that I write to the duke himself, although his formal demand leaves me free to write to the prince 405 or to one of his courtiers.[48] He extorted this from me beyond what was prescribed. Then when I had promised the kind of polite letter that one could be expected to write to such a great prince and which would not bring dishonour to me, he asked that I add certain sentences. This also he asked beyond the terms of the agreement. In the third place, he asked in 410 the late afternoon that he have the completed letter the next morning, which meant that I would have had to write the letter at night in bed. I ask you, did the arbitrators ever dream of anything of the sort? Fourth, he demanded the preface at the same hour. For what reason, except that he could show it around, as if he suspected that I would not do as I promised. This too 415 was conceded to his unprincipled demands. In the fifth place, he wanted me to give him the letter to the prince to read and to have it sealed in his presence by my servant so that there would be no chance of fraud. What an unfriendly gesture to be immediately so distrusting! But what a stupid gesture also. If I had wished to deceive him, could I not have sent another 420 letter by another messenger?

But if they think this is worthy of applause, that is, to have been able to extort so many concessions, they should for the same reason congratulate brigands who force a good man who wishes neither to kill nor to be killed to hand over his purse and to swear under oath that he will not seek revenge. 425 Who withdraws more from an agreement, one who demands more than he has contracted or one who gives less than promised? As soon as my secretary brought in the letter, Eppendorf began to upbraid him as if he had written the letter, for he did not have the least evidence that I had written it. And where is that promised forgetting of all suspicions and offences? 430

* * * * *

47 For what follows cf Ep 1950.
48 Cf Ep 1934:509–11.

Moreover, whether the rumour is true that in meetings and banquets he inveighed against my name at full tilt, his fellow tipplers will know best! If what they boast of is true, then that is true perfidy. I am not referring to refusal to abide by some article of the agreement but to acting against that which is the heart of the agreement. I am not accusing Eppendorf on this   435
count, rather I am on his side. But at all events, he has told the story about reducing me to conditions to which he himself would not descend for many thousands of ducats to too many people for him to deny it.

From these conjectures who would not conclude that he became reconciled under false pretences, but when he had failed in his hope for mone-   440
tary gain he looked for another kind of revenge? Nevertheless, I have interpreted everything honestly. Yet his simplicity, trustworthiness, and integrity are vaunted, while I, after conceding so many things that were beyond what was stipulated and after interpreting in a good light so many instances of bad faith, have perfidiously violated a pact! I do not yet repudiate the agree-   445
ment, but I fight against those who talk without seriousness about a matter that they do not understand and in so doing do more harm to the reputation of the one they wish to appear to support than to mine. Therefore I have written these things for Eppendorf, not against him. For I think that according to the terms of the agreement it is my duty to restore and protect his   450
honour and fame to the best of my ability and in so far as he will allow me.

I have sent this letter to you, distinguished sir, so that you may have something to respond to these blabbermouths, who as soon as they have satisfied their stomach and what is below the stomach have nothing to do but speak ill of everyone and thus enjoy evangelical freedom. Farewell.   455
Given at Basel, 1 May 1528

1993 / From Erasmus Schets   Antwerp, 4 May 1528

The autograph of this letter, which was first published by Allen, is in the University Library at Basel (Scheti epistolae 14). On Erasmus Schets and his role in the management of Erasmus' financial affairs, see Ep 1931. Erasmus' reply to this letter is Ep 1999.

CORDIAL GREETINGS
When your servant Quirinus arrived here around the beginning of April,[1] sent by you from Germany, there was a rumour of the declaration of war

* * * * *

1993
1 Talesius; see Ep 1955 n1.

by the alliance of the kings of France and England against the emperor in
Spain.[2] This turn of events has alarmed all of us here as it has Quirinus, and   5
the journey to England was not safe. In the end, the rumour became more
subdued; it was understood that the English did not want any confrontations
with the emperor and wished to adhere to their old treaties. We all breathed
more easily, and so Quirinus attempted the journey and crossed over to
England. He will report to you what he has seen and heard there and will   10
take care of your affairs.

Concerning the money that had passed into the hands of Weldanck,[3]
it has been ascertained that you wrongly suspected Birckmann.[4] For Weldanck, being less familiar with the transactions of exchange with which Tunstall had charged him, ended by giving the money back to Tunstall.[5] He, not   15
yet sufficiently informed about your repeated instructions to deliver the
money to Luis de Castro,[6] gave it to certain Italians. The money remained

* * * * *

2 Following his repudiation of the Treaty of Madrid, Francis I entered into the
anti-imperial League of Cognac with the papacy, Venice, Milan, and Florence
(Epp 1931 n11, 1932 n12). Under the guidance of Cardinal Wolsey, Henry VIII
tried to keep England aloof from these developments, hoping to play a key
role as honest broker in the negotiations between Francis and Charles. On the
other hand, the sack of Rome in May 1527 (Ep 1987 n1) turned the pope into
a virtual prisoner of the emperor and thus robbed him of his freedom to ac-
commodate Henry in the matter of his divorce from Queen Catherine, the emperor's aunt. So, for a time, 'honest brokering' consisted of siding with Francis in his negotiations with Charles and attempting to compel the emperor to
accept peace terms advantageous to Francis and Henry. On 21 January 1528
an English herald actually delivered a declaration of war to Charles at Burgos
(LP 4 no 3827). In late March, war seemed imminent (LP 4 nos 4108–12). But
Henry and Wolsey, neither of whom had any intention of direct participation
in fighting on the continent, quickly decided to pursue their aims via diplomatic means (LP 4 no 4153). See also J.J. Scarisbrick Henry VIII (University of
California Press 1968) 198–202.
3 The 90 angel-nobles of the annuity from Archbishop Warham for 1527; cf
Ep 1931:14–15 with n5. If these were actual gold angel-noble coins, this sum
would have been worth £33 15s 0d after the debasement of November 1526
(Appendix Tables 2–3, 464–76 below). But Erasmus Schets indicated in Ep
2001:5–14 that the nobles to which he was referring were not the gold coins
but instead a money-of-account, still worth 6s 8d or 80d, so that three such
'nobles' had a value of one pound sterling (in silver). And, if the nobles in this
letter were also this money-of-account, this sum would have been worth £30
sterling.
4 Cf Ep 1931:23–9.
5 On Tunstall, see Ep 1726 introduction.
6 Cf Ep 1764:4–6.

in their hands for some time. Finally, through Tunstall a document called
a bill of exchange, worth fifty Flemish pounds, eleven shillings, and eight
pence,[7] was sent to Pieter Gillis, who deposited this sum of money into my   20
account.[8] Quirinus, now returned from England, says that Tunstall told him
that he paid fifty pounds sterling to these same Italians. The money received
here did not correspond at all to that sum, since there is a difference of one
third. We must write back to Tunstall to inform him of this error. I shall
give this task to Pieter Gillis; I shall also write to Luis so that the matter   25
may be brought to a satisfactory conclusion. Some fate or other has pursued
this money from the beginning; it is now more than a year that it is wandering around in uncertainty. At last the matter will come to a clear and honest
solution.

Luis de Castro also writes me that he received from the same Quirinus   30
thirty-five pounds sterling.[9] Quirinus will explain where they originated.
I see that your English pension has diminished because of the devaluation
of money, in this case the pound, caused by the increase in the value of
gold. For where previously they paid you in angels or gold nobles (three of
which at that time were equivalent to one pound sterling, but now because   35

* * * * *

7 For the bill of exchange or draft, see Ep 1934 n85. On the basis of the relative
  exchange values of the English angel-noble – valued at 90d sterling and 119d
  groot Flemish – the sum of £50 11s 8d groot Flemish would have then been
  worth £38 4s 8d sterling, not the £50 that Tunstall had reportedly paid to the
  Italians. As Schets notes, 'there is a difference of one third.' See n14 below,
  which indicates that the sum, when exchanged into English pounds sterling,
  was worth £39 sterling. See Appendix Table 3, 476 below.
8 Pieter Gillis (Ep 184). Though his leading role in the management of Erasmus' financial affairs in the Netherlands and England had been taken over by
  Schets (Ep 1931), Gillis' friendship with Erasmus persisted (cf Ep 1972:9) and
  he continued to concern himself with Erasmus' well-being.
9 For the relative values of £35 sterling, see Ep 1965 n4. Schets' statement that
  the increase in the value of gold was responsible for the devaluation of the
  pound sterling is largely correct. For the current rise in international gold
  values during the 1520s, and for its impact on Henry VIII's debasements of
  August 1526 (gold alone) and November 1526 (gold and silver), which also
  resulted in the introduction of gold crowns (single-rose crown in August, and
  double-rose crown in November), see the Appendix 440–5 with Tables 1–3,
  457–76 below. As Schets correctly notes, three angel-nobles (at 6s 8d or 80d)
  used to be worth exactly one pound sterling; but he was incorrect in stating
  that three such nobles were now worth £1 4s 6d (*ad libram cum solidis quatuor
  cum dimidio*). After the two debasements had raised the value of the angel-
  noble to 7s 6d or 90d sterling, they were worth instead 270d = £1 2s 6d (ie
  two shillings less). See also Epp 1866 n3, 1931 n8.

of the increase in the value of gold they are worth one pound, four and a half shillings), they continue to pay you in pounds, adding to these pounds, the denomination in use, an amount that corresponds to the increase in the value of gold. That is the reason why you receive less gold than usual for the same number of pounds, as I think I have explained to you on other 40 occasions in my letters. Take note how it is that you receive less in England, since your pension is reckoned in pounds, than you are accustomed to receive in the denomination of angels or gold nobles. For at one time a pound sterling was worth twenty-eight Flemish shillings, whereas now it is worth not more than twenty-five.[10] I wished to explain this to you so that 45 you would understand how this came about and why it is that you receive less from your English pension than usual. I will see to it that the thirty-five pounds sterling that Luis de Castro received from Quirinus be exchanged here with the least possible interest.

In addition, Master Jan de Hondt[11] has arranged to pay me at the fair in 50 Bergen[12] the pension of sixty-five florins that became due after the feast of

* * * * *

10 According to Schets, the English pound sterling was worth 28 shillings groot Flemish before Henry viii's two debasements of August and November 1526. By relative gold values (when, previously, the angel-noble had been worth 80d sterling and 116d groot Flemish), the pound sterling should have been worth exactly 29 shillings, though likely only 28 shillings when foreign exchange fees are taken into account. After those two debasements, however, the exchange value of the English pound sterling necessarily fell to about 25s groot Flemish, according to Erasmus Schets. That is confirmed by the fact that the new double-rose crown, issued with the November debasement, valued at 5s 0d or 60d sterling, was worth 76d groot Flemish in the Low Countries. Thus four rose crowns were worth exactly one pound sterling and just over 25s groot Flemish (304d groot Flemish = 25s 4d groot Flemish). See the Appendix 440–50 with Tables 2 and 3, 464–76 below.

11 Jan de Hondt (Ep 751) had replaced Pierre Barbier (Epp 443, 1294) as the canon in possession of the Courtrai prebend that had been conferred on Erasmus (Epp 436, 443) and was thus responsible for the payment of the annuity to Erasmus. Since, however, payment had to be made first to Barbier and then to Erasmus, there were endless difficulties; see Epp 1094 (introduction and nn3, 6), 1605 n1, 1621 n3. Pieter Bietenholz's article on Barbier in CEBR I 94 includes a useful summary of the whole complicated business of Erasmus' Courtrai annuity, which still awaits investigation by an expert.

12 The town of Bergen-op-Zoom (now part of the Dutch province of North Brabant) had two annual fairs, the first of which was held at Eastertide (see Ep 1671 n4). In 1528 Easter fell on 12 April, and the spring fair that year is known to have taken place from 9 April to 6 May (see Allen's note at lines 50–1).

the Purification.[13] I shall collect this sum and keep it with the other money, both received and to be received, and according to your directions I shall keep it until you decide what should be done with it. Whatever you command shall be executed.   55

After settling these matters I met Pieter Gillis. I inquired of him what he knew of the money that Tunstall said he gave to an Italian in England, who gave him in exchange fifty pounds, eleven shillings, and eight pence in Flemish money. He said that he had spoken to the Italian and understood from him that the money Tunstall gave him in England did not exceed thirty-nine pounds sterling, which sum is equivalent to fifty pounds, eleven shillings, and eight pence of this currency, which have been deposited here by the Italian. And so it seems that for the said thirty-nine pounds sterling (paid in nobles, three of which equal one pound) ninety nobles, equivalent in value, were given which have been unaccounted for all this time. It seems that Tunstall has now augmented these with another twenty-seven nobles to make one hundred seventeen nobles, which converted into pounds amounts to the said sum of thirty-nine pounds sterling.[14]

* * * * *

13 2 February. Again, the type of florin is not specified. Erasmus Schets, writing from Antwerp, may have meant the current Hapsburg Flemish gold florins, popularly known as Carolus florins (after Emperor Charles v), containing 1.700 g fine gold, which had a current 'rate' or exchange value of 42d groot Flemish = 25d or 26d sterling = 247d tournois. By Henry viii's royal proclamation on exchange rates, dated 6 July 1525, the Carolus florin was given an official rate of 25d sterling; but no such rates on foreign gold coins were provided after the two English debasements of August and November 1526, which produced an increase in the value of English gold coins and undoubtedly led to a rise in market prices for Carolus and other florins. (See the Appendix 440–50 with Table 3, 476 below). Erasmus did not, however, use the term 'gold,' and he usually presented values of pensions and annuities in some money-of-account. He most likely meant the current florin money-of-account, in which one florin had a slightly lesser value, of 40d groot Flemish, so that six florins equalled one pound groot; cf Ep 1934 n6. Hence 65 such florins had a value of £10 16s 8d groot Flemish. To earn this sum, an Antwerp master mason, paid an average daily wage of 10d groot, would have had to work for 260 days, or 1.24 years (at 210 days a year). See also Ep 1965 n4.

14 See n7 above. According to Schets, this sum of £50 11s 8d groot Flemish had been exchanged in England for £39 sterling; but earlier in his letter (line 22 above) he had noted that the value was instead £50 sterling – an amount whose value he had then queried. His current valuation is based, however, upon the fact that sum was paid in English nobles, whose type is not specified. Before the debasements of August and November 1526 (see Ep 1931 n8 and nn3 and 9 above), gold angel-nobles were worth 80d sterling – three to the pound –

Bedyll,[15] who mentioned the sum of one hundred forty nobles to Quirinus, seems to have given a wrong report. Nevertheless Pieter Gillis and I will   70 write to England to obtain more certain information about the matter, lest our carelessness result in having you suffer losses.

May God grant you the health that I desire for myself. My wife, who has recovered well from a recent childbirth, sends her greetings. A great number of friends ask me, each in turn, to send their greetings whenever I   75 get the chance to write you. Do keep your friends and me informed about your health, when you can.

Farewell from Antwerp, 4 May 1528.

Your dear friend Erasmus Schets

To the most learned Erasmus of Rotterdam, my distinguished friend,   80 one and only light of all literature

1994 / From Gerard Morinck   Louvain, 8 May 1528

Gerard Morinck (d 1556) of Zaltbommel on the Waal studied at Louvain, receiving his MA in 1513. Staying on in Louvain to lecture in arts and theology (licentiate in 1527), he became a close friend of Maarten van Dorp (Ep 304), president of the College of the Holy Spirit, who died on 31 May 1525. By the end of that year Morinck had been appointed a lecturer in theology at Holy Spirit. In 1529 he seems to have become a tutor at the abbey of St Gertrude at Louvain, and in 1533 his services were engaged by the abbot of the Benedictine abbey of St Trudo at St Truiden, where he remained until his death. Although a theological conservative and opposed to the Lutheran reformers, he was attracted to humanism and admired Erasmus, whose faith in biblical scholarship as the path to reform he shared. He wrote biographies of his

*****

so that £39 sterling had a value of 117 such nobles, not 90 nobles, as stated in this letter. Those two debasements together raised the exchange value of the angel-noble from 80d to 90d, so that £39 sterling would have been worth fewer such nobles: 104 angels. To complicate matters even more, however, Schets subsequently indicated, in Ep 2001:5–14 (as already noted in Ep 1931 n8 and n9 above) that these were not gold coins but a notional money-of-account by which three nobles are worth a pound sterling, and that money-of-account would not have been affected by the 1526 debasements. Nevertheless, even that mode of reckoning still provides a sum of 117 'nobles,' in money-of-account. See also the Appendix 440–50 with Tables 2–3, 464–76 below.

15 Thomas Bedyll (Ep 387), secretary to Archbishop Warham and thus responsible for the transferral to Erasmus of his annuity

friend Dorp, St Augustine (the occasion of this letter), Pope Adrian vi, and others, as well as a number of exegetical works.

The letter was first published by Förstemann/Günther (Ep 86) from the autograph in the Burscher Collection at Leipzig (Ep 1254 introduction).

GERARD OF MORINCK TO ERASMUS OF ROTTERDAM, GREETING
In recent days, most learned sir, our friend Heemstede communicated to me a letter of yours to him,[1] mainly for the reason that many things in it were relevant to me. You say in it that you heard that I have written with great care a life of Augustine. You say also that if I should be willing to send   5
it to you, perhaps to be added to your volumes on Augustine,[2] because it is not your intention to dedicate your learning to this task, it would be an outstanding memorial of me in such a splendid work. Assuredly, most kind sir, I am immensely grateful for such kindness towards one who has not yet merited it, since you offer of your own accord what many would wish to   10
purchase at a great price, to be borne not without praise upon the lips of men. I have no way of repaying this attention bestowed on me, but I shall never incur the charge of ingratitude.

To inform you in a few words of the origin of this story, there were, I must tell you, among the Bethlehemites in Louvain[3] holy men and fer-   15
vent initiates in the study of good letters, who greatly encouraged me to undertake this project last summer. There was no limit or moderation to their demands until they finally compelled me to take up my writing tablet. Their motive was that many traditions concerning Augustine are quite open to suspicion. Their desire is to seek out something conclusive from Augus-   20
tine's own works and present it in a modern idiom. While we have such vivid portraits of other saints, they feared that the life of this greatest of saints might fall into complete neglect. I had already completed some pages, albeit in great haste, when word went round that you were dedicating your great learning to restore the works of Augustine with great care and judg-   25
ment, so that there was hope that they would soon be published with universal acclaim. When I learned of this I immediately stopped work on my undertaking, having no doubt that as in the magnificent tribute you paid

* * * * *

1994
1 Not extant, but probably answering a reply to Ep 1900. On Jan of Heemstede, of the charterhouse at Louvain, see also Ep 1646.
2 The Froben Augustine of 1529 (Ep 2157)
3 A house of Augustinian canons at Hérent, on the north side of Louvain

to Jerome at the beginning of that work,[4] you would likewise celebrate Augustine,[5] since he had merited no less of Christianity, nor had he advanced 30 the cause of sacred letters with less industry. And from there the rumour reached you. Then again, when I take serious thought of my abilities, I see that the task clearly surpasses my limits and requires a specialist who has a thorough knowledge of Augustine's works, which I do not have. I have some knowledge, but not enough that I should dare construct a portrait of 35 Augustine.[6] But I know also that the work must be completed quickly and bides no delay, because they say that everything will be published by the time of the next fair.

Wherefore, most learned sir, you would do better if you did not refuse to undertake this pious work, especially since you can accomplish it quickly 40 and successfully. For you have the time, I think, and you are possessed of a rapid facility of the pen like no other man in this century and, finally, you have a minute knowledge of the subject. If you do not do it, you will disappoint the expectations of many who assume that you will produce something similar to what you did in the edition of Jerome, especially consid- 45 ering that these two are by general admission the greatest Doctors of the church, or; and it would be fitting if those who merited equally of the church should be celebrated equally. But you will also give room for suspicion (if you will pardon me for saying so) that you are less well disposed to Augustine, for they will silently think that it was not by chance that you omitted to 50 lend your eloquence to praise him while you honour Jerome with so much praise. But if you can be persuaded by entreaties, all scholars would fervently implore you not to give the impression by preferring to remain silent of neglecting one whom the consensus of all the world holds in highest esteem. Reflect upon this within yourself, I earnestly pray you, and do not 55 disappoint the hopes of scholars. This will be worthy of your great learning; it will be worthy of Augustine, who, a great man himself, demands that he be represented by a great man, lest someone like me detract from rather than enhance the dignity of such a subject. Do what you think to be most proper to your high office, I beg you. 60

* * * * *

4 Fols a^5–β^8 in the first volume of Erasmus' edition of 1516
5 The Froben Augustine of 1528–9 contains (1 595–610) only the life of Augustine written by his pupil Possidius.
6 Morinck's own biography of Augustine was completed in 1531–2 and published at Antwerp in August 1533, with a dedication to the Bethlehemites of Louvain (see line 15 with n3 above).

I read your book *On The Bondage of the Will*[7] from beginning to end
with as much attention as I could. But I do not know what could be more
perfect or in which no one except perhaps Momus himself could find fault.[8]
You put things before our eyes with such clarity, with the use of apt comparisons, that it would be clear even to the blind.[9] Moreover, everything is   65
so learned that I doubt if anyone in this age has cut more to the quick, as
they say.[10] To sum up, there is almost no writing of yours, in the judgment of many, in which you speak more circumspectly considering the
morals of the times or which leaves less room for calumny, so much so
that even your enemies are forced to admit it. Continue, most learned sir,   70
to bring succour to these troubled times in this same manner. You will earn
among men everlasting memory and with God a reward worthy of your
merits.

As far as I understand, your Lordship has written to Frans, a friar minor, to tell him to abstain from injuring your name in a very offensive man-   75
ner in public lectures.[11] I should write more openly about this matter save
that I do not have the time I would wish. I shall postpone it to a future occasion. You will hear not only by word of mouth but also in printed volumes
that the young man, whose beard has just grown in, is contending with you,
although he conceals and represses his thoughts like an officiant at the mys-   80
teries of Eleusinian Ceres,[12] no doubt so that he will be less embarrassed

* * * * *

7 Morinck absent-mindedly writes *De servo arbitrio*, which is the title of Luther's
    book. He means *De libero arbitrio*, Erasmus' *Discussion of Free Will*.
8 Cf *Adagia* I v 74. Momus (or Momos) was the Greek god of mockery, fault-
    finding, scoffing, and carping criticism as well as the patron deity of writers
    and poets. He found fault with Aphrodite for talking too much and for wear-
    ing sandals that creaked (though her naked body escaped criticism). This sort
    of behaviour led eventually to his being banished from Olympus.
9 *Adagia* I viii 93
10 Here 'cut to the quick' (*ad vivum resecare*) means 'be meticulous.' See *Adagia* II
    iv 13.
11 Ep 1823 to Frans Titelmans, which was answered by Ep 1837A
12 The Eleusinian mysteries, dedicated to Demeter (Ceres in Latin) and held an-
    nually at Eleusis (near Athens), were the most sacred in ancient Greece, at-
    tended only by initiates who were under solemn vow not to reveal what took
    place at them. The principal officiant was the hierophant ('displayer of sa-
    cred things'). Chosen for life from the hieratic clan of the Eumolpides, he
    alone was permitted to enter the sanctuary where the objects sacred to Deme-
    ter were kept. At the climactic moment in the celebrations, he displayed the
    sacred objects to the initiates present.

if his rash bravado should break a string.[13] I read a sample of his work;[14] I would have read it more closely if I could have got hold of a copy to read it more carefully. But there is nothing there that should concern your Lordship. It is all of such a nature as you would expect from such a person, that is, ridiculous and childish things worthy of the nursery. They are not worthy of your Highness' attention unless you think that you must attack the university itself. I shall give you an example of these writings as soon as I can. But in the meantime I should like you to promise that you keep these things secret, for I wish not to suffer any hostility, if that is possible.

Our friend Goclenius is having a letter of mine sent to you,[15] for what reason I do not know. I ask that it be torn up as soon as it is read. Do the same with this one lest if it is thrown away it may fall into someone's hands. With this I say farewell, most learned and kindest of men. May the good God long keep you healthy, strong, and unharmed, and may he grant that your efforts contribute to the public good.

Yours truly, Gerard Morinck

To the consummate theologian Erasmus of Rotterdam, at Basel

1994A / From Conradus Goclenius   Louvain, 10 May [1528]

The autograph of this letter, which was first published by Allen, is in the University Library at Basel (Goclenii epistolae 15). Allen initially assigned the year-date 1529. By the time he realized, on the basis of the clear connection with Epp 1972 and 1994, that the letter belonged in 1528, the letters for that year had already been published in volume 7. So he numbered the letter 1994A, and it appeared in volume 8 lvii–lxix.

Conradus Goclenius (Ep 1209) was professor of Latin at the Collegium Trilingue in Louvain, where he was much admired for his fine teaching. He was not only Erasmus' most reliable contact in Louvain but also one of his closest friends, always ready to render devoted service in both scholarly and practical matters. To him Erasmus entrusted his autobiography, the *Compendium*

* * * * *

13 *Adagia* II vi 36: *Ne in nervum erumpat* 'For fear it break the string.' Erasmus notes that the metaphor 'is taken from archers who, by drawing their bowstring with excessive force, sometimes snap it, not without great risk to themselves' (CWE 33 309).

14 Possibly a manuscript copy of the *Collationes quinque super epistolam ad Romanos* (Antwerp 1529), in which Titelmans defended the authority of the Vulgate against Lorenzo Valla, Lefèvre d'Etaples, and Erasmus.

15 Cf Ep 1994A:16–17. The letter is not extant. On Goclenius see Ep 1994A.

vitae, along with the request that Goclenius help with the publication of his
collected works after his death (Ep 1437). Goclenius was also one of those for
whom Erasmus made provision in his will.

It seems likely, on the basis of Ep 1973:27–8, that this is Goclenius' reply to
a letter from Erasmus written on or about 20 March 1528.

Cordial greetings. For some time now I have wished to inform you about
the stupidities of a petty little monk of the Franciscan order so that I could
convince you in very fact, as I have written to you many times, that there is
no one more despicable, more childish, more removed from common sense
than this young man.[1] But despite all my vigilant efforts to find the right   5
opportunity, I have had no success so far except that Gerard Morinck gave
me some hope of obtaining his little book,[2] since he divined who it was that
wrote that nonsense. And just when we arrived at the critical moment, he
was suddenly called back to his home town because of some urgent business.
But he solemnly promised me his cooperation on his return and I think he   10
made that same promise to you in a letter.[3] I have no doubt that he will
fulfil his promise as long as he understands that you will be very grateful
for this service and is assured that this can be done without incurring any
harm to himself among his fellow countrymen, whom he fears rather than
loves. On the first point you may give me your opinion; for the second I   15
have taken full responsibility myself. I have sent you a letter from that same
Morinck to I know not whom.[4] You see that it bears the mark of one who
has a close affinity with the studies whose revival is owed to your efforts
alone.

I added a humorous letter with an addendum by a monk from Lille. He   20
was jokingly asked by my student, Jocab,[5] a well-educated young man with
a sharp wit, whether it was right for him to lecture on your *Enchiridion* to the
boys he was instructing. He had no other design in doing this than to have
that buffoon, who was continually shouting abuse from the pulpit against
the name of Erasmus, betray himself by his own evidence and accomplish   25
his own undoing. A good many of us read his answer with great pleasure.

* * * * *

1994A
1 Goclenius' letters to Erasmus about Frans Titelmans (Ep 1823) are not extant.
2 See Ep 1994 n14.
3 Ep 1994
4 See Ep 1994:91–2.
5 Unidentified

I had no time at all to reread the *Adages*[6] because, in order to be of more benefit to literary studies to the best of my abilities, I doubled my lecture time; I cannot leave the stage without disgrace before the play is over, once I have entered upon it.   30

I have to take it in good part that Hieronymus Froben did not publish *De officiis*,[7] although I had hoped otherwise. I lectured on some lighter subject matter, waiting to hear his answer after the Frankfurt fair, since you wrote to me that he would not undertake the task until he had dealt with the vendors at Frankfurt. But since he has not indicated his decision to take   35 advantage of this opportunity, I conclude that it is not to his liking or that he is not in agreement with his partners. Accordingly, since I cannot remain idle, especially in the face of such remote and uncertain prospects, circumstances compelled me to make some plans and obliged me to lecture on Livy, of whom I happened to have copies. But if Froben has decided other-   40 wise, I shall not be lacking in the duties of a friend. Even if he would have done me a great favour and would have gained some advantage for himself, in my opinion, I take it in good part if in an unpromising situation he preferred to model himself on a Quintus Fabius rather than a Minucius.[8] Your conjecture *medium Ianum* in the second book of *De officiis* I consider an   45 oracle of learning or even of the Muses.[9] I have no doubt that Cicero him-

* * * * *

6 Erasmus was now collecting material for the enlarged edition of September 1528 (Epp 2022–3).

7 There is a 1528 Froben edition of Cicero's *De officiis* edited by Erasmus and Goclenius. It appears, however, that it was not published until later in the year, probably in time for the autumn fair.

8 Quintus Fabius Maximus Verrucosus (c 275–203 BC), a Roman politician and soldier, was called 'Cunctator' because of his preference for delaying tactics during the Second Punic War. In that same war Minucius launched a precipitous attack on Hannibal and had to be rescued by his rival, the 'Cunctator' Fabius.

9 In a passage (2.24.87) that deals with acquiring and investing money, Cicero observes that this is a matter more appropriately discussed by financial experts than by philosophers. The earliest printed editions of the work, following the available manuscripts, described the experts as 'quibusdam optimis viris ad *ianuae* medium sedentibus' (certain worthy gentlemen located at the middle of *the door*), which made no sense. Pietro Marso, whom Erasmus had known in Italy (Epp 152:23n, 1347:278–82), was the first to suggest that *ianuae* was an error for *Ianum*, the reference being to the central archway east of the Roman forum, named for the god Janus, where Roman money changers plied their trade. The first edition of *De officiis* to incorporate this correction was that published at Venice by Giunta in 1525. The Cratander Cicero (Basel, March 1528) still had *ianuae*, but the Froben edition of the autumn of 1528 (see

self, if he were to come back to life, would acknowledge only that reading as genuine.

Franz Dilft passed by here on his return journey but did not stop off.[10] Therefore I have not been able to learn anything from him up to now. I hope 50 he gained enough wisdom in this odyssean journey that he will not regret the waste of effort and the financial loss.

Concerning the climacteric year,[11] if it were someone else who was troubled by it I would not marvel at his foolishness, not to say impiety. But if you are the man I have always thought you to be by general assent of 55 all good men, there is no power of the fates that can stand in the way of the immortality of the name of Erasmus. Such is your service to the whole human race that you will live in men's memory forever. I do not see what purpose you had in writing that,[12] unless perhaps you wanted to make fun of magic superstition. 60

Edward Lee had a magnificent reception at the imperial court, if you know what I mean.[13] Quirinus[14] is bringing the little book to you.[15] Cornelis

* * * * *

n7 above) had *Ianum*, which seems to have been a correction made independently by Erasmus. Not until the discovery of manuscripts unknown to Erasmus and his contemporaries would this conjectural correction be confirmed by documentary evidence.

10 See Ep 1942 n1.

11 Astrologists regarded the sixty-third year of a person's life as a 'grand climacteric' year, ie the crucial year in the person's life and one in which a major event was to be expected. If one takes 1466 as the year of Erasmus' birth, he would be entering his grand climacteric in October 1528.

12 Perhaps in the letter to which this is the answer

13 Edward Lee (Ep 765) was Henry VIII's ambassador at the court of Emperor Charles V in Spain in the years 1525–30, which were a period of increasingly hostile relations between the English and imperial courts. On Erasmus' previous relations with Lee, see Ep 1341A:823–30. Goclenius' reference to Lee's 'magnificent reception' at the imperial court is an ironic reference to the uproar in January 1528 caused by an ineptly worded statement in which Lee seemed to say that the French king was more trustworthy than the emperor. This was followed by an indignant response from the imperial side and by Lee's effort to explain away his gaffe. Lee's statements and the imperial response were soon published. See n15 below.

14 Talesius, see Ep 1955 n1.

15 Allen thought that this was a reference to the 'scurrilous attack' on him that Erasmus attributed to Lee (Ep 1744:133–5). It is much more likely, however, that Goclenius is referring to the small book entitled *Exhibita quaedam per Eduardum Leum, oratorem anglicum in consilio Caesareo ante belli indictionem. Responsio cordatissima nomine Caesareae Maiestatis ad eadem*, published by Johannes

de Schepper has returned from Spain, having been dignified by the emperor
with the rank and income of a knight.[16] He holds the office of ambassador
here and is a true friend of good letters, which he defends vigorously at   65
court against calumnies. When I paid him a visit recently, he asked that I
inform him when a messenger would be leaving here in your direction, for
he wishes to write to you. But when Quirinus returned he was in the most
distant part of Flanders, so I could not accede to his wishes. My own situation is practically unchanged. I am still involved in a lawsuit in Antwerp,   70
with no little loss of time, for I often have to appear before the judge. But I
think it will turn out well.[17]

My present conditions are beginning to weigh heavily upon me, and I
pretty well regret having passed up so many opportunities that presented
themselves to me over the years.[18] The College does not support me, nor   75
can it. I can expect no other remuneration than my daily bread. The burdens

* * * * *

Grapheus at Antwerp in 1528. The booklet contains three items: a statement
by Lee urging the emperor to accept the peace terms offered by the French
king; a second statement by Lee exhorting the emperor to keep the peace; and
an anonymous response to Lee on behalf of the emperor. All evidence points
to Alfonso de Valdés (Ep 1807), the emperor's Latin secretary, as the author of
the imperial response, and it is likely that Valdés took the initiative in publishing the three pieces. It is worth noting that in Valdés' response, Lee is pil-
loried not only as the ambassador of a once-friendly country turned enemy
but also as a known enemy of Erasmus. The many 'Erasmians' at the imperial court clearly did not like him. Through them, Erasmus knew that Lee was
doing his best to sow opposition to Erasmus in Spain (cf Ep 1814 n39). See
Erika Rummel 'Political and Religious Propaganda at the Court of Charles
v: A Newly-Identified Tract by Alfonso Valdés' Historical Research 70 (1997)
23–33.

16 In 1526, Schepper (Ep 1747 n23) had embarked on a long and distinguished
   career as a trusted administrator and diplomat for Emperor Charles v. Though
   it is doubtful that Schepper and Erasmus ever met, they had many friends
   in common, including Goclenius and the imperial chancellor Gattinara, and
   Erasmus consequently viewed Schepper as an influential ally.
17 In April 1525, Goclenius was appointed canon of Our Lady's in Antwerp. But
   the appointment was contested by a rival candidate who had the backing of
   the curia, and the result was a lawsuit that dragged on for more than eight
   years. See Epp 2352, 2573, 2587, 2644, and Henry de Vocht History of the Foundation and the Rise of the Collegium Trilingue Lovaniense, 1517–1550 Humanistica
   Lovaniensia 10–13 (Louvain 1951–5) III 95–103.
18 Cf Ep 1765:19–23. On Goclenius' discontent with his situation at the Collegium
   Trilingue, cf Epp 1388:3–5, 1435:1–6, 1457:3–8.

I have to bear are, willy-nilly, such that, even adding what I receive for religious functions to the salary from the college,[19] it comes to twenty-five
Flemish pounds.[20] I can hardly get by. This is the very reason why Rutgerus
established a family,[21] since he lives more cheaply at home than living freely   80
at the college in the midst of crowds of visitors, which, because of the reputation of the college, it is impossible to escape unless we flee the college.
I am given some hopes again about a position at court, concerning which I
will seek your advice when I have more exact information about it.

The tragic farce about Franz Birckmann is now on everyone's lips.[22] I   85
would have wished, certainly, for your sake that it had come to an end. For
those who do not know of your honesty and generosity, I might also add
for your enemies, it generates some kind of suspicion. He defends himself
no less strenuously and loquaciously than you accuse him unceasingly. I
neither have nor have had any dealings with him except through you, and   90
I shall take care that none exist in the future. I do not plead his cause, nor
does he seek my advocacy. But I am sorry that it provides an opportunity
for calumny to your enemies. They claim repeatedly that for the slightest
injury you snarl like a dog and demand openly and strenuously that he be
sent to the gallows. I thought it was my duty to tell you these things out   95
of my respect for you, lest in this region among those who are ignorant of
your very just motives, or simply do not even hear about them, there be any
diminution of your prestige, acquired by the exercise of so many virtues.

Farewell, unique glory of religion and letters.

Louvain, sixth day before the Ides of May   100

Your most devoted friend Conrad Goclenius

To the supreme adornment of the age, Desiderius Erasmus of Rotterdam. At Basel

* * * * *

19 On the payments to Goclenius from the Collegium Trilingue, see *Literae virorum eruditorum ad Franciscum Craneveldium, 1522–1528* ed Henry de Vocht,
Humanistica lovaniensia 1 (Louvain 1928) Ep 95 introduction.
20 An annual salary of £25 groot Flemish was worth about 143 Carolus gold
florins, at 42d groot each (CWE 8 350 Table B; CWE 12 649–50 Tables 3C and
D), equivalent to about £15 9s 6d sterling, if the value of the Carolus florin is
taken as 26d sterling (see Ep 1993 n13). In Antwerp, a senior master mason,
paid 10d groot Flemish per day (annual mean of summer and winter wages),
would have had to work 600 days or 2.86 years (210 days per year) to earn an
equivalent income.
21 See Ep 1882.
22 See Epp 1931:23–9, 1972:5–8.

1995 / From Hermann von Wied   Brühl, 27 May 1528

First published in the *Opus epistolarum*, this is Archbishop Hermann's reply to
Ep 1976.

HERMANN, BY THE GRACE OF GOD ARCHBISHOP OF COLOGNE,
PRINCE ELECTOR OF WESTPHALIA, AND DUKE OF ENGER, ETC,
TO ERASMUS OF ROTTERDAM, GREETING

Esteemed and dear sir, a few days ago your letter was delivered to us, in
which with the greatest kindness and learning you saw fit to invite us into   5
your friendship, attributing to us as well in your goodness certain qualities
that we suspected are owed more to your affection than to any right judgment. Nonetheless, we shall gladly allow ourselves to be praised by you in
the way in which a certain Cyrus was by Xenophon,[1] so that we may be
able to perceive more clearly through your advice what are our duties to   10
Christendom and to ourselves. Hence there is no need for you to appeal so
earnestly to us for our friendship. For as soon as we heard your name, which
has brought such glory to good letters, we were immediately seized by a
strong impulse, as it were, of devotion towards you. Indeed it is my wish
that you should have every blessing, even if perhaps it is not in our power   15
to provide them all immediately. Of this you can be certain, that we consider nothing more important than that Christendom together with good letters should flourish freely and securely, after the thorns have been torn out
by the roots. This is what men of learning strive for daily, but often without fruit, since there is always that one who resists their efforts and sows   20
tares among the good crops at night,[2] and to do more harm makes thorns
grow, by which the good seed of God is choked.[3] But you must continue
to the best of your ability to cleanse the threshing floor of darnel and straw
with the winnowing fan of gospel teaching.[4] As far as we are concerned, we
shall gladly lend our support in this task, hoping with the grace of our Lord   25
shining upon us to secure peace one day among Christian princes. Without this he labours in vain who labours to tear out the roots of error. In the

* * * * *

1995
1 The reference is to Xenophon's *Cyropaedia*, a pseudohistorical account in eight
  books of the life of Cyrus the Great. An idealized portrait of a monarch guided
  by Socratic principles, it was hugely popular with the Romans.
2 Ie the devil; see Matt 13:24–30, 36–40.
3 Matt 13:7
4 Cf Matt 3:12, Luke 3:16.

meantime we ask that you help us by your prayers to devote our energies
faithfully and usefully to the task that has been committed to us.

From our castle at Brühl, 25 May 1528   30

1996 / From Hector Boece   Aberdeen, 26 May 1528

> First published as Ep 62 in Enthoven, the autograph of this letter is in the
> Rehdiger Collection of the University Library at Wrocław (Rehd 254.31).
>   Hector Boece (Boethius), c 1465–1536, a Scott from Dundee, was a co-resident
> with Erasmus at the Collège de Montaigu in the 1490s. Ep 47, addressed to
> Boece, served as the preface to Erasmus' *Carmen de casa natalitia Iesu*. Boece
> left Paris in about 1496 to become principal of the College of St Mary (later
> called King's College) at the newly founded University of Aberdeen. This let-
> ter is evidently the first contact between Erasmus and Boece since their time
> together in Paris. Erasmus answered it in 1530 with Ep 2283.

HECTOR BOECE TO THE EMINENT ERASMUS OF ROTTERDAM,
CORDIAL GREETINGS

On a recent business trip to Aberdeen, Hans Bogbinder,[1] a considerably
learned young man of Danish blood, who has the greatest respect for you,
said he did not so much marvel as rejoice to have found in the farthest cor- 5
ners of the world devoted admirers of yours engaged in the study of literature. To his great delight, he saw in Aberdeen scholars of sacred learning
with your *Paraphrases* of the gospel of Christ always in their hands. These
works, which you published for the sake of instructing youth in good letters
and morals, are so eagerly devoured by the young that whoever does not 10
strive to the best of his abilities to imitate Erasmus, by general consensus the
glory of this age, and does not pore over his books diligently is accounted
by his fellow students as having no desire to learn.

Eagerly inquiring into the reasons for this cult of Erasmus, Hans discovered that the leading figures of Aberdeen University had once been your 15
disciples. And to tell you the truth, I was in my small way among the first to
lay the foundations of this institution. When I was with you in Paris thirty-
two years ago at the religious college of Montaigu, where you interpreted
certain sacred texts, an admiration of your learning and your exceptional
modesty of soul took hold of me, which has remained with me and increased 20
day by day as the renown of your name grew. For, besides your outstanding

* * * * *

1996
1 Ep 1883

Hector Boece
Artist unknown
Marischal Museum, Marischal College
Historic Collections, University of Aberdeen

command of the Greek and Latin languages, how much philosophy and theology you know! I understood that you were devoted from the beginning
to this most sacred discipline. Then there is such fervour in your teaching,
such lucidity in your writing, such zeal for the defence of true piety, that   25
you seem to be some divine being dwelling among men! I do not think there
is any place in the world accessible to human habitation that is ignorant of
this. You are an object of admiration to all the learned world; you find favour
with all those who profess the Christian religion. Your piety is so consonant
with your learning that one can see from your writings that all your joy, all   30
your care, all your leisure and hours of work seem to be devoted to the cultivation of sacred letters. Since you are regarded and are the most learned of
the learned, your spirit is, in the judgment of all, worthy to enjoy the most
honourable tranquillity in this life and, after you have fulfilled your earthly
mission, the immortal reward that God has reserved for those who love him.   35
    But a future age will hear of your praises, greater, certainly, than any
of us can imagine, when a great many will judge that our age was fortunate that you led such a fruitful existence in it. For myself, since I do not
have the learning or the personal prestige to be able to attain to even a tiny
fraction of your praise, I shall take care, as far as in me lies, that as better   40
studies revive throughout the world chiefly through your efforts, those who
are taught good morals and humane disciplines at Aberdeen will hold you
as the unrivalled father of literary studies, will cherish and venerate your
name, and will forever sing of your glory worthy of immortal fame. Since
the huge distance that separates us does not allow me to offer any other ser-   45
vice, I shall render you at least the benevolence of mind that is owed to you
and the gratitude of which I am capable for the superabundance of your
benefits to me.
    Farewell and acknowledge as your own the University of Aberdeen,
attached more than all other mortal men to the volumes you have published.   50
    Aberdeen, 26 May 1528

1997 / To Willibald Pirckheimer   Basel, 28 May 1528

This letter (= Ep 1174 in wPB) was first published in the *Pirckheimeri Opera*.

Cordial greetings. I think you received the letter I sent you some days ago,[1]
in which I alerted you against the rumour that Eppendorf seems to have

* * * * *

1997
1 Ep 1992

spread throughout Germany, as vicious as it was false. For the present I
shall explain in a few words what I should like to ask of you.

Opsopoeus[2] published a Greek edition of the letters of Basil and Gre-   5
gory Nazianzen.[3] I took it upon myself to translate them in order to gratify
the wishes of the Polish bishop of Cracow,[4] who gave me an honorarium of
sixty ducats.[5] But I found that the letters were terribly edited. Right on the
title page he wrote πατρῶν for πατρός. For πατρῶν is not used in Greek.[6] In
the first letter I presume the reading was βαττακάρᾳ, meaning 'with a droopy   10
head';[7] he wrote βαθεῖ κάρῳ, which is neither Greek nor Latin. Concluding
from these samples that there would be others, I refrained from translating.
Therefore I ask you that, if Opsopoeus has a manuscript copy, you would
request him to send it to me.[8] If this can be done in time, I shall issue the
book before autumn; if not, at the first opportunity. At the same time, it   15
must not be allowed that such a great author be so poorly edited. Young
men of this type, more daring than learned and more concerned with their
own profit than with the public good, are a great plague to literary studies.
I hope you are in the best of health.

* * * * *

2 Vinzenz Heidecker (or Heydnecker), who took the humanist name Vincentius
  Opsopoeus (Obsopaeus, Obsopius) because he was the son of a cook, was an
  important figure in the editing and translating of Greek texts. He matriculated at Leipzig in 1524 and almost immediately launched a series of translations of Luther's German works into Latin and his Latin works into German,
  all published by Secerius in Haguenau. He settled for a time in Nürnberg,
  where he made his first translations from the Greek, including two books of
  the *Iliad* (1527). It was there also that Pirckheimer lent him the manuscript of
  the letters of Basil and Gregory of Naziansus (cf following note). In 1528 his
  learning and his sympathies for the Reformation led to his appointment as
  rector of the new Latin school in Ansbach, where he continued his activity as
  editor and translator until his death in 1539. See Heinrich Jordan *Reformation
  und gelehrte Bildung in der Markgrafschaft Ansbach-Bayreuth: Eine Vorgeschichte
  der Universität Erlangen. 1. Teil (bis 1560)*. Quellen und Forschungen zur bay-
  erischen Kirchengeschichte 1/1 (Leipzig 1917) 115–32.
3 *Basilii magni et Gregorii Nazianzeni theologorum Epistolae Graecae, nunquam antea
  editae* (Haguenau: J. Secerius 1528)
4 Piotr Tomicki (Ep 1919)
5 See Ep 1953 n2.
6 This form of the genitive plural is in fact found in the *Odyssey* 4.687 and 8.245,
  as Allen notes. The usual Attic form is πατέρων.
7 *Adagia* IV ii 79
8 See Ep 2028, where Erasmus reminds Pirckheimer of this request. Since there
  is no mention of such a manuscript in the preface (Ep 2611) to Erasmus' edition of Basil (1532), one must infer that Pirckheimer was unable to fulfil the
  request.

Given at Basel, 28 May 1528   20
To the distinguished Master Willibald Pirckheimer, councillor of his
imperial Majesty

1997A / To Maarten Davidts   [Basel, c May 1528?]

This letter was first published, without date, in the *Opus epistolarum*. The recipient, Maarten Davidts (d 1535) was a canon of the collegiate church at Brussels
with whom Erasmus had stayed in 1516 (Ep 532:35n). It was at Davidt's request
that Erasmus wrote the epitaph for Philippe Haneton that is appended to this
letter. Haneton, seigneur of Lindt, was from 1500 to 1522 principal secretary
and *audiencier* (officer in charge of government documents) of the Grand Council at Mechelen and from 1520 treasurer of the Order of the Golden Fleece.
It is known that he died on 18 April, but the year of his death has remained
uncertain, some sources giving 1522 and others 1528. Allen argued for 1522
and published the letter as Ep 1280, but Cornelis Reedijk, in his edition of the
The Poems of Desiderius Erasmus (Leiden 1956) 341–2, has argued more persua-
sively for 1528 (cf CWE 86 548–50). So we have placed the letter here, at the
end of the letters for May 1528. The Latin epitaph with a prose translation of
it by Clarence Miller can be found in CWE 85 158–9 no 75. The metrical translation offered here, which turns the iambic senarius of the original into iambic
pentameters, is the work of Charles Fantazzi, with help from Alec Dalzell.

ERASMUS OF ROTTERDAM TO MARTIN DAVIDTS, GREETING
Although intent on other things, I willingly undertook this little task, both
for you, my host – for among men of old the right of hospitality was especially sacred – and in memory of an excellent man, whom I have always
found to be a person singularly well disposed towards me and most solici-   5
tous of my welfare. If you are pleased with the epitaph, well and good, but
if not, it will be no trouble for me to rework it. Farewell.

> Here in this place Philippus Haneton
> Lies in his grave, a famed and gilded knight
> Who served King Philip[1] and the emperor Charles   10
> As audiencer, winning great acclaim.

* * * * *

1997A
1 The reference is to Philip the Handsome, duke of Burgundy, husband of
  Joanna of Castile and father of Charles v. Shortly before his sudden death
  in 1506, he and Joanna were proclaimed queen and king consort, hence the
  title given him here.

The holy order of the Golden Fleece
Selected him to be its treasurer.
In this one man, such was his faithfulness,
His generous heart, and courtesy towards all,   15
That Virtue left no place for Jealousy.
By high and low alike his loss will be
Uniquely felt, but he in heaven dwells.

1998 / To Henry VIII   Basel, 1 June 1528

First published in the *Opus epistolarum*, this is Erasmus' reply to Ep 1878.

ERASMUS OF ROTTERDAM TO HENRY, KING OF ENGLAND,
GREETING
Although the providence of eternal God, O most serene King, exercises and
tries his people with various afflictions, nevertheless his goodness so tempers the harshness of the remedy, often intermingling the happy with the   5
sad, that human weakness can bear up under it. As Paul says, he gives us
with the temptation the means to overcome it.[1] He cuts and burns in such
a salutary manner that by mixing comfort with torment he mercifully as-
suages our ills, pouring the pungent wine upon our wounds but at the same
time adding oil. For just as I was on the verge of collapse, both as a result of   10
my unremitting labours to advance the cause of learning and because of my
ruinous state of health (a heavy burden even if the feebleness of old age were
not yet upon me),[2] but also distressed still more by the incurable dissensions
in the church and the frenzied attacks of evil men – lo and behold! beyond
all expectations your Majesty's letter was delivered to me with the kind in-   15
vitation to come to England, as though from shipwreck on a storm-tossed
sea to a nearby peaceful harbour, offering me everything, not as befitted my
merits – for they are nought – but as was proper to a most clement prince.
     I can scarcely say, illustrious prince, how much strength, how much
exhilaration I experienced from this so courteously written letter. I was flat-   20
tered by the opinion your Majesty seems to have conceived of me. Again
and again I wished that I was such a one who either by my counsels or my
services could gratify such a Christian prince. But my spirit sinks each time
I perceive that my ability does not correspond to your expectations or my

* * * * *

1998
1 1 Cor 10:13
2 See Ep 1934 n7; see also lines 35–6 below with n5.

desires. And yet my spirit, despite the many reasons that called me back,   25
eagerly desired to set sail for England. What deterred me were my age, becoming more burdensome day by day; my health, more fragile than glass,
which I barely manage to protect by keeping to my house; the long journey,
no longer safe from the attack of brigands; and, to add to this, the difficulties of a sea journey and the terrifying rumours of war. And report usually   30
exaggerates what has been learned.

    These and other things that I cannot entrust to a letter discourage me
from making this journey, but I nonetheless sent a servant ahead so that I
would not find things totally unprepared.[3] After his departure, just before
Easter,[4] I was stricken with a sickness which so prostrated me that it seemed   35
it would bear me off to a happier life.[5] I recovered from it gradually, but
in such a way that my scant strength is much more enfeebled than before.
After this my servant returned to tell me that the situation in both Germa-
nies[6] was such that if none of the obstacles that I mentioned were present,
and if matters in England were perfectly at peace, still no part of the jour-   40
ney would be safe. No place is free of bands of soldiers who spare neither
friend nor foe. And the duke of Gelderland is a menace everywhere.[7]

    Therefore I give the one thing I could give, most excellent king: I ren-
der you thanks for your singular devotion towards me and feel myself no

* * * * *

3 Quirinus Talesius (Ep 1955 n1)
4 12 April 1528
5 See Ep 1989 n4.
6 'Germany,' most of which lay within the boundaries of the 'Holy Roman Empire of the German Nation,' was conventionally (and roughly) divided into
   Upper Germany (*Germania superior, Oberdeutschland*) in the south and Lower
   Germany (*Germania inferior, Niederdeutschland*) in the north. There was a corresponding distinction between the dialects of High German (*Hochdeutsch*) and
   Low German (*Niederdeutsch*). The Netherlands belonged geographically and
   linguistically to Lower Germany while, at the other end of the Rhine, Basel
   and Strasbourg were in Upper Germany.
7 Cf Ep 2024:36–7. From 1492 until his death in 1538, Karel van Egmond, duke
   of Gelderland, offered bitter resistance to the efforts of the Hapsburg government of the Netherlands to deprive him of his duchy. To that end, he became an ally of Francis I against Charles V. Renewed conflict between him
   and Charles in the spring and summer of 1528 led eventually to negotiations
   that in October produced the treaty of Gorkum (Gornichem), by which Emperor Charles finally recognized Karel van Egmond as the duke of Gelderland.
   Only following the death of Egmond and the disputed succession of William
   of Cleves in Gelderland did Charles V succeed in subduing the duchy to Hapsburg rule (1543). See P.J. Meij 'Gelderland van 1492–1543' in *Geschiedenis van
   Gelderland, 1492–1795* ed J.J. Poelhekke et al (Zutphen 1975) II 13–78.

less indebted than if I had been the recipient of all the benefits you offered   45
to me in your kindness; and I feel all the more obligated the more I recognize that I am not entitled to them. I shall not implore you not to take offence at my declining your kind invitation. The goodness of your nature is
well known to me. I know that far from being angry with me it will grieve
you that I have such valid reasons for declining. We are driven by the fates;   50
to the fates we must yield. If, however, I can please your Majesty in any
way that can be accomplished in a written work, I shall refuse nothing that
lies within my power. In the meantime, I shall not cease to pray for the
tranquillity that your piety and virtue deserve.

I did not entrust this letter to my servant,[8] since I thought it better to   55
be silent than write in an ambiguous way.

Given at Basel, 1 June 1528

1999 / To Erasmus Schets   Basel, 13 June 1528

First published by Allen, using the autograph in the British Library (MS Add
38512 fol 25), this letter is Erasmus' response to Ep 1993. Ep 2014 is Schets'
reply.

Cordial greetings, my good friend. The error concerning the fifty pounds
sterling is due to my servant.[1] As to what Pieter Gillis said about the thirty-
nine pounds sterling,[2] it is certain that the bishop gave Tunstall forty pounds
at the current exchange of three nobles to a pound, since ninety and thirty
make one hundred and twenty.[3]   5

* * * * *

8 See n3 above.

1999
1 Quirinus Talesius (Ep 1955 n1); on the error cf Ep 1993:21–4.
2 Cf Ep 1993:58–69.
3 On the money that Warham gave to Tunstall to arrange to have delivered to
  Erasmus, cf Epp 1965:29–43 with n4, 1993:12 with n3. Before the English debasements of August and November 1526, as indicated in previous notes, three
  gold angel-nobles, then worth 8od each, had the value of one pound sterling
  (240d). After these two debasements, which required an increase in the value
  of that gold noble from 8od to 9od, three such nobles were now worth £1 2s
  6d; conversely, £40 sterling would now be worth 106.67 angel-nobles, rather
  than 120 nobles. However, in his reply to this letter (Ep 2001:5–14), Schets
  indicates that he was referring not to the actual gold angel-noble coins, but
  rather to a notional money-of-account that, despite the 1526 debasements, had
  retained its former value: three nobles to the silver-based pound sterling. For

Pieter Gillis has two promissory notes, of which he can show you one. And so for the year 1526 the bishop has paid in full; for the year 1527 he paid ten pounds; twenty pounds are still owed.[4] And this year 1528 starts from the feast of the Annunciation in the season of Lent that has just passed.[5]

The Courtrai pension for the whole year will be due this month on the feast of St John the Baptist.[6] I have written to Jan de Hondt.[7] Do not involve Pieter Gillis in my affairs, as far as you can.[8] Send my best wishes to your wife and family.

Don't give any money to my servant Nicolaas Kan,[9] if he should ask you for it. He has enough and more than enough. Farewell, most dear friend.

At Basel, 13 June 1528

Yours, Erasmus of Rotterdam

At the next fair or through my servant,[10] if he is returning here, send a receipt for the money that you have in my name.

Don't let the English know that my money remains with you. Have them believe that it was sent to me. The same goes for Pieter Gillis.

I send this letter of the archbishop[11] so that you can see the sum of money that was sent.

To the distinguished gentleman Erasmus Schets, at Antwerp

2000 / From Johannes Fabri   Prague, 17 June 1528

First published as Ep 87 in Förstemann/Günther, the manuscript of the letter was in the Burscher Collection at Leipzig (Ep 1254 introduction). On Fabri, see Ep 1926 n10.

* * * * *

the monetary details, see also Epp 1931 n8, 1993 n9, 2001 n4; and the Appendix 440–50 with Tables 2 and 3, 464–76 below.

4 This shows that Warham's yearly pension to Erasmus, perhaps including the parish at Aldington (Ep 255 introduction), was £30.

5 Annunciation, 25 March, fell within Lent (25 February–11 April) in 1528. In England, the new year began on 25 March.

6 24 June; see Ep 1993 n11.

7 On de Hondt, see Ep 1993 n11. The letter mentioned here is not extant.

8 Cf lines 20–1 below.

9 Kan (Ep 1832) was the intended bearer of this letter, but there was subsequently some confusion about whether it had in fact been delivered by Kan or by Quirinus Talesius, as Schets, perhaps mistakenly, reported. See Epp 2014:66, 2015:15–16.

10 Probably Kan

11 See n3 above.

Cordial greetings. I would be afraid, most learned Erasmus, that you might interpret this inordinately long intermission of my correspondence in a far different manner than is actually the case, if I were not convinced that both you and I experienced long ago the whirlwind activities and waves to which one is exposed once he has destined himself for a life at court. For after so 5 many and such royal, which is to say important, missions, to which I dash off hither and yon, first in lower Pannonia[1] and now in Bohemia, I have scarcely been able to purloin enough time to send greetings to Erasmus. Therefore, in your kind indulgence you will more readily forgive me if I have not written to you as often as you perhaps would desire. I should wish 10 to assure you that, at least as far as I am concerned, my feelings which, if I am not mistaken, you have realized are anything but callous, have not changed one iota in your regard. In reality that friendship, even if it is mutual, would be quite lukewarm if it could immediately be shattered when the courtesy of a greeting is occasionally neglected. I remain therefore as 15 I was, a staunch supporter of my friend Erasmus. Proof of this is that I have obtained from the most serene and most Christian King Ferdinand,[2] my most gracious lord, the promise that he would award you a pension of four hundred florins,[3] on condition, however, that as soon as possible you pack your belongings and your literary paraphernalia and betake yourself 20 forthwith to Vienna. This would mean, not that you would have to take up a professorship of humanities, but only that you would be an inestimable adornment to his royal Majesty and the other leading men of the court and also to the humanities themselves and to the entire university. We all know how important it is where the great Erasmus resides, the celebrity whose 25 name and incomparable learning are today exalted throughout the world.

* * * * *

2000
1 Hungary
2 Ep 1935 n5. The dedication to Ferdinand of Erasmus' *Paraphrase on John* (Ep 1333, 5 January 1523), to which Ferdinand responded graciously and generously (Ep 1343), opened a period in which Erasmus felt secure in Ferdinand's good favour.
3 The type of florin is not specified; but if the pension that Ferdinand of Austria offered Erasmus was to be paid in Vienna, the florins are probably those of the Four Imperial Electors, currently worth about 40d sterling, 59d groot Flemish, and £1 10s 0d tournois each. If so, this pension would have been worth £66 13s 4d sterling, £98 6s 8d groot Flemish, and £600 tournois. An English royal proclamation of 6 July 1525 on exchange rates had given the Rhenish florin an official value of 39d sterling. But, as noted earlier (cf Ep 1993 n13), no exchange rates on foreign gold coins were provided after the two English debasements of August and November 1526, which did increase the values of English gold coins. See the Appendix 440–50 with Tables 2 and 3, 464–76 below.

Many things conspire, my good Erasmus, to tear you away without regret from your beloved Basel. First, the scoundrels associated with the filth
of Oecolampadius and Zwingli (one could hardly imagine anything more
unbearable) torment you, as we know, in the most spiteful manner;[4] then the   30
envy of the fates has recently carried off Froben himself from these lands,
by a premature death;[5] with him gone I do not see what can hold any attraction for you in Basel. On the other hand think of the advantages you
will enjoy here if you consent to the king's plans. First there is the salubrious climate of Vienna, so much to be recommended that for that rea-   35
son it may be regarded as preferable to Plato's Academy. To this is added
the advantage that, since crops are so abundant, the cost of living is very
cheap. What shall I say of the profuse liberality of the bishops who have
their sees not only in Hungary but in Poland, from which source I promise
you rich profits? Furthermore, without mentioning other things, certainly   40
an entire chorus of learned men will rival each other to flock to you as if
to a sacred anchor.[6] Then also all students of the humanities will pay such
homage to your name that by this means alone you will gain immortality.
How many do you think there will be who, as soon as they know that Erasmus has come, will wish to dedicate themselves to the higher disciplines,   45
even if they had renounced them previously? Through the generosity and
piety of the king there has been a reorganization of things so that professors'
salaries have been increased substantially. His principal aim in this was to
have those learned in Greek, Latin and, on equal terms, Hebrew, wherever
they may be, to be called here to hold these positions and drive out the   50
sophists.[7]

* * * * *

4 Johannes Oecolampadius (Ep 224:30n), long Erasmus' associate in humanist
   scholarship, was now the principal leader of the evangelical reform movement in Basel and a partisan of Zwingli in the 'sacramentarian controversy'
   with the Lutherans (Epp 1928 n9, 1930 introduction). In January 1528 he and
   Zwingli had participated in the disputation that led to the triumph of the
   Zwinglian reformation in Bern (Ep 1988 n1) and greatly emboldened the advocates of reform in Basel. In December and January 1528/9 public agitation,
   culminating on 9 February in an outbreak of iconoclasm in the city churches,
   led to the banning of the Catholic mass. The Reformation Ordinance (*Refor-
   mationsordnung*) of 1 April 1529 established an evangelical church order in
   the city. See Locher 372. It was these developments that precipitated Erasmus' move to Freiburg im Breisgau in April 1529; see Allen Ep 2149 introduction.
5 See Ep 1900.
6 *Adagia* I i 24
7 Following his consecration as bishop of Vienna in 1530, Fabri himself established the Collegium Trilingue of St Nicholas at the University of Vienna.

But where are my ramblings taking me? I shall see to it personally that the king write to you very soon in his own hand.[8] I wish with this letter of mine to give you previous notice so that you in turn, as quickly as possible, will inform me of your intentions. Be of good health and write back.   55

Given at Prague, 17 June 1528

Yours sincerely, Fabri

To his friend Erasmus of Rotterdam, paragon of learning, at Basel

2001 / From Erasmus Schets   Antwerp, 24 June 1528

This letter was first published by Allen from the autograph in the University Library at Basel (Scheti epistolae 15). Erasmus' answer is Ep 2015. On Schets, see Ep 1931.

Cordial greetings.

I wrote you most recently during the month of May through your carrier Quirinus,[1] who I believe and hope has reached you safely. From that time I have awaited a letter of yours, which thus far has not come.

I described to you the whole series of events concerning the money that   5
was deposited in London with Weldanck; how Tunstall finally recovered the money and changed it through the agency of a certain Italian to be given to Pieter Gillis – I refer to the ninety nobles that had disappeared for such a long time in the hands of Weldanck. These were added to the other twenty-seven, amounting together to the sum of one hundred and seventeen nobles   10
of the kind of which three are equal to one pound sterling, not of those struck in gold.[2] So the one hundred and seventeen nobles in question come to thirty-one pounds sterling, which Tunstall exchanged for fifty pounds, eleven shillings and eight pence in Flemish money.[3]

From these figures it is clear that the payment of your English pension   15
occurred after the devaluation of gold.[4] It would not be a bad idea if you

* * * * *

8 Cf Epp 2005:23–4, 2007:12–13. The letter is not extant.

2001
1 The letter in question was Ep 1993.
2 Ep 1993:12–21, 66–8
3 For these transactions, and the nature of the 'noble' (as money-of-account and not a gold coin), see Epp 1866 n3, 1931 n8, 1993 nn3, 7, and 14, 1999 n3.
4 The term 'devaluation' as used here (*auri diminutioni*) is, paradoxically, accurate, for an increase in the official values of gold coinages, even when they remained physically unchanged, was a debasement, and in that sense,

gave me a detailed account of your English pensions. I could then instruct
Luis de Castro, who could politely ask for them each year in your name.
That would be a relief for you and for those who are desirous of giving you
this money, since perhaps it is a burden for them to take care of obtaining   20
a good exchange for the money they are giving. Luis is perfectly willing to
do this and is eager to help.

Concerning the rest of the money I received in your name, you have
an account in the letter I sent with Quirinus.[5] The total amount of money received until now that I have in my possession is six hundred forty Braban-   25
tine florins.[6] Whatever I subsequently receive I shall add to that and then at
last carry out your instructions.

On another occasion I commended to your good will Karel Uutenhove,
who is going to Basel to study.[7] I send you together with this several letters addressed to him. I ask you to give them to him together with my   30

* * * * *

a 'devalution.' For Henry VIII's two linked debasements of August (gold only)
and November (gold and silver) 1526, see the Appendix 440–50 below.

5 See n1 above.

6 In Ep 2014 (lines 34–5 and n5), Erasmus Schets refers to 'six hundred and
forty florins in our money,' for which 'six florins equals one pound' (*quorum
sex conficiunt vnam libram*). Presumably he means similar florins here: that is,
the Flemish and Brabantine money-of-account worth 40d groot Flemish (cf Ep
1934 n6), and not the gold Hapsburg Carolus florins, then worth 42d groot
Flemish. If so, this sum was worth £106 13s 4d groot Flemish (= 609.52 Carolus
florins). A master mason then employed in Antwerp (in Brabant) would had to
work for 2,560 days or 12.19 years, with 210 days' annual employment, at 10d
groot per day, to earn the value of 640 florins, in money-of-account. For the
Carolus florins, see the Appendix Table 3, 476 below; and CWE 8 350 Table B;
CWE 12 650 Table 3D.

7 A native of Ghent, Karel Uutenhove (documented c 1524–77) had by 1524 attended the Collegium Trilingue in Louvain. At this point he was on his way to
Basel, where Erasmus received him into his household and took an immediate
liking to him (Epp 2015:14–15, 2062:42–4, 2065, 2077, 2078). In 1529 Erasmus
dedicated to him his edition of *Opuscula* by St John Chrysostom (Ep 2093) and
made him a speaker in the colloquy Ἀστραγαλισμός sive *Talorum lusus* 'Knuck-
lebones, or The Game of Tali.' Following two years of study in Italy, 1529–31,
Uutenhove returned to Ghent, by which time Erasmus had come to regard
him, with great disappointment, as a man of good family but mediocre education and little inclination for study. Nonetheless, their correspondence continued until 1535. Elected alderman at Ghent in 1539, Uutenhove had to retire
from public life following his participation in 1539–49 in the city's rebellion
against the regent, Mary of Hungary. In later years his Protestant leanings
were a source of trouble. He withdrew for a time to Paris (1556–67) and then
apparently retired to Jülich-Cleves to live with his son, also named Karel.

greetings. Remain in good health, and when you have time tell me how you
are keeping. For our health depends very much on yours.

Antwerp, 23 June 1528

To the incomparable savant of sacred letters Master Erasmus of Rotterdam, at Basel   35

2002 / To Ferry de Carondelet   Basel, 25 June 1528

This is the preface to an edition of the writings of Faustus, bishop of Riez in
fifth-century Gaul, published by Johann Faber Emmeus at Basel in 1528 (*Fausti
episcopi de gratia Dei et humanae mentis libero arbitrio opus insigne, cum D. Erasmi
Roterodami praefatione*). Erasmus' contribution to the project appears to have
been limited to the writing of this preface.

On Ferry de Carondelet, archdeacon of Besançon, see Epp 1350 n6 and 1749
introduction. He died two days after this preface was dated (Epp 2010:6–7,
2012:15–23).

TO THE MOST HONOURED FERRY DE CARONDELET, ARCHDEACON
OF BESANÇON, FROM ERASMUS OF ROTTERDAM, GREETING
Why should I call down curses upon the common cold, loathsome and relentless enemy of the dedicated scholar, which suddenly sprang up while I
was with you and interrupted the longed-for pleasure of your sweet com-   5
pany and caused annoyance to you and your friends, to whom I wished to
be congenial?[1] Now, even if my health permitted me to fly from the nest
without risk, it would not be possible because of the locusts that beset the
countryside everywhere, much more dangerous than the ones in Egypt that
only devastated the crops, while these spare neither a man's purse nor his   10
life.[2] All that remains for us to do is to converse in this way.

I send together with this letter something from the hunt.[3] 'Is it yours?'
you will ask. Certainly not. The tortoise will sooner catch the hare, as the
proverb has it.[4] It belongs to Aquila. Who? You will say. I do not doubt
that you have heard the name of the excellent gentleman, Count Hermann   15

* * * * *

2002
1 A reference to Erasmus' visit in 1524 to Porrentruy and Besançon in Burgundy,
  during which he suffered from poor health: see Ep 1956:9–23 with n1.
2 Ie the 'bands of soldiers' referred to in Ep 1998:41–2.
3 Ie a hunt for books; cf Ep 182:1–2.
4 *Adagia* I viii 84

von Neuenahr,[5] provost of the church of Cologne, who, although he merits acclaim from his long line of ancestors, is nevertheless so pre-eminent by virtue of his native talent, his shrewd judgment, his uncommon learning, his purity of life combined with a rare wisdom, his rare loftiness of spirit joined with an admirable mildness of character that even without the 20 recommendation of his ancestors he could not but be celebrated and illustrious. Since in place of the gambling table and whoring he cultivates the love of literature, he discovered this book in an old library,[6] as one would find prey lurking in a thicket. He captured his prey and sent his catch here. What was sent to a single individual I have made accessible to all. Too bad 25 he did not send it to me before I wrote *De libero arbitrio* against Luther![7]

There seems to have been a council held in Gaul at which the heresy of Pelagius was condemned.[8] It is amazing how quickly this spread throughout Africa. It probably took rise in Gaul, since we learn that Pelagius was a Briton.[9] It was already beginning to weaken when Julian,[10] a very learned 30 and eloquent man, reinstated it. Augustine in several learned tomes came to grips with it.[11] From this one can learn how dangerous it is to spread new dogmas since there is nothing too absurd that it does not find its followers.

* * * * *

5 Ep 1926 introduction. In Latin 'Neuenahr' is *Nova Aquila*.
6 Possibly during his visit to Spain; cf Ep 1926:1–2, 5–7.
7 Epp 1419, 1481
8 Erasmus appears to be referring to the synod of Arles (473), but he is confused about the heresy dealt with there: see lines 37–41 below with n13.
9 Named for the British (probably Irish) theologian Pelagius, who taught at Rome in the late fourth and early fifth centuries, Pelagians held that human beings can, of their own free will and by their own efforts, unassisted by divine grace, take the initial and crucial steps towards salvation. By 418 Pelagianism had been condemned as a heresy by both Emperor Honorius and Pope Zosimus, but it did not quickly disappear. Its influence persisted longest (into the sixth century) in Gaul and in Britain.
10 Julian (c 386–454), the erudite Pelagian bishop of Eclanum in Apulia, who engaged Augustine in a bitter debate over human nature and divine grace
11 It was against Pelagius that Augustine developed most fully his doctrines of the fall of man, original sin, and predestination. He maintained that since the fall of Adam all human beings are so mired in sin and evil that they can be rescued only by the grace of God who, in his inscrutable wisdom, has predestined some to receive his unmerited mercy. Augustine's single most important work against Pelagianism was *On the Spririt and the Letter* (412). The issue raised in this controversy – just how much is to be attributed to human will and/or divine grace in the scheme of salvation – continued to agitate theologians in the centuries that followed and, as the debate between

What is more insane than the teaching of the Manichaeans? Yet even so
learned and perceptive a man as Augustine dedicated himself to this doc-   35
trine.[12]

Meanwhile in your wisdom you will note the truly Christian tolerance of the bishops of that period, who required nothing more of the priest
Lucidus (for he had professed the doctrines of Pelagius) than that he give
his supporting signature to the condemnation of the articles of belief with-   40
out having to be present.[13] Furthermore, you will take notice of that apti-
tude to teach that Paul requires of a bishop more than any other.[14] Not content merely with condemning, they teach; and not only do they set forth
the authority of the council but they also use persuasion through the citing of the Sacred Scriptures. With what caution and discretion do they as-   45
sert the doctrine of free will while not at the same time attributing anything to our merits! There are some who say that Faustus, who wrote this
book, once shared the beliefs of Pelagius.[15] For that reason in the *Decreta*,

* * * * *

Erasmus and Luther in the 1520s showed, was still the subject of heated debate
in the sixteenth century. Cf nn13 and 15 below.

12 Named for its founder Mani or Manes (c 216–75), Manichaeism was a dualistic
religion that combined a Persian Zoroastrian concept of God with Christian
elements. Manichaeans posited an eternal struggle between light and dark-
ness, the former identified with spirit and good and the latter identified with
matter and evil. The sect spread rapidly in the Roman Empire and was popular in fourth-century North Africa, where the young Augustine adhered to it
for a time. Cf Epp 1451 n8, 1738 n59.

13 Lucidus, a priest in fifth-century Gaul about whom nothing is known apart
from the condemnation of his views by the synod of Arles in 473, was not a
Pelagian. Quite the contrary, he was an extreme predestinarian, holding that
God has predestined some to eternal death and others to eternal life, in such a
way that salvation is to be attributed to divine grace alone with no contribution
whatever by human effort. He taught further that, because the non-elect are
destined for hell, Christ did not die for them. Ordered by bishop Faustus to
retract these views, Lucidus gave written notification to the synod at Arles of
his submission.

14 1 Tim 3:2

15 In his *Liber de ecclesiasticis scriptoribus* § 190, Johannes Trithemius writes that
the 'learned and elequent' Faustus was 'tainted' with Pelagianism but that,
'censured and corrected by [St] Fulgentius,' he abandoned his erroneous views
and subsequently (c 490) wrote against them in the *De gratia Dei*. In so doing
however, as Trithemius does not report, Faustus expressed views that were
soon condemned as 'semi-Pelagian.' While not denying the necessity of grace
for salvation, he nonetheless maintained that the first steps towards salvation
are to be taken by the human will and that grace comes into play only later. For
this reason, the work was declared heretical by the Synod of Orange in 529.

distinction fifteen, the writings of a certain Faustinus of Riez in Gaul are
believed to be apocryphal (although he is here called Faustus).[16] That it is   50
an ancient work, even without the authority of the chroniclers, who date
it to the year 490,[17] is indicated by the style itself. You can easily detect
the Gallic turn of phrase in it. It is florid and rhythmical and pleasant
rather than forceful. It resembles the diction of Eucherius and Sulpicius.[18]
For Hilary, whose works I have dedicated to your brother, the archbishop   55
of Palermo,[19] is more fiery but less clear. This Faustus is clearer than Hilary, simpler than Eucherius, more unadorned than Sulpicius. He adopted
a style that was most appropriate for teaching – lucid, transparent, concise
– but not for that reason disagreeable. When citing from the Old Testament he adds a Latin translation of the Septuagint, lest anyone skim lightly   60
over the Scriptures. St Jerome wrote somewhere that studies long flourished in Gaul,[20] all the more reason that we strive to have them flourish again as they have already begun to reburgeon. The work will commend itself to you even more because a Gaul will come face to face with a
Gaul.   65

I will know if you were pleased with this little gift if you recompense
me in the near future; a little letter, however brief, will be ample compensation.

I wish your Highness unending happiness.

Given at Basel, 1528 on the day after the feast of St John the Baptist   70

* * * * *

16 Part 1 distinction 15 c 3 §74 of the *Decretum* of Gratian incorporates the list
  of 'books to be received and not to be received' that is found in the so-called
  Decretum Gelasianum (early sixth century). Included among the works 'to be
  avoided by Catholics' because they were 'written or preached by heretics or
  schismatics' are the works, not of 'Faustinus' but of 'Faustus of Riez in Gaul.'
  Like all the other works thus proscribed, those of Faustus are labelled *apocrifa*,
  a term that clearly meant 'harmful' or 'heretical' and not simply 'uncanonical,'
  as the word 'apocryphal' is used today. The misnomer 'Faustinus' was presumably either an error in the text of the *Decretum* that Erasmus used or else
  a mistake in his recollection of it.
17 So Trithemius (cf n15 above)
18 Eucherius (d 449), bishop of Lyon, wrote exegetical works and ascetic treatises. The *editio princeps* was published at Basel by J.W. Brassicanus in 1531.
  Sulpicius Severus (c 360–c 420), who lived in southern Gaul, was the author
  of an influential life of St Martin of Tours and of a chronicle of sacred history from creation to the year 400, written in classical style and using pagan
  as well as Christian sources.
19 Jean (II) de Carondelet; see Ep 1334.
20 See Jerome Ep 125.6.

2003 / From Alonso de Fonseca   Madrid, 29 June 1528

On Alonso de Fonseca (1475–1534), archbishop of Toledo and primate of Spain, see Ep 1748 introduction.

First published in the *Opus epistolarum*, this is Fonseca's answer to Ep 1874. The surviving manuscript, a rough draft in what may be a secretary's hand, is in the Real Academia de la Historia, Madrid (MS Est 18, gr 1.5 fol 23). This letter was part of a packet of letters from Spain that also included Ep 2004 and was delivered to Erasmus in the first week of March 1529; see Epp 2125, 2126. Erasmus' reply is Ep 2134.

ALONSO DE FONSECA, ARCHBISHOP OF TOLEDO, PRIMATE
OF SPAIN, TO THE THEOLOGIAN ERASMUS OF ROTTERDAM,
GREETING

That you consider my letter a consolation amidst the toils and hostile criticism by which you are exercised would be a source of great joy to me,   5
both for my sake and also to a certain extent for yours, if it were not,
conversely, also a cause for sorrow that you, a man whose whole lifetime
has been spent in reviving and soothing the spirits of others with real and
lasting consolation, should be so involved with persons entirely unworthy of your attention that you have need of such consolation yourself.[1] I   10
have long thought that you have so managed your affairs that you should
not be excessively perturbed by events of this kind and should not seek
any other solace, if they press hard upon you, than that which comes from
a right and sincere conscience. Yet in your kindness and benevolence of
heart you bring it about that in giving so much importance to the efforts   15
of your friends you do them great honour with such words of commendation.[2] And would that there were forms of service besides letters by which
it were possible to deliver you altogether from these cares. Believe me, you
would no longer be suffering from these adversities. And yet we must not
altogether regret the efforts expended in your behalf up to now, since it   20
seems that the tempest that arose last year not only rages with less violence but even has gradually subsided. If it quiets down altogether, as I
hope, it may be of some benefit that it was stirred up. It is important in
this type of seditious strife that the adversaries understand that they will
have to follow proper legal procedure rather than engage in wholesale acts   25

* * * * *

2003
1 On the hostile criticism of Erasmus in Spain, see Ep 1926 n4.
2 Ep 1875:18–24.

of violence and oppression. This you seem to have fully achieved up to now.

We have read your defence,[3] but – as in other matters – in a great hurry. I particularly enjoyed the moderation that you exhibited for the most part (for with certain persons it was impossible to do so) as well as the restraint 30 that I hoped you would exercise in this matter, and had personally taken it upon myself to recommend to you. [4] As for the rest, I cannot judge: Erasmus will always be true to himself. Continue, therefore, what you are doing, meriting more of Christendom day by day and at the same time preparing immortal praise for yourself, which, far from being tarnished by the un- 35 scrupulous manoeuvres of your enemies, is worn bright by them and thus shines ever more radiantly.

Your emended version of the works of Augustine, in which I hear you are engaged, is a task distinctly worthy of you.[5] He seemed to be the only remaining classical author who was to be reborn with Erasmus as the mid- 40 wife; and because I have nurtured from my earliest years an inborn incli- nation to revere and admire this hero, he is the one author whom I most wished to be restored.

But among your many labours, why do I not exhort you to the best of my ability to finish that work to which I know many have invited you 45 and which you of your own will began so felicitously? Since you have hith- erto devoted so much energy in affirming and revindicating Christian stud- ies, why not do as much now in confuting new errors or, I should say, old ones that have sprouted up again? We see them like poisonous herbs putting out dense growth day by day, infecting the vineyard of the Lord, in which 50 you exert your manful efforts. Already they impede the growth of buds and young shoots so that there is danger that if they continue to grow to- gether they will dry up and choke the legitimate stock with their defective nature. You will perform a deed worthy of your learning and your piety; you will bring aid to your Germany, infected with so many sects, ridden 55 with so many errors, tottering and falling under the weight of so many dis- sensions and seditions. Even if Christian piety were the least consideration (which, as a matter of fact, we know to be your chief concern), still the ex- cellent majesty and splendour of this Empire should inspire not only you but all leading citizens to confront this evil. If it should prevail, there is no 60

* * * * *

3 Ie the *Apologia adversus quosdam monachos Hispanos* (Ep 1967)
4 See Ep 1813:23–4.
5 Ep 2157, the dedicatory letter in the ten-volume Froben Augustine of 1529, was addressed to Fonseca.

doubt but that your commonwealth will be reduced from its present glory as the most flourishing of all and become the most pitiful and desperate of all.

It is useless for you to make the usual excuse of feeble health or dearth of knowledge. There is no one who is not convinced that Erasmus is the one 65 and indeed the only one who is equal to such a great task, not only through the resources of your eloquence and learning, whose efficacy is known to all the world, but also because of the confidence and authority you inspire in everyone. In order to be effective in this cause, we need a man who owes nothing to the benefits of the great of this world, who has of his own will 70 renounced all access to future advancement, who is attracted to this contest not by the malady of adulation or the vice of avarice or ambition, but is drawn into the arena by zeal for religion. Scarcely any other man could come forward who would not be thought to serve the interests of his class, or cater to the power of the few, and in the end to indulge those vices that 75 were the kindling wood for this fire.

But the task is full of danger, full of difficulties, for one must either shamefully flatter the powerful or incur their dislike by criticizing their moral conduct. What, then, shall we do? Shall we, in the face of this difficulty, abandon the defence of true piety and allow the vices of men to im- 80 pair the purity of the church so that she must pay for our wrongdoings? Would it not be possible to manage this affair so that the false beliefs of our adversaries and the corrupt morals within our own ranks might be censured with a twofold reward for our efforts, namely that the latter return to a more sane mind and the former to a sane one, and that, when some day 85 peace is established among princes, public affairs begin to be established and arranged without tumult or disorder?

But why should I speak of these things to you, who have a much better grasp of them than I? We willingly accept the reasons you give for not being able to make the journey here, since there was no other possibility. 90 I am also aware that you can make better use of your well-earned leisure than by undertaking a voyage abroad, and that through your unremitting scholarship the advantages deriving from this decision will be extended to a greater number of people. For the furtherance of your studies I have provided that a bill of exchange be sent to you.[6] The time will come when I will 95 be able to show you more generosity.

* * * * *

6 In the sum of 200 ducats; see Ep 2004:40. Since these are indeed gold coins and not the Spanish ducat money-of-account (= 375 maravedís), they may be Spanish *excelente* coins, which Ferdinand and Isabella introduced in 1497, as close

Farewell and keep us in your affection.
Madrid, 29 June 1528

2004 / From Juan de Vergara   Madrid, 29 June 1528

This is Vergara's response to Ep 1875. Erasmus' reply is Ep 2133. The manuscript, a rough draft in the same hand as that of Ep 2003, is in the Real
Academia de la Historia, Madrid (MS Est 18 gr 1.5 fol 22). It was first published, with the omission of lines 1–7, by A. Helferrich in the *Zeitschrift für
historische Theologie* NF 23 (1859) 597–8, with mistaken attribution to Mercurino
Gattinara.

On Vergara, who was now secretary to the archbishop of Toledo, Alonso de
Fonseca, see Epp 1277, 1814.

I delayed somewhat in replying to your two letters, one dated 2 September
and the other 15 October, [1] most honoured Erasmus, because I did not wish
you to receive my letter without that of my prince.[2] Besides, I think it less
an obligation to seek pardon for a long silence from a friend so seriously
occupied and so deluged by letters from all sides than for the too frequent   5
exercise of this duty,[3] especially when that person would never shirk his
duty when faced with more pressing needs. That you should not only think
well of the coarseness and clumsiness of my style but even, if you please!
think it worthy of praise I can only consider as an expression of your good
will towards me.   10
Since your opinion cannot but be impartial, I do not ask that you offer it, nor do I think it in my interest that it be expressed. Concerning your
court case, I cannot do other than approve of all that you write in your letters. They are things that would find anyone's approval, not to say mine,
since there is nothing that you write that does not have my approval. After   15

* * * * *

imitations of the Venetian ducat (3.74 grams, 23.75 carats fine). Two hundred
such coins, or other close European imitations of the ducat, would have been
worth about £46 13s 4d sterling, or £66 13s 4d groot Flemish, or £455 tournois.
For the bill of exchange, see Ep 1934 n85. See also Peter Spufford *Money and
its Use in Medieval Europe* (Cambridge and New York 1988) 322 Table 6.

2004
1 Ep 1875 is dated 2 September 1527. The letter of 15 October is not extant; it
  undoubtedly accompanied Ep 1885.
2 Ep 2003 from Archbishop Fonseca
3 Cf Ep 1985 n2.

that first burst of fury with which they plotted to expose you to the blind
prejudices of public ill will came to nothing, your enemies wage the campaign with a leaden sword,[4] so that it seems that the more prudent among
them almost regret their intemperance. Some, the vilest among them, are
still barking, so that it seems best to treat this whole faction with disdain   20
rather than to provoke them. The trial seems to be adjourned for a hundred years, as in the Areopagus,[5] since there is no mention of it. I think
the judges have adopted a similar policy concerning the publishing of your
Apologia.[6] So far they merely abstain from judgment, lest by giving formal
permission they seem prejudiced against your enemies or by forbidding its   25
publication seem prejudiced against you. But if the book suddenly bursts
on the scene without warning, I hope it will be welcomed with all the more
enthusiasm. And yet I think there will be some who will try to stir up unpopularity against you for its outspokenness against judges of such high
rank. I have no doubt, however, that the reading of this book will curb the   30
presumption of many, encourage the fainthearted, and gain many followers for you even from among those who had aligned themselves with your
accusers.

My archbishop displays his usual zeal in defending your honour. The
opposing faction strives to divert against me all the hatred arising from this   35
favour, at times resorting to threats. For my part I devote myself to your
cause and will continue to do so in ever greater measure, as I have begun.
The most reverend archbishop learned through a letter of yours to me about
your great labours and expense in restoring to us the text of Augustine,[7]
and he immediately allotted two hundred gold ducats to help defray the   40
expenses; the bill of exchange is herein enclosed.[8] His greatest desire, as
you will see from his letter, is that you devote most of your energies to
the refutation of the heresies in your part of the world.[9] It is his conviction
that he who has laboured so hard in the Lord's vineyard, working the soil,
inserting the grafts, and completing all the other demands of cultivation,   45
cannot pass over with impunity the weeding of the crops, without which
the rest of the labour will almost have been in vain.

* * * * *

4 *Adagia* II v 10; on Erasmus' conservative opponents in Spain, see Ep 1926 n4.
5 We have not been able to trace the source of this seemingly proverbial saying,
   which is not found in the *Adagia*.
6 See Ep 1967.
7 The Froben Augustine of 1529, dedicated to Archbishop Fonseca; see Ep 2157.
8 Cf Ep 2003 n6. For the bill of exchange, see Ep 1934 n85.
9 Ep 2003:54–63

    I know that many others have already approached you about this and
I do not doubt that you have reasons for your strategy. Nevertheless, you
should wish to have the approval, if not of everyone, at least of your special   50
friends.

    My brother Francisco, who had been stricken with a long and grave
illness, recovered miraculously after reading your letter and has regained
some of his strength while staying with me; but he has not returned to his
former vigour and liveliness of mind and body. Perhaps he will write you a   55
letter.[10] My brother Tovar also intends to write to you so there will be none
of us who does not intrude upon your leisure.[11] The only one left is my
sister Elizabeth,[12] a young woman not indifferent to the Muses, who first
enjoyed those of your books that were translated into our native tongue
but now peruses them in Latin, not without considerable profit from your   60
learning and piety. She enjoins me to convey her cordial greetings to you
in my letter.[13] Bear in mind that we are all, each one of us, your faithful
followers.

    Farewell.

    Madrid, 29 June 1528   65

2005 / To Ferdinand of Austria   Basel, 15 July [1528]

    On Ferdinand, see Ep 1935 n5.

    This letter was first published in the *Opus epistolarum*, but there were roughly
    contemporary manuscript copies (c 1529/30) of it and of Ep 2006 on page 344
    of a commonplace book written by Gallus Knöringer, prior of the Benedictine
    monastery of St Mang in Füssen. In 1907, when Allen examined the manu-
    script volume, it was in the private possession of the Freiherr von Ponickau.
    For more on the history of the volume, see Allen's introduction. Its current
    location, if indeed it still exists, is unknown; efforts by German archivists to
    find it have so far proved fruitless.

    * * * * *

10 Francisco (Ep 1876 introduction) did write in response to Ep 1885 (see Ep
   2125), but the letter is no longer extant.
11 Bernardino Tovar, Vergara's half-brother and an ardent Erasmian (Ep 1814
   n14). No correspondence between him and Erasmus survives, but Erasmus
   was wont to send him greetings and compliments when writing to Vergara;
   see Epp 1875:212–13, 1885:207–8.
12 Isabel de Vergara (documented 1528–33). In 1533 she was denounced to the
   Inquisition as a Lutheran, but it is not known what happened to her as a result.
13 Erasmus returned these greetings in March 1529, using the occasion to praise
   learned women; see Allen Ep 2133:102–11.

The Füssen manuscript and the *Opus epistolarum* text diverge radically in the dating of this letter and Ep 2006. For reasons that can only be guessed at, Knöringer placed both letters in January 1529, a date ruled out by the clear association of Ep 2006 with letters that have a confirmed year-date of 1528 (Epp 2000, 2008, 2028). On the other hand, the *Opus epistolarum*, which is fairly frequently wrong about year-dates, puts the letter at 15 July 1527 (see line 26 below). Given that King Ferdinand is known to have written to Erasmus at about mid-July 1528 (Epp 2000:53–4, 2007:11–13) and that no other reply from Erasmus survives, given also that this letter and Ep 2006 are placed together in Knöringer's manuscript, and given finally that the surviving letters from 1527 give no indication of a similar correspondence between Erasmus and Ferdinand, Allen concluded that the year-date in the *Opus epistolarum* had to be corrected to 1528. Though the invitation to Vienna is not specifically mentioned here, Erasmus is clearly turning down the offer of a signal honour and, here as in Ep 2006, on grounds of health.

TO THE INVINCIBLE FERDINAND, KING OF HUNGARY AND
BOHEMIA, INFANTE OF SPAIN, ARCHDUKE OF AUSTRIA,
DUKE OF BURGUNDY, MARQUIS OF MORAVIA, COUNT OF TYROL,
AND LIEUTENANT-GENERAL OF THE EMPIRE[1]

If I did not rejoice wholeheartedly at the successes of the prince who has be-   5
stowed so many favours on me and showed me such good will, illustrious
King Ferdinand,[2] I should deservedly be called the most ungrateful of men.
If, moreover, his prosperity, on which the good fortune of all Christianity
in great part depends, were not a source of great joy to me, I should be
regarded as worse than impious. For although all human felicity proceeds   10
from God, its author, he nevertheless often revives and raises up his people
through good princes when he is propitiously inclined towards them, and
afflicts them through evil men when he has been offended. Therefore I deserve no praise in this case if I do what it would be the greatest infamy
not to do. What grieves me is that I do not see what I can offer your High-   15
ness at my age and in my present state of health beyond my good wishes
and my sincere devotion. My poor health would be an intolerable burden
in itself even without the added disadvantage of old age. At any rate, what-

* * * * *

2005
1 The fullness of this list of titles, including that of 'king of Hungary and Bohemia,' is probably Erasmus' response to the advice received from Caspar Ursinus Velius in Ep 1917:19–29.
2 See Ep 1935 nn5, 8.

ever I am capable of contributing with what is left of my mental powers
and strength I shall, with God's help, contribute unfailingly to my last day.   20
He in his great goodness, even without my help, will deign to prosper the
deeds and achievements of your Majesty for the good of the Christian commonwealth and the concord of the church. This we never cease to implore
in our most fervent prayers. For the favour you show me in your most kind
letter,[3] although this is nothing new coming from you, I am most grateful.   25
          Given at Basel, 15 July [1527]
          Erasmus of Rotterdam

2006 / To Johannes Fabri   Basel, 16 July 1528

> First published in the *Opus epistolarum*, this is Erasmus' reply to Ep 2000. On
> the manuscript copy at Füssen, see Ep 2005 introduction.

TO THE ILLUSTRIOUS JOHANNES FABRI, COUNSELLOR OF THE MOST
SERENE KING FERDINAND, CORDIAL GREETINGS
I have never doubted your continued good will towards me. The good intentions of the prince[1] I welcome and admire greatly. I am familiar with the
subterfuges of the people you mention;[2] I am contemplating escape but I see   5
no haven.[3] My health is in such a state that my only hope is in God. I do not
shrink from death but from prolonged torment. I have either a stone in the
bladder or an ulceration of the bladder;[4] both maladies are worse than many
deaths. You know what it is like to transplant an old tree. You call me to Vienna, that is, to a new world, when I am already dying. There too, I think   10
there are deranged theologians and perverse monks who hearken neither
to pontiffs nor to princes. You know about the Spanish melodrama.[5] The
revered faculty of Paris has dared to condemn some of my books, in particular the *Colloquies*, without being able to find a single example of impiety.[6]

* * * * *

3 Not extant; cf Epp 2000:52–3, 2007:12–13.

2006
1 King Ferdinand
2 Ep 2000:28–30
3 See Ep 1926 n8.
4 See Ep 1989 n4.
5 See Epp 1926 n4, 1967.
6 The faculty of theology had censured Erasmus' *Colloquies* in May 1526 and
   a number of his other works in December 1527. Then, on 23 June 1528, the
   entire university ratified the faculty's censure of the *Colloquies*, which was

There are some there under the leadership of Béda who are raving mad.[7]　15
My conscience alone holds me back from the Lutherans: otherwise I would
tell those furies what sort of people they are.[8]

I am not too concerned about financial matters in planning my move
from here. Elsewhere professors of languages are hired at high salaries,[9] but
now there is no audience: this new gospel has brought in so much laziness.　20
Even if there were nothing to discourage me from coming to Vienna, what
god will take me there? Movement is fatal to this illness of the bladder, and
any change of diet is dangerous for me. What shall I do in Vienna, a proud
city, as I am told, and thoroughly German? My health cannot even sustain
the formal greetings of learned men.[10] Finally, it is of no great importance　25
where I station this weak little body. A visit to Vienna is more of a wish
than a hope. Farewell.

At Basel, 16 July 1528

2007 / To Bernhard von Cles　　　　Basel [c 16 July] 1528

First published in the *Opus epistolarum*, this letter is probably contemporary
with Epp 2005–6 and 2008, which accounts for the conjectural month-date assigned by Allen. The year-date is confirmed by the publication of the second
edition of Irenaeus (lines 3–4) in 1528. Some indication of the content of the
letter to which this is the reply can be found in Ep 2030:43–6.

* * * * *

incorporated into a decree issued by the rector (see Epp 2033 n15, 2037 introduction). The text here, taken from the Füssen manuscript, seems to indicate that Erasmus had not yet learned of the action of the entire university,
although news of it would soon reach him (see Ep 2021:129–32). When the letter was published in the *Opus epistolarum* (1529), Erasmus altered the sentence
in question to read as follows: 'By an edict of the rector of Paris, masters are
forbidden to teach my *Colloquies* to boys in schools, even though nothing of .
their content has so far been shown to be less than pious.'

7 On Béda, see Ep 1943 n6.
8 The extreme compression of Erasmus' language here makes it difficult to understand his intended meaning. It was Erasmus' constant complaint that his
conservative critics wanted to push him into the Lutheran camp and that it
was only his conscience that kept him true to the Catholic church (see, for example, Ep 1906). So the sense here is that only his conscience keeps him from
joining the Lutherans in their condemnation of 'those furies' in Paris.
9 As in Nürnberg, for example; see Epp 1901:21–3, 2008:39–40.
10 The word here translated as 'formal greetings' is *salutationes*, the plural of *salu-
tatio*, the Roman word for the formal greeting that etiquette required clients
to render at the house of a distinguished patron.

Ferdinand of Hapsburg's most trusted adviser since 1521, Bernhard von Cles (Epp 1357, 1738) had now become his supreme chancellor. A reliable friend and patron of Erasmus, Cles had already offered him residence at Trent on generous terms (Epp 1409, 1771:13–16) and would repeat the offer in later years. It seems that he was also instrumental in helping Erasmus settle in Freiburg in 1529.

ERASMUS OF ROTTERDAM TO BERNHARD, BISHOP OF TRENT, GREETING

Reverend Bishop, so that you will know that your guardian spirit has brought good fortune to Irenaeus,[1] he is being printed again at the urgent demand of the booksellers. Would that these young men who dedicate 5 any old book to anyone at all would not inscribe anything to great prelates of the church except what is worthy of their high positions! On the public office that has been bestowed on you[2] I do not congratulate you so much as I do Ferdinand. The greater the extent of his rule, the greater his need of such counsellors. And yet he seems destined to have far greater power still. 10 I pray that it bring fortune and favour to him and to the Christian world. I recognized with delight the hand of your Highness in the letter of the king and I kissed it with all due reverence.[3] May the Lord prosper your deeds.

At Basel, 16 July 1528

2008 / To Caspar Ursinus Velius   Basel, 16 July 1528

The manuscript of this letter, in the Royal Library at Copenhagen (GKS 95 Fol, fol 198), is an autograph rough draft with seven corrections in Erasmus' own hand and with a heading in a secretary's hand. The letter actually sent and the version published in the *Opus epistolarum* both incorporated Erasmus' corrections, but Allen adopted the unrevised text 'as revealing what was in Erasmus' mind.'

The Silesian poet and jurist, Caspar Ursinus Velius (see Ep 1810 n6), held the chair of rhetoric at the University of Vienna and was the official historian to King Ferdinand (Epp 1917:15–18, 1935:70–1), whom he had accompanied on his campaign in Hungary in 1527–8. This letter answers one from Prague, c 28

* * * * *

2007
1 The first edition of Irenaeus had been dedicated to Cles in 1526 (Ep 1738), much to the delight of the prelate (Ep 1793).
2 The supreme chancellorship at Ferdinand's court
3 The letter is not extant; cf Epp 2000:52–3, 2005:23–4.

June 1528 (see AK Ep 1269:14–15), in which Ursinus had made some criticisms
of the *Ciceronianus*.

TO URSINUS VELIUS
Cordial greetings. The *Paraphrase on John* was published last autumn. Although I had dedicated it to Ferdinand before he was made king, I changed
the title of my own accord and added the name of the king, without yet
knowing how it would turn out.[1] The theologian Hesychius, of whom you   5
write, has already been published.[2]

Far be it from me to prescribe rules for you, but love sometimes reminds even one who needs no reminding. I see that there is nothing more
safe than to write nothing. You made it known to me with great elation that
you had been assigned the role of an historian but gave not the slightest in-   10
dication that you wished this to be kept secret. It is the sort of thing whose
publication brings no dishonour to the king and even confers great honour upon you, but now you complain that something has been made public
which you did not wish to be divulged.[3]

It was not my intention in the *Ciceronianus*[4] to pass everyone in re-   15
view. Ten examples were sufficient, and I erred more in naming so many
than in omitting some.[5] Nor did I include some writers in order to praise
them. Nosoponus denies the name of Ciceronian to all of them,[6] although
I did accord some praise in passing. I treated Beatus very candidly, just
as he deserves, but I was not going to publish it before showing him the   20

* * * * *

2008
1 The first edition of the *Paraphrase on John* was published in February 1523
(Ep 1333), before Archduke Ferdinand had achieved the status of king. No
surviving copy of any authorized edition of the *Paraphrase* contains the change
of Ferdinand's title indicated here. One must assume that this edition of 1527
has completely disappeared.
2 *Isychii presbyteri Hierosolymorum in Leviticum libri septem*, edited by Johann
Sichard and published at Basel by Cratander in March 1527. This commentary on Leviticus (PG 93 787–1180), which exists only in Latin and is based on
the Vulgate rather than the Septuagint, is not an authentic work by Hesychius,
the fifth-century presbyter of Jerusalem.
3 The complaint appears to have been that the history of the war in Hungary,
which Ursinus was now beginning, had been mentioned in the *Ciceronianus*
see CWE 28 428.
4 Ep 1948
5 Velius had complained of Erasmus' failure to mention Vives; see Epp 2040:14,
2056:26–7.
6 Nosoponus is the character in the dialogue via whom Erasmus satirizes the
Italian Ciceronians.

passage.[7] I know his sensitive character. Later he came to see me seemingly to discuss whether it was to his advantage to be mentioned. I answered that I would do as he wished. 'Perhaps' he said, 'it would be better not to be mentioned.' 'So shall it be,' I said and with that he left. There are some people whom I would not wish to deal with unless they give their consent. I should be inclined to place Vives among this number.[8] Haio Herman Phrysius never published anything and I have not seen anything of his except for a few letters to me.[9] You are right in saying that there could be nothing more agreeable. I would certainly have mentioned Sauermann if he had come to mind.[10] I did not know whether Brassicanus was still alive nor did he ever publish anything worthy of note, as far as I know.[11] Need I say more? I was foolish to mention so many. I would have been much more foolish if I had made it appear that I did not omit anyone, not even the mediocre and the insignificant. In some cases, however, I gave some consideration to friendship. And when I was getting the book ready, or rather when it was in the process of being printed, along came Eppendorf, making dire threats. I knew they would come to nothing. But I could not convince Beatus or Baer about this until they themselves perceived the blustering of the man from their own experience.[12]

I am afraid that Vienna will suffer the same fate as Nürnberg.[13] Professors are hired at great expense but there are no students. And I do not know by what trick of fate those who teach literature there are tainted with Lutheranism. But I have written to Johannes Fabri about this.[14] I ask that you give Gabriel Saucius my warm and sincere greetings.[15] Farewell.

Given at Basel, 16 July 1528

How cruel of you to have confined so many kings, emperors, and popes into such a narrow space![16]

* * * * *

7 On Beatus Rhenanus see Ep 1933 n2.
8 Vives had taken offence at the omission of his name from the *Ciceronianus*, and his relations with Erasmus had now become rather cool: see Epp 2026:3–6, 2040, 2061.
9 See Epp 1978, 2056.
10 On Georg Sauermann see Ep 1342 n88.
11 On Johannes Alexander Brassicanus see Ep 1146.
12 See Epp 1933 and 1934.
13 See Epp 1901:21–3, 2006:19–20.
14 Ep 2006
15 Saucius has not been identified.
16 Evidently a reference to Ursinus' *Monosticha Regum Italiae, Albanorum, Romanorum, & virorum illustrium, tum Caesarum usque ad nostram aetatem. Monosticha Summorum Pontificum Rom. a Petro usq[ue] ad Clementem Septimum* (Vienna: Johannes Singren, March 1528), which was dedicated to Bernhard von Cles (Ep 2007).

2009 / To Jean de Guise, cardinal of Lorraine   Basel, 16 July 1528

This letter was first published in the *Opus epistolarum*. The surviving manuscript is an autograph rough draft in the Royal Library at Copenhagen (GKS
95 Fol, fol 196).

Jean de Guise (Epp 1841, 1911), cardinal of Lorraine and bishop of Metz,
was an influential adviser to King Francis I of France and a patron of humanist scholarship whom Erasmus had enlisted in his efforts to prevent the
condemnation of his works by the Paris faculty of theology.

TO THE REVEREND LORD JEAN, CARDINAL OF LORRAINE
Cordial greetings, most excellent prince. When I learned from letters of my
friends that your Highness gives unstinting support to humane studies, and
on that account to Erasmus, and was encouraged by those same friends to
present you with some token of my gratitude, I dedicated a little book to   5
your name,[1] not one that befits your high office but something that I happened to have ready. And it seemed to me that my act of homage would
have been amply rewarded if you had accepted my devotion in good part.
But since, beyond every expectation and merit of mine, you have in your extraordinary kindness honoured me with a gift that exceeds my worthiness   10
in the same measure that this little book is unworthy of your nobility, it was
much more gratifying to me to be honoured by the recognition of such a
great prelate than to be enriched by a gift. As far as my personal feelings
are concerned, I derive great joy from your kindness, esteeming any gift
that you would wish to give me as already given. But I have nothing that I   15
can show as a proof to others.

I do not know the reason for the delay. You wrote that you had given
this commission to your treasurer. Men of this profession are often of the
opinion that money given to studies is not well invested. And they produce many excuses: 'It slipped my mind'; 'I was too busy with other mat-   20
ters'; 'The goldsmiths did not keep their word'; 'I had no messenger by
whom I could send it.' Whatever the case may be, so far not even a rumour
concerning the vases has reached me.[2] I do not know what happened. Perhaps someone thinks that my service has been amply rewarded in the prolonged pleasure I had from my expectation. If you wish that I be content   25

* * * * *

2009
1 Erasmus' translation of St John Chrysostom's *Commentary on Galatians*, the
  preface to which was Ep 1841
2 See Ep 1962:19–23.

with that, I shall be glad to do so, since before your promise I considered myself fortunate that your Highness had thought well of my endeavour. I have no doubt but that in your kindness you promised this gift sincerely, without being called upon to do so and with no expectations from the
recipient.   30

But this is more than enough about these trivialities to such a great
prince. I am grateful that you have helped me by your favour in the eyes
of all and ask again and again that you continue to do so. May the Lord
prosper all the undertakings of your Highness; I hope your humble servant
has merited your commendation.   35

Given at Basel, 16 July 1525

2010 / From Christoph von Carlowitz   Besançon, 16 July 1528

First published as Ep 63 in Enthoven, the autograph of this letter is in the
Rehdiger Collection of the University Library at Wrocław. Only the last sheet
has survived.

On Christoph von Carlowitz, see Ep 1951 n7.

... and he[1] asked me not to mention this matter to him again. I did not
wish to conceal this from you so that you would know what you might
expect concerning his sentiments towards you. If anything else arises that
I think it will be in your interest to know, I shall gladly inform you of it
out of my great regard for you, as soon as I have someone to convey the   5
message. At the moment there is nothing else to report save that in recent
days your friend Carondolet passed away,[2] though I do not doubt that you
have already learned of this.

Besançon, 16 July 1528

I have moved to Besançon, not that I have left Dôle entirely, but in   10
order to sequester myself for a while from the company of the Germans,
who are present there in great numbers, and so that I could apply myself to
improving my French.

Again farewell, and if you ever have the occasion to write to the duke
of Saxony, do recommend me to him again.[3]   15

Christoph von Carlowitz

* * * * *

2010
1 Perhaps Ludovicus Carinus; see Ep 2063:1–34.
2 On 27 June 1528; see Epp 2002 introduction and 2012:15–23.
3 Cf Ep 1924:47–50.

To the illustrious Master Erasmus of Rotterdam, theologian and friend
justly deserving of the greatest reverence

2011 / From Johann Henckel   Sopron, 18 July 1528

> The autograph of this letter is in the Rehdiger Collection of the University
> Library at Wrocław (MS Rehd 254.84). It was first published by Gusztáv Bauch
> in *Történelmi Tár* (1885) 353 and then as Ep 64 in Enthoven.
>   On Johann Henckel, confessor to Queen Mary of Hungary and ardent ad-
> mirer of Erasmus, see Ep 1672.

Greetings. With your indulgence, most holy Erasmus, my high esteem and
unmatched affection for you compels me once again to write to you. If I do
wrong in this, for the importunate demands of good will are never without
fault, you may impute it to our friend Antonin,[1] who first corrupted me, or
to your kindness, which reinforced this corruption in a very solemn letter.[2]   5
I resort once more to this kindness, although I would rather have as my advocate and intercessor with you the person whom I consider to be the author
and instigator of my effrontery, if there were any way to enlist the services
of this excellent man. I cannot mention this without tears. For, in case you
are not aware of it, Antonin has been taken from us – or rather from him-   10
self, since he is still alive and conscious – by a terrible attack of madness that
seems incurable. It is believed that he fell victim to this through his excessive study of medicine in his effort to live up to his reputation, which was
outstanding everywhere. In the beginning it was so violent that for a long
time he had to be handcuffed so that he would not commit some act of vio-   15
lence against himself or his domestics. The doctors who had been hired from
the start almost treated the matter lightly, and had great hopes that with the
coming of spring (for the sickness had occurred in the winter) the treatment
would have better results. But we are no closer to a true cure than previously.
He is slightly less deranged now but still mentally unbalanced. To put it suc-   20
cinctly, he has been reduced to such a state that we who had often hoped
that he might be granted more than one lifetime now pray for his death.[3]

* * * * *

2011
1 Jan Antonin (Ep 1953 n1). It was Antonin who first drew Henckel to the attention of Erasmus and fostered contact between them: see Ep 1660:14–44.
2 An apparent reference to Ep 1672, which Erasmus had written in response to
   a letter from Henckel that is no longer extant (see Ep 1660:15–16)
3 This malady persisted for some time. In June 1529, Erasmus expressed his joy
   at learning of Antonin's recovery (Ep 2176).

But these tidings are too distressing to relate to you in greater detail. I am certain that you have already been far too much saddened by the unhappy fate that has befallen such a dear friend. I shall say a few words about myself and what it is that I should wish to obtain from you. I beg of you again and again not to be unwilling to hear my request. To begin with the most recent events, I returned lately to my mistress the queen, whom I was forced to leave because of the disastrous and turbulent events here, in order to perform my accustomed duty, that is, to preach the word of God at court.[4] You could hardly find another court more peaceful, more orderly, or more devoted to true piety than this one, which is a result of the discipline of an excellent princess. If you saw her at home, you would say that she was not in her apartments but in school. Books are always in her hands; she teaches, she learns; and she consoles her widowhood with holy readings. So mindful is she of the ancient writers that what others find difficult to read in the midst of prosperous times, she has learned in the midst of tears and mourning. Your *Paraphrases*, which are her favourite reading, she read previously in German translation,[5] but now she reads them in Latin, just as you wrote them, and turns them over again and again in her mind and absorbs their meaning. She is so singularly devoted to you because of your holy labours that she could not be more devoted.

Why, therefore, my dear Erasmus, could you not oblige her with some small gift? You have the opportunity and the subject matter, one that has not been written about and which is altogether appropriate, her own person. I do not mean that you should praise her, since she cannot be sufficiently praised in accordance with her merits. But just as all wives are greatly indebted to you because of one queen who is a wife,[6] so all widows, of whom there is a great number surviving in this kingdom after that great disaster, if anywhere in the world, and especially at this court, may feel

* * * * *

4 In 1524 Henckel was appointed chaplain to Queen Mary, but following the defeat and death of her husband, Louis II, at Mohács in August 1526, he first accompanied the queen from Buda to Bratislava and then left her service, returning to his former parish in Košice. In 1528 Queen Mary recalled him to her service, where he remained until 1531, when she left to become regent of the Netherlands.

5 By 1523, a complete German translation of the *Paraphrases* on the Epistles by the Swiss reformer Leo Jud was available. The following year saw the publication of excerpts from the *Paraphrase on Matthew* (translated by Petrus Tritonius) and the complete *Paraphrase on John* (translated by Michael Rischen). See Heinz Holeczek *Erasmus Deutsch* 1 (Stuttgart-Bad Cannstatt 1983) 296–7.

6 Catherine of Aragon, to whom Erasmus had dedicated his *Institutio christiani matrimonii* in 1526 (Ep 1727).

forever honoured and obliged to Erasmus because of one queen who is a widow.[7] You will render this act of homage to the high regard this serene heroine has for you and to my prayers, if I so merit. For this service you will find her neither ungrateful nor unmindful,[8] and me forever indebted to you as I have long been your devoted follower. Enjoy the best of health,   55 most esteemed Erasmus.

At Sopron in Hungary, 18 July in the year of our salvation 1528

Johann Henckel, pastor of Košice, counsellor and preacher of the widow Mary, most serene queen of Hungary and Bohemia, etc

I have sent you a second copy of this letter as a precaution against   60 those who have made it a practice of intercepting letters.

To the prince and champion of all good learning, the excellent and eminent Erasmus of Rotterdam

2012 / From Hieronymus Artolf   Besançon, 22 July 1528

First published as Ep 88 in Förstemann/Günther, the autograph was in the Burscher collection at Leipzig (Ep 1254 introduction).

A native of the Grisons in Switzerland, Hieronymus Artolf (d 1541) studied at Basel (BA 1511, MA 1513, followed by sporadic medical studies) and became a schoolteacher there. In addition to teaching, he appears also to have done work for Johann Froben and other Basel printers. He probably had more con-tact with Erasmus than can be documented from the three letters (this and Epp 2907–8) that constitute their surviving correspondence. Later, in the years 1537–40, he was once or twice dean of the faculty of arts, and in 1538–9 he was rector of the university.

HIERONYMUS ARTOLF OF GRISONS TO ERASMUS OF ROTTERDAM, GREETINGS

I have tried on numerous occasions, most learned Erasmus, to write a few lines to you so that you might come to know me, although Rhetus[1] has long

* * * * *

7 Erasmus responded in 1529 with *De vidua christiana*, dedicated to Mary (Epp 2100, 2110).
8 Erasmus took this as a hint that he was to receive a gift; see Allen Ep 2110:12–18.

2012
1 Rhetus, ie a native of Rhaetia, the Latin name for the Grisons. This appears to be the name by which Artolf was known to his friends (cf Ep 440:17).

been known always and everywhere as a sincere and loyal herald of your   5
praises and strong supporter of Erasmus. But I have been held back until now from writing to you, glory of all true learning, partly through a
feeling of shame, and partly through the consciousness of my ignorance
and dull intellect, lacking the grace of Minerva. Finally, the necessity of
fate has won out, forcing me to wipe away all shame and present my-   10
self to you in a masked guise as if to invite your ridicule. I should have
wished that I could have communicated a more auspicious message to you,
which would have made my letter more pleasing to your Excellency. But
since the gods have willed otherwise, we must accept what has happened
as best we can. In brief, the archdeacon of Besançon, a most devoted pa-   15
tron of yours, as you know, has departed this life in recent days.[2] A stone
that had formed in his bladder a long time ago, made up of very tiny
stones, blocked his urine for almost eleven straight days to such an extent that it flowed back up to the mouth of his stomach and forced him
to vomit it forth. You may readily understand how cruel and painful this   20
death was, which took its origin from the lowest parts, as it were, while the
more vital parts of the human body were affected only by contact with the
malady.

If I have informed you of this later than I should have, it was for lack
of messengers and also because I learned only in Dijon that he had been   25
your patron. In addition, so that I may allay any suspicion of rumour that
may happen to arise there, let me tell you what happened to Nicolaus Episcopius on his journey.[3] En route to Dôle he happened to fall into a band
of horsemen, by whom he was detained in chains for a few hours together
with his entourage. But in the end he had only to tell them the intent of   30
his journey and treat them to a lavish feast to secure his release unharmed.
The reason is that the marshal in charge of the whole region of Burgundy
is keeping close guard there these days.[4] I did not wish to keep this news
from you so that you would not suspect that any more serious incident had
befallen him. Finally, most learned Erasmus, if there was anything incorrect   35
or unpleasing to you in this message, as there surely is, please do not be
offended. In the meantime, may you enjoy vigorous health.

Given at Besançon, 22 July 1528
To Erasmus of Rotterdam, champion of true and pure theology

* * * * *

2 Ferry de Carondelet; see Ep 2002 introduction.
3 On Episcopius, son-in-law and business partner of Johann Froben, see Ep 1714
   introduction. The purpose of his journey to Dôle at this time is not known.
4 The marshal has not been identified.

2013 / To Mercurino Gattinara   Basel, 27 July 1528

On Gattinara, grand chancellor of Emperor Charles v and ardent champion of
Erasmus and of Erasmian reform, see Epp 1150, 1643. Pleased to have such an
influential friend and patron at the imperial court, Erasmus appealed to Gattinara for help in securing the payment of the arrears of his imperial pension
and in silencing the attacks on his orthodoxy by the theologians of Louvain,
with success on both counts: see Epp 1700, 1747, 1757, 1784A, 1785, 1815. In
his most recent letter to Gattinara (Ep 1872), Erasmus had urged moderation
in dealing with the Lutherans. This letter of introduction for Frans van der
Dilft is the last of Erasmus' correspondence with Gattinara to survive. Gattinara died in Innsbruck in 1530, on his way to attend the imperial diet at
Augsburg. The manuscript, in a secretary's hand but corrected, signed, and
addressed by Erasmus, is in the Real Academia de la Historia at Madrid (MS
Est 18 gr 1.5 fol 13). The letter was first published in the *Opus epistolarum*.

Cordial greetings, excellent sir. Though exposed to mortal danger and oppressed by a stone in the bladder,[1] which recently caused the death of
Ferry, archdeacon of Besançon,[2] brother of the reverend Lord Archbishop of
Palermo,[3] nevertheless we still live on in hope of peace, knowing that the
hearts of kings are in the hands of God,[4] who can suddenly turn them in   5
whatever direction he wishes.

Frans van der Dilft,[5] the young man who bears this, was born of a
high-ranking family in his native land. He is a young man of exceptional
ability and fully worthy, in my opinion, of receiving the best education and
a solid moral training at the imperial court. He is known to me from his   10
long residence in my household. He has an upright and fortunate nature that
should not be wasted in indolence and carousing. If in your wisdom you
do not reject my judgment, as I hope you will not, I should very much wish
that you would find a place for him at court, which your influence can easily
accomplish, and that he may be given some duty suitable to his years. I hope   15

* * * * *

2013
1 See Ep 1989 n4.
2 Ferry de Carondelet; see Epp 2002, 2010:6–7, and 2012:15–23.
3 Jean (II) de Carondelet (Ep 1276)
4 Cf Prov 21:1.
5 See Ep 1942 n1. Dilft was now planning to set out from the Netherlands to
  seek his fortune in Spain and had solicited this letter of recommendation from
  Erasmus; see Ep 2026:9–11.

that the youth will obtain this favour from you by his own good qualities. I
know how many swarms try to force their way into the emperor's court, but
this aspirant by reason of his family, comeliness, learning, and integrity is
not one to be judged according to ordinary standards. Although I am already
most indebted to you on many counts, you would certainly place me under   20
much greater obligation to you by this service. I hope that your illustrious
Highness enjoys the best of health.

Given at Basel, 27 July 1528

The Luther fever is abating day by day to the point that Luther himself
is writing palinodes on his doctrines virtually one after the other and on   25
this account is looked upon by others as a heretic and a madman.[6] But I
am afraid that the stolid immorality of certain monks may start up a new
tragedy.

Again farewell.

The humble servant of your illustrious Highness Erasmus of Rotter-   30
dam

Signed in my own hand

To the illustrious Lord Mercurino Gattinara, supreme chancellor of his
imperial Majesty. In Spain

2014 / From Erasmus Schets   Antwerp, 27 July 1528

This is Schets's response to Ep 1999. The letter was first published by Allen,
using the autograph in the University Library at Basel (Scheti epistolae 16).

* * * * *

6 Allen speculated that this might be a reference to such works as Luther's *Von
  der Wiedertaufe an zwei Pfarrherrn* (February 1528) and *Vom Abendmahl Christi
  Bekenntnis* (March 1528). Both, however, were vigorous assertions of Luther's
  teaching that could not possibly be described as 'palinodes,' ie retractions or
  recantations (see *Adagia* I ix 59: *Palinodiam canere* 'To sing a palinode'). What
  Erasmus had in mind was the Saxon Visitation Articles that had been written
  by Melanchthon in 1527 and published, with an important preface by Luther,
  in 1528 (see Epp 1944 n1, 1981 n9). Because of the cautious and moderate approach in the Articles to traditional doctrines and practices (eg the stipulation
  that Christians should confess their sins to a priest as well as to God), there
  were some who jumped to the conclusion that the Wittenbergers were creep-
  ing back to Rome. This charge came not only from critics within the evangelical camp like Johannes Agricola (Ep 1981 n9) but also from adversaries in
  the Roman camp who, in the words of Luther in the preface to the published
  Articles, 'boast that we have regretted our teaching and are retreating and re-
  canting' (LW 40 272); see Wengert 109–14, 141. Here Erasmus adds himself to
  the list of those 'boasters.' Cf Epp 2049:33–5, 2059:71–2.

Cordial greetings. I last wrote you this past month.[1] Afterwards I received your letter[2] as well as another from the archbishop of Canterbury, with an announcement that forty English pounds sterling had been deposited in England.[3] This sum, entrusted into the hands of Italians by Tunstall, was converted into fifty pounds, eleven shillings and eight pence of our money 5 and reached Pieter Gillis in a single exchange transaction.[4]

I am thus relieved of two uncertainties, first that pounds are paid to you in England at the current rate of exchange, as I have written you several times; second, that for the fifty pounds, eleven shillings and eight pence in our money received here, which are worth at least thirty-nine sterling, forty 10 sterling were given in England. From this it is clear that the money suffered a loss and erosion of one pound. I don't know whether this is attributable to those in Canterbury or London who transferred the money to the Italians or to the Italians themselves, who perhaps permitted themselves a usurious rate of exchange. This could have been avoided if they had simply given 15 whatever money they wished to be exchanged at a normal rate to Luis de Castro. If they were to do this, you would not have to be burdened by these financial worries.

I have received the Italians' written bill of exchange from Pieter Gillis – for it was through him that I received the money from the Italians – and 20 it contained nothing but the aforesaid sum I received from them, so that I could not demand more. If the contract had stated clearly that these Italians had received forty pounds in England with a guarantee to exchange them at their value here, I would have been able with clear evidence to ask them to account for their rate of exchange and to have avoided this excessive 25 interest.

In addition, you write that you do not wish to involve Pieter Gillis in your affairs and that I should take care that no Englishmen or anyone else should know how much money you have deposited with me. I shall look after this so that you will not have to do so. As a matter of fact, no one has 30 known about this and no one will know.

You also ask that I send you a receipt of the money you have deposited with me. I recently sent you a summary account: that I have in my possession

* * * * *

2014
1 Ep 2001
2 Ep 1999
3 See Ep 1999 n3.
4 For the conversion of this sum of £40 into £50 11s 8d Flemish pounds groot, see Ep 1993 nn7, 14.

six hundred and forty florins in our money,[5] of which I shall now give you
a detailed statement.   35

In the first place I received in the bill of exchange I mentioned, delivered to me by Pieter Gillis, fifty pounds, eleven shillings, eight pence in our
money, which, converted into florins, amount to three hundred three and a
half florins.[6]

In addition, Luis de Castro received in England from the hands of   40
your servant Quirinus thirty-five pounds, which Luis at a very honest rate
of exchange converted into forty-five pounds, five shillings, six pence in our
money, which make two hundred seventy-one florins and thirteen stuivers.[7]
In addition, I received from Master Jan de Hondt half of his annuity, sixty-
five florins. It is evident therefore that these revenues amount to the said six 45
hundred forty florins and three stuivers. To this sum Frans van der Dilft has
recently added twenty-eight florins.[8] So in total I have deposited with me six
hundred sixty-eight florins and three stuivers. I shall add to that whatever
I receive from other sources and will dispose of the whole amount as you
shall instruct me. This letter will serve as a written contract or receipt. I 50
could not explain or review your holdings more clearly.

I shall see to it that Master Jan de Hondt consigns what he still owes
from the elapsed annuity as soon as possible. I have written to Luis de Castro asking him to speak to the most reverend archbishops of Canterbury
and London and tell them not to give your money to anyone but him if they 55
wish it to be delivered to you at a proper rate of exchange. I also asked him
to recall to them in a discreet way the twenty pounds still remaining from
the year 1527.[9] I am certain that he will take care of all your interests with
great competence as long as he knows what is expedient.

* * * * *

5 The 640 florins 'in our money' are clearly not the Flemish-Hapsburg gold coins
  (Carolus florins) but rather the traditional money-of-account worth 40d groot
  Flemish, so that six florins equals one pound (*quorum sex conficiunt unam libram*); and thus this sum was worth £106 13s 4d groot Flemish. Cf Epp 1934
  n6, 1993 n13, and 2001 n6.
6 The sum of £50 11s 8d was thus also worth, by this ratio of six florins to the
  pound, as Schets correctly stated, 303 and a half florins money-of-account.
7 The sum of £35 sterling was converted into £45 5s 6d groot Flemish = 271.65
  florins money-of-account (again, at six florins to the pound); or, as stated here
  271 florins and 13 stuivers = 26d groot. The stuiver was the former double
  groot silver coin (2d), also known as the patard; see CWE 1 327, 331; and Ep
  1934 n6.
8 Cf Ep 2015:1–2.
9 See Ep 1999:8.

I saw from the letter of the archbishop[10] what regard the king and 60
the primates of England have for you and what support they give to your
writings and studies; this afforded me great pleasure. You are urged by
them with great insistence to move to England; but if you had to move, you
could not in my judgment move anywhere more tranquilly and find a more
peaceful home than here with us. 65

Your servant Quirinus,[11] who recently brought your letter here, has set
out for Holland, where he is remaining for a little while. I do not know
what his business was there. If another messenger presents himself, I will
not hold this letter up any longer. I have nothing more to say except to send
you my sincere greetings and to wish you health and prosperity. 70

From Antwerp, 27 July 1527

To the great man and eminent authority in sacred letters Master Erasmus of Rotterdam

At Basel

2015 / To Erasmus Schets   Basel, 30 July 1528

This letter was first published by Allen, using the autograph in the British
Library (MS Add 38512 fol 27). It is Erasmus' reply to Ep 2001. Schets's reply
to this letter is Ep 2024.

Cordial greetings. Frans van der Dilft writes me that he paid you twenty
gold florins that he owed me.[1] If he gave you silver florins it would be to my
loss. Here florins have their usual value. Crowns have diminished somewhat
in value; they are worth hardly a third of a stuiver.[2] When payment is made

* * * * *

10 Ep 1965
11 Possibly a mistake for Kan (Cannius); see Ep 1999 n9. But cf Allen Ep 2924:3–5.

2015
1 Dilft's letter is not extant, but see Epp 2014:46–7, 2024:17–19. These may be
  gold Rhenish or Imperial florins (of the Four Electors) rather than Flemish
  Hapsburg Carolus florins, or Florentine florins, or any of their close imitations.
  For the current values of all these florins, see CWE 1 316–19; CWE 12 650, Table
  3D; and Appendix Table 3, 476 below.
2 For silver florins, see North and Munro 'Money and Coinage' (Ep 1934 n51).
  The crowns are presumably the recently issued English rose noble crowns,
  worth 5s or 60d sterling, in England, with the debasement of November 1526.
  See the Appendix 440–50 with Tables 2–3, 464–76 below.

in crowns in England there is a great loss, for there they have a high value, 5
but much less where you are. But if they are received there and sent here,
some gain is made.

I am surprised that Jan de Hondt is late with his payment.[3] I have a
suspicion about what is the cause. Pierre Barbier is staying with him, the
dean and theologian; he is always hungry and filches whatever he can from 10
friend and foe alike.[4] If he has not paid yet, I shall send a special messenger. I regret that I wrote to him[5] not to make pension payments to Marcus
Laurinus.[6] I would prefer that he pay him rather than anyone else.

Karel Uutenhove has his letters. He is living with me, a well-
disciplined young man.[7] I wrote in a letter delivered by Kan what it was that 15
I wanted.[8] If he returns, do not give him any money in my name.[9] Farewell.

Basel, 30 July 1528

Yours truly, Erasmus

To the honourable Master Erasmus Schets, Antwerp banker. At Antwerp

20

2016 / From Levinus Ammonius   Sint Maartensbos, 31 July 1528

Like Ep 1463, which was also from Levinus, this letter was first published
by Allen from a manuscript in the Bibliothèque municipale at Besançon (MS
599 page 179). In the earlier letter, Levinus, a Carthusian in the monastery
of St Maartensbos, west of Brussels, sought to initiate a correspondence with
Erasmus but received no reply. This second attempt, after an interval of four
years, was a success. Erasmus answered with Ep 2062, and five more letters in their subsequent correspondence survive (Epp 2082, 2197, 2258, 2483,
2817).

Ammonius was an excellent classical scholar whose letters tended to be vir-
tuoso performances. His Latin is splendidly fluent and vigorous. In this letter,
moreover, as in Epp 2082 and 2817, he shifts from time to time into excellent

* * * * *

3 See Ep 1993 n11.
4 Barbier (Epp 443, 1294) was now dean of Tournai (Ep 1862). Erasmus, to whom
  Barbier owed a considerable sum of money, knew of the latter's chronic penury
  (Ep 1862:8–15), all of which fed his suspicion that Barbier was cheating him
  on his annuity. Cf Epp 1548:21–7, 1993.
5 de Hondt
6 See Epp 1849:11–15, 1866:1–3.
7 See Ep 2001 n7.
8 Ep 1999
9 Cf Ep 1999:14, 18.

Greek. Here the first ten lines, as printed in Allen, as well as a dozen more
lines spread through the remainder of the letter, are in Greek.

LEVINUS AMMONIUS SENDS CORDIAL GREETINGS TO DESIDERIUS
ERASMUS OF ROTTERDAM, THE MOST GENUINE OF THEOLOGIANS
If there is anyone who has shown his thorough displeasure and irritation
with my confrère Cousturier,[1] who has been stirring up trouble for you and
hurling insults vindictively upon your innocent head, both speakable and   5
unspeakable, and all of this rashly and without foundation, dear friend and
true delight of our age, Erasmus, true to your name as universally beloved,
then be assured that it is my kinsman, Johannes de Molendino, canon of
Tournai,[2] an eloquent supporter of yours, whom you once accurately called
in one of your letters a man of refined taste.[3] I have written to him often   10
and at great length about this matter,[4] venting my anger at Cousturier rather
candidly – for it was not safe to do this among my confrères – since I was
moved to indignation by this situation and could not suffer in silence that
his silly lunacies should distract you from your studies, which are so useful and salutary to Christendom. What could be more shameful than that   15
the anxious and avid expectations of so many thousands of good people
should be delayed by the interference of a single crazed individual? I have
also discovered that the prior of the Carthusian monastery, primate of the
whole order,[5] was requested in the letters of certain people to impose silence upon this cursed individual,[6] who, in my opinion, is better suited to   20
mend shoes[7] than to emend books, as he presumes to do. They said of him
that he was solely responsible for blackening with his cobbler's black all that
is spotless; he is without a doubt the disgrace not only of our order but of
the name of theology. With his insufferable abusiveness, he would outstrip
all indulgence, and his inarticulate loquacity would exhaust the patience of   25
any reader. It would be unseemly for me to put in writing what curses and

* * * * *

2016
1 Ep 1943 n7
2 Molendino, also known as Jean Molinier (Ep 371), shared his kinsman's admiration for Erasmus (Ep 1763). A friend of Pierre Barbier, the dean of Tournai
  (Ep 2015 n4), he was frequently involved in the handling of Erasmus' income
  from the canonry at Courtrai (see, for example, Epp 1470:2–3, 1471:18–20).
3 Ep 806:19–21
4 Ep 1763
5 Willem Bibaut (Ep 1687)
6 Erasmus himself made such a request in Ep 1687.
7 A pun on Cousturier's Latin name Sutor (sutor = 'shoemaker,' 'cobbler').

maledictions I called down upon that impious head, especially when I read
what you wrote,[8] justly lamenting that you have been distracted from your
work, *De modo concionandi*,[9] which we await with great interest, by his senseless ravings. And even if I did write these things to you I am quite sure that   30
in your good nature you would take pity on him, although he is worth no
good man's pity. May God restore him to his senses.

I do not think you have need of my crude sketch, since I am certain
that with your skilled brush you have depicted him among others in his
true colours in your catalogue of ill-omened names, which you have long   35
promised us.[10] Otherwise I would easily find it in me to paint a portrait of
Cousturier from head to foot, as they say,[11] since I am familiar with his idle
talk, having followed it at close hand. I do not doubt that you focused a bit
more on his portrait and, not simply content with limning some slight detail,
did not lift your brush too quickly from the canvas. On the contrary, you   40
did not omit the least feature that you thought appropriate for him, so that
you could present us with a finished portrait that exhibited all his qualities.
And surely there is no reason that should prevent you, out of regard for our
order, from treating him in the manner he deserves. Let people be offended
as they will. What is this to you or to me? Such persons give clear proof   45
of their depravity. At the same time everyone will know that not all the
members of our order are evil, but that there are some, though they be few,
who hate evil.

I remember that some years ago when he[12] was a prior in Paris, a
member of our order happened to be returning there and had with him the   50
Psalms of David in Greek, which I had once copied out. You yourself had
seen and praised it at Louvain, if my informant is not mistaken. It had been
left on the table by chance and our friend Cousturier happened to come in
and picked it up. When he saw that it was written in Greek he shook his
fingers convulsively, as if he had touched a snake, and pointing his finger   55
at the other person menacingly said 'Aha! You too are one of them!'[13] And
immediately he bolted out the door cursing such an impiety, namely, that
he had found a Greek Psalter in a Carthusian monastery. Yet, clever fellow

*****

8 In the penultimate sentence of the *Apologia adversus Petrum Sutorem* LB IX 804E
9 Ie the *Ecclesiastes*; see Ep 1932 n25.
10 The promise is in Ep 1858:393–415 and the list itself (though without names)
   is Ep 2045.
11 *Adagia* I ii 37
12 Cousturier
13 Cf Matt 26:73.

that he is, in the book he wrote against the Anticomarites – I don't know
who they are, unless they are the ones who criticized the *comaron*, that is,   60
the arbutus or strawberry tree (the fruit of which Cousturier goes wild over
as a delicacy)[14] – he suddenly began to speak Greek,[15] so help me God! And
it was in the angelic salutation.[16] But whom do you call Anticomarites, my
good Cousturier? Why don't you say Antidicomarians (for you seem to have
some grievance against them) if you have something to say, you who are   65
so learned that you cannot even use the correct name for those whom you
have chosen to attack? But perhaps you are making a saving, like the rustic
in Plautus who said, 'For the people of Praeneste the *ciconia* is a *conia*.'[17] I
would write more to you about that book (ye Gods! What a book and what
a size!), my dear Erasmus (since he makes I know not what threats against   70
you in it,[18] but he fights with a wooden sword,[19] as usual). I know you will
never read it, and I did not want to bother you with such trifles. Of course,
it is so elegant and urbane and full of such exquisite gems of rhetoric that,
if I had it in for anyone, it would be punishment enough if I were to force
this book on him as his daily grind.   75

But why dwell on him so long? Will my whole letter be concerned with
this rare creature? Not at all! Yet I purposely began with these anecdotes to

* * * * *

14 *Apologeticum in novos Anticomaritas praeclaris beatissimae virginis Mariae laudibus
    detrahentes.* (Paris: J. Petit 1526), a denunciation of those who, in Cousturier's
    opinion, were detractors of the Virgin Mary. The word *Anticomaritas* in Cous-
    turier's title is a solecism that earned the ridicule of both Levinus and Eras-
    mus. Given that his subject was Mary, Cousturier should have written *anti-
    mariani* or *antidicomariani* (names used at the time of Augustine and Jerome to
    describe those who denied the perpetual virginity of Mary). Here Levinus ob-
    serves sarcastically that Cousturier's target must be critics of the strawberry
    tree (*comaron*). In the colloquy *Synodus grammaticorum* 'A Meeting of the Philo-
    logical Society' CWE 40 831–41, Erasmus' parody would exploit (among other
    things) the word *maritae*, which means either 'wives' as a noun or 'married'
    as an adjective. Thus *anticomaritae* (in which *co* = *quo*) presumably meant 'girls
    with feeble old men as husbands.'
15 Allen cites the *Apologeticum* fol vi, but provides no further information.
16 The angelic salutation to Mary in Luke 1:28
17 In Plautus's *Truculentus* (680–91), one of the characters asks the eponymous
    crude rustic why he says *rabonem* when he means *arrabonem* (from *arrha* 'pledge
    money'). Truculentus replies that the omitted 'a' is his saving, just as when
    the people of Praeneste in their dialect say *conia* when they mean *ciconia* (a
    stork).
18 Allen reports that, though Cousturier's *Apologeticum* contains much fulmina-
    tion against those who diminish the praise of the Virgin, there is no mention
    of Erasmus by name.
19 Literally, a figwood sword, as in *Adagia* II viii 63

show you what my sentiments are towards you and towards him. Certainly, if I had been able to do so freely and had not been prevented through fear of those who are more powerful and have also been associated with this 80 beast, the whole world would have known in what veneration I hold the name of Cousturier. And you would have no suspicions about the tree in the vision, as far as I am concerned.[20] You know what I mean and I need not remind the mindful.[21]

I wrote you another letter about four years ago, dear Erasmus, in which 85 at the end I modestly asked that you would see to the publication of some work by St John Chrysostom in his own language.[22] That you have now done so is most gratifying not only to me, although I am particularly grateful, but to all men of learning.[23] I would have thanked you long ago for such a great benefaction save that I was ashamed to approach such a great man empty- 90 handed a second time. But Christ shall give you full recompense in heaven to make up for all of us. Now, in addition to the elegant homilies *De laude precationis, De fato et providentia Dei*, and on Paul's Epistle to the Philippians, we have also read the beautiful books *De episcopi dignitate* and *De divi Babylae martyrio*.[24] In translating the latter book the man they call Oecolampadius 95 made some bad errors in various passages,[25] but especially in this one: 'He had decided to put an end to the war and to live a peaceful life and resolved to make this good decision binding by a strong law and secure conditions.'[26] He translates δόξαν as 'glory' instead of as an impersonal participle which, as not only you (what ever escapes your eye?) but even one only slightly 100 versed in Greek would see immediately, should have been translated in an entirely different manner.[27]

* * * * *

20 Allen says 'Cf Dan. 4. 10 seq.' The reference is to Nebuchadnezzar's vision of the tree as described in that chapter, but the relevance of that vision in the present context is not apparent.
21 Adagia I ii 12
22 Ep 1463:159–61. Levinus adds in the margin here: 'I believe, however, that others as well asked the same thing.'
23 See Ep 1463 n11.
24 For Erasmus' editions or translations of the works by Chrysostom mentioned here, see Epp 1563 (*De laude precationis* = *De orando Deum libri duo*), 1661 (six sermons *De fato et providentia Dei*), 1734 (two homilies in Greek on the Epistle to the Philippians), 1558 (*De episcopi dignitate* = *De sacerdotio*), 1856 (*De divi Babylae martyrio* = *De Babyla martyre*).
25 Cf Epp 1817:44–54, 1835:11–14; on Oecolampadius, see Ep 2000 n4.
26 Levinus cites the passage in Greek.
27 In *Chrysostomi Psegmata quaedam* (Basel: Cratander, March 1523) page 14, Oecolampadius' translation reads as follows: 'Gloriam fore, omisso bello; ociosam dein vitam agere. Itaque decreuit bonum hoc consilium stabili lege et securis

But I shall leave that for another time. In that letter, therefore, I expressed my devotion to you, since I had no other way of communicating with you. And I promised that if I could do you any favour, you should not 105 doubt that I would do so with both hands.[28] And so to acquit myself of my promise, I pray you through Christ, dear Erasmus, whom we hold most sacred, that you believe that what I have done has been done out of the greatest affection for you. Through the gift of a friend I have finally had access in this year 1528 to your book of St Jerome's *Epistles*, which you divided 110 into three books and published in 1524.[29] I was able to peruse them with more leisure than in other copies that I had seen before, which are owned by others here in the monastery, and was able to make notes and excerpt at leisure what I thought would be of use to me or to others. In so doing I happened to come across some passages that I could briefly point out to 115 you without prejudice, out of my sincere devotion to you. I was inspired to do this partly so that through my attentive reading of the text I might be of some help to your studies, which are worthy of immortality, and partly so that neither now nor in future will these captious critics who examine your works with jaundiced eye, detecting these same errors, stir up another great 120 furore against you. They would exaggerate everything in their usual manner, although this[30] is no crime but merely a sign of a lapse of memory or a lack of attention. There is nothing surprising in this, nor can it be reckoned as a fault if in such a varied work the mind is not always alert but sometimes sleep creeps in unawares, to which we easily fall victim when we are 125 peacefully secure and out of range, as the saying goes.[31] The sincerity of St Jerome himself suggested this audacity to me. He praises Pammachius and Domnio for having, either by letter or by having sent him carefully ordered excerpts from a volume, requested that he either correct or explain them.[32]

* * * * *

confirmari terminis.' In English this would be: '*It would have been a source of glory for him* to end the war ...' etc, which is a mistake for '*He had decided* to end the war ...' This was an easy error to make, given that the noun 'glory' and the aorist participle 'decided' have the same form, δόξαν.

28 Ep 1463:118–19; cf *Adagia* I ix 16.
29 See Ep 1451 introduction. The reference is to the second printing of the Froben edition of Jerome, in which the letters were edited by Erasmus. The first edition was in 1516; see n33 below.
30 Ie Erasmus' having made small errors
31 *Adagia* I iii 93
32 Jerome Ep 50.3 (to Domnio, written in 394). St Pammachius (c 340–410) was a Roman senator of the Furian family to whom Jerome dedicated several of his works, including his commentaries on the minor prophets (406) and Daniel

I admit, Erasmus, that if you consider my worthiness I cannot be com- 130
pared in any way to Pammachius or Domnio. Nevertheless, I have good
hope that I shall not incur your disfavour in this little service, since I have assumed this task with the same feelings towards you as they had for Jerome,
namely, in a spirit of great friendship. If perhaps at some later date you
should publish a new edition, you may wish to give a little thought to my 135
suggestions and, if they are of any value, you may change or explain these
passages. But if you do not wish to do this, or my comments do not convince
you, I pray you by the same Christ that you immediately cast them into the
fire and that henceforth they be known to no man but be totally obliterated.
That you may do this in all safety, I promise in good faith that I shall never 140
show anyone what I have written down in my notebooks. What is more, lest
they be seen by others, I shall immediately consign them to the flames as
soon as I know your wishes. Far be it from my intentions to seek out dishonest glory for myself from your labours, as if I discern more than you do.
I have put these notes together merely through a collation of passages and 145
in the light of my own judgment, which, in my opinion, is not altogether to
be despised, wishing only to consult your best interests. For there is nothing here that pertains to the Christian faith or the doctrines of the church,
on which matters, if I am not mistaken, we are perfectly in agreement. It is
merely a question of the reliability of a reading or the citation of sources. 150
Furthermore, lest anyone think I have done anything without due reflection,
I carefully compared this edition with the first edition printed in 1516,[33] and
I found there all the same mistakes that were not corrected in the edition
of 1524. Nothing has been changed in this second edition except that indexes were added and a few passages were expanded. This being the case, 155
I thought it not inappropriate to alert you to these things privately and in
a friendly manner. Receive then this offering as a token of my gratitude to
you, through whose holy labours in both languages I gladly acknowledge,
not only to you, that I have derived much profit. And I wish you to believe
me when I say from the bottom of my heart that I am no less lacerated by 160
the insults that certain individuals vie to heap upon you than I would be if

* * * * *

(407). After the death of his wife, he took the monastic habit and devoted himself and his fortune to works of piety. Pammachius' contemporary, St Domnio
(d after 394), was a Roman priest and diligent collector and editor of books
much admired for his holiness and learning by both Augustine and Jerome.
In his home Jerome found rare books useful for his biblical scholarship and
dedicated to him his commentary on Ezra (394).

33 See Ep 396.

they fell upon my own head. But I am consoled, as you can also be, by the knowledge that in the course of human affairs the best have always been at the mercy of the worst. Think how St Jerome himself, not to mention others, had to contend, like a second Hercules, with so many monsters and for 165 so long! And with all his armour he was barely able to withstand their attack. But now he enjoys tranquil peace with Christ and reaps the great reward of a brief test of fortitude, such as we hope with all confidence awaits you at the end of this troubled existence. Do not let the wickedness of slanderers break your spirit, I beg you. Christ Jesus, sole font of all innocence, 170 was not able, or at least did not wish, to avoid the abuse of the wicked, so that he might provide the perfect example of tolerance for his followers. He was called a violator of the Sabbath,[34] a violator of the law,[35] a glutton and a drunkard, a friend of publicans and of sinners,[36] and finally a Samaritan and one possessed by demons.[37] And in the end, after such malignant abuse, 175 he was led away to an ignominious death upon the cross.

But I am really stupid to give you advice! It is easy for the healthy to give advice to the sick.[38] It is easy to say 'Bite on the bit,'[39] 'Ignore them,'[40] 'Do not return evil for evil,'[41] but this is more easily said than done. 'If you were in my place,' the character says, 'you would feel otherwise.'[42] So 180 then, we must ask Christ that he deign to grant us the meekness of which he gave the most perfect example and which he prescribed for his followers. Without his continued favour all our attempts are in vain. We may readily believe that he will not hesitate to grant his favour when we ask for what he himself ordained. 185

To return to myself, there is absolutely no reason for your having any doubts about my sincere affection. But if you can still entertain some doubts, put me to the test as you wish, and if you do not find me to be completely sincere, I give you permission to treat me in whatever way you please. But I am certain you will never find anything to give you doubts. Wherefore, 190 in my turn, I have good hope that in your perfect integrity you will take all of this in good part and will number Ammonius at least among the lowest ranking of your friends. I assuredly shall cede to no one in my loyalty and

* * * * *

34 John 5:15–18
35 John 19:7
36 Matt 11:19, Luke 7:34
37 John 8:48
38 Terence *Andria* 309
39 Ie accept the situation: *Adagia* I iv 14
40 The source of 'Ignore them' (*Dissimules facito*) has not been found.
41 Cf Rom 12:17.
42 Terence *Andria* 310

constancy towards you. Nevertheless, as bright as is my hope that you will
receive these notes in the spirit in which they were written, I know that if I   195
could give them to you in person, from one hand to the other, as they say,[43] I
could more easily persuade you by my demeanour, my eyes, and the whole
expression on my face how grateful I am to you and how much veneration
I have for you, as no other can claim. But as things are, I am compelled to
offer them to you from a distance, by letter delivered by someone else and   200
perhaps not at an opportune moment and without the necessary courtesy
(which failing I should be careful to avoid if I delivered them in person),
since I have no other choice.

Therefore, dear Erasmus, I beg of you through our common hope for a
better life that, if I have been lacking in the obligations that I owe to you on   205
numerous counts, your good nature and affability, known throughout the
world, may make amends for my failings. I wish you to know, however, that
for a little while I shall not be without fear that I shall earn hostility rather
than favour, until you confirm by letter the hope I have conceived and assure
me that my fears have been in vain. I implore you to do this in whatever way   210
you deem appropriate. May Christ Jesus, the true Samaritan,[44] preserve you
unharmed for the advancement of his church and deliver you from wicked
and unscrupulous men, so that you may continue your pious works.

From Sint Maartensbos, from the convent of the Carthusians of the
same name, near Geeraardsbergen in Flanders, 31 July 1528   215

2017 / To John Longland   Basel [c 1] August 1528

This is the preface to the *Concionalis interpretatio, plena pietatis, in psalmum 85*
(Basel: Froben, August 1528). On John Longland (1473–1547), bishop of Lincoln, distinguished preacher, and friend of Erasmus, see Ep 1535.

TO THE MOST REVEREND FATHER IN CHRIST, JOHN LONGLAND,
LORD BISHOP OF LINCOLN IN ENGLAND, FROM DESIDERIUS
ERASMUS OF ROTTERDAM, GREETING
It is an ancient saying and a true one, most honourable Bishop, that 'A re-
quest from the powerful exacts compliance';[1] but far more persuasive is the   5

* * * * *

43 Adagia II viii 8
44 Cf Luke 10:25–37.

2017
1 See *Adagia* v i 46 *Preces armatae* 'Requests backed by force,' at the end of which
Erasmus attributes this saying to 'that famous mime' (*ille mimus celebris*), by

request of one who merits our gratitude. Not to defer to the wishes of one more powerful involves some risk, but not to comply with the wishes of a benefactor is the height of shame. Ingratitude is a more detestable fault by far than indiscretion.

Furthermore, when a request is made by one who has the right to com- 10 mand, it has more authority for the very reason that he does not order but requests. Indeed, if it is a sign of defiance to refuse a command, it is gross inhumanity to refuse a request. When one who by his authority can command and by his merits demand his due makes a simple request in compensation for his services, and this in such a way that it seems no request 15 at all, then his request has all the more efficacy. As a result, modesty often obtains what importunate demands would not have obtained.

Since, then, you besiege me with so many engines of war, reverend Father – your authority, your merits, the modesty of your request – I was less fain to make excuses, since you almost suggested one yourself. Indeed, 20 my excuse was neither single nor of one kind, and it was perhaps more just than you might wish, but I could not refuse a prelate of such great eminence who was so deserving and who made his request in such a way.[2] So here you have the psalm, such as it is, but all the same a testimony of my unqualified esteem and devotion. The intention merits your approval if the 25 ingenuity does not. You cannot despise the attempt even if the result is less than satisfying. I shall not keep you any longer from the psalm. Farewell.

Basel, August 1528

2018 / To Alfonso de Valdés   Basel, 1 August 1528

Printed at the end of Erasmus' *Concionalis interpretatio* of Psalm 85 (see Ep 2017 introduction), this is Erasmus' reply to Ep 1807. It is devoted almost entirely to Valdés' inquiry about the meaning of Erasmus' motto *Concedo nulli* 'I yield to no one.'

On Alfonso de Valdés (d 1532), Latin secretary of Charles v and 'imperial secretary' to Chancellor Mercurino Gattinara, see Ep 1807 introduction.

* * * * *

which he meant Publilius Syrus. This saying and many others besides were falsely attributed to him. See O. Friedrich *Publilii Syri sententiae* (Berlin 1880) 97.
2 In Ep 1535, in which Erasmus dedicated his exposition of Psalm 4 to Longland, Erasmus wrote (lines 3–6): 'You were the first to encourage me to produce a commentary on the Book of Psalms and in frequent letters since then you have returned again and again to the same theme.' The 'frequent letters' referred to do not survive.

ERASMUS OF ROTTERDAM TO THE MOST DISTINGUISHED ALFONSO
VALDÉS, SECRETARY TO HIS ROYAL MAJESTY, GREETING

What you signify to me in your usual discreet manner I have also very
clearly learned in letters from others,[1] that there are some who find a cause
for slander in the figure of the god Terminus on my signet ring, protesting   5
that the accompanying device 'I yield to no one' betrays an intolerable arrogance.[2] What else is this but a symptom of that fatal disease of finding fault
with everything? Momus is ridiculed for having criticized Venus' sandal;[3]
but these people who have found something to nibble at in a ring outdo Momus himself. I would call them Momuses, but Momus criticizes only what   10
he has first carefully examined. These fault finders, or rather trouble makers, carp with eyes closed at what they neither see nor understand, such is
the potency of the disease. And in the meantime they think of themselves
as the pillars of the church, when they do nothing but betray their own stupidity, joined with an equal malice, is more known the world over than is   15
good for them. They imagine that the words 'I yield to no one' spoken by
Erasmus. But if they were to read my writings they would see that there is
hardly anyone, no matter how mediocre, to whom I should prefer myself,
more ready to concede to everyone than to none.

Those who know me more closely through friendly conversation will   20
attribute any other vice to me but arrogance. They will declare that I resemble more the Socratic 'I know one thing, namely, that I know nothing' than
'I yield to no one.' But let them imagine, if they will, that I am so insolent
as to put myself before everyone; do they also think that I am so stupid
that I would proclaim this in a motto? If they had any Christian sentiments,   25
they would interpret these words either as not being spoken by me or as

* * * * *

2018
1 Not extant
2 In 1509 Erasmus was given a ring containing an antique gem carved with
   a figure identified as that of the god Terminus (cf lines 61–6 below). There
   was no motto on the ring itself. But in 1517–18, Erasmus, having adopted Terminus as his personal emblem, had a seal made with the head of the young
   god bordered by the inscription *Cedo nulli* 'I yield to no one.' For pictures
   of both the ring and the seal, see page 242. Erasmus customarily signed important documents with this seal. See, for example, his first will (1527), CWE
   12 548:127. On the vexed question of the meaning of the motto *Concedo nulli*,
   which Erasmus had not always understood as he explains it here, see Edgar
   Wind 'Ænigma Termini' *Journal of the Warburg Institute* 1 (1937) 66–9. See also
   James K. McConica 'The Riddle of "Terminus"' *Erasmus in English* 2 (1971)
   2–7.
3 Momus was the god of carping criticism and mockery; see Ep 1994 n8.

Top
Left: Wax impression of ring containing an antique gem carved
with the head of a figure identified as Terminus, gift of Alexander Stewart,
archbishop of St Andrews, to Erasmus in 1509
Right: Wax impression of seal with Terminus figure, plus the inscription *Cedo nulli*
'I yield to no one,' engraved for Erasmus at his own request
Bottom
The figure of Terminus on the reverse of the medal of Erasmus
made by Quinten Metsys in 1519
Historisches Museum, Basel

having some other meaning. They see that carved image, the stone beneath and a young man above with his hair fluttering in the breeze.[4] Does this bear any resemblance to Erasmus? If that is not enough, they see carved in the stone 'Terminus.' If you end the verse with this word, the verse will be an iambic dimeter acatalectic: 'Concedo nulli Terminus.' But if you begin with this word, it will be a trochaic dimeter acatalectic: 'Terminus concedo nulli.' What if I had painted a lion and added as a motto: 'Flee, unless you wish to be torn apart'; would they assign these lines to me instead of to the lion? But what they do has no more sense, for I look more like a lion than a stone, if I am not mistaken.

They will say: 'We did not notice it was in verse, and we do not know who Terminus is.' Therefore in future will it be a crime to compose in verse because they did not learn the rules of metre? In any event, since they knew that in mottoes of this kind one should always try to discover some enigma, which is meant to elicit the conjectures of those who see it, if they did not know who Terminus was – although they could learn this from Augustine or Ambrose[5] – they should have sought the answer from those with experience in such matters. At one time the boundaries of fields were marked by some sign. It was a stone that rose up out of the ground, which ancient laws declared to be irremovable. One of these prescriptions is reported in Plato: 'Do not take away what you have not put down.'[6] A superstitious belief was added so that the ignorant crowd would be deterred from the audacity of taking it away, for it was believed that one violated a god in the stone. The Romans call him Terminus, to whom a shrine and a feast, the *Terminalia*,[7] were dedicated. This god Terminus, according to Roman chronicles, was the only one who refused to yield to Jupiter; because when the birds of augury allowed the deconsecration of all shrines they made an exception for the shrine of Terminus. Livy reports in the first book and again in the sixth book of *Ab urbe condita* that 'when after due observance of the auguries the Capitoline was divested of its gods, Juventas and Terminus refused to

* * * * *

4 Although Erasmus is ostensibly discussing his seal, the reference here to 'hair fluttering in the breeze' more closely corresponds to the image of Terminus found on the medal cast by Quinten Metsys in 1519 (Epp 1092:4–6, 1408 n17), and it is clear from the lines that follow that he is indeed describing the medal. See the picture of it on page 242; and cf lines 73–5 below.
5 Cf Augustine *De civitate Dei* 4.29, 5.21, 7.7. Allen could find no mention of Terminus in the indexes to Ambrose, and an electronic search of the *Patrologia Latina* database has confirmed that there is none.
6 *Laws* 11.1 (913c)
7 23 February

be removed.'[8] This omen was received with great joy because they thought that it portended the perpetuity of the Roman Empire. Juventas is useful in war and Terminus is unmovable.

At this they will probably cry out: 'What do you have to do with a god of fable?' It came to me by chance, I did not solicit it. When Alexander, titular archbishop of St Andrews, was called back to his native land from Siena by his father, King James of Scotland, he summoned me from Rome and, like a grateful and loving pupil, made me a present of several rings as a souvenir of the time we had spent together.[9] Among these was one with Terminus sculpted upon the gem. Previously I did not know who it was, but an Italian,[10] who was a connoisseur of antiquities, identified him. I took it as an omen and interpreted it as a warning that the boundary of my life was not far off. I was about forty years old at the time.[11] Lest this thought escape my mind, I began to stamp this image on my letters. I added a line of verse, as I said previously.[12] And so I made myself a motto from this profane god, which exhorted me to a reform of life. For death is the true bourne that yields to no one. That cast image, moreover, bears the inscription in Greek: 'Behold the end of a long life'; the corresponding Latin proverb is: 'Death is the ultimate boundary of things.'[13] They will say: 'You could have inscribed that on a skull.' Perhaps I would have accepted that one if it had occurred to me, but I liked the one I chose, first because it came about by chance, and then because it had a double attraction: on the one hand, its allusion to an old and celebrated history and, on the other hand, its obscurity, which is the property of mottoes.

There you have the apology concerning Terminus or, I should say, about goats' wool.[14] And would that these people would finally put a terminus to their calumnies! I would gladly make a pact with them to change my motto if they would change their mania. In that way they would be acting more in the interests of their authority than by claiming that it is under-

60

65

70

75

80

85

* * * * *

8 1.55.3–5; 5.54.7. Juventas was the Roman equivalent of Hebe, the goddess of youth.
9 This was in the early months of 1509; see Ep 604:4n.
10 Unidentified
11 If one accepts 28 October 1466 as the most likely date of Erasmus' birth, he would have been forty-two in the early months of 1509.
12 See lines 30–3 above.
13 Horace Epistulae 1.16.79. These mottoes are found on the Metsys medal (see n4 above), not on the seal.
14 Ie about questions of no importance, such as whether goats have wool or hair. See Adagia I iii 53.

mined by those who study the humanities. The desire to harm their reputations is so far from my mind that it gives me great pain to see them present
themselves as a laughing stock to the world with their foolish calumnies
and not be ashamed of being confuted time and time again and made ob-
jects of derision. May the Lord preserve you unharmed in body and in soul,   90
dearest friend in Christ.

Given at Basel, 1 August 1528

2019 / From Polidoro Virgilio   London, 2 August 1528

This is the preface to Virgilio's translation of Chrysostom's *Comparatio regii po-*
tentatus et divitiarum ac praestantiae, ad monachum in verissima Christi philosophia
acquiescentem (Paris: G. Morrhy, March 1530). Erasmus had published the Greek
text, dedicated to Virgilio, in 1526 (Ep 1734). On Virgilio, who was court historian to Henry VIII of England, see Ep 531:456n and the introductions to Epp
1175, 1666, 1702.

POLIDORO VIRGILIO OF URBINO TO HIS FRIEND ERASMUS OF
ROTTERDAM, GREETING
I have finally undertaken the task that you assigned me of translating the
little work of St John Chrysostom on the perfect monk and the evil prince,[1]
for I have recently returned to the study of Greek, which I had left off long   5
ago to write the history of England.[2] I suppose you were reluctant to assume this task in order not to curry the favour of the monks, because of
their hostility towards the humanities, and not to expose yourself to the hatred and resentment of kings. But you did well. Since the tyrant of Chrysostom had nothing in common with our princes, who are honourably born   10
and trained from childhood to virtue, justice, and beneficence, and since a
good part of present-day monks differ greatly from the ancient fathers in
learning, morals, and holiness of life, there is no reason for me to fear that
this barbarous version of the little book will get me into trouble. If they are
wise when they read this, monks will exert all their efforts and energy to   15
imitate that perfect monk, and princes will take every care that they will
have nothing in common at any time with the evil prince. As far as you are
concerned, since by common accord you are by virtue of your exceptional

* * * * *

2019
1 Ep 1734:13
2 The *Anglica historia*, on which he had been working since 1505 but would not
  publish until 1534

learning already in heaven, you will understand how much influence your
authority has with me as well, since I entered without reluctance upon this   20
task that you had assigned me, even if it was one that involved much work
but little praise, especially for a Latinist who likes always to be his own
master.

Farewell. At London, 3 August 1528

2020 / From Girolamo Aiazza   Chambéry, 5 August 1528

This letter was first published as Ep 64 in Enthoven. The manuscript is in the
Rehdiger Collection of the University Library at Wrocław (MS Rehd 254.2).
Girolamo Aiazza (c 1472–1538) of Vercelli, who signed himself Hieronymus
Agathius in Latin, had recently (March 1528) become grand chancellor of Duke
Charles II of Savoy and was still in office in 1535. Otherwise nothing is known
of him except that he is buried in the church of San Bernardo in Vercelli.
Erasmus' somewhat perfunctory reply is Ep 2041.

JESUS

Setting out on his return trip to Basel, the secretary who is the bearer of
this letter[1] spoke so highly of your name that he urged me to write to
you as one who had so often drawn pleasure from reading your works,
even though I was writing to someone I did not know, and as a person of   5
no learning to one of great learning. I made the excuse that I had nothing to write about, but he answered: 'Write what the ancient writers used
to write: "If you are well, it is well; I am well."[2] Since he is the kindest of men, he will be happy to receive anything you write to him.' 'Why
don't I take as my subject,' I said, 'the bizarre miracle that they say took   10
place in Turin?[3] Since our Erasmus is a staunch defender of the faith, he
will take the opportunity to write something against the Lutherans and

* * * * *

2020
1 Probably Joachim Zasius (d 1540), the oldest son of the famous jurist Udalri-
  cus Zasius. Since 1524 Joachim had been a ducal secretary in Savoy with special responsibility for relations with the German states, in which capacity he
  visited Basel several times.
2 'If you are well, it is well' (*si vales, bene est*), and 'if you are well, I am well' (*si
  vales, ego valeo*) were epistolary formulae commonly found at the beginning of
  Roman letters, often abbreviated as SVBE and SVEV.
3 Whatever the miracle was, Erasmus clearly thought it was an imposture devised by dishonest monks; see Ep 2041:3–4.

the renewers of ancient heresies.' Therefore I send you a little letter enclosed with mine which, though not elegant, is filled with interesting facts.
A friend of mine, a man of proven trustworthiness, sent it to me from Turin.   15
You will see from it that the opinion we faithful believers have of purgatory is the absolute truth. Although from the reading of Gregory's *Dialogues*
we can detect many things that lead us to this belief,[4] still it will be no
small thing to add this to the ancient authors in defence of the Christian
religion.   20

As a man of little culture and even less learning, I shall end my brief
note, lest I assail your ears with my unpolished words. But first I should like
you to know that I am your zealous and loyal follower, and often, when I
have some moment of freedom from the duties of the courtroom and public
affairs, I immerse myself in the reading of your works.   25

As a Jeromian yourself, please regard with Christian charity this
Jerome, who loves and cherishes men of learning; for I revere and respect
you with the eye of the mind, and if I am able to do anything to please you,
I shall gladly do it in deeds rather than words.

From Chambéry, 5 August 1528   30

Your faithful follower, Girolamo Agathius, in his own hand

To the most venerable and learned Erasmus of Rotterdam, as to a
brother

2021 / From Germain de Brie   Gentilly, 12 August 1528

This letter and Erasmus' response to it (Ep 2046) are concerned with the furore
that had broken out in Pariš following the publication of the *Ciceronianus* (Ep
1948), in which the character Nosoponus (the voice of Erasmus' Italian critics)
rates the Paris scholar-publisher Josse Bade above the great French humanist Guillaume Budé as a Ciceronian. The offending passage reads as follows
(CWE 28 420–1): 'I would allow him [Bade] to compete for this glorious title [of
Ciceronian] sooner than Guillaume Budé. On the whole, Bade's endeavours
have met with considerable success, though they would have met with more

* * * * *

4 In the fourth book of his *Dialogues*, Gregory the Great (c 540–604) made a
major contribution to the medieval conception of purgatory as a place where
the souls of those who have died in the grace of God expiate their unforgiven
venial sins and undergo whatever punishment is still required for forgiven
sins before they enter heaven. He supported this view with numerous tales
of those who had been favoured with visions of souls in the afterlife.

if domestic worries [a large family] and his commitment to making money hadn't interfered with the quiet detachment that accords with literary studies, which any candidate in this competition must be able to enjoy. That's the situation, however much Budé's exceptional and manifold gifts of intellect compel our imagination.'

Although intended as a left-handed compliment to Budé, whose views of the excesses of fanatical Ciceronianism were much the same as those of Erasmus, the passage was taken as a deliberate insult to Budé in particular and to French scholarship in general. In letters now lost, Louis de Berquin and Germain de Brie wrote to Erasmus concerning this perceived indiscretion, and Erasmus replied, asking them to avoid calling attention to the matter (see lines 2, 129 in this letter; Epp 2046:3–4, 89–90, 344–5; 2047:27–9; 2048:2, 13–14). But Budé's friends immediately took note, producing stinging epigrams at Erasmus' expense (see Ep 2027:27–30 with n14). When Brie (in the present letter) and Gervasius Wain (in Ep 2027) provided further details of the hostile reaction in France, Erasmus decided to act on Brie's suggestion (lines 98–109 of this letter) that he publish a letter proving to the French that he was not envious of Budé's 'glorious reputation.' So he hastily composed Ep 2046 and published it, together with the present letter and three other long letters (Epp 1891, 2037, 2045) that were essentially *apologiae*, in the *Selectae epistolae*, which was in print by 16 September 1528 (Epp 2050–1). Epp 2021 and 2046 were also printed at Paris in 1528 and in the *Opus epistolarum* of 1529; for the details, see Allen's introduction.

Erasmus altered the offending passage in the second edition of the *Ciceronianus* in 1529 (see CWE 28 587 n676), but Budé was not placated and never wrote to Erasmus again. For Bade's reaction to the *Ciceronianus*, see n4 below.

Germain de Brie (c 1490–1538) was a French humanist and priest who, having won the favour of the French royal house (particularly the queen, Anne of Brittany), accumulated sufficient wealth to be able to lead a life of leisured devotion to his studies. In 1508, while still in his teens, he had met Erasmus in Venice, and their subsequent friendship is reflected in the correspondence that began with Ep 569 in 1517 and continued until Erasmus' death. When Brie became involved in a controversy with Thomas More (1519–20), Erasmus intervened to help achieve a truce (Epp 1117, 1133). When in 1525 Brie manifested a particular interest in John Chrysostom, Erasmus persuaded him to translate several of the saint's works for his *Chrysostomi lucubrationes* (Basel: Froben 1527); see Epp 1733, 1736, 1800. In the *Ciceronianus*, Erasmus expressed his admiration for Brie (see n6 below), who would now do his best to reconcile him with his French critics.

GERMAIN DE BRIE TO ERASMUS OF ROTTERDAM, GREETING
I come to that part of your letter,[1] which, since it pertains especially to you,
is in a certain way common to us both, for by right of our close association I cannot but share automatically in anything that involves your reputation, whether it be good or bad. My greatest wish, most beloved Erasmus (I   5
cannot use a more sacred word in the circumstances) is that no cloud, especially at this time, which is antagonistic enough to the humanities, should
arise by which the splendour of your friendship with Budé might be obscured. Budé, as you are aware, is a man so admired by all of us that all
men of learning here regard him as a god. This is due not only to his loyalty,   10
honesty, and authority but also to his age, genius, and learning. He is a man
of such talent that there is nothing you might wish to learn that he cannot
teach you. To me he is and always was what Aristo was to Pliny.[2] Whenever
I am looking for some abstruse fact, Budé is my treasure. To sum it up, he
is to the French what Erasmus is to the Germans. The greater, then, is the   15
indignation that comes over all our minds when, being of this opinion for
just cause, we think that you not only compared him with Bade but ranked
him lower. I know that Bade is not altogether a stranger to the Muses;[3] but
whatever his qualities, his reputation among us to the present is such that
whenever there is any discussion of learned men among learned men, there   20
is no mention of Bade. His goal is merely profit, not eloquence, as you will
not deny.[4]

* * * * *

2021
1 Erasmus' letter replying to Berquin; see line 23 below and cf Epp 2046:337,
  2047:27–9, 2048:10, 2077:8–10.
2 Titius Aristo was one of the great lawyers of his day and legal adviser to the
  emperor Trajan. He was much admired by Pliny the Younger, who wrote to
  him seeking legal advice. See Pliny *Epistles* 1.22, 8.14.
3 *Adagia* II vi 18
4 On Bade (1462–1535), see Ep 183. Until 1515, when Erasmus established his
  connection with Froben, Bade was one of Erasmus' favoured printers. Bade
  had on occasion complained that unauthorized versions of Erasmus' works
  were causing him to lose money (see, for example, Epp 263 and 472). But the
  charge, advanced by both Erasmus and Brie, that Bade was more interested
  in profit than eloquence was motivated largely by Bade's lucrative position as
  a *libraire juré* of the University of Paris, in which capacity he published traditional medieval and scholastic texts in addition to works of humanist scholarship. Seeing in Erasmus' comments a contemptuous dismissal of his career as
  a scholar and publisher, Bade responded indirectly in 1529 in the preface to
  his edition of Cicero's *Philippics*. Flatly denying that money was his principal

I did not have need of a copy of the letter to so-and-so[5] to be better prepared to undertake your defence. For many reasons, however, I should not wish not to have read that letter. All of us know what I said openly right from the start, for many people complained bitterly to me following the publication of the *Ciceronianus* because of many things in it that did not please everyone, especially the wound (that is how they put it) that you dealt Budé. In order to win me to their side, these same persons put the worst possible interpretation on the judgment your Nosoponus made of me.[6] 'Hold on,' I said, 'You are not paying attention to what deserves your most careful attention, that Erasmus expresses one opinion when Nosoponus is the speaker and another when Bulephorus is speaking.[7] Moreover, in the whole work the author's one purpose was not to find fault with the eloquence of Cicero (that would be completely senseless) but to mock and execrate the almost superstitious affectation of Ciceronian diction – which we see that no ancient author ever attempted – that some advocate. If my judgment does not fail me, anyone who is prudent and patient enough to read the whole of the *Ciceronianus* attentively before pronouncing judgment on it after a cursory reading will find that Erasmus has treated this subject with great felicity and indeed in a Ciceronian manner, that is, with great skill and corresponding eloquence and invention. How perverse, how preposterous it is to condemn, not what you have failed to understand (that would be a lesser evil), but what you have never read and never intend to read!' For I remember, my excellent Erasmus, that many have been led astray by this same kind of recklessness to condemn various books of yours in the past.

* * * * *

motivation, he argued that classical learning, which he had done much to promote, needed to be guided by tradition and authority if Christianity were to be kept free of error. Hence the need to publish traditional texts, even if they did not meet the high standards of classical eloquence. See Mark Crane 'The Rule of Faith Over the Rules of Grammar: Josse Bade and the Development of a Conservative Theory of Textual Criticism' in *Rule Makers and Rule Breakers* ed Joseph Goering et al (Ottawa 2006), 43–56, especially 52–5.

5 Ie Berquin; cf line 2 above. Since Berquin was suspected of heresy (see Ep 2027:1–16), Brie probably thought it prudent to suppress his name.

6 Asked whether Brie can be counted as a Ciceronian, Nosoponus replies (CWE 28 422): 'He has not yet completed the course. He has achieved richness and clarity, but in quite a number of points he is unlike Cicero. Even so he justifies our having high hopes of him, if he maintains his present devotion and enthusiasm. In the mean time we are glad to cheer one who is running well.'

7 In contrast to Nosoponus, who is the voice of the Ciceronians, Bulephorus voices Erasmus' views.

I am neither able nor willing to rehearse here all the things I have
put forward to defend your cause. But as far as the outward expression
of my sentiments towards you is concerned, in refuting their arguments I   50
did not become more friendly towards you than I was previously but was
much more earnest in manifesting my friendship. For even if it did not seem
possible that my affection for you could be increased, when this dispute
arose among us concerning the publication of the *Ciceronianus* I defended
your honour not indeed with greater zeal but more fiercely, more openly,   55
more cogently. In the end I defended it so strongly that now I need some
defender who will plead my case with them. I am called to trial because I
am too favourably disposed towards Erasmus. An eloquent witness to this
is Thomas Lupset,[8] our mutual friend, who together with me is your firm
supporter and who is much distressed that your reputation has suffered   60
such great detriment here because of this affair.

But to return to their discussions and complaints, as I listened to them
our long-standing friendship certainly prompted me to take care not to give
anyone reason to suspect that I had taken offence at Nosoponus' judgment
of me. Thus this disturbance, or rather open animosity, forced me to take   65
greater care to prevent anyone from thinking that there had been any less-
ening of my affection for you. In that regard I confess myself to be of such
a character that I make my own judgments about myself and have no anxiety or ambition for external praise. For we are mindful how much greater
pleasure there is when the fruits of our talents and learning are stored away   70
in our conscience rather than in worldly renown.

Well, dearest Erasmus, as I have defended you before others, I now
make some accusations against you in your presence (my outspokenness
with everyone and my affection for you, which is unique and outstanding,
give me the right to take this liberty) – yes, you stand guilty on several   75
counts: in my view, you seem to have stooped too low, in quite an indiscreet manner, in making that comparison we are speaking about. I wish that
the damage had been repaired, even at the risk of my own reputation, or
that you had suppressed the name of Budé in the *Ciceronianus* altogether, or
had given your opinion of him somewhere else, or had matched him with   80
anyone else but Bade. That one comparison is so offensive to all of us that
it has alienated many well-disposed persons from you, since they consider
that to compare Budé with Bade is equivalent to comparing Achilles and

* * * * *

8 Cf Ep 2052:14–15. In 1528 Erasmus' friend and former student, Thomas Lupset
  (Ep 270:69n) was in Paris as tutor to Cardinal Wolsey's natural son Thomas
  Winter.

Thersites.[9] This is the unanimous opinion they have of Budé and Bade. Yet when I first mentioned this matter to Budé, he seemed to be completely in-   85
different. He is a man endowed with such wisdom and greatness of spirit that he refers everything that pertains to him to his conscience, not to vain-glory. He seeks his reward not in the words of this person or that but in scholarship itself. There are some, however, who tell me that he is some-what offended by all of this, but since I have not seen him for many days, I   90
cannot verify that.

Therefore, although I do not think that the feelings of the majority should be regarded as right judgment, I would nevertheless not deny that some consideration should be given to people's opinion, especially since I see that you great orators take such great pains that your speeches will find   95
favour with the crowd and desire that you receive applause, acclamation, and sometimes even flattery from the people rather than hissing and guf-faws. Similarly, I think you would do much for your reputation among us if you would take it upon yourself, either by changing the passage pertaining to Budé, or by adding an appendix to the work, or by addressing a letter   100
to someone which you will then publish, to prove to our French colleagues and indeed, I would greatly wish, to everyone, including myself and, if I am not mistaken, to Budé himself, who is the chief one concerned, that you are not envious of his glorious reputation.[10] Of this I am quite convinced (for you are equals, while envy is a sign of inferiority), that when you men-   105
tioned Budé and Bade in the same breath you did not wish to refer to Budé's learning and eloquence in a way that many have wrongly interpreted (for I would not accuse them of malice). It pertains to your own glory that your equal should appear as great as possible.

This seems to me to be the state of the whole case. I leave it to you   110
to decide whether it should be brought to court and pleaded or whether it should be withdrawn. I wished to write these things to you in a simple and friendly manner, because it was right by reason of our mutual affection that you should know not only my defence of your cause but also my advice in your cause. I thought that I must demonstrate sufficiently not only my   115
devotion to you but also my judgment of you, for I saw that I had to bear in mind not so much what an honourable person would approve in the present circumstances but what he would approve at any time.

* * * * *

9 Achilles, hero of Homer's *Iliad*, was the greatest of the Greek heroes in the Trojan war. Thersites, by contrast, was the ugliest man in Troy, and was killed by Achilles for jeering at him for his supposed love for the dead queen of the Amazons, Penthesilea.

10 Ep 2046 was Erasmus' response to this suggestion.

It is now up to you, excellent Erasmus, to write back to me with the
same simplicity and friendship, whether you prefer to follow my advice or   120
disagree with it. If I shall seem to you to be a false counsellor, please explain
the nature of my error. Although I am prepared to yield to your authority in
every matter and on every subject, in this case, in which feelings of affection
are less compelling with me than with you, I nevertheless think it more just
to be outdone by you in reason rather than in authority. But I am confident   125
that you will be in complete agreement with my opinion and will bring it
about that neither shall I regret having given you advice nor will you regret
having accepted it.

As far as concerns the edict[11] mentioned in your last letter, what else
can I say but that they have wished it to be stipulated in this edict that   130
your writings are meant for old people and not children, since they have
ordained that only children should be prohibited from reading your works?
But joking aside, although this is no laughing matter, I feel sorry for the
writers of our time, since I see that it is not enough for them to avoid danger
to their reputation, and sometimes their lives, by infusing sanity into their   135
writings, but that they must also find readers of sound mind everywhere.
They are clearly paying the penalty for other people's malignity or madness,
or rather both. The thought of this indignity, which returns again and again
to my mind, most learned Erasmus, makes me give up hope sometimes,
even though I try diligently to lift myself from the ground, and resolve   140
for the rest of my life to vow myself to Harpocrates and impose perpetual
silence upon myself.[12]

But more about this on another occasion. I am greatly disturbed by
your poor health,[13] especially because (I do not mean to flatter you, Erasmus) it is not one man but literary studies themselves and all the humanities   145
in one man that seem to undergo the greatest danger. Therefore I beg and
beseech you to take thought for my anxiety through frequent letters and
take diligent and attentive care of your health. This will be of profit to all
men of learning and a source of great joy to me.

But I shall end, lest I go much beyond the limits of a letter, which I   150
have already exceeded. But if you do not write me a return letter of equal

* * * * *

11 This was the formal condemnation of the *Colloquies* by the University of Paris
on 23 June 1528; see Ep 2037 introduction. Erasmus' 'last letter' is mentioned
in Epp 2046:342–3, 2048:13–14; it was perhaps contemporary with Ep 2009.
12 Harpocrates, the god of silence, was represented as holding one finger to his
mouth, indicating that the mysteries of religion and philosophy were not to
be revealed to ordinary people.
13 See Ep 1989 n4.

length, if your health permits you to do so, you may expect only brief notes from me in future.

From our gardens at Gentilly, 12 August 1528

2022 / To the Reader Basel, 13 August 1528

> This is the preface to the new, enlarged edition of the *Adagiorum opus* pub-
> lished by Froben at Basel in September 1528. The new edition also featured a
> special dedication (Ep 2023). For the preceding edition of 1526, see Ep 1659.
> For indications of the progress of the printing of this edition, see Epp 1986:20
> and 1991:76.

DESIDERIUS ERASMUS OF ROTTERDAM TO THE SCHOLARLY READER
I fear, friendly reader, that some may find me lacking in good faith and consistency, since we promised in the preceding edition that it would be the last,[1] and now we have augmented it with more new entries than ever before. Relying on this promise, certain publishers have printed the *Adagia*, 5 not without care, certainly, and not without good results, and, it is hoped, with some profit! We sincerely approve of the benefits that accrue to those who by their industry advance the cause of good letters, provided that the pursuit of gain does not exclude the honesty and respect owed to learning. Those who, to avoid expense, do without the services of a learned proof- 10 reader and offer us books of the ancient writers painfully adulterated, mutilated, mangled, and corrupted, are worthy in my opinion of graver punishment than those who profane and pillage holy places. You will wonder at this point what excuse I shall use to extricate myself from this situation. Shall I respond with Agesilaus:[2] 'If it is just, I promised; if it is unjust, I 15 merely spoke' and say that what is useless for learning is not just?[3] I am not so impudent as to say with the jurisconsults: 'No action arises from a simple promise.'[4] Or shall I clear myself with a proverb, 'Better the second

* * * * *

2022
1 See Ep 1659 n1.
2 King Agesilaus II of Sparta (400 to 359 BC) was renowned for his many military victories over the Persians and Sparta's Greek enemies and came to symbolize the Spartan virtues of simplicity, piety, and self-reliance.
3 This is the fourth of 79 apophthegms attributed to Agesilaus by Plutarch (*Moralia* 208D). Erasmus provides a fuller and clearer version of it in book 1 of his *Apophthegmata* (LB IV 94C): 'Of course, if indeed what you ask is just, I promised; but if not, then I spoke, but I did not promise.'
4 Ulpian *Digest* 124.42

time,'[5] claiming that the wise man should not think it debasing to change
his plans for the better when an occasion presents itself. I shall act simply: 20
I acknowledge my error, I beg to be excused from the charge of breach of
promise.

   When I promised that edition would be the last, I spoke truly, although
I did not speak the truth. I said what I felt in my heart and what I thought
would definitely be the case. Later, when Galen and several other authors   25
not available in print were published,[6] and there was hope that still others
would appear, I changed my mind, not for my own benefit – that is not
my standard of judgment – but for the common good of learned studies.
There is a great deal of difference between plucking adages from the very
gardens of the original authors, where they were born, and taking them   30
from collections, naked, sometimes even corrupted, so that often you cannot
understand the meaning or the way they are used. But if the authors are
published, would it be accounted foolish to enrich what is deficient, explain
what is obscure, correct what is corrupted? I for one do not think so.

   You will say, 'They could have been put into an appendix.' They could   35
have, and this would be more convenient for the scholarly reader; would
it were so for the printers! 'But there should be more consideration for
the world of study than for private gain, if the interests of both cannot be
equally satisfied.' When we learned that this work was being published in
Lyon,[7] we wanted to put off this edition until a later time, but preparations   40
at the Froben press had progressed to the point that publication could not
be deferred without a substantial loss. There is no reason for me to be envious of another man's profit; I am no potter in this respect.[8] There was no
more honest soul than Johann Froben, although once or twice he followed
the promptings of some swindlers.[9] Hieronymus Froben has succeeded this   45
great man. As he formerly relieved his father while he was alive of a great
part of his labours, so now he sustains on his shoulders the whole vast undertaking with such honesty, vigilance, and fervent passion for the study of
letters that not only do you not miss Johann Froben but you feel that the energy of the admirable old man has been rejuvenated, as it were, in his son.   50

            * * * * *

5 *Adagia* I iii 38
6 See Epp 1594 nn3–4, 1746:2–4.
7 By Gryphius in 1528, a reprint of the Froben edition of February 1526 (Ep
   1659). See Ferdinand Vander Haeghen *Bibliotheca Erasmiana: Bibliographie des
   oeuvres d'Érasme* 12 vols (Ghent 1897–1950) 4 109.
8 Ie not a jealous rival (*Adagia* I ii 25)
9 See Ep 1526:31–7.

If someone should now harass me with the celebrated saying 'It is shameful for the wise man to say "I hadn't thought of it,"'[10] I should defend myself in as many words: 'I am not one of that class of heroes.'[11]

If I have succeeded in appeasing the printers, who for that matter should be less irate, since he who enriches them is already preparing his journey hence,[12] then I think scholars should no more be angry with me than polite guests with a host who after telling his guests, 'Enjoy what you have before you and don't expect anything further,' then sets a pheasant or a cake before them, especially since no one is obliged to eat if he does not want to. And in my opinion it is fitting that the guest at my table should be somewhat more fair-minded than the one invited to that other one, because the trickery employed there is suited to luxury, but mine to learning. I do not wish to call to my defence the peculiar character of the subject, which demands to be nourished and to increase with daily reading. If the most approved writers took this liberty in any subject whatever, in those days when manuscripts copied by hand could only be acquired at great expense, why shall I not take this same liberty myself in the *Adagia* in these times when books are bought at less cost perhaps than is expedient for the study of letters. It was not the last edition to be published, as I said it would be. Perhaps this, which I dare not say will be the last, will be the last.[13] I have so deceived others that now I do not believe myself.

Farewell.

At Basel, 13 August 1528

2023 / To Charles Blount   Basel, 13 August 1528

This is a new preface, printed at the end of the introductory sheets to the new edition of the *Adagia* (Ep 2022). As Allen observes, it was probably added as an afterthought, to keep the page from being blank.

* * * * *

10 Cicero *De officiis* 1.23.81
11 *Adagia* II v 48 CWE 33 263: 'I'm not one of that class of heroes, not one of those people, that is, who are more given to doing an injury than a service. Taken from the spirits who, once roused, often bring destruction and rarely are of any help. Hence this adage was in use among those who were promising to do good, not harm.'
12 An apparent allusion to the fierce attacks of the stone that had plagued Erasmus since Easter. See Ep 1989 n4.
13 It was not to be the last; see Ep 2049:23–5, where Erasmus is already requesting 'annotations for the next edition,' which would be published in 1533 (Ep 2726).

Charles Blount, fifth Baron Mountjoy (1516–44), was the son and heir of Erasmus' friend and patron, William Blount, the fourth baron (Ep 79). Erasmus, who took an interest in the boy's education, dedicated to him not only this and later editions of the *Adagia* (See Allen Epp 2215:212–4, 2295:24–7, 2726, 2830, 3092) but also his edition of Livy in 1531 (Ep 2435). Like his father, whom he succeeded in 1534, Charles was closely associated with the English court and was a patron of humanist scholars.

DESIDERIUS OF ROTTERDAM TO THE ILLUSTRIOUS YOUNG BOY
CHARLES MOUNTJOY, GREETING

If you really wish to be the true son of your most distinguished father, to be the true heir of his possessions, my dear Charles, you must take care that you do not fall away from your father's excellent qualities and that you pre- 5
pare yourself to be a successor of your father more in virtue than in possessions. Although he is illustrious through the ancient lineage of his ancestors and is blessed with an abundance of riches proper to the magnificence of his ancestry, nevertheless, if you were to esteem his true worth, he is far more illustrious and opulent because of the adornments of literature and 10
virtues than because of pedigree or possessions. With regard to other possessions, neither custom nor law allows children to succeed their parents until they have departed this life, but as for those that are one's chief blessings, it is right that children should claim them as their inheritance from their most tender years. This the loving affection of your father desires with 15
fervent prayers, and splendid foundations have been laid for that purpose, as you have been initiated into the rudiments of both literatures,[1] at least as much as befits your age. And on every side you have incentives and spurs that never become dull to continue in your progress: first of all, your father himself, then the noble young girl of almost your same age, Princess 20
Mary,[2] born of a learned king and a queen no less pious than learned, who can already write in good Latin letters that show forth innate good qualities worthy of her race.[3] Then there are the many daughters of the family of More,[4] like a chorus of Muses, so that I do not think it is necessary for me to spur on one already running on his own initiative. 25

* * * * *

2023
1 Ie both Latin and Greek
2 The future queen, born (like Charles) in 1516
3 On the education of princess Mary, see Ep 1727 n4.
4 See Epp 999:187–8 with n28, 1402:37–9.

I meant only to suggest to you that since I dedicated the *Adages* to your father long ago,[5] you too should associate yourself in the sharing of this possession. This will not detract any praise from your father, it will add no little lustre to the work, and will procure for you, unless I am deluding myself, very tangible benefits. It is nothing new that the same work be dedicated to several persons; and if it were new, I would answer that a father and a son so like his father should be thought of as one person rather than two. For what is a son but the father who finds youth again in another self? And perhaps your father does not have time in his duties at court to attend to such concerns and now like a spent runner hands on the torch to you.

Therefore read this book, my dear Charles, dedicated to your father, and in your reading think that Erasmus, once your father's teacher, is speaking to you. May the Lord Jesus protect you and make you prosperous throughout your life, illustrious child.

Given at Basel, 15 August 1528

2024 / From Erasmus Schets   Antwerp, 14 August 1528

This is Schets's response to Ep 2015. The letter was first published by Allen, using the autograph in the University Library at Basel (Scheti epistolae 17).

Cordial greetings. I wrote to your kind self in another letter what the current circumstances required.[1] I have nothing else to write save that another letter of yours arrived through a messenger from Basel at the same time as your servant Quirinus arrived from Holland.[2] Either because of the pleasantness of being in his native land or perhaps because of business affairs he was detained there until now and was not able to return here sooner. He will give you a report of any news that he has collected here and there.

After sealing my other letter, I received another half of your pension in the sum of sixty-five florins from Jan de Hondt, which I added to your assets as detailed in my previous letter. I now have in total seven hundred thirty-three florins and three stuivers.[3] I shall retain this sum that has accumulated

* * * * *

5 Ep 126

2024
1 Ep 2014
2 Probably the letter mentioned in Ep 2014:66.
3 The total of 733 florins and 3 stuivers is expressed in the Flemish Hapsburg 'florin' money-of-account (in which 6 florins = 1 pound groot), so that this sum

to you and do with it as you direct me. You need not be worried about Jan
de Hondt; he will continue to contribute what he owes you. I instructed him
to pay the pension every year to a friend of mine in Courtrai so that he will
not hesitate, giving the excuse that he does not know to whom he should   15
pay the money.

You will not suffer any loss in receiving the twenty gold florins from
Frans van der Dilft. I have received them in gold and they are worth twenty-
seven of our florins. You will receive them either at the current rate of exchange or in gold, as they were received.[4]   20

Concerning crowns or any other species of money in which they pay
you in England, I do not know what loss you may incur. The exchange rate
determines the value of the money, worth more there and less here. As you
say, however, you may be able to make some profit on their money by having it exported. But there is the obstacle of the interdict, which specifies that   25
no money can be exported without the risk of confiscation, not to mention
that the money is exposed to the hazards of the sea and thieves en route.
Therefore it will be safer to resort to exchange transactions for this money.[5]

* * * * *

was worth £122 3s 10d (ie 4d plus 6d for the 3 stuivers). To earn such a sum,
an Antwerp master mason would have had to work for 2,932 days (almost 14
years). See also Ep 2014:44–51.

4 The 20 florins from Frans van der Dilft were undoubtedly Rhenish or Imperial
gold florins, currently worth about 59d groot Flemish, compared to a value of
42d groot for the Flemish Hapsburg Carolus gold florin. Thus (by the ratio of
59:42), 20 Rhenish florins would have been worth 28 Carolus florins – but we
would also expect a deduction of one florin for the money changer's fee. These
20 Rhenish gold florins would also have been worth 29.5 florins, in the previously mentioned Flemish Hapsburg money-of-account, in which 6 florins = one
pound groot; and thus 29.5 florins = £4 18s 4d groot Flemish. Cf Ep 1934 n6.

5 The 'crowns' are the rose crowns, which, as imitations of the French crowns
(*écus à la couronne au soleil*), were introduced into England with Henry VIII's
debasements of August and November 1526: the first (August) was the single-
rose crown worth 4s 6d or 54d sterling (probably containing 3.208 grams fine
gold); and the second (November) was the heavier double-rose crown worth
5s 0d or 60d sterling (containing 3.404 grams fine gold). For their introduction,
and the debate about their composition, see the Appendix 440–50 with Tables
2 and 3, 464–76 below; and see also Ep 2027 n9. Note that from January 1364,
England's Parliament had forbidden the export of any English coin, as well as
all forms of gold and silver bullion, except by a royal licence; see Statute 36 Edward III, stat 1 c 2 in Great Britain, Record Commission *The Statutes of the Realm*
ed T.E. Tomlins, J. Raithby et al, 6 vols (London 1810–22) I 383. In May 1663,
Parliament repealed its provisions concerning bullion exports; see Statute 15
Charles II c 7 in *Statutes of the Realm* v 451 sec 9. But the prohibition against

There are no new developments of which I can write optimistically, since everything here is in a state of great unrest and seething with the tu- 30 mult of war. Italy, not having been sufficiently devastated by the sword, is now ravaged by famine and a fearsome epidemic. They say that the French army besieging Naples has been almost annihilated by this pestilence.[6] I know not how to express it, but we see the emperor's interests being protected and defended more by divine power than by arms. We are enjoying 35 a truce with the French here, but we are at war with Gelderland, and it is going quite well up to now.[7]

The emperor and the French king exchange hateful words both in person and by letter. The emperor reviles the French king for his breach of an oath and the French king in turn openly vilifies the emperor, accusing him of 40 being a liar. The emperor, trusting in the truth and deeming nothing so odious as a lie, has challenged the king of France to single combat,[8] with the firm

* * * * *

the export of any English coins was maintained until Peel's Act of April 1819 (Statute 59 George III c 23). In this respect, England was a monetary anomaly. While virtually all later medieval and early modern states and principalities banned the export of bullion (ie precious metals to be delivered to the domestic mint), most such countries, unlike England, freely permitted the export and import of all legal-tender coins. Such bullionist export prohibitions – along with the attendant risks of piracy and losses at sea – were the fundamental reason why, from the later thirteenth century, European merchants engaged in bill-of-exchange transactions instead of transporting precious metals abroad. See Munro 'Bullionism and the Bill of Exchange' (Ep 1934 n85); John Munro 'Billon – Billoen – Billio: From Bullion to Base Coinage' *Revue belge de philologie et d'histoire / Belgisch tijdschrift voor filologie en geschiedenis* 52 (1974) 293–305; and Albert Feavearyear *The Pound Sterling: A History of English Money* 2nd rev ed by E. Victor Morgan (Oxford 1963) 28–36, 95, 220–1. Almost three decades earlier, on 27 January 1500, Erasmus had experienced a costly and humiliating experience of this nature when, on his departure from England (Dover) for the continent, English customs officials had confiscated almost all his money, in the form of English coins, to the value of twenty pounds sterling. See Ep 119 to Jacob Batt (Paris, February 1500), especially 9n. As the note rightly states, 'Erasmus never forgot the loss of the money on which he had counted to continue his studies.' But Cf Ep 279:16–21 to William Gonnell (Cambridge, November 1513), in which Erasmus almost makes light of this incident, in stating that 'I had lost all I had in the world at once, but I was so undismayed that I went back to my books all the keener and fuller of energy; and presently, a very few days after this, out came my book of proverbs.'

6 Pastor 10 23–5
7 See Ep 1998 n7.
8 On 18 March 1528, the emperor sent a message to Francis I challenging him to a duel. Ten days later Francis accepted the challenge. But when Charles sent a herald to France to conclude arrangements for the duel, Francis refused to

hope that through the death of one of them all these disasters may come to an
end. The latter is required to choose the weapon, the other the place of combat. This is something almost unheard of and truly unworthy of such princes.   45
I do not see how, with such passions ignited, this madness can cease, unless
someone come from heaven, sent by the God of peace, who in his mercy will
deign to soften the hearts of these princes with feelings of charity and join
them together into a peace and concord worthy of the embrace of Christ.

Farewell from Antwerp, 14 August 1528   50
Your good friend Erasmus Schets
To the incomparable and learned Erasmus of Rotterdam, unsurpassed
interpreter of the sacred page

2025 / From Adrianus Cornelii Barlandus   Louvain, 14 August [1528]

An old friend of Erasmus and one of his most enthusiastic supporters in Louvain, Barlandus (Epp 492, 1584) was now professor of eloquence at the university (Ep 1694).

The autograph is in the Rehdiger Collection of the University Library at
Wrocław (MS Rehd 254.17). Allen notes that it was first published in 1923
as entry B 290 in the *Bibliotheca Belgica: Bibliographie générale des Pays-Bas* 2nd
series, ed Ferdinand van der Haeghen (Ghent/The Hague 1891–1924). In the
new integrated edition of both series in 7 volumes prepared by Marie-Thérèse
Lenger (Brussels 1964–75; repr Brussels 1979) entry B 290 is found in vol 1
page 176. Allen assigned the year-date because the letter falls between the *Ciceronianus* (Ep 1948) and the edition of Augustine (Ep 2157), and is clearly
contemporary with Ep 2026.

The arrival of your servant, Nicholas,[1] brought me great joy, most learned
sir, for he delivered a letter from you and announced that you were in excellent health.[2] I swear on my life that this is more joyous news than if I had

* * * * *

allow him to carry out his mission. The Council of Castile declared that by
refusing the emperor's challenge the French king had once again demonstrated
that he was no gentleman.

2025
1 Kan; see Epp 1999 n9, 2026:1. He was expected to return to Basel shortly; see
  Epp 2039:5–6, 2063:35–8.
2 The letter is not extant. It was probably written c 13 June and carried by
  Kan with Ep 1999 on his journey to the Netherlands. But cf Ep 1999 n9 on
  the confusion over the identity of the carrier of that letter. On the temporary
  improvement in Erasmus' health, see Ep 1998:36–7.

received the announcement of the accession of a huge inheritance. I am not
unaware how much the higher studies that we profess will gain in distinc-   5
tion the longer you live, although nothing is long or lasting that has an end.

I read your *Ciceronianus*, in which as you wing your way over the
world you reach even Zeeland. You include me there not among men of
learning, which is the most I could expect, but among men of eloquence.[3] I
could hardly acknowledge such an honour, but nonetheless I was delighted   10
by this judgment coming from such a great man.

I am sending with Nicolas[4] two orations of Cicero with commentary
for the use of those who are studying rhetoric here with me.[5] I am now
interpreting the *Philippic* in defence of Sulpicius.[6] I would like to have your
interpretation of some orations of Cicero in which you would also analyse   15
the rules of rhetoric. Such a work of yours, believe me, would encourage
the reading of Cicero in all schools where now only his letters are read,[7] in
which young students can learn eloquence of speech, but not the abundant
and opulent style of oratory. If I could succeed in obtaining this favour from
you, at least in the speech in behalf of Pompey,[8] which is usually the first one 20
to be read, I shall consider that you would have rendered me the greatest
courtesy and that I would be forever in your debt. Not many years ago
you wrote a commentary on Cicero's *De officiis*.[9] I beg that we may have
something of Erasmus on the speeches of the prince of eloquence.

Concerning matters here, I have nothing worthy of a letter, since I do   25
not approve in any way of what happens here from day to day nor of the
initiatives that are taken.[10] All scholars here are eagerly awaiting your critical and emended edition of Augustine.[11] You will live on with that forever, as you deserve, since you have rescued his beautiful writings from the
damage wrought by ignorance. Farewell, most kind master and teacher.   30

* * * * *

3 See CWE 28 424.
4 See line 1 above.
5 Seventeenth-century bibliographers attributed to Barland commentaries on *In
   Catilinam* 1 and *Philippics* 9, but no printed editions are known. See Etienne Dax-
   helet *Adrien Barlandus, humaniste belge, 1486–1538* (Louvain 1938) 193 with n3.
6 *Philippics* 9
7 Between 1504 and 1517 there were six editions of *Quaedam epistolae* of Cicero
   published at Deventer and one at Antwerp, all evidently intended for use in
   schools. See Wouter Nijhoff and Maria Elizabeth Kronenberg *Nederlandsche
   Bibliographie van 1500 tot 1540* 3 vols (The Hague 1940) II nos 2647–52.
8 *Pro lege Manilia* or *De imperio Gnaei Pompeii*
9 See Epp 152, 1013.
10 Perhaps a reference to the complaints about the Collegium Trilingue reported
   in Ep 1899:87–96
11 Published in 1529; see Ep 2157.

Louvain, on the vigil of the Assumption
Yours ever, Adrianus Barlandus
To the pre-eminent theologian Master Erasmus of Rotterdam

2026 / From Conradus Goclenius   Louvain, 16 August [1528]

First published by Allen, the autograph is in the University Library at Basel
(Goclenii epistolae 13). Allen assigned the year-date on the basis of the movements of Dilft (lines 2–3).

On Goclenius, see Ep 1994A.

Cordial greetings. I have nothing to write for Kan to bring to you.[1] In fact,
since the departure and the return of the messenger whom Frans van der
Dilft sent here,[2] nothing worthy of mention has happened. I know nothing
of Vives' plans except what I learn from your letters. He is too disdainful to
communicate anything to us, and, following your advice, I have no relations   5
with him except for a polite association.[3] There are no manuscripts of Seneca
here,[4] to my knowledge, but I shall investigate more diligently and shall
write to Lips as soon as a messenger is available to go to that forsaken place
in which he lives.[5] Frans van der Dilft hopes that through your letter of
recommendation he will find welcome in Spain.[6] He is now busily preparing   10

* * * * *

2026
1 See Epp 1999 n9, 2025 n1.
2 The letter carried by the messenger in question had reached Basel by 30 July;
  see Ep 2015:1. On Dilft see Ep 1942 n1 and cf lines 9–10 below, Ep 2063:52–5.
3 Allen read this passage as evidence that Vives' coolness towards Erasmus at
  this time (see Ep 2040 introduction) had been extended to Erasmus' friends
  as well. But it can just as well be read as evidence that Vives was preoccupied
  with his own work and that Erasmus had advised his friends to leave him
  alone. In the absence of further information about the situation and what Erasmus actually said, one cannot know for sure. Certain it is, however, that communication between Erasmus and Vives had remained perfectly civil, with no
  evidence of 'disdain' on either side.
4 Erasmus was working on the new edition of Seneca that would be published
  in March 1529 (Ep 2091).
5 Maarten Lips, the distinguished patristic scholar who had helped Erasmus
  with the edition of Augustine (Ep 1547), had left Louvain in 1525 and taken
  up residence in the Augustinian nunnery of Croix-à-Lens-Saint-Rémy, Liège;
  see Ep 2045 introduction.
6 Erasmus' letter of recommendation was Ep 2013. For more on Dilft's journey
  to Spain in search of employment, see Epp 1663 introduction, 2063:52–7, and
  Allen Ep 2109:1–24.

himself for the journey. If there is any other news I shall write at the time
of the next fair.

At Louvain, 16 August.

Yours, Conradus Goclenius

To the prince of all learning, Master Erasmus of Rotterdam   15

2027 / From Gervasius Wain   Paris, 16 August 1528

The autograph of this letter, first published as Ep 89 in Förstemann/Günther,
was in the Burscher Collection at Leipzig (Ep 1254 introduction).

A doctor of theology at Paris, Gervasius Wain of Memmingen (Ep 1884)
was an active member of the Collège de Sorbonne and of the English-German
nation. He also had close connections to the court of Francis I, whom he would
serve on diplomatic missions in the early 1530s. He visited Erasmus in the
spring of 1527 (Ep 1827:15–16) and was one of his most reliably informative
contacts in Paris.

Berquin is in very poor repute with the Parlement of Paris.[1] In recent
days the supreme pontiff, *motu proprio* (as the bull puts it),[2] has issued a

* * * * *

2027
1 Louis de Berquin (Ep 925:17n) was a gifted young humanist whose admiration for Luther and Erasmus would cost him his life. Tried in 1523 for possessing condemned works of Luther and Melanchthon, Berquin had escaped
   punishment by means of a solemn abjuration of all Lutheran heresy. He then
   got into trouble because of his translations into French of *Querela pacis*, *Encomium matrimonii*, and other works of Erasmus that the faculty deemed to
   be tainted with heresy. In February–March 1526, Berquin was tried again on
   these charges and others by a special, papally appointed tribunal of judges
   delegate (cf Ep 2038 n14) who, supported by the Parlement and guided by the
   findings of the faculty of theology, declared that he was a relapsed heretic and
   thus liable to the death penalty. Only the direct intervention of the king prevented the imposition and execution of the sentence. Released from prison in
   November 1526, Berquin, still under the protection of the king and his sister,
   Margaret of Angoulême, decided to appeal the sentence of the judges, which
   had not been invalidated by his release. This led to his fatal third trial (see
   n5 below). The history of Berquin's troubles up to this point can be traced
   in greater detail in Epp 1579:200–19 with nn44–5, 1599 introduction and n1,
   1692, 1875:96–114. Further developments in 1528 are reflected in Epp 2048,
   2066, 2077. For a new account of Berquin's three trials that corrects a number
   of errors in the standard works on the subject, see Farge 'Berquin.'
2 *Motu proprio* (of his own accord) is the generic name for certain rescripts (see
   following note) issued by the pope for reasons he himself deems sufficient,

rescript[3] in which he takes away the power of judging Berquin from the judges delegate[4] and gives and confirms the power he had bestowed two years ago to the judges who found Berquin guilty of heresy, on such terms that there will be no right of appeal.[5] You can imagine, I am sure, to what peril Berquin is now exposed. If he had listened to your advice,[6] this whole predicament and no little expense would have been avoided, and he would have protected his honour. I am inclined to think that under the name of Berquin the faculty of theology has evil designs against you. They think that the two of you are in complete agreement,[7] although I have removed that suspicion from many persons. Believe me, through Berquin's imprudence in spreading stories about you he has greatly increased hostility towards you.

* * * * *

without taking the advice of the cardinals or others. Usually in the form of decrees, *motu proprio* rescripts are not sealed or countersigned as a bull would be. Wain's use of the word 'bull' here is thus, strictly speaking, inaccurate.

3 Papal rescripts are the written response of the pope to the queries or petitions of individuals. Rescripts dealing with the administration of justice (eg the appointment of judges or the interpretation of law) were common.

4 'Judge delegate' is the canonical term for a judge appointed by the pope to deal with a case locally.

5 King Francis, acting in concert with the pope, had assigned jurisdiction in the Berquin case to a new commission of judges delegate composed entirely of jurists, including Guillaume Budé. The indignant protests of the Paris theologians moved Pope Clement VII to issue a rescript revoking the authority of the new commission and transferring the case back to the panel of judges delegate that had found Berquin guilty in 1526. But, as Berquin himself subsequently reported to Erasmus, this revocation remained without effect (Ep 2066:31–2). The reason was that the papal legate, who bore the brunt of the king's fury at this interference with royal prerogative, decided, on the advice of the royal chancellor Duprat, not to publish the papal revocation. Consequently, the recently appointed panel of judges delegate remained in charge of the case and, in the end, condemned Berquin to death. See Farge 'Berquin' 68–70.

6 Ie to refrain from stirring up trouble; see Epp 1599:13–14, 2077:26.

7 The theologians' campaign against Berquin overlapped with its investigation of the works of Erasmus. In May 1525, the faculty condemned French translations of four works of Erasmus (*Encomium matrimonii, Inquisitio de fide, Querela pacis*, and selections from the *Paraphrases* on Matthew and Luke) that were nonetheless published in the following October. Already in May, Béda (Ep 1943 n6) informed Erasmus that Berquin was suspected of being the translator (Ep 1579:200–11). In June, Erasmus replied that the books had been translated without his knowledge and that material might have been added that was not attributable to him (Ep 1581:835–42). In August he wrote to Berquin, urging him not to publish French translations of his works on controversial topics (Ep 1599).

Every single religious order here, and even the women, denounce Berquin
as an enemy of God and of the church. You know how the common crowd   15
vents its fury upon those suspected of heresy.

His reverend Lordship, the cardinal of Lorraine, has taken care that
what he promised be provided.[8] You may be certain that the Cardinal's
treasurer, will send you the sum of two hundred écus.[9] Toussaint Hossey,
the cardinal's secretary,[10] played no small part in this. He has asked to be   20
remembered to you in my letter. In your kindness would you please send
him a little letter, making mention of me, if this is not to impose too much
upon your friendship.

You have stirred up an amazing commotion here by writing that Bade
comes closer to Cicero's style than Budé.[11] Budé has his followers here, and   25
they are tearing you to shreds in epigrams.[12] But they are not worthy of
Caesar's anger.[13] I have heard that Lascaris, that old Greek, stung you with
a pungent epigram.[14]

* * * * *

8 Ep 2009 had been a gentle reminder to Cardinal Jean de Guise-Lorraine that
   a promised gift had not yet arrived.
9 The écu had been France's principal and internationally renowned gold coin
   from its first issue by Charles v in 1385, as the *écu à la couronne*. Its successor,
   the *écu au soleil*, first struck by Louis xi in 1475, continued to be struck, in
   various forms, until 1640. See CWE 1 315; CWE 12 650 Table 3D and Appendix
   Table 3, 476 below; and Ep 2024 n5. In 1528 its official exchange value was £2
   tournois, so that this sum was worth £400 tournois = £63 13s 4d groot Flemish
   = £46 13s 4d sterling. Erasmus had earlier assumed that the gift would be in
   plate rather than in money; see Ep 2009:17–23.
10 Toussaint Hossey of Valenciennes (d 1563) had studied at Louvain (MA 1514),
   where he reportedly shared accommodation and meals with Erasmus for a
   time and formed a friendship with Juan Luis Vives as well. He remained the
   cardinal's secretary until 1543, when he was made bishop of Toul.
11 See Ep 2021.
12 See Epp 2038, 2040, 2046, 2047, 2048, 2077.
13 The phrase *Caesaris ira* or *principis ira* occurs frequently in Ovid's *Epistulae ex
   Ponto* and the *Tristia*, which were written from Tomis on the Black Sea, whither
   he had been banished by Caesar Augustus.
14 Born in Constantinople, Janus Lascaris (Ep 269:55n) became a noted scholar
   and diplomat in Italy and France and did much for the diffusion of Greek
   texts in the West. In 1508–9, while French ambassador to Venice, he helped
   Erasmus with the Aldine *Adagia* (*Adagia* ii i 1). Erasmus, who admired him as
   one of the few Greek exiles who had real skill in Latin (Ep 1347:259), seems
   to have tried to win him for the Greek chair at the Collegium Trilingue (Ep
   836). Having cultivated good relations with Lascaris (Epp 1736:43–4, 1794:7–
   10), and having spoken well of him in the *Ciceronianus* (CWE 28 416), Erasmus
   was bitter about the criticism referred to here; see Epp 2038, 2040, 2048, 2077.

I wrote this before supper. Towards the end of supper they brought me Lascaris' epigrams. I include them herewith so that your pen may answer our stupid Gauls and Gaulasters. Budé has a book in press with Ascensius entitled, as I understand, *On the Properties of Greek and Latin Style.*[15] Rumour has it that you are mentioned in the book.[16] I was not able to procure a copy of the censures of the faculty against your books.[17] They are in the possession of one man, Berthélemy, a theologian of the Sorbonne.[18] There are those who think that the mountains are in labour.[19] Take my word for it, they will not easily publish what they think should be published.[20] Farewell, my excellent friend.

Paris, 16 August 1528

Your Gervasius. In haste

To the great Erasmus of Rotterdam, doctor of Sacred Scripture. At Basel

2028 / To Willibald Pirckheimer   Basel, 25 August 1528

This letter (= Ep 1190 in wpb) is in sequence with Ep 1997. It was first published in the *Pirckheimeri Opera.*

Cordial greetings. I think you received the letter in which I asked that you send me the manuscript of the epistles of Basil and Nazianzen.[1] I am eager to have it for very good reason and it will be at no harm to you. But I await word from you at the coming fair.[2]

Ferdinand wrote me a most flattering letter inviting me to Vienna at a salary of four-hundred florins, on the condition that I take up residence

* * * * *

15 Budé was in fact working on a philological treatise on Greek words, not one on both languages (see Ep 1794 n2). It was published as *Commentarii linguae graecae* by Josse Bade (Ascensius) in 1529.

16 Cf Ep 1794:16–24.

17 See Ep 2037 introduction.

18 Jacques Berthélemy (d 1543) had sat on committees that examined works of Luther and Erasmus as well as the French translations of Erasmus by Berquin. Together he and Béda secured the censure of Erasmus' *Colloquies* in June 1528 (see Ep 2037 introduction).

19 *Adagia* I ix 14: *Parturiunt montes, nascetur ridiculus mus* 'The mountains labour, forth will creep a mouse.'

20 The censures were in fact not published until 1531; see Ep 2033 n15.

2028

1 Ep 1997

2 Ie at the autumn book fair in Frankfurt

there.[3] But I have no intention of moving to another world.[4] If you assure me that you are in good health it will give me the greatest pleasure. Farewell, my distinguished friend.

Basel, 25 August 1528

Your Erasmus of Rotterdam, writing extempore

To the illustrious Willibald, councillor of his imperial Majesty

2029 / To Christoph von Stadion   Basel, 28 August 1528

First published in the *Opus epistolarum*, this is Erasmus' reply to a letter, now lost, from Christoph von Stadion, bishop of Augsburg.

Born not far from Ulm to parents of knightly status, Christoph von Stadion (1478–1543) took his BA and MA at Tübingen (1491, 1494) before studying theology at Freiburg (1494–7) and law at Bologna and Ferrara (1497–1506). In 1506, having completed his doctorate in law at Ferrara, he became a canon of the cathedral at Augsburg. By 1512 he had become official to the bishop and in April 1517 he was elected bishop. As a churchman, he was an advocate of reform who, while loyal to the Catholic church, recommended moderate treatment of the Lutheran reformers. At the Diet of Augsburg in 1530, for example, he took an active part in the ultimately futile efforts to effect a rapprochement between the religious parties. He had, moreover, an interest in learning that was reflected in the dedication to him of works by (among others) Johann Maier of Eck, Johannes Cochlaeus, and Vincentius Opsopoeus (see Allen's introduction).

Given his views on reform and his esteem for scholarship, it was only natural that Stadion should be attracted to Erasmus. It was he who initiated contact between them with the letter to which this letter is Erasmus' reply. Their correspondence, from which eleven letters in addition to this are still extant (Epp 2064, 2070, 2332, 2359, 2362, 2480, 2592, 2787, 2856, 3036, 3073), lasted until Erasmus' death. Early in 1530, Stadion travelled to Freiburg specifically to meet Erasmus and to present him with valuable gifts. While Stadion found in Erasmus inspiration and support for his moderate and conciliatory views, Erasmus saw in Stadion one of the few bishops who were genuine supporters of learning and of reform. Erasmus dedicated to him the Froben edition of St John Chrysostom in 1530 (Ep 2359) and of the *Ecclesiastes* in 1535 (Ep 3036).

Faithful to the end to his Erasmian irenicism and enthusiasm for Catholic reform, Stadion was nonetheless unable to stem the progress of Lutheranism

* * * * *

3 See Ep 2000:16–21 with n3.
4 In Ep 2005 Erasmus politely declined the invitation.

Christoph von Stadion, bishop of Augsburg
Hoher Dom zu Augsburg
Bistum Augsburg

in his own diocese, particularly in the city of Augsburg. In 1537 he was compelled to remove his chapter from Augsburg to the town of Dillingen. He died in 1543 while attending the imperial diet in Nürnberg.

ERASMUS OF ROTTERDAM TO CHRISTOPH VON STADION, GREETING

Since I could not do so in your presence, I kissed your sacred hand in the letter written by your fingers,[1] distinguished Bishop. But with much greater reverence I kissed the spirit of piety, sincerity, and purity that your letter, brief though it is, emanates. This was more vividly portrayed to me as in a 5 painting and presented to the eyes of the mind in the words of Augustinus Marius.[2] It gives me great joy that he is both known to you and esteemed by your Reverence. He is much appreciated by all good men for his Christian learning and the remarkable kindness and candour of his character, but there is no clearer evidence of his piety than that he inspires the hatred of 10 the worst elements of mankind. He readily convinced me of the paternal affection and profound charity that your Reverence bears towards me, and I received these words with great enthusiasm. But this joy was tempered to a great degree by a mixture of sorrow and shame when I compare your high opinion of me and the favour you have shown me with my own merits. 15 And yet I find some consolation for my faintheartedness in the judgment of such an upright and learned prelate, flattering myself with the thought that a man of such fine discretion cannot be entirely deluded and that one so honest and upright does not deceive.

This turmoil in the church torments my spirit more than one could 20 imagine. It is not that my conscience accuses me but that I am grieved by this public calamity that has befallen the Christian religion, for I was the first and almost the only one to resist this budding evil. I was a truer prophet than I would wish when I said that this play that began with applause in every corner of the world would come to this end. And we see verified 25 before our very eyes what usually happens in dangerous maladies, partly through the ignorance of doctors and partly through the intractability of patients, namely that the disease has reached the stage where it is no longer able to be cured. And in the meantime the monarchs of the world contend endlessly with one another and gratify their own best interests. The monks 30 for the most part pursue their own interests as well, not those of Jesus Christ.

* * * * *

2029
1 Not extant
2 A native of Ulm who had been suffragan bishop of Basel since 1527. One letter to him from Erasmus (Ep 2321) survives.

Their aim is not that Christ may reign in the hearts of men but that they may safeguard their own supremacy. They place their greatest hope of victory in stirring up tumults among the people and in barefaced calumny, in which some of them are past masters. Some theologians through hatred of Luther condemn even those things that were said with pious intent, which were not invented by me but handed down by Christ and the apostles. Thus it comes about that through their insensible audacity many remain attached to the faction who would otherwise have withdrawn, and many join who would not have joined. What stone have they left unturned and what do they not do in order to push me finally into the Lutheran camp now that I am worn out by their abusive treatment? And yet the course of events tells us clearly that this tempest has been sent upon us by God, offended by our wrongdoing, as he once sent down frogs, locusts, dogflies, and other plagues upon the Egyptians. Nevertheless, no one, in acknowledgment of his own misdeeds, calls upon God's mercy. Everyone deludes himself and casts guilt upon his neighbour. If we seek after human causes, nothing is easier than to indicate through whom this evil took rise and through whom it has increased in fury.

Lately I hear that many are convinced that this whole tempest in the church has come about through my writings. The chief author of this unfounded rumour was Girolamo Aleandro, a man, to say nothing more, who has no scrupulous regard for the truth. Alberto, prince of Carpi, more Aleandro's close ally than a partisan of his views, is of the same opinion.[3] Meanwhile no one, Lutheran or Antilutheran, has appeared who could clearly demonstrate even one unapproved doctrine in my writings, although so many cohorts have risen up with this one goal in mind. All they can adduce are affinities, similarities, scandals, suspicions, and sometimes superb lies. It is quite often the case that they have not read what they are criticizing or, if they did read it, do not understand it. As if anything at all could be written with such circumspection that it could not be converted to the uses of calumny by such methods if a prejudiced interpreter were to put his mind to it, or as if it were fair that I should be declared a heretic because they have not learned Greek and Latin.

That what I say is not without foundation you in your wisdom could ascertain in my apologies. But to give you something to laugh about, I shall add something that recently happened in Spain. In Madrid there is a physician by the name of Suárez, very learned in both languages, who supports

* * * * *

3 On Aleandro and Pio see Epp 1987, 2042:18–21, 2066:63–70, 2077:54–62, 2080.

my cause.[4] The Dominicans instigated one of their flock to approach this man for the purpose of deterring him from reading my volumes. Since he got nowhere, as a last resort he declared that my books were not worthy of being read by pious men because they cast obscene slurs upon the prelates of the church. To prove this he had my little book on Christian matrimony brought forth,[5] in which he said I called bishops sodomites and denounced them for having four or five concubines. The book was brought in, and he pointed out the passage, which reads: 'Someone who has unwisely married a woman who is not a virgin is said to have shared his body with her, whereas someone who has slept with a host of harlots has not shared his body, as if he were pure and wholesome (τέλειος, the Greeks say) and, if he wishes, is appointed to four or five bishoprics.'[6] At first the doctor was astounded but then burst into laughter at the man's stupidity. Ancient laws called what was exceptionally pure *purus putus*. *Putus* is equivalent to *purgatus* 'purged,' so that we speak of pruning (*putare*) a vine, and we call the cuttings *putamina*. But in Spain and Italy they call a boy who consents to obscene sexual acts a *putus*.[7] Then since the word *episcopatus* is neither Greek nor Latin,[8] I preferred to say *episcopa*, the word that Paul used: 'He who desires a bishopric' etc, ἐπισκοπή.[9] But he thought *episcopus* and *episcopa* were used like *dominus* and *domina*.[10] What could be more stupid? And yet the Dominicans regard this man as learned. Of the same sort are almost all those who publicly and privately engage in frenzied attacks against the name of Erasmus with such perverse obstinacy that neither the emperor nor the archbishops of Toledo and Seville,[11] who through their sense of fairness are on my side,

* * * * *

4 This same story is retold in Ep 2045:250–84. The physician in question has not been identified. See CEBR III 296 sv 'Suárez.'
5 *Institutio christiani matrimonii* (Ep 1727)
6 Cf CWE 69 299, where the passage is rendered somewhat differently.
7 In Spanish the word *puto* retains the same meaning, but it appears never to have been used that way in Italian.
8 The word *episcopatus* (ie the office and dignity of a bishop) is found in the Vulgate (Ps 108:7, 1 Tim 3:1), in Tertullian *De baptismo* 17, and in Ammianus Marcellinus 27.3.12, as well as in countless medieval texts. But it is not found in classical Latin.
9 1 Tim 3:1, where Paul uses the Greek word *episcope*, for which Erasmus coins the Latin word *episcopa*.
10 *Dominus* 'lord' or 'master'; *domina* 'lady,' 'mistress,' or 'sweetheart (concubine).' So the Dominican understood *episcopa* to mean bishop's concubine, though to follow Erasmus' logic, it would have meant a female bishop.
11 Alonso de Fonseca (Epp 1748, 2003) and Alonso Manrique de Lara (Epp 1846, 1967)

have been able to control them. My own personal loss is of little importance; I should wish that all the results of my lucubrations be obliterated if I were to perceive that they give rise to impiety. What grieves me is to see that the 95 house of God is propped up by these beasts, as on the shoulders of multiple Atlases.

I recognize in your kind offer the ardour of your good will towards me, and I am eager to fly off from here to some other place,[12] but my debilitated health holds me here. The emperor invites me to Spain, Ferdinand 100 to Vienna, Margaret to Brabant, the king of England to England, Sigismund to Poland, Francis to France, and they offer lavish stipends;[13] would that, as they can give me these things, they could also give me my youth and a flourishing good health!

I wrote this on the spur of the moment while engaged in many occu- 105 pations; I am anxious that you read it if only in order that you may know from this piece of evidence that I believe with my whole heart what Augustinus Marius told me of your exceptional kindness. May the Lord Jesus keep your reverend Highness without harm.

Given at Basel, 26 August 1528 110

2030 / To Andrzej Krzycki   Basel, 26 August 1528

This letter was first published in the *Opus epistolarum*. It is the first of six letters answering the group of letters sent from Poland in February 1528 (Epp 1952–4, 1958). The letter from Krzycki to which this replies is not extant, but it would have had the same date as the others, c 18 February 1528.

On Krzycki, since April 1527 bishop of Płock, strong opponent of the Reformation, admirer of Erasmus, and accomplished Latin poet, see Ep 1629. Erasmus praised him highly (under his Latinized name Andreas Critius) in the *Ciceronianus* (CWE 28 428).

ERASMUS OF ROTTERDAM TO ANDRZEJ KRZYCKI, BISHOP OF PŁOCK, GREETING

Your letters have the special qualities, illustrious Bishop, of banishing all sadness from my mind and bringing to it a certain joy. The reason for this is not hard to find. Your uniquely good-natured and friendly spirit breathes in 5

* * * * *

12 See Ep 1926 n8.
13 Epp 1431 n25 (Spain); 2000 and 2005 (Vienna); 1408:11–12, 1553:23–4, and 1871 (Brabant); 1878 and 1998 (England); 1952 (Poland); 1375 and 1805:164–6 (France). Cf Epp 1938 n4, 2037 n40, 2054:4–28.

them. Astrologers seek favourable and adverse constellations in the heavens. Sorcerers attribute fortunate or unfortunate events to good or evil spirits. But I am more of the opinion that a man's fate lies in men. We see that some people are born for the destruction of certain other people. Here we should have use of an astrolabe so that we might recoil from men of ill omen, allying ourselves with kind and friendly people. That people to whom I have been of no little help by my labours and to whom I have done no harm should rant hysterically against me leaves me utterly bewildered. I marvel at the obtuse stupidity of these men, who in spite of suffering defeat so many times, feel no shame. They set no bounds to their campaign of calumny, even though they see that they accomplish nothing more than to reveal their own malice joined with a matching stupidity, which by now is more than sufficiently well known to the world. My own personal loss is slight. What causes me heartfelt grief is that the church is supported by these Atlases, and even worse, that these abscesses must be tolerated and even nourished by the Christian people. They are polyps weighing upon the eyes.[1] I console myself with the thought that God wishes to cleanse me by these afflictions of any bit of empty glory that may have crept into my soul. Come now, it is the Lord, let him do what he thinks best,[2] for he sees more than we.

I am not unaware of how much I owe you for your devotion towards me. Since you do this discreetly, it is not only I who am in your debt but also the Christian religion and good letters, which I make great efforts to advance in my small way. Your nephew, Andrzej Zebrzydowski, who lives under my roof and shares my board, provides me profitable and pleasant company.[3] I wish I could be of as much use to him as I ought and wish to be! On the other hand, as far as my health and my distracting occupations permit, I am not lacking in my duty. I show him the way, I spur him on, although he is already well on his way, and sometimes I exercise him in conversations. He is applying himself manfully to the study of both languages so that there is good hope that he will return to you the kind of young man we both wish him to be. He has me to exhort him to the study of literature,

* * * * *

2030
1 Cf *Adagia* II viii 65: *Ut fici oculis incumbunt* 'As warts grow on the eye.' The idea of a growth that cannot be removed without risk is here applied to 'those people who, though a grievous and intolerable burden, cannot be forcibly removed without great public mischief.' Among those Erasmus includes the 'irreligious and idle flocks of monks' in the mendicant orders; see CWE 34 74–6.
2 1 Sam 3:18
3 See Ep 1958 n1.

but he has a much greater teacher in frugality, for what he receives from us is a very meagre and frugal diet. He respects me like a father and relieves me of a great deal of boredom by his agreeable and pleasant company. He told me how it was that your gift did not reach me.[4] But in my view you sent me a precious gift in sending your dear nephew to me. I hope that he does not regret his coming here any more than I do not tire of his company. 40

I am sorry about the calamity in Hungary,[5] although Bernhard, bishop of Trent and high chancellor of King Ferdinand, recently wrote to me that things have turned out so successfully that it is plainly evident that a propitious divine power is at work.[6] But what part of the world today is not shaken by warlike tumults? And day by day the wrath of monarchs grows more violent and we do not recognize that God is angry with us. They say the pope is in Nice, a city on the coast of Savoy, and that he is trying to bring about a state of peace between the French and the emperor.[7] Would that he could be this time at least the sovereign pontiff or, to put it better, the greatest and best! Julius found ready obedience when he called men to war;[8] I fear the present pontiff will not meet with this same compliance when he exhorts to peace, if indeed he is engaged in what he is supposed to be doing.[9] 45 50 55

The letter I wrote to King Sigismund, once it appeared in print, won me considerable unpopularity at the court of Ferdinand because of one little word: I added the word 'king' to John's name.[10] I did not know that it was

* * * * *

4 In Ep 1803:92–7, Leonard Cox had suggested that a letter of encouragement to young Zebrzydowski would not go unrewarded by his uncle. Erasmus had obliged with Ep 1826, and that may have elicited the gift referred to here.

5 Ie the military conflict between Ferdinand of Hapsburg and John Zápolyai, rival claimants to the throne of Hungary. See Ep 1935 nn5, 8.

6 Bernhard von Cles; see Epp 1357, 2007. The letter referred to here is not extant.

7 There appear to have been widespread reports that the pope would go to Nice in the attempt to secure a peace: see LP 4 no 4319 (2 June 1528) and Epp 1987:53–4, 2038:28–30, 2042:17. But he did not do so. Peace between the emperor and the king of France would not be restored until the conclusion of the peace of Cambrai in August 1529.

8 In 1510–11, Pope Julius II had taken the lead in forming the Holy League (with Venice, the Swiss Cantons, Ferdinand II of Aragon, Henry VIII of England, and Emperor Maximilian I) for the purpose of driving the French 'barbarians' out of Italy.

9 As Ep 2038:29–30 shows, Erasmus has doubts that peacemaking was the pope's real intent.

10 Ep 1819:153. John Zápolyai was Ferdinand's rival for the kingship of Hungary. The reference to him as 'king' was thus an affront to Ferdinand. Erasmus made

in my letter and I would not have believed it if I had not consulted my
draft copy. I feel that some are rather angry with me because I express my   60
abhorrence for war every chance I get and exhort to peace.[11] Evidently the
one thing lacking to our woes was not to be permitted even to utter a sigh
of lament in these calamitous times.

To return to your Geta,[12] who will be hit with another tribute to be
paid, I fear that if this tempest does not subside,[13] the annates, as they are   65
called, will be doubled.[14] They are now demanding that these taxes, which
were formerly due within three years, must be paid promptly, which is
a great burden to the churches and a great detriment to the very person
in whose interest these settlements are made.[15] He would act more peacefully and more properly if he did not have the means to maintain a palace   70
guard and armed forces. But since every bishop almost without exception
looks after his own interests, there is little consideration for the public good.
The torrent of human affairs carries downstream many things of this kind,
which it is easier to censure than to correct.

I shall write to the king, but in a few words.[16] As you inspired him to   75
this generosity with your words, would you be so kind as to thank him in
my name if my words were not adequate to express the magnificence of the
gift[17] or the warmth of my feelings. May the Lord preserve your Highness
free from harm, most distinguished Bishop.

Given at Basel, 26 August 1528   80

* * * * *

amends in the list of titles placed at the head of Ep 2005. Moreover, when he
published Ep 1819 in the *Opus epistolarum* (1529), he amended the text so that
it referred to 'John, who has usurped the title of king.' Cf Ep 1819 n24.
11 Cf Ep 2032:1–3.
12 Terence's comedy *Phormio* opens with the slave Davos describing the unhappy
   lot of his fellow slave Geta who, as a typical have-not unfairly fleeced by the
   rich, finds himself compelled to buy gifts for members of his master's family
   when they marry, have a child, and so on. It seems that Krzycki had applied
   the name Geta to himself in consequence of having had to pay further annates
   on his translation from the see of Przemyśl to that of Płock in March 1527.
13 As the context here makes clear, the 'tempest' that Erasmus is referring to is
   not the theological turmoil of the time (cf Ep 1926 n6) but rather the wars in
   Italy, in which the pope was deeply involved.
14 'Annates,' (also known as 'first fruits'), consisted of the first year's revenue of
   an ecclesiastical benefice (or a specified portion of that revenue), paid to the
   papal curia in return for appointment to that benefice. It was an onerous levy
   and much resented by those who had to pay it.
15 The pope
16 Ep 2034
17 Evidently the gift of 100 gold ducats that accompanied Ep 1952

2031 / To Justus Decius   Basel, 26 August 1528

This is Erasmus' reply to Ep 1958. It was first published in the *Opus epistolarum*.

ERASMUS OF ROTTERDAM TO JUSTUS, SECRETARY OF THE KING OF
POLAND, GREETING

I am affected by the advantages and disadvantages that befall my friends in
no other wise than I am by things that happen to me. I was concerned about
your difficulty;[1] now that it has been settled, I am exceedingly happy, for   5
I number my Justus among my truest friends. I can hardly put into words
how distressed I am at the poor health of Antonin.[2] Who was more sincere
of heart? Who showed himself more a friend? I should feel less grief if he
had exchanged life for death.

A similar malady seized R.P. in Italy, where he was discharging an   10
embassy in his king's name.[3] The doctors in despair counselled a change of
climate. He returned to England; after much time he finally regained his
health and was restored to his former state. It gave me particular joy since
beyond all expectation I had recovered such a great friend. But behold yet
another evil! Through the workings of a certain important personage he   15
was thrown into jail, because it is said that he wrote some rather unguarded
things against this man in his usual offhand manner. But I think he is now
free.[4]

Would that I could hear that our friend Antonin has also been here
restored to us and to himself! In his last letter he threatened to make me   20
some gift or other,[5] which I could not disregard. He said he would send
it through a person he had in his service here named Josephus,[6] if I am
not mistaken. I would wish to suffer the loss of many gifts if I could recover such a friend. It seems to be a fatal illness.[7] Here in the house of a
friend four girls and several servants were stricken with it; one of them   25

* * * * *

2031
1 Whatever this was, Decius made no reference to it in Ep 1958. It was presumably reported in person by Andrzej Zebrzydowski (Ep 1958 n1).
2 Jan Antonin (Ep 1953 n1). On his illness, see Ep 2011:10–22.
3 A reference to Richard Pace; see Epp 1955 introduction and 2033:66–9.
4 The 'important personage' was Cardinal Wolsey; cf Ep 2033:69–73.
5 In Ep 1916:2–5 Erasmus gratefully acknowledges Antonin's 'threat' to present
  him with a 'grand and extravagant' (but unspecified) gift. Antonin's letter,
  possibly written in answer to Ep 1825 (May 1527) is not extant.
6 Probably Tectander, Antonin's brother-in-law; see Epp 1810:20 with n7 in line
  21, 1916:45–6.
7 By June 1529, Erasmus had learned of Antonin's recovery (Ep 2173).

died.[8] Johann Froben, a man worthy of immortality, was taken from us by a paralysis.[9] He could have lived several years longer if he had not been so ashamed to be ill.

Andrzej Zebrzydowski delivered with good faith all that he had received.[10] With him sharing my household I now find consolation for my poor health and my toils. I pray that you continue to hold this belief: not to judge my sentiments from my fulfilment of the duties of letter-writing. Farewell, my very good friend.

Given at Basel, 26 August 1528

2032 / To Krzysztof Szydłowiecki   Basel, 27 August 1528

This letter was first published as Ep 12 in Horawitz I. The surviving manu-script is a sixteenth-century copy in the same volume in which Allen found Ep 1113. The volume is now in the Forschungsbibliothek Gotha (MS Chart B 20 fol 52 verso). The letter appears to have been written in response to a let-ter from Szydłowiecki that would presumably have been contemporary with Epp 1952–4, 1958.

Szydłowiecki (Epp 1593, 1752, 1820) was grand chancellor of Poland and a lavish patron of art and literature.

Greetings. What you find so pleasing in my writing some, to whom this constant preaching of peace seems to be an insult to princes, who are end-lessly at odds with one another find offensive.[1] And yet I do not condemn all war – at times it is necessary – nor do I rebuke any prince. Neverthe-less, it cannot be denied that wherever there is war there is wrongdoing on one side or the other and sometimes on both. But God judges the hearts and motives of princes, not I.

The letter they printed in your country[2] has won me considerable un-popularity, not with Ferdinand himself,[3] who is a model of fairness, but

* * * * *

8 This evidently took place in the Froben house 'Zum Sessel,' in which Hierony-mus Froben appears to have lived with his wife Anna Lachner until 1531. Hi-eronymus' stepfather, Johann Herwagen, may also have moved in with his wife, Gertrude Lachner, Johann Froben's widow. Cf Ep 2033:63–4, 73–5.
9 See Ep 1900.
10 Ie the one hundred ducats sent by the king; see Ep 2033:1–2.

2032
1 Cf Ep 2030:60–1.
2 Ep 1819
3 Ferdinand of Austria (Ep 1935 n5)

with some of the leading men at his court, because of one little word which   10
I did not know was there; I gave John the title of 'king,'[4] since I had no
other at the time. I received with great joy of spirit Sigismund's letter,[5] full
of kindness and religious feeling, and his gift as well, not without some
embarrassment.[6] As I did not merit it, so I did not expect it.

The tumults of war and faction grow more violent each day, and I   15
see no end of this evil unless the leaders of the church together with kings,
laying aside their personal feelings, commit themselves entirely to the divine will, and unless the people, changing their lives for the better, appease God's wrath and flee to him for mercy. If the new sects are over-
thrown only to give new life to the tyranny of unscrupulous monks, or   20
if those who under the name of the Roman pontiff have up to now done
whatever they pleased, this will serve to change the plague, but not to
get rid of it. Things must be regulated by the authority of bishops and
princes so that Christ may conquer and piety triumph, not the wickedness of men. In this matter I ask that you steadfastly maintain the spirit   25
you have shown up to now and do not deviate to right or left. I pray that
your Highness is in excellent health, most illustrious sir and outstanding
patron.

Given at Basel, 27 August 1528
Your Highness' most faithful servant, Erasmus of Rotterdam   30
I have signed this in my own hand.
To the illustrious Master Krzysztof Szydłowiecki, castellan and captain
of Cracow and chancellor of the kingdom of Poland

2033 / To Jan (II) Łaski   Basel, 27 August 1528

This is Erasmus' reply to Ep 1954. The manuscript was in the same ill-
fated folio volume as that of Ep 1954. It was first published in *Materyaly do
dziejów piö miennictwa Polskiego* ed Teodor Wierzbowski 1 (Warsaw 1900) 37–8
(no 63).

LETTER OF ERASMUS TO THE MOST REVEREND LORD PROVOST
Andrzej Zebrzydowski, whom I am pleased to have as a guest in my
house, paid me one hundred Hungarian ducats in the name of the king
and paid forty ducats in your name to Glareanus, who happened to be

* * * * *

4 John Zápolyai, Ferdinand's rival for the kingship of Hungary; see Ep 1819:153;
  cf Ep 2030:56–60.
5 Ep 1952 .
6 For the gift, and Szydłowiecki's part in securing it, see Ep 1954:15–19.

present.[1] If such a windfall were to come his way from time to time he   5
could procure a divorce from his poverty. Consider that this gift has been
given to studies and to a man who is not ungrateful. Beatus expects nothing from you but mutual good will, and his financial circumstances are
not straitened.[2] If you have decided to send him something, send him a
symbolic gift pleasing in its novelty rather than anything of value. I am   10
extremely happy that my devotion meets with the archbishop's approval.[3]
Concerning his pledge of a gift, you make profuse excuses for his busy life,
as if it required much freedom from affairs to say: 'Send him a hundred
ducats.' But, joking aside, my dear Łaski, I am perfectly content that I have
his support. I would wish that this excellent old man had a nephew and you   15
a brother who was a little more fortunate.[4] But there has never been any
family that did not have its canker.

If you regret your purchase of the library I shall refund the money you
paid.[5] I surely have no regrets; but I should like you to know that in the
meantime the value of the books has increased by seventy or eighty florins.[6]   20
To give you an idea of this, the Galen alone is sold here for thirty florins.
Your Mercury,[7] tired of Poland, as it appears, is working with Froben. He
complained that he was not treated kindly and he tried to extort some money
from me; nothing is ever enough for types like him.

Everywhere the phalanxes of the monks are diligently at work, but   25
they are never satisfied. The instigator of the Spanish melodrama secretly
does everything in his usual manner; his is a nature born for virulence and
for sowing discord. And he is the ambassador of reconciliation among kings

* * * * *

2033
1 On the payments see Epp 1952:35–6, 1958:1–2, 12–13. On Zebrzydowski see
   Ep 1958 n1; on Glareanus, Ep 1977 n29. For Hungarian ducats, see Epp 1934
   n51, 1953 n2, 1958 n2.
2 On Beatus Rhenanus see Ep 1933 n2.
3 Ep 1954:23–31
4 A reference to Hieronim Łaski (Ep 1341A:1218–69) who, following the battle of
   Mohács in 1526, had taken sides with John Zápolyai, Ferdinand of Hapsburg's
   rival for control of Hungary.
5 In 1526, Łaski had made arrangements to purchase Erasmus' library under
   terms that left him in use of it for the rest of his life. Cf CWE 12 542:32–5
   (Erasmus' first will).
6 The type of florin is not specified; and no gold florins are indicated. While
   these may be Imperial gold florins, Erasmus, though writing in Basel, may
   again have meant the Flemish Hapsburg money-of-account, by which six
   florins equals one pound groot Flemish. See Ep 1934 n6.
7 Possibly the messenger 'George' of Epp 1915:57, 1916:6–7

whereas, given his character, he would sooner have created war from peace.[8]
Strenuous efforts are being made in England as well,[9] but I have the king,   30
queen, the archbishop of Canterbury, More, and Tunstall, bishop of London
and grand inquisitor,[10] firmly on my side. You know the opinion of me in
Italy.[11] In Brabant they are becoming more lenient.[12] In Savoy a certain Franciscan began to inveigh against me with might and main, but I silenced him
with letters written to him and to his prince.[13] Since I made Béda a public   35
laughing-stock he has wanted to have his revenge.[14] By his doing it came

* * * * *

8 On Erasmus' conviction that Edward Lee (Ep 1994A n13) had instigated the investigation of him by Spanish monks that ended in the inconclusive Valladolid
Conference in 1527, see Epp 1744 n19, 1814 n39, and cf Ep 1994A n15.

9 Cf Ep 1697:26–30, 90–7, where Erasmus complains to Cardinal Wolsey that
virulent attacks on him by Dominicans were freely for sale in England while
his own harmless *Colloquies*, so it was rumoured, had been banned. Before
dispatching the letter, however, Erasmus learned that the rumour concerning
the *Colloquies* was untrue and that there was no official effort to ban them; Ep
1697:124–6.

10 'Grand inquisitor' is not a title but rather an ironic description of Tunstall's
leading role in actions against heresy at this time. In November 1527 Cardinal
Wolsey commissioned a panel of eight bishops, including Tunstall, to investigate charges of heresy in the diocese of London. The conduct of the proceedings soon fell into the hands of Tunstall, who proved himself reluctant to practise great severity. He displayed similar mildness when, starting in February
1528, he undertook an investigation into the origin of the heretical books that
were reaching Oxford in large numbers. See Charles Sturge *Cuthbert Tunstal*
(London 1938) 136–43.

11 A reference to Erasmus' Italian detractors, against whom his latest sally had
been the *Ciceronianus* (Ep 1948).

12 Ie in Louvain. It is not clear exactly what Erasmus means here. But he did point
out more than once that the Louvain theologians, in contrast to those in Paris
(see n15 below), had never issued a formal condemnation of the *Colloquies* (Epp
1697:26–8, 2077:39–40). Moreover, with the deaths of both Nicholaas Baechem
and Vincentius Theoderici in 1526 (see Ep 2054:19–20 with n10), Louvain lost
its status as a leading centre of opposition to Erasmus.

13 The Franciscan was Jean Gachi. See Ep 1891 to him and Ep 1886 to Charles III,
duke of Savoy.

14 On Noël Béda see Ep 1943 n6. By the spring of 1527 Erasmus had rendered
Béda 'beside himself with anger' (Ep 1905:17–19) by publishing no fewer than
three replies to Béda's criticisms of him: briefly in the *Prologus in supputationem
calumniarum Natalis Bedae* (Ep 1664; LB IX 484D–485D), and *In N. Bedae censuras
erroneas elenchus* (LB IX 495–514), both of 1526, and then in much greater detail
in the *Supputatio errorum in censuris Bedae* (LB IX 515–702) of March 1527 (cf
Epp 1902:336–40, 1905:113–15). Moreover, he had also written to Francis I (Ep
1722, 16 June 1526) asking for royal intervention to curb the attacks on him and

about that the sacred faculty came together on alternate days and, of the articles that he had collected from all my writings, condemned five at each session, so that they could exercise their authority over me. And now they have condemned some articles from my *Paraphrases* in which there were quotations from the Gospels, but they were presented as if they came from me.[15] I answered and sent one copy, with accompanying letters, to the Parlement of Paris and to the sacred faculty.[16] The tragic commotion has abated but I have no doubt that it will break out somewhere else. I wonder what the intentions are of that faculty, which once earned the world's respect. They are awaiting my death, and every year they celebrate my obsequies with their tongues.

Augustine is approaching the end;[17] no one would believe how many gross errors I have uncovered in it. This winter, if the Lord grants me some free time, I will prepare my notes for the *De concionando*,[18] and already magpies and jackdaws are squawking about it. 'What?' they say, 'Is he going to teach us how to preach when he has never preached in his life?' With the effort I expended on the Augustine I could have completed all my works. Froben, of happy memory, imposed this task upon me, although I fought against it tooth and nail,[19] and no amount of money would have made me

* * * * *

other humanist scholars by Béda and Pierre Cousturier (Ep 1943 n7). Francis responded by ordering the Parlement of Paris to withdraw Béda's *Annotationes* from sale until further notice, but the faculty denounced Erasmus' letter as favourable to heresy, wrote to the king in justification of their action, and persisted in their campaign against Erasmus. See Farge *Orthodoxy* 192–4.

15 In September 1527, the faculty, which had already censured the *Colloquies* in May 1526, resumed its omnibus examination of Erasmus' works. On 16 December 1527 it condemned 112 propositions drawn largely from the *Paraphrases* on the New Testament and from Erasmus' books against Béda. Then, on 23 June 1528, the entire university endorsed the faculty's condemnation of the *Colloquies*. See Ep 2037 introduction and Farge *Orthodoxy* 194–6. The Paris censures were not published until 1531; Erasmus' response, *Declarationes ad censuras Lutetiae vulgatas*, followed in 1532.

16 The letter to the faculty of theology was Ep 1902 (12 November 1527) and that to the Parlement was Ep 1905 (14 November 1527). With each letter Erasmus included 'brief responses to certain articles' under consideration by the faculty (Epp 1902:336–8, 1905:111–13, 1922:45–6) as well as a copy of his *Supputatio* (see n14 above), the most detailed of his responses to Béda's *Annotationes* (Epp 1902:338–40, 1905:113–15).

17 The Froben Augustine, published in 1529 (Ep 2157)

18 Ie the work on preaching that would eventually be published in 1535 as *Ecclesiastes*; see Ep 1932 n25.

19 Literally 'with hands and feet' (*Adagia* I iv 15); cf Ep 2046:416–18.

change my mind. But now the port is in sight. The little book without a title[20] received the treatment it deserved; I have completed it, having made note of the errors.[21] I did not undertake the job of correcting Ambrose,[22] and I did not read all of it but gave part of it to the proofreader Sigismundus,[23] a learned man with good judgment, but indolent. No one was in more need 60 of an amender; but this will be completed at some other time. As far as the press is concerned, I hope it will fare better than when Froben was alive. Hieronymus Froben and the new husband of Froben's wife are in charge of the press.[24]

I can hardly express how distressed I am at Antonin's illness.[25] It is 65 a deadly malady. A year ago Richard Pace, who was fulfilling an embassy in Italy, was stricken with insomnia; that was followed by delirium.[26] The doctors gave up hope and he was brought back to England. Finally, he returned to health there. But a worse evil followed upon the previous one.[27] He had written something rather outspoken against the cardinal. When this 70 circulated through the court, it gave too much pleasure to many. He was thrown into jail, although the king was not much angered. But I hope he is now free. Some time ago two sisters of Froben's wife were stricken by a type of this mania, a terrible sickness. Some men were stricken with it also and several of them died.[28] 75

No message could bring greater happiness to my spirit than the news that Antonin has been restored to himself and to us.

I would have written at greater length if you had not indicated to me in a recent letter that you were considering a trip to Spain.[29] May you, together with all of your dear ones, be of good health. 80

* * * * *

20 Apparently something in the Augustine edition. Possibly the brief *Liber Meditationum* in volume 9 474–505, where Erasmus, who doubted the ascription to Augustine, noted: 'I have added the title.' See Allen 51–2n.
21 Presumably, having prepared a list of errata
22 *Liber de apologia David*, published by the Froben firm in 1529 (Ep 2190)
23 Gelenius; see Ep 1702 n1.
24 Froben's widow, Gertrude Lachner (Ep 419:17n) had married Johann Herwagen (1497–c 1558), the Strasbourg publisher who had just moved to Basel. At first he was a partner in the Froben press, but in 1531 he went into business for himself and occupied the house that until 1529 had been Erasmus' residence.
25 Cf Ep 2011:10–23.
26 Erasmus' date is off by two years. Pace's illness began in 1525. See Ep 1955 introduction.
27 On this, see Ep 2031:10–19.
28 See Ep 2031:24–6.
29 Ep 1954:32–3

Given at Basel, 27 August 1528
You will recognize your friend's hand.

2034 / To Sigismund I   Basel, 28 August 1528

This is Erasmus' reply to Ep 1952. The manuscript, a sixteenth-century copy,
is in the Zamoyski collection of the Polish National Library in Warsaw (Ep
1952 introduction): MS BN BOZ 2053 vol 8 fols 245–8 verso. The letter was first
published in the *Opus epistolarum*.

ERASMUS OF ROTTERDAM TO SIGISMUND, KING OF POLAND,
GREETING

In the midst of so many exertions that we endure besides the tribulations of
ill health and old age, in the midst of so many troubles and annoyances by
which we are assailed on this side and that, the letter of your Majesty, King   5
Sigismund, glorious among all sovereigns, brought us no ordinary consolation, breathing in its every line a remarkable kindness and a special regard
for us. And indeed, although Solomon writes, 'A king's wrath is the messenger of death,' the same writer also says, 'In the gladness of a king's coun-
tenance there is life.'[1] Your letter exhibited that joyful and benevolent coun-   10
tenance. Although I perceive not at all in myself the qualities that would
merit the favour you show me, nonetheless, to be truthful, it is gratifying to
be praised by a king so much praised himself and to gain further incentive
for my efforts, whatever their worth. For my part I felt that I would have received abundant reward for my services if your Majesty had looked kindly   15
upon my boldness. Now I see that all has turned out well, since through
my act of boldness I have been able to have direct experience of your truly
kingly generosity and piety, of which I had heard such great acclaim. Your
generosity was demonstrated by your warm feelings of friendship for my
humble self and by the weighty testimony with which you deigned to hon-   20
our my meagre talents, not only in a most kind letter but also in the form
of a magnificent gift.[2] Your piety is made manifest in that you attribute the
prosperity of your kingdom not to your own powers and design but to the
goodness of God.

Who would not cherish such pious and Christian sentiments uttered   25
by such a great king? Solomon wrote truthfully 'The heart of the king is

* * * * *

2034
1 Prov 16:14–15
2 One hundred gold ducats; see Ep 1952 n3.

in the hands of God and he shall incline it wherever he will.'[3] But true praise belongs to those kings who in turn incline their hearts to God, the king of all kings, relying on the assent of him without whose good auspices no human enterprise achieves its end, and who dispose all their actions in the knowledge that whatever they do is done before the eyes of him who is judge no less of kings than of the common people. But by virtue of your Christian modesty, illustrious King, you do not fail to win praise but rather make it rightfully your own. You would lose it if you did not acknowledge him to whom all glory is due. Nothing can truly be called prosperous, nothing happy, which has not received the blessing of him who is the dispenser of all happiness. Those things are done with best auspices and most favourable auguries that are done according to the prescriptions of him who said: 'Through me kings rule and lawgivers make just judgments; through me princes govern and the mighty ordain justice.'[4] This was spoken by eternal wisdom, which is the Son of God. What does wisdom prescribe for kings? 'Mercy' it says, 'and truth protect the king, and his throne is strengthened by clemency.'[5] He shows mercy in relieving the oppressed, truth in judging without bias, clemency in tempering the severity of the laws.

The primary function of kings, which they profess even by oath when they accede to power, is to assist widows, to come to the aid of orphans, and to repel violence from all those who are unjustly oppressed. Truth has two attendants, wisdom and steadfastness. Wisdom illumines the eyes, by which we perceive what is right and what is not, what is useful to the state and what is not. Through steadfastness the mind rises above all passions and is not diverted from rectitude by either anger or love or hate. Clemency tempers necessary severity with leniency. The law prescribes fairness for everyone, but not everything is suited to everyone. This moderation in the administration of public justice, which is called equity, is sought from the heart of the king as from an oracle, if it has been rightly said by wise men that the king is the living law.[6] The law is limited to few words, but the circumstances of persons and situations are infinite. In these, therefore, the king speaks in place of the law, but his pronouncements are no different

* * * * *

3 Prov 21:1
4 Prov 8:15–16
5 Prov 20:28
6 A commonplace of ancient political thought, found (for example) in Aristotle *Politics* 3.8.2, Cicero *Laws* 3.1.2, and Plutarch *Moralia* 780c–E. Cf *The Education of a Christian Prince* CWE 27 264.

from what the law would say if it could answer to every case. Clemency   60
consists in not immediately venturing upon war when cause for war is given
but rather in leaving no avenue untried if matters can be settled without
war. Sometimes it is wiser to pretend not to notice an injustice than to seek
vengeance by force of arms. Clemency consists, if war cannot be avoided
by any other means, in waging it in such a way that there will be the least   65
possible shedding of human blood and that it will be finished as quickly
as possible. It was this wisdom, which brings all good things with it, that
Solomon prayed for to assist him always in his exercise of power as his
faithful and dependable counsellor.[7]

This was seen also by the ancients as through a cloud. For we read   70
that the Egyptians used to represent the image of the king in hieroglyph-
ics by adding an eye to the sceptre. By the sceptre they signified a morally
right, impartial, and unswerving spirit; by the eye they signified wisdom,
which distinguishes between good and evil. They commended these same
virtues in other symbols, placing on the top of the sceptre an eagle and at   75
the bottom a hippopotamus. By the eagle was meant clear perception and
contempt for lowly things, by the hippopotamus suppression of wrath and
ferocity by reason, for this animal is wild and untamed.[8] Moral rectitude
cannot exist except in a spirit that is truly sublime and perspicacious, superior to all human passions, which often drown out the voice of reason.   80
Since these qualities shine out in you, invincible King Sigismund, they become truly yours only if you ascribe them to God, as you do, from whom
flows whatever good there is in us. In the case of material goods, what we
transfer to another ceases to be ours; with spiritual goods the opposite is the
case: what we attribute to God begins to be truly ours.   85

But I am carried along further than the length of a letter allows. It
remains for me to pray Christ, all good and almighty, to protect these gifts
in you and continue to increase them continuously with new ones, and may
he inspire the same mentality in all princes, so that, being of one accord and
under the guidance of heavenly wisdom they may decide on those measures   90

* * * * *

7 1 Kings 3:9, 2 Chron 1:10
8 Erasmus' principal source here is *The Hieroglyphica of Horus Apollo*, generally
  known as the *Horapollon*, 1.56. An ancient Greek work of uncertain date, it offered fanciful, allegorical interpretations of Egyptian hieroglyphs. Following
  the discovery of the manuscript in Greece (c 1420), the work aroused much
  interest among North Italian humanists. First published in 1505 by Aldus in
  Venice, it went through more than thirty editions in the sixteenth century, including the Latin translation of Bernardino Trebazio published by Froben at
  Basel in 1518.

that will promote the common good and receive Christ's approval, so that at
long last this tempest in human affairs may one day be turned into peace.[9]
I willingly accept the favour that your clemency kindly offers beyond my
merits and am immensely grateful for it. I do not see what I can promise
in return, save for a mindful and grateful spirit and whatever homage a   95
humble servant can provide for a powerful king. May the Lord Jesus bestow
his favour on all your undertakings.

Given at Basel, 28 August 1528

Your most serene Majesty's humble servant Erasmus of Rotterdam.
Written in his own hand   100

2035 / To Piotr Tomicki   Basel, 31 August 1528

This is Erasmus' reply to Ep 1953. The autograph is in the Zamoyski collection of the Polish National Library at Warsaw (Ep 1952 introduction): MS BN
BOZ 2053 vol 9 fols 13–14 verso. The letter was first published in the *Opus
epistolarum.*

Cordial greetings. Most honoured Bishop, you will receive a rather laconic
letter from me in response to yours, since I am more overwhelmed than occupied by tasks that are not particularly grand or important but burdensome
nonetheless. I am extremely happy that the boldness I displayed in disturbing your Highness with my writings turned out well. In so doing, I deferred   5
more to the wishes of Antonin than to my own inclinations.[1] Though your
letter is brief and, as you say, laconic, it breathes a prolix good will towards
me. I should consider myself singularly fortunate if I could identify any
merits in me that could justify the enthusiastic devotion shown towards me
by such a pious, learned, and distinguished prelate. Certainly I shall strive 10
to bring it about that you will not seem to have conferred this favour on an
ungrateful person or one who does not merit it.

But just as your letter delineated a likeness of your spirit, so Andrzej
Zebrzydowski, a young man worthy of his line who is valiantly struggling

* * * * *

9 Sigismund was currently engaged in efforts to mediate a peace in Hungary
between King Ferdinand and his rival John Zápolyai. These bore fruit in a
one-year truce signed in 1530.

2035
1 Jan Antonin (Ep 1953 n1) had encouraged Erasmus to write to Tomicki; see Ep
1919.

with Greek and Latin literature and whose daily company in my house-   15
hold is a great solace and ornament to me, has depicted and portrayed you
so completely in frequent conversations that, if I were in your presence, I
don't think I should have a clearer picture of you.[2] May Christ, all good and
almighty, allow many such bishops to grace the church of God. It would then
be possible to hope for a period of serenity to follow on this violent tempest   20
in the affairs of men. There would be reason to congratulate the Christian
world as we now congratulate the kingdom of Poland, a great kingdom, but
alone in its tranquillity. As far as I am concerned, I have a special veneration for such great men, even if they have done me no personal favour. In
the present case I understand what affection I owe you, who did not think   25
it enough to testify to your exceptional good will towards me in a letter but
also wished to demonstrate it by a pledge in gold. And so I anxiously look
about me to see what proof I can give of my gratitude, although I know that
in your generosity you are content with a sign of reciprocal affection.

Your relative Andrzej delivered sixty Hungarian ducats to me in your   30
Highness' name.[3] I shall not try to express my profuse thanks but prefer
to render thanks in some tangible way. May the Lord keep you safe and
prosper all that you do, most respected Bishop.

Given at Basel, 31 August 1528

Erasmus of Rotterdam wrote this in his own hand and affixed his sig-   35
nature.

To the most reverend Lord and renowned Prince Piotr, bishop of Cracow and vice-chancellor of the kingdom of Poland. In Poland

2036 / To Bonifacius Amerbach   [Basel, August 1528]

The autograph of this letter (= AK Ep 1270) is in the University Library at
Basel (MS AN III 15 12). It was first published in C.A. Serin *Epistolae familiares* (Basel 1779) no 39. Erasmus wrote it while Andrzej Zebrzydowski (line
4) was living in his house and the arrival there of Daniel Stiebar (line 2) was
expected. Stiebar had arrived in Basel c September 1527 (see Ep 2069 introduction) and Zebrzydowski, having departed Cracow in February 1528 (Ep 1958),
had taken up residence in Erasmus' house sometime before 26 August (Epp
2030–1, 2033). Both departed Basel in September 1528 (Epp 2065:23–4 with n3,
2069). Allen set the conjectural month-date at July/August, when basil and
thyme are in bloom (line 8); AK, eschewing such subtleties, put the date at
'summer 1528.' On Amerbach, see Ep 1933.

* * * * *

2 Zebrzydowski (Ep 1958 n1) was Tomicki's great-nephew.
3 Cf Ep 1953 n2. On their value see Ep 1934 n51.

Cordial greetings. I am not eager to have boarders nor am I in search of income, but seeing that Daniel[1] is a young man possessed of very humane qualities, I shall provide for his meals at least. I have no bedrooms available. The Polish gentleman[2] is happy that he is coming. I cannot accept less than three florins a month.[3] I would like him to offer three and a half, which is   5 what the Polish gentleman gives. If he does not wish to specify the sum, let him at least say that he will give what I ask.

If your garden has basil and thyme, I should like to have a little. Return to Daniel his letter and his little book. I have read both of them carefully.

Farewell.   10

To Master Bonifacius Amerbach

2037 / To John Longland   Basel, 1 September 1528

This letter was first published in the *Selectae epistolae*, where it is incorrectly addressed to Jean Gachi (see Ep 1891). Allen found the correct address to Longland in the index to the *Opus epistolarum*.

Longland (Ep 2017) had evidently written to Erasmus urging him to mitigate the hostility of his severely orthodox critics in England by revising some of his works, particularly the *Colloquies*. There had been rumours of such criticism of the *Colloquies* two years earlier (see Ep 1697:26–89). In this letter Erasmus first replies to Longland in detail and then, starting at line 147, reports on the similar treatment of his books in Paris where, on 23 June 1528, the entire university had endorsed the faculty of theology's condemnation of the *Colloquies* and other works (Epp 1697 n8, 1784 n2, 1875 n26, 1902 introduction, 2006:12–14, 2033 n15).

ERASMUS OF ROTTERDAM TO BISHOP JOHN, GREETING

Most honoured Bishop, my servant Quirinus brought me two letters of yours.[1] In one of them you repeat to me the old refrain about the grievances of certain theologians. I should like to assure you that I was very pleased

* * * * *

2036
1 Stiebar (Ep 2069)
2 Zebrzydowski; see Ep 1958 n1.
3 Again, these are probably not gold coins but rather the Flemish money-of-account, in which six florins equals one pound groot Flemish. See Epp 1934 n6, 2033 n6.

2037
1 Quirinus Talesius had been in England in April; see Ep 1955 n1. The letters are not extant.

to receive this admonition, since I recognize that it proceeds from a lov- 5
ing heart. In a spirit of piety you encourage me to follow the example of
Augustine; that is exactly what I have been doing on my own for some
time now, deleting or correcting whatever I find that needs correction, although Augustine, after publishing his *Retractations*,[2] left many things that
were simply heretical, if one would wish to examine them now. And the 10
judgments of mortal men are so varied that you will hardly find three persons who have the same opinion. There are certain people of such perverse
opinion that if I were to enter into deliberation with them I would have
to delete the best parts of my writing and the things most conducive to
piety.   15

As to the articles which you enumerate as cited by these critics for
condemnation, I could answer simply that there is nothing of the kind in
my *Colloquies* and that no young boys become worse by reading them. But
these are the fabrications of men who one would say were born for the sole
purpose of spreading calumny. I would not wish this to be taken as an insult 20
to their orders.[3] But in human affairs there is no body that does not have its
cankers. Up to now they have exercised their tyranny over those of tender
age and unqualified idiots; now it irks them that young people are learning
things they do not know. Hence those tears![4]

In my *Colloquies* there is nothing obscene or lascivious, although they 25
might also treat chastely things that are lascivious by nature, for example the
colloquy of 'The Suitor and the Young Girl,'[5] or of 'The Young Man and the
Harlot.'[6] I think I have taken every precaution that those of tender years do
not imbibe loose morals from my writings. Concerning pilgrimages, what
is it that I teach, I pray you, but that men avoid superstition in them, of 30
which the world was full everywhere to the point of madness, with greater
gain accruing to the caretakers of the churches than to religion?[7] The *Collo-*
quies approve of confession, which drives those who advertise themselves as
evangelicals into a rage. I make fun of a soldier who approaches confession

* * * * *

2 In the *Retractations*, which were written towards the end of his life (426–7),
   Augustine reviews his works in chronological order, explaining the circumstances and the principal ideas in each and correcting those things in them
   that he had come to regard as erroneous.
3 More often than not, Erasmus found himself doing battle with Franciscan and
   Dominican friars.
4 Terence *Andria* 126; *Adagia* I iii 68
5 *Proci et puellae* 'Courtship' CWE 39 256–78
6 *Adolescentis et scorti* CWE 39 381–9
7 *Peregrinatio religionis ergo* 'A Pilgrimage for Religion's Sake' CWE 40 619–74

in the way the common crowd does.[8] They take offence because I say at one 35
point that the confession one makes to God is what counts, and the young
man intimates that confession is a human institution,[9] but he does not assert it emphatically. I talk about the form of confession now in use, which I
do not condemn anywhere. That it was instituted by Christ is neither probable nor has anyone been able to prove it. If anyone can do so, I will be the 40
first to applaud him. In the meantime I teach that it should be preserved as
if Christ instituted it.

In the book *De modo confitendi*[10] I do not argue that we should not
confess but that we should confess in a useful manner. I could not write
this book without making certain troublesome assertions, which I do not at- 45
tribute to confession but to the shortcomings of those who confess and their
confessors.[11] Although the whole world is full of stories about the scandals
and crimes that are committed under the cover of confession, these detractors reproach me with indignation because I touched on some of these matters in a very restrained manner. They do not consider how many things 50
whose very mention could taint the mind of the reader I passed over in silence with a Christian sense of propriety. But many monks encourage this
form of confession, not through love of piety but because they reap a rich
harvest from it, while they hold sway in the houses of the rich, whose secrets they know, while they assist the dying, while they nibble away at wills. 55
Let them consider the Lerna of evils[12] that has sprung from confessions up
to the present day and let them cease to wonder that I made some recommendations about the correct manner of confessing. Let them consider also

* * * * *

8 Thrasymachus in the colloquy *Confessio militis*, also known as *Militaria* 'Military
Affairs' CWE 39 53–63

9 In the colloquy *Confabulatio pia* 'The Whole Duty of Youth' CWE 39 96:31–97:9

10 Ie in the *Exomologesis* of 1524 (Ep 1426)

11 Erasmus views on the sacrament of confession, which included doubts about
its institution by Christ and the necessity of private confession as well as sharp
criticism of the abuses of confessors, were a favourite target of his conservative critics, who accused him of being in agreement with Luther. The *Exomolo-*
gesis, his first treatise devoted entirely to the subject, did not placate his critics.
So in March 1530 he issued a revised version of it (Basel: Froben) that was
almost twice as long as the original. In it he attempted to placate his opponents, going as far as he could, for example, to find divine institution for the
sacrament.

12 *Adagia* I iii 27. The swamps of Lerna near Argos were home to the hydra,
the many-headed serpent that grew two heads to replace every one that was
cut off. Hercules eventually killed it with the aid of his nephew, Iolaus, who
cauterized the neck-stumps as soon as Hercules had cut off the heads.

how much superstition there was in the worship of the saints, how much
pestilence from ceremonies instituted by men, and they will see that my   60
admonition was very necessary.

The saints are pleased by the veneration offered to them if one imitates
their lives; all the same, no more certain example of living can be sought
from anyone more than from Christ himself. I advocate true veneration. But
superstitious cult was more profitable to these wretches, hence the loud out-   65
cries. I do not condemn ecclesiastical ceremonies either there or anywhere
else, but I indicate what use should be made of them and I propose a better
form of worship. If this is the teaching of Christ and the blessed Paul, if it
is a pious and holy thing, why these outcries against me? But some cry out:
'Who did not know that the goal of piety should not consist in ceremonies?'   70
On the contrary, who does not know that all religion up to now has been reduced to ceremonies and that the old evangelical vigour has practically been
eliminated through them? That was indeed more useful for the prestige and
profit of certain people. But Christ thirsts for another kind of gain.[13] And
it is his dignity that must first be taken into consideration. Let these people   75
commend themselves by true piety; if that is not present, what is the pomp
of ceremonies but pure hypocrisy?

Concerning the choice of foods, I gave ample response to Noël Béda,[14]
though he hasn't the decency to admit it. If the truly pious man should consider this matter attentively, he would prefer that it should be a question   80
of exhortation rather than obligation. Considering the times, there would be
fewer snares and more people who fast out of genuine religious feeling,
especially if some example of Christian abstinence and temperance would
shine out in the lives of priests. In France, according to a written report, two
people are in danger for no other reason than that they ate meat on two days   85
during Lent, constrained to do so because of illness.[15] Do you see what effect ceremonies have? That because of man-made regulations we violate the
precepts of God, considering fratricide less serious than contradicting the
law of bishops. And yet no bishop has forbidden any sick person to consume
what is required for his health.   90

I am not the only one to condemn the excessive number of feast days,[16]
especially since nowadays more sins are committed on feast days than on

* * * * *

13 Matt 16:26
14 Béda (Ep 1943 n6) had criticized *De esu carnium* (Ep 1341A:1306–11) and Erasmus had responded in the *Prologus supputationis* (Ep 2033 n14).
15 Cf lines 248–50 below.
16 Cf Ep 1039:190–209.

any other days. I heartily approve of a moderate number of feast days, but
I should wish that they be dedicated to the sacred purposes for which they
were instituted, not for sinful pleasures. The Christian religion today does   95
not depend on miracles, and it is no secret how many false beliefs have
been brought into the world through men who are clever in procuring their
own gain with the aid of fabricated miracles. We will believe much more
firmly in what we read in the Scriptures if we do not believe in any old
tales invented by men.   100

Already now men are appearing who revive the old tricks. In one place
a ghost was seen that demanded absolution from a priest because he had
died without confession, not because he did not want it but because access to
a priest had been denied him. What is the lesson here but that those who do
not confess can be absolved and that after this life there is need of a priest   105
for those who were denied the opportunity of confessing even though they
desired it?

In another place a certain pastor, just before the sabbath, secretly put
live crabs in a cemetery and placed burning candles on their shells. As they
crept among the tombs a frightening spectacle was seen in the night and   110
no one dared to draw near. Terrible rumours resulted. With everyone in a
state of shock the pastor taught the people from the pulpit that these were
the souls of the dead who demanded to be liberated from their torment by
masses and almsgiving. The trick was discovered when a few crabs were
found among the rubble, carrying the extinguished candles, which the pas-   115
tor had failed to collect.

The same man contrived another ruse. His niece was living with him,
a woman with a fair amount of money. He used to sneak into her bedroom
in the dead of night, wrapping a sheet around himself and pretending to
be a ghost. He uttered strange sounds, hoping that the woman would send   120
for an exorcist or would talk about the occurrence. But she, with a man's
courage, secretly asked one of her relatives to hide himself and spend the
night with her in the bedroom. He armed himself with a club for exorcisms
and, having quaffed a good many drinks so that he would be less afraid,
hid himself in the bed. The ghost appears in the usual way, bellowing some   125
doleful sounds. The exorcist wakes up. He springs forward, still feeling
the effects of his drinking, and assaults him; thereupon the ghost tries to
scare him off with sounds and gestures. But the drunk man said, 'If you
are the devil, I'm his mother,' and grabbing the impostor, lets him have it
with his club. He would have killed him if the ghost, changing his voice,   130
had not cried out, 'Spare me, I am not a spirit, but Master Johannes.' Recognizing the voice, the woman jumped out of bed and put an end to the
struggle.

These are just the beginning. Even though I always thought it was a pious act to pray or offer masses for the dead, I never gave much credence to such tales about bogeymen even if there were no trickery, which is hardly ever absent. At any rate, Chrysostom thinks that these are all tricks of demons.[17] If young people nowadays are more prone to neglect these practices, which we do not wish to be neglected but to be observed in a holier way, why don't people think that they got this from the books and sermons of the Lutherans rather than from my writings? Finally, since in these times everything is contaminated, who can write anything with such circumspection that it will not be seized upon by some people as a pretext for satisfying their own desires? Many things would have to be deleted from the sacred texts if we are ready to remove whatever has been to many an occasion of sin. Let anyone produce one sentence that is less than Christian from all my writings and I shall be the first to eliminate it. Certain theologians had condemned some passages, albeit voicing personal opinions, but they were all of such a nature that they either did not understand what I had written or what they adduced was blatant calumny. They censured some gospel passages from the *Paraphrases* as if they were spoken by me.[18] How many lies I pointed out in Béda's book, how many calumnies, how many ravings of a deranged mind![19] They show no shame and, as if no response had been given, they continue on their merry way. They allow young boys to be taught Fausto's *Elegies* and Poggio's *Facetiae* translated into every language, as well as other works of priapean obscenity.[20] But, without giving any valid reason for doing so, they refuse to tolerate my *Colloquies*, a work designed to perfect the Latin of young boys, or my *Encomium of Matrimony*, an imaginary exercise, modelled after the example

* * * * *

17 Homily 28.3 (on Matt 8:23–4)
18 See Ep 2033:39–41 with n15.
19 See Ep 2033 n14.
20 While 'priapean obscenity' is an apt label for the lascivious *Facetiae* (first published in 1470) of Poggio Bracciolini, it hardly fits Fausto Andrelini's *Elegiae* (1494), which sing the praises of Christ and the Virgin Mary. It is possible that Erasmus was really thinking of Andrelini's youthful work *Amores sive Livia* (first printed in 1490 at Paris), which sings the praises of Venus and Priapus in explicitly erotic language. Cf Epp 1104:12–18, 1111: 68–70, where Erasmus remembers Andrelini (d 1518), his former friend from Paris days, as a man of mediocre learning who had railed against theology, had been a rake, and had lectured on 'that rubbish the *Priapeia*,' an ancient anthology of witty but extremely obscene poems.

of the declamatory school.[21] They take refuge in the protection of authority 160
and numbers. The sacred faculty and the honoured university are used as
pretexts – as if we did not know by what schemes these senate decrees are
sometimes passed.

Everywhere the dishonesty of a certain few has more power than the
integrity of the others. The leader and the stage director of such specta- 165
cles have a few sworn followers.[22] Each of these draws in whomever he
can by entreaty, money, dishonour, force. And this flock has the good fortune of having the kind of rector they desire.[23] The ideal moment is sought,
care is taken that those are present who will give their assent or at least
give in; those are excluded whose judgments they know are in the service 170
of good rather than of the perverse cupidity of this or that person. In that
way an edict is passed that serves their best interests.[24] The rest is handled by their sworn friends and the rector, whom they have won to their
cause. Bravo! Thus piety wins the day, thus triumphs the Catholic church.

* * * * *

21 First published in 1518 under the title *Declamatio in genere suasorio de laude
matrimonii*, the *Encomium matrimonii* (as it quickly became known) eventually
became part of *De conscribendis epistolis* (1522), where it was included as an
example of a 'letter of persuasion' (CWE 25 129–45). From the beginning, the
work drew the fire of conservative theologians, who thought that Erasmus had
praised marriage too highly and that his intent was to deny the superiority of
priestly celibacy to marriage (Ep 1341A:846–9). Erasmus' defence was always,
as here, that the work was merely a rhetorical exercise and that he had also
written a counter-argument, a 'letter of dissuasion,' against marriage (cf Ep
1341A:650–9). But the view of marriage expressed in the *Encomium* was genuine and was strongly reasserted in 1526 in the *Institutio christiani matrimonii*,
dedicated to Catherine of Aragon (see CWE 26 528–9 n1).
22 Béda and Berthélemy (Ep 2027 n18). There is a more detailed narrative of the
events recorded here in Allen Ep 2126:139–48.
23 Allen, following volume 6 of Du Boulay's *Historia universitatis parisiensis* (1673),
indicated that the day of Béda's appearance before the entire university to secure the condemnation of Erasmus' books, 23 June 1528, was also the day on
which Bertinus Myss was elected as the new rector. But James Farge has established, on the basis of the university archives, that Myss was not elected until
the following day, 24 June, which means that it was his predecessor as rector,
Nicolas Boissel, who presided over the meeting of the university. Just before
the election took place, the faculty of arts took the unusual step of thanking
Boissel, a theologian, for his labours in the domain of literature, an apparent reference to the preceding day's condemnation of the *Colloquies*. See James
Farge's article on Boissel in CEBR I 160.
24 Ie the condemnation of Erasmus' books on 23 June; see Epp 2021:129, 2042:24.

And furthermore, they exploit the authority of princes and pontiffs, given   175
to them for the suppression of heresy, to avenge private grievances and to
destroy the humane studies that they have never learned, and this they do
against the will and desire of monarchs and pontiffs. The intention of the
latter is that those who are legally convicted of impiety should be healed
with Christian compassion, if they are curable, and that the ultimate pun-   180
ishment should not be invoked except when every other expedient has been
tried, especially since this deadly evil has spread so widely. But for those
who zealously devote their energies to restoring higher studies to the light,
who rescue good authors from decay or textual error, who inflame men's
minds to sincere piety, they wish that they be held in honour and be the   185
object of gratitude. Many not only feel this gratitude but show it concretely.
    Those people are disturbed that scholastic subtleties are no longer in
vogue. What, I ask you, lasts forever in human affairs? At one time there
were no schools of theology and Augustine was regarded as an invincible
dialectician because he had read Aristotle's *Categories*. Finally, theological   190
studies reached their highest point, not to say went beyond it. Sacred Scripture, together with the ancient authors, went out of favour. Nor were Peter Lombard's collected works read, save only by the few.[25] A great part of
the age was wasted in sophistic and superfluous questions. Now the world
scene is moving in another direction, but they hold on grimly to their ha-   195
bitual pursuits, venting their fury against everything they have not learned.
Who does not admit that much honour is owed to monks? Give us true
monks and honour will not be lacking. But where are they? All they have is
the habit and the tonsure, except for a very few. I scrupulously avoid saying that there are none. I beseech you, a lover of piety, to make a tour of the   200
monasteries of your region and see how little Christian piety you will find
there, how little spiritual vitality, especially among those who call them-

* * * * *

25 Although Peter Lombard (c 1100–60) wrote commentaries on the Psalms and
   the Pauline Epistles, his fame rests on his last work, the *Four Books of Sentences*
   (*Sententiarum libri quatuor*), a lucid, comprehensive, and systematic survey of
   Christian doctrine that represented the triumph of the dialectical approach to
   theology characteristic of medieval scholasticism. By the thirteenth century,
   the *Sentences* had become the standard textbook of Catholic theology in all
   universities and were the subject of lectures and commentaries by virtually
   every theologian of repute. Erasmus thought that the scholastic theologians
   of his day failed to measure up to the standards set by the 'Master of the
   Sentences,' who at least directed his attention to serious questions, and he
   claimed to have encountered some who had never even read the *Sentences* (Ep
   456:271–5).

selves mendicants. In our region they exercise an incredible tyranny. Again
and again I must testify that I do not say these things to insult any order,
but I refer to those who are an utter disgrace to their order. Although they 205
recognize the reasons why they are hated by many, they do nothing to correct their failings but rather strive to prevail through dishonesty, violence,
and intrigue.

Would that you had enough time to read my responses to Béda and
the Spanish monks![26] You would see from what trivial nonsense they have 210
stirred up such great disturbances. Yet they are not ashamed of their ignorance, falsity, calumny, malice. This is their strategy: 'Let us all shout out
before the people whatever can be said against the most wicked of men;
let us not be silent at banquets, in secret confessions, in intimate conversations, at court, before the greatest and the lowliest, but especially before 215
the unlearned, who cannot read Erasmus' books. We must especially be on
our guard that nothing of his be translated into the vulgar tongues, for that
would immediately lay bare our lies.[27] In that way we are sure to win.'
What could be more wicked than such animosity? and this is the piety of
monks. Augustine says that nowhere does one live more virtuously than in 220
the monasteries and nowhere is error more dangerous,[28] and yet he is speaking of those who lived together not bound by vows, at least not perpetual
vows. What would he say now if he saw many monasteries that differ in no
way from public brothels? What would he say of many convents of monks
in which the last thing you will find is chastity? I am speaking of monas- 225
teries in my country.[29] And in those that are privileged with the name of
the Observance,[30] good God! How few there are in which you will observe
the sincerity of the Christian soul! And yet we build new monasteries every day. They pretend I am their enemy, if you please, although in all my
writings I do nothing but exhort them to true religion. If this is so dear to 230
their hearts, as they wish it to appear, how is it that they do not welcome my
work? Through their stupidity and unscrupulousness, matched by an equal
malice, I foresee that this tumult to which Luther gave rise will be followed

* * * * *

26 On Erasmus' responses to Béda see Ep 2033 n14. On the *Apologia adversus
monachos* see Ep 1879.
27 Cf Ep 2048:25–6.
28 Ep 78.9
29 Ie in Holland, of which Erasmus could speak from personal experience. As
Allen suggests, this remark was probably inserted out of deference to possible
English susceptibilities.
30 See Ep 1967 n10.

by another much more grave tumult unless the authority of princes and
bishops exercises vigilance in time.   235

Already certain Dominicans and Franciscans are raising up their heads
and venting their rage upon those they hate whenever the occasion offers
itself; their hatred is directed against all those who favour good letters and
truer piety. Recently in France they threw three people into jail, of whom
one would have been burned at the stake unless the justice of the king   240
had delivered him, referring the case to Paris. Do you want to know the
charge? A monastery was being built there at kingly expense. This man,
who for that matter was totally alien to Lutheranism, said: 'These outlays of
money would perhaps be better spent on orphans, widows, and the poor.'
The monks considered these words as an act of *lèse-majesté* against their or- 245
der and demanded that this upright and learned man be sent to the stake.
The torches were already in their hands, the pyre was heaped up, the final
sentence pronounced.[31] Two others were seized, for grave reason, of course.
Their crime? Constrained by illness, they had eaten meat on two days during Lent, and they did not deny it.[32] These are the preludes of monastic   250
tyranny. Unless this be checked, what is the prognostication for the future?
For you are an excellent prophet, a man of wisdom. The best prophet is
the wise man. The indignation of the people will break out into a fiercer
storm.[33] The mendicants alone – I blame certain unscrupulous ones among
them, not the orders themselves – were the source and origin of all this evil, 255
and the world will not be at peace until they are brought into line. It is in
their own interest that this should be done. The better part, if not the greater
part, of monks should desire this. It is an act of violence to suppress monasteries, which has been attempted in some places.[34] A better solution is that
monasteries become schools of sobriety, chastity, modesty, and true piety.   260

* * * * *

31 Cf Ep 2038:36–40. According to James K. Farge (private communication to the
   annotator), there is no record of such a case having come before the Parlement
   of Paris. It might possibly have come before the papally appointed judges
   delegate (Epp 2027 n1, 2038 n14), but the records of that tribunal are no longer
   extant.
32 Cf lines 84–6 above and Ep 2038:34–6.
33 The most recent 'storm' had been the Peasant's Revolt in Germany, 1524–5.
34 It is not clear what 'attempts' Erasmus has in mind here. By 1528, the process of
   dissolving monasteries or turning them into schools or hospitals had already
   been under way for several years in the Protestant territories of Germany
   and Switzerland. But the context here suggests that Erasmus was referring to
   attempts by Catholic authorities to deal with wayward monks by suppressing
   their houses. In Ep 1547:23–30, he describes the suppression of a house of
   Augustinian canons in January 1525 by the city of Basel, which had not yet
   officially gone over to the Reformation.

I shall indicate elsewhere by what methods this should be done. For the moment, I should merely like to suggest in passing that it would enhance the reputation of the monks if they were prohibited by law from attracting young boys and girls into their ranks through blandishments and threats, and if it were proven that some were drawn into the order through guile, they should be restored to liberty by the authority of bishops and their kidnappers[35] brought to justice; if provision were made that serious and upright men stimulate the spiritual growth of professed religious, both men and women, with the food of heavenly doctrine and that no one be allowed to live a life of leisure. It would contribute in no small way to the concord of the church if, as far as possible, the immense variety of titles, habits, and rites were done away with: it would suffice if their vesture were poor and simple and their facial expression and seemly behaviour gave evidence of the monk rather than the colour or shape of the amice; and if, in addition, they were to lay aside the diplomas with which they are armed to excess against monarchs, bishops, magistrates, and the common people – and even more against themselves[36] – and acknowledge what their bishops and the leaders and founders of their orders did and wished them to do.

But I will expand on this subject at another time. I shall now return to the point where I left off. If something is to be corrected, let that moderation be employed which befits Christians and which we see was demonstrated by those of earlier times, whose learned piety successfully fought against the battle formations of so many heresies.[37] What do they think they will attain with senseless tumults, vicious alliances, poisonous slander, scurrilous impudence, warlike audacity, manifest lies? The church, Christ's dove, is not in the habit of defeating malice with malice, stupidity with stupidity, or

* * * * *

35 Kidnappers (*plagiarii*) are on the list of lawless sinners in 1 Tim 1:9–10. Cf Ep 447:68–70, 751, where Erasmus had also used *plagiarii* (translated as 'body-snatchers' and 'slave-dealers') to describe those who lure youngsters into religious orders.
36 In the pre-Tridentine church, one of the principal obstacles to monastic reform, and indeed to religious reform in general, was that so many religious orders possessed documented exemptions or immunities from the ordinary jurisdiction of the bishops as well as from secular jurisdiction, and also that individual religious houses (or groups of them) were often exempt from the disciplinary authority of their order. Cf Ep 1875 n36.
37 This refers in particular to the Dominicans, founded in 1215 with the express purpose of the learned refutation of heresy and preaching against all deviations from Catholic orthodoxy. First on the list of heresies to be combatted was that of the Albigensians of southern France, where the order was founded. The sentences that follow are a reminder that Erasmus was not pleased with the tendency of latter-day members of the order to find heresy in his works.

impiety with impiety, but has learned to overcome evil with good.[38] No one
can be in doubt about my feelings. I could have been a high-ranking leader
in the Lutheran church;[39] I preferred to incite the hatred of all of Germany
against me rather than to withdraw from the community of the church. I   290
could have been the initiator of a new sect. I recruited no disciple to my
side but delivered as many as I could to Christ, preferring to have fellow
disciples rather than disciples. I seek no fortune, although I am invited on
all sides by the greatest princes,[40] and they are not few in number. I might
seem to be speaking arrogantly, but let it be known that I am speaking the   295
truth. I continue in my modest circumstances and I do not allow my poor
health[41] and old age to discharge me from unending and excessive labours.

These things make clear how much I abhor heresy. But certain things in
my writings give offence. My adversaries do not observe how much greater
offence was given by the things that my admonitions seek to cure. Concern-   300
ing my attempt to recall scholastic theology to the scriptural sources and to
the reading of ancient authors, to speak frankly, I have no regrets as yet,
especially every time I think of the frivolous sophistries into which it had
fallen. But if they wish to restore it to its former dignity, let them not do
so by lashing out against others but by exhibiting a reasonable theology,   305
worthy of Christ, as has begun to be done in some schools. Piety and conscience compelled me to make some reproaches against monks, although
even here I made many concessions to the name of religion and to Christian
modesty. They will better restore their former authority if they show that
they are true monks by their pious and holy conduct rather than by heaping   310
abuse on the reputation of others by their stupid lies. And if they truly wish
to uphold the dignity of their orders, let them restrain those rabble-rousers
whose words and deeds do them dishonour, and let them return to the purity of morals by which they once won for themselves such great favour in
the whole world.   315

* * * * *

38 See Rom 12:21.
39 Erasmus, who usually speaks of the Lutheran 'sect,' faction,' 'conspiracy,' and
   so forth, here writes *Lutherana ecclesia*. Cf Ep 1485:7, where, writing to the Strasbourg reformer Wolfgang Capito, Erasmus refers to 'that church of yours' (*ves-
   trae ecclesiae*). In the following sentence of the present letter Erasmus capital-
   izes *Ecclesia* in the phrase 'community of the church.' His use of 'church' in
   'Lutheran church' is thus, as always, ironic.
40 Since the invitations noted in Ep 1938 n4, new ones had arrived from Sigismund I of Poland (Ep 1952) and Ferdinand of Austria (Epp 2000, 2005). See
   Ep 2029:98–104.
41 See Ep 1989 n4.

In brief, with sincere devotion we must strive that Christ be the victor in this tumult and that the triumph be secured for him alone, not for human passions, which we see vying on both sides to seize the victory for themselves. Let the pope and the cardinals win, but only if their vision is directed towards Christ; let even the monks win if they serve the cause of Christ. But if they look to their own glory, their bellies,[42] profit, and power, we are no longer fighting for Christ but for the world. The evil is not taken away, but taken elsewhere; the disease is not cured but changed, perhaps for the worse. What is good in the teachings and counsels of Luther let us follow, not because he gave these counsels but because they are right and accord with Holy Scripture. I see the danger that we may not reach a just equilibrium but, as often happens, may change our course to the opposite direction. Just as previously there was much superstition in the cult of the saints, now these zealots will add many things in order to distance themselves further from Lutheran belief. Moderation had to be used, not excess. The people had to be taught that images were nothing more than symbols, provided for the minds of the ignorant; that saints are to be venerated, not adored with *latria*, as it is called;[43] that it is more perfect to lift up our minds to God without corporeal images than through images; and that it is more perfect to ask of Christ whatever we wish to obtain. It would be safer to propose Christ for our imitation rather than any of the saints. The saints are most truly venerated by the imitation of their good deeds. Not all images are appropriate for use in church; measure and decorum must be observed in the choice of them. Not to go on too long, if in other things one would not give vent to excess but would observe temperance, we could hope for a happy issue from this present turmoil.

But this will never be unless princes and the leaders of the church remove private feelings from their decisions and look only to the glory of Christ and the common good of the Christian religion. If we were to act in this way, God would be present to us and would turn these tumults into peace. It is sufficiently clear that this tempest in human affairs has been sent upon the earth not without the will of God, just as he inflicted various plagues upon the Egyptians so that they would regain their senses.[44] The wisest course would be that we all take refuge in God's mercy, and that each should admit his guilt. As things are, we all cast the blame on one another;

320

325

330

335

340

345

350

* * * * *

42 See Ep 1980 n1.
43 Catholic theology distinguishes between the 'worship' (*latria*) owed to God and the 'veneration' (*dulia*) owed to the saints. The Virgin Mary receives *hyperdulia*.
44 Exodus 8–11

no one acknowledges his own guilt. We do not seek a remedy for our ills, but revenge.

As far as I am concerned, I shall not take it too badly if all of my works sink into obscurity. If they are harmful to piety, I would not even wish them to survive. If they add to piety but it is God's will that they perish, whether it be my fault or someone else's, let the will of him be done who can only wish what is best. Let them show me some doctrine that is contrary to Christian piety; if I do not correct it immediately, let them cry out that I am a bad Christian. What am I to do in the face of the suspicions, perversities, calumnies, and lies of the stupid, the malevolent, and the uninstructed? I can wish them a better mind, but I cannot cure them. Would that I could do that also! Christ will cure them when he thinks it best.

Your friend Aldridge assumed much work for himself for my sake in collating manuscripts,[45] but I have nothing with which to repay him since he is so far away. I ask that in your kindness you will repay him for me.[46] I am very happy that he enjoys your favour. May the Lord Jesus keep you free from harm.

Given at Basel, 1 September 1528

2038 / To Hermann von Neuenahr Basel, [c 1 September] 1528

This letter was first published in the *Opus epistolarum*. The year-date is confirmed by the reference to the uproar in France over the *Ciceronianus* (Ep 2021). Allen assigned the conjectural month-date on the basis of the points of contact with Ep 2037, which immediately precedes this letter in the *Opus epistolarum* and is dated 1 September. On Count Hermann, see Ep 1926.

ERASMUS OF ROTTERDAM TO HERMANN NEUENAHR, GREETING

I had planned to move elsewhere before this winter,[1] but Augustine,[2] my Mt. Athos,[3] detains me. In my *Ciceronianus*[4] I do not condemn the style of Ci-

* * * * *

45 For the new edition of Seneca; see Ep 2056 n5.

46 This request may have had something to do with Aldridge's appointment to a prebend in Lincoln in 1528.

2038

1 See Ep 1926 n8.

2 The Froben edition of 1529 (Ep 2157)

3 Ie my source of trouble and weariness; see *Adagia* IV iv 39: *Aetna*, Athon 'An Etna, an Athos.'

4 See Ep 1948.

cero – whom I have always regarded so highly that if other writers, no matter how eloquent, are compared to him, they seem to me to be mute – but the 5
foolish affectation of Ciceronian language. I pass in review many learned
men, whom Nosoponus does not include in the list of Ciceronians, in order
to console himself with the thought that he shares with so many other men
the distinction of not being a Ciceronian.[5] I name none without praise. But
certain followers of Budé are said to be furious that I compared Budé with 10
Bade, although I compare them only with respect to that facile Ciceronian
fluency which I point out is to be regarded as of no consequence and which
Budé himself expressly despised.[6] And lest anyone could misinterpret this,
I add, 'although Guillaume Budé is to be admired for many other excellent
qualities.'[7] There is no serious work of mine in which I do not speak of him 15
more respectfully than any Frenchman ever did. And yet if the rumour is
true, Budé's friends are so furious it is as if I had urinated on his father's
and mother's ashes. They exclaim, 'O heaven and earth! Budé with Bade!'
They claim that I envy Budé's fame and they tear me apart with numerous
epigrams, among which some are thought to be by Joannes Lascaris.[8] Him 20
also I mention very respectfully in this book, and I never mention his name
elsewhere save with a flattering introduction. Who would think there was
so much stupidity in France? The case was brought to the attention of the
king. When he wished to know the cause of this disagreement, he was told
that Budé had criticized me in one of his works and that, offended by this, I 25
sought revenge and compared him with Bade.[9] I see that such commotions
can arise in the realm of higher studies as they can in religion.

It is said that the great high priest is in Nice, making efforts to establish peace between the two monarchs,[10] but I am afraid it is vendetta that
he is after.[11] It is a fatal evil, of which I see no end. If the Lutheran faction 30

* * * * *

5 Nosoponus is the voice of Erasmus' Italian critics.
6 See Ep 1812:122–40.
7 For the text of the offending passage, see Ep 2021 introduction. For similar
   accounts of the uproar, see Epp 2040:14–29, 2044:10–27.
8 See Ep 2027:27–8.
9 Cf Epp 2046:347–51, 2048:16–18.
10 See Ep 2030:48–55.
11 In the immediate wake of the sack of Rome in May 1527, the pope's family,
   the Medici, were expelled from Florence and replaced by a republican regime.
   Clement's diplomatic efforts were henceforth aimed not only at his own safe
   return to Rome, which took place in October 1528 (Ep 1987 n1), but also at the
   restoration of the Medici dukes to Florence. Following the formal reconciliation between Clement and Charles in the treaty of Barcelona (June 1529), the

deteriorates, which they themselves are working to bring about, an intolerable tyranny of pseudomonks will arise.[12] Here they are in command.[13]
They have won in France also, I hear, through the favour of the king's
mother[14] and the chancellor, now a cardinal.[15] In one of the provinces two
men were captured and risk losing their lives because, constrained by sick-   35
ness, they ate meat for two days during Lent.[16] A third person would have
been burned at the stake if the king had not intervened. The case has been
referred to Paris.[17] He[18] said that the excessive sum spent for the build-
ing of a monastery could have perhaps been put to better use to help orphans, widows and the poor. These are preludes; you can surmise the rest.   40
Farewell.

I do not respond to your archbishop because his letter provided me
with no subject to write about.[19]

At Basel, 1528

* * * * *

Emperor's forces laid siege to Florence and restored the Medici (1529–30). See
Pastor 10 chapters 2–3.

12 Ie the friars. Cf Epp 1238:110n, 1582:108, 1926:8
13 It is not immediately clear what Erasmus means by 'here' *apud nos*. He can
   scarcely mean 'here in Basel,' where the already foreseen victory of the
   Zwinglian Reformation would cause him to leave the city in the spring of
   1529 and resettle in Freiburg im Breisgau. The more likely meaning is 'here
   in Germany.' If so, the sentence is probably an expression of Erasmus' long-
   standing dismay at the tendency of Ferdinand of Austria to engage in the violent suppression of heresy, a tendency behind which he was inclined to see the
   influence of the friars. See Epp 1924:25–42, 1926:18–20, 1977:50–2, 1983:3–9.
14 As regent for her son during his captivity in Spain (1525–6), Louise of Savoy
   had allowed the Paris conservatives to pursue more vigorously than before
   their campaign against Berquin, Lefèvre d'Etaples, and others accused of
   heresy. Among other things, she complied with their request that she establish, in cooperation with the pope, the tribunal of 'judges delegate' that in due
   course found Berquin guilty of relapse into heresy. See Epp 1692 n9, 2027 n1.
15 Antoine Duprat (1463–1535) was a doctor of civil and canon law whose career
   prospered under the patronage of Louise of Savoy and her son, the future
   Francis I. On the latter's accession to the throne in 1515, Duprat was made
   chancellor of the realm. In holy orders as early as 1516, Duprat was appointed
   archbishop of Sens in 1525 and was named a cardinal in 1528. Entrusted by the
   king with virtual control of ecclesiastical policy, he moved it, as noted here,
   in a firmly conservative direction (cf Epp 2042:17–19, 2053:20).
16 See Ep 2037:84–6, 248–50.
17 See Ep 2037:239–48.
18 The person accused
19 Cf Ep 1995 from Hermann von Wied.

Antoine Duprat
Detail of the portrait of Francis I with his children and advisers (see xv above)
Musée Condé, Chantilly

2039 / To Erasmus Schets   Basel, 2 September 1528

This letter was published by Allen, using the autograph in the British Library
(MS Add 38512 fol 29). On Schets, see Ep 1931.

Cordial greetings. I pray you to see to it that my package is delivered to
England,[1] and the letter to Valdés to Spain.[2] I have written concerning the
pensions.[3] For the year 1527 twenty pounds, that is, sixty nobles, are owed
me in England;[4] by the feast of St Michael they will owe me forty-five nobles.[5] The entire Courtrai pension was due on last St John's Birthday.[6] My   5
servant Kan has not returned.[7] I suspected this would happen. If you and
all of yours are in good health, I have great reason to rejoice.
    Given at Basel, 2 September 1528
    You will recognize your friend's hand.
    To the honourable Master Erasmus Schets. At Antwerp   10

2040 / To Juan Luis Vives   Basel, 2 September 1528

This letter was first published in the *Opus epistolarum*. Vives' reply is Ep 2061.
As the content of both letters indicates, there was now a certain coolness in the
relationship between Erasmus and Vives. One reason may have been Vives'
growing independence as a scholar (cf Ep 2026 n3). Another was probably
Erasmus' reluctance to come openly to the defence of Vives's patron Catharine
of Aragon, in the matter of Henry VIII's desire to divorce her (see lines 45–7
below). But the principal reason was doubtless continuing friction arising out
of misunderstandings over Vives's edition of Augustine's *De civitate Dei* for
Froben; see Epp 1309 introduction, 1531:41–6, 1889:19–28).

* * * * *

2039
1 The package contained Ep 2037, probably other letters as well, and possibly a
  presentation copy of the *Concionalis interpretatio in psalmum* 85 (Ep 2017)
2 Not extant, dated 31 August 1528; see Allen Ep 2109:2.
3 Either to his English patrons about the method of paying the sums owed him,
  as Schets had advised (Epp 1931:31–4, 2014:15–18), or (in a letter no longer extant) to Schets himself in response to the latter's suggestion in Ep 2001:15–22.
4 Cf Epp 1999:7–8, 2014:56–8. These are not the gold angel-nobles (or any other
  nobles), but instead the 'noble' money-of-account, in which three nobles = one
  pound sterling. See Epp 1866 n7, 1931 n8, 1993 n3.
5 The first half of the pension from Warham for 1528, due by 29 September (in
  England the year began on 25 March); cf Ep 1999:7–9 with n3.
6 Cf Ep 1999:10–11.
7 Ep 1999 n9

ERASMUS OF ROTTERDAM TO JUAN LUIS VIVES OF VALENCIA,
GREETING

If you have nothing of Seneca but the notes by Aldridge in the copy that
was in More's possession for quite some time,[1] it will be of no use; I have
things of a very different sort. But if you have come upon some ancient   5
manuscripts, which I sincerely hope you have, I do not ask that you send
them here, for perhaps it would get here too late; they are already at work
here. But when you have perused my edition, you may polish up your own
if you wish. I could not abandon mine. The first one that appeared was not
mine.[2] I never brought greater disgrace upon myself in anything than in   10
trusting that imbecile, who I thought had some degree of common sense.[3]
This was a task suited to you or another Spaniard[4] or some learned man,
whatever his origins. But I was not able to tolerate this indignity.[5]

Velius complains that I passed you over in the *Ciceronianus*,[6] although
it was a simple matter of forgetfulness. If they think it cannot be condoned   15
in consideration of my old age, certainly it should have been condoned because of what might better be called the turmoils rather than the toils of
my studies.[7] And yet I was more fortunate in omitting your name than in
mentioning Budé's. Although I treat him most respectfully in all my writings and no less in that dialogue, all the followers of Budé are nevertheless   20
furious, according to report, because I compared him with Bade, although
the comparison had to do with a quality of style that I teach is worthy of
contempt and that Budé himself genuinely despises. Nevertheless, lest anyone misconstrue my words, I added: 'although he is admired for his many
excellent qualities.'[8] What insulting language! The French, joined also by   25

* * * * *

2040
1 A copy of Erasmus' edition of the Froben Seneca of 1515 that Erasmus had
   asked Robert Aldridge to collate with a manuscript at King's College, Cambridge and have sent to him via More; see Ep 1656:11–14, 95–8. Cf Epp 2056:1–
   12, 2061:1, 12–14.
2 Erasmus blamed the defects in the Froben edition of 1515 on the friends he
   had left in charge of the printing in Basel; see Ep 325.
3 Wilhelm Nesen; see Epp 1341A:447–63, 1479:99–102.
4 Because Seneca himself was a Spaniard. Vives did not act on this suggestion.
5 Ie the appearance of the defective first edition of Seneca under his name
6 In a letter to which Ep 2008 was the reply: see Ep 2008:15, 24–6.
7 Though clearly insulted by the omission of his name, Vives accepted this apology; see Ep 2061:15–28. To make amends, Erasmus inserted a complimentary
   reference to Vives in the second edition of the *Ciceronianus*; see CWE 28 429.
8 Cf the similar accounts in Epp 2038:10–27, 2044:10–22. For the offending passage in the *Ciceronianus* and a more detailed account of the uproar that it
   caused, see Ep 2021 introduction.

Joannes Lascaris – which I can hardly believe, since I have mentioned him with great respect in all my writings, including this dialogue – think this affront must be avenged with abusive epigrams.[9] A fatal affliction has befallen both religion and the world of study.

Hieronymus[10] showed me your letter.[11] You plead quite a cogent case with him. You try to persuade him that the *City of God* is selling well. How he wishes this were true![12] If he did not have so many volumes left over, there would be no need of your exhortations or mine. Events themselves would require that the work be reprinted. 'But damn that liar!' you say. Who is that liar? Pseudocheus[13] said that everything had been sold and the new edition was already in preparation. But Johann Froben and Hieronymus Froben say that many copies remain. Show us who the liar is. When I urged Hieronymus to print your *Declamations*,[14] he answered that he still had forty copies of your work in stock, which he had printed at my instigation.[15] If these are all lies I do not know what to say. Your name is celebrated already and I have no doubt that some day it will be very celebrated,[16] especially if you make your name with some work of practical interest, like the one published by Lazare Baïf.[17] I have urged Hieronymus to write to you himself, for he is a bit lazy.

God forbid that I meddle in the affair of Jupiter and Juno,[18] especially since I am not well informed about it. I would more readily award two

* * * * *

9 See Ep 2027 n14.
10 Froben
11 Not extant
12 Cf Epp 1532:41–3, 1889:19–21.
13 Pseudocheus is the double-dealing liar in Erasmus' colloquy *Pseudochei et Philetymi* 'The Liar and the Man of Honour,' first published in 1523 (CWE 39 344–50). His real-life counterpart was Franz Birckmann, the Antwerp bookseller and printer's agent about whose underhanded business methods Erasmus had often complained; see Ep 1931 n6. Vives had instantly recognized that Pseudocheus was Birckmann (Ep 1513:46–50).
14 The *Declamationes Syllanae quinque,* published by Hillen at Antwerp in 1520 with a preface by Erasmus (Ep 1082)
15 Froben had reprinted Vives' *Somnium* in March 1521; see Ep 1108 n28.
16 Indeed, most of the works that established Vives' fame as the greatest Spanish humanist and educational theorist of the sixteenth century were published in the decade that commenced in 1529. See CEBR III 412.
17 *De re vestiaria*; see Ep 1962 introduction.
18 Ie of Henry VIII and Catherine of Aragon, whom Henry was eager to divorce (Ep 1932 n11). It seems that Vives, a strong supporter of Queen Catherine, had asked Erasmus for an expression of opinion about the divorce and that

Junos to one man than take one away. I had confided a letter to Nigro,[19] but unsealed and included in the letter to him,[20] leaving him the option of delivering or destroying it. The servant[21] who sealed it blurted out something imprudently to someone.[22] The queen sent me a gift.[23] But that person took 50 a lot away from its pleasure by delaying its arrival.[24] He detained my servant for six full weeks, seeking every opportunity to send him off empty-handed. The queen gave a gift; he usurped it. He is so lacking in generosity that he is not willing to give a gift that was given by another.

Farewell, 2 September 1528.   55

2041 / To Girolamo Aiazza   Basel, 3 September 1528

First published in the *Opus epistolarum*, this is Erasmus' reply to Ep 2020.

ERASMUS OF ROTTERDAM TO GIROLAMO AIAZZA, GREETING
Most distinguished sir. I think it is an act of piety to pray or offer masses for the dead, but if I have any intuition at all, the tale of the ghosts is a concoction of the monks,[1] who have the intention to lie but not the ability. They have an extraordinary love for the fires of purgatory because it is very 5 useful for their kitchens. I see that, as things now stand, this victory will go not to Christ but to the desires of certain people who serve their own

* * * * *

Erasmus here takes refuge by referring to a letter he had written on the subject earlier; see n20 below, and cf Ep 2061:84 with n15.
19 This is doubtless a somewhat cumbersome pun on the name of Thomas More. A mulberry or a blackberry was a *morum* (neuter), and a *morus* (feminine) was a mulberry tree. Horace writes of *nigra mora* 'blackberries' (*Satires* 2.4.22). As Allen observed, More was the obvious person to whom Erasmus would have committed an important letter.
20 Allen conjectures that the letter in question was a letter to Queen Catherine, sent with Ep 1804 (to Thomas More) and apologizing for his indiscretion in mentioning divorce in his *Institutio christiani matrimonii* (1526); see Ep 1804:313–15, and cf Ep 1727 introduction.
21 If the conjectures in the preceding note are correct, this would have been Nicolaas Kan, who left England in April 1527 without waiting for Mountjoy's letter (Ep 1816:11–13).
22 Evidently Mountjoy, who was a member of the queen's household
23 In acknowledgment of the *Institutio christiani matrimonii*; see Ep 1816:13–17.
24 Cf Ep 1966:11–13.

2041
1 See Ep 2020:9–13.

interests rather than those of religion. But Christ will see to this, whose favour we do not yet deserve.

You call me jokingly a Jeromian;[2] but, not to keep you in the dark, I am now more of an Augustinian, since I am emending all his works with immense effort, while of Jerome's opus I had undertaken only the *Epistles.*[3] The Augustine has now in great part been published.[4] I am grateful for your devotion to me, which I can only repay with mutual good will.

Farewell.

At Basel, 3 September 1528

2042 / To Pierre Toussain   Basel, 3 September 1528

This letter was first published in the *Opus epistolarum*. Pierre Toussain (Epp 1559 introduction, 1618:20–5, 1619), canon of Metz and Greek scholar, had studied in Basel (1514–15) and subsequently (1524–5) lived there with Johannes Oecolampadius (Ep 2000 n4), whose antipapal views he shared. Back in Metz in 1525, he was frustrated in his desire to preach his evangelical message. In the summer of 1526, having left Metz in search of greener pastures, Toussain joined the entourage of the sister of Francis I, Margaret of Angoulême (Ep 1615), who in 1527 would become Queen of Navarre, and established contact with Lefèvre d'Etaples and other members of the Meaux circle. At this point he was still resident at Margaret's court, and he still enjoyed Erasmus' affection as a man of learning despite his attachment to the views of Oecolampadius, Guillaume Farel (Ep 1341A n305), and others with whom Erasmus disagreed.

ERASMUS OF ROTTERDAM TO PIERRE TOUSSAIN, GREETING

There is no reason, my dear Pierre, that you should apologize to me for your temerity or your somewhat hurriedly written letter.[1] I know that what you write comes from very sincere feelings. Nor is there reason for you to fear that you may reap some unpopularity from it. Your letter was faith-

* * * * *

2 Ep 2020:26
3 See Ep 396 introduction.
4 The printing of the ten volumes of the Froben Augustine took nearly two years, commencing in the autumn of 1527 and concluding in the summer of 1529. See Allen Ep 2157 introduction.

2042
1 Not extant

fully delivered to me, and I shall not divulge it. And even if it were made public, it contains nothing unworthy of a pious man. You will not be one bit less congenial to me because you had some association with Berquin, whom I consider a learned and erudite man. I regret only that, trusting in his own feelings, he has exposed himself to the greatest peril.[2] If he had kept quiet after his first victory,[3] he would be enjoying peace and quiet now. But he preferred to follow his own impulses rather than my advice.[4] If the unpopularity he caused for me[5] had been of profit to him, I would be consoled that the inconveniences I suffered were compensated by the benefit accruing to a friend, but now we are a burden to each other and he listens to no advice.

I hear the pope is in Savoy,[6] and I also hear how much zeal the cardinal of France shows for the church and how much value he places in theologians and monks.[7] I suppose Alberto Pio, prince of Carpi, is there, a great friend of Aleandro,[8] who in a book he sent me tries to prove that I am the cause of all this tumult.[9] I can see the tyranny that is going to arise. I fear that worldly interests will triumph. This is due to our crimes.

I am still of the opinion that it is better for me to maintain silence, if they do not add anything to the edict.[10] I have replied so many times: I have exposed to the Cousturiers and the Bédas their lies, calumnies, insanities, and ignorance; they have lost all sense of shame.[11] Their whole hope of victory lies in hullabaloo, insults, bulls, and bombast, the collusion and favour of princes. What are your plans, excellent sir? to go into retreat? You must retreat into yourself to find peace of mind.

I beg you to commend me to your illustrious queen,[12] whose pious prudence and prudent piety I greatly admire. If you write more rarely, you

* * * * *

2 On Berquin's situation at this time, see Ep 2066 introduction.
3 Ie his release by order of the king during his first trial for heresy in 1523
4 Cf Ep 2027:7–9.
5 See Ep 1599:1–4.
6 See Ep 2030 n7.
7 Duprat; see Ep 2038 n15.
8 On Pio and Aleandro, see Ep 2029:51–4. Erasmus subsequently learned from Berquin that Pio was indeed in France and living in Paris (Ep 2066:64–6).
9 The 'book' was Pio's response to Ep 1634. Dated 14 May 1526, it circulated in manuscript before being published in January 1529 as *Responsio accurata et paraenetica* (Paris: Bade). Pio had sent Erasmus a copy of it. See Epp 1634 introduction, 1987 n2, 2066 n19.
10 Ie the edict condemning Erasmus' *Colloquies*. See Ep 2037 introduction.
11 See Ep 1943 nn7 (Cousturier) and 6 (Béda).
12 Margaret of Angoulême

will deprive me of your pleasant company but will remain equally dear to me. May the Lord preserve you, dearest friend in the Lord.

At Basel, 3 September 1528

2043 / To Nicolas Le Clerc

Basel, 5 September 1528

Nicolas Le Clerc (d 1558) was a leading member of the faculty of theology at Paris, active in the defence of the faculty's prerogatives and in the furtherance of its campaigns against heresy. From May 1525 to January 1527 he had been one of the members of the special inquisitorial commission established by the regent, Louise of Savoy, the pope, and the Parlement of Paris to deal with cases of heresy. This letter was first published in the *Opus epistolarum*.

ERASMUS OF ROTTERDAM TO THE THEOLOGIAN NICOLAS LE CLERC, GREETING

When I hear that you are a learned, upright, and thoughtful man, I am astonished, if what I have learned from quite trustworthy men is true, that in sacred sermons you often disparage my name as if I were a heretic and worse than Luther. There is of course the example of Guillaume Duchesne, of happy memory;[1] but St Paul admonishes us to rival one another in good.[2] That man understands better now whether he was right in denouncing me as a heretic and an Antichrist before the ignorant multitude. Certainly Ludwig Baer, a man, as you know, of outstanding integrity and no ordinary learning, and also a good friend of yours, who knows me from close at hand and on familiar terms, thinks very differently of Erasmus than you preach.[3] I have no doubt that if you were to read my writings and become acquainted with me you would feel and speak otherwise about me.

* * * * *

2043
1 Duchesne (Ep 1188 n15), who died in 1525, was a member of the faculty of theology who regularly served on faculty committees. According to Erasmus, Duchesne, 'a little oldish man full of venom,' had (with Noël Béda) been a leading participant in the faculty's examination of Luther in 1520 and 1521 (Ep 1188:33–54) and had then become Béda's chief collaborator in the Paris proceedings against him: see Epp 1664, 2053:31–2; *Supputatio* LB IX 447–52; *Spongia* CWE 78 138–9. Again according to Erasmus, Duchesne was similarly involved in the proceedings against Louis de Berquin (Allen Ep 2188:97–8).
2 Gal 4:18
3 Baer (Ep 1933 n3) wrote to Le Clerc at about this time and apparently received an answer from him; see Ep 2065:60–1.

If you were to see how many evils I suffer at the hands of these de-   15
fenders of factions, you would consider my steadfastness, patience, or if you
prefer, misfortune, worthy of some favour. For a long time now I have offered myself to you so that I might be admonished concerning anything in
which I deviated from piety;[4] no one corrects me, no one teaches me, but the
whole thing is carried on by raising outcries among the people, detraction,   20
and conspiracies. 'But,' you say 'Béda gave admonition.' Does admonition
consist in directing a barrage of lies and blatant calumnies against a fellow
Christian? The church of Christ, distinguished sir, does not usually achieve
victory by means of contumely and deception but by truth; it does not seek
the destruction of those in error but their cure. If you have Christ before   25
your eyes, he will be present to you in your endeavors, but if you pay heed
to human passions, you serve the interests of the world, not of Jesus Christ.
It is clear that this tempest has been sent upon the world by God to urge
us to reform our lives. Now pious men must insure that the victory go to
Christ, not to this or that group of men, most of whom pursue their own   30
interests, not those of Jesus Christ.

If what has been reported to me is true, I urge you to change your
language and your manner of thinking. If it proves false (which I would be
more willing to believe), consider that this was never written to you. May
the Lord direct your thoughts to all good works.   35
Given at Basel, 5 September 1528

2044 / To Pierre Danès   Basel, 5 September 1528

Pierre Danès (c 1497–1577), who had studied with Guillaume Budé, was currently a member of the circle of young scholars associated with the human-
istically oriented press of Josse Bade. In 1530 Danès was appointed to teach
Greek at the king's new college of royal lecturers and thereafter advanced in
royal service. In 1546 he was appointed to be one of Francis I's representatives at the Council of Trent and in 1549 he became tutor to the sons of Henry
II. In 1557 he served on a commission to reform the University of Paris and
in the same year received papal confirmation as the bishop of Lavaur.

It was evidently Danès' connection with both Budé and Bade that prompted
Erasmus to write this letter, which is part of his attempt to calm the uproar

* * * * *

4 In his controversy with the Paris theologians, Erasmus' had repeatedly offered
to correct any real errors found in his works; see Epp 1571:1–5, 20–6; 1664:336–
9; 1723:30–2.

in France over the supposed insult to Budé, who in the *Ciceronianus* (Ep 1948)
is declared inferior to Bade as a Ciceronian (see Ep 2021 introduction). Danès
apparently intended to reply (Ep 2065:61) but no such letter is known. There
is no evidence of any other correspondence between Erasmus and Danès.

This letter was first published in the *Opus epistolarum*.

ERASMUS OF ROTTERDAM TO DANÈS, GREETING

As I am greatly chagrined to see that in many parts of the world the Muses,
terrified by this tumult in human affairs, are either completely silent or have
lost all their vitality, so I had great cause for rejoicing that your country
of France offers them a peaceful and pleasant haven. For Italy, long the   5
parent and homeland of great geniuses, has long been at the mercy of cruel
Mars. Nor is Spain at peace. Germany proliferates with those who under the
guise of evangelical piety labour to bring about the extinction of all liberal
learning.

But my joy has been vitiated somewhat by the tumult that has arisen   10
there in France concerning my *Ciceronianus*, although the subject matter was
significant enough that Budé himself promised me in a letter that he would
write something against these apes of Cicero.[1] My sole purpose in writing
this treatise was that those who are eager to appear as Ciceronians should
not be content with reproducing some features or vocabulary of Ciceronian   15
style but truly represent all of Cicero. And I compared Budé with Bade not
in any or every characteristic, but only in that aspect which Budé genuinely
despises and which I teach in that dialogue is worthy of scorn. Nor do they
take notice that these things are said by Nosoponus, not by Erasmus. Lastly,
so that no spiteful person might criticize the comparison, I added that Budé   20
is to be admired for many other excellent qualities.[2] And yet these people
found the subject worthy of insulting epigrams.[3] It is of great importance
for the future of studies that those who fight for the cause of polite letters
should join ranks against the enemy battalions, which are never more united
than when they suppress the emerging study of language and good letters.   25
I am afraid that the fickleness of some will bring the same contagion to
humane studies as that which has been visited upon the Christian religion.

I do not know you either in person or in writing, but I admire your
dedication to the Muses and to all the Graces. Serious men of learning have

* * * * *

2044
1 See Epp 1812:123–4, 2046:63–5.
2 For the text of the passage in question, see Ep 2021 introduction.
3 See Ep 2027 n14.

given me a description of you in their letters to me. I did not wish, my   30
dear Danès, that these sentiments of mine be unknown to you; you may be
certain that they are free of any pretence. Farewell.

Given at Basel, 5 September 1528

2045 / To Maarten Lips   Basel, 5 September 1528

Allen thought that this letter might perhaps have been the outcome of Erasmus' promise in Ep 1858:393–416 to publish in a *brevis libellus* (a brief pamphlet) a catalogue of the names of all his malicious critics. As Allen himself
points out, however, the letter is scarcely long enough to constitute a *libellus*,
and none of the critics is named. All that one can say with certainty is that the
letter was ostensibly written at the instigation of Lips (see lines 3–7), that it is
indeed a catalogue of many of the critics already dealt with in Epp 948, 1126,
1144, 1858, 1967, and 1985, and that it was thus suitable for inclusion in the
Selectae epistolae, in which all the other letters except Ep 21 (ie Epp 1891, 2037,
2046) had also been written as *apologiae*.

Like Erasmus, Maarten Lips (Epp 750 and 1837), was an Augustinian canon
regular and a largely self-taught classical and patristic scholar. He was Erasmus' principal collaborator on the great Froben edition of Augustine (Ep 2157).
In 1525, Lips left the priory of St Maartensdal in Louvain, where conflicts had
arisen because of his friendship for Erasmus, and moved to Lens-Saint-Rémy
in the province of Liège, where he became chaplain of the Augustinian nunnery of Croix-à-Lens.

DESIDERIUS ERASMUS OF ROTTERDAM TO HIS FRIEND MAARTEN
LIPS, GREETING
Although your heartfelt devotion to me cannot but be most gratifying, yet
I should not wish that you do serious battle with such rabble, and I am
not greatly interested in knowing what this or that individual is blathering   5
about. 'They must be exposed to public scorn,' you say. But why do you
look for someone to expose them when no one exposes them better than
themselves? If I were truly their enemy – but God forbid that any Christian
would wish evil on another Christian – I would desire no other revenge than
that in this way they subject themselves to the hatred, scorn, and ridicule   10
of all good persons. I bear up with my own lot with considerable restraint,
consoling myself with the example of David, reflecting within myself: 'What
if the Lord imposed it upon them to speak ill of me and by that remedy
wished to cleanse in me what was displeasing in his eyes? Perhaps in the
past I was too susceptible to the applause of learned men; certainly I must   15
confess that I took great pleasure in the friendship of men of learning. This

bitter medicine is a good antidote to this pleasure. And given that the abyss of the divine plan is inscrutable,[1] what if God is procuring the salvation of both parties? For me, so that warned by the abusive attacks against me I may turn completely to Christ; for them, so that after exposing to everyone their prodigious stupidity, joined with a malice to equal it, they will be forced to return to their senses one day?' What astounds me is that they are so devoid of good sense and shame that after being confuted, caught in the act, ridiculed, and hissed off the stage by the judgments of sensible men so many times, they do not cease to enact this same performance. What is it that supplies them with such confidence if not the ignorance of the people, the willingness of women to listen to them, the scarcity of those who are learned and possessed of good judgment? That's a fine rock that gives them support, but this rock is not Christ, whom they pretend is their brother.

When my emended edition of Jerome was issued,[2] they persuaded a certain female monarch,[3] among others, that I did not like Jerome's style and that I had taken on this work to put into more elegant language what he had expressed in his words. What could be more stupid? As if I could say more elegantly what Jerome had said! or that I was so out of my mind as to think I should undertake such a huge labour in order to change someone's style! Those responsible for this were not from the rank and file, but one was a Dominican, another a Franciscan, both of them bishops.[4] I don't think either of them found anything offensive in the emendations of Jerome, since they had never read anything of his.

When the New Testament appeared, how certain preachers ranted stupidly from the pulpit that there was someone who dared to correct the Magnificat, the Lord's Prayer, and the Gospel of John. How satisfied they were with themselves! how they gloated in triumph! while in the meantime they offered themselves as an object of derision to learned men and all men of good sense.[5]

I heard my praises sung with my own ears. At Antwerp the Prior of the Carmelites, a doctor of theology, was delivering a sermon in his monastery.[6]

* * * * *

2045
1 Cf Ps 35 (Vulgate):7.
2 See Epp 541:99–104, 948:225–38, 1805:42–4.
3 Catherine of Aragon
4 The Dominican was Jorge de Ateca, the queen's confessor; see Ep 948:226n. The Franciscan was doubtless Henry Standish, bishop of St Asaph; cf n9 below.
5 See Epp 541:92–9, 948:99–113, 1126:21–48, 1805:44–7, 1967:156–61.
6 For this sermon, preached on 31 May 1517 by Sebastiaan Craeys, see also Epp 948:114–21 and 131–8, 1967:161–70.

The only proof of his status was his violet-coloured hat. Otherwise, far from being familiar with the Sacred Scriptures, he did not know a word of Latin. There was a great crowd because it was the feast of Pentecost. While he was   50 reciting with as much ignorance as stupidity some inane snippets that he had learned, he happened to spot me and accused me of two sins against the Holy Spirit, one that I dared to correct the Magnificat, and the other that I had said that preachers do not know their subject since they take their text from the sacred writings handed down by the inspiration of the Holy Spirit.   55 As if there were no difference between the Holy Spirit and a monk like him, who seemed more like a blockhead than a man – you should have heard the guffaws! not only of learned men but of some women too who knew me, for I was living in the neighbourhood.[7]

The occasion for this utterance was as follows. A few days previously,   60 a certain old man of the same order had given a sermon in that very place.[8] His theme was from 1 Peter 1:4, 'Be prudent and vigilant in prayer.' Then he said many things taken from his notes about the virtue of prudence, which in Greek is σωφρονήσατε (which has more the meaning 'be sober'). Sobriety, which is the opposite of luxury, and vigilance, which forbids sleepiness, the   65 companion of luxury, go together with prayer. I had said this at a banquet without wishing to offend anyone and without hostility. For this old man did not seem to me to be a bad fellow. I was just sorry that he was not a little more educated.

What shall I say of that person who in the presence of a king, sur-   70 rounded by leading men of the court, got down on his knees, threw his hands into the air, and begged the aid of the prince in suppressing the books of Erasmus?[9] When he was asked to produce what he had found in my writings that was opposed to piety, he counted on his fingers with in- credible hauteur three articles: that I denied the resurrection of the body,   75 that I criticized marriage, and that I likewise criticized the Eucharist. When proof was demanded, he brought forward with the same stupidity a pas- sage from First Corinthians, chapter 15, 'We shall all rise,' to which corre- sponds a passage in Thessalonians 1:4, 'Then those of us who live, who, etc.' Since I point out a variant reading there, without condemning any particu-   80 lar reading, this fellow, in a marvellous display of dialectic, concluded that

* * * * *

7 Probably with Pieter Gillis, with whom Erasmus seems to have lived whenever he was in Antwerp; see Epp 471:29–30, 476:27–33, 532:33, 534:63, 584. Gillis was present at the sermon with Erasmus; see Ep 948:135–7.
8 See Ep 948:121–31.
9 Henry Standish; see Epp 1126:99–192, 1127A:24–44, 1581:382–9.

I denied the resurrection if those who were alive on the last day would be changed into immortality without the intervention of death. At this point, constrained by the arguments of learned men in the audience and trying to evade the issue, he answered that the apostle Paul had written to the   85
Corinthians in Hebrew! This statement was greeted by much laughter; but the prince, mild man that he is, was merciful and felt embarrassed for the man, who was a recipient of his favour, while the man himself felt no shame at all. This man too was not of the rank and file, but a professor of theology, and now even a bishop. These days audacity is much more successful   90
than wisdom.

There was another man very similar to this one, a great theologian in the judgment of many, the very greatest in his own eyes, a solid pillar of the church.[10] He had long inveighed publicly against my New Testament, saying that the final destiny of the church was at hand, and that Antichrists   95
and their precursors had arrived. When we were together without anyone present, I asked him to produce anything that he found offensive in the New Testament. When he remained silent, I pressed him for an answer. Finally this paragon of modesty answered that he had never read my Annotations. Would a Nomentanus[11] or a buffoon have answered differently?   100

The other man, a bit more modest and also more elevated in rank[12] on two separate occasions had approved my Annotations without reservation as a learned and pious work. A little later on I complained that he approved of Lee's calumnies although previously he had approved of my work without reservation after having read it from beginning to end, as he said. The reply   105
of this august personage was that he had indeed read it but not carefully enough.[13]

* * * * *

10 Nicolaas Baechem (Egmondanus), the Carmelite; for the incident reported here, see Epp 948:141–8, 1225:59–63, 1581:265–9.
11 Horace *Satires* 1.1.102. Nomentanus was proverbial for extravagance and riotous living.
12 Jan Briart of Ath, acting chancellor of the University of Louvain (Epp 670, 1571 n4)
13 For Erasmus' claim that Briart had given his full approval to the second edition of the New Testament Annotations, see Epp 1225:66–84, 94–101, and 124–34, 1571:8–14, 1581:69–85. According to the parallel account in the *Apologia qua respondet invectivis Lei*, Ath turned aside Erasmus' complaint that he approved of Edward Lee's harsh criticisms of the first edition with assurances that he had not changed his mind and that he did not at all disapprove of the work; see CWE 72 11–12.

This same man made some odious comments about me before a crowded classroom without mentioning my name but in such a way that no one failed to understand who it was he was attacking. When I com- 110 plained to him in private, he solemnly swore that I was the last person he had in mind. He merely had a few scruples about the *De matrimonio*. When we discussed this among ourselves he admitted that every time I used the word *coelibatum* he understood it to mean a chaste and virginal life. He did not deny that when he read the title *Declamatio*, he understood it to 115 mean a church sermon.[14] I asked him whether he thought it just that I was charged with heresy, although certain of the accusers had not learned Latin. He smiled but said nothing. I think you know the persons to whom I am referring.

You also must know Bucenta,[15] who, in addition to the many other ab- 120 surdities he uttered in private conversations, thought it was intolerable that in one of the Annotations I had written of St Thomas Aquinas that the age in which he lived was not worthy of such a great genius.[16] Obviously I said this to praise him, imputing blame, if anywhere, to the age into which he was born. But that grammarless theologian thought 'not worthy of' meant 125 'detestable to.' There is a new enthymeme[17] for you: 'Bucenta does not know grammar; ergo Erasmus blasphemes against St Thomas.' That same person had noted a passage in which through a comparison I magnify the evil of malicious detraction, which has the same effect as a defamatory book – indeed it does more harm. He thought I was giving approval to a defamatory 130 book, as if one could be said to approve of adultery if in a similar comparison he exaggerated the evil of murder.[18] He noted down a passage[19] in which, after citing the opinions of ancient writers who seem to attribute to the Virgin Mary some actual sin,[20] I add: 'and we absolve her entirely of all sin.' I wished to indicate, of course, that the opinion of certain modern writ- 135 ers differs a great deal from that of the ancient commentators. He thought

* * * * *

14 See Ep 1967:171–4.
15 Vincentius Theoderici (Ep 1196). On the origin of this pseudonym, which comes from the Greek word for an oxherd or a rustic ploughman, see Ep 1196 n48.
16 See Epp 1126 n38 and 1196:45–51.
17 Ie an incomplete syllogism
18 See Ep 1196:52–8.
19 See Ep 1196:58–71.
20 Ie a concrete, specific sinful act, as opposed to 'original sin,' which is sinful human nature in general

that I had declared in my own name that the Virgin Mary was free from original sin, and he was going to include this among my errors.[21] And he uttered many other statements more foolish than these, which I prefer not to mention.   140

He was intent on vengeance but his style was not up to it. So he began to read Virgil, Juvenal, and the *Margarita poetica*[22] to polish up his style. He found three assistants for this purpose. Through this cooperative effort the brilliant work was finished. He was dying to have it published but he did not gain the permission of the vicar of the order. At last he secretly   145 gave birth to his asinine offspring under a feigned name. It was a slim little book.[23] You could not imagine anything more ignorant, insipid, or insane; but in this small book I have counted seventy manifest lies.[24] I have no doubts about who the authors were. My friends sent me a long letter informing me that one of them, Cornelis of Duiveland, wrote to Lee. In it he   150 divulges the mystery of this stupid affair. Since the printer got into trouble and the judge forbade the book to be sold, they sent out some Dominicans with packsaddles to sell them secretly hither and yon. Isn't that a clever trick, worthy of such a sacred order? After that was over they immediately

* * * * *

21 Only since 1854 has the Immaculate Conception, ie the miraculous preservation of the Blessed Virgin from the taint of original sin, been official Catholic doctrine. In Erasmus' time that was still a controversial question among theologians, with the Franciscans in favour and the Dominicans (like Theoderici) opposed. Erasmus himself was inclined to accept the Franciscan view, though he thought it imprudent to assert too much on a matter not yet authoritatively settled by the church. See Ep 1126 n40 and CWE 40 1020–2 n51.

22 An anthology of excerpts from classical and Renaissance authors by Albrecht von Eyb (1420–75), first printed at Nürnberg in 1472. Eyb, a German churchman (canon in Würzburg from 1462), had studied law in Italy and been deeply influenced by Renaissance culture and humanism. Among other things, he published German translations of works by Boccaccio and Plautus and a treatise on marriage.

23 The *Apologia* (1525) by the pseudonymous 'Godefridus Ruysius Taxander' attacking Erasmus' *Exomologesis* and *De esu carnium*. By the time he wrote this letter, Erasmus had learned that 'Taxander' was really Theoderici and three other Dominicans, one of whom was the Cornelis of Duiveland referred to in line 150. For details, see Ep 1571 n14.

24 The Latin is *manifesta mendacia*, which was the title that Erasmus gave to the reply to 'Taxander' that he wrote but decided not to publish. The manuscript, which is preserved in the Royal Library at Copenhagen, has been deciphered by Erika Rummel, who was the first to show that the apologia was aimed at 'Taxander.' Her English translation, *Manifest Lies*, is found in CWE 71 113–31, 165–71 (notes).

vanished from sight, one to Zeeland, another to Gelderland, a third I know 155
not where. Rabinus alone stayed where he was, except that shortly afterwards he departed from the land of the living.[25] One exploit was enough to
earn immortality for his name. And the deviser of these machinations was
my mortal enemy because I showed little favour to his order, of which he
obviously was a great ornament. 160

In Bruges a certain suffragan bishop ranted and raved against Luther
and Erasmus for a whole hour, obviously to convince the people that there
was an alliance between us.[26] And he would have succeeded except that
the people had learned from these very examples not to be readily taken
in by such fictions. Since this had not gone too badly, the suffragan, taking 165
advantage of the absence of the dean,[27] obtained permission to speak once
again from the precentor,[28] his drinking-companion, and he had the gall to
say openly from the pulpit that there were heretical things in my books. As
he came down from the pulpit he was stopped by a remarkably learned man,
at that time a pensionary of the republic, now elevated to a higher office.[29] 170
Despite the efforts of the preacher to escape, his challenger insisted that he
cite a single passage. How do you think he got out of it? As buffoons do,
he said that he had never read any of my works. He merely had intended
to read the *Moria*, but he found there such profound Latinity – these were
the words he used – that he was afraid I might slip into some heresy.[30] 175

When the *Letters of Obscure Men* first appeared, they were welcomed
with great applause by the Franciscan and Dominican monks in England,
who were convinced that they were written seriously to insult Reuchlin and

* * * * *

25 *Rabinus* 'the rabbi,' ie Theoderici, who died on 4 August 1526. 'Rabbi' (Master)
was a term that Erasmus often used to denigrate scholastic theologians; see,
for example, Ep 1126:374–8 with n45, where he uses it at the end of a long
narration of some of his early encounters with Theoderici in Louvain.
26 Nicolas Bureau, a vigilant heresy-hunter who also attacked Juan Luis Vives in
much the same manner described here; see Ep 1144:43–53 with n12
27 Erasmus' friend Marcus Laurinus (Ep 1342), dean of St Donatian's at Bruges
since 1519
28 Gisbert van Schoonhove, precentor at St Donatian's from 1514 until his death
in 1524 (Ep 1012 n4).
29 Frans van Cranevelt (Ep 1145), who in 1515 was appointed pensionary (legal
consultant) to the city of Bruges and in 1522 became a member of the Grand
Council at Mechelen
30 In Epp 1581:433–9 and 1967:154–6 Erasmus similarly names the *Moria* (*Praise of
Folly*) as the work in question. But in earlier accounts he had named the *Paraphrases* as the work beyond the comprehension of the bishop; cf Epp 1144:51,
1192:43.

to favour the monks.[31] When a certain very learned man with a sharp wit
pretended that he was somewhat offended by the style, they consoled him.   180
'Don't look at the outer covering of the style, my good man,' they said, 'but
the substance.' They would not have understood them even today, had not
somebody added a letter warning the reader that they were not to be taken
seriously.[32] Afterwards in Brabant a certain Dominican prior, a doctor of
divinity, wishing to make a name for himself among the fathers, bought up   185
a pile of these books, to send them as a gift to leading men in the order, not
doubting for a moment that they had been written to honour the order.[33]
What mushroom could be more stupid?[34] But these men are, as they think
themselves to be, the Atlases of the tottering church. From among them
experts on church doctrines are selected; they pronounce on the books of   190
Erasmus, and they judge whether we are Christians or heretics.

From that same congregation there rose up a standard-bearer of theologians who boasted that he had Erasmus by the waist and he could not
escape.[35] He said, 'He wrote that Jerome was not a virgin.[36] Behold, Jerome
himself declares that he was a virgin.' 'Where?' 'In the book to Eustochium   195
he says, "We do not merely praise virginity, but we preserve it." '[37] In triumph he said, 'What is more clear? No one preserves what he has lost.'
When Jerome says 'preserved,' he means that he prescribes the way to preserve it, just as one who writes on military discipline is said to prepare soldiers for combat. What applause he received from his drinking-companions!   200

* * * * *

31 The first edition of the *Epistolae obscurorum virorum* appeared in 1515, with enlarged editions following in 1516 and 1517. The work, written anonymously
by the humanists Johannes Crotus Rubianus and Ulrich von Hutten, was a hi-
larious lampoon of the scholastic theologians who had denounced the famous
Hebraist Johann Reuchlin for his opposition to the campaign of the Jewish
convert Johann Pfefferkorn to have all Jewish books confiscated. The work
consisted of letters, written in barbarous Latin by fictitious critics of Reuchlin, that were addressed to a real person, Ortwin Gratius, one of the Cologne
theologians.
32 The reference is to the very last of the letters (II 70), from 'Magister Maleolus'
to Ortwin Gratius, in which satire is abandoned in favour of direct scorn and
derision of Reuchlin's critics.
33 Cf Ep 808:15–21. The prior was Jacobus Remigli (Ep 808:19n).
34 See *Adagia* IV i 38.
35 Cf *Adagia* I vi 96: *Medius teneris* 'You are gripped by the middle.' The standard-
bearer was quite possibly Vincentius Theoderici again; cf Epp 1858 n56, 1967
n20.
36 Cf Erasmus *Life of Jerome* CWE 61 48–9.
37 In the letter to Eustochium (Ep 22.23); see CWE 61 168.

But what laughter, what snorts of disdain, what sneers from learned men!
No day goes by without their perpetrating stratagems of this sort, of which
you give examples yourself.

In a nearby region of France a Franciscan who was endowed with
amazingly strong vocal chords never stopped crying out against me at the   205
top of his voice, in public, in private, at banquets and from the pulpit.[38] I
voiced my complaints to the man in a lengthy letter and at the same time I
alerted the ruler of this region to curb the man's impudent aggressiveness,[39]
saying that it was in the interests of the public tranquillity of the region.
The preacher wrote back to me,[40] solemnly swearing that he never spoke   210
about me except in the most respectful terms. He repeated the same thing
emphatically to certain noblemen who had heard his blasphemies so many
times with their own ears. But the sacred cowl of Francis covers over many
things of this kind.

A certain Dominican was guilty of a similar act of shamelessness. He   215
lashed out against a certain prince in a slanderous preface, venting his fury
in a torrent of verbal abuse.[41] At the insistence of his friends he wrote a palinode in his own hand in which he swore that he had never harboured any
ill feeling concerning the count but had always regarded him as a learned
and pious man. Yet in that same palinode he repeated words from the pref-   220
ace which could refer to no one else but the count. I have a copy of the
palinode.[42] How do you wish to interpret this, as incredible stupidity or a
scurrilous act of impudence? And yet he was the light of his order, an outstanding expert in matters of the faith, and an incomparable professor of
theology. What do you think those rank and file confrères say and do, to   225
whom it is enough to say *ipse dixit* and they immediately applaud, acclaim,

* * * * *

38 Jean Gachi (Ep 1891 introduction)
39 Ep 1891 to Gachi and Ep 1886, addressed to Charles II, Duke of Savoy
40 The letter is not extant.
41 In 1519 the Dominican theologian of Cologne, Jacob of Hoogstraten (Ep 1299
   n25) published his *Apologia secunda* against Johann Reuchlin and his defenders. In the preface to the *Apologia* Hoogstraten heaped abuse on Hermann von
   Neuenahr (Ep 1926) for his part in the publication of a volume of letters (*Epistolae trium illustrium virorum*) in defence of Reuchlin; see Ep 1006:52–73, 162–4.
   The count and his family took umbrage and sought revenge. Starting with Ep
   877:18–35, Erasmus took great delight in telling and retelling the story (only
   hinted at here in the lines that follow) of Hoogstraten's consequent expul-
   sion from Cologne by Hermann's relatives; see also Epp 889:42–6, 1892:56–62,
   Allen Ep 2126:115–28, and CWE 36 324–5 (*Adagia* IV vii 64).
42 Cf Ep 1892:59–61. The document is not extant. On palinodes, ie retractions, see
   Ep 2013 n6.

and to a man give their approval.[43] In Spain a certain member of the Franciscan order, a man held to be learned and pious, also denounced articles excerpted from my books. One of these was worse than heretical, namely, that I had written in the *Enchiridion* that the apostles had a true and gen- 230 uine theology. He cried out at the top of his voice before the people: 'Who could put up with this writer? He says there is no true theology anywhere but in Germany, whereas that country is rife with heresies.'[44] He denounced another no less dangerous article. In the fifth chapter I had written that it was of no great value to be buried in the Franciscan cowl, and that the habit 235 would be of no advantage if you had not imitated the life of St Francis.[45] In this he said I agreed with Montanus, who said that the fallen could not return to the state of grace;[46] as though I had said that there can be no return to grace except through the Franciscan cowl, or that the cowl confers a good state of mind upon a person. He condemned a passage in the *Para-* 240 *clesis* where I say that I wish all women should read the gospel and the epistles of the apostles.[47] This seemed to him to be heretical, even though there are two extant epistles of John to a woman.[48] But on what grounds did he prove it heretical? He said: 'He contradicts a precept of Paul, who in 1 Timothy 2 says 'Let a woman learn in silence with all subjection, etc.'[49] As if a 245 woman were not allowed to open her mouth at home, or as if it were the same thing for a woman to speak in church and to read something silently at home! This leading light of the Franciscan clan had collected and made public thirty articles of this kind.

* * * * *

43 *Ipse dixit*, meaning 'He said so himself,' is the secular equivalent of 'Thus saith the Lord.' It attributes to the speaker an authority so great that what he says must be believed without question, even if no reason is given; see *Adagia* II v 87.

44 On this incident and the meaning of *germanam*, see Ep 1967:181–8.

45 *Enchiridion*, 'Fifth rule'; see CWE 66 72.

46 The Montanists, named after the second-century Montanus of Phrygia, were (among other things) extreme in their demands for holiness of life. The most famous Montanist, the church Father Tertullian, taught that those guilty of mortal sin could not be reconciled with the church.

47 *Desiderius Erasmus Roterodamus: Ausgewählte Werke* ed Hajo Holborn (Munich 1933; repr Munich 1964) 142:15–16; *Christian Humanism and the Reformation: Selected Writings of Erasmus* ed and trans John C. Olin (New York 1965; repr New York 1975) 97.

48 Only 2 John is addressed to a woman, ie 'to the elect lady and her children' (which modern scholars take to be a symbolical reference to a local church and its members).

49 1 Tim 2:11

Recently a certain Dominican prior,[50] regarded as a learned man among   250
his confrères, accosted a certain physician,[51] who was conspicuously learned
in both languages and an ardent follower of mine, wishing to turn him away
with deceptive talk from his devotion to Erasmus. When he made no head-
way but rather incited the doctor to feel even greater admiration for me
and to express it in words, the theologian, forgetting his feigned restraint,   255
began to give vent to his real sentiments, declaring that the books of Erasmus were not worthy to be read by decent people, since they were filled
with obscene insults. When the doctor asked for an example he said: 'Read
the book he recently wrote on matrimony.'[52] 'What's there?' 'He calls bishops sodomites and says that they have four or five concubines each.' At   260
this the doctor burst into laughter, saying: 'You must have a good eye, because I read the book twice and didn't see what you saw.' But the theologian, sure of himself, said, 'Bring me the book and I'll show you.' The book
was brought forth, and the passage was pointed out in which I discuss the
fact that today a man is not accepted into the priesthood if unknowingly   265
he has married an unchaste woman instead of a virgin, whereas one who
has sexual relations with many prostitutes is not only received into the dignity of the priesthood but can be awarded four or five bishoprics. These
are my exact words: 'Someone who has unwisely married a woman who
is not a virgin is said to have shared his body with her, whereas someone   270
who has slept with a host of harlots has not shared his body and, as if he
were pure and wholesome (τέλειος, the Greeks say), and if he wishes, is appointed to four or five bishoprics.'[53] In wonder, the doctor said: 'Where is
that sodomite? Where are the five concubines?' In the end he understood
from the man's answers what a raving idiot he was. The Spaniards, like the   275
Italians, commonly call an effeminate boy or a male prostitute a *putus*,[54] just
as they call female prostitutes *putanas*.[55] But the ancient writers, according
to the custom of an ancient law, used the expression *purus putus* to mean
unblemished, for from the word *putus* we say *putare*, meaning 'cleanse' or
'purify.' That accounts for your sodomite. But where do the five concubines   280
come from? He thought *episcopa* was related to *episcopus* just as *domina* is to

* * * * *

50 Ep 2029:67–89
51 Suárez; see Ep 2029:68.
52 *Institutio christiani matrimonii* (Ep 1727)
53 Cf CWE 69 299, where the passage is rendered somewhat differently.
54 In Spanish the word survives as *puto* and has the same meaning, but the word
   does not exist in Italian.
55 In Spanish the word is *puta*; in Italian *puttana*.

dominus.[56] But since *episcopatus* is neither Greek or Latin,[57] I preferred to use the same word Paul did, ἐπισκοπή.[58] Those who betray their own stupidity with such examples complain that I do harm to their authority.

But I have an even more gross tale to relate.[59] In a certain monastery the prior of the Dominicans had distributed my works among the monks in order to list the errors in them. My edition of Jerome fell by chance to one of them. Since he knew as little about Jerome as he did about Erasmus, he began to talk indiscriminately of whatever gave him offence, whether in Jerome or in my commentary. He had amassed a huge pile of errors. When each one presented his findings at an assembly, this man counted it as the highest praise if he could bring forward more articles than anyone else. Finally someone with a little more sense perceived that the man made no distinctions between Jerome and Erasmus; and so in place of his hoped-for praise he won ridicule. This case proved that more errors can be gleaned from any orthodox writer than from my books, if a person brings such prejudices to reading them as these men do to mine. Indeed I vow that I can produce more plausible calumnies from the Epistles of St Paul than they can draw from my writings, provided that the name and authority of the writer are removed.

Must I repeat here the story about the English theologian who, when it was being discussed in an assembly whether it was clearly stated in the Sacred Scriptures that a heretic should be submitted to capital punishment, cried out in the words of Paul, 'After a first and second admonition, shun the heretic'?[60] When he repeated this refrain again and again, causing the others to wonder what he meant, one more shrewd than the rest understood that his error consisted in thinking that *devitare* 'shun' meant *e vita tollere* 'take away his life.' What was the result? Some were ashamed that such a shameful aberration could exist in an old man and a theologian. Such is the extent of the error that engulfs those who without grammar and without the study of the sacred books wish to be regarded as theologians.

* * * * *

56 *Dominus* 'lord' or 'master'; *domina* 'lady,' 'mistress,' 'wife.' The Dominican thus understood *episcopa* to mean 'bishop's concubine.'

57 The word *episcopatus* (ie the office and dignity of a bishop) is found in the Vulgate (Ps 108:7, 1 Tim 3:1), in Tertullian *De baptismo* 17, and in Ammianus Marcellinus 27.3.12, as well as in countless medieval texts. But it is not found in classical Latin.

58 1 Tim 3:1; Erasmus coined the word *episcopa* to translate Paul's ἐπισκοπή.

59 This incident may have been recent. At all events, it is not mentioned in any of the letters enumerated in the introduction.

60 Titus 3:10. This story is told also in the *Moria*; see CWE 27 146–7.

What I shall say now originates with a professional body of the highest renown.[61] It was revealed in a written work that has not yet been made public. In the colloquy entitled *Symbolon* I call God the Father simply the 'author of all that is,' meaning, of course, that he is the sole beginning without beginning.[62] Commenting on this, my theologian friend – I shall not reveal his name – added on his own 'things,' where I had written 'of all that exists,' and he explains that the three Persons are distinct things, so that I cannot get away with it. Then he postulates that 'author' and 'cause' and similar words impart to the words they qualify a distinction of substance or essence, not to mention one of things or persons.[63] This is the language he uses. He supports this, saying that in the time of Gerson[64] a theologian at Paris who said in a public speech that the Father is the cause of the Son was forced to make a public retraction, although he merely meant that the Son proceeded from the Father, etc. (To make a comment in passing, why did a person who makes accusations of calumny concerning the word 'cause' dare to say that the Son proceeds from the Father when we attribute this procession properly to the Holy Spirit?)[65] But to get to the point, what deity indicated to him that it makes no difference whether you say 'author' or 'cause'? And I shall not say anything about the word 'cause,' which I did

315

320

325

330

* * * * *

61 Ie the faculty of theology at Paris. See Allen Ep 2466, addressed to the Paris theologian Nicolas Maillard, where in lines 105–202 Erasmus recounts the same incident described here and refers to his critic as *quidam e tuo sodalitio* 'a certain person from your sodality.'

62 By *Symbolon*, ie 'Creed,' Erasmus means his colloquy *Inquisitio de fide* 'An Examination concerning the Faith,' which is a commentary on the Apostles' Creed. For the passage in question, see CWE 39 428:30–41. As the editor, Craig Thompson, points out in his notes, the word 'author' in English does not have the force of *auctor* in Latin, which includes the meaning 'maker' (*factor*). See also *De utilitate Colloquiorum* 'The Usefulness of the Colloquies' CWE 40 1108:32–1109:4.

63 The accusation, in other words, was that Erasmus had denied the doctrine of the Trinity, which holds that the three Persons of the Godhead – Father, Son, and Holy Spirit – are one substance. The Nicene Creed describes the Son as 'begotten not made, being of one substance with the Father, by whom all things were made.' On the basis of his far-fetched interpretation of Erasmus' description of the Father as 'author' of all things, the Paris theologian claims that Erasmus had made the Father the 'cause' of the Son, thus implying that the Son was of a substance distinct from that of the Father.

64 Jean Gerson (1363–1429), the great Paris theologian

65 In the theology of the Western church, as formulated in the Nicene Creed, the Son is 'begotten of the Father' and the Holy Spirit 'proceeds from the Father and the Son.'

not use. He shudders at the word 'cause,' as if 'beginning' or 'origin' or any other word were appropriate for divine things. And what are those similar words he talks about? are they 'beginning,' 'origin,' 'source,' and the like? At any rate the word 'author' is used correctly to designate the source from which something flowed. And Hilary attributes a special authority to 335 the Father because in him is the highest and absolute principle of beginning.[66] Nor did Augustine shy away from the word 'author' in his dispute with the Arian Maximinus.[67] When the Arian said: 'We adore the Father as author,' Augustine interprets 'author' as the beginning of the Son and the Holy Spirit. Does it seem just to you that I should be accused of speaking 340 irreligiously about God because that theologian had not learned Latin and had not read Hilary or Augustine?

Why should I mention here the sayings of Christ and St Paul condemned in my name, although in the *Paraphrase* they are spoken by another person?[68] In the writings of Lee, Zuñiga, and Béda, how many preposter- 345 ous statements, examples of ignorance, malice, calumnies and lies I expose, how many blasphemies also, if one were to press the argument closely, as they contrive calumnies against me on matters of vocabulary![69] Although it is they themselves who devise these schemes, they blame me because they suffer ill repute in certain quarters. Let them see to their reputation them- 350 selves; as for myself, as far as in me lies, I shall not suffer the glory of Christ to be obscured by the passions of men. Then and only then shall we truly and happily exult, if we exult in him. What else is accomplished by all these altercations, verbal abuse, detractions, deceptions, ruses, lies, distortions except that their own authority, which should have been very weighty, 355 is undermined? The minds of listeners and readers, which should have been stimulated to piety, are poisoned. Christian concord, without which we are not Christians, is torn asunder. My temperament rebels against this sort of conflict in such a manner that I should prefer to maintain complete silence about all these charges rather than to go forth into the arena time after time 360 as a gladiator,[70] except that I knew it would be impious to admit the crime of impiety when my mind is free of any feeling of impiety. I am determined to follow a right conscience and in these stormy times not to divert my eyes from Christ. Let him see to the outcome. As for yourself, if you will hearken to my words, do not contend too much with this rabble, lest they interfere 365

* * * * *

66 *De Trinitate* 2.1
67 *Contra Maximinum* 2.5
68 See Epp 2033:39–41 with n15, 2037:150–2.
69 See Epp 1341A:823–30 (Lee) and 868–927 (Diego López Zúñiga), 1943 n6 (Béda).
70 Cf Ep 1934 n1.

with your happy tranquillity, the fruit of your disdain for this world, your meditation on the sacred writings and your contemplation of heavenly bliss. May the Lord Jesus protect you.

Given at Basel, 5 September 1528

2046 / To Germain de Brie   Basel 6 September 1528

First published in the *Selectae epistolae*, of which is it the centrepiece, this letter is Erasmus' reply to Ep 2021. On Germain de Brie and the controversy to which this letter belongs, see Ep 2021 introduction.

DESIDERIUS ERASMUS OF ROTTERDAM TO GERMAIN DE BRIE, GREETING

You had informed me some time ago,[1] my excellent friend Brie, that the publication of the *Ciceronianus* had stirred up ill feeling against me there. I easily foresaw that this would be the case, but only among those who were afflicted by the same superstition that I attribute to Nosoponus,[2] desiring through the characterization of this one person to provide a remedy for all. But never did I expect that someone from the world of learning would think that this little book, designed to be of general utility for scholarly pursuits, should be the object of epigrams in the style of Hipponax.[3] This is what I am told by friends there, whose word is to be trusted. And to give me a taste of them they sent me three or four examples, as undeserved as they were unlearned, and they did not conceal their authorship.

I frequently lament that nowhere in the world is Christian piety not at risk because of this deplorable scourge of dissidence. But I fear that a similar scourge may now beset humane learning, which for a long time has flourished with reasonable success in many regions, but nowhere more successfully than in your country of France.[4] In Italy, frightened by the tumult of war,[5] the Muses are silent and inactive. As far as I am concerned, although I am by nature far removed from the character of those who are so attached to this or that nation that they almost hate all others, if there was any nation

* * * * *

2046
1 In a no longer extant letter written soon after the publication of the *Ciceroni-anus*; see lines 89–90 below and Ep 2021 introduction.
2 The character in the *Ciceronianus* who is the voice of the Italian Ciceronians. Cf lines 71–3 below.
3 See Ep 2027:25–8. Hipponax was an ancient Greek poet who loved to tear his victims to pieces in bitter and scurrilous attacks; see *Adagia* II ii 56.
4 Cf Ep 1840:13–19.
5 See Ep 1935 n10.

to which I felt more favourably disposed, it was always France. Witnesses
to this are those who have lived with me, as well as my own writings, in
which I gladly dwell on the praises of the French people, specifically in the
Panegyric, in which I congratulate Prince Philip on his return from Spain.[6] 25
For this reason I am all the more distressed by this fatal dissension, which
for so long now separates the two most powerful monarchs of the world.
Since I saw that in Germany the study of the liberal arts was either extinct
or reduced to a state of inertia, and in Italy amidst the clash of arms did
not dare to raise its head, I rejoiced that in France at least the Muses had a 30
peaceful and pleasant abode. But it was of the utmost importance that there
should be a consensus of feelings and interest among those who champion
humane letters. We could have taken our model from the foes of literary
studies, who we see are wonderfully united in serried ranks against these
studies. We should not take into account in what region each one was born. 35
All those who were trained in the same studies are fellow citizens and fellow initiates. So what is the use of creating such a great fuss out of so trivial a matter and affording this delightful spectacle to those who hate us as
much as they do our studies so that they are spurred on all the more to engage in what they are already doing on their own with great zest. 'Oil on 40
the fire,' they say.[7]

    'But you gave them a pretext,' they will say. What pretext, I ask? Un-
less we want to close our eyes altogether, what more does that book do than
expose the superstitious, pedantic, foolish, and defective emulation of Cicero and advocate the true imitation of that author? What learned or sen- 45
sible man would not approve of this? What is more useless to true learning than that youth should spurn all writers who differ from Cicero's style
and take him as their sole model? And the only thing they try to reproduce of his is what is of least importance. This disease had taken root first
in Italy, and the ones who raised the greatest rumpus there were those 50
who were least like Cicero. Then the contagion began to flare up among
not a few of our writers, especially those who returned from a trip to
Italy.[8]

*   *   *   *   *

6 The *Panegyric for Archduke Philip of Austria* (Epp 179–80), in which Erasmus described the reception given to Archduke Philip on his progress from Flanders
   to Spain in 1501–2 (not his return from Spain, as indicated here); see CWE 27
   21–3, and cf Ep 1840:20–1.
7 *Adagia* I ii 9
8 Here Erasmus doubtless had Christophe de Longueil primarily in mind; see
   Ep 1948 introduction.

Since I saw that this was utterly useless both to solid learning and to
Christian eloquence, I spent a few days on this little work to rid the minds   55
of young persons of this superstition, which draws them away from the
very thing it pretends to accomplish, since they regard with disdain many
authors worthy to be read while at the same time they do not succeed in
emulating the one model they propose for themselves. It is not that I am
so blind as not to perceive that Marcus Tullius is so much the prince of   60
eloquence that all others, no matter how eloquent, when compared to him,
seem to lapse into silence.[9] Therefore I do not understand why this subject
offends them. I urged Guillaume Budé in a letter to undertake this subject,[10]
and he indicated that he intended to deal with this sort of people when the
occasion presented itself.[11] If the subject was not displeasing to Budé, what is   65
the meaning of all this hysteria among those who wish to be seen as zealous
followers of Budé?

But perhaps it is not the subject but the manner of treatment that gives
offence, since Nosoponus denies almost everyone the honour of the name of
Ciceronian. But they should have borne in mind that it was Nosoponus who   70
was speaking, not Erasmus. Nor is the speech of Bulephorus to be taken literally, because he pretends to be afflicted with this same malady in order
that he may cure others.[12] For that reason he allows this honour to be denied well-reputed writers so that Nosoponus will not be too discouraged if
he does not attain his goal. Therefore no censure is implied of those who are   75
denied the title of Ciceronians, especially according to the criteria and opinion of Nosoponus. On the contrary, it was my purpose to prove that there
were many writers gifted with such learning and eloquence that they could
rival Cicero with equal, if not identical talents. But they would be far removed from the outer covering and veneer of Ciceronian style, which is the   80
only thing some aspire to. It was not my intention to disparage anyone's reputation. Even if I introduce a character whose judgment is limited, I never
depart from proper decorum, not mentioning anyone without giving him
his due praise, at least as far as that was possible, *en passant* and incidentally.
I did not attempt to pronounce praise or censure of all writers. Ten examples   85

* * * * *

9 Cicero's full name was Marcus Tullius Cicero, which frequently led to his
being called 'Tullius' in Latin or 'Tully' in English. In the paragraph following this one, Erasmus refers several times to 'Tully' and calls his imitators
'Tullians,' but we have kept the more familiar 'Cicero' and 'Ciceronians.'
10 Not extant
11 See Epp 1812:123–4, 2044:10–13.
12 The character Bulephorus in the dialogue is the voice of Erasmus.

were sufficient for my purpose. But I thought I might earn the gratitude of
some whose names I mention, and indeed such was the case. Then I thought
that these varied assessments would be useful for young men who aspire to
a learned eloquence. You yourself seemed in a previous letter to be of that .90
opinion.

But some are offended that Budé did not receive honourable treatment.
How so? Because Nosoponus, still not free of his prejudices, removes him
from the list of Ciceronians? Budé himself admits this openly, since he does
not affect what Nosoponus prescribes and he condemns this exclusive imi- 95
tation of one writer.[13] Yet removal from Nosoponus' list does not mean that
anyone is removed from the rank of learned or eloquent writers, since in the
same dialogue I point out that there can exist a man who is more learned and
more eloquent than Cicero and yet be very different from him in matters of
style. Therefore where is that alleged affront to Budé? Let them claim that 100
he is more learned than Marcus Tullius, he will not be denied that praise;
let them claim he is more eloquent, Nosoponus' eulogy will not stand in
the way. But they say I devote few words to his praise. The nature of the
subject did not allow for copiousness of language, but in the *Annotations* to
the New Testament and in the *Adages* I not infrequently strive to find scope 105
for enlarging on his praises, even if there is less of this in my letters.[14] Unless perhaps they will also consider it an outrage to Budé that he is praised
by Erasmus not only frequently but also in serious writings of his that may
perhaps outlive their author by several centuries.[15]

However they judge this matter, I was motivated by the desire to give 110
honour to Budé. At the same time I was not unaware that his modesty did
not desire the testimony of my pen, nor did his fame have need of my commendation, since he had within himself the qualities that would render him
dear and famous throughout the world, even if he were not yet the celebrity
that he is now. But at the time I thought it would be beneficial to learned 115
studies and, I readily admit, to myself. I have always had so much regard
for Budé that I considered his friendship a great honour to me, and I thought
the mere mention of his name, like an adornment of precious stones, would
add some dignity to my books. I read with great pleasure the praise that
you lavish upon him in your letter, rejoicing that at least among you due

* * * * *

13 See lines 63–5 above.
14 See the annotations on Matt 20:2; Luke 1:4, 13:9, and 16:26 in the *Novum Instrumentum* of 1516, and cf Ep 1794:11–15. See also Ep 1334:295–305. There are
   no praises of Budé to be found anywhere in the *Adagia*.
15 Cf lines 178–81 below.

honour is given to his outstanding merits and that a man who has claim to   120
our greatest gratitude and adds to his merits with each passing day for his
contributions to learning should be revered like a god.[16] Since I have always
entertained these feelings for Budé and still do, what drives them to invent
suspicions of envy and hatred?

But they proclaim that I have committed an unforgivable crime in com-   125
paring Budé with Bade. First of all, I do not cite the names of learned men
in pairs, as Quintilian compares Greek and Latin writers,[17] but by region. It
happened by chance that their two names coincided, since both are French
and both live in Paris. Unless perhaps they also think it intolerable that
Budé and Badius should figure in the same list. Those who feel this way are   130
very far from the sentiments of Budé, unless I completely misunderstand
his character. 'But you compare one to the other,' they say, 'a camel to an
ant.' 'No,' I respond, 'it is Nosoponus who compares, not I.' Very well. I
shall not resort to the excuse of a literary personage to make my defence,
at least in the passage in question. Let us suppose that Erasmus wrote this   135
and that he wrote it to express his true feelings; was there a single word
that might damage Budé's reputation? I make a comparison, but on what
point? On the illustriousness of their ancestry, on worldly goods, on rank,
on learning or eloquence? None of these. Merely on the outer covering and
veneer of Ciceronian style, which Budé openly regards as of no consequence,   140
and in my book I teach openly that it must be disregarded and demonstrate
that it was disregarded by the best and most respected writers. I compare
Budé to Badius just as I compare Leonardo Aretino to Quintilian, Filelfo to
Pliny.[18]

'But you almost give Bade first place,' they say. Of course I prefer him   145
in that aspect in which he is to be preferred, but by assigning him this preference I do not take away from the fame of Budé. The point of my argument
is that the most celebrated writers differed from Cicero. Therefore the more
Budé surpasses Bade in learning and eloquence and the further Bade is left
behind, the more apt is this example for my purpose. I am astonished that   150
there are learned men there who do not see this; and if they do see it, I am
the more astounded that some raise this uproar and think this is a matter
worthy of insulting verses. Finally, so that no evil-minded person should

* * * * *

16 See Ep 2021:9–10.
17 10.1 §§ 101, 105, 123
18 As Allen noted, these comparisons are not found in the *Ciceronianus*. It is
   Lorenzo Valla whom Erasmus compares to Quintilian and Ermolao Barbaro
   whom he compares to Quintilian and Pliny (CWE 28 415–16).

seize the opportunity from the unequal comparison to indulge in slanderous talk, I add: 'however much Guillaume Budé's exceptional and manifold   155
gifts of intellect compel our admiration.'[19] Is there any word here that does
not emphasize his superiority? I attribute 'manifold gifts' to him; this was
not enough in my opinion: I add 'exceptional'; and I did not say that he is
'endowed with' but that they 'compel our admiration,' preferring him not
only to Bade but to almost all writers. One whom all look up to is more than   160
just a little elevated above all the rest.

Since these things are clearer than day, what is the meaning of this
blindness of judgment, so that, although I have treated Budé so respectfully,
causes them to grumble and complain as if I had spat in his face? They say (if
it please the Muses!) that I harass the living and the dead,[20] although I pass   165
over no one in that book without praise except myself. Even the very person
who is said to amuse himself writing verses against me receives honourable
mention in the dialogue,[21] and I never mention his name anywhere without
a flattering preamble. Another person chimes in: 'He favours his own equal
more.' I do not consider this statement insulting to me, but I don't know if   170
Bade would take it calmly that he is compared to Erasmus. Others are free
to judge Bade as they wish; I have always counted him among those whose
learning, talent, and eloquence are not to be despised, although I am willing
to admit that he would have been a greater man if a more kindly fate had
given him the leisure and tranquillity to pursue his studies.[22]   175

But such things are beside the point. As my comparison is respectful
to Budé, so it does not detract anything from Bade. But where are the proofs
that I am envious of the praises accorded to Budé? Was it envy that impelled
me to speak of him so often in terms of affection and respect in my works,
which are not insignificant but destined to live on,[23] as I hope, in such a man-   180
ner as I think no one else has done, not even a Frenchman? Am I accused
of jealous rivalry there in France when I have faced the grave envy of Rome
by preferring him even to the Italians in my letters?[24] My dear Germain, I
congratulate rather than envy such men, who not only promote the study of
good letters by their efforts but adorn them by their great eminence. I don't   185

* * * * *

19 CWE 28 421
20 Cf Ep 2048:20.
21 Joannis Lascaris (see Ep 2027 n14); cf *Ciceronianus* CWE 28 416.
22 The relevant passage on Bade in the *Ciceronianus* is quoted in the introduction
    to Ep 2021.
23 Cf lines 105–8 above.
24 See Ep 1794:40–50.

think there is any vice from which I am further removed than envy. Who
ever felt that I displayed any annoyance at being regarded as inferior even
to the most mediocre of writers? Would that I were equally exempt from
all other vices! At one time we had some epistolary skirmishes for the sake
of practising the pen (at that time he was more partial to Jacques Lefèvre),   190
but these little clashes confirmed rather than diminished our friendship.[25]
Later it was said that he had conceived some ill feeling towards me because
I seemed in some of my writings to make disparaging remarks against the
French. There is one place in the *Colloquies* where a character promises that
he would be able to show where he could get as much money, either gold or   195
silver, as he wanted. Then he deluded the eager expectations of his hearer
saying: 'From Budé's *De asse*.'[26] What could be more harmless than this
quip? Or what else does it tell the reader but that Budé wrote a weighty
tome called *De asse*? Would Lazare Baïf have reason to be angry with me
if someone in the *Colloquies* made fun of a man dressed in rags, promising   200
him that he would show him a place where he could get any kind of clothes
he wished, and when the man expressed his eagerness to know where, he
answered: 'In Baïf's *De re vestiaria*?'[27] Such scrupulous regard is not even
shown towards sacred writings.

I shall not repeat other stories of this same kind, lest I become prolix,   205
especially since I have appeased Budé on this matter by letter.[28] Will it not be
permitted me to say anything against the French even in jest under the guise
of any fictional character without all of France charging me with the crime
of *lèse-majesté*? How many nations will be angry with me whose character
is censured in the *Adages*?[29] But you may judge my sincerity in this matter   210
from this: I would never have persuaded myself that Budé was irritated with
me on this account unless he himself had indicated his displeasure (which
he seems to have quickly forgotten) with his usual frankness in a letter to
me.[30] I don't think there are any human friendships so happy that once in a

* * * * *

25 See Epp 744, 778, 810, 869, 896, 906, 915, 930; on Jacques Lefèvre d'Etaples see
   Ep 315.
26 In *De captandis sacerdotiis* 'In Pursuit of Benefices' CWE 39 48:24–36. *De asse* was
   Budé's magisterial treatise on ancient coinage.
27 On Baïf and his *De re vestiaria*, see Ep 1962 introduction.
28 Ep 2047
29 The *Adagia* contain Erasmus' reflections on many 'nations': Brittany (II iv 48),
   Corsica (III i 74), England (II i 1, II ii 68, I iv 54), France (II i 1, III vi 50, III viii
   5), Germany (I ix 44, II i 1, II vi 23), Holland (III i 1, III i 26, IV vi 1), Italy (IV
   iv 54), Picardy (I vi 93, II viii 53, III ii 41).
30 Not extant; answered by Ep 2047

while some little clouds like this do not appear. But such slight feelings of   215
resentment are often a renewal of affection.[31]

Finally, after the publication of the *Ciceronianus* I was urged in letters
from my friends to write some sort of apology to mollify his feelings in case
he had taken offence. This seems also to have been the intent of your letter.
But it did not occur to me what I should write or to whom I should write. I   220
was so convinced of Budé's wisdom and integrity that, rather than fearing
that he would be offended, I expected his thanks for mentioning him. I was
so acquainted with his magnanimous spirit and human qualities, of which
you speak, that even if it happened that I had said something a little indiscreet I thought he would either disregard it or interpret it in a good light.   225
And so since my feelings towards him were those one should entertain towards an old friend and a leading figure in the literary world, and since the
passage was so far from being unseemly that in a few words it paid him
great homage, how could I be induced to believe that Budé was offended?
Should I have written to one of his friends? Whomever I would have cho-   230
sen I would have blackened his opinion either of me or of Budé or of both
of us. Of me, as if I were a man of such impudence that without provocation I should take up my pen against such a man, one whom for the sake of
humane letters I cannot but love even if there were no friendship between
us (I will go further, but just as truly, he not only had little respect for me   235
but also spoke disparagingly of me). Of Budé, for who would consider him
so ill-tempered a person as to repay a sincere compliment with resentment?
Of both of us, for who would think that I have such delusions about myself
that I should undertake to compete in reputation for learning with that man
whom I have always placed beyond the uncertainties of the times and lo-   240
cated with those famous heroes of old, or that Budé would be so petty as to
deign to engage the likes of me in combat? For the moment no one will persuade me that Budé is any less my friend until he confesses his annoyance
in a letter, which I do not think he will do.

As for those who amuse themselves writing foolish little verses,[32]   245
whose reputations do they hurt more, mine or Budé's? As far as I am concerned, the text itself exonerates me. Thus whatever blame exists will fall
upon Budé, on whom they cast suspicion for becoming angry with a friend
for no reason or for choosing such stupid friends – unless they do this without his knowledge. You had more reason to be angry with Erasmus, my dear   250
Brie, since I give you a more cool treatment than I do Budé.[33] And yet I had

* * * * *

31 Terence *Andria* 555
32 See lines 166–8 and n21 above.
33 See CWE 28 422.

no fears at all about you, since I have long known your rectitude of judgment and your good-natured character. How alien to the Graces and the
Muses are those who tried to incite you against me with slandering words
when they should have appeased your anger! What does such inhuman con-   255
duct have to do with humane letters? You exhort me prudently and lov-
ingly to look out for my own reputation. Farewell to all reputation if this
contagion has attacked those who cultivate humane studies! In what manner shall I treat this argument without harming the reputation of those who
are seething with anger about nothing? I compared Budé to Bade. What if   260
I had compared Budé's wine flask with Bade's wine flask; would they cry
out that it was a supreme insult to Budé's name? This comparison did no
more damage to Budé's fame than if I had compared a wine flask to a wine
flask.

There remains one more thing, if it so please the gods, namely, to de-   265
fend myself against the charge of envying Budé – as if the respectful mention of his name scattered throughout so many of my works did not declare
how I envy him! We envy those whom we hope we can equal. Budé is so
many miles ahead of me that I look up to him and admire him rather than
rival him. When in your kindness you put Budé and Erasmus on the same   270
level, saying that I am to Germany what Budé is to France,[34] that is an example of graceful rhetoric, but you err no less gravely than if I had compared Budé with Bade without qualification. We are more unequal than dis-
similar, Erasmus and Budé. And as it is a sign of grateful appreciation that
France venerates and acknowledges theirleader of the Muses,[35] so there are   275
not lacking in Germany those to whom this honour is owed rather than to
Erasmus. 'The one whom you equal should be the pinnacle,' you say. How
will those who make me the equal of Bade take this unless they accord the
same indulgence to the acclamations of their friends as it is said that Venus
accords to the perjuries of lovers?   280

But to return to the charge of envy, I beseech you, what syllable do they
find in my books that breathes of envy for Budé? Or what writer at all will
they cite, great or mediocre, whose industry I do not favour? Have I ever
taken up my pen against anyone who did not first assail me? You also indicate as a remedy that I omit mention of Budé in the next edition or separate   285
him from Bade. That is very easy and I shall gladly do so.[36] But what new
calumnies will they invent who have already invented this calumny? If I do

* * * * *

34 Cf Ep 2021:14–15.
35 Ie Apollo
36 For the altered version of the passage on Budé in the second edition of the
   Ciceronianus, see CWE 28 587 n676.

not mention him, they will attribute it to jealousy. If I correct it they will
recall the memory of the previous comparison that had stirred up animosity
in the first place. Nevertheless, I shall do as you advise. As this advice pro- 290
ceeds from a sincere heart, I hope that it will have success. Although I never
doubted the sincerity and loyalty of your feelings towards me, nevertheless
it is most gratifying to me that you gave further evidence to everyone of
your devotion to me. I merely hope that it does not arouse ill will against
your reputation, you whose exceptional learning and unblemished character 295
have won you everyone's favour and no one's jealousy.

But I ask you, great advocate that you are, how good and how strong
a case have you taken upon yourself to defend? It is true that the worst
cases are usually assigned to the best lawyers, but I suspect these people
have more need of a good doctor than a good lawyer. What charge do they 300
bring but 'He compared Budé to Bade,' and this is their constant refrain:
'He compared Budé to Bade.' And among them they say there are those who
formerly seemed to be friends and who did not have a bad opinion of our
studies. After I compared Budé to Bade, they suddenly take away any good
quality they previously attributed to me – talent, learning, eloquence, good 305
judgment, and even common sense. Friendship that can cease was never true
friendship.[37] What kind of friendship can that be which for such frivolous
reasons is turned into hostility? Indeed, which repays a good service with
insult? The wicked need only the opportunity, as the proverb goes.[38] But
worse are those who use an act of kindness as an occasion for wickedness 310
and seek an opportunity for revenge where they ought to show gratitude.
Such behaviour as this, worse than Scythian,[39] is totally opposed to humane
learning.

It was my misfortune that some people brandished the point of their
styluses against me. But whom did I ever attack for so frivolous a reason? 315
I dare say that one could not easily find a writer in whose works you will
encounter as many flattering references as in mine. In this very book, in
which I introduce a character of perverse opinion, the subject itself, a discussion of the varieties of style, invited me to disclose what I liked or dis-
liked in individual styles. In doing so I observed such moderation in my 320
strictures that no one, if I am not mistaken, could justly say that I was lacking in good will. This exercise was of no small advantage for the progress
of the young. But I preferred to be less useful to everyone than to offend

* * * * *

37 See *Adagia* ii i 72, citing Aristotle *Rhetoric* 2.13.4.
38 *Adagia* ii i 68
39 The Scythians were proverbial for their barbaric cruelty; see *Adagia* i v ix 85.

anyone. I imagine there are foreigners[40] there who are nettled by my statement that nothing can be eloquent which is not Christian.[41] These persons   325
probably use the comparison of Budé with Bade to conceal their own resentment, which they are ashamed to admit, and they sow the seeds of dissension, seeking to thrust someone forward to avenge their resentment. I think
you know the meaning of the saying: 'to have a keen nose.'[42] But against
these people, who under the name of good letters promote the re-sprouting   330
of paganism,[43] I had to take a firm stand. If we are true Christians, nothing should seem learned, elegant, or refined that does not express the spirit
of Christ, whenever the subject demands it. I know some clandestine supporters of paganism who, if they rouse my anger, will receive the welcome
they deserve. They will learn that in defence of Christ I am not timorous; in   335
other cases I am not reluctant to concede to anyone.

Certainly with regard to the letter that I had written to someone, in
which I gave free rein to my feelings in confidence to a friend,[44] although it
contained nothing that was not true or was offensive to Budé, still I would
prefer that it had not fallen into other hands. I had written to one person,   340
whose loyalty was known to me, and I did not think that in your wisdom
you needed someone to advise you, although I did caution you in a later
letter.[45] So little intention did I have of publishing it that I wrote it to be
read only by two persons.[46] Therefore I ask you that this matter not progress
any further, although already I hear that the rumour of this feigned conflict   345
has reached the ears of our Most Christian King. Of course he had nothing
else to do without having to occupy himself with this nonsense too! I have
learned by letter that when the king inquired what was going on between
us, a member of court answered him. He said that Budé was annoyed that
I often made attacks against the French in my writings and that I in turn,   350
wishing to make retaliation, compared him to Bade.[47] Whoever said this, if
my sources are accurate, did me no favour. It is the most blatant falsehood
to say that I ever attacked the French, even if Budé, because of his ardent
patriotism, had nourished suspicions and displeasure in this regard. But

* * * * *

40 Italians, in particular
41 In the concluding paragraphs of the *Ciceronianus*; see CWE 28 447–8.
42 *Adagia* I vi 81
43 See Ep 1948 introduction.
44 In his reply to Berquin; see Ep 2021 n1.
45 See Ep 2021:129.
46 By Berquin and by Brie, to whom he sent a copy; see Epp 2048:35–7, 2077:8–10.
47 Cf Ep 2038:24–7.

this, whatever its importance, has nothing to do with the present case. It   355
is very human that sometimes false suspicions and silly little annoyances
can occur between close friends, but if you take a closer look, they quickly
disappear. This is all part of the human comedy.

To conclude, I always thought that Budé was too great a man for me
to envy, if indeed I were able or accustomed to envy anyone, and I consider   360
him too good a man to approve of these foolish disputes. Moreover it would
be completely absurd for me to prefer Bade to a man whom I often compare
to Ermolao Barbaro and the Plinys.[48] I shall not consider it a just reason for
breaking our friendship if at any time Budé has different views than I, provided that in observation of ancient custom he refrains from insulting talk   365
and allows me to defend my cause with similar moderation if I think my
cause is just. You joke about my old people's *Colloquies*.[49] People want children always to be children and to do nothing but be sung to sleep. They
are so solicitous that they prefer them to read Poggio's *Facetiae*[50] rather than
imbibe some straightforward notions about morals and piety from my *Col-*   370
loquies. I hope I prove to be a false prophet, but I foresee a more terrible
tragedy than the Lutheran one arising in the future unless the authority of
princes curbs the tyranny of certain men who, blind in battle and insolent in
victory, are already with gladiatorial hearts[51] preparing their attack against
good letters and those who cherish them. I hoped that the outcome of this   375
deplorable conflict would contribute to the glory of Christ; now I fear human passions will seize for themselves what was owed to him and a new
war will take rise from the old one, worse than the one that was already
disastrous enough. At this point I do not see what we can do besides pray.
There is no reason, my most learned Brie, why this fatal tempest should de-   380
ter your spirit from promoting higher learning. Though you see that this
age has shown little gratitude for my labours, perhaps posterity will be less
ungrateful. Rather, you can blame my fate, since I seem to have something
in common with Hercules, to speak in grandiose terms about a very minor subject, who earned nothing for his labours but envy and whose last   385
struggle with the hydra was the most difficult of all. Born under a more
benign star, you will pursue your career under more favourable auspices,
made more cautious by my example. You have nothing to fear if you confine
yourself to the green meadows of the Muses. Would that I had done so!

* * * * *

48 See Ep 1794:49–50.
49 See Ep 2021:129–33.
50 Cf Ep 2037 n20.
51 See Ep 1943 n4.

Lazare de Baïf has given us an elegant little book on the different types   390
of vesture and soon will publish one on culinary utensils.[52] Those who now
tyrannize with their censures do not have any jurisdiction over these subjects, which bring much pleasure and support to the study of polite letters.

I am bearing up quite well with my poor health; Christ, who teaches
me not to fear death but rather to desire it, gives me strength. To my mind   395
I have lived long enough, and one must have an inordinate desire for life
who refuses to leave this turbulent world when there is good hope that we
will pass to a happier abode. But 'what is this I hear, my excellent friend?
Will all the humanities be in peril at the death of one man? If your complete
sincerity were not well known to me, I would say that you were engaging   400
in mere pleasantries or rhetoric. You challenge me to write you letters of
equal length, making dire threats if I do not conform.[53] What crueler threat
could you make than to send me merely laconic letters in the future? I do
not refuse the challenge, if you would only give me equal health, equal
leisure, and the gardens of Gentilly.[54] I do not know whether I have equalled   405
your letter; perhaps in the number of lines, but how could I match your
elegance?

A rumour has reached here that the kings have concluded an agreement.[55] But the more fervently I wish it is true the less I dare to believe it. If
it comes about, I would like to revisit France before my last day.[56] You can   410
imagine how much I envy you your seclusion, your friends, gardens and
leisure, greatest boon of all.

You would pardon my feelings of envy if you could see in what a
treadmill I find myself. I have to supply material for seven presses to print.
Augustine especially is killing me,[57] since I am emending all his works,   415
while with Jerome I took on only the letters.[58] Although I resisted this task
tooth and nail, it was thrust upon me by Johann Froben of blessed memory,[59] to whom I was so devoted that I could not refuse him anything even

* * * * *

52 See Ep 1962 introduction and lines 15–18, and cf lines 199–204 above.
53 See Ep 2021:151–3.
54 On the gardens, cf Ep 2021:154.
55 The rumour, whatever its source, was false. By this time, the French disaster
   in Italy was nearly complete, but a peace settlement was not concluded until
   August 1529 at Cambrai.
56 For the impediments to this that peace between Francis I and Charles V would
   remove, see Ep 1408:22–5.
57 Ie the Froben Augustine that would be published in 1529 (Ep 2157)
58 See Ep 396 introduction.
59 Cf Ep 2033:54–5.

if he ordered me to lead a rope dance in the public square.[60] He died in this
labour, which I fear will consume me also; at any rate it has almost ruined   420
my vision.[61] There is no end or limit to these volumes; the same things have
to be read and reread so many times. The obscurity of the subject matter, the
subtlety of style, often drawn out into long periodic sentences, require an
attentive reader and do not allow your attention to flag for a single instant.
I have found so many errors that no one would believe it unless he com-   425
pared it with the original, and it is strange that no one has complained of
this previously. I did not add any commentary except in those cases where
some word needed comment to avoid future corruptions; I only removed
errors, relying on the evidence of ancient manuscripts. I arranged the material in a suitable order; I briefly indicated spurious works, with the loyalty   430
and conscientiousness that is owed to such a pious, learned, and eloquent
champion of the church. I did not add his life, which we see he took care
of himself.[62] He preferred to be his own biographer. I can see the harbour
but it is still far off. If it is given to me to survive this labour, then it will be
right that you congratulate your friend Erasmus, just as we do in the case   435
of friends long despaired of when their prow touches the native shore after
a long and perilous voyage. Farewell.

Given at Basel, 6 September 1528

2047 / To Guillaume Budé   Basel, [6 September] 1528

First published in the *Opus epistolarum*, this letter was written after the composition of Ep 2046 but before the *Selectae epistolae* had made it through the press
(lines 5–6). Evidently, therefore, it was sent to Paris along with Epp 2042–4,
2046, and 2048, which supports the month-date assigned by Allen. A brief reference to the lost letter from Budé to which it is the answer is found in Ep
2046:211–14.

Erasmus' soothing words failed to have their desired effect on Budé. On
19 October, Daniel Stiebar (Ep 2069) in Paris wrote to Bonifacius Amerbach

* * * * *

60 In ancient Rome, young people engaged in a kind of chain dance in which the
   participants stayed together by taking hold of a rope. Terence *Adelphi* 4.7.34;
   Livy 27.37.
61 But not so seriously as to require the use of spectacles; see Allen Ep 2275:25–8
   (February 1530): 'My eyes, thank God, are not failing – many people wonder that I have not gone completely blind long ago. So far I have never used
   spectacles, either in daylight or in lamplight.'
62 Vives had urged Erasmus to write a life of Augustine for the edition, but he
   used instead the life that had been written by Possidius, Augustine's friend
   and disciple.

(AK Ep 1303:26–9): 'Erasmus was so far from appeasing Budé by his letters that they do not hesitate to say that Budé has not yet unsealed them, never mind read them. I have not made mention of this to Erasmus; if you think it is wise to do so, you may tell him.'

ERASMUS OF ROTTERDAM TO GUILLAUME BUDÉ, GREETING
See what magnificent confidence I have in your fairness, most learned Budé, that I chose none other to be my advocate in this case than the one against whom I am charged with a crime and whose defamation these men seem to be avenging. I send this letter to you, since my collection of letters is   5
still in the hands of the printers,[1] although there is nothing additional in it that pertains to this matter. So far is it from my mind to entertain any envy or ill will towards you that, when I heard that the fruits of your labour were published, I rejoiced wholeheartedly both for the sake of learning in general and for my own sake as well as for you, under whose guidance   10
and leadership Roman and Greek literature is flourishing so in France. And for this reason you in your wisdom will devote yourself all the more to preventing the scourge of discord from contaminating this good fortune.

What kind of example is it, I pray, to spread defamatory verses about a matter of such insignificance?[2] As if I could not amuse myself in composing   15
such verse if I felt like indulging a similar madness! I have no doubt but that you find these things offensive, mindful of the truth of that ancient saying: 'Good will untimely differs not from hate.'[3] This fever first took rise in Rome through those who did not tolerate that a Frenchman or German should be praised; you see how far it has progressed.   20

I think you have laid aside the suspicion that you seem to have conceived about me – but, believe me, an absolutely false one – namely, that I intentionally attack the reputation of the French. Although this vexation of yours was the cause of no little unpopularity for me among the French, nevertheless, since I know that it proceeded more from an ex-   25
cessive sense of patriotism than from personal animosity, I endure what has happened with more equanimity. In the letter I wrote to Berquin there is neither any voluntary falsehood nor, I think, anything injurious to your reputation.[4] Nonetheless I was apprehensive that it might fall into the hands of more than two persons. It certainly will not be published   30

* * * * *

2047
1 The *Selectae epistolae*, which was in print by 16 September (Epp 2050–1).
2 See Ep 2027:27–8 with n14.
3 *Adagia* I vii 69
4 See Ep 2021 n1.

by me.[5] One must write in one way for one's friends, in another way for the public. I trust that if in your wisdom you do not think that what I ask is owed to our friendship, then surely you will concede it to the public tranquillity of humane studies. But I am sure that in your kindness you will see to it that I am obliged to you on both counts. Farewell.   35

At Basel, in the year 1528

2048 / To Louis de Berquin   Basel, [c 6 September] 1528

Because of its connection with Epp 2066 (Berquin's reply to this letter) and 2077 (Erasmus' reply to Berquin), this letter has to be placed among those sent to Paris in September. It was first published in the *Opus epistolarum*. On Berquin, see Ep 2027 n1.

ERASMUS OF ROTTERDAM TO LOUIS DE BERQUIN, GREETING
Your letter,[1] of which you desire a copy, doesn't wish to materialize for the moment; if I find it, I'll send it to you. If I remember correctly, you write in it that the one thing that offended you was the comparison of Budé to Bade, since they have nothing in common apart from a few letters. Then,   5
when you urged me to write an apology to Budé, you indicated clearly that you were afraid he might be offended. Although I am well acquainted with Budé's character,[2] I am not convinced that he could have been offended by that reference.

I truly regret that the letter I wrote you has been circulated,[3] although   10
not even there is anything said in a derogatory way about Budé. If there were, it would have been an unintentional slip. I didn't think you needed someone to caution you. In a later letter I advised Brie to keep this matter silent so that no commotion would result,[4] although I had faith in his discretion even if he were not forewarned. But things turned out in the usual   15
human fashion. Of course the king does not have enough to do without having to know about these inanities. The one who gave the answer to the

* * * * *

5 Erasmus sent a copy of it to Germain de Brie but did not intend it to be published; see Epp 2048:35–7, 2077:10–12.

2048
1 The one that Berquin wrote after first seeing the *Ciceronianus*; not extant. Erasmus' reply to it is mentioned in line 10.
2 Cf Ep 896 introduction.
3 See Ep 2021 n1, and cf line 35 below.
4 See Ep 2021 n11.

king's inquiry that you mention was an enemy.[5] But they are writing play-
ful epigrams about it too, which no doubt are very clever and ingenious.
Among these is one who says that I harass the living and the dead.[6] And   20
yet, apart from never being mentioned by me except in a respectful manner, I do not provoke him at all in that particular book![7] I see that exactly
the same kind of disturbance will arise in humane studies as we see among
kings and professors of theology.

Concerning translation,[8] they will readily respond that books can be   25
read with less danger by the learned than by the ignorant. And perhaps they
will make other charges against you. I applaud your confidence of victory,[9]
but what worries me is that it so often eludes us. The pope has come back
to life;[10] he has his cardinals, who are both powerful and loyal to him. The
Dominicans and Franciscans are beginning to wage a vigorous campaign,   30
and I hear that jurisdiction has been restored to the judges who pronounced
sentence against you.[11] I admit writing that all your efforts come to naught,[12]
but not without regret, my Berquin. Would that the circumstances could
warrant another kind of language.

I never dreamed of publishing the letter.[13] I sent it to Brie so that he   35
would be better prepared to defend me if someone were to make some
protestation. What good it would do me to answer the theologians I have no
idea, since they do not read my writings.[14] And certain Béda-ites are making
moves against me with murderous intent.[15] I don't know what hope I have in
rulers; if they were to show great favour to me, they would be overwhelmed   40
by the unprincipled hordes. If only my response had succeeded in making
people mistrust the judgment of the theologians, for I have already thrown
so many lies, so many blatant calumnies, and so much ignorant nonsense in

* * * * *

5 Cf Epp 2038:23–7, 2046:347–51.
6 Johannes Lascaris: Epp 2027 n14, 2038:19–23
7 Ie the *Ciceronianus* (Ep 1948)
8 For Berquin's translations into French of works by Erasmus, see Ep 1599 n1,
  and cf Epp 1678:59–61, 1692:1–5, 1722:60–3, 1875:101–4.
9 Cf Ep 1875:111–14.
10 The pope had recovered from the effects of the sack of Rome in May 1527
   and was about to return to Rome from his exile in Orvieto. See Ep 1987 n1.
11 See Ep 2027:2–5.
12 It is not known where Erasmus said this.
13 Ie Erasmus' reply to Berquin; see line 10 above and cf Epp 2047:27–31, 2077:
   8–10.
14 Cf Ep 2053:3–5.
15 On Béda, see Ep 1943 n6. This sentence is adapted from a line in Terence
   Phormio 5.7.71.

Béda's face,[16] both of whose books are said to have received the approbation
of the most revered faculty.[17] I would prefer that the faculty would so mod-   45
erate its judgments that all would believe them rather than that I should bring
it about that no one believes them, even if I could do that. How shall I be able
to teach what the faculty or the university is when I am equally ignorant of
both? I am embarrassed to have written so many apologies. I would rather
defeat this hydra by publishing good books that will live on in posterity.   50

I am much obliged to you for what you write about the leaders of these
excesses.[18] I shall carefully consider my answer. Besides my bad health[19] and
exacting labours, I am tormented by certain hoodlums that those evangelicals set upon me one after the other. Now in addition to that Thraso[20] I have
to deal with a viper, a young man who has lost all shame and reason, vic-   55
tim of some foul disease.[21] There is no dog so mangy that it cannot do harm
when things are so ulcerated. I consider it less burdensome to fight with the
whole faculty of theology than with such dungheaps.

Farewell.

I shall write more perhaps to send with Anton.[22] A friend writes to   60
me that you are making boastful threats, as if you wished to strike terror
into the theologians in my name.[23] Whatever your intention, if indeed you
are doing this, you are fueling their hatred. I am not interested in cures for
illness. I have lived long enough, not to say more than long enough. This is
all I could answer to your letter.[24] Farewell.   65

Basel, 1528

* * * * *

16 For Erasmus' response to Béda's criticisms, see Ep 2033 n14.
17 One of these books would certainly have been the *Annotationes* of 1526 (Ep
   1642 n5), which were approved by the faculty on 16 May (Farge *Registre* 152B).
   As Allen notes, the second might have been the *Apologia adversus clandestinos
   Lutheranos* of 1529, which Béda would put together in October 1528 (see fol
   9 recto of the *Annotationes*) and which the faculty might thus already have
   been aware of. But the faculty did not grant permission to publish it until 2
   December (Farge *Registre* 249D).
18 Possibly Berthélemy (Ep 2027 n18) and Le Clerc (Ep 2043) in addition to Béda.
   Cf Ep 2037:164–72.
19 See Ep 1989 n4.
20 Eppendorf; see Epp 1934 and 1992. Thraso is the bombastic soldier in Terence's
   Eunuchus.
21 Quite probably Ludovicus Carinus; see Ep 2063 nn1, 3.
22 Bletz, a professional courier; see Ep 1784 n1.
23 Possibly, as Allen suggests, Pierre Toussain who, in a letter now lost, had
   written to Erasmus concerning Berquin (see Ep 2042:1–16). Or, perhaps more
   likely, Gervasius Wain in Ep 2027:1–16.
24 Not extant

2049 / To Joachim Martens   Basel, [c 16 September] 1528

First published in the *Opus epistolarum*, this letter answers one that is no longer
extant but is mentioned in a letter of Bonifacius Amerbach to Jacopo Sadoleto
written c 11 October 1528 (summary published as AK Ep 1300). This is the only
one of the letters exchanged between Martens and Erasmus to have survived.

Apart from what can be learned from references to him in the correspondence of Erasmus, little is known about Joachim Martens of Ghent (documented 1527–c 1540). On 15 September 1527 he matriculated at Montpellier
(*Matricule de Montpellier* 52), and in the following summer or early autumn
he was at Carpentras with Sadoleto, to whom he subsequently dedicated his
only published work, a Latin translation of Galen's *De alimentorum facultatibus*
(Paris: S. de Colines 1530). Sometime in the autumn of 1528, Martens moved
to Paris, where he may have done battle against Noël Béda and his supporters
(see Ep 2077:50–2). Erasmus subsequently praised him as a medical scholar
of great promise (Allen Ep 2274:20–2). In August 1532 he visited Erasmus in
Freiburg and Amerbach in Basel, expecting to go on to Italy but changing his
mind and returning to his ailing mother in Ghent.

ERASMUS OF ROTTERDAM TO JOACHIM, PHYSICIAN OF GHENT,
GREETING

I had already collected some proverbs from Galen when your first letter arrived; a little later I received another dealing with pretty much the same material. Your solicitude was most gratifying to me, for it demonstrated your   5
singular devotion towards me. I had excerpted those proverbs not in a continuous reading but as I came across them by chance, which I suppose you
did as well. In many we were of one mind, save that I had accumulated
more; among yours there were two that had escaped me.[1] Obviously you
admire Galen very much, and rightly so; but I am distressed that such an   10
important author is published at such great expense in such faulty editions
as those which are now being produced in Italy.[2] See what the cursed thirst
for gold can do![3] What a sacrilege is committed for the few gold coins with
which a learned proofreader could be hired.

Jacopo Sadoleto is not unknown to me, since I have received from him   15
once and again letters brimming with kindness. I barely have the time to

* * * * *

2049
1 Allen could find no reference in the next edition of the *Adages* (1533) of any
  contribution by Martens of proverbs from Galen.
2 See Epp 1698:10–15, 1707:5–11, 1713:29–32; cf Ep 1746 n1.
3 *Aeneid* 3.57

write him now.[4] I was scarcely able to write this letter to you, whom I cherish deeply, partly because of your exceptional learning, partly because of your generosity, which I believe I detected in your letter and from this service you have rendered me.[5] I shall consult your notes on the introductory   20
essays of Galen that I have translated,[6] when I get the chance. Right now I am so weighed down by Augustine, a writer so inexhaustible that I seem to be supporting Etna and Athos on my shoulders.[7] The *Proverbiorum chiliades*, enriched with many new additions, are being published.[8] I would be most pleased if you would wish to make some annotations for the next edition.   25
I shall send you a copy of the *Chiliades* as a gift if I can find a trustworthy person to deliver it. I published also a little homily on Psalm 85.[9] The Augustine is coming to an end. When I am freed of that I shall embark on a greater project, although the obstinate growlings of the Zoiluses leave me little leisure time.[10]   30

As soon as Luther stepped on to the stage to enact his drama, I, all too accurate a prophet, predicted that the matter would come to this pass. No one believed me. Now, having learned by experience through the example of stupid persons, he is showing such moderation that he is almost singing a palinode.[11] But the Phrygians learn wisdom too late.[12] On the other hand   35
the mendicant tyrants,[13] and some theologians with them, bitterly hostile to good letters as well as to heresy, engage in such perverse manipulations that I fear a greater conflagration will break out. Since I call for moderation, that is, to have Christ as our goal, I am criticized by both sides. And the struggle is fiercer with friends than with enemies. I am afraid that human passions   40
will seize for themselves the victory due to Christ. The only thing left to us is to pray for a happier outcome of these tempests.

* * * * *

4 On Sadoleto and his relations with Erasmus, see Epp 1511, 1555, 1586. Erasmus would soon resume their correspondence with Ep 2059.
5 Ie in collecting the adages from Galen; see lines 3–12 above.
6 See Ep 1698.
7 The Froben Augustine of 1529 (Ep 2157); see Ep 2038:2–3 with n3.
8 Since 1508, editions of the *Adagia*, originally called the *Adagia collectanea*, were called the *Adagiorum* (or *Proverbiorum*) *chiliades*, ie *Thousands of Adages*. On the new edition see Epp 2022, 2023.
9 See Ep 2017.
10 Zoilus (c 400–c 320 BC), was a Greek rhetorician and philosopher who denounced Homer as a purveyor of fables and criticized Isocrates and Plato as well. His name was synonymous with 'carping critic.'
11 Ie making a retraction. See Ep 2013 n6.
12 *Adagia* I i 28
13 Ie members of the mendicant orders, Franciscans and Dominicans

It gave me great pleasure to hear mention of those who have an un-
biased opinion of my studies. This is the one thing that consoles me in the
midst of the ingratitude of men, that I have on my side all the most impor-   45
tant and most upright men, and this is true of almost every region – England, Brabant, Spain, Germany, France, Hungary, Poland. I could give you a
long list of them if I were not afraid to sound like a braggart. And they testify to their good will not only in letters that render me great homage but
also by the promise of princely terms and gifts freely sent.[14] The learned   50
almost everywhere are with me, except those who are strongly attached to
the new factions and are led not by good judgment but by their feelings.
I pit the good will of so many great men against the likes of Lee, Zúñiga,
Cousturier, and Béda.[15] And you also, my dear Joachim, I gladly number
among my sincere friends.   55

Like you I was a friend of Hilarius, both in the past and now more
intensely since I know he is so close to you.[16] I am sorry that he is playing
the vagabond,[17] and there are murmurings about his taking a wife;[18] I am
afraid he does not manage his affairs very well. I shall write to Alciati if I
have the time.[19] Convey my personal thanks and greetings to the governor,[20] 60
Maecenas of humane studies, and also to the great man, d'Oraison,[21] and
to the bishop of Maguelonne.[22] The illustrious physician is on his way to

* * * * *

14 For the most recent invitations, see Ep 2037 n40.
15 See Epp 1341A:823–30 (Lee) and 868–927 (Zúñiga), 1943 n7 (Cousturier), and
   1943 n6 (Béda).
16 Erasmus' one-time servant and courier, Hilarius Bertolph (Ep 1712 introduction), was a native of Ledeberg near Ghent.
17 For 'vagabond' Erasmus writes aleten, from the Greek ἀλήτης, a word much
   used of beggars in the Odyssey (as at 17.420).
18 In 1527, Bertolph, after having lived for a time in France, returned to Ghent,
   where he got married in 1528.
19 See Ep 2051.
20 Johannes Nicolai (Jean de Nicolai, d 1533), bishop of Apt (Vaucluse) and papal governor of Avignon from 1519. A doctor of both laws and a patron of
   humanist learning who instituted public lectures on the Epistles of St Paul,
   he was a friend of both Andrea Alciati and Jacopo Sadoleto. This is the only
   known reference to him by Erasmus.
21 Antoine Honorat, sieur d'Oraison (documented 1503–44), who had some sort
   of royal commission in Provence. In 1528 Andrea Alciati described him as an
   old friend who had requested him to write a legal treatise on duelling (AK Ep
   1261). Erasmus also sent him greetings in Epp 2296 and 2442)
22 Guillaume Pellicier (c 1498/9–1567) who, in 1527 or 1528 and with the help
   of Margaret of Angoulême, succeeded his uncle (also Guillaume Pellicier) as
   bishop of Maguelonne (near Montpellier). By 1528 he was a councillor to King

Venice.[23] No one approves this man's morals, few his medicine. For my part,
I would not like to have such a man either as friend or enemy.

Farewell. At Basel, 1528   65

2050 / To Petrus Decimarius   Basel, 16 September 1528

On Petrus Decimarius, see Ep 1986. This letter, clearly the answer to one from
Decimarius, was first published in the *Opus epistolarum*.

ERASMUS OF ROTTERDAM TO PETRUS DECIMARIUS, GREETING
I consign this letter also to the winds and make it short so that there will be
less of a loss if it goes astray. To those who stir up trouble concerning Terminus I give answer in the appendix to the Psalm.[1] I send you that little book.
The book *On Pronunciation* is not read by many and is more successful for   5
that reason.[2] Whereas the *Ciceronianus*, which is snatched up by everybody,
is creating quite a furore in Paris.[3] You will find out about the affair in my
letter to Brie, of which I send you a printed copy.[4] There is no happiness in
human affairs without some admixture of pestilence.

Carvel has written to me from Lyon.[5] I can plainly foresee that a new   10
conflagration will break out because of these magpies and jackdaws, birds
of evil omen. Arising from the stupid clamours of these men against good
letters it returns to its source, as I see.

* * * * *

Francis I. A conscientious if not perfect bishop (he fathered five children by a
Greek woman and, in the 1550s, had to be cleared of charges of heresy and
treason), he distinguished himself by his interest in scholarship. A serious
student of the elder Pliny, he was known particularly for his knowledge of
medicine. He actively promoted medical studies at the University of Montpellier, where Erasmus had a circle of admirers around Petrus Decimarius (Ep
2050).
23 Allen and, following him, CEBR, state that the reference is probably to Paracelsus (Ep 1808), whom Erasmus had consulted on medical matters in 1527. But
there is no warrant for applying to Paracelsus the negative sentiments expressed here. So the identity of 'the illustrious physician' remains a mystery.

2050
1 Ie in Ep 2018, which was printed at the end of *In psalmum 85*
2 See Ep 1949.
3 See Ep 2021 introduction.
4. Ep 2046, which was published in the *Selectae epistolae*; see Ep 2021 introduction.
5 See Ep 1986 n4.

You need not concern yourself with pomegranates or anything else. I
do not crave such delicacies and this type of commodity is not easily ex-   15
ported. I get my supply of wines from nearby Burgundy.

I shall write to the illustrious bishop[6] when I have time. When you
write that I am very busy, you do not tell the whole truth. You should have
said that I am overwhelmed. Give my best regards to Alexander, Antonius,
Diego of Burgos, and Jacques Ferrand.[7] Beatus Rhenanus is in Sélestadt.[8]   20
Glareanus and Amerbach send you their sincere greetings.[9] There is an incredible scarcity of learned men here. The evangelical fever holds many in
its grip. Farewell, my excellent friend.

Given at Basel, 10 September 1528

2051 / To Andrea Alciati   Basel, 16 September 1528

On the famous Milanese jurist and champion of the humanist approach to the
study of law, Andrea Alciati, see Epp 1250 and 1706. Although Erasmus and
Alciati corresponded over a long period of time, starting in 1521, their principal contact was via their mutual friend, Bonifacius Amerbach (Ep 1933), who
had studied with Alciati (1518–21) during the latter's first period of teaching at the papal university in Avignon. In 1527, following several years of renewed residence in Milan, Alciati returned to his professorship at Avignon,
where he remained until moving to a professorship at Bourges in 1529.

First published in the *Opus epistolarum*, this letter was dispatched to Alciati by Bonifacius Amerbach, along with his own letter to Alciati, dated c
11 October 1528 (AK Ep 1301:25–6; cf Ep 2049:59–60). In his reply, dated 22

* * * * *

6 Pellicier (Ep 2049 n22)
7 Allen, who did not know who Decimarius was and thought that the name
  might be a pseudonym for Alonso de Valdés (see Ep 1986 introduction), speculated fruitlessly on the names of the persons to whom Erasmus sent greetings in this sentence. 'Alexander' is unidentified. 'Antonius' is possibly Antonius Cameranus, who had matriculated at Montpellier on the same day as
  Decimarius; see *Matricule de Montpellier* 49 no 825. 'Diego of Burgos' does not
  match the name of any of the three men from Burgos in Old Castile who are
  known to have matriculated at Montpellier in the 1520s; see *Matricule de Montpellier* 47 nos 796–8. Jacques Ferrand matriculated at the University of Montpellier on 26 October 1516 and received a medical doctorate on 10 February
  1527; see *Matricule de Montpellier* 29 no 485, 51 no 854.
8 He was still there on 24 September 1528, when he wrote AK Ep 1292 (= BRE
  267) to Bonifacius Amerbach.
9 On Glareanus, see Ep 1977 n29; on Amerbach, Ep 1933.

November, Alciati stated that he had received the letter and was answering it
(AK Ep 1312:73–4), but the reply has not survived.

ERASMUS OF ROTTERDAM TO ANDREA ALCIATI, DOCTOR OF LAWS,
GREETING

Amerbach, a man of exquisite refinement, read aloud to me the passage in
your letter that made mention of me in a manner that betokened friendship
more than mere courtesy.[1] This kind of generosity, most learned Alciati,   5
would be appropriate for all those who cultivate the liberal disciplines; but
there is nothing so auspicious in human affairs that some foul disease does
not gradually creep in. I greatly admire the style and talent of Longueil, although at times I find him lacking in this warmth. Nevertheless I am grieved
that this talent has been taken from us prematurely.[2] I am compelled to say   10
that I miss sometimes that same virtue also in Budé, in other respects a most
learned and upright man. You will know my feelings from the letter I wrote
to Brie that is contained in the little book I am sending you.[3]

Your natural disposition, your admirable learning, your moral character purer than snow, were altogether worthy of being treated with like   15
kindness by fortune; yet why should I lament your fate when present conditions are the same for everyone?[4] I admire and commend your strength of
character, excellent sir, but I would rather praise your moderation in prosperity than your courage in adversity. Would that fortune raged so fiercely
against me as to weaken its powers! I have to do battle with a host of   20

* * * * *

2051
1 On 28 August 1528, Alciati had written to Amerbach from Avignon as follows (AK Ep 1282:40–4): 'I have learned with great pleasure that Erasmus is
there with you and is hard at work on new and heroic things; otherwise he
would have written to me. I know, my dear Bonifacius, how much I owe
that man and am not so insensitive as not to be aware that he gave me
the greatest thing that can to given to any mortal man, namely, fame and
eternity.'
2 Erasmus had already mentioned Longueil's premature death in earlier letters
to Alciati (Epp 1675:15–18, 1706:4–6), but here he may well have been alluding to the ambiguous (and much criticized) faint praise of Longueil in the
Ciceronianus (CWE 28 345).
3 Ep 2046, published in Selectae epistolae; see Ep 2021 introduction.
4 In a letter to Amerbach of 26 May 1528, Alciati had deplored the general turmoil of the times and particularly the unhappy fate of his home, Milan, in the
Italian wars (AK Ep 1261:13–16). On the course of the Italian wars at this time,
see Ep 1935 n10.

ANDREAS ALCIATVS, ME-
DIOLANENSIS.

Eloquio Ius Romanum lucebat & arte, id
Turba obscurarant barbara Legulei.
Andreas prisco reddit sua Iura nitori,
Consultosque facit doctius inde loqui.

F 4

Andrea Alciati
Philippe Galle *Virorum doctorum de disciplinis benemerentium effigies* (Antwerp 1572)
Metropolitan Toronto Reference Library

snakes, breathing their lethal poison not from seven but from thousands of heads.[5]

This is a laconic epistle, but I am afraid that, worn out by my inept handwriting, you will say it is too long. There is reason to congratulate Boniface: the distended womb of his wife gives him promise of the long- 25
desired name of father.[6] Farewell, distinguished adornment of this age. Do not judge my sentiments towards you, I pray, by my diligence in writing letters. You would call this a long letter if you knew by what toils I am oppressed and to how many people I must respond.[7]

Given at Basel, 16 September 1528   30

2052 / To Germain de Brie   Basel, 21 September 1528

This letter was first published in the *Opus epistolarum*. On Germain de Brie, see Ep 2021 introduction.

ERASMUS OF ROTTERDAM TO GERMAIN DE BRIE, GREETING
In his preface to the works of Cyril, Oecolampadius made reference to me without good reason, to you with more reason, but it was temperate in tone.[1] A certain party has begun transcribing the *Psegmata graeca* by way of experiment, but ineptly, as is obvious.[2]   5

* * * * *

5 Doubtless a reference to the Lernaean Hydra, the mythical, multi-headed, poisonous sea monster with seven (or more) heads. Killing it was one of Hercules'
   seven labours. Cf Ep 2046:383–6.
6 His daughter Ursula was born on Christmas Day 1528 and died on 20 June
   1532 (AK Epp 1556 n9, 1661 n1).
7 Cf Ep 1985 n2.

2052
1 The reference is to the Latin edition of the works of St Cyril of Alexandria
   (*Opera . . . in quibus habes non pauca antehac Latinis non exhibita* (Basel: Cratander,
   August 1528), edited by the Basel reformer Johannes Oecolampadius (Ep 2000
   n4) with translations by various hands. In his preface (cited at length in Allen's
   note), Oecolampadius protested against unfair critics, having in mind particularly Brie, who had criticized Oecolampadius' Latin translation of St John
   Chrysostom's *De sancto Babyla* as incompetent and aimed at the subversion of
   true religion (see n2 below). Oecolampadius complained, without rancour, that
   Brie was engaging in slander over petty errors and that it was unreasonable to
   expect all translators to measure up to the standards set by Brie and Erasmus.
2 In March 1523, Cratander at Basel had published *Divi Ioannis Chrysostomi Psegmata quaedam*, a collection of short pieces (*psegmata* 'shavings') by St John

I didn't know More was in Paris.[3] I should like to know what passed
between you. I hear and rejoice that Budé's *On the Eloquence of Greek Style* has
been published.[4] They say that there is mention of me in it – not very flattering, I am told, but I expect better things from Budé.[5] If he disagrees with me
or makes some reasonable corrections, I shall never interpret it as an insult.   10
Truly, I never heard anything more senseless than such views.[6] But something else is disturbing certain people who consider nothing elegant that is
not pagan. They would not want good letters to utter the name of Christ.[7]

Give my greetings to Lupset;[8] I surmise from the fact that he does not
write to me that he is very busy, and for that reason I have hesitated to write   15
to him. Farewell, my kind friend Brie. I am surprised that there is no certain
news of Jacques Lefèvre.[9]

At Basel, on the feast day of St Matthew 1528

The bearer of this letter is the Pole Andrzej Zebrzydowski,[10] a young
man of noble lineage in his country. He was drawn away from my company   20
by his desire to see France, resplendent with the light of so many learned
men. I hope you will be so kind as to give him audience from time to time.
Again farewell.

* * * * *

Chrystostom translated into Latin by Oecolampadius. Among the pieces included was Chrysostom's *De sancto Babyla*, the Greek original of which Erasmus would publish (under the title *De Babyla martyre*) in 1527 (Ep 1856).
When Brie published his own translation of the work (Paris: Simon de Colines, March 1528), the title, *Liber contra gentiles, Babylae Antiocheni episcope
... vitam continens*, included the extension *Contra Ioannis Oecolampadii transla-
tionem*. Included in the volume, moreover, was a list of Oecolampadius' errors
of translation (*Insignium Ioannis Oecolampadii erratorum ... elenchus*). See Epp
1817:44–54, 2062:26–7.
3 In late August, Thomas More had been chosen to be the delegate from England at negotiations in Cambrai between France and the emperor that were
to commence on 4 September. But the mission was called off and More apparently did not leave England (LP 4 no 4579, Appendix 196, 198–9). Erasmus
may have heard a false rumour arising out of reports of the intended mission.
4 It was not in fact published until September 1529, under the title *Commentarii
linguae graecae* (Paris: Josse Bade); cf Epp 1794 n2, 1812 n1, 2077:66–8.
5 Cf Epp 1794:17–24, 2077:68–9.
6 Ie the views of the French Ciceronians
7 See Ep 1948 introduction.
8 See Ep 2021 n8.
9 Following his return to France after taking refuge in Strasbourg (Ep 1717:34–7),
Lefèvre, still fearing his enemies among the Paris theologians, had kept quiet;
cf Ep 2077:36–8.
10 Ep 1958 n1

2053 / To Nicolaus Vesuvius   Basel, 21 September 1528

Nicolaus Vesuvius (Ep 1784) was chaplain to Michel Boudet (Ep1612), bishop
of Langres, who was closely associated with the French court, a friend of Guillaume Budé, and a supporter of humanist scholarship. Apart from his correspondence with Erasmus in the years 1527–8, Vesuvius is undocumented. The
letter was first published in the *Opus epistolarum*.

ERASMUS OF ROTTERDAM TO NICOLAUS VESUVIUS, GREETING

I see that Béda and his cohorts are setting out with gladiatorial hearts to
make trouble for me.[1] Some people[2] urge me to make an open all out attack
on the faculty. This does not seem well-advised to me and, even if it did, I
do not have the time. I have heard that the bishop is a man of exceptional   5
wisdom;[3] I should like to hear his oracular pronouncement on this matter.

The person who sent me the French adages seems to me to be a pious man and the one who sent me the sayings a man of congenial spirit.[4]
Greet them both for me; I had no time to write to them. The one who added
a preface to the Donatus shows his true colours, as stupid and boorish as   10
ever.[5] He does not merit anyone's wrath. This is the misfortune of the times
in which we live, that even the most contemptible people can do whatever
they wish. The audacity of the evangelicals provokes princes to find a remedy for this evil. But I am afraid this medicine will not be beneficial to either
party. Perhaps they will apply the knife and cautery to one another.   15

I should hope, if possible, that the royal privilege be given at least for
the Augustine.[6] The assets of the children of Froben depend on this work.
I donate my own work virtually free of charge,[7] but otherwise I would not

* * * * *

2053
1 Cf Ep 2048:37–50. On 'gladiatorial hearts,' cf Ep 1943 n4.
2 Including Berquin; see Ep 2048:37–8, 52–3, 60–2.
3 Boudet; see introduction.
4 Apparently friends of Vesuvius who had offered material for the next edition
  of the *Adagia*
5 The contributor of the preface is unidentified. Allen's suggestion that it might
  be Pierre Vitré (Ep 66) seems wide of the mark, since Erasmus remained on
  friendly terms with him all his life and remembered him in his will (cf Ep
  2062:32–8 with n13). The fourth-century *Ars grammatica* of Aelius Donatus was
  the most widely used Latin grammar all through the Middle Ages and into
  the early modern period.
6 The Froben Augustine of 1529 (Ep 2157). On earlier privileges granted to
  Froben, see Ep 1341 n4. On the currently sought privilege for the Augustine,
  see Ep 2075.
7 Cf Ep 1900:54–6.

take on such a task for two thousand florins.[8] A religious sense of duty demanded it of me. I hear that the cardinal of France is not very amenable.[9] 20
Perhaps some are whispering inauspicious things into his ears that will prejudice him against me. There is nothing of my own in this work except that
I removed textual errors as far as I could, indicated spurious works, and
divided up the book according to subject matter. The preface will contain
nothing that will be offensive to anyone. If your bishop has any influence 25
with the king, I wish that at least in this work he will grant us the royal
privilege. I am sending a little book of *Epistles*,[10] assuming that Anton[11] will
be willing to carry such a heavy load.

Farewell.

Given at Basel on the feast day of St Matthew 1528 30

They write me that Nicolas Le Clerc is ranting against my name,[12] following the example of Duchesne.[13] A new kind of preaching! And yet they
say he is regarded as a man of outstanding honesty and sobriety. I am loath
to believe it.

2054 / To Erard de la Marck   Basel, 1 October 1528

Erard de la Marck (Ep 738), cardinal-prince-bishop of Liège and zealous Catholic reformer, had been a correspondent and patron of Erasmus since 1517. In
the 1520s their relations had been marred more than once by mistrust and misunderstanding (see Epp 1268 n9, 1341A:1716–22, 1482:9–16) and there would
be more trouble in the 1530s. At this point, however, common opposition to
Luther and concern for Catholic reform had restored tolerably good relations
between them. In 1527, in the preface to the fourth edition of the New Testament, Erasmus had paid tribute to Erard's wisdom and perceptivity (LB VI ***3
verso), and in this letter as well as in Ep 2382 (7 September 1530), the last two
in their surviving correspondence, Erasmus addressed Erard with the courtesy due to someone whose patronage (for Haio Herman and the Collegium
Trilingue) was being sought.

* * * * *

 8 Since this is purely speculative, and probably hyperbole, there is no way of
knowing what kind of florins Erasmus meant: gold Florentine or Rhenish (Imperial) or Hapsburg Flemish, or the Hapsburg Flemish money-of-account (six
florins = one pound groot). But certainly Erasmus meant a very large sum of
money.
 9 See Ep 2038 n15.
10 The *Selectae epistolae*; see Ep 2021 introduction.
11 Bletz, a professional courier; see Ep 1784 n1.
12 See Ep 2043.
13 See Ep 2043 n1.

First published in the *Opus epistolarum*, this letter belongs to a group of several that were carried by Felix Rex (Ep 2068 n1). This letter was sent together with Ep 2055 to Haio Herman, to whose discretion was left the final decision concerning their delivery (Ep 2056:40–1).

ERASMUS OF ROTTERDAM TO THE BISHOP OF LIÈGE, GREETING
Some time ago I sent a letter and the second book of the *Hyperaspistes* to your Highness through the agency of a certain Michael Borman.[1] I do not know whether he brought them. I have long been thinking of taking flight from here,[2] but I don't know to what nest. King Ferdinand calls me to Vienna with a princely salary,[3] but it is to another world. The king of England invites me in a very friendly letter,[4] but I have a horror of sea voyages. Sigismund, king of Poland, invites me, and has already sent me an honorary gift of no small value.[5] I am invited by several bishops,[6] but I should prefer, let us not say to grow old – for I am already old – but to take my rest in Brabant. But I see no prospects of a salary there, although it has been promised;[7] besides, too much liberty is allowed to certain stupid monks and theologians, who under the pretext of the Catholic faith wage war against good letters and those that practise them, and some against the gospel itself.

Paris has its Béda,[8] though he is not the only one,[9] and Brabant too has its share of people like him. In the books that I have published up to now they have not been able to find a single sentence that is contrary to Christian doctrine, and through their spitefulness they have made me have a better opinion of my work. Egmondanus and Vincentius have gone to

* * * * *

2054
1 Allen could not identify this messenger. He was possibly the Michiels Borman who was canon of the collegiate church of St Denis at Liège, whose will is preserved in the archives there (CEBR I 173). Erasmus' letter is not extant, but doubtless was written in early September 1527. On *Hyperaspistes* 2 see Ep 1853.
2 See Ep 1926 n8. On the royal invitations noted here, cf Epp 1938 n4, 2029:99–104, 2037 n40.
3 See Epp 2000, 2005.
4 Ep 1878, answered in Ep 1998
5 See Ep 1952.
6 See Epp 1562:3–6, 1409, 1771:13–15, 1814:483–91.
7 When Margaret of Austria made the resumption of Erasmus' imperial pension conditional on his return to Brabant, she also offered him support in excess of his pension; see Ep 1380 introduction.
8 Ep 1943 n6
9 There were also Cousturier (Ep 1943 n7) and Berthélemy (Ep 2027 n18), among others.

their appointed place,[10] but there is no lack of those to succeed them. I hear 20
that in Mechelen there is someone who is railing against my name in public
from the pulpit,[11] in open contempt of the imperial edict[12] and, worse yet,
of the command of Christ.[13] And the court closes its eyes to all of this; and
Erasmus carries away this reward for all the labours by which he attempts
to aid the cause of good letters and the Christian religion. They pretend that 25
they still doubt whether I am sincerely in the Catholic camp. And yet they
could convince themselves of this by noting that all the sects share a more
than deadly hatred for me.

Perhaps it is not new to you there that Johannes Oecolampadius has
publicly taken a wife, a very comely young woman.[14] The Augustinian 30
preacher did the same,[15] and so did the Franciscan preacher recently.[16] This
is their way of condemning the heresy of those who despise marriage. One
of these was a bachelor who some time ago, having been condemned by the
magistracy, was flogged in the public square and, wearing an iron collar
around his neck, was conducted outside the gates by the executioner to be 35
banished into perpetual exile. Ejected with him was a baker, with whom he
was staying, and his wife, whom he had persuaded with exceptional cunning to sleep apart from her husband and then slept with her himself, with
the partial connivance of the husband.[17]

* * * * *

10 Egmondanus, ie Nicolaas Baechem (Ep 1254 n6), and Vincentius Theoderici
(Ep 1196) both died in August 1526.
11 Cf Ep 2055:3–6. Almost certainly Jan van Paesschen (documented 1503–32),
Carmelite at Mechelen and ally of Baechem. Following Baechem's death, Paesschen had evidently taken the latter's place as vociferous public critic of Erasmus and the Collegium Trilingue; Epp 1788:28–9, 1806:6–10.
12 See Ep 1690 n11.
13 Matt 7:1–3; Luke 6:37, 41–2
14 See Ep 1977 n33.
15 Thomas Gyrfalk (d 1560), who since 1524 had been preacher at the Augustinian house in Basel. A strong supporter of Oecolampadius, Gyrfalk in 1529
became second minister (after Oecolampadius) at the cathedral.
16 Johann Lüthard (d 1542), a native of Lucerne, first appears in the records in
1520 as the preacher of the Franciscan house at Basel. His adherence to the
reform party caused trouble with his superiors, but the civic authorities supported him and in 1529 he was confirmed as minister to the Franciscan church
and to the hospital. He took as his wife a former Franciscan nun named
Elisabeth.
17 The bachelor, Peter Frauenberger (documented 1520–8), was a native of Alsace
who registered at the University of Basel in 1522 (MA 1523) and in the same
year took over the Basel parish of St Alban. Expelled from Basel in November 1525 for his reformist views, he returned to the city (and possibly to St

Let me tell you another tale.[18] In a country district called the Old Vil- 40
lage there was a certain peasant in the inn, who as he was mocking the Eucharist, suddenly expired. Witnesses testified that it happened in this way.
A rustic sacristan was carrying a little receptacle filled with consecrated
bread, which they call hosts. Together with him was another peasant who
had formerly been a sacristan. When they got to the village I mentioned,   45
they felt like having a drink. Once inside the inn the companion asked the
sacristan to give him a host. When the latter hesitated, he took it and as
a joke began to consecrate it. The innkeeper's wife, seeing this, upbraided
him, but the peasant said, 'It's none of your business, go get us some wine.'
When the woman returned, she found the man prostrate on the floor. She   50
asked what was wrong with him. Those drinking at another table responded,
'Perhaps he fainted?' The woman brought some vinegar, they put it to his
lips, but to no avail, he was obviously dead. This is no idle tale. I have
heard other reports, but I did not want to write things of which I was not
certain.   55

A young man by the name of Herman of Friesland[19] has moved to
Mechelen, a man of a distinguished family in his country, of exceptional
learning and blameless life, who would be a great adornment to your court
if you were to grant him your favour. If he is not yet known to you, I ask
your most reverend Highness to deem him worthy of your acquaintance.   60
If you do know him, please try to get to know him more personally and
to welcome him into your friendship, as he deserves, with your habitual
generosity. For although outstanding virtue is sufficient unto itself among
philosophers, nevertheless, in order to be of benefit to many, it sometimes
has need of the support of princes. The court has need of many services;   65
to this end young men whose character affords great promise should be
encouraged. But perhaps your kindness is already attending on its own to
what I ask. I shall add that Erasmus has not changed in his sentiment towards you, and I have no doubt that you will continue to be the Maecenas

* * * * *

Alban's) in 1527, only to expelled again the following year, along with the
baker Johann Varnower (documented 1528–9), with whom he had been staying, and Varnower's wife. In May 1529 Varnower was granted a divorce from
his wife, who had borne a child assumed to be Frauenberger's. There is a brief
allusion to this scandal in Erasmus' *Epistola ad fratres Inferioris Germaniae* cwe
78 339.
18 This incident too is briefly recounted in the *Epistola ad fratres* cwe 78 339; cf
n17 above.
19 Haio Herman, whom Erasmus always referred to as Hermannus Phrysius; see
Epp 1978, 2056, and cf Ep 2055:21–8.

you have always been when the circumstances demand it. I wish you the   70
greatest felicity.

Given at Basel, 1 October 1528

2055 / To Jean de Carondelet   Basel, 1 October 1528

Jean (II) de Carondelet (Ep 1276), who was archbishop of Palermo (a see that
he never visited) as well as dean of Besançon and provost of St Donatian in
Bruges, had risen to prominence in the service of the Hapsburgs in the Netherlands. He resided at Mechelen and was a leading official at the Netherlands
court during the regencies of Margaret of Austria (d 1530) and Mary of Hungary. In 1531 he became president of the privy council of the Netherlands.
Erasmus, who had dedicated his edition of St Hilary (Ep 1334) to Carondelet,
considered him a staunch friend whose support could be relied on.

First published in the *Opus epistolarum*, this letter, like Ep 2054, was entrusted to Haio Herman for use as he saw fit.

ERASMUS OF ROTTERDAM TO JEAN, ARCHBISHOP OF PALERMO,
GREETING

Although I combat the new sects at such great personal risk, I hear there
is someone in Mechelen who with clownish impudence delivers frenzied
tirades against my name.[1] His imperial Majesty has prohibited it many   5
times,[2] and there still is no one who has been able to demonstrate in all
my numerous volumes a single sentence in opposition to the true faith, although it has been attempted by Lee and Zúñiga, and recently by Béda and
the Spanish monks.[3] Their unscrupulousness takes advantage of your leniency. What can come of these clamourings but some new uprising? I can   10
tolerate in one way or another the withdrawal of the imperial pension,[4] but
I do not think I deserve this reward.

Here things have reached the point that it is no longer safe for me
to remain in this country. King Ferdinand calls me to Vienna with great

* * * * *

2055
1 See Ep 2054:20–2 with n11.
2 See Ep 2054:22 with n12.
3 See Epp 1341A:823–30 (Lee) and 868–927 (Zúñiga), 1943 n6 (Béda), 1967 (the
   Spanish monks).
4 Payment of this pension (cf Ep 2054 n7) was now long in arrears and would
   never be resumed: see Epp 1408:11–12, 1434, 1585:10–19, 1700:5–9 with n3,
   1703.

promises,[5] but I would prefer to retire in Brabant more than any other place 15
if I were not impeded by certain unprincipled individuals who, whenever
they see fit, respect neither the emperor nor God nor men.[6] Here I am reduced to silence, the heated rooms are detrimental to my health,[7] and it is
not fitting that an old man live in a foreign country; last of all, my years
and my health for a long time now require peace and quiet. 20

I think your Highness knows Herman of Friesland,[8] a young man born
of a good family in his native land, of innate good qualities and exceptional
learning, who in my opinion would be a great ornament and asset to your
court if you would show him the favour of your friendship. I would ask
more insistently that you do this if I did not know that such are the young 25
man's gifts that he will amply commend himself to you on his own merits. I
know that you will be grateful to me if you deign to get to know the young
man more personally. May the Lord preserve you free of harm.

Given at Basel, 1 October 1528

2056 / To Haio Herman   Basel, [c 1 October 1528]

First published in the *Opus epistolarum*, this letter is obviously contemporary
with Epp 2054 and 2055, which were delivered with it (see lines 40–1).

ERASMUS OF ROTTERDAM TO HAIO HERMAN OF FRIESLAND,
GREETING
They have set to work on Seneca,[1] for we had a good number of manuscripts
for the *De beneficiis*. In the meantime I have sent this messenger at my own
expense solely for the purpose of having him bring back your manuscript to 5
me.[2] You need have no apprehensions about it; no one will touch it besides
me. Cover it with paper wrapping with an outer covering of a waxed linen
cloth. It will be sent back with the same care. I shall have an opportunity

* * * * *

5 See Ep 2005.
6 Cf Ep 2054:19–23.
7 Erasmus had a strong aversion to German stoves. Johann Froben had a fire-
   place specially installed in the house that Erasmus occupied in Basel. See Epp
   1248 n5, 1258 n18.
8 Haio Herman; see Ep 2054 n19.

2056
1 Erasmus' second edition of Seneca, published by Froben at Basel in March
   1529 (Ep 2091)
2 A copy of the Treviso Seneca (1478) that had belonged to Rudolph Agricola
   and was profusely annotated by him; see Allen Epp 2091:108–18, 2108.

in the preface to make honourable mention of your name, if you will allow
me.[3] I don't know what manuscripts Vives saw,[4] unless perhaps it was yours   10
or one that was collated by a friend of mine at the home of Thomas More.[5]
But I have collected such a mass of annotations that I have no fear of his
manuscript or of yours.

I should gladly leave this task to anyone at all if shame did not compel me to clear myself of the disgrace contracted through the stupidity and   15
perfidy of a friend.[6] In the first edition we were both guilty: he accepted to
do what he was absolutely incapable of doing, but it was I who entrusted
the task to him. We are both equally to blame, save that it is more shameful not to know oneself, and it borders on the disingenuous to have a better
opinion of a person than he deserves. But it was solely his fault that when   20
he heard that I was complaining about the edition he removed the part of
the copy that had the most annotations so that he would not be found out.
Apart from this, I have more than enough to occupy me.

My *Ciceronianus* offended quite a few Italians, which I suspected would
be the case; it also offended the French, which I never expected.[7] You will   25
become aware of this from the little book I am sending you.[8] Velius remonstrates with me because I left you out[9] – as if I had to pass judgment on everyone, even those who have not yet become famous through
their writings. As far as that is concerned, he has good reason to admire
the agreeable eloquence of your style. It is of great importance, my dear   30
Herman, how you present yourself to the world in your first writings.
Choose a subject that is not so much ambitious as likely to win favour
and popularity, but most of all one that commends itself by its usefulness.
Since I have been unsuccessful in this, I recommend it more confidently to
others.   35

I beg of you with great insistence that you ensure that this courier
does not return to me empty-handed. The work is in progress and cannot

* * * * *

3 A promise kept in Ep 2091 (see preceding note).
4 See Ep 2061:1.
5 The friend was Robert Aldridge, whom Erasmus asked to collect the variant readings from manuscripts of Seneca at King's College and Peterhouse in
  Cambridge and forward them via Thomas More; see Epp 1656, 1766:95–102,
  1797, 2040:3–4, 2061:12–14.
6 Wilhelm Nesen, whom Erasmus held largely responsible for the 'somewhat
  unfortunate' first Froben edition of the *Senecae lucubrationes* in 1515; see Epp
  1341A:449–63, 1479:99–102.
7 See Epp 1948, 2021.
8 Evidently the *Selectae epistolae*; see Ep 2021 introduction.
9 In a letter to which Ep 2008 was the reply; see Ep 2008:26–8.

be interrupted without great expense.[10] If there is anything that you wish me to do for you in return, I assure you that you will not find me wanting in gratitude. I have written to the bishops of Palermo and Liège.[11] It is up 40 to you to decide whether the letters should be delivered.

Basel, [1529]

2057 / To Erasmus Schets   Basel, 1 October 1528

On Schets, see Ep 1931. The letter was first published by Allen using the autograph in the British Library (MS Add 38512 fol 31). The first sentence of Ep 2115 indicates that it never reached Schets.

Cordial greetings. I have many remedies against the stone, but I have lent them to a person who is in danger of death. This past March I was deprived of a dear friend, Ferry, archdeacon of Besançon, brother of the archbishop of Palermo, who used to supply me with Burgundy wine.[1]

One[2] has to observe a moderate diet, especially at supper; avoid be- 5 coming cold, and especially do not let your feet get cold. One should not wear a belt or clothes that are too tight around the kidneys, and eat light food, like lamb or chicken. One should abstain from food that is too hot or greasy, like fried food, from strong wines, and from too much bread, especially stale bread. One should urinate often.   10

Against pain I have found nothing more effective than the following.[3] Put some camomile and parsley into a linen pouch and boil them in a clean pot until half of the water has evaporated. Then taking out the pouch, drain off all the water immediately (that can be done easily with two wooden disks) and then the pouch is applied immediately to the loins, where the 15 pain is, until it becomes lukewarm. Then it is put back into the same boiling water, taken out again and applied. This can be done twice or more, lying down on a bed. Then, putting the palm of the hand on the painful area, one

* * * * *

10 The printers were already at work on the new edition of Seneca; see line 3 above.
11 Epp 2055 to Jean de Carondelet, 2054 to Erard de la Marck

2057
1 Ferry de Carondelet (Ep 2002 introduction) had been Erasmus' chief source of the Burgundian wine that he considered essential to keeping his kidney stones under control; see Epp 1316 n7, 1359 n5, 1510:109–12, 1749:16–23. He died on 27 June 1528. On his brother Jean de Carondelet see Ep 2055 introduction.
2 Ie anyone afflicted with kidney stones
3 Cf Ep 1558:69–116.

should fall asleep for a while. Then one should try to urinate. This method
has hardly ever failed me.   20

I shall send you other remedies if I get back what I lent. But there is no
end of remedies; the best remedy is diet. One should avoid drinking freshly
brewed beer, especially if it is full of sediment; one may have some light
red wine.[4]

I ask that you send the letter addressed to Flanders to the person to   25
whom I wrote it.[5] For you, my dear Schets, your excellent wife and all of
your family, I send every best wish.

Given at Basel, 1 October 1528
To the honourable Erasmus Schets, merchant
Yours, Erasmus of Rotterdam   30

2058 / To Johann von Riedt   Basel, 1 October 1528

This letter was first published in *Briefe und Documente aus der Zeit der Reformation im 16. Jahrhundert* ed Carl and Wilhelm Ludwig Krafft (Elberfeld c 1875)
164, from a seventeenth-century copy that had disappeared by the time Allen
was preparing his edition.

Johann von Riedt (d 1535), who belonged to a patrician family of Cologne
and studied at the university there (matriculation in 1484), was a member
of the Cologne city council from 1514, serving several terms as burgomaster
before his death. He represented Cologne at the imperial diets of 1529 and
1530. Known to have supported reform of the University of Cologne, he was at
the same time equally opposed to the Lutheran reformers and the conservative
scholastic theologians.

TO JOHANN VON RIEDT

Cordial greetings. I had not forgotten Johann von Riedt, but nonetheless it
was very pleasant that you revived the memory of our old acquaintance.[1]
Christoph von Carlowitz, a young man of great promise, as you write, is

* * * * *

4 The Latin is *vinum subrubrum*. On the translation of *subrubrum* as 'light red'
  rather than 'rosé,' see Ep 1749 n5.
5 Possibly Ep 2060

2058
1 It is not known when or where Erasmus and Riedt became acquainted. As
  Allen points out, Erasmus visited Cologne a number of times in the years
  1515–20. It is also possible that Riedt went to Paris to study sometime in the
  years 1495–1505.

living in Dôle;[2] I shall do as you command by letter. I like Joachim very 5
much.[3] He came to see me twice. I shall invite him to dinner and if there
is anything in which I can oblige him, I shall gladly do so, even if only for
your sake.

I don't know what the monks and the theologians in your region are
up to. In Paris and in Spain they have simply gone mad.[4] This tyranny has 10
come about through the violence of Luther while he attempts perversely to
restore everyone to liberty.

Whatever you do for Jacobus Ceratinus you do both for a man emi-
nently worthy of it and for your university;[5] but, as I see it, you are deliberating too much about his salary. I wish for you, my very dear friend, and 15
all of yours the best of health.

Given at Basel, 1 October 1528

2059 / To Jacopo Sadoleto   Basel, [1 October] 1528

This letter was first published in the *Opus epistolarum*.

Shortly before the sack of Rome in 1527, Sadoleto (Ep 1511), long Erasmus' most consistent defender and advocate in the papal curia, had gone to
his bishopric of Carpentras in southern France, where he would remain until
1536. With this letter Erasmus resumes, possibly in response to the prompting of Joachim Martens (Ep 2049:15–17), a correspondence that had evidently
been interrupted and of which there was no surviving trace after Ep 1586.
Sadoleto's reply to this letter is Ep 2074, where the opening lines confirm the
month-date assigned here.

* * * * *

2 On Carlowitz see Epp 1951 n7, 2010. His acquaintance with Riedt had probably been made during his visit to Cologne in 1527. In Ep 2010:9, which Erasmus perhaps did not receive or had forgotten, Carolwitz reported that he had
  moved from Dôle to Besançon.
3 Joachim Sterck van Ringelberg of Antwerp (c 1499–after 1531) studied Latin
  and Greek, rhetoric and the sciences at Louvain and then, in 1527, ventured
  abroad, visiting Cologne, Mainz, and Heidelberg on his way to Basel. There he
  published his *Institutiones astronomicae* (V. Curio, 31 October 1528), for which
  Erasmus supplied two poems (CWE 85 158–9 nos 76–7). By the end of the
  year, Erasmus identified Ringelberg with the public agitation of the reformed
  party in Basel (Ep 2079:44–5) and was less enchanted with him than he is
  here. By April 1529 Ringelberg had departed Basel for the Netherlands and
  then France, where an edition of his *Opera* was published at Lyon in 1531 (S.
  Gryphius).
4 Cf Ep 2006:10–15.
5 Ceratinus (Ep 1951 n6) was evidently being considered for a position at the
  University of Cologne that he ultimately did not get.

ERASMUS OF ROTTERDAM TO JACOPO SADOLETO, BISHOP OF
CARPENTRAS, GREETING

How many calamities this fatal tempest in human affairs brings with it,
most distinguished Bishop! What shall we lament or whom shall we console? What part of the world can escape this violent blast? Or who among   5
the forces of good is not himself in need of a consoler? We have seen Rome
sacked more cruelly than it was in ancient times by the Gauls or by the
Goths.[1] We have seen the leader of the church, Clement, treated with greatest inclemency,[2] and we still see the two most powerful monarchs of the
world set at variance by irremediable hatred and, if the rumour be true,   10
challenging each other to single combat.[3]

In such a great uproar we had great fears for you and Bembo,[4] in whom
more than in anyone else and almost alone, it seems to me, that moral integrity and blameless piety of old have survived. I have always esteemed the
outstanding gifts of you both. Yours I have come to know not only through   15
the acclaim of your friends and your letters to me but also from your excellent book,[5] which continues to enjoy great favour among those who appreciate the combination of moral perfection with good letters.[6] I began to esteem
and admire Bembo with greater intensity after I read the letters published
by Longueil,[7] who once was the recipient of the kindness of both of you.   20

* * * * *

2059
1 The emperor's mutinous troops brutally sacked Rome in May 1527.
2 During the sack, Clement took refuge in the Castel Sant'Angelo, where he
  remained a virtual prisoner of the emperor for several months. Cf Ep 1987 n1.
3 See Ep 2024:38–45 with n8.
4 The great Venetian humanist, Pietro Bembo (1470–1547), was a close friend of
  Sadoleto, together with whom he had served Pope Leo x as secretary before
  retiring to a villa near Padua in 1521 to devote himself to his studies. Up to
  this point, Erasmus appears to have had only the slightest acquaintance with
  Bembo or his works and no great interest in either. This letter, together with
  the reference to Bembo in the *Ciceronianus* (see n7 below), is the first sign of
  a new and lively interest that would, starting with Ep 2106 in 1529, blossom
  into a warmly friendly correspondence interrupted only by Erasmus' death.
5 His commentary on Psalm 50 (Rome: Franciscus Minutius Calvus 1525)
6 In the letter acknowledging receipt of a copy of the commentary, Erasmus
  lauded Sadoleto's successful combination of humanist scholarship and style
  and genuine piety, contrasting it favourably to the pagan tone that he found
  in the works of most Roman humanists: Ep 1586:1–14.
7 At this point, Erasmus does not seem to have been familiar with any of the
  works that Bembo himself had published: in the *Ciceronianus* (cwe 28 435) he
  complains that 'there is nothing of Bembo's available.' But in the same passage
  (ibidem 435–6) he goes on to heap praise on both Bembo and Sadoleto for
  their achievement of a Ciceronian eloquence that did not preclude the use of

I saw how important it was for the scholarly world and for religion
that such spirits were saved from this fire. Concerning Bembo, I have not
yet laid aside my anxiety, since I am uncertain of his fortunes. But I congratulate you particularly, whom some divine power propitious not only to
you but also to higher studies and religion has rescued from the storm –   25
and would that it had rescued you entirely! I hear that a great part of you
has perished, namely, your library rich in rare works in both languages.[8] I
can draw a home-grown conclusion[9] about how grave a loss this has been
to you, especially since it is irreparable.

What unheard-of barbarity! Was there ever such savagery among the   30
Scythians, the Quadi, the Vandals, the Huns, or the Goths that, not satisfied
with plundering whatever riches they could find, would in their fury burn
books, a sacred possession? In this event I grieve not only for the plight
of a friend but for my own as well. Consider that whatever was lost there
was taken from me and from all men of learning. The catastrophe that be-   35
fell the city of Rome was the catastrophe of all nations, since it was not
only the citadel of the Christian religion and the nurturer of men of talent and, if I may say so, the tranquil domicile of the Muses, but also the
common mother of all peoples. Who, indeed, even if he were born in another world, was not received, nurtured and brought up in the peaceful bo-   40
som of that city? Who, though coming from the most remote corner of the
world, thought of himself as a stranger there? Further still, to how many
was that city dearer, sweeter, and happier than their own native land? Or
what person is so uncivilized that that city does not send him back to us

* * * * *

ecclesiastical Latin where the proper treatment of Christian topics required it.
As Erasmus here indicates, that favourable judgment of Bembo was based on
his reading of letters by him found in the posthumous edition of the works of
Christoph de Longueil (on whom see Ep 1948 introduction) published by Philippus Junta at Florence in December 1524 (repr Farnsborough, Hants: Gregg
1967): *Christophori Longolii orationes duae pro defensione sua in crimen lesae maiestatis [etc]*. The volume includes four books of Longueil's own letters to Bembo,
Sadoleto and others, as well as a fifth book of letters by Bembo and Sadoleto
to Longueil, to one another, and to Guillaume Budé (among others).
8 The library had been lost, not in the sack of Rome, as Erasmus evidently assumed (see next paragraph) and as Sadoleto himself subsequently reported
(Ep 2074:31–3), but on the voyage to France. When the plague broke out on
ship among the carriers and Sadoleto's own servants, they were put ashore
empty-handed and the ship sailed off to 'unknown lands' with nearly all of
Sadoleto's library, including precious Greek manuscripts. For Sadoleto's own
description of the mishap, see Allen's note.
9 Ie one based on his own experience; see *Adagia* I x 48.

PETRVS. BEMBVS.

Pietro Bembo
Artist unknown
Biblioteca Ambrosiana, Milan

more peaceful and civilized? Or who has ever lived there for any period of   45
time who did not leave reluctantly, who did not gladly seize the opportunity to return there when it was offered him or try to find it if it was not
offered? Assuredly this was more truly the destruction of the world than
of a city.

Shaken by so many differences of opinion, the Christian religion is tot-   50
tering. The fury of Bellona is present everywhere,[10] and in the midst of so
many dissident and tumultuous voices the Muses and the liberal disciplines
either lie helplessly prostrate and are paralyzed or they remain silent, terrified. And, as if this were not enough of a catastrophe, added to this are
pestilence, famine, and a scarcity of everything. Nor in the midst of this   55
surging sea is there any port of good hope on the horizon; sky and sea surround us.[11] And yet I think that Clement, the leader of the church in such a
turbulent storm, will show himself a courageous and outstanding pilot. This
evil requires a skilful doctor, which even the name Medici seems to promise
us in him;[12] these animosities among rulers require some great counsellor,   60
who will recall their exasperated spirits to clemency. And the well-omened
name of Clement VII conveys this. I have no doubt that God's power will
assist his piety if only the Christian people, recognizing the hand of God
urging them to correct their lives, and confessing their sinfulness, will take
refuge in his mercy with hearts unfeigned. Otherwise it is to be feared that   65
the same thing will happen to us as happened to the Egyptians who, unable to be healed by so many extreme remedies,[13] were swallowed up in
the sea.[14]

This evangelical fever – as it pleases them to call it – is abating
and gives good hope of returning to sanity. What Luther is publishing   70
now seems almost to have the semblance of a palinode;[15] and this so displeases his disciples that they call him, if you please! a heretic, maintaining that he is devoid of the evangelical spirit and that his human
spirit is deranged.[16] Not a few citizens and cities are returning to their

* * * * *

10 The Roman goddess of war, variously represented as the wife, sister, or daughter of Mars
11 Virgil *Aeneid* 3.193
12 Cf Ep 335:91–6, addressed to an earlier Medici pope, Leo x.
13 Ie the ten plagues described in Exodus 7–11
14 Exod 14:26–30
15 Ie a retraction. See Ep 2013 n6.
16 See Ep 2013:24–6 with n6, and cf Epp 2049:31–5, 2062:40–2.

senses.[17] But I am afraid the disease will break out again through the ac-   75
tions of certain people. 'Who are they?' you will say. Those same individuals
through whose perverse counsel and hysterical clamours this evil both took
rise and progressed to this point. They strive to claim for themselves the
victory due to Christ, and they do not think their triumph is grand enough
unless they see not only heresies crushed but also good letters trodden un-   80
der foot, seeing that they attack those who cultivate them with more violence than the heresiarchs themselves. But I am confident that the fairness of
the sovereign pontiff, bishops, and princes, in opposition to their insolence,
will lend support to good and learned men.

    Farewell. At Basel, 1528   85

2060 / To Omaar van Edingen   Basel, 1 October 1528

    This letter was first published in *Illustrium et clarorum virorum Epistolae se-
lectiores* ed Daniel Hensius (Leiden 1617) 305. The autograph is now in The
Pierpont Morgan Library, New York (MA 376).
    Omaar van Edingen of Ghent (c 1488–1540) was clerk of the council of Flan-
ders from 1525 until his death. He was a kinsman of Karel Uutenhove (Ep 2001
n7), who was currently living with Erasmus at Basel (Epp 2062:42–4, 2065:23),
and a close friend of Levinus Ammonius (Epp 2016, 2062), whose enthusiasm
for Erasmus he shared. Following Erasmus' departure from Basel in 1529,
Edingen eagerly offered him spacious accommodation either at his house in
Ghent or at his nearby country estate (Allen Ep 2197:102–11).

Cordial greetings, and I beg of you with great earnestness to ensure that
the enclosed letter[1] is delivered to Levinus Ammonius, your most devoted
client; in asking this I consider myself also in your debt, but a debt that I
contract gladly to both a good and a learned man, as I am told. Therefore
in future count Erasmus in the number of your friends.   5
    Farewell. 1 October 1528
    Erasmus of Rotterdam, in his own hand
    To the most distinguished Omaar van Edingen, clerk of the Council of
Flanders, in Ghent

    * * * * *

17 See Ep 1988:8–13 with nn5–6

  2060
1 Ep 2062

2061 / From Juan Luis Vives Bruges, 1 October 1528

This is Vives' reply to Ep 2040. It was first published in volume 2 of Vives'
Opera omnia (Basel: Episcopius 1555).

VIVES TO ERASMUS

What I have on Seneca are annotations:[1] some of which I took from ancient
manuscripts, others are my own based on what I was able to derive partly
from the meaning of the words, partly from the nature of the subject matter.
But whatever their worth, I prefer that that author, who so much deserves 5
to be read and to be known, come into the hands of readers emended by
you rather than by me. I have no doubt that it will be an edition worthy
of your name if you will be willing to direct the work personally and be
present with your assistance; do not entrust to anyone else a project in which
your own reputation is at stake as well as the great benefit of the readers. In 10
the present state of things neither the Sibyls themselves nor an interpreter
of dreams could elucidate the text.[2] I had never heard the name Aldridge
before reading your letter. At More's house I did not see any edition of
Seneca that had even a single correction.[3]

I sampled rather than read your *Ciceronianus*. I myself have received a 15
letter from a person who is not only my friend but a distant relative, who
exhorts me to read nothing but Cicero and to imitate him in sententious sayings, words, and figures of speech, and in this way I will leave Longueil
and many others behind me.[4] I laughed at this childish idea of imitation,
which has taken possession of the minds of many, like a form of madness. 20
I would have been very pleased if you had mentioned my name. But I readily pardon this slip of your old age even if you purposely passed over my
name, since I am certain you did not do it out of personal enmity.[5] It is no

* * * * *

2061
1 Epp 2040:3–5, 2056:10–11.
2 Sibyls were priestesses who prophesied in a trance. The most famous of them
  was the Sibyl of Cumae, who is said to have written her predictions on palm
  leaves. These were collected at Rome, entrusted to a college of priests, and
  consulted in times of crisis. Although Sibylline prophecies were regarded as
  unquestionably true, they were also notoriously opaque and ambiguous. Cf
  Adagia I vii 91.
3 See n1 above.
4 Ep 1948 introduction
5 See Ep 2040:14–18.

wonder that you forgot me, since you were occupied in collecting names from every rank and file, so that, as I was skimming through it, it reminded me of what Atticus said to Cicero in his review of orators.[6] And yet I don't think you have forgotten about me, but attribute your decision to the nature of your plan.

I am quite astonished that Budé or anyone else who is familiar with the art of the dialogue could have taken grave offence at your words,[7] even though this discord between you is not new, in my opinion, but long-standing.[8] After that first reconciliation it was made worse by words and letters but, having been kept in check for a while, it now manifests itself on this occasion disguised under another cloak. So Alecto and Ate infest the affairs of men,[9] leaving nothing public or private untouched: wars among princes, dissension in the world of letters, mad frenzy in human nature it-self, differences in the unity of religion, hatred and cruelty in the love of piety. Would that Christ, looking upon us with more indulgence, would deign one day to put an end to such great evils and bring peace and seren-ity to the troubled state of things. And yet if it befitted anyone to be of one mind, it is we, who are devoted to the study of those arts and disci-plines that are hated and attacked by many, who have the support of great authority and great power.

Please give Hieronymus[10] my greetings. If he does not like writing, he need not bother himself to respond to my letters. I am sorry that my works caused a loss or were not lucrative to his enterprise.[11] In future I shall make every effort not to cause him any trouble and to further his interest, if I can; I gladly take it upon myself to do this to the best of my

* * * * *

6 Cicero *Brutus* 269. In the course of the dialogue, as Cicero is enumerating vari-ous orators of the past, he omits the name of Marcus Servilius, of whom virtu-ally nothing is known. When asked by Atticus, another speaker in the dialogue, why he had done this, Cicero responds that the omission was unintentional.

7 See Ep 2021 introduction.

8 Vives was right about this. The relations between Budé and Erasmus, which were conducted entirely by letter, had from the beginning been fraught with conflict, misunderstanding, and bitterness. See the summary of their corre-spondence by Marie-Madeleine de la Garanderie in CEBR I 215–16.

9 Alecto was one of the three Furies in Greek mythology, unceasing in her anger. Ate was the goddess or daimon of blind folly and mad impulses.

10 Froben

11 Hieronymus had refused to reprint Vives' edition of Augustine's *De civitate Dei*; see Ep 2040:30–40 and cf Ep 1665:2–7.

ability. The reason for my writing to him was a certain Franciscan who was
in Basel recently to see you.[12] He told me that Froben wished to print some   50
of my works. But I would not be surprised if he were lying, since many
who come here from there are liars. To your question of who this liar is,[13]
it is the person who says one thing here, and another there, as you write
to me.

But, please, my revered teacher, let us not talk any further about   55
these matters, neither I to you nor you to me, if you so approve. For I
have the impression that every time you enter into this discussion you do
so with some annoyance.[14] Do not think that I am so anxious about being named; I should prefer to be of use to a few persons by my good
qualities than that my name, whatever its renown, be spread throughout   60
the world without benefit to others. I am not unaware how unjustified is
that glory which does not pay regard to merit, so vain and insubstantial
that you can enjoy it no longer than that moment when you are trans-
ported by the applause and acclamation that surround you; you see and
hear things that are foreign to you; it is not you, for when you return   65
to yourself you find nothing. How much gall is mixed in with this drop
of honey! If from nowhere else, certainly I could take you as an example
and illustration in this. In the end we must reflect that we are pilgrims
on this earth, or rather are on our way to an appearance in court, in a
short time to appear before a judge, no matter how many detours we try   70
to make. There human ignominy will not silence the defendant, nor will
glory (like the testimonials or eulogies of the people of a province) promote
his cause. But he whom the Lord commends will receive favour. I see no
one so ablaze down with glory that he will not be cooled down by these
reflections.   75

Therefore I pray you, my good master, not to write to me in future
about renown and glory. For I declare to you under oath that I am far less
sensitive to these words than you can imagine. I am more concerned with
the public good. I will gladly lend my support in this cause if I can do so,
and I think those people are happy who have contributed to the public good.   80
I think that a truer glory and praise will be yours when I see that one is
made better by reading the works of your great genius than when you hear
all those titles: 'most eloquent, most learned, most excellent.'

* * * * *

12 The Franciscan is unidentified.
13 Ep 2040:34–5
14 As in Ep 2040:30–44

Would that Jupiter and Juno[15] would make offerings not to the ancient goddess Venus but to Christ, the converter of hearts![16] My greetings   85
to Rhenanus,[17] and to Cantiuncula,[18] if he is in Basel.

My very best wishes of good health

Bruges, 1 October 1528

2062 / To Levinus Ammonius   Basel, 2 October 1528

First published in the *Opus epistolarum*, this is Erasmus' answer to Ep 2016.
Forwarded to Ammonius by Omaar van Edingen in accordance with Erasmus'
instructions in Ep 2060:1–2, it reached Ammonius on 4 November. His delight at receiving it is expressed in a letter to Edingen of 10 November that
Allen found in the Bibliothèque municipale at Besançon and published in his
introduction for this letter. Ammonius' reply to Erasmus is Ep 2082.

ERASMUS OF ROTTERDAM TO THE CARTHUSIAN
LEVINUS AMMONIUS

Your first letter inspired me with such affection for you, my friend, as I
scarcely feel for anyone else.[1] It was not by design but by necessity that
I did not answer it. There are so many who demand letters from me that   5
I barely have enough time for this one occupation.[2] And among them are
some whom it is not safe to deny. Even more pleasing was your most recent
letter, which, besides a singularly pious and fraternal affection, conveys a

* * * * *

15 See Epp 1932:69 with n11, 2040:45 with n18.
16 Vives here applies the ancient cult title *Venus Verticordia* to Christ.
17 Beatus Rhenanus was currently in Sélestat; see Ep 2050:20 with n8.
18 In 1524, Erasmus' friend and admirer, Claudius Cantiuncula (Epp 852:85n,
   1616 and 1636 introductions, 1674 n18, 1732 n18, 1841 n3), had resigned
   his professorship of civil law at the University of Basel and left the city,
   unable to tolerate the tensions arising out of the city's growing commitment to the Reformation. After a brief period in his native city of Metz,
   he entered the service of Jean de Guise, cardinal of Lorraine and bishop
   of Metz (Epp 1841, 2009), becoming his chancellor in 1527. In 1532 he
   moved to Germany to become a member of the Reichskammergericht (imperial supreme court) and then in 1533 entered the service of Ferdinand of
   Austria.

2062
1 See Ep 1463.
2 Cf Ep 1985 n2.

readiness to give service as well;[3] nothing could be more acceptable than
this. Only one thing caused me a slight displeasure, namely that you are 10
so careful not to offend me, as if I were such a barbarian that not only
do I become angry when treated wrongly but am even offended by such
expressions of fealty.

Would that the material had come in time![4] There is nothing contained
there that is not of great importance for my work; I clearly rushed that work 15
into print. If there is anything in which I may be of service to you in return,
I shall give proof of how far I was from being offended by what you call
your self-assurance. I beg you all the more that, if you have other material
of that nature, you do not hesitate to communicate it to me. Whatever you
send to Erasmus Schets in Antwerp will reach me safely,[5] but send carefully 20
sealed whatever you think should be sent.

The *Adagia* have come out again enriched with numerous additions.[6]
Froben, at my suggestion, has found Greek characters that are a considerable
improvement.[7] If seven presses were not barely sufficient for the polygraph
Augustine,[8] a modest work of Chrysostom in Greek would appear at the be- 25
ginning of spring.[9] Germain de Brie has translated *Babylas* and launched a
full-scale attack against Oecolampadius,[10] to the delight of the theologians.
He is ready to translate what is left of the *Psegmata*.[11] I expect this will
produce a new comedy.

I am offended by 'the shoemaker,'[12] not so much for personal rea- 30
sons as for the Christian religion, which puts its faith in such buffoons.
He has as his counsellor a schoolmaster, whom I fed when he was dying
of hunger in England, taught when he was devoid of any learning, recommended with letters when he was utterly destitute – the most stupid and

* * * * *

3 Ep 2016
4 Ie the notes on Jerome mentioned in Ep 2016:103–76
5 On Schets, see Ep 1931.
6 See Epp 2022, 2023.
7 Ie larger Greek characters, first used in the *Epistolae floridae* of 1531 (cf Ep 2080
 introduction).
8 The Froben Augustine of 1529 (Ep 2157)
9 Erasmus' next publication of Chrysostom in Greek, *Aliquot opuscula divi Chrysostomi Graeca*, was in fact published by Froben in 1529 with a dedicatory letter
 dated 1 February (Ep 2093).
10 See Ep 2052 n2; and for Ammonius' own attack on Oecolampadius' competence
 as a translator of Chrysostom, see Ep 2016:95–102.
11 The title of Oecolampadius' volume of translations of Chrysostom; Ep 2052 n2
12 The epithet is in Greek; it refers, of course, to Pierre Cousturier (Ep 1943 n7),
 whose Latin name was Sutor 'cobbler'; cf Ep 2016:3–5.

ridiculous specimen of humanity you could imagine, a Norman by birth.[13]   35
It is from this man that my blabbermouth friend learned whatever he vom-
its forth against me as if it were documented fact, though there is no living
creature more fatuous than this scoundrel. Béda and his followers rage fu-
riously in Paris[14] and the hordes of Spanish monks are no less ferocious.[15]
This tyranny of halfwits is the end result of Luther's violence. Now he is   40
coming forward with moderate proposals as if it were as easy to remedy
evil actions as it is not to commit them.[16] Karel Uutenhove amply commends
himself to me by his very temperate character and I shall never allow myself
to have appeared lacking in my duty towards him.[17]

This is a letter in my own hand, which I am afraid you may not be   45
able to read, but in your generosity you will interpret this also as proof of
my warm friendship.

May the Lord preserve you, my dear Ammonius, and enrich you with
all the gifts of the Spirit.

Basel, 2 October 1528   50

2063 / From Conradus Goclenius   [Louvain], 7 October [1528]

This letter was first published by Allen, using the autograph in the University Library at Basel (Goclenii epistolae 16). The year date is confirmed by the
movements of Kan, Dilft, and Schepper. For Goclenius, see Ep 2026.

Cordial greetings. I could hardly believe from your letter that Carinus has
lapsed into such a degree of shamelessness or madness as to have committed
such a dishonourable misdeed against himself, against letters, and against
the prince of letters.[1] I would not have believed it unless a former student

* * * * *

13 Allen tentatively identified the 'Norman by birth' as Pierre Vitré, but that is
just as unlikely as the similarly tentative identification of Vitré at Ep 2053:9–
10 and for the same reasons (see n5 in that letter). Ammonius took this to be
a reference to Gervasius Amoenus (Ep 209:63n); see Allen Ep 2082:240–6.
14 See Epp 1943 nn6–7, 2006 n6, 2037.
15 See Epp 1926 n4, 1967.
16 See Ep 2013:24–6 with n6, and cf Epp 2049:31–5, 2059:70–1.
17 See Ep 2001 n7.

2063
1 In the absence of Erasmus' letter, which is not extant, it is not possible to say
what the 'dishonourable' misdeed was. On the likely motives for Ludovicus
Carinus' anger at Erasmus, see n3 below.

of mine gave me assurance of it: on his return here from Dôle he told me   5
practically the same things about this monstrous behaviour of Carinus that
were contained in your letter, and when I expressed my disbelief produced
an autograph letter of Carinus.² The gist of it was that he was being continually exposed to scorn among good men in their daily conversations and in
your letters.³ He said that he would no longer tolerate this injurious treat-   10
ment and that he had found a way to avenge himself and would accomplish
this revenge even though he knew that he would make enemies of all the
followers of Erasmus. I was greatly astonished at his fury and I feel as much
pity for him as sadness that your noble person will be the object of attack of
these dogflies. Whatever kind of gladiatorial contest this will be, it will pro-   15
vide a very pleasant spectacle for the enemies of literary studies. Therefore
I hope it will be settled by any means possible. I truly think that if Beatus
Rhenanus or Amerbach or Glareanus⁴ would endeavour to divert him from
his purpose he would not be so out of his mind as not to yield to the counsel
and admonitions of men of such calibre.   20

As far as I am concerned, if I were in Erasmus' place, that is, a Roscius
on the stage of the world,⁵ I would prefer to pay him ten talents of gold
for the ounce of fame that he falsely believes to have lost because of you
than to endure the vexation caused by the ingratitude of your dogs barking
at you. This would be better for him as well, so that he not brand himself   25
forever with the stigma of being an ingrate. I know I may be justly accused
of temerity for saying this to you. But the shamefulness of all this disturbs
me; I am saddened that the enemies of good letters derive pleasure from it,
and I am saddened that your sacred labours are obstructed. For the glory
of the name of Erasmus is too great for the attacks of Carinus to diminish it   30
even in the least. I am ashamed of Carinus that he has become so blind as not

* * * * *

2 Allen speculates that the 'former student' might have been Christoph von Carlowitz (Ep 1951 n7), who had studied briefly with Goclenius (Ep 2026) at Louvain in 1527 and was now studying at Dôle, but there is no evidence that
  Carlowitz had 'returned' to Louvain, even briefly.
3 Carinus' friendship with Eppendorf may well have been a motive; see Ep
  2048:54–6 and Allen Epp 2101:49–52, 2111:27–31, 2120:3–6, 2129:28–33. Another
  may have been Erasmus' repeated criticisms of Carinus' old teacher, Wilhelm
  Nesen, in connection with the Seneca edition of 1515; see Ep 2056 n6 and Allen
  Ep 2085:5–18.
4 All three of these had been mediators between Erasmus and Eppendorf; see
  Ep 1934 introduction.
5 Quintus Roscius Gallus (c 126–62 BC) was a famous actor at Rome, esteemed
  particularly for his mastery of comedy. Actors have been known to style themselves 'the new Roscius' and the name can be used generically simply to mean
  'distinguished actor.'

to see into what disgrace he is about to plummet. I can wish him nothing better than that he return to his senses. If it were in my power, I would rather restrain him with chains than allow him to commit such an effrontery.

I am surprised that Kan has not yet arrived there.[6] He left here on about 16 August, if my memory does not fail me, and was certain of arriving in Basel in a few days before Hieronymus Froben departed for the Frankfurt fair. Perhaps he fell in with a travelling companion who was in no hurry, or became ill.

I think you have heard about Nicolaas van Broeckhoven and Johannes Munterus and some other priests in the College of Antwerp, who last August, after secretly selling or packing up all they possessed, disappeared and are still missing.[7] This incident once again gave the enemies of good letters a rich opportunity for detraction, because Nicolaas was regarded as not unlearned in good letters, and now he is proclaimed as most learned in them even by his enemies in order to strengthen the accusation that no one versed in letters can be free of the perverted opinions of the day. It is not yet being openly proclaimed but only rumoured that they took wives and made off.[8] The rumour does not seem to me to be without foundation, for since Luther became the high priest of this sacred rite it has come to be almost an article of faith that no one without a wife can be a Christian.[9]

Around the first of September our friend Dilft went off to Zeeland with the intention of crossing over to Spain on the first fleet of ships that assembled there.[10] But up to now he was forced to remain there since the wind from the north was not blowing. It is possible to pass through the English Channel only with this wind. It is the fifth day now that it has been steadily blowing. Therefore I think he has set out on his voyage. Wary and my colleagues Rutgerus Rescius and Campen send their greetings.[11]

* * * * *

6 See Ep 2026 n1.
7 Nicolaas van Broeckhoven (c 1478–1553), who had been head of the College (Latin school) of Antwerp, soon turned up in Bremen and adhered openly to the Reformation. In 1540 he became rector of the Latin school at Wesel. He died as a pastor at Blankenburg in the Harz; cf Ep 616:15n. 'Munterus' is most likely Jan de Munter of Ghent (documented 1510–28?). He matriculated at Louvain in 1510 and was in orders by 1515. Like Broeckhoven, he was a friend of Adrianus Cornelii Barlandus (Ep 2025). He disappears from the historical record at this point.
8 Broeckhoven had married (or soon did) and had several children.
9 Luther had married in June 1525; see Ep 1624:15–17.
10 Cf Ep 2026:9–11.
11 On Nicholas Wary of Marville, since 1526 second president of the Collegium Trilingue, see Epp 1806A and 1856. Rescius (Epp 546, 1758 n10) was the first professor of Greek at the Trilingue. Jan van Campen (Ep 1257 n12) was professor of Hebrew at the Trilingue.

The Franciscan is now in Antwerp to bring forth his offspring, but the
leading theologians are opposed to it, as I have learned. But you need have 60
no fears of him.[12]

Farewell, the 15th of October.

Yesterday Cornelis de Schepper, imperial ambassador returning from
Poland,[13] and Claudius Cantiuncula, who took care of some business of his
prince at our court,[14] journeyed here. Both of them are so devoted to you that 65
I can hardly believe anyone else can rival them in their loyalty to Erasmus.

Again farewell.

I had no time to reread the letter since the messenger was in such a
hurry. So if there are any errors, please pardon them.

Yours, Conrad Goclenius 70

To Master Erasmus of Rotterdam, at Basel

2064 / From Christoph von Stadion   Dillingen, 8 October 1528

This letter was first published as Ep 13 in Horawitz I. The autograph is in
the Württembergische Landesbibliothek Stuttgart (Cod hist 2° 47 fols 1–2). On
Christoph von Stadion, see Ep 2029, to which this letter is his reply. Erasmus'
response is Ep 2070.

CORDIAL GREETINGS

I received on 1 September the letter you sent on 26 August, and as the daily
reading of your works affords me incredible delight, so I can hardly express
how much I appreciate a letter written in his own hand by the prince of
learning and a beloved friend. What you say about the Luther affair is both 5
all too well known to me and all too true. Not only theologians but also
leading dignitaries of the imperial court condemn Lutheran writings even
if they are in agreement with the Gospels. And what perturbs me more is
that they strive to defend and protect everything that has been observed in
the Christian religion to this day even if it is devoid of all reason. It is too 10

* * * * *

12 Probably Frans Titelmans (Ep 1823), whose *Collationes quinque* (Ep 1994 n14)
would be published at Antwerp in 1529; see Allen Ep 2089:1–4.

13 Schepper (Ep 1747 n23) was on his way back to Spain from an embassy on behalf of Charles v to King Sigismund of Poland. For a detailed documentation
of his itinerary, see Allen 61n.

14 On Cantiuncula see Ep 2061 n18. 'His prince,' Jean de Guise, cardinal of Lorraine (Epp 1841, 2009), was at this time involved in negotiations at the Burgundian court in Mechelen (LP IV 4580).

evident to require any proof that there are many human constitutions mixed
in with the gospel writings that have little accord with them. The one reason,
and in my opinion the most important, that prevents these tumults within
the church from being restored to peace and concord is this: everyone seeks
his own interests and is driven by his own passions; no one has the common   15
good and the Christian religion at heart. Unless God in his boundless mercy
disposes otherwise, I do not see any hope for peace and concord.

As to the assertion of some that this tumult within the church took
rise from your writings, believe me, most learned Erasmus, they spread this
talk not out of love for religion, of which they are the enemies, not through   20
respect for virtue, which they have never savoured, but through envy, resentment, and ill will. It is a great stimulus to envy to be outdone by others. They inevitably conceive a great hatred for those who, equipped with
secure knowledge, transmit the precepts of the gospel in simple and clear
terms and inevitably take issue with those who lack the knowledge. What   25
others derive from your writings I know not; I can sincerely say that I have
drawn from your works more than from the writings of any others. There
is nothing at all in your writings that displeases me. On the contrary, by
reading them I become better and more instructed every day; they show me
the true Christian way of life. I speak sincerely, not merely from personal   30
feeling. It is no wonder that you are denounced for no reason or for the
slightest pretext as if you had erroneous ideas about the Christian faith; this
race of men has always exercised its tyranny and violence against good and
learned men through hatred and envy rather than through regard for religion. They regarded the very learned man Lorenzo Valla suspect in matters   35
of faith because he said that the *Catholicon* or Hugutio and others never explained a word correctly unless they found it already explained elsewhere,[1]
or because it is self-evident that there are three categories, not ten; three elements, not four; three internal senses, not five; the concrete does not differ
from the abstract; there are no pure elements except those we see and touch;   40
the sea is not deeper than the earth; there is one transcendent, not six.[2]

* * * * *

2064
1 The *Catholicon* was a Latin grammar and dictionary assembled c 1286 by the Dominican Giovanni Balbi and published by Gutenberg at Mainz in 1460. Uguc-
   cio of Pisa (d 1210) was a bishop of Ferrara and canonist whose *Liber deriva-
   tionum* was an enlargement of the glossary compiled by the eleventh-century
   Lombard, Papias. Erasmus thought they were 'ringleaders of barbarism'; see
   Ep 26:96–100.
2 Most of these 'self-evident' propositions are found in Valla's *Repastinatio dialec-
   tice et philosophie*. In the edition of Gianni Zippel (Padua 1982), see pages 112–

Now you see, my excellent Erasmus, what they did not hesitate to pretend or invent as calumnies against upright and learned men so that they could denounce them as guilty of the crime of *lèse-majesté*. But I cannot see what they could bring against you on the charge of heresy, since you could show your faith not only by your teaching but by your actions, whereas they could not. Not only is their life contemptible but their reputation also, not to mention those of them who are deranged and completely mad.

I wished to write this to you so that you may know that these words, which our friend Augustinus Marius[3] wished to communicate to you in my name, proceeded not from my mouth, but from my inmost being.

May Christ in his great goodness and power keep you unharmed as long as possible.

Given at Dillingen, 8 October 1528

Christopher, bishop of Augsburg, in his own hand

To the prince of learning, Master Erasmus of Rotterdam, theologian, dearest and beloved friend

At Basel

2065 / From Philippus Montanus   Paris, 13 October [1528]

The autograph of this letter, first published as Ep 67 in Enthoven, is in the Rehdiger Collection of the University Library at Wrocław (MS Rehd 254.109).

Philippus Montanus (c 1498–1576) was born at Armentières in Flanders (now in the French Département du Nord). He matriculated at Louvain in 1518 but no more is known of him until the summer of 1528, when he visited Erasmus at Basel and stayed in his house until early September, when he departed for Paris, carrying with him letters that Erasmus had asked him to deliver. In Paris Montanus settled down as a teacher of Greek and worked on the Greek Fathers, first at the Collège de Lisieux (until 1536) and then at the Collège de Tournai. In 1562 he returned to Flanders, where he became rector of Queen's College at the newly founded University of Douai. Erasmus commemorated Montanus' visit to Basel by

* * * * *

15, 363–85 (three categories); 21–30, 373–7 (concrete/abstract); 115–24, 415–35 (pure elements); 12–21, 36–41, 366–73 (one transcendent). For further information, see Peter Mack *Renaissance Argument: Valla and Agricola in the Tradition of Rhetoric and Dialectic* (Leiden 1993) 31–51.

3 See Ep 2029 n2.

giving the name Philip to one of the characters in the colloquy *Impostura* 'The Imposture,' first published in 1529 (CWE 40 860–2), and in his will he bequeathed Montanus 150 gold crowns. Although the two continued to exchange letters (Montanus is known, for example, to have sent Erasmus a detailed eyewitness description of the execution of Louis de Berquin in April 1529), the present letter is the only one in their correspondence to have survived.

In the letter Montanus describes his journey from Basel to Paris and renders account of the delivery of the letters that Erasmus had entrusted to him. On the journey Montanus was one of a party of four: the other three were Daniel Stiebar (line 24), Stiebar's servant Lawrence (line 24), and the unnamed brother of Anton Bletz (line 14).

Cordial greetings. You will wonder perhaps, my most revered teacher, at my long silence. Do not, I beg of you, ascribe my not writing to you until now to negligence but rather to the scarcity of couriers. I was impatient to write to you about our affairs even in the midst of my journey, if there had been someone to take the letter to you. If only someone had at least of- 5 fered his services when, with the help of the gods, we arrived here safely. At that point I would have been able to tell the whole tale with more precision, since the memory of places and events was still fresh in my mind and in more detail. Now, because of my public appointment as professor at the Collège de Lisieux as a result of the petitions, both opportune and 10 importunate, of its principal,[1] a post that I had long refused in vain, and because of the unexpected departure of Anton,[2] I do not have the opportunity to write as fully as I would have wished. I had heard from his servant that he was to leave within eight days, but on the very next day his brother, who was our companion on the journey, informed me that he was prepar- 15 ing to set out for the Basel fair; therefore if I wanted him to deliver a letter, I would have to hurry. When I heard this I decided that it would be better to give a cursory account of things here in a haphazard fashion rather than write nothing at all, hoping that you would take in good part (considering your great kindness) whatever was sent to you with good intention. 20 But, as I began to say, the passing hour prompts me to review briefly our most significant news.

* * * * *

2065
1 Jean de Tartas, documented 1524–35
2 Presumably the courier, Anton Bletz (Ep 1784 n1).

The day our Polish friend and Karel left us,[3] we arrived successfully towards evening at Thann,[4] but on the next day Lawrence, Daniel's[5] servant, began to complain that he felt something in the sole of his foot that gave 25 him pain. And little by little the pain increased to such a point that we had to look for a horse for him in a village a few miles away. To arrive more quickly at our destination we hired three horses to carry Daniel and me as well as Lawrence. At times we made use of vehicles also and completed the journey in this way, not always as you used to say jokingly, in your de- 30 lightful way, 'in the name of the Lord,' but sometimes in carriages and on horses unless perhaps on mares, which the peasants palmed off on us instead of horses. When we got to Bayon,[6] a town situated about two miles from Saint-Nicolas,[7] Daniel bought a horse for Lawrence, and so with two on horseback and two on foot we headed for Saint-Nicolas. But before ar- 35 riving there one of the shoes on Lawrence's horse fell off. This, however, was only a slight mishap; what happened afterwards was worse. At Saint-Nicolas a blacksmith changed the horse's shoes but attached them so firmly that he nailed one to the flesh as well as the hoof; the horse's limp got worse on the way to Paris, so much so that those on foot had to wait for those 40 on horseback, and the horse that had been bought for five crowns was sold for barely one crown. This incident was a bit troublesome, but the rest went smoothly enough. We arrived safely in Paris by the grace of God on the fifteenth day after our departure, where the first thing I did was to fulfil punctiliously the commissions your Excellency had entrusted to me. 45

I delivered almost all the letters to their addressees personally.[8] Budé was not at home, but his son assured me that he would return that night. I gave the letter[9] to his son and asked him to give it to his father when he re-

* * * * *

3 The 'Polish friend' was presumably Andrzej Zebrzydowski (Ep 1958 n1) and 'Karel' can only have been Karel Uutenhove (Ep 2001 n7). It seems that these two set out with Montanus and Stiebar (see n5 below) to keep them company for a time before returning to Basel. Zebyzdowski set out again for Paris circa 21 September, bearing Epp 2052–3 together with another letter, now lost, to Budé (see lines 49–50 below), Uutenhove, on the other hand, was still living in Erasmus' house in December (Epp 2077–9).
4 In Upper Alsace
5 Daniel Stiebar (Ep 2069)
6 In the valley of the Moselle, twenty-four miles south-south-east of Nancy
7 Saint-Nicolas-de-Port, on the Meurthe, 8 miles south-east of Nancy. The distance between it and Bayon is approximately 13 English miles.
8 Epp 2042–4, 2046–8
9 Ep 2047

turned. After a few days I went back to his house together with the Pole,[10] and when he received your letter from the Pole, I asked him whether he had received the one I had delivered a few days ago;[11] he replied that he had and asked if he could help, as is his habit. Vidoveus, the chaplain of the bishop of Langres,[12] was not in Paris. I looked for him two or three times and was told that he would be back shortly. But when I saw that there would be no end to my waiting, I entrusted your letter to a priest to be delivered to him. He pledged that he would make sure that it would be delivered into his hands. Today I went to see whether he had returned, in order to know if he had received your letter, and at the same time to indicate to him that Anton was soon to return to Basel, but they said that he had not returned. Master Nicolas Le Clerc[13] said that he had written back to Baer.[14] Pierre Danès[15] said that he would respond to you. I did not think it was necessary for me to tell Budé, Berquin,[16] and Brie[17] about the departure of Anton, because I knew that they had received a copy of the *Letters*[18] from him. I think they had been informed by him about this matter.

If there is anything, my dear teacher, that you wish me to take care of here, you may safely confide it to your friend Philippus as to your Excellency's most devoted servant. I wish you to judge him according to his modest or rather insignificant ability, assured of his loyalty and diligence, which will never be found lacking to your good will. So much for this.

The letter written to Berquin gave offence to many.[19] By contrast, the one you recently sent to Brie[20] found good reception among a great majority of people and will surely calm, I hope, the tumult that seemed ready to break out in the world of studies.

* * * * *

10 See n3 above.
11 Allen surmised that this would have been a letter of introduction to Budé for Zebrzydowski.
12 Montanus means Nicolaus Vesuvius, who was chaplain to the bishop of Langres and to whom Ep 2053 was addressed. On the bishop, Michel Boudet, see Ep 1612.
13 To whom Ep 2043 was addressed
14 On Baer see Ep 1933 n3.
15 Addressee of Ep 2044
16 Recipient of Ep 2048
17 Recipient of Epp 2046, 2052
18 The *Selectae epistolae* (Ep 2021 introduction)
19 See Ep 2021 n1.
20 Ep 2046

Many who long to have your thoughts on preaching await your book 75
on the subject,[21] for they know how successfully you can treat it, just as
you do many others. In your wisdom you know that the common good
depends in great part on preaching. Therefore those who have the interests of the common good at heart are anxious that we have expert preachers. If you do this no one doubts but that all those who have long been 80
under obligation to you will be all the more devoted to you, not to mention (although it is of the greatest importance) how blessed and auspicious
it is to have been faithful to the talents that God in his goodness has bestowed upon us. But why am I saying this to you? It's like the sow teaching Minerva.[22] I know dear master, that you have no need of a counsellor. 85
Yet I, together with all men concerned with religion, desire so much that
you finish this work that I could not but join my prayers to the wishes of
others.

Concerning commonplaces or the proper meaning of words,[23] which
you promised in your great kindness when I was boarding with you, I beg 90
you to give me some reply if you have the time.

Farewell, Erasmus, my master and most revered teacher, and may you
always consider Philippus as one of those most devoted to your Excellency,
whom you once accepted into the number of your disciples and servants,
not indeed through any merits of mine but solely through your kindness. I 95
for my part shall make every effort never to seem to have given even the
slightest opportunity for my name to be erased from the list of your friends.

François Dubois[24] thanks you for the *Letters*[25] you sent him and wishes
your Honour every blessing. The principal of the College of Lisieux,[26] with
whom I now reside, asked that I send your Excellency his greetings. He 100
regards and speaks of you in the highest terms.

Paris, 13 October

Yours sincerely, Philip Montanus

To the eminent professor of Sacred Scripture Master Erasmus of Rotterdam, his most revered teacher, at Basel   105

* * * * *

21 The waiting would continue until 1535, when the long-promised work would
   finally be published under the title *Ecclesiastes sive de ratione concionandi*; see
   Ep 1932 n25.
22 *Adagia* I i 40
23 Perhaps *De pueris instituendis*, which would be published in September 1529
   (Epp 2189–90)
24 See Ep 1600
25 See n18 above.
26 See n1 above.

2066 / From Louis de Berquin   [Paris, c 13 October 1528]

This is Berquin's reply to Ep 2048; Erasmus' response to it is Ep 2077. The manuscript, an autograph in the ill-fated Burscher Collection at Leipzig (Ep 1254 introduction), was incomplete, only the first leaf having survived. Berquin's authorship is established by the identity of the hand with that of Ep 1692. It was first published by Förstemann/Günther who, having initially overlooked the letter, found it in time to place it among their notes, on pages 351–2.

As this letter illustrates, Berquin (Ep 2027 n1), heedless of the counsel of his friends, was now recklessly engaged in the provocation of his foes that would lead to his death in April 1529.

The letter probably reached Erasmus with Epp 2065 and 2069, the latter of which Erasmus replied to (Ep 2078) on the same day that he replied to this one: 23 December.

Cordial greetings. I read the defence of your *Ciceronianus*,[1] which I think found favour with many, even with Budé himself.[2] I think it was your express intention to show that all excellent and celebrated writers were so different from Cicero that they made no effort to imitate him, and consequently, that Budé himself, distinguished with so many other tal-   5
ents, had so avoided striving after Cicero's style that Bade should be included in this list rather than Budé. But our friends understood this to mean that almost all those whom you criticize there had aspired to imitate Cicero's style with great earnestness but ineffectually, among whom even Budé himself had vainly attempted this but had to yield the palm   10
to Bade, inferior to him in so many other accomplishments. Nosoponus plays the part of those who are affected by this superstition; for that reason he magnifies this quality, which no one among so many luminaries had ever attained, but which he believed he had achieved. On the other hand, in his role as critic Nosoponus represents the personage of Erasmus.[3]   15

* * * * *

2066
1 Ep 2046, probably the actual letter sent to Brie, since the version printed in the *Selectae epistolae* had not yet arrived (line 16 below).
2 See Ep 2047.
3 This was the root of the furore over the *Ciceronianus* in France. In the dialogue it is the character Bulephorus who is the voice of Erasmus, while Nosoponus is the voice of the excessive Ciceronianism that Erasmus wanted to parody. But the French, as Berquin notes, insisted on equating Nosoponus with Erasmus. See Ep 1948 introduction.

I would like to have the rest of the *Letters* which you sent if they are now finished.[4]

You write that my enemies will readily answer that your books are read with less harm by the learned than by the ignorant.[5] I will not allow myself to be convinced of this. On the contrary, I dare to affirm, and I hope 20 to make it public, that the French works are read by the ignorant with less resulting harm than the Latin works that are read by the others. I don't see what they can lay to my charge apart from having provided translations, unless perhaps they objected to some marginal annotations. They imitate Momus who found fault with Venus' sandal, since he could not criticize 25 anything else.[6] But in the same way they will be able to charge me with whatever I noted in the Iliad of errors of Béda.[7] In the conduct of my life I have sufficiently shown how far I am from the crime of which they have accused me. I have no doubt of the victory, which would have come more quickly if I had not preferred to make it more spectacular. I had no need of 30 a papal document except to expose their blasphemies. It is utterly false that jurisdiction was restored to the judges who condemned me.[8] And even if it were true, they still will never have any power over me.

I see that you are not going to respond to the theologians,[9] and perhaps it is best to ignore them for a while, at least as long as these mad- 35 men keep themselves under control. Whoever reads the records of my trial will easily understand what kind of people my critics are, even if they do not read the descriptions you so often give of them. I hear that the authorities in Louvain have pronounced the same edict,[10] no doubt so that

* * * * *

4 This is an odd sentence. The word for 'letters,' *epistolae*, is capitalized in the text, which seems to indicate that it is being used as a title. If this is the case, then Allen was probably right to take the sentence as a (none too clear) reference to the *Selectae epistolae* (Ep 2021 introduction) and to conclude that this letter was written before Berquin's copy of the volume was delivered to him by Anton Bletz (Ep 2065:63–4).

5 Ep 2048:25–6, where the issue is Berquin's French translations of works by Erasmus and others

6 On Momus, see Ep 1994 n8.

7 Cf *Adagia* I iii 26: *Ilias malorum* 'Iliad of troubles.' The reference is perhaps to marginal notes in a copy of Béda's *Annotationes* against Erasmus and Lefèvre (Ep 1943 n6).

8 See Ep 2027:1–6.

9 Cf Epp 2048:35–50, 2053:3–5.

10 Ie the edict of 23 June 1528 condemning the *Colloquies* (Ep 2037 introduction). In Ep 1697:26–8 and again in Ep 2077:39–40, Erasmus denies that any such condemnation had ever been issued in Louvain; but see Epp 1537:27–32, 2077:40–2.

they will not miss the chance of aping the Parisians, although I think they   40
have been plotting this for a long time. One good thing is that although
the theologians have condemned the *Complaint of Peace* as well as the *Declamation on Marriage*, the university made no pronouncement on the former.
Noël Béda is striving with all his might that that little book of *Twelve Articles of Béda's Faith*,[11] which had been sent by the king to the university   45
for their approbation or condemnation,[12] be condemned by the authority of
the university and that Béda himself be judged orthodox in his opinions
and writings.[13] And although he has so many conspirators on his side, he
has not been able so far to have all his articles approved.[14] Some protest
that it is too evident that Béda condemned Christ and the Gospels. I think   50
you have already received a letter and the little book of an anonymous
friend who, if he could, would combat this outrageous behaviour single-
handed.[15]

* * * * *

11 The reference is to the anonymous *Duodecim articuli infidelitatis magistri Natalis
   Bedae ex libro suarum Annotationum excerpti, reprobantur et confutantur* [Paris:
   Josse Bade 1527], a booklet containing twelve articles excerpted from Béda's
   Annotations, each one of which was found to be heretical in the accompanying
   confutation. Erasmus and Béda both thought that Berquin was the author of
   the work, an attribution duplicated in the literature (including CEBR I 138) ever
   since. Recently, however, James Farge has argued convincingly that the real
   author was another enemy of Béda, the Paris theologian Jacques Merlin. See
   Epp 1875 n30, 1902 introduction and n7, and Farge 'Berquin' 67–8, with n68.
12 King Francis sent the work to the four faculties of the University of Paris for
   their verdict. See Ep 1902 introduction, which includes the text of the king's
   letter to the university.
13 There could be little doubt of what the faculty of theology's verdict would be.
   It had issued its *nihil obstat* for the entire contents of the *Annotations* in advance
   of their publication. See Epp 1664 n1 (especially page 28), 1721 introduction.
14 Béda wanted the book itself condemned, but he wanted the twelve articles
   cited and confuted in the book to be approved. In the end, the faculties responded simply by denouncing the anonymous author of the book, which they
   judged to be dangerous and offensive to Christian piety.
15 The letter is not extant. Erasmus, who received neither the book nor the letter,
   did not know the identity of 'the anonymous friend' to whom Berquin that
   was referring. He speculated that Berquin might have had in mind the 'someone from Ghent' (possibly Joachim Martens; Ep 2049) who had reportedly
   displayed great courage 'in the tumult caused by Béda's followers'; see Ep
   2077:49–52. For his part, Allen speculated that 'the anonymous friend' might
   have been Lefèvre, but the latter, preoccupied at this time (1526–30) with translating the Bible into French, did not, as far as we know, produce a book of any
   size on any other subject. See *The Prefatory Epistles of Jacques Lefèvre d'Étaples*
   ed Eugene F. Rice Jr (New York 1972) xiv, 487–512.

I don't know what that person meant who wrote to you that I wish to
terrify the theologians by using your name.[16] Perhaps when that edict was is- 55
sued I may have answered that Erasmus would not remain silent and would
treat them as they deserved. But as far as my trial is concerned, I accused
the faculty itself to their faces of their calumnies, heresies, and blasphemies.
I recited to them the propositions that they had falsified, sentences from
the gospel and Christ's own words which they had declared heretical. They 60
made no response to this.[17] What could they have responded when their own
written documents testified that they had done this and their calumnies and
heresies were so evident that they could not resort to subterfuge?

You write[18] that you answered the letter of Alberto Pio, prince of
Carpi,[19] who is living here, but that you did not send the *Response*[20] be- 65
cause you did not know where he was living. But he has already circulated
his book here among many, and I do not know if he would have published
it if, after receiving your last letter, I had not succeeded in having one of
his close friends advise him not to hasten publication until Erasmus had answered. It is clear, unless I am mistaken, that in certain matters he thinks 70
differently than he writes. In your case, this vainglorious individual, true to
the Italian character, wished to make it appear that he could find fault with
Erasmus. As far as the writings of Luther are concerned (I am not speaking about all of them), it seems that he has not understood a great many
things, and certainly that he has interpreted many of them perversely and 75
in a defamatory manner, especially what Luther wrote concerning faith and
good works. On this point he interprets consistently as if Luther preaches
a useless faith, which, like the fig-tree cursed by the Lord, stands out for
its foliage but bears no fruit.[21] I do not say these things because I favour
Luther but because I abhor calumny no matter who is its object. 80

* * * * *

16 See Ep 2048:60–2.
17 There are no surviving records of the trial against which to measure Berquin's
   account here.
18 Allen suggests that this might have been in a postscript added to the fair copy
   of Ep 2048 but not preserved in the rough draft on which the *Opus epistolarum*
   text was based.
19 The reference is to Pio's *Responsio accurata et paraenetica*, which was in the form
   of a letter and was dated 14 May 1526. It was not published until January 1529
   (Paris: Bade) but it circulated in manuscript and Pio sent Erasmus a copy of
   it. See Epp 1634 introduction, 1987 n2, 2042 n9.
20 Evidently an early version in manuscript of what became Erasmus' *Responsio
   ad epistolam Alberti Pii*, published by Froben in March 1529
21 Mark 11:13–14

If you have decided to publish or send him your *Response*, see to it (as you usually do) that you do not injure his self-love or seem to flatter him too much. He is a man who enjoys great favour with the pope and with his nephew, Cardinal Salviati,[22] his envoy here ...

2067 / From Benedikt Burgauer   Schaffhausen, 16 October 1528

First published as Ep 90 in Förstemann/Günther, the autograph of this letter was in the Burscher Collection at Leipzig (Ep 1254 introduction). Benedikt Burgauer (1494–1576) of St Gallen took holy orders in 1515. In 1519 he became parish priest in St Gallen, where he allied himself with the reformers. But his hesitation in deciding between the Lutheran and Zwinglian positions and his retention of a number of traditional Catholic views caused him so much trouble that in 1528 he happily moved to a parish in Schaffhausen. There he was soon in trouble again, this time for allegedly erring too much on the side of Lutheranism. In 1536 he lost his position at Schaffhausen and, after a few years of wandering from post to post, moved to Isny in the Allgäu, where he remained until his death.

GRACE AND PEACE FROM THE LORD
Letters have been brought to me through my brother,[1] most learned and excellent Erasmus, that were smuggled out of Spain,[2] as I understand. I could not have found a more trustworthy courier to deliver them to your Eminence. When you wish to reply to them in the future through this same 5 messenger, confide them to me. My brother has asked me to suggest to you to have them sent there as quickly as possible via the Fugger bank. He is willing to take all this upon himself without charge. I desire that your Worthiness count me among the number of those who wish to serve and oblige you, who think of Erasmus as the glory and most meritorious defender of 10 all of Germany and the church, praise him, and magnify the gifts of God. With this letter I promise that I lay myself under obligation to do the will

* * * * *

22 Giovanni Salviati (1490–1553) was the nephew of Pope Leo x, who created him cardinal in 1517. He served Clement VII as legate to France from September 1526 to August 1529.

2067
1 Possibly the Dominik Burgauer who is known to have studied at Freiburg, Basel, and Wittenberg
2 Possibly answers to Epp 1968–71

of your Lordship. If it is not asking too much, I desire as my most fervent
wish to have and to see the handwriting of Erasmus so that I can recognize
that my letter was delivered to you. Farewell.   15

From Schaffhausen on the feast of St Gall, 1528

Benedikt Burgauer, pastor of Schaffhausen, most loyal servant of your
Eminence

To the illustrious and universally learned Desiderius Erasmus of Rotterdam, prince of theologians, resident in the famous city of Basel, most   20
revered in the Lord

2068 / From Tielmannus Gravius   Cologne, 16 October 1528

This letter was first published by Allen from the autograph in the Rehdiger
Collection of the University Library at Wrocław (MS Rehd 254.65). Tielmannus
Gravius (Epp 610:50n, 1829 introduction) was employed in the chancellery of
the archbishops of Cologne from about 1503 and had close ties to Archbishop
Hermann von Wied (Ep 1976). Owner of a fine library and a patron of scholars, he may have met Erasmus when the latter passed through Cologne in
1518. Their correspondence, which began in 1527 with Ep 1829, lasted until
Erasmus' death. Erasmus dedicated to Gravius his edition of Lactantius' *De
opificio Dei* (Ep 2103).

Cordial greetings. When Felix left here for Brabant, Erasmus, my incomparable patron, I immediately gave him a letter for you,[1] in which, since at
that moment my mind was occupied with both foreign and domestic concerns, I described in fewer words than I wished the tragicomedy of his trip.
I had the desire, for my own gratification, as one very busy man to another,   5

* * * * *

2068
1 The letter is not extant. Felix Rex of Ghent (d 1549), nicknamed Polyphemus,
  had recently entered Erasmus' service as famulus and letter-carrier. Though
  inclined to wander in search of other employment, Rex nonetheless remained
  in Erasmus' service until the summer of 1532. On his present journey, he must
  have left Basel on about 2 October, carrying Ep 2058 to Cologne and probably
  also a letter to which this is the reply. From Cologne he went first to Brabant
  to deliver Epp 2054–7, 2060, and then to Holland. Returning via Antwerp with
  a letter from Schets (see Ep 2072:1), he was again in Cologne on 16 October
  and received this letter for delivery. He then travelled with Adolf Eichholtz
  as far as Niederheimbach (Ep 2071 n1) and then, shortly before 9 November,
  reached Basel (Ep 2072).

to recount a few bagatelles to you. If what I have provided is pleasing to
your ears, you must not give thanks to me but rather your friend Polyphemus, whose plight induced me to write this amusing tale to you. If you do
not find it entertaining, the sterility of the subject can be blamed on him.

When he returned to us from his native city he told us that his wife   10
had died in childbirth together with her child. Now that he is completely
free from the halter of matrimony, he seems to have placed such hope in
your authority that he does not wish to act rashly in entering upon any way
of life unless you strongly encourage him to undertake it. I do not know
the man at all, therefore I neither wish nor am able to give any testimony 15
about him. But as far as I can divine from an acquaintance of a few days
with him in my house, he appears to be extraordinarily sincere. You will
easily be able to be of help to him through your influence, which is powerful
everywhere, but particularly with princes. And he seems worthy of enjoying
better fortune than he has hitherto enjoyed.   20

I hear that the works of Augustine that have been restored through
your effort, will be offered to the public at the next fair.[2] I hope this will
come about with good auspices so that we may reap the abundant fruits of
your splendid achievement and your pious labours. In the meantime may
Christ the Lord preserve you safe and unharmed for us.   25

Given at Cologne, 16 October 1528

Your Tielmannus Gravius

To the most learned Desiderius Erasmus of Rotterdam, theologian
without equal

2069 / From Daniel Stiebar   Paris, 18 October 1528

This letter was first published as Ep 91 in Förstemann/Günther, using the autograph that was in the Burscher Collection at Leipzig (Ep 1254 introduction).
Erasmus' reply is Ep 2079.

Daniel Stiebar von Buttenheim zu Sassenfurth (1503–55) belonged to a noble family of Franconia. After a period of study at the University of Erfurt,
Stiebar in 1517 became canon of the cathedral chapter at Würzburg, where the
bishop, Konrad von Thüngen (Ep 1124), encouraged his ambitions for an administrative career in the ecclesiastical principality. Given leave to further his
studies, Stiebar registered at the University of Basel in the summer of 1527.

* * * * *

2 The Froben Augustine in ten volumes, published in 1529 (Ep 2157)

He seems to have made a particularly good impression on his professor of law, Bonfacius Amerbach, who in August 1528 asked Erasmus to let Stiebar live in his house. Having no bed to spare, Erasmus nonetheless offered the young man a place at his table (Ep 2036) and quickly formed a high opinion of him. A month later, Stiebar left for Paris in the company of Philippus Montanus (Ep 2065), probably carrying Epp 2046–8. In 1529 he returned to Würzburg via Antwerp and, after further study at Freiburg (1529–30), where he lived with Erasmus, he commenced his administrative career in Würzburg, often attending diets and conferences where the religious division of Germany was on the agenda. His correspondence with Erasmus lasted until the latter's death.

Greetings. I see that I acted rightly and more wisely than I thought when, in leaving you recently, I said that I would not write to your Excellency until you promised that you would forgive any barbarisms that might occur. If that agreement had not been reached, a certain sense of embarrassment would have absolutely deterred me from writing to your Excellency even if 5 I were tempted to do so. But when I recall our agreement and your indescribable kindness and good will towards me, I no longer feel any shame. And it almost seems that once you have thrown off the restraints of shame you are no longer ashamed of anything. Such is the case with your friend Stiebar, who relying, as I said, on your kindness will not be afraid to blurt 10 out whatever comes into his head.

There is no reason for me to bother you, excellent Erasmus, concerning our journey. By the grace of God, we arrived in Paris safely, one and all.[1] The only trouble we had in the whole trip was that I had to buy a little horse for five crowns for my servant, who wasn't used to physical hardship.[2] The 15 climate was very mild and we were not harried by excessive cold or heat or rain. That part of France and Lorraine which we traversed in our journey is not subject to the raids of highwaymen. In any case we suffered no harm. As far as Philippus[3] and I were concerned, things went quite well. Although we were somewhat fatigued by the length of the journey, this was compensated 20

* * * * *

2069
1 The four participants in the journey were Stiebar, his servant Lawrence, Philippis Montanus, and the unnamed brother of Anton Bletz; see Ep 2065 introduction.
2 Cf Ep 2065:34–42.
3 Montanus (Ep 2065)

for by other advantages. Philippus behaved in such a way towards me and those who accompanied me that I have no other wish for the moment than to have the occasion of doing him some good service in return. I am staying with a barber here in order to learn the French language as best I can. His stories, even though I don't understand them, amuse me so that I almost die laughing. For the time being, I have decided to put my boys[4] through a mill, since at the school named St Barbara[5] they are grinding away at their assignments.

Enough for now about the journey and the new life I have begun. What can I say of your affection and solicitude for me? For the life of me, dear Erasmus, I cannot express in words how indebted I am to your Excellency for the unheard-of kindness and good will you have shown towards me. Believe me, as I considered it the summit of happiness to have lived on familiar terms with one of the world's greatest philosophers, I now count it as one of my greatest miseries that, by reason of necessity, I have had to leave you so quickly. But what can one do? One must yield to time and to necessity. What more have I to say? Nothing, my dear Erasmus, except to express my earnest desire to convince you that I shall bear witness, even from afar, to your good will towards me. For I have inculcated it into my mind that only through mutual affection can we return thanks to those who formed our minds through literature and virtue and who love us sincerely. Not only shall I never cease to respect and love you from the bottom of my heart, but I hope also that I may be able to add something more to this if my meagre fortunes permit it. I ask of you that you retain me among the number of your friends, into which you have recently admitted me. Farewell, glory of the world of letters.

Paris, 18 October 1528

Your friend Daniel Stiebar

Brie instructed Philippus to send you his personal greetings in Philippus' own words; he could not write to your Lordship because of a burning fever. I write this at Philippus' behest. He would have written this himself except that his letter was already sealed.[6]

To the illustrious Erasmus of Rotterdam, friend and teacher, at Basel

* * * * *

4 Not mentioned in Ep 2065 as companions on the journey. Possibly a group that he had been asked by someone at home to look after
5 The Collège de Sainte-Barbe, a constituent college of the faculty of arts at Paris, across the street from the Collège de Montaigu
6 Ep 2065

2070 / To Christoph von Stadion   Basel, 22 October 1528

First published in the *Opus epistolarum*, this is Erasmus' response to Ep 2064.

ERASMUS TO CHRISTOPH VON STADION, BISHOP OF AUGSBURG,
GREETING

I greatly admired in your letter the Christian piety worthy of a great prelate.
I cannot discern in myself what you attribute to me with such exceptional
kindness; I know myself too well. But I interpret your praise as a conso-   5
lation against the malicious and perverse judgments of certain people, not
to mention the deadly traps that certain adherents of the new factions are
laying for me with amazingly covert stratagems.

The Augustine is almost killing me,[1] and added to that is the Seneca,
an insuperable task,[2] in addition to the burden of writing letters;[3] and yet   10
the magnitude of my studies is the least part of my fatigue. I admire your
patience for being able to read through the psalm that I treated cursorily
and of which I could only produce a sketch, as it were, because of my many
occupations.[4] I recognized from your Highness' letter to the Reverend Augustinus Marius[5] that you had read it through. I think I have treated the   15
fourth psalm with a little less incompetence.[6]

This is all I could write for the present since I am overwhelmed with
work; I shall write more copiously on another occasion. May the Lord Jesus
keep watch over your most revered Highness.

Given at Basel, 22 October 1528   20

2071 / From Adolf Eichholz   Heimbach, 23 October 1528

This letter was first published as Ep 92 in Förstemann/Günther, using the autograph that was in the Burscher Collection at Leipzig (Ep 1254 introduction).

On Adolf Eichholz, who taught canon law at Cologne, see Ep 866 introduction.

* * * * *

2070
1 The ten-volume Froben Augustine of 1529 (Ep 2157)
2 Erasmus' second edition of the works of Seneca, published in March 1529 (Ep
2091)
3 Cf Ep 1985 n2.
4 See Ep 2017.
5 Not extant
6 See Ep 1535.

✝

Cordial greetings. As I was about to set out not long ago to the wine harvest in a village called Heimbach,[1] my dear sir, renowned far and wide, I
ran into a companion on the way who was highly recommended to me by
Tielmannus Gravius,[2] our great mutual friend. I speak of Felix Rex (alias
Polyphemus) of Ghent,[3] a man, by God, whom I found, through our conver-   5
sations on various subjects in Greek, Latin, French, and Italian in six days
on board ship together and in hostelries, to be quite learned, practised, and
experienced in history and literature and languages. When I learned from
Tielmannus that he is one of your couriers and servants whom you prize
more than the rest, I immediately welcomed him with open arms,[4] as they   10
say, all the more readily, and treated him with particular kindness to the
best of my abilities throughout our journey. For that reason I could not allow him, loaded down though he was with a great bundle of letters from
various parts of the world that he was carrying to you, to return to your
Reverence without these little trivialities from me. I wished first of all to   15
assure you that I am in good health and also to respond at least extempo-
raneously, if not with the requisite elegance, to the letter you sent very recently to your friend Adolf (in which you promised that you would write
at greater length at some later time).[5] Under the circumstances I would ask
that in your kindness (which you possess in great abundance) you would   20
look not to the elegance of style, since my muse is rather coarse, but to the
sincerity of my sentiments towards you and your kind forbearance.

But let us return to our journey. When I finally landed in Boppard,[6] I
went together with Felix to meet the customs officer, Christoph . . .[7] who I
know is a very loyal friend of yours, so that he might send a letter to you   25
if he had the time to do so. (Your friend Johann Flaming was not present at
the time.)[8] Excusing himself on account of the shortness of time at his disposal, Christoph asked Felix to send his best regards to you and his cordial
good wishes. After that, in homage to your great name, he honoured both

* * * * *

2071
1 Niederheimbach, on the middle Rhine between Koblenz and Bingen
2 See Ep 2068 introduction.
3 See Ep 2068 n1.
4 *Adagia* II ix 54
5 The letter is not extant.
6 On the left bank of the Rhine, 10 miles south of Koblenz
7 Christoph Eschenfelder (Ep 879). Eichholz left a gap in the manuscript for the
   surname, but did not manage to recall it before dispatching the letter.
8 See Ep 867:62n.

of us with an excellent customs officer's wine[9] for the sea journey. Finally I   30
offered hospitality to Felix in our town of Heimbach so that I could have a
more opportune occasion to write to you. But not to seem too loquacious, I
shall close with a few words and gladly give way to the more elegant and
learned letters addressed to you by others.

Farewell then, our great and gracious Maecenas, and may you live   35
happily to the age of Nestor,[10] and welcome with favour your friend Eichholz, who is forever dedicated to you, and treat him as though he were your
servant.

From the town of Heimbach amidst the occupation and commotion of
the wine harvest, 23 October in the year of grace 1528   40

Your friend, if ever there was one, Adolf Eichholz of Cologne

You will have an abundance of news from Felix and others.

To the most eloquent Desiderius Erasmus of Rotterdam, by far the
prince of theologians, his ever revered teacher

2072 / To Erasmus Schets   Basel, 9 November 1528

Allen was the first to publish this letter, using the manuscript in the Royal
Library at Brussels (KBR MS II 3012). The first line of Ep 2115 shows that the
letter did not reach Schets (on whom see Ep 1931).

I received the letter you sent me through Polyphemus[1] and the one you
sent through Bernard.[2] Nothing is owed to me in England besides the pension that the Archbishop of Canterbury regularly sends me.[3] The bishop of
London often sends me something, but he owes me nothing.[4] Similarly the
bishop of Lincoln sends me fifteen angels every year,[5] but out of kindness   5

* * * * *

9 Cf Epp 867:58–9, 879:12–13.
10 Homer's Nestor, king of Pylos, lived three whole generations, which some ancients reckoned at 300 years but was more probably something close to ninety,
assuming thirty years for each generation.

2072
1 Felix Rex (Ep 2068 n1); the letter is not extant.
2 Unidentified
3 William Warham; see Epp 1999:7–8, 2039:3–5.
4 Cuthbert Tunstall; see Epp 1726, 1750:1–2, 1781:1–2.
5 John Longland; see Ep 1758:5–6 with n6. These gold angel-nobles, valued at
90d sterling from November 1526, were worth £18 15s 0d sterling = about £24
16s 0d groot Flemish = £152 10s 0d tournois. To earn such an income, a master

and not that he owes me anything. I asked that they pay the money to Luis
de Castro if they wish to send anything.[6] Keep the money until I write to
tell you what to do with it. And may you keep well, my excellent friend,
together with those dear to you.

9 November 1528   10

To the honourable Erasmus Schets at Antwerp

2073 / To Haio Cammingha   Basel, 12 November 1528

This letter was first published in the *Opus epistolarum*.

Born into a noble family in Friesland, Haio Cammingha (d 1558) studied in
Louvain and may have attended classes at the Collegium Trilingue. In 1528 he
joined his friend Viglius Zuichemus (see n9) at Dôle but soon tired of the place
and wrote to Erasmus applying for admission to his household. By February
1529 he was installed as a paying guest (Ep 2108), remaining until the end of
January 1530. When he left, he owed Erasmus money, a debt that he promised
to settle with Erasmus Schets at Antwerp. He also declared his intention to
return to Erasmus in the spring. But Cammingha did not return and he did
not settle his debt until November 1531, which earned him the enduring wrath
of Erasmus. Cammingha made efforts to appease Erasmus, but the surviving
correspondence offers no evidence of success.

ERASMUS OF ROTTERDAM TO HAIO CAMMINGHA OF FRIESLAND,
GREETING

It must be that at our birth there was some conjunction of the stars or some
secret affinity existed between our personal geniuses, dearest Haio, since
from our brief correspondence,[1] although you were completely unknown to   5
me and I was known to you only by name, I immediately felt a strong attachment to you, and events have proven that you had the same experience.
If that were not so, you would never have sought to be on familiar terms
with me in a letter written with such affection and, if I might say so, eagerness to please, since at Dôle you had so many colleagues of noble rank who   10
provided pleasant company by their community of interests and similarity

* * * * *

mason at Cambridge would have had to work for 750 days (at 6d per day) or
3.57 years. See Epp 1993 nn3, 7, and 9, 1931 n8.
6 Epp 1590 n2, 1765:4–6

2073
1 Not extant

of life. It is an old and common saying that like with like most easily flock
together;[2] but with us it must be some new secret force of nature, like a mag-
net attracting metal. Not any person whatsoever is suitable to share in the
life of my household, my distinguished young man. My assiduous labours,   15
sometimes beyond my strength, in addition to my age, which weighs heavily on me, and above all my failing health, which often reminds me of my
mortality, force me to be a man of few friends, although it is my character
to gratify everyone in every need, if I can. But if my feelings about you do
not deceive me, if your letter did not present a false image of your nature, if 20
those who know your character through knowledge and experience tell me
the truth, I shall not be reluctant to admit a person of such disposition into
the close association of my household, hoping that you will add distinction
and joy to our little family.

These are my sentiments; now it is up to your discretion to take prac-   25
tical measures and determine what is most to your advantage, in which regard, my dear Cammingha, I should not wish you to sacrifice anything on
my account. You will have a table seasoned more with literary conversations
than with gastronomic delights. So far is it from luxury that it is not much
more lavish than that of Pythagoras or Diogenes whenever they dined at   30
home.[3] You will be inclined to say that you have come to the school of frugality or have been welcomed into the mess halls of the Spartans. No one
seems to me to live a happier or more luxurious life than someone who is
always abstemious: he enjoys both tranquillity of mind and health of body,
and when he rises from the table he is refreshed more by fruitful discourse 35
than by feasting, having appeased his hunger in such a way that his stomach is not growling nor his body so heavy with food that it weighs down
the spirit when he has to attend to studies or some other serious matter.

What is more unpleasant than those banquets, or I should say more
aptly, drinking bouts,[4] one great pandemonium filled with crude outbursts, 40
where the guest is forced to drink the amount prescribed, and each one
does harm to himself in order to drag another into harm. If there is no sense
of pleasure when the body is prey to sickness, what pleasure can there be

* * * * *

2 *Adagia* I ii 22
3 The celebrated philosopher and mathematician Pythagoras was famous for his
  frugality and his preference for the simplest food and clothing. For his part,
  the Cynic philosopher Diogenes embraced poverty, boasted of it, and lived in
  a tub.
4 Cf Epp 76:15–16, 643:37–8, 1033:224–8.

when wine has completely robbed you of your senses? It would be hard
to say what is more inhuman, to deprive one who is thirsty from drinking   45
or to force one who is not thirsty to drink. Is that a banquet, I ask, or a
torture? I won't speak of the brawls and fights and other misdemeanours
that drunkenness usually brings with it; I won't mention the waste of money
(there is no more unseemly way of losing it), how irretrievable a waste of
time, the most precious commodity we possess. This senseless pleasure is   50
followed the next day by real suffering: the mind is lethargic, the stomach
is in agony, and the head is spinning. Sometimes a resultant fever exacts the
penalty for intemperance, and the brief pleasure, if indeed it can be called
pleasure, is expiated by prolonged suffering. There are those too who lure
young persons of better character to their own habits. You might say that   55
they have gone to school for no other reason than to interfere with other
people's studies.

   You are very dear to me, my excellent Haio, for these reasons: since
you have the commendation of a line of illustrious ancestors; since you are
possessed of a patrimony sufficiently ample to afford luxury if you so de-   60
sired; since you have not yet, I believe, entered upon your twentieth year;
and, finally, since you have Friesland as your native land, where, in general,
luxury is almost regarded as a virtue and frugality a vice, and yet you so
recoil from these bestial pleasures that nothing is sweeter to you than a frugal and sober life. You remember that you set out for the university so that   65
you might return home as from a rich market richly endowed with the precious wares of good letters to adorn in your turn the lineage of your family
and to add more lustre to it than you received. These things are proof to
me of a singularly noble character born to virtue. As it was once said with
as much shrewdness as truth, whoever is virtuous in Athens must be ex-   70
ceptionally virtuous elsewhere,[5] so it takes an extremely virtuous character
to resist being corrupted by so many provocations to vice.

   Since I have clear proof that you are a person endowed with such
moral character from the letters and reports of many people who are well
acquainted with you, I could not but congratulate you, and at the same   75
time I have the firm hope that through your writings and your exemplary
life you will make your Friesland more celebrated. It has become famous
for men of great talent. Not to mention men like Canter and Langen,[6] who

* * * * *

5 *Adagia* IV i 53
6 Jacob Canter of Groningen (Ep 32) and Rodolf von Langen of Münster (Ep
  70:52n)

is more divine than Rodolphus Agricola?[7] Successor to his glory is Haio
Herman,[8] a young man of great promise who will one day transmit the   80
torch of this glory to you. As for Viglius,[9] I am happy that he is hasten-
ing vigorously, as you write, along this course. These things prove that
there is some truth in the common saying that Friesland is the fertile parent of men of great talents but that life's pleasures prevent many of them
from making their way to the highest virtue.[10] There is hardly any other   85
vice that is worse adapted to the Muses and Minerva than luxury and
intemperance.

Therefore, since I know that nothing gives you more pleasure than
the study of letters, you will, if it will be beneficial to you, be received
as the most welcome of my guests. You will come to a philosophical ta-   90
ble and even, if you will, a healing table. It has restored several guests
of precarious health to a better state of health; at any rate (may Nemesis not hear my words)[11] none of my table companions has ever become
sick. They are always very few in number; my sole purpose in this is
at meals and in the hours after repasts[12] – in which I generally refrain   95
from study unless there is some urgent necessity – to beguile the tedium
of solitude with pleasant stories, which however we do not allow to be
completely foreign to the Muses. If you wish to be of this number, I shall
ensure that you do not regret having chosen our company. But if circumstances counsel otherwise, I wish that you be persuaded that this letter,   100
like a bill of exchange, will be a guarantee that, wherever you or I may
be, Erasmus is and will always remain one of those who sincerely wish
you every blessing and from whom you will ask nothing in vain provided it be of such a nature that it is within my power to be of service.
Farewell.   105

Given at Basel, 12 November 1528

* * * * *

7 Ep 23:58n
8 Ep 1978
9 This is the first reference in Erasmus' correspondence to Viglius Zuichemus
   (1507–77), who was currently studying law at Dôle and would eventually have
   a distinguished career as a legal scholar in Germany and as a councillor and
   diplomat for Charles v and his successors as rulers of the Netherlands. He
   will enter Erasmus' life with Ep 2101 in February 1529.
10 Cf Ep 1237:13–18.
11 Nemesis was the spirit of divine retribution against those who succumb to
   hubris.
12 Cf Epp 1759:59–61, 1805:294–5, 1833:15–17.

2074 / From Jacopo Sadoleto   Carpentras, 20 November 1528

This is Sadoleto's reply to Ep 2059. First published in the *Opus epistolarum*, it
was also published in the edition of the *Sadoleti epistolae* prepared by Sadoleto's nephew Paolo Sadoleto (Lyon: Gryphius 1550). There is extensive vari-
ation between the two texts although, as Allen observes, none of them produce any important changes in the sense. The *Opus epistolarum* text would have
been based on the letter actually received by Erasmus, while the 1550 text was
presumably based on the rough draft that remained in Sadoleto's possession.
This means either that the rough draft was greatly revised before dispatch to
Erasmus or that his nephew Paolo himself revised the letter when preparing
his edition. At all events, Allen's text, while noting the 1550 variants in his
critical apparatus, printed the *Opus epistolarum* version, which is the basis of
our translation.

JACOPO SADOLETO, BISHOP OF CARPENTRAS, TO ERASMUS OF
ROTTERDAM, GREETING

I received your letter from Basel dated 1 October, in which it was added
in your own hand that you had previously sent another copy,[1] which I did
not receive. This one too was brought here quite late, so that I received it   5
only in mid-November. It gave me the greatest pleasure, most learned Erasmus, to receive it, for it placed before my eyes the image of your eminent
virtue and great kindness, which I love and admire, and it gave testimony
of your singular good will towards me. The fact that you took such great
care to learn about my well-being and continued to show your solicitude   10
until you were certain of my fate and that I had returned to my dwelling
is great evidence of your singular affection and good will towards me. In
this regard, upon my life, my dear Erasmus, I shall not allow you to outdo
me in affection. I have always loved and admired your many qualities and
perhaps most of all your intellectual abilities, your learning, your copious   15
style, and, above all, that you have dedicated all the distinctions of your
great learning to zeal for religion and to celebrate the name of Christ. Although I am equal in sentiment to the great love you bear towards me, I cannot articulate it in the words of a letter, so eagerly do I desire to express my
feelings of obligation towards you. My style and the power of speech are   20

* * * * *

2074
1 Possibly with Ep 2049. The handwritten addendum did not make it into the
   published text of this letter.

inadequate, which you with your experience will be able to perceive better than I.

As far as I am concerned, my salvation and freedom from harm were granted to me by some miraculous divine favour, since twenty days before that horrible disaster struck the city of Rome I had left the city to journey to my diocese.[2] I had already bound myself before God to abandon everything else and to set out and reside there for the rest of my days. It was because of that good intention alone, I think, that God judged it worthy that I should be saved. For the rest of my life is of such a sort that I should confide in God's mercy, not his justice. But the fewer my merits the more the gratitude I owe to God's great clemency and goodness. I lost all my fortunes in that terrible pillage, including my library which I had filled with Greek and Latin books acquired from all parts of the world.[3] In all the harm I suffered I felt this one great loss, which you esteem to be a serious one and I agree, but all of this must be accepted with resignation.

Concerning my friend Bembo you need not worry.[4] While Leo was still alive,[5] Bembo, seized by illness, betook himself to Padua for a change of climate and took up residence there.[6] He is still living there now, totally dedicated to literature and study, in complete communion with the Muses. I think he is composing something that will redound to his praise and fame and will be of great usefulness to others.

As for the fate of Rome, no other voice other than your own can worthily deplore it. It is incredible how much calamity and destruction have been visited upon the human race in the ruin of the city. If there were some vices present in it, virtue still ruled over a great part of it. That city was always the abode of civilization, hospitality, and all prudence and wisdom. If there are any who are happy at its fall they are to be accounted not as men but as savage wild beasts. But I think there

* * * * *

2 The sack of Rome by the emperor's troops began on 6 May 1527. Sadoleto's departure from Rome can thus be put at c 16 April. On the basis of Sadoleto's letters, Allen determined that Sadoleto had sailed to Nice from Civitavecchia and had then arrived at Carpentras in Provence, not far from Avignon on 3 May.

3 Sadoleto's statement here that his library was destroyed in the sack of Rome does not jibe with his description elsewhere of its loss on the voyage to Carpentras, which commenced several days before the outbreak of the violence in Rome. See Ep 2059 n8.

4 See Ep 2059:12.

5 Leo x died on 1 December 1521.

6 In his villa near Padua, in the summer of 1521

were few people who did not feel sorrow at the destruction of the no-
blest and most important of all cities, or who, even if they were so driven   50
by a mad fury as to desire its downfall and annihilation, would not now,
after their hatred has subsided, be moved by repentance for their madness
and by the unpredictability of human affairs. But let God see to them. You
wrote that it seems that they are already coming to their senses, which I
hope is the case, and I shall never cease to pray God to that end. For I do   55
not hate them; I merely wish they would return to sanity. But God will
see to it.

To have you as my companion in the sorrow that we have both felt
at the shameful calamity that has befallen the leading city of the world is
no small consolation to me, and I form an excellent opinion of your ad-   60
mirable character and spirit. If only some common approach to peace and
concord might come from it! Oh, that some day there might be some reason for us to console ourselves and have high hopes for the common good!
In these circumstances you write with great wisdom, and I fully understand that with all hope completely removed, there is no place left for good   65
letters and sacred studies unless God has decided otherwise. Yet we must
neither lose spirit nor become tired, but rather all of us who have been
imbued and instructed in the best studies must offer help in this time of
calamity and universal loss, each according to his own powers, and in our
books devote ourselves to the cause of peace and piety, even if we can-   70
not do so in the conduct of public affairs. I myself am engaged in this activity, and I see that you have long ago won such renown that there is
scarcely anyone who can compete with you, not to say have any hopes of
equalling you. For what we struggle to attain with great labour and much
time is not at all suitable or accomplished, while you with no trouble, in   75
the briefest amount of time, publish things that are so quickly and perfectly executed that the brilliance and fluency of your style seems the result not of careful workmanship but of natural endowment. Wherefore it
should come as no surprise to you that there are many who criticize and
envy you, for your praise has been greatly exalted. Not all men are drawn   80
by your virtue to love you; some rather are moved to spitefulness by your
widespread reputation. Such men should be despised by you and esteemed
of no account. They are not worthy that your spirit should suffer the least
perturbance because of their malice. As for me, as your love for me and my
nature and the duties of friendship demand, I shall always remain a pro-   85
moter of your renowned virtues and a staunch admirer of your dignity and
renown.

Farewell.

At Carpentras, 20 November 1528

2075 / To Nicolaus Vesuvius [Basel, c November 1528]

This letter, which answers one now lost, was first published by Allen, using the autograph that is now in the Goldast collection of the Staats- und Universitätsbibliothek Bremen (MSA 0008/007). It falls between Ep 2053, in which the proposal for the privilege was first made, and the letters of 23 December (2077–80), which were carried by Anton Bletz (Ep 1784:1).

On Nicolaus Vesuvius, see Ep 2053.

Cordial greetings. I do not quite understand what you mean when you write that the matter concerning the privilege[1] has been taken care of unless by that you mean that it has been categorically denied. If there is no hope, I do not want you to wear yourself out on that account. If there is some hope, I should like to be informed of it. Some are muttering their opposition 5 because Erasmus had a hand in it.[2] Would that someone else had put his hand to it! for I am afraid this task will be the death of me. There are so many errors in this author,[3] who goes on forever. I don't know if anyone else could have done it more learnedly. I hardly think there is anyone who would put up with so much tedium. I am not adding any *scholia* as I did 10 with Jerome. I merely remove the errors. Where possible I put the material in order and indicate what belongs to another hand. Therefore they have nothing to fear about the interference of my hand.

Bérault is staying in Orléans. I wrote to him.[4] I send my regards to the Lord Bishop.[5] I shall write a longer letter via Anton.[6] 15

To the most distinguished gentleman Nicolaus Vesuvius, chaplain of the bishop of Langres

2076 / From Maarten Lips [Lens-Saint-Remy?] [December] 1528

On Maarten Lips and his current place of residence, see Ep 2045.

The autograph of this letter is in the Rehdiger Collection of the University Library at Wrocław. It was first published as Ep 90 in Horawitz v. Allen

* * * * *

2075
1 Ie a copyright for the Froben Augustine; see Ep 2053:15–16.
2 Cf Ep 1309:47–65.
3 Augustine
4 The letter is not extant. On Nicolas Bérault see Ep 1284.
5 Michel Boudet, bishop of Langres (Ep 1612)
6 Bletz (see introduction)

assigned the approximate month-date on the basis of the reference in lines 1–2.

In Erasmus' edition of Ambrose, published in August 1527 (Ep 1855), the table of contents for volume 4 announces four books of *Interpellationes*, ie *De interpellatione Job et David libri quatuor* (On the Prayer of Job and David, four books). But there are only three, numbered I, III, IV. Also announced is an *Apologia David* in one book, with no mention of a second book. Lips reports here that he has sent to Conradus Goclenius at Louvain for transmission to Erasmus at Basel the following:

1/ a copy of what he considers to be book 2 of the *Interpellationes*, based on a manuscript belonging to a certain Pascasius, with variants from another manuscript.

2/ collations for the other three books, doubtless from the same manuscripts, with references to a printed edition, presumably that of Erasmus.

3/ a copy of a second book of the *Apologia David*, together with collations for book 1.

Erasmus, who doubted the ascription of these texts to Ambrose, nonetheless printed them in *De pueris instituendis* of September 1529. In his preface (Ep 2190) he makes no mention of the manuscripts nor, perhaps in deference to the wish expressed here in lines 34–5, does he acknowledge the contribution of Lips. In 1531 Lips tried again to persuade Erasmus that he had in fact found the genuine book 2 of the *Interpellationes*, for which he now had three or four manuscripts (Allen Ep 2566:139–60), but Erasmus refused to be convinced, and volume 4 of the next Froben edition of Ambrose (1538) still showed only three books. The texts that Lips had supplied were included in the same volume, but separate from both the *Interpellationes* and the *Apologia David*. Later scholars, however, have accepted the authenticity of both works. See *Patrologiae cursus completus ... series Latina* ed J.-P. Migne (Paris 1882) 14 849–66, 929–60.

* * * * *

Cordial greetings. I sent this to Goclenius around the second Sunday of Advent.[1] Accept it with your usual kindness. Let us know, I pray you, how you are faring and what you are doing.

Meaning of the abbreviations in the second book of *Interpellationes*: *Pasc.* (You know who that is);[2] *al.* = another copy. The rest is clear. Abbre-   5
viations in the three other books of the *Interpellationes* which I have edited: first I give the page number, then sometimes I add: *ver. a princ. cap.*, that is,

* * * * *

2076
1 December 1528
2 Possibly Paschasius Berselius of Liège (Ep 674). Cf line 35 below.

a given line from the beginning of the chapter, and then you begin numbering the page from the beginning of the chapter. Sometimes I add to the page
number *ver. a fine cap.*, and then you must count from the end of the chapter   10
to arrive at the designated line without error. In most cases you will read:
'such and such page, such and such line,' sometimes 'such and such line
from the end of the page,' and I think you will understand how to number
the pages.

Of what use would it have been to send you the second book when   15
the others were so corrupt? But the first book was more mutilated than the
others. Now, if nothing else, the books will be published more free of errors
than before, and a second will no longer be missing. Therefore, as I said,
accept it as genuine and leave it at that!

At the same time, by the same messenger, I entrusted to Goclenius the   20
second book of the *Apology of David* and my corrections of the first book. The
first book (which previously was thought of as the only book) was published
in a fairly correct form, but I have no doubt that you will approve of at least
some of my annotations. I did not seal the second book the way I did the
others. I sent it, but only wrapped it. And I know that Goclenius will not   25
send this *Apology* unless he finds a messenger to whom he can freely entrust
the package. The rest he will send, if I am not mistaken, by whomever he
can find, in the form of a letter.

Perhaps you will be surprised that I speak of a second book when
hitherto there was only one and no one mentioned a second book. I shall say   30
nothing against that except that you should test it yourself. Almost nothing
else seems as genuine a work of Ambrose as that *Apology*. It exceeds the
second book of *Interpellationes* in size.

Farewell, my dearly beloved Erasmus, and be sure not to make any
mention of me to Pascasius. 1528   35

Yours devotedly, Lips

To establish the pagination and the line numbers I asked Goclenius to
lend me his Ambrose, for your sake. He did so but, as I heard, reluctantly.
No wonder; he was afraid it might be damaged in the journey here and back.
It would be right that I send him my thanks, but I cannot. Please exercise   40
this duty in my behalf, if you would.

To the eminent professor of sacred theology Desiderius Erasmus of
Rotterdam, residing at Basel

2077 / To Louis de Berquin   Basel, 23 December 1528

This is Erasmus' response to Ep 2066. It was first published in the *Opus epistolarum.*

ERASMUS OF ROTTERDAM TO LOUIS DE BERQUIN, GREETING

Even if Nosoponus were playing the part of Erasmus,[1] there was no reason
for Budé to become angry. I cannot marvel enough at this perversity of
judgment. Italy sent us this fever so that no part of the world would be free
of discord.[2] Driven out of Rome, they infest France,[3] and I think that from a   5
single heresy many will be generated.[4] So I intend to declare a holiday from
studies after Easter,[5] especially now that Froben is dead.[6]

It is unfortunate that the personal letter that I wrote you, and which I
would not have communicated to Brie unless he was to keep it to himself,
is passing from hand to hand as if it were meant for publication.[7] I can   10
scarcely be led to believe that Jacques Toussain is of such insensible and
boorish character that for no reason at all he should wish to vent his fury
in defamatory verse against the name of a man who has never uttered an
injurious word against him.[8] But I wonder even more at the Greek, if the
verses attributed to him are truly his;[9] unless perhaps they are both eager   15
to enter into the good graces of men like Cousturier and Béda.[10]

As regards yourself, my dear Berquin, I cannot but return your loving
devotion towards me, but this devotion of yours, no matter how you justify
it, puts an intolerable burden of hostility upon my shoulders. You exhibit the
letter[11] in which I confide to your ears things that one can say and things that   20

* * * * *

2077
1 See Ep 2066:15.
2 The 'fever' of Ciceronianism and the attendant criticism of Erasmus; cf Ep
  2047:19–20.
3 Erasmus is doubtless thinking in particular of his most formidable critic Alberto Pio, who in June 1527, a month after the sack of Rome, was sent by
  Clement VII to the French court to represent the interests of the Holy See (CWE
  84 xxviii). Erasmus was unaware of Pio's presence in Paris until informed of
  it by Berquin (Ep 2066:64–6); cf lines 54–7 below and Ep 2080.
4 Apart from indicating that Erasmus expected more trouble from his critics,
  this passage is obscure. It may refer to something in the missing portion of
  Ep 2066.
5 28 March 1529, by which time, no doubt, he hoped that his work on the Froben
  Augustine (Ep 2157) would be finished
6 Ep 1900
7 Cf Epp 2047:27–30, 2048:10–12 and 35–7.
8 Toussain (Ep 810:497n) was a devoted member of Budé's circle and would
  soon (1530) become royal professor of Greek. See Ep 2119 (13 March 1529), in
  which Erasmus remonstrates with Toussain on this matter.
9 Janus Lascaris; see Ep 2027 n14.
10 Epp 1943 nn7 (Cousturier) and 6 (Béda)
11 Cf lines 8–10 above.

one cannot say.[12] You make it known that I shall not be silent.[13] There was, believe me, no need of these provocations for those who are already more than inflamed against me without need of prompting. I would appreciate your loyalty if I did not see that it has such disastrous consequences. Everything you have done so far has had the opposite effect of what was intended. You made public your victory against my advice;[14] see how it has turned out. As for those misbegotten translations of yours, which you thought were the only way of appeasing hatred, I ask you, what good did they do? One bishop alone began to feel a little more well-disposed towards me.[15] What was obtained by the letter? or the diffusion of the Twelve Propositions?[16] These served no other purpose than stirring up a hornets' nest. You have good, solid reasons for all of this, but they do not further the cause of either of us. You preferred a brilliant victory to a swift one. I applaud your confidence, but either it deceives you or my foreboding deceives me.

From letters of my friends I get wind of some terrible plot being hatched by the Béda faction. Proof of this is that a well-known former friend of mine, frightened by their threats, does not dare to write me a single word.[17]

In Louvain the edict against my *Colloquies* never appeared. Therefore that was an empty rumour.[18] For a long time they have privately prevented anyone from lecturing on them formally in the colleges, in order to please the monks.[19]

* * * * *

12 Erasmus puts 'things that one can say and things that one cannot say' in Greek: ῥητὰ καὶ ἄρρητα.

13 Ep 2066:55–7

14 Allen says that the 'victory' in question was Berquin's release from prison at the king's command in 1526, following his condemnation as a relapsed heretic (cf Ep 2027 n1). But Erasmus' later statements that Berquin had 'flaunted this success in writing,' 'in a triumphal little book' clearly refer to the outcome of the first trial in 1523; see Allen Epp 2158:103–4, 2188:107–10. No such book exists.

15 Berquin claimed that allowing ordinary people to read his works in French was the best way to counter misguided antagonism directed at him, and he cited the example of an unnamed, poorly educated French bishop who had abandoned his hostility to Erasmus after reading Berquin's French translation of the *Querela pacis*. See Allen Ep 2188:130–9.

16 See Ep 2066:44–50.

17 Most likely Lefèvre d'Etaples; cf Ep 2052:16–17 with n9.

18 See Ep 2066:38–9.

19 See Ep 1537:27–32.

I learn that Béda in a public ceremony called a *resumpta*[20] made honourable mention, first of Luther, second of Erasmus, and third of Lefèvre. He has no shame! He parades about in his regalia and triumphs in *resumptae*,[21] as if the world were populated only by imbeciles. I hear that Lefèvre has secretly withdrawn from public light but I think it is an empty rumour.

I have received neither a pamphlet nor a letter from the anonymous friend.[22] Simon Riquinus,[23] who I think is known to you, told me about someone from Ghent who showed himself to be a man of courage in the tumult caused by Béda's followers.[24] I don't know whether he is the one. If you sent it, I am surprised that you did not say who the courier was.

I shall respond to Alberto Pio, but only by letter. I wonder what his plan is in circulating that pamphlet.[25] He pleads a case against me in shame-

* * * * *

20 A *resumpta* was a public ceremony in faculties of theology at which someone who had been awarded a doctorate engaged in a disputation on a biblical subject. Until he had done his *resumpta* the doctor could not preside at faculty disputations unless granted a dispensation to do so. In theory, the *resumpta* was supposed to take place soon after the awarding of the doctorate, but in practice it was not uncommon for it to be postponed for years, with dispensations being granted as needed in the interim. Farge *Registre*, for example, records fourteen cases (none involving Béda) in which the faculty granted a dispensation to one of its members to preside at a disputation *resumpta non facta* (61A, 62A, 123A, 142A, 154B, 215A, 229A, 241B, 242A, 247D, 251A, 262A, 314A, 319D). This report by Erasmus seems to indicate that Béda, who received his doctorate in 1508, did not do his *resumpta* until twenty years later, in 1528.

21 Erasmus may be playing on the literal sense of *resumere*, which here would mean to put on again garments that had been discarded.

22 See Ep 2066:50–3.

23 Simon Riquinus (Rychwyn, Reichwein), documented 1519–1547/8, whom Erasmus may have met in Cologne in the autumn of 1520, was headmaster of a school at Diest in Brabant from 1525 until 1528. This letter indicates that he was now, or had recently been, in Paris and had apparently had some sort of contact with Berquin. He soon moved on to Louvain, where he seems to have completed his medical studies. In 1529 he left Louvain to become the personal physician of Duke John III of Cleves, at whose court he had close contact with Erasmus' friends Konrad Heresbach (Ep 1316) and Johann von Vlatten (Epp 1390, 1948). His personal correspondence with Erasmus commenced from there with Ep 2246. By 1533 he had moved to Trier, where he became personal physician to the elector.

24 Possibly Joachim Martens, physician of Ghent, who had moved to Paris sometime in the autumn of 1528; see Ep 2049, which is addressed to him.

25 See Ep 2066:64–70.

less arguments and is openly hostile, doing his utmost to teach that I was the occasion, the cause and the instigator of this whole affair.[26] Aleandro does the same in his *Racha*,[27] astonished that I am still alive when so many thousands of men have been slaughtered in Germany. I am not unaware of the close bond of friendship that exists between Alberto and Aleandro.[28] He wages a campaign against Luther in such a way that he seems to be colluding with his adversary.

The point that offends you in the Psalm is nothing.[29] We do not seek eternal salvation from any man but solely from God, however much we are helped by the suffrages of the saints.[30]

I hear that Budé's book *On the Diction of the Greek Language* is being printed.[31] I frequently encouraged him to do this and I am very happy on this account. I hear mention of me is made in it. If he does so with the courtesy worthy of learned men, he will not offend me. If otherwise, which I do not think is the case, I should like to have a copy as soon as possible. He would have an answer in kind before Easter, but nothing that would destroy our friendship.

If there is anything you want me to know, send someone at my expense or hire him with the agreement that he receive two crowns from you and the same amount from me.[32] But see to it that he solicits letters from other friends.

Karel Uutenhove,[33] truly the kind of person you describe him to be, is a great consolation to me through his presence in my household. May he derive equal benefit from me! This letter would have reached you earlier if Anton had not delayed his departure beyond all expectations.[34]

Farewell.

Given at Basel, 23 December 1528

* * * * *

26 Ie the German Reformation
27 See Ep 1717 n18.
28 See Ep 1987:6–11.
29 Perhaps the recently published *In psalmum 85* (Ep 2017). Berquin's point is not made in the surviving portion of Ep 2066.
30 This position is clearly stated in *In psalmum 85*; see CWE 64 14, 44.
31 Cf Ep 2052:7–9.
32 The two crowns are presumably the English double-rose crowns, struck from November 1526, worth 5s od sterling each, rather than the current French crowns (ie the *écus à la couronne au soleil*). See Appendix 440–50 with Tables 2 and 3, 464–76 below.
33 Ep 2001 n7
34 Anton Bletz (Ep 1784 n1); cf Epp 2078:27–8, 2079:75.

2078 / To Andrzej Zebrzydowski   Basel, 23 December 1528

Zebrzydowski (Epp 1826, 1958 n1) had now been in Paris since the autumn; see Epp 2052:19–21, 2065:23. The letter was first published in the *Opus epistolarum*.

ERASMUS OF ROTTERDAM TO ANDRZEJ ZEBRZYDOWSKI,
GREETING

My very distinguished young man, my feeling of loss at your absence is greatly alleviated by the knowledge that both your trip and your stay in Paris have gone successfully, especially since you write that your studies 5 there are progressing better than here; which I foresaw would certainly be the case. That city has many men gifted with exquisite learning. One would say that all the Muses driven out of Italy by the din of armour have migrated to France.[1] I have no doubt that you will apply yourself vigorously there so that you will not seem to have gone to such a rich emporium of literary 10 studies in vain. Although here too, I know not by what decree of fate, there is a great uproar of those professing to teach.[2]

Glareanus is now much more attached to you than he was before.[3] That petty quarrel reconciled you, as sometimes from a bad beginning a great friendship is born. There is no need for you to excuse your silence. 15 I consider the letter sent to Karel Uutenhove[4] to have been written also to me. I have another boarder who is not lacking in wit.[5] Karel cannot tolerate stoves.[6]

About your return to us, I don't know if you are joking. When will Paris, which entices its guests more and more once they have breathed 20 its perfumes, let you go? Nevertheless, if you think it will be to your profit, you will be more welcome here than ever. In any case, you will not find me a worse host but one who is perhaps even more accommodating, because in a short time I am going to shake off these labours.[7] I am

* * * * *

2078
1 The wars between Francis I and Charles V were being fought in Italy rather than France (or Spain), which meant that Paris currently provided a more hospitable environment for the Muses than did any of the major centres in Italy.
2 Cf Ep 2079:42–4.
3 On Glareanus see Ep 1977 n29.
4 On Uutenhove, see Ep 2001 n7.
5 Hubertus Barlandus; see Epp 2079:65–8, 2081.
6 Neither could Erasmus; see Ep 2055 n7.
7 Cf Ep 2077:6–7 with n5.

surprised that I have not had a word from Poland.[8] If you have any news,   25
let me know.

That you are receiving this letter so late is Anton's fault, who put off his
departure longer than usual and longer than I expected.[9] Baer, Bonifacius,[10]
Hieronymus,[11] Glareanus, and the rest of your devoted friends send their
greetings. If you do not mind, please relay my best greetings to Marcin   30
Dąbrówski.[12]

And may you enjoy the best of health.

Given at Basel, 23 December 1528

2079 / To Daniel Stiebar   Basel, 23 December 1528

First published in the *Opus epistolarum*, this is Erasmus' reply to Ep 2069.

ERASMUS OF ROTTERDAM TO DANIEL STIEBAR, GREETING

Come now, my dear Stiebar, rid yourself of any timidity and refresh my
spirit with your witty and congenial letters, 'not afraid' of the majesty of
Erasmus, as you write.[1] Some people are so modest that through a feeling of
shame they are deterred from performing their duty. What could be more   5
gratifying to me than letters that recall to me a very dear friend and mitigate the desire for one who is absent? Fate took you from me when I barely
knew you. Undoubtedly, it was your sense of propriety, which was altogether fitting for your age and your nobility of birth, that did me harm. As
a result of this, I made your acquaintance too late, since from personal ex-   10
perience of the unscrupulousness of some of them I regard all men of this
rank with mistrust.[2]

* * * * *

8 Erasmus was expecting replies to Epp 2030–5, written in August. They eventually arrived but are not extant. Erasmus' replies to them were written in
   June 1529: Epp 2173–8.
9 Anton Bletz (Ep 1784 n1); cf Epp 2077:79–80, 2079:75.
10 On Ludwig Baer and Bonifacius Amerbach see Ep 1933.
11 Froben
12 Marcin Słap Dąbrówski, a young Pole who was travelling with Zebrzydowski
   as his companion. His own extant correspondence with Erasmus begins in July
   1530 with Ep 2351.

2079
1 See Ep 2069:10–11, where the word 'majesty' is not found.
2 Allen observes that Erasmus' experience with Heinrich Eppendorf had made
   him suspicious of all knights. But Erasmus knew that Eppendorf's knightly
   status was bogus. So this is much more likely an allusion to Erasmus' bitter
   experience with Ulrich von Hutten, who was a real knight. See Ep 1934.

Philippus Montanus painted a delightful picture of the tragicomedy of your trip.[3] He will be much more endeared to me in future since he rendered you such good services, as you write.[4] You are wise in enrolling 15 yourself in a school of chattering, the barber-shop, in order to learn French, where for a while you will maintain a Pythagorean reserve.[5] What else can you be there but a listener? And yet one French girl will contribute no less to your mastery of the language than thirty men. The most certain road to progress is to learn by heart the inflections of the nouns and verbs, then to 20 read books written in good French, but with a good male teacher or, if you prefer, a female teacher. I would encourage you to sprinkle a little Greek into your studies so that you may return home *tetraglottal*.[6] I approve and am glad that you have given yourself some freedom.[7] In the meantime look to your own advancement, while you can. 25

The rest of the letter, in which you discourse copiously on our close ties and on your unceasing devotion to me, although they were unnecessary – especially since I have so many proofs of your devotion – gave me great delight all the same. I am happy to revive memories of so dear a friend now and again, since this addition to the number of my friends, in my opinion, 30 has been of no minor importance in adding to my happiness, if there is such a thing. Besides mutual affection and the exchange of letters, I ask nothing of you, my distinguished young man.

But you in the abundance of your love threaten to offer me, in addition to what is essential in friendship, some incidental benefits as well; as if it 35 were of no account that you left with me at your departure a golden pledge of your affection.[8] Therefore whatever that promise is, I release you from it entirely. Do you wish to add to your kindness to me? Strive to distinguish yourself to the utmost degree in humane studies. Now that you are mine by right of friendship, I shall consider every good thing that accrues to you to 40 have accrued to me also.

* * * * *

3 In Ep 2065
4 In Ep 2069:21–3
5 Ie remain silent; see *Adagia* I v 29.
6 Ie quadrilingual, knowing four languages; the word is Greek in the text.
7 Ie by sending the boys to school; see Ep 2069:26–8.
8 The Latin for 'golden pledge' is *aureum pignus*. Erasmus could have been referring either literally to something made of gold or metaphorically to something
'golden' in the sense of 'precious.' Allen, who took *aureum* literally, speculated
that the pledge may have been a gift of money, noting that no gift from Stiebar
is found in the 1534 inventory of Erasmus' gold plate (see Sieber 5–6). It is
equally possible, however, that the pledge was not gold at all but something
else that Erasmus nonetheless found precious.

So that you will not be altogether ignorant of what goes on here, in Basel there is a great hubbub caused by those who are giving public lectures.[9] A great outcrop of them has suddenly sprung up. Among them is Joachim from Antwerp,[10] a man born for this. A certain old doctor taught in a public lecture what Christ's testament was. Although I always thought that it was 'Peace I give to you,'[11] he has shown that it is 'Increase, and multiply and fill the earth.'[12] He fulminates against those who are continent, especially nuns, greatly irritated that such fertile fields are not cultivated. The retention of seed, he says, causes heart attacks, dizzy spells, and other mental aberrations, which are very widespread at present. This Silenus of ours,[13] they say, is soon to marry a nun so that he won't suffer any dizzy spells.

Another man of the same profession told another story.[14] He kept a woman servant with him because he suffered from nightmares. A priest seduced her for himself. When the doctor had no success with writing love-letters, he spread the rumour that the priest had married the girl. The priest, thinking that this rumour might diminish his revenues (for he was, or at least wished to be seen as, a Catholic), brought the doctor to court. The love-letters, in which he miserably lamented that he was so prostrated by longing for the girl that he could not eat or sleep, were read aloud to the great amusement of the judges and the audience. I need not elaborate. The priest won, the doctor was forced to recant – twice defeated, since neither Venus nor Mercury favoured his cause.[15]

Karel Uutenhove[16] has gained a congenial boon companion, which makes me very happy. He is a learned doctor and at the same time delightfully witty.[17] If you wish to know his name, it is Hubertus; his country, he is from Barland.[18] So we pass part of the day in laughter and in light-hearted stories.

* * * * *

9 Cf Ep 2078:10–11.
10 Ringelberg; see Ep 2058 n3.
11 John 14:27
12 Gen 1:22
13 Silenus, the oldest satyr, was the faithful companion and teacher of the wine-god Dionysus. When drunk, which was most of the time, he possessed much wisdom and could reveal important secrets to mortals.
14 Erasmus corrects himself in lines 73–4 below.
15 Venus was the goddess of love; Mercury the god of eloquence.
16 Ep 2001 n7
17 Cf Ep 2078:17.
18 See Ep 2081.

I would like to have chatted with you longer, my very dear Daniel, but   70
Seneca calls me back to the treadmill.[19] He all but kills me in a task that
never ends. My best wishes for your good health.

I had misunderstood the story about the doctor. There are not two but
only one, who danced both shows. You will receive this letter a bit late.
Anton is to blame, since he put off his departure longer than usual.[20] Once   75
again, farewell, my dearest Stiebar.

Given at Basel, 23 December 1528

2080 / To Alberto Pio   Basel, 23 December 1528

This letter was first published by Erasmus himself in the *Des. Erasmi Roterodami*
epistolarum floridarum liber unus antehuc nunquam excusus (Basel: J. Herwagen,
September 1531).

On Alberto Pio, prince of Carpi, and his emergence as Erasmus' most
formidable Italian critic, see Epp 1634 and 1987, and see also Nelson Min-
nich's introduction to CWE 84. Erasmus was moved to write this letter by
the information received from Louis de Berquin that Pio, about whose whereabouts he had been uncertain, was now living in Paris and planning to publish
an attack on him (Ep 2066:64–70; cf Ep 2077:54–7).

ERASMUS OF ROTTERDAM TO ALBERTO PIO, PRINCE OF CARPI,
GREETING

When your little book[1] was delivered to me, illustrious Prince Albert, I had
begun immediately to sketch some sort of response, but in the meantime the
chaos caused by the destruction of Rome[2] has stricken the hearts of all. Vari-   5
ous rumours have reached here about you; and even if accurate information
had been available about where you were, there were no roads passable for
the transport of letters. Recently I learned through the letters of friends that
you were fulfilling an embassy at the court of the Most Christian King and
that your little book was circulating among many persons and that it would   10

* * * * *

19 The Froben Seneca (Ep 2091), on which Erasmus had been at work for some
    time (Ep 2040).
20 Anton Bletz (Ep 1784 n1); cf Epp 2077:79–80, 2078:26–7.

2080
1 The *Responsio paraenetica* of May 1526. It was not published until January 1529
   (Epp 1987 n2, 2066 n19), but a manuscript copy reached Erasmus in the summer of 1526; see Ep 1744:137–8.
2 The sack of Rome in May 1527

not be long before it would be published. I would have thought of looking
after this myself long ago, in the hope that the prestige of your name, or
the fairness of your argument, or the suavity of your language might charm
some people into leading a better life, except that you attacked me so vio-
lently and relentlessly. For since your aim is my destruction, it is of no great   15
importance what civility of language is employed, as if a prince were to condemn you to death with honorific language. I wish you had challenged me
to a battle in which I could have engaged you solely in a test of intellect and
eloquence. I would have counted it a great glory to have contended with Alberto, even if I were to retire in defeat. As things stand, you bring such a   20
case against me that if I keep silent I admit guilt of a capital offence, but if I
answer I can hardly do so, first of all, without hurting you; second, I would
be moving Camarina, which it would have been better to leave alone,[3] since
the situation everywhere is more than sufficiently aggravated. As for the
rest, I advise you not to hasten the publication of that little book, or if you   25
do not want your efforts in that enterprise to be lost, tone down the part
that deals with me.

　　If this courier had alerted me even three days before he set out, I
would have reread your little book and sent my *Response*,[4] but I shall do
that through another courier when a reliable one is available. After reading   30
it you will decide in your wisdom what you think will be best for both of
us. It is scarcely safe to commit anything whatever to a letter. But if there
were either some chance of a personal colloquy, or if you were to have business in this region, then either my opinion of you is completely mistaken or
you would think that you must support Erasmus with your favour rather   35
than burden him the more by chiming in with the calumnies of others.

　　Farewell.

　　Given at Basel, 23 December 1528

2081 / From Hubertus Barlandus　　　　　Strasbourg, 30 December 1528

First published as Ep 69 in Enthoven, the autograph is in the Rehdiger Collection of the University Library at Wrocław. Erasmus appears to refer to this
letter at the end of Ep 2172.

　　Hubertus Barlandus (d 1544) was a native of Baarland in Zeeland and
a kinsman of Adrianus Aelius Barlandus (Ep 760:16n) and Jan Becker of

* * * * *

3 *Adagia* I i 64
4 The *Responsio ad epistolam Pii* (CWE 84 1–103), which did not appear in print
　until March 1529; cf Ep 2066 n20.

Borsele (Ep 291). He studied humanities with Becker and Vives at Louvain but then devoted himself to the study of medicine at Louvain, mathematics at Paris, and medicine again in Montpellier in 1526. Following a journey to Italy, he returned north in 1528 via Basel and Strasbourg. In Basel, he stayed with Erasmus, whom he had met at the College of the Lily in Louvain. Erasmus' delight in his company is expressed in Ep 2079:66–70. At Strasbourg, where this letter was written, Barlandus edited the *Medicinales epistolae* of Giovanni Manardo (J. Schott, 17 February 1529) and sent a copy to Erasmus, who thanked him in Ep 2172. By 1531 he was back in the Netherlands, where he spent the remainder of his life as a physician and medical scholar.

May Jupiter bring destruction upon the fifth element and astrology.[1] It is on account of them that I spare no expense and suffer some hardship, and yet I do not progress as I expected. Similarly, I do not know what curses to call down upon my parents who, ever more tardy in answering and sending me money, have kept me in continual suspense for the whole duration of   5
this stay. If it were not for them, I would not have remained here so long. No more than eight miles distant is Tübingen,[2] where the glory of our age in mathematics, Johann Stöffler,[3] is giving public lectures. I would have set out for there long ago if I did not have to wait for the letters my friends were to send me, which prevented me from moving farther away. I am so   10
eager to get started that I will not be at peace until I either find someone who will live up to my expectations or can settle into a permanent position from which it would not be very easy to escape afterwards. I do not wish it to be understood that I am wasting all my time, but that I am not making the progress I desire.   15

* * * * *

2081
1 Barlandus writes 'upon the fifth element and astrology' in Greek. In Aristotelian science, the 'fifth element' was ether (aether) which, in contrast to the four terrestrial elements of earth, air, fire, and water, was the substance that filled the universe above the terrestrial sphere.
2 The text does indeed say 'eight [Roman] miles' (*octo milibus passuum*), which is nonsense. As the crow flies, the distance is roughly 80 English miles or about 129 kilometres.
3 Johann Stöffler of Justingen (1452–1531) was a famous mathematician and astronomer as well as a prolific astrologer (cf Ep 1280A n21). In 1511 he was called to a chair in mathematics at Tübingen, where Philippus Melanchthon was one of his students. The first sentence of this letter seems to indicate that Barlandus was interested chiefly in Stöffler's skills as an astrologer.

Johann Stöffler
From *Bibliotheca chalcographica* (Heidelberg 1650)
Universitätsbibliothek Tübingen

The day before yesterday that little man came to visit us, a very good and dear friend of mine.[4] Yesterday we delivered the letters to each addressee. The one and only Eppendorf[5] invited us to dinner today. The little man left for Haguenau around midday, since he had found pleasant companions for the journey. So I stayed behind, wondering whether I should go alone to dine with Eppendorf. Some friends of yours here who are solicitous of your honour persuaded me to go. They were somewhat afraid that he might take umbrage and think that it was an insult to him that after one person set out on a journey the other should also not appear, since he knew that we are both devoted to the name of Erasmus. So I went to see the man and dined with him, and was received royally. We made mention of you and I spoke of your distinctions without his ever seeming to evince any sentiment that was less than friendly towards Erasmus. He confided to me among other things that he is expecting an answer from you any day now;[6] when he receives it he will move to France or to the court of his prince.[7]

But I have gone on too long. I shall write more often as long as I do not annoy you with my uncouth style. I commend myself always to your great dignity, Erasmus, our soul, as devoted to you as one can ever be. I pray God, all good and all powerful, to preserve your excellent self for length of days.

A heartfelt farewell from Strasbourg, 30 December 1528

To the eminent theologian and leader of the republic of letters, Master Erasmus of Rotterdam, ever revered teacher. At Basel

* * * * *

4 Allen speculated that this might have been Felix Rex Polyphemus (Ep 2068 n1), stating as his reason that in the colloquy *Cyclops* he 'seems to be represented as small.' But the passage in question (CWE 40 865) indicates that Cyclops (ie Rex) is taller than the other interlocutor, Cannius (Nicolaas Kan, Ep 1999 n9). Besides, both 'Polyphemus' and 'Cyclops' were the names of giants. If the 'little man' was indeed Rex, Barlandus may have been engaging in irony.

5 Ep 1934

6 Probably an answer to the letter of June 1528 (which Erasmus claimed not to have received) in which Eppendorf complained that Erasmus had not yet kept his promise to dedicate a work to him; see Ep 1934 introduction. Erasmus did not write to Eppendorf again until about January 1529 (Ep 2086).

7 Duke George of Saxony

THE COINAGES AND MONETARY POLICIES
OF HENRY VIII (r 1509–47)

Coinage debasements
The coinage changes of Henry VIII

JOHN H. MUNRO

The infamy of Henry VIII's Great Debasement, which began in 1542 and was continued by his successors for another six years after his death, until 1553, has obscured the previous monetary changes of his reign, especially the two linked debasements of 1526. Certainly the Great Debasement was by far the most severe ever experienced in English monetary history and was one of the worst experienced in early-modern Europe.[1] The 1526 debasements and related monetary changes are of interest not only to economic historians but also to readers of the *Correspondence of Erasmus*, since many of the letters discuss financial transactions that were affected by them.

Coinage Debasements

Coinage debasement is a complex, arcane, and confusing topic for most readers, and indeed for most historians. Put simply, however, we may say that it meant a reduction of the fine precious metals contents, silver or gold, represented in the unit of money-of-account. That generally also meant (though not always) a physical diminution of the precious metal contents in the affected coins. Thus the nature and consequences of coinage debasements depended on the relationship between coins and moneys-of-account, that is, the accounting system used to reckon prices, values, wages, other payments, receipts of income, and so forth.

THE RELATIONSHIP BETWEEN COINS AND MONEYS-OF-ACCOUNT

The English money-of-account, closely based on the monetary system that Charlemagne's government had established between 794 and 802, was the

* * * * *

1 The four classic accounts of Henry VIII's debasements, are, in chronological order: Frederick C. Dietz *English Government Finance, 1485–1558* University of Illinois Studies in the Social Sciences IX (Urbana, Ill 1920) 137–59, 175–91; Sir Albert Feaveayear *The Pound Sterling: A History of English Money* 2nd ed revised by E. Victor Morgan (Oxford 1963) 46–86; C.E. Challis 'The Debasement of the Coinage, 1542–1551' *Economic History Review* 2nd series 20/3 (December 1967) 441–66; and J.D. Gould *The Great Debasement: Currency and the Economy in Mid-Tudor England* (Oxford 1970). See also Christopher E. Challis and C.H. Harrison 'A Contemporary Estimate of the Production of Gold and Silver Coinage in England, 1542–1556' *English Historical Review* 88 no 349 (October 1973) 821–35; C.E. Challis *The Tudor Coinage* (Manchester and New York 1978); C.E. Challis 'Lord Hastings to the Great Silver Recoinage, 1464–1699' in *A New History of the Royal Mint* ed C.E. Challis (Cambridge and New York 1992) 179–397; and C.E. Challis *Currency and the Economy in Tudor and Early Stuart England* Historical Association pamphlets no 4 (London 1989).

pound sterling.[2] This particular money-of-account, with 12 pence (d) to the shilling (s), and 20 shillings to the pound (and thus 240 pence to the pound), remained the most prevalent in western Europe until the French Revolution. The new Carolingian pound, as a money-of-account, was worth one pound of silver in the corresponding new Carolingian weight (displacing the old Roman pound), which contained 12 ounces (489.506 grams).[3]

The only coins struck were, however, the silver penny and its subdivisions (half and quarter pennies, and even smaller coins). Larger denomination, full-bodied silver coins, those that Carlo Cipolla called *moneta grossa* – known as *grossi* in Italy and *gros* in France – were not struck until the later twelfth century, accompanying a major inflationary expansion in European silver mining.[4] Many of these *grossi* and the French *gros tournois* (of 1266) represented the shilling: that is, they were worth 12 pence in the local money-of-account. In England, the first coin larger than the penny did

* * * * *

2 'Money and Coinage of the Age of Erasmus' CWE 1 328–9, 330–1, 347 Appendix E.

3 See Etienne Fournial *Histoire monétaire de l'Occident médiéval* (Paris 1970) 24–7, whose arguments are quite complex. The new Carolingian pound weight of 489.506 grams was designed to be 1.5 times the weight of the old Roman pound of 12 ounces (or 18 Roman ounces), which, according to Fournial, had once weighed 327.453 grams but had diminished slightly to 326.337 grams by the ninth century. These weights have been challenged by other numismatists (by even more complex arguments), who offer alternative weights for the Carolingian pound: 408.0 grams, 411.36 grams, 459.36 grams, and 483.33 grams. For a summary, see Willem Blockmans 'Le poids des deniers carolingiens' *Revue belge de numismatique et de sigillographie* 119 (1973) 179–81. In support of Fournial's view is the fact that the later *livre de Paris* (16 *onces*) also weighed exactly 489.506 grams; and the *marc de Troyes*, the mint weight used in France and most of the Low Countries, with half its weight (8 *onces*), weighed 244.753 grams. For these weights, and documentary analyses, see John Munro 'A Maze of Medieval Monetary Metrology: Determining Mint Weights in Flanders, France and England from the Economics of Counterfeiting, 1388–1469' *The Journal of European Economic History* 29/1 (Spring 2000) 173–99.

4 Subdivisions were as small as the Flemish mite = $^{1}/_{24}$th of a penny. The first *grossi* were issued in Genoa in or about 1172 (worth 4d); then in Venice in 1192 (worth 26 *denari*); in Florence, in 1237 (*fiorino*); in Milan, about 1250; in France, with Louis IX's great monetary reform of 1266 (silver *gros tournois* = 12d *tournois*); in Flanders, from 1275 (the *groot*, imitating the *gros tournois*); and in England, from 1279 (the *groat* = 4d sterling). See Carlo Cipolla *Money, Prices, and Civilization in the Mediterranean World: Fifth to Seventeenth Century* (New York 1967) 14–15 (quotation), 42–51; Peter Spufford *Money and its Use in Medieval Europe* (Cambridge and New York 1988) 109–62 and 404–6 Appendix 1; Fournial *Histoire monétaire* (n3 above) 78–80.

not appear until Edward I's recoinage of 1279: the groat, worth only 4d sterling.[5] The shilling coin (worth 12d) did not appear, at least as a regular issue, until the reign of Henry VIII: the *testoon* of May 1542 (issued with the commencement of the Great Debasement).[6]

* * * * *

5 Nicholas J. Mayhew 'From Regional to Central Minting, 1158–1464' in *A New History of the Royal Mint* ed C.E. Challis (Cambridge and New York 1992) 120–8

6 Also known as 'teston,' 'tester,' and 'sovereign groat.' When the testoon was first issued is still the subject of much vexatious dispute. Several monetary historians have contended that the initial issues took place in or about 1504, under Henry VII (r 1485–1509); see Feavearyear *Pound Sterling* (n1 above) 439 Appendix III.ii; W.J.W. Potter and E.J. Winstanley 'The Coinage of Henry VII' *British Numismatic Journal* 30 (1961) 262–301, 31 (1962) 109–24, especially 109–112 ('shillings'), and 32 (1963) 140–60; and E.J. Winstanley 'The Sovereign Groat of Henry VII' in R.A.G. Carson *Mints, Dies, and Currency: Essays Dedicated to the Memory of Albert Baldwin* (London 1971) 161–4 (very inconclusive: the coin in question may be a fraud). See also Challis *Tudor Coinage* (n1 above), 48–9, 60–1. While admitting that there is no documentary evidence for its issue under Henry VII, Challis states that 'it does seem reasonable to suppose that the three "sovereign type" denominations – the penny, groat, and sovereign [shilling] – stemmed from the decision to introduce new designs in 1489,' when indeed the gold sovereign, worth 20s or £1, was first struck (Tower Mint indenture of 28 October 1489, which mentions no silver coins at all). Arguing in favour of this thesis on numismatic grounds, while also citing dubious evidence from some chroniclers (Robert Fabyan, Polidoro Virgilio, Raphael Holinshed), Challis presents a photograph of a silver testoon, purportedly issued under Henry VII, dating from c 1504 (48 fig 13). The first problem for such a dating is that two royal proclamations on coinage, issued on 5 July 1504 and 27 April 1505, do not mention any such coins worth 12d, but only groats (4d), half groats (2d), and pennies (1d); and the same is true of four later monetary ordinances, issued on 25 May 1522, 24 November 1522, 6 and 8 July 1525. They are all published in *Tudor Royal Proclamations* ed Paul L. Hughes and James F. Larkin 2 vols (New Haven and London 1964) I: *The Early Tudors (1485–1553)* no 54 (pages 60–1); no 57 (pages 70–1); no 88 (page 136); no 95 (page 141); no 102 (page 145); no 103 (page 146). The second problem is that no mint indentures (instructions) of Henry VII issued from the time of the gold sovereign of 1489 make any mention of silver coins worth 1s. The Tower mint indenture of 22 November 1505 lists only groats (4d), and coins worth 2d (half groats), 1d, ½d, and ¼d (farthings), as do all the subsequent mint indentures before the Great Debasement. Thus the first extant mint document to list specific issues of the 'testoon' or shilling coin is the Tower Mint indenture of 16 May 1542. Since this coin was issued at the commencement of the Great Debasement, the testoon was struck not of sterling silver but of 9 oz 5 dwt fineness. See Christopher E. Challis 'Appendix 2: Mint Contracts, 1279–1817' in *A New History of the Royal Mint* ed C.E. Challis (Cambridge and New York 1992) 717–21. (Challis gives a fineness of 9 oz 2 dwt; but see 450–1 and nn65–72 below). The first

The relationship between the silver coinage and the Carolingian-style moneys-of-account that so commonly appear in the correspondence of Erasmus – for example, the English pound sterling, the French *livre tournois*, the Flemish *pond groot* (*livre gros*) – is a simple one. The silver penny coin always equalled in value one penny (d) in the local money-of-account, so that the value of one pound in the local money-of-account always equalled the value of 240 currently circulating silver pennies (*deniers*), irrespective of the changes in their silver contents that had resulted from centuries of debasements.[7]

METHODS OF COINAGE DEBASEMENT IN MEDIEVAL AND EARLY MODERN EUROPE

A coinage debasement, whether for silver or for gold, was implemented by one or more of three techniques: 1/ a reduction in fineness, so that less silver or gold and consequently more base metal (usually copper) composed the coin's alloy; 2/ a reduction in weight; and 3/ an increase in the nominal or money-of-account value of the coin. An increase in the nominal value of a gold coin – of the English gold noble, for example, from 6s 8d (80d) to 7s 4d (88d) – constituted a debasement in that a lesser quantity of precious metal (in this case, fewer grams of gold) was represented in the unit of money-of-account.

The third method was applied to silver coinages only rarely in continental Europe, and never in England. Because most silver coinages were rigidly tied to their respective moneys-of-account, so that, as just indicated, the penny coin always represented one penny (d) in the money-of-account, increases in nominal coin values were necessarily applied only to those high-value silver coins whose silver contents remained unchanged when the penny coin and its subdivisions were subjected to debasements that

* * * * *

mention of 'testons' in Hughes and Larkin *Tudor Royal Proclamations* I is no 302 (page 420) for 10 April 1548: 'calling in testons because of counterfeiting.'
7 Peter Spufford 'Coinage and Currency' in *Cambridge Economic History of Europe* ed M.M. Postan et al III: *Economic Organization and Policies in the Middle Ages* (Cambridge 1963) 576–602; Spufford *Money and Its Use* (n4 above) 411–14 Appendix 2, 'Money of Account'; Hans Van Werveke 'Monnaie de compte et monnaie réelle' *Revue belge de philologie et d'histoire* 13 (1943) 123–52, reprinted in Hans Van Werveke *Miscellanea mediaevalia: Verspreide opstellen over economische en sociale geschiedenis van de middeleeuwen* (Ghent 1968) 133–58; Herman Van der Wee *The Growth of the Antwerp Market and the European Economy, 14th to 16th Centuries* 3 vols (The Hague 1963) I: *Statistics* part 1, chapter 3: 'Money and the History of Prices' (pages 107–36).

reduced their fine silver contents.[8] The same was true for gold coins when their precious metal contents remained unchanged, especially following a debasement of the silver coinage. When silver coins were debased, the relative or exchange values of the gold coins almost always increased, as market forces drove up their values, which were expressed in the silver-based money-of-account. Princes then had no alternative but to raise the money-of-account values, or exchange rates, on their gold coins in order to maintain the same equilibrium between the mint's value and the market values for precious metals, so that merchants would not export gold coins and bullion to foreign markets.

For English silver coins, therefore, we may focus on the first two methods – reductions in fineness and in weight – both of which necessarily increased the number of coins of a given denomination struck from a pound weight of pure silver. The English term 'debasement' indicates an adulteration of the coin's fineness, a change in the ratio of the two components in its alloy, silver and copper. All coins contained at least some copper to serve as a hardening agent in order to provide greater durability and thus to reduce wear and tear on the silver or gold, both very soft metals. Most medieval and early modern princes could not resist the temptation to add more copper to their coins, thus reducing their silver or gold contents. Before and after the Great Debasement of Henry VIII and Edward VI, the English monarchy provided a rare exception to continental practices. Indeed, the purity or fineness of England's silver coins remained among the best in Europe, as 'sterling silver,' with 11 ounces 2 dwt (pennyweight) of silver and 18 dwt of copper, for a total of 12 Troy ounces, so that the silver fineness or purity was 92.50 per cent.[9] Historically, that

* * * * *

8 An early and prime example was the fate of Louis IX's *gros tournois*, struck from 1266 with commercially fine silver (*argent-le-roy* = 23/24 or 95.833 per cent pure silver), worth 12d *tournois*, during Philip IV's debasements of the petty silver *deniers*, from 1295. The *gros* itself was then left untouched so that its relative value (relatively higher silver contents) rose, as did its nominal value, from 12d to 20d by 1301. See Fournial *Histoire monétaire* 87–9.

9 According to Mayhew 'Central Minting' (n5 above) 109–10 and nn79–81, English mint documents provide proof that pennies and groats were struck from sterling silver, with 18 dwt copper, as early as 1279–80. But these documents, published in *The De Moneta of Nicholas Oresme and English Mint Documents: Translated from the Latin* ed Charles Johnson (London 1956) do not precisely confirm that statement. Thus the *Tractatus Nove Moneta* of c 1280 (page 66) states that English 'Sterlings' contain 18.5 dwt of copper (*de cupro pondus xviii sterlingorum et oboli*); and the *De cuneo et monetario* (The St Edmunsbury Trial Plate) of c 1280 states (page 86) that 'the pound must contain 11 oz 2¼ dwt of fine silver (*de fin argent xi unces, ii esterlings, et j ferling*), and the rest alloy

became the official 'standard' of silver fineness. The only prior and temporary exception had taken place in 1335, when Edward III's government reduced the fineness to 10 ounces of silver (83.333 per cent fine), and then only for halfpennies (no full pennies were struck). The Great Debasement thus marked the second and final exception, when the penny's fineness was reduced, ultimately, to just 3 ounces of silver (25.00 per cent fine) in April and October 1551, and again, finally, in June 1553 (Table 1 part 1 below).[10]

For gold coins, the English fineness standard was the almost universal one of 24 carats, with subdivisions in grains. From the introduction of the gold florin in December 1343, and then of its replacement, the gold noble, in July 1344, English gold coins were as fine as any others – as fine indeed as the Florentine florins and Venetian ducats – at 23.875 carats (99.479 per cent pure).[11] Only with Henry VIII's monetary changes of 1526 was that standard reduced for gold coins: initially, to 22 carats (91.667 per cent fine). Debasements of both coinages by such reductions in fineness were far more common in medieval and early modern Italy, the Low Countries, Spain, and France, where the more appropriate term was *affaiblissement* (French) or *indebolimento* (Italian), meaning enfeebling or weakening the coinage, and were more commonly undertaken concurrently with reductions in the coin's weight.

* * * * *

(ie 17.75 dwt copper). See also Johnson's introduction xxvii and n2. For the silver mint standard in France and the Low Countries (*argent-le-roy*) see nn3 and 8 above, and also CWE 1 312, 330.

10 Challis 'Mint Contracts' (n6 above) 700 (July 1335) and 728 (June 1553)

11 See CWE 1 313, 314, 316, 325–6. There was no European uniformity in using grains to indicate gold fineness, not even in England, where grains were reckoned either out of 4 or out of 12. Thus the fineness for gold nobles at 23 carats 3.5 grains (out of 4) was often also given as 23 carats 10.5 grains, both meaning 23.875 carats. J.D. Gould, in his *Great Debasement* (n1 above) 12 Table II (on the gold coinages of 1526–60), failed to recognize this anomaly, incorrectly believing that all gold grains were reckoned in terms of a total of 12, and thus providing an incorrect lower fineness for coins described as 23 carats 3.5 grains. Italian florins and ducats were never struck with a full 24 carats, but were comparable to English nobles, for, as noted in the text, all coins required at least some copper as the requisite hardening agent. See Mario Bernocchi *Le monete della Repubblica fiorentina* 5 vols (Florence 1974) III: *Documentazione* 55–75, 110–20 (tables of fineness 1252–1531, when the *fiorino d'oro* was last struck). See also Frederic C. Lane and Reinhold C. Mueller *Money and Banking in Medieval and Renaissance Venice* (Baltimore and London 1985–97) I: *Coins and Moneys of Account* 229–30: usually 'better than 23¾ carats,' and thus often better in fineness than many Florentine florins.

In England, the standard mint weight, from the era of William the Conqueror to the monetary changes of Henry VIII in 1526, was the Tower Pound, which weighed 11.25 Troy ounces (349.914 grams) and contained 5400 Troy grains (480 grains to the ounce).[12] The earliest reliable documents for English silver coinage come from the reign of Henry III (r 1216–73), with more or less continuous mint accounts from 1235.[13] These and other documents indicate that 242 silver pennies were then struck from the Tower Pound – close to the Carolingian standard of 240 to the pound – so that each penny weighed 22.314 Troy grains (1.446 grams). With a fineness of sterling silver, it contained 1.337 grams of pure silver. In England as in most European countries, the historic monetary pattern was a periodic but continuous loss of the penny's silver contents. The final English silver coin issued (in February 1817), with the standard sterling silver fineness, had a weight of 7.273 Troy grains (0.471 grams), and thus it contained only 0.436 grams of fine silver.[14] Hence, over almost six centuries the English silver penny lost almost two-thirds – 64.95 per cent – of its fine silver contents.

That six-century reduction in silver contents was in fact considerably less than that incurred during the Henrician Great Debasement of 1542–53, which finally removed 83.10 per cent of the penny's silver contents.[15] Seven years after the Great Debasement had ceased (June 1553; see Table 1 part 1 below), Elizabeth I imposed a *renforcement* or 'strengthening' and partial restoration in the renowned Recoinage of November 1560. The traditional

* * * * *

12 CWE 1 332
13 Christopher E. Blunt and John D. Brand 'Mint Output of Henry III' *The British Numismatic Journal* 3rd series 39 (1970) 61–5, for London and Canterbury, including some partial accounts from July 1220. See also Mayhew 'Central Minting' (n5 above) 99–107.
14 Feaveayear *Pound Sterling* (n1 above) 439 Appendix III.ii; Blunt and Brand 'Henry III' (n13 above); Challis 'Mint Contracts' (n6 above) Appendix II
15 Between May 1542 and April 1551 the silver content of the English penny was reduced from 0.639 gram fine silver (as established by the recoinage of November 1526) to just 0.108 gram. In October 1551 the silver contents were restored to 0.477 gram, then reduced to 0.216 gram in December 1551. In June 1553 they were increased to 0.259 gram, in August 1553 to 0.475 gram, and then slightly increased again to 0.480 gram with the Elizabethan Recoinage of November 1560. The silver coinage then remained untouched for four decades, when, in July 1601, its fine silver content was reduced to 0.464 gram. Thereafter, the silver penny remained unchanged until the final debasement, of 6 February 1817, by which the penny's pure silver content was diminished to 0.436 gram. See Challis 'Mint Contracts' (n6 above) 721–58 and Table 1; Feaveayear *Pound Sterling* (n1 above) 435 Appendix I; 439 Appendix III.ii. See Table 1 part 2 below.

monetary standard of sterling silver (11 oz 2 dwt) was fully restored (from 3 oz of silver in June 1553, and then from 11 oz of silver in August 1553), but the silver penny's weight was restored to just 8.000 Troy grains (0.518 gram), much less than the 10.667 grain weight (0.691 gram) prescribed for Henry VIII's silver coinages from 1526 to 1542. Thus, combining changes in both weight and fineness, we find that Elizabeth's reformed coinage of 1560 contained only 75.12 per cent as much silver as did Henry VIII's coins from 1526 to the onset of the Great Debasement: 0.480 gram vs 0.639 gram pure silver. From the 1560 Elizabethan Recoinage to the final silver coinage issued in 1817, the penny lost only 9.17 per cent of its pure silver contents.[16]

That loss may usefully be compared with the 11.11 per cent reduction in the penny's fine silver contents that took place with Henry VIII's debasement of the silver coinage (but not his first debasement), in November 1526. As large as that may appear to be, it was much less than the 20.00 per cent reduction in fine metal contents that Edward IV had imposed in the previous silver debasement, of August 1464, and obviously far less than the 83.10 per cent reduction experienced during the Great Debasement of 1542–53.[17]

THE MOTIVATIONS FOR COINAGE DEBASEMENTS

The first major difference between the 1526 debasements and the Great Debasement of 1542–53 was the former's very modest reduction in the penny's fine silver contents (11.11 per cent) and the drastic, indeed unprecedented, reductions in the latter debasement (83.10 per cent), though the differences in the debasements of gold were more modest (see Tables 1 and 2 below). The second major difference was in what motivated them. The 1526 debasements were undertaken as a purely defensive monetary policy, designed to protect the English money supply and the economic viability of the royal mints. In sharp contrast, the Great Debasement was implemented and maintained for eleven years as an aggressive fiscal policy, designed to increase the king's mint profits.

* * * * *

16 Challis 'Mint Contracts' (n6 above) Appendix II; Feavearyear *Pound Sterling* (n1 above) 439 Appendix III.ii
17 See Table 1 part 1 below. For Edward IV's debasement and the associated monetary changes of 1464–5, see John H. Munro *Wool, Cloth and Gold: The Struggle for Bullion in Anglo-Burgundian Trade, 1340–1478* Centre d'Histoire Économique et Sociale (Brussels and Toronto 1973) 157–63; Christopher E. Blunt and C.A. Whitton 'The Coinages of Edward IV' *British Numismatic Journal* 5 (1948) 53–6; Nicholas Mayhew 'The Monetary Background to the Yorkist Recoinage of 1464–1471' *British Numismatic Journal* 44 (1974) 62–73.

1/ Aggressive fiscal policies and inflation

One of the most powerful incentives for medieval and early modern coinage debasements was the lust for greater mint revenues, derived from the ruler's princely prerogative to exact a seigniorage tax on minting. In an era when many princes found that their feudal incomes were severely limited (often by custom) and taxes difficult to impose and collect, seigniorage revenues often provided them with very substantial incomes.[18] As the fourteenth-century French philosopher Nicholas Oresme contended in his famous treatise *De Moneta*:

> I am of the opinion that the main and final cause why the prince pretends to the power of altering the coinage is the profit or gain from which he can get from it; it would otherwise be vain to make so many and so great changes ... Although all injustice is in a way contrary to nature, yet to make a profit from altering the coinage is specifically an unnatural act of injustice.[19]

Oresme, it should be noted, never admitted the possibility that some debasements were defensive in nature (for reasons to be explained later); nor did he observe that the necessity underlying most debasements now regarded as 'aggressive' was financing warfare (including defence).[20]

* * * * *

18 See Hans Van Werveke 'Currency Manipulation in the Middle Ages: The Case of Louis de Male, Count of Flanders' *Transactions of the Royal Historical Society* 4th series 31 (1949) 115–27, reprinted in Hans Van Werveke *Miscellanea mediaevalia* (n7 above) 255–67; Arthur J. Rolnick, François R. Velde, and Warren E. Weber 'The Debasement Puzzle: An Essay on Medieval Monetary History' *Journal of Economic History* 56/4 (December 1996) 789–808; Munro *Wool, Cloth, and Gold* (n17 above) 11–41 Appendix I, 202–08 Tables F–I. See also nn20–1 below.

19 Quotations from the editor's translations in Johnson *De Moneta* (n9 above) chapter 15 page 24 (first quotation) and chapter 16 page 25 (second quotation). The official title of Oresme's treatise is *Tractatus de origine, natura, jure, et mutacionibus monetarum*. On the importance of Oresme (c 1320–82) see Johnson ix–xviii; Spufford *Money and Its Use* (n4 above) 295–305.

20 Johnson *De Moneta* (n9 above) xi makes the point that a common motive for debasement was 'the wear of current coin,' although this was not mentioned by Oresme. See 437–40 below for the explanation. For the link between warfare and coinage debasements – beginning with Philip IV of France (r 1285–1314) – see Spufford *Money and Its Use* (n4 above) 289–318; and John Munro 'Coinage Debasements in Burgundian Flanders, 1384–1482: Monetary or Fiscal Policies?' in *Comparative Perspectives on History and Historians: Essays in Memory of Bryce Lyon (1920–2007)* ed David Nicholas, James Murray, and Bernard Bacharach (Kalamazoo, Mich) in press.

The medieval opposition to such aggressive coinage debasements stemmed from the all too visible consequences: rising prices – that is, inflation – and the consequent loss of purchasing power, especially for those living on fixed incomes. While wage earners almost always suffered from inflation, the most vocal, or rather the most effective, opponents of debasements were the landed nobility, whose rents and feudal dues were chiefly defined, by the later Middle Ages, in money-of-account, rather than in kind (harvest shares) and labour services. Some historians argue that inflation resulted from the combined responses of those producers, tradesmen, and merchants who sought to compensate for the loss of precious metals received in the debased coin by raising prices. But most economists, rightly noting that debasements increased the quantity of coins (of a given denomination), contend that inflation resulted instead from the increase in the money supply.

My own recent research indicates, however, that inflation, if almost always the inevitable result of coinage debasements, was never proportional to the extent of the debasement, or indeed as much as the monetary mathematics and the traditional Quantity Theory of Money would indicate. First, the common notion that, say, a ten per cent debasement would lead to a ten per cent increase in the coinage supply is fallacious, because it ignores the reciprocal nature of the two changes involved: that is, the reduction of the quantity of precious metal, silver or gold, in the money-of-account units (the penny, shilling, and pound) and the increase in the money-of-account value of the coinage struck from a pound of fine silver or gold.

The mathematical formula to express this reciprocal relationship is $\Delta T = [1/(1-x)] - 1$. In this formula, the letter T is the *traite*: the total money-of-account value of the coins struck from a pound of pure gold or silver, as the case may be.[21] The Greek letter Δ means the percentage rate of change in that *traite* value; and the letter x represents the percentage reduction in the gold or silver contents of the pound sterling (or, for silver, in the penny coin linked to the penny and pound in money-of-account). If we take the ex-

* * * * *

21 The alternative term 'mint equivalent' was first introduced in Gould *Great Debasement* (n1 above) 13 and has been used by many other Anglophone monetary historians since then. But the term used in all of the mint accounts of late medieval and early modern Low Countries is *traite*. The formula for computing its value is: *traite* = $N.V/F$ = number (N) of coins struck per pound times the coin's official face value (V) divided by the percentage fineness (F) of the coins. The comparable French term was *pied de la monnaie*. See Fournial *Histoire monétaire* (n3 above) 30–1 (with a much more complex formula).

ample of Henry VIII's silver debasement of November 1526, which reduced the fine silver contents of the penny by 11.111 per cent (one-ninth), and use that number is this equation, we find that: $[1/(1-0.111)]-1 = 0.125$, or 12.50 per cent. That means that the *traite* or total coined value of a Troy pound of silver increased by 12.50 per cent, a calculation that is verified in Tables 1 and 2 below.

This silver debasement probably did not, however, produce a corresponding 12.50 per cent increase in the aggregate English money supply, for several reasons. If the bimetallic mint ratio was not correspondingly adjusted – and it was not, in November 1526 – such a debasement would have led to some outflow of the gold coinage. At the same time, the debasement may not have succeeded in reminting all the former issues of silver coins, some of which may have been hoarded or exported. Furthermore, the effects of these coinage changes, and related economic changes (see below) on the supply of credit, an important component of the money supply, cannot possibly be calculated.

Nor may we assume, even if the aggregate money supply had increased by 12.50 per cent, that such an increase would have led to a proportional increase in the price level, as the traditional Quantity Theory of Money indicates. Any inflationary increase in the money supply may have been offset, to some degree, by both a reduction in the velocity or 'turnover' of the circulating units of money (coins and credit instruments) and by any subsequent increase in the volume of production and trade, especially in response to rising prices. Those changing relationships can be seen in the formula for the revised Quantity Theory of Money, $M.V = P.y$, in which the four components are calculated in annual aggregate 'national' terms. M is the aggregate value of the money supply, V is the income velocity of money circulation (the rate of turnover for a unit of money), y is the net value of total national output (and thus total national income), and P is the price level, usually measured by the Consumer Price Index (CPI), as the best measure of inflation.[22]

* * * * *

22 The letter Y is the Keynesian symbol for the value of the Net National Product or Net National Income, in the formula $Y = C+I+G+(X-M)$; it represents the sum of total consumption (C), government expenditures (G), investment (I), and the difference between the values of exports and imports ($X-M$). Lowercase y is Y deflated by the CPI. For a further analysis of debasement and inflation, see Munro *Wool, Cloth, and Gold* (n17 above) 11–41; Munro 'Coinage Debasements' (n20 above); Spufford *Money and Its Use* (n4 above) 289–318 ('The Scourge of Debasement').

The CPI used here for England is the well-known Phelps Brown and Hopkins 'Basket of Consumables' Index, with the base 100 calculated as the average of all prices in the basket for the period 1451–75.[23] In the case of the Great Debasement – if we allow three years for the monetary changes to have taken their full effect – the rise in the CPI that followed the overall reduction of 83.10 per cent of the penny's fine silver contents was 123.04 per cent: from the CPI index number of 163.21 in 1541 to the CPI of 364.03 in 1556. But the mathematical formula for the reciprocal relationship between a debasement and the rise in prices (discussed 433 above) produces a far higher expected inflation of 491.72 per cent. If we measure the inflation by five-year averages (quinquennial means), beginning with the quinquennium preceding the Great Debasement, we find that the CPI rose from a mean of 153.69 in 1536–50 to one of just 272.12 in 1551–5, an increase of only 77.06 per cent. This historical observation, contradicting a common view that any potential mercantile gains from debasement were eliminated by inflation,[24] helps to explain why so many debasements were successful in achieving their fiscal motives.

The mint master or 'moneyer' may also have had an incentive to promote debasements in that he could have augmented his revenues from the 'brassage' levy, the fee or tax that allowed the 'moneyer' to realize a profit, as the residual amount after recovering his costs: for wages, copper and other materials, mint dies and other tools.[25] But much evidence from not

* * * * *

23 E.H. Phelps Brown and S.V. Hopkins 'Seven Centuries of the Prices of Consumables Compared with Builders' Wage-Rates' *Economica*, *Economica* 23/92 (November 1956) 296–314, reprinted in E.H. Phelps Brown and Sheila V. Hopkins *A Perspective of Wages and Prices* (London 1981) 13–59. For a recent recalculation of all of their index numbers from their working papers, now located in the British Library of Economic and Political Science (LSE Archives), Phelps Brown Papers, Box 1a.324. see the Excel file online at: http://www.economics.utoronto.ca/munro5/ResearchData.html. The index numbers used here, based in part on the money-of-account values of the annual baskets, are from that file.

24 Rolnick, Velde, and Weber 'The Debasement Puzzle' (n18 above) especially 803–4. They rely principally on assertions in Harry Miskimin *Money, Prices, and Foreign Exchange in Fourteenth-Century France* Yale Studies in Economics 15 (New Haven 1963) 53–82 (especially 81–2), based on wheat prices, an analysis that fails to provide adequate proof for the view that inflation was normally proportional to the extent of coinage debasements and that such inflation ensued quickly after such debasements.

25 The capital costs of constructing and maintaining the mint were, however, normally borne by the ruler. Sometimes the ruler 'farmed' or sold the right to

just English but a wide range of continental records strongly indicates that in an 'aggressive' debasement the ruler's fiscal motives prevailed over those of the mint masters.

How debasements achieved these fiscal goals is rather complex. In essence, a properly designed debasement attracted more bullion to the mints by offering merchants a greater quantity of coins having the same nominal value than that received before the debasement. That 'offer' is known as the mint price, that is, the price that the mint pays to merchants who deliver bullion for coinage. In accounting terms, it is the total money-of-account value of the coins struck from a pound weight of pure silver (or gold), that is, the *traite* value (see 433 above), minus the total money-of-account value of the mint charges (the combined fees for seigniorage and brassage).

No debasement could have succeeded without such an increase in the mint price (in nominal or money-of-account values). Implicit in that condition is the requirement that the merchant had to receive coins with initially a greater purchasing power than that previously offered by the domestic mints and currently offered by competing foreign mints as well. So long as the merchants spent all those coins before the almost inevitable, if never proportionate, inflation ensued they would reap substantial profits. To the extent that inflation did ensue, the public paid the price – in what economists rightly call the seigniorage tax – for the gains reaped by the merchants and the prince. Since the prices of necessities – food, clothing, shelter – generally rose the most during such inflations, the poorer strata of society suffered the most.[26]

Most successful 'aggressive' debasements did result in dramatically increased mint outputs: first by requiring merchants to surrender their old

* * * * *

operate the mint to such 'moneyers,' but evidently not in medieval England. See Philip Grierson *Numismatics* (Oxford 1975); *Later Medieval Mints: Organisation, Administration, and Techniques* ed Nicholas J. Mayhew and Peter Spufford, Eighth Oxford Symposium on Coinage and Monetary History, British Archeological Reports International Series no 389 (Oxford 1988); Munro *Wool, Cloth, and Gold* (n17 above) 1–41.

26 The value of the debased coins that the merchant received also had to compensate him for the mintage fees on older coins delivered to the mint. See the Flemish evidence in Munro 'Coinage Debasements' (n20 above), and also in John Munro 'The Usury Doctrine and Urban Public Finances in Late-Medieval Flanders (1220–1550): Rentes (Annuities), Excise Taxes, and Income Transfers from the Poor to the Rich' in *La fiscalità nell'economia Europea, secoli XIII–XVIII / Fiscal Systems in the European Economy from the 13th to the 18th Centuries* ed Simonetta Cavaciocchi, Fondazione Istituto Internazionale di Storia Economica 'Francesco Datini,' Atti delle 'Settimane de Studi' e altri convegni no 39 (Florence 2008) 973–1026.

(and better) coins for recoinage, indeed by demonetizing them;[27] and second, by offering them such substantial gains from spending debased coins that they brought other, new, and often foreign sources of bullion to the ruler's mints. Obviously, the increased flow of bullion into the mint and thus its increased coinage outputs provided the prince with his chief source of gain, by augmenting his seigniorage revenues even if the rates remained unchanged. Most princes also sought a further gain by increasing their seigniorage rate; but higher rates necessarily lowered the mint price, thus reducing the incentive to bring bullion to the mint. A fundamental test to determine whether or not a debasement was aggressive (fiscal motive) or defensive (monetary motive) was whether or not the seigniorage or combined mint fees increased as a percentage of the bullion's value when coined (see Tables 1 and 2 below).

2/ Defensive monetary policies and Gresham's Law
The most obvious 'defensive' motive that many princes cited for debasement was protection against a neighbour's aggressive debasements, and in particular against what is known as Gresham' Law. As just noted, most successful aggressive debasements depended on luring not just domestic but foreign bullion and coins to the aggressor's mint. Such tactics proved all the more successful if the aggressor minted debased imitations of its neighbours' coins, and England had long been beset by influxes of debased counterfeit sterling coins, and even debased gold nobles.[28] If merchants succeeded in

* * * * *

27 Most medieval and early modern monetary ordinances implementing a debasement required, under penalty of law, the surrender of old coins, which were thus *demonetized*, to be reminted. But the fact that an old, pre-debasement penny would continue to circulate only as a penny, with the same value of 1d, meant that anyone spending old (good) pennies instead of spending new (debased) pennies would lose value: the potential loss in not receiving more 'bad' pennies for the old 'good' pennies. The merchant's alternative was to melt down the old coins as bullion and hoard them, or to export them to foreign mints or markets as bullion, in either case driving them out of circulation. See nn29–30 below on Gresham's Law.
28 Nicholas J. Mayhew 'The Circulation and Imitation of Sterlings in the Low Countries' in *Coinage in the Low Countries (800–1500): The Third Oxford Symposium on Coinage and Monetary History* ed Nicholas J. Mayhew, British Archeological Reports, BAR International Series 54 (Oxford 1979) 54–68; Feavearyear *Pound Sterling* (n1 above) 12–20; John Munro 'An Aspect of Medieval Public Finance: The Profits of Counterfeiting in the Fifteenth-Century Low Countries' *Revue belge de numismatique et de sigillographie* 118 (1972) 127–48, reprinted in John Munro *Bullion Flows and Monetary Policies in England and the Low Countries, 1350–1500* Variorum Collected Studies series CS 355 (Aldershot, Hampshire

spending counterfeit coins at the same face value as 'good' coins, they would then cull the good coins from circulation and export them, often melted down as bullion, to the offending mints abroad. Hence the essence of Gresham's Law: 'Bad money drives out good.'[29] That 'law', a commonplace observation attributed to the Tudor financial agent and diplomat Thomas Gresham (c 1519–79), was well known to fourteenth-century mint officials and was cited in most French and Flemish debasement ordinances, which were, of course, always presented as purely 'defensive' measures.[30] In the long run, the domestic consequence of Gresham's Law was a continuous deterioration of the circulating standard, that is, the mean (average) precious metal contents of the domestic coinage stock.

Such coinage deterioration was further exacerbated by both normal 'wear and tear' in circulation over many years and by the nefarious but all too common practices of 'clipping' and 'sweating' the coins. 'Clipping' was undertaken by using shears to cut off small pieces from the coin's normally imperfect edges; 'sweating' was undertaken by rapidly shaking a group of coins together inside a leather bag. Friction would remove some surface metal and cause it to adhere to the leather, and the metal could then be scraped and removed from the bag.

The success of these techniques was based on the crudity of medieval minting using the techniques of 'hammered coinages.' First, the moneyer placed the coin 'blank,' a disk cut from a thin sheet of alloyed metal, on the reverse die (bottom), and then he used the obverse die (top) as a hammer to imprint the required designs or inscriptions on each side of the blank. The hammered coin was then trimmed with shears to give it the approximate shape of a circle. The result was that no two 'good' coins were identical, nor were they observably different from bad 'clipped' or 'sweated' coins.[31]

* * * * *

and Brookfield, Vt 1992) essay no II; Munro 'A Maze of Medieval Monetary Metrology' (n3 above) 173–99.

29 See John Munro 'Gresham's Law' in *The Oxford Encyclopedia of Economic History* ed Joel Mokyr et al 5 vols (Oxford and New York 2003) II 480–1.

30 Munro *Wool, Cloth, and Gold* (n17 above) 28, 33, 35, 40, 44, 58, 60, 74, 87, 101, 150, 161, 169, 179; Munro 'Coinage Debasements' (n20 above). The principles of Gresham's Law can also be found in treatises of the Polish scientist Nicholas Copernicus (1473–1543), but not in the original texts of Oresme's *De Moneta*. As noted in Johnson *De Moneta* (n9 above) xii, the text in question has been added later, possibly by Flemish mint officials.

31 In 1662 the Royal Mint adopted the water-powered screw press, which created more perfectly circular coins with milled edges that could not be so readily clipped, sweated, or counterfeited; but these problems were not finally resolved until the adoption of Boulton's steam-powered coin press, developed

Several historians have estimated that England's medieval and early modern silver coinages lost about one per cent of their fine metal contents a year from a combination of counterfeiting, 'clipping,' 'sweating,' and normal wear and tear in circulation (not including unretrieved hoards, shipwrecks, etc). Nicholas Mayhew, with a more conservative estimate (0.2 per cent per annum), contended that during every decade in the fourteenth century 'seven tons of silver vanished into thin air.'[32] For the viability of the prince's mint, the true economic significance of continuous physical deterioration of the coinage from all such causes has to be understood in terms of the difference between the value of precious metals as bullion and as coins.[33]

Official, legal-tender coins could circulate only so long as they commanded an *agio* or premium in value over their bullion contents; and only so long as current coin issues commanded that *agio* would merchants continue to deliver bullion to the mint. This premium normally equalled the

* * * * *

between 1787 and 1810. See Thomas J. Sargent and François R. Velde *The Big Problem of Small Change* (Princeton and Oxford 2002) 53–64, 273–90. Continental experiments with mechanized screw presses and cylinder coin presses began in sixteenth-century France. Far higher costs of production explain why they did not readily supplant hammered coinage. In England, screw-press milled coins and hammered coins coexisted after 1662, and up to the Great Recoinage of 1696. See also Angela Redish 'The Evolution of the Gold Standard in England' *Journal of Economic History* 50/4 (December 1990) 789–805; George Selgin 'The Institutional Roots of Great Britain's "Big Problem of Small Change"' *European Review of Economic History* 14/2 (August 2010) 205–34.

32 For the higher estimate, see C.C. Patterson 'Silver Stocks and Losses in Ancient and Medieval Times' *Economic History Review* 2nd series 25/2 (May 1972) 205–35. For the lower estimates, see Sir John Craig *The Mint: A History of the London Mint from AD 287 to 1948* (Cambridge and New York 1953) xvi, 60; and Nicholas J. Mayhew 'Numismatic Evidence and Falling Prices in the Fourteenth Century' *Economic History Review* 2nd series 27/1 (February 1974) 1–15. See also Philip Grierson 'Coin Wear and the Frequency Table' *Numismatic Chronicle* 7th series 4 (1964) iii–xii, republished in Philip Grierson *Later Medieval Numismatics (11th–16th centuries): Selected Studies* Variorum Reprints no 19 (London 1979). He adds the factor of chemical erosion to precious-metal losses in circulation.

33 For the following arguments, see Feavearyear *Pound Sterling* (n1 above) 10–20; John Munro 'Bullionism and the Bill of Exchange in England, 1272–1663: A Study in Monetary Management and Popular Prejudice' in *The Dawn of Modern Banking* ed Fredi Chiappelli, Center for Medieval and Renaissance Studies, University of California (New Haven and London 1979) 169–239, reprinted in John Munro *Bullion Flows and Monetary Policies in England and the Low Countries, 1350–1500* Variorum Collected Studies series cs 355 (Aldershot, Hampshire and Brookfield, Vt 1992) essay no IV.

combined values of the mint charges (brassage and seigniorage). It was economically justified by the greater exchange value of coins over bullion in
obviating the significant transaction costs involved in weighing and assay-
ing bullion, including non-legal tender coins, to ascertain their true intrin-
sic precious metals contents. That cost-saving benefit in turn allowed coins,
with the prince's official stamp or insignia, to circulate by tale, that is, at
face value, and not by their bullion value.

When the currently circulating coins had suffered a continuous, ob-
servable diminution in their average silver contents, merchants responded
to that loss by discounting the entire coinage: not by refusing to accept coins
by tale, but by bidding up prices, including the market price of silver bullion, in money-of-account terms, thereby reducing and finally eliminating
the necessary premium on coinage.[34] In similar fashion, the bullion contents
in any newly minted coins of the official standard would have enjoyed a
relatively higher value, similarly eliminating the *agio*, so that, in accordance
with Gresham's Law, those newly minted coins would have been culled
from circulation and exported (or hoarded) as bullion.

Under these adverse circumstances, princes had no alternative but to
reduce the fine silver (or gold) contents of newly minted coins to the currently prevailing inferior standard of the circulating coins. They had to engage in a purely defensive coinage debasement, with low mintage fees as
well, lest precious metals be lost to foreign mints and their own mints become idle. That chronic phenomenon explains why virtually all European
coinages experienced long-term, continuous debasements until the era of
precious-metal commodity moneys came to an end in modern times.

The coinage changes of Henry VIII

The two debasements of 1526 were defensive in nature. They must be understood, first, in the light of an unusual monetary ordinance that Henry

* * * * *

34 To accept coins by 'tale' (face value), rather than by weight and fineness, with
high measurement costs, was to recognize the commercial advantage of coins
over bullion, especially the savings in transaction costs. The arguments in Rolnick, Velde, and Weber 'Debasement Puzzle' (n18 above) 800–1, to the effect
that coins were accepted only by weight (and presumably fineness), and not
by tale, are completely untenable, and not supported by any known monetary
historian other than Miskimin (see n24 above). For a more modified view,
by one of this article's co-authors, see Sargent and Velde *Big Problem of Small
Change* (n31 above) 16–19, 22, 322. For royal statutes requiring acceptance of
coins by tale, except those very badly impaired, see nn53–4 below.

had issued on 25 May 1522, one that abrogated a long-standing ban on foreign gold coins.[35] It permitted the free, legal-tender circulation of the most internationally prominent gold coins: 'ducats' (presumably both Venetian ducats and Florentine florins) and French 'crowns' (*écus à la couronne* and *écus à la couronne au soleil*).[36] A similar ordinance of 24 November 1522 authorized the legal-tender circulation of certain imperial gold coins: the *carolus* florin and some other unnamed 'base florins' (presumably both the Burgundian-Hapsburg Philippus florins and imperial Rhenish florins).[37] Possibly the ordinances on foreign gold coins were a requirement of Henry VIII's current if temporary anti-French alliance with the Hapsburg emperor,

* * * * *

35 For English prohibitions dating from 1275 against the importation of foreign coins, see Munro 'Bullionism and the Bill of Exchange in England' (n33 above) 216–20 Appendix A. That ban may not have been complete, for a statute of January 1504 (19 Henry VII c 5), had granted or recognized the legal-tender status of 'coyne of other landys nowe currant in this Realme for grotes or for foure pense [4d]' that were not clipped or impaired. See Great Britain, Records Commission *Statutes of the Realm* ed T.E. Tomlins, J. Raithby, et al 6 vols (London 1810–22) II 650.

36 Hughes and Larkin *Tudor Royal Proclamations* (n6 above) I no 88 (page 136). The Italian ducats and florins were given an exchange rate of 4s 6d sterling: they contained 3.536 to 3.559 grams of fine gold; the *écus au soleil* were given a rate of 4s 4d sterling: they contained 3.296 grams of fine gold; the *écus à la couronne*, a rate of 4s 0d sterling: they contained 3.275 grams of fine gold. See CWE 1 336 Appendix A; Challis *Tudor Coinage* (n1 above) 68; and Table 3 below.

37 Hughes and Larkin *Tudor Royal Proclamations* (n6 above) I no 95 (page 141). The exchange rates for Italian ducats and florins and French *écus* were confirmed at the rates given in the previous ordinance (in n36 above). The Hapsburg coin of 'fine gold,' called the *carolus*, was given a rate of 6s 10d sterling, which seems very high for the Carolus florin, which, furthermore, had a fineness of only 14 carats gold (at this time worth just 42d *groot* Flemish). Perhaps the ordinance meant the *real d'or*, of 23 carats 9.5 grains = 23.792 carats gold, containing 5.275 grams fine gold, and worth three times as much: 127d or 10s 7d *groot* Flemish. Thus the unnamed 'base florins' may refer to the actual *Carolus* florin, first struck in February 1521, at 14 carats, containing 1.700 grams fine gold, and the imperial Rhenish florins (of the Four Electors) of 18 carats 6 grains = 18.50 carats, containing 2.527 grams fine gold. These 'florins' were granted exchange rates of 2s 1d sterling and 3s 3d, respectively. The rate for the Rhenish florin, at 39 sterling, is confirmed in Erasmus' correspondence with his banker, Erasmus Schets, in Ep 1681, dated 17 March 1526 and Ep 1758, dated 2 October 1526. For a confirmation of the rate for the Carolus florin, at 25d sterling, see CWE 12 646–51 Table 3, especially 650. See also CWE 12 697–9 Table 17; CWE 8 349–50 Tables A and B; and CWE 1 314–18 and 338–39 Appendix A.

Charles v.[38] Those official rates for these foreign gold coins were recon-firmed in royal ordinances of 6 and 8 July 1525,[39] but the legal-tender status of foreign gold coins did not survive the second debasement of 1526.

HENRY VIII'S DEBASEMENT OF AUGUST 1526: GOLD AND THE GOLD COINAGES

An unusual, and indeed unprecedented, feature of Henry VIII's first de-basement, imposed on 22 August 1526, was that it involved only the gold coinage, and was not, as had always been the case in the past, combined with a debasement of silver. This debasement did not prescribe any physical change in the coins, but a revaluation that was (for reasons explained ear-lier) nevertheless a genuine debasement (see 427 above). That revaluation was the result of recommendations from a royal commission, established on 24 July 1526, under the leadership of Henry's chief minister, Thomas Cardi-nal Wolsey (1475–1530), with instructions 'for increasing the sterling value of the coinage to an equality with the rates of foreign currency.'[40]

The August 1526 ordinance required three steps to achieve this objec-tive.[41] The first was an increase in the value of all existing English gold de-nominations by ten per cent: the gold sovereign (1489), issued as the 'pound' coin, rose in value from 20s 0d (240d) to 22s 0d (264d) sterling; the ryal or rose noble, from 10s 0d (120d) to 11s 0d (132d); the angel-noble, from the traditional 6s 8d (80d) to 7s 4d (88d). The second was, not surprisingly, a less than commensurate increase in the value of legal-tender foreign gold coins: Italian ducats and florins from 4s 6d (54d) to 4s 8d (56d), an increase of 3.70 per cent, and the French *écus au soleil* from 4s 4d (52d) to 4s 6d (54d), an in-crease of 3.85 per cent. No mention was made of the other recently current

* * * * *

38 J.D. Mackie *The Earlier Tudors, 1485–1558* (Oxford 1957) 308–12 (treaties of 25 August and 24 November 1522). By 1523, England was at war with France, but the Anglo-Hapsburg alliance effectively ended with England's truce with France, 15 August 1525; see Hughes and Larkin *Tudor Royal Proclamations* (n6 above) 1 no 104 (page 147).

39 Hughes and Larkin *Tudor Royal Proclamations* (n6 above) 1 no 102 (page 145); no 103 (page 146)

40 *Letters and Papers, Foreign and Domestic, of the Reign of Henry VIII Preserved in the Public Record Office, the British Museum, and Elsewhere in England* ed J.S. Brewer, J. Gairdner, and R.H. Brodie, 36 vols (London 1862–1932) 4 part 1 (1870) no 2338 (page 1046)

41 Hughes and Larkin *Tudor Royal Proclamations* (n 6 above) 1 no 111 (pages 156–8); and Challis 'Mint Contracts' (n6 above) 720; Challis *Tudor Coinage* (n1 above) 67–9

gold coins. The third and most striking step was the introduction of a new English gold coin, the 'crown of the rose,' to have the 'like fineness, poise, and goodness' of the current French 'crown of the sun,' the *écu à la couronne au soleil*, and the same value (4s 6d).

Neither the fineness nor the weight of the new crown was otherwise specified. Its fineness was presumably, however, not that of the *écu*, 23 carats (95.833 per cent pure), but the same as that of all subsequent issues of English crowns, 22 carats (91.667 per cent pure).[42] The weight is more problematic, in the absence of any documentary evidence. Albert Feavearyear (1963) offered the first of two estimates: 54 grains (3.499 grams).[43] Ignoring that estimate, Christopher Challis (1967, 1978, 1992) offered a lower one of just 51 grains (3.305 grams).[44] Feavearyear's estimate is to be preferred on the grounds of logic: exactly 100 coins of 54 Troy grains could have been struck from a Tower Pound of 5400 Troy grains, whereas 51 Troy grains would have yielded the awkward number of 105.882 coins. Since the new crown was intended to supplant the French *écu au soleil*, Feavearyear's estimated weight is again more convincing because it is closer to that of the current French *écu* (as struck from July 1519), 3.439 grams. While the new English crown would have been very slightly heavier than the *écu*, its inferior fineness meant that it contained less fine gold: 3.208 grams (according to Feavearyear's weight estimate) vs 3.296 grams in the *écu* (Table 2 part 2, Table 3 below).[45] Challis's weight estimate would have meant a fine gold content of only 3.029 grams fine gold, far too low to allow the English crown to serve as an acceptable substitute for the *écu*.

In speculating on the origins of the August gold debasement, and the introduction of the English crown, Feavearyear contended that financing

* * * * *

42 Hughes and Larkin *Tudor Royal Proclamations* (n 6 above) I no 111 (page 157). See also the text in *Letters and Papers . . . of Henry VIII* (n40 above) 4 part 2 (1872) no 2423 (page 1085), for the royal proclamation of 22 August 1526 that 'a new coin is about to be made in England, called the crown of the rose, of the same weight and value,' 4s 6d, as that of the French 'crown of the sun.' See the text above and nn43–4 below.

43 Feavearyear *Pound Sterling* (n1 above) 438 Appendix III

44 Challis *Tudor Coinage* (n1 above) 311 Appendix III; Challis 'Mint Contracts' (n6 above) 720

45 For the 1519 *écu au soleil*, see Adrian Blanchet and Adolphe Dieudonné *Manuel de numismatique française* 2 vols (Paris: 1916; reissued 1988) II: *Monnaies royales françaises depuis Huges Capet jusqu'à la Révolution* chapter 20 page 314. Note that the weight and gold contents of the *écu au soleil* given in CWE 1 336 Appendix A are for the earlier version of 1475 (3.369 grams).

England's two-year war with France (1523–5) had required excessive precious-metal exports and very substantial loans from Flemish and Italian bankers, both of which had led to a fall in exchange rates and thus to a sharp rise in the market value of ducats and other foreign gold coins. According to this author, English merchants were then accepting ducats for as much as 5s 2d, well above the 4s 8d rate set in the August ordinance.[46]

The recent rise in the value of gold was a far more widespread and far more profound phenomenon than Feavearyear had indicated. Evidence for free-market gold prices at Antwerp during this period show that the value of gold had risen from a very stable £91.979 *groot* Flemish per kilogram in the period 1500 to 1511 to £95.785 *groot* Flemish per kilogram by 1520, by which time it had exceeded the official Hapsburg mint price (rising from 96.84 per cent to 100.85 per cent). Then it rose far more rapidly: to £112.461 *groot* Flemish per kilogram by 1525 (109.23 per cent of the official mint price), an increase of 17.23 per cent in just five years.[47] Such circumstances had already forced King Francis I of France to debase (revalue) his gold coinage in May and again in July 1519; and Emperor Charles V to do the same for the Low Countries' coinages in February 1521 (when he introduced the *Carolus* florin), and to raise the gold rates again in August 1521.[48] It is thus significant to observe, in Henry VIII's August 1526 ordinance, that

> in Flanders as in France, the price of money and gold ... is so much enhanced in the valuation thereof that not only strange [foreign] golds, as crowns and ducats, but also the gold of this realm, as nobles, half nobles, and royals, by merchants as well strangers resorting hither ... for the great gain and lucre that they find thereby daily, be transported and carried out of this realm to no little impoverishing thereof, and finally to the total exhausting and drawing out of all the coins out of the same, unless speedy remedy be provided in that behalf ...[49]

This is a traditional, pre-Gresham exposition of Gresham's Law.[50]

* * * * *

46 Feavearyear *Pound Sterling* (n1 above) 48–9
47 See CWE 12 644–5 Table 2; and Van der Wee *Antwerp Market* (n7 above) I 133–4 Table 16.
48 For France, see n45 above; for the Hapsburg Low Countries see CWE 8 348–50 Tables A and B.
49 Hughes and Larkin *Tudor Royal Proclamations* (n6 above) I no 111 (page 156)
50 Virtually the same rendition of Gresham's Law was used to justify Henry VIII's aggressive, profit-seeking debasement of 16 May 1544. See Hughes and Larkin *Tudor Royal Proclamations* I no 228 (page 327).

What was responsible for this rise in the relative value of gold (an increase in the bimetallic ratio)? There are only two possible reasons: either the gold supply had contracted or the silver supply had expanded. In either case, gold would have become relatively more expensive, as demonstrated when its value was given in any silver-based money-of-account. The answer is clearly the latter, in the light of the South German-Central European silver mining boom that had commenced in the 1460s and reached its peak in the late 1530s. As contended in earlier publications, that mining boom was produced by radical technological innovations in both mechanical and chemical engineering, which were devised in response to the deflationary 'silver famines' of the mid-fifteenth century. This region's mined output of pure silver more than quadrupled: from an annual mean of 12,973.44 kg in 1471–5 (when data first become available) to an annual mean peak of 55,703.84 kg in 1536–40 (minimum estimates based on available if incomplete data). The major event of this era was the opening of the vast Joachimsthal mines in Bohemia in 1516, which in 1521–5 produced an annual mean output of 9,703.24 kg of fine silver.[51]

As a reflection of this rise in the market's bimetallic ratio, that is, with the fall in the relative value of silver, the August 1526 ordinance raised the official Tower mint ratio in favour of gold from 11.158:1, which Edward IV had established in March 1465, to 12.274:1.[52]

* * * * *

51 John Munro 'The Monetary Origins of the "Price Revolution": South German Silver Mining, Merchant-Banking, and Venetian Commerce, 1470–1540' in *Global Connections and Monetary History, 1470–1800* ed Dennis Flynn, Arturo Giráldez, and Richard von Glahn (Aldershot, Hampshire and Brookfield, Vt 2003) 1–34, especially 8–9 Table 1.3. See also John Munro 'The Central European Mining Boom, Mint Outputs, and Prices in the Low Countries and England, 1450–1550' in *Money, Coins, and Commerce: Essays in the Monetary History of Asia and Europe (From Antiquity to Modern Times)* ed Eddy H.G. Van Cauwenberghe, Studies in Social and Economic History (Leuven 1991) 119–83; John Nef 'Silver Production in Central Europe, 1450–1618' *Journal of Political Economy* 49 (1941) 575–91; John Nef 'Mining and Metallurgy in Medieval Civilisation' in *The Cambridge Economic History of Europe* 2: *Trade and Industry in the Middle Ages* 2nd rev ed, ed M.M. Postan and E.E. Rich (Cambridge 1987) 691–761 (1st ed published in 1952). From Joachimsthal is derived the German monetary term *thaler*, the Dutch *daalder*, and the American *dollar*.
52 Computed from data in Tables 1 and 2 below. The bimetallic ratio expressed here is the ratio of the *traite* or coined value of a pound (or kilogram) of silver to the *traite* coined value of a pound (or kilogram) of gold. Since gold coins were valued in the silver-based sterling money-of-account, the only way to express a falling value of silver was by an increase in the money-of-account

HENRY VIII'S GOLD AND SILVER DEBASEMENTS OF NOVEMBER 1526
Henry VIII's government evidently soon decided that these monetary measures were insufficient. On 5 November 1526 Henry VIII issued a new monetary ordinance (repeating the version of Gresham's Law in the August 1526 ordinance), with four components to achieve the previously announced objective to 'provide an equality with the rates of foreign currency,' and hence to obviate 'Gresham's Law': another increase in the value of current English gold coins; the issue of new, higher valued English gold coins; the denial of legal-tender status to foreign gold coins; and previously mentioned debasement of the silver coinage (see 431 above).[53]

The value of current English gold coins was raised by another 2.27 per cent, for an over all increase of 12.50 per cent (one-eighth). Thus the value of the gold sovereign was raised to 22s 6d; that of the ryal or rose noble to 11s 3d; and that of the angel-noble to 7s 6d (see Table 2 part 2, Table 3 below).

The first new gold coin was the crown of the double rose, struck at 22 carats fineness, with a weight of 57.313 Troy grains (heavier than the former rose crown), and a pure gold content of 3.404 grams; it was given a value of 5s 0d sterling or 60d (compared to 4s 6d for the former single-rose crown). Half crowns were also struck, with proportional weights and values (2s 6d). The other new gold coin was the St George noble, which received the old noble's traditional value of 6s 8d sterling (three to the pound sterling) and its traditional fineness of 23.875 carats, but with a weight of only 71.111 Troy grains, thus containing 4.584 grams fine gold. Half nobles, with proportional weights and values, were also struck.[54]

The denial of legal-tender status to foreign gold coins, so that they no longer enjoyed fixed legal exchange rates, was based on the valid observation that so many 'ducats' were being struck, in various continental principalities, 'of divers fineness and weights' – that is, of inferior quality – that many people, 'not being expert in knowledge of the fineness ... might take great loss and be deceived therein.' No mention was made of

* * * * *

value of the gold coins – by a rise in the value of the sovereign, for example, from 20s to 22s sterling.

53 Hughes and Larkin *Tudor Royal Proclamations* (n6 above) I no 112 (pages 158–63). For the wide variety of ducats and florins, see CWE 1 314 and 339 Appendix A, Table D; and John Munro 'Money and Coinage: Western Europe' in *Europe 1450 to 1789: Encyclopedia of the Early Modern World* ed Jonathan Dewald et al (New York 2004) IV 174–84.

54 See also Challis 'Mint Contracts' (n6 above) 720; Challis *Tudor Coinage* (n1 above) 68–71.

the French gold coins, but clearly Henry VIII's government under Cardinal Wolsey would not have allowed them to compete with the new English double-rose crowns. Henceforth, all 'ducats as other coins of gold of outward parts not named' were to be treated as bullion, to be sold or traded 'at such value as the payer and receiver of them can agree' or delivered 'unto the King's mint' for recoinage. This provision was both novel and significant, since in the past royal ordinances had forbidden any free-market exchanges in foreign coins and stipulated that all such coins be delivered to the mint as bullion.[55] Equally remarkable was another provision permitting the Burgundian-Hapsburg silver 'carolus' or 'double placks' (struck from 1521) to 'be current in receipts and payments for 4d sterling the piece, as they now be.'[56]

The defensive nature of this first debasement, of the gold coinage, is revealed by the very modest increase in the official values of the gold coinages, which, according to the available evidence (given above) was still less than the current rise in the market prices for gold, at home and abroad. Further proof that the 1526 debasement of the gold coinages was purely defensive can be found in the exceptionally modest rate of mintage fees (Table 2 part 3 below): just 0.51 per cent, on all gold coins. The fees had declined from a rate of 12.00 per cent in Edward IV's initial gold debasement of August 1464, to a more modest fee of 4.63 per cent in Edward's second debasement of March 1465, and to a rate of 0.56 per cent set in November 1492, when the Tower mintage fees were last changed. The principle adopted was simple:

* * * * *

55 Hughes and Larkin *Tudor Royal Proclamations* (n6 above) I no 112 (page 161). On 27 March 1538, however, Henry VIII again permitted the legal-tender circulation of ducats, at 5s 0d sterling, of *écus au soleil*, at 4s 8d, and of other French *écus* (crowns) at 4s 0d sterling; ibidem no 178 (pages 261–2). See also Munro 'Bullionism and the Bill of Exchange' (n33 above) 187–96, 216–20 Appendix A; John Munro 'Billon – Billoen – Billio: From Bullion to Base Coinage' *Revue belge de philologie et d'histoire / Belgisch tijdschrift voor filologie en geschiedenis* 52 (1974) 293–305; reprinted in John Munro *Bullion Flows and Monetary Policies in England and the Low Countries, 1350–1500* Variorum Collected Studies series CS 355 (Aldershot, Hampshire and Brookfield, Vt 1992) essay no III.

56 Hughes and Larkin *Tudor Royal Proclamations* (n6 above) I no 112 (page 160). See also CWE 8 349–50 Tables A and B. Presumably the coin meant was the *réal* or 'double carolus' struck at almost *argent-le-roy* fineness (93.40 per cent pure), containing 2.875 grams pure silver, compared to the 2.556 grams of pure silver in the new English 4d groat. That privilege was not granted to the other Burgundian-Hapsburg silver coins, all of inferior fineness. The ordinance recommended, however, that all these Burgundian-Hapsburg coins be surrendered to the king's mint.

low mintage fees permitted a higher mint price, which should have attracted more gold bullion to the royal mints.

As Table 2 part 2 below also indicates, the two gold debasements, as measured by the diminution of grams of fine gold in the pound sterling, amounted to 9.091 per cent in August 1526 and a further 2.222 per cent in November 1526, for an overall reduction of 11.111 per cent. The seeming paradox that such a debasement led to a 12.50 per cent increase in the value of gold coins can now be readily resolved by the previously discussed formula relating debasements to reciprocal changes in money-of-account values (see 433 above): $\Delta T = [1/(1-x)]-1$, so that $[1/(1-0.111)]-1 = 0.125$, or 12.50 per cent.

As indicated earlier, this second debasement, of November 1526, involved not just gold, but also the silver coinages. It reduced their pure silver contents, by weight alone – retaining the traditional sterling silver fineness – by one-ninth: 11.111 per cent (Table 1 part 1 below). We can more readily understand its purely defensive nature when we realize that more than sixty years had passed since the last silver debasement and recoinage of August 1464, under Edward IV, during which time all the previously discussed circumstances – 'clipping,' 'sweating,' counterfeit coin imports, and the operations of Gresham's Law – had combined to diminish the average silver contents of currently circulating coins, undoubtedly by well more than ten per cent. Indeed, as early as 1504, Henry VII's Parliament had contended, in enacting a statute on the coinage, that

> his Coyne, and specially of Sylver, is sore ympeyred as well by clippyng therof as counterfettyng of the same and by bryngyng into this Realme of the Coyne of Irelond, by occasion wherof gret rumour and variance daly incresith amongis his subjettis for takyng & refusyng of the same.

The statute declared that all legal-tender coins, 'beyng Sylver and not clypped, mynesshed, or otherwyse empeyred, except for reasonable weryng, albeit they be cracked,' were to be 'curraunt through all the seid Realme for the somme as they were coyned for' (that is, at face value, 'by tale').[57] Such complaints and corresponding measures can be found in subsequent royal proclamations, up to the 1526 debasements.[58]

A further test revealing the purely defensive nature of the silver debasement of November 1526 is once more the mintage fees, set at the ex-

* * * * *

57 *Statutes of the Realm* (n35 above) II 650, statute 19 Henry VII c 5
58 Hughes and Larkin *Tudor Royal Proclamations* (n6 above) I no 54 (pages 60–1, no 88 (page 136), no 95 (page 141), nos 102–03 (pages 145–7)

ceptionally low rate of 2.22 per cent (Table 1 part 3 below).[59] In contrast, when Edward IV debased the silver coinage in 1464, he had exacted a high mintage fee of 12.00 per cent, one that indicates that even though his debasement had also been the first in over fifty years (since 1411–12), it was primarily an aggressive, profit-seeking measure. Over the next three decades, however, Edward IV and then Henry VII were forced to lower the mintage fees, by stages – to 2.67 per cent by 1492 – in order to raise the mint price and thus to attract more bullion.

BIMETALLIC MINT RATIOS AND THE NEW TROY POUND
Remarkably, when we compare the gold and silver coinages that Henry VIII struck in his debasements of August and November 1526 with the previous coinage issues, those that Edward IV had struck in his debasements of 1464–5, we find that the overall percentage debasement of Henry's gold coinages (that is, the total reduction in the gold contents of the pound sterling in money-of-account) was precisely identical to the percentage debasement of the silver coinage (that is, the reduction in the penny's silver contents): 11.111 per cent for each of the two coinages. Consequently, the November 1526 mint ordinances nullified the previous change in the bimetallic ratio (to 12.274, in August 1526), thereby restoring the ratio that Edward IV had established in March 1465, that is, 11.158:1 (see 445 above). While the bimetallic ratios were slightly altered during the rapid and often drastic changes the Great Debasement of 1542–53, that same ratio of 11.158:1 was re-established with Elizabeth I's Recoinage of November 1560, and it remained unchanged until the new coinages of 1601.[60]

This is one of the most puzzling features of the 1526 debasements, for the first one had been undertaken, in August, with the intention of altering the mint ratio more in favour of gold in order to retain gold in England. The bimetallic mint ratio is, in fact, an aspect of Gresham's Law. For if the official mint ratio undervalues one metal and thus overvalues the other metal in relation to market and foreign mint ratios, the relatively cheaper metal (here, silver) will drive out the other (gold). Or more simply, merchants will choose to have each metal coined in the mints that offer higher values. Along

* * * * *

59 Only the total mintage fees are supplied in this table, because most of the English Tower mint accounts and mint indentures provide only that total, not separate rates for brassage and seigniorage.
60 Calculations of the official bimetallic mint ratios, based on mint data supplied in Challis 'Mint Contracts' (n6 above) 720–57, indicate a rise from 12.109 in 1601 to 13.363 in 1612, to 13.348 in 1623, to 14.485 in 1660, to 15.210 in 1718 (remaining at this level until 1815).

with the undisputed importance of the Central European silver-copper mining boom, and then, from the 1550s, of the even greater silver inflows from Spanish America, England's unaltered bimetallic mint ratio helps to explain why England, which had minted predominantly gold before 1526, came to mint predominantly silver thereafter, especially as the market ratio continued to rise in favour of gold.[61] In 1521–5 silver constituted only 38.96 per cent of the total value of English mint outputs; in 1531–5, 68.41 per cent; and in the second half of the century, silver accounted, on average, for 82.84 per cent of the total value of steadily mounting mint outputs (even well after the end of the Great Debasement).[62]

Another significant feature of the mint and monetary ordinances of November 1526 was the change from the traditional, historic Tower Pound, containing 11.25 Troy ounces (5400 Troy grains = 349.914 grams), to the Troy pound, with 12.00 Troy ounces (5760 Troy grains = 373.242 grams).[63] Possibly such a change, relatively minor though it may have been, helped to obscure the extent of the coinage debasements. In the tables for this study, all of the pre-1526 monetary and mint data have been converted from the Tower pound to the Troy pound, to permit direct comparisons of the monetary changes from 1464.

THE GREAT DEBASEMENT OF 1542–53: SOME NEW OBSERVATIONS

From November 1526, England's gold and silver coinages, mintage fees, and mint prices remained unchanged until the onset of Henry VIII's Great Debasement in May 1542. Since Erasmus died almost six years earlier, in July 1536, the Great Debasement cannot be the focus of this study. But there remains, surprisingly, considerable confusion about when it began as a profit-

* * * * *

61 See John Munro 'South German Silver, European Textiles, and Venetian Trade with the Levant and Ottoman Empire, c. 1370 to c. 1720: A Non-Mercantilist Approach to the Balance of Payments Problem' in *Relazioni economiche tra Europa e mondo islamico, secoli XIII–XVIII / Europe's Economic Relations with the Islamic World, 13th–18th Centuries* ed Simonetta Cavaciocchi, Fondazione Istituto Internazionale di Storia Economica 'Francesco Datini,' Atti delle 'Settimana di Studi' e altri convegni no 38 (Florence 2007) 907–62; K.N. Chaudhuri 'Treasure and Trade Balances: the East India Company's Export Trade, 1660–1720' *Economic History Review* 2nd series 21 (December 1968) 480–502.
62 See Munro 'Monetary Origins' (n51 above) 22–3 Table 1.6. For the Central European silver mining outputs, see 8 Table 1.3; for the outputs of the Spanish American silver mines and for imports of silver into Seville, see 4–5 Table 1.2.
63 CWE 1 332. The Troy pound was first mentioned in a parliamentary statute of 1414: 2 Henry IV Stat 2 c 4, concerning the Goldsmiths, in *Statutes of the Realm* (n35 above) II 188.

seeking enterprise: in 1542 or in 1544. That debate needs to be resolved. Furthermore, the significance of the 1526 monetary changes as a purely defensive debasement can be better understood by demonstrating that the aggressive, profit-seeking aspects of the Great Debasement were present from very onset of the coinage changes, in May 1542.

The best known authorities on the Great Debasement are Frederick Dietz, Albert Feavearyear, Christopher Challis, and J.D. Gould.[64] Gould evidently followed Dietz in contending that the initial change in the silver coinage, undertaken from 16 May 1542, was relatively minor. In their incorrect view, it reduced the silver fineness from the traditional sterling silver standard of 11 oz 2 dwt to 10 oz (with 2 oz of copper).[65] Dietz explicitly stated that 'this debasement was not a financial expedient; it was defensible on purely economic grounds, as a necessary measure to prevent the export of gold and silver from England.'[66] Gould states that this 'first debasement ... offered no incentive to remint silver coins of the 1526–42 issue, except on Government account.'[67]

Gould's statement, published in 1970, surprisingly ignored earlier criticisms of Dietz's views published in Feavearyear's *Pound Sterling* (1963) and in Challis's 'Debasement of the Coinage' (1967).[68] Gould evidently also ignored the relevant mint documents. To be sure, the mint ordinance does seem to indicate a new silver fineness of 10 oz. As Feavearyear notes, however, the mint instructions (indenture) for this date explicitly state that the new silver coinage was to be 'of the standard of 10 oz sterling silver and 2 oz of allaye' – that is, not 10 oz of pure silver, but silver of only 92.50 per cent purity.[69] For some inexplicable reason, however, Feavearyear then

* * * * *

64 See the sources cited in n1 above.
65 Gould *Great Debasement* (n1 above) 11 Table 1, text on page 43; Dietz *English Government Finance* (n1 above) 175
66 Dietz *English Government Finance* (n1 above) 175–6. That incorrect view was endorsed in Mackie *Earlier Tudors* [n38 above] 412. The only partial justification for Dietz's statement is that (according to Feavearyear *Pound Sterling* [n1 above] 51) the current market price for silver was 3s 8½d per ounce, compared to a mint price of 3s 8d, by the 1526 indenture. Nevertheless, all the evidence presented here indicates that this debasement was aggressive, and marked the true beginning of the Great Debasement.
67 Gould *Great Debasement* (n1 above) 43
68 Feavearyear *Pound Sterling* (n1 above) 50–2; Challis 'Debasement' (n1 above) 441–66, especially 442. There is no justification, however, for Feavearyear's assertion that 'the silver money was not coined according to the [mint] indenture.'
69 See Feavearyear *Pound Sterling* (n1 above) 52. The quotation, however, is from *Letters and Papers ... of Henry VIII* (n40 above) 19 part 1 (1903) li (Preface):

concluded that pure silver fineness was 'only 8.3 oz in the pound' (69.167 per cent fine), an impossibly low estimate, whose calculation is not explained.[70] Since sterling silver already contained 18 dwt (of 20) copper (7.5 per cent of 12 oz), this mixture, by one calculation – simply by adding 2 oz of copper and displacing 2 oz of silver, for a total of 2 oz 18 dwt copper – would have produced an alloy of 24.167 per cent copper and thus only 75.833 per cent pure silver, that is, with a silver fineness of 9 oz 2 dwt copper.[71] Alternatively, 10 oz of sterling silver plus 2 oz copper could be seen as 77.0833 per cent pure silver, that is, $11.10/12.0 * 10/12 = 0.925 * 0.8333 = 0.770833$, which converts to a measure of 9 oz 5 dwt fine silver.

Challis, who treated the mint documents with far more care than either Dietz or Feavearyear, stated that both interpretations are possible, suggesting that the mint instructions may have been deliberately ambiguous to disguise the extent of the debasement. He chose the first estimate, of 9 oz 2 dwt silver, one that he retained in all his subsequent publications on Tudor coinage.[72] But this lower estimate is far too close to that established in the next step of the Great Debasement, implemented on 28 May 1544, which reduced the fineness to 9 oz pure silver (75.00 per cent pure) – a fineness, it must be noted, substantially higher than Feavearyear's inexplicable estimate for the 1542 debasement.

* * * * *

'Note on the Debasement of the Currency,' declaration of the account of Sir Martin Bowes and Thomas Skipwith. Feavearyear's citation of this source is inaccurate.

70 Feavearyear *Pound Sterling* (n1 above) 52. He notes, from the mint document *Letters and Papers . . . of Henry VIII* 19 part 1 (n69 above) lii (34 Henry VIII), that 5,513 Troy lb of copper alloy were used to strike 22,053 Troy lb of the debased coinage, an amount equal to 25 per cent of the total, thus indicating a fineness of at least 9 oz fine silver.

71 Challis, 'Debasement' (n1 above) 442, citing another mint document (National Archives [Public Record Office], Exchequer, E101/303/8): 'every pound weight of these moneys of silver aforesaide shall holde tenne ounces of sterling silver and twoo ounces of alloye in every pownde weight of troy aforesaide. That is to say to hold twoo ounces of alloye more in the pound weight of troy thanne doothe the sterling money . . . before the date of this indenture.' See also Challis *Tudor Coinage* (n1 above) 83–5, and 312 Appendix III; Challis 'Mint Contracts' (n6 above) 721. As Challis notes, the Great Debasement was preceded by debasements of the Irish silver coinages in March 1536 and July 1540.

72 Challis 'Debasement' 442–3, *Tudor Coinage* 83–6, 312 (mint indenture), and 'Lord Hastings to the Great Silver Recoinage' 288 (all n1 above); and Challis 'Mint Contracts' (n6 above) 721

The major problem with Challis's lower estimate for the 1542 coinage, as may be seen in Table 1 part 3 below (penultimate column), is the adverse mint price calculated for that fineness, for it is *higher* than that offered in the next debasement, of May 1544. In other words, the 1544 mint price would have been uncompetitively *lower* than the 1542 mint price: £2.619 sterling for a Troy pound of pure silver in 1544 vs £2.637 per pound Troy in 1542. But the mint price calculated for the second estimate, a 1542 coinage of 9 oz 5 dwt, would have been suitably lower than that subsequently offered in 1544: £2.619 lb sterling for a Troy pound of pure silver in 1544 vs £2.595 lb sterling in 1542. The 'golden rule,' so to speak, for the success of any coinage debasement is that the mint price for bullion offered to merchants for any newly debased coinage had to be higher than that offered by the previous mint indenture, and also higher than the current market price for bullion.[73] If we accept the second and higher estimate for the fine silver contents of the 1542 coinage, we can see from Table 1 part 1 below that the Great Debasement had begun, in May 1542, with a reduction of 21.88 per cent in the silver contents of the penny (coin) and pound sterling (money-of-account), almost double the reduction imposed on the 1526 coinage (and also greater than that in Edward IV's 1464 debasement). The 1542 debasement of the gold coinage, as indicated in Table 2 part 1 below, was a more modest 9.69 per cent: that is, a reduction from 13.752 grams to 12.420 grams of fine gold in the pound money-of-account based on the gold sovereign, the rose noble, and the angel-noble.

Further evidence that the Great Debasement had commenced as early as May 1542 as a profit-seeking, aggressive, fiscal enterprise, and not as a merely defensive measure, can be found in the mintage fees. For silver, as Table 1 part 3 below demonstrates, the total mintage fees prescribed in 1542 were 16.67 per cent of the metal coined (per Troy pound of silver), compared to just 2.22 per cent in the defensive debasement of 1526. By the fourth debasement, of April 1545, the mintage fees on silver had risen to 61.11 per cent; and thereafter, until 15 April 1551, they remained above 50 per cent with only one exception (45.83 per cent in July 1550 debasement).

* * * * *

73 See 436 above. That dictum does not hold with the reverse coinage change, a *renforcement*. As Table 1 part 3 below also indicates, the mint price offered merchants with Elizabeth I's Recoinage of November 1560, at the equivalent of £3.162 for a Troy pound of pure silver, was lower than that previously offered, £3.191 (with debased coinage). That explains why a *renforcement* was so much more difficult to achieve than a debasement, requiring an effective ban and demonetization of all previous coin issues.

After the Great Debasement for silver effectively ceased in June 1553, the mintage fees suddenly and precipitously dropped to just 2.50 per cent, and did not change with the Elizabethan Recoinage of November 1560.

For the several debasements of the gold coinages (for which the worst degree of fineness, in 1546–7, was 20 carats = 83.33 per cent fine), the mintage fees were more modest than those for silver, though still high enough to justify labelling them as aggressive. As Table 2 part 3 below indicates, for the first debasement, of May 1542, the mintage fees exacted were 4.17 per cent of the gold metal coined, compared to just 0.51 per cent charged in the 1526 gold coinages (that is, 8.2 times higher). Those mintage fees peaked at exactly 15.00 per cent of the gold metal coined in 1546, fell to just 3.33 per cent in 1547–8, temporarily rose to 5.73 per cent in 1550, but then fell to 0.38 per cent in 1551. From the end of the Great Debasement in 1553 up to and including the Elizabethan Recoinage of November 1560, the mintage fees were a commendably modest 0.56 per cent for coins of traditional purity, 23.875 carats, and 0.61 per cent for those of what became the permanent alternative standard of 22 carats (91.167 per cent fine), including crowns and, later, guineas.[74]

There is no mystery about the causes of the Great Debasement: the fiscal necessity of financing Henry VIII's many wars, especially those with France, when other royal revenues, including those gained from land sales following the dissolution of the monasteries (1536–40), had been virtually exhausted.[75] According to Challis's estimates, now widely accepted, the net profits from the Great Debasement (from the mints of Canterbury, Southwark, York, and London Tower I and Tower II, but excluding the Irish mints) amounted to at least £1,157,407 sterling, as recorded in the accounts of the Under-Treasurers, and a further profit £94,418.913 (again excluding the Irish mints), as indicated in the accounts of the accounts of the High Treasurer. If the Irish mints are included, the total mint profits from July 1542 to Michaelmas 1551 amount to about £1,285,000.[76]

* * * * *

74 From October 1551, gold sovereigns, angel-nobles, and rose nobles ('ryals') were struck in two finenesses, 23.875 and 22.00 carats, but crowns were struck at only 22 carats. The last gold coins to be struck at 23.875 carats were issued in July 1660; and thereafter only coins of 22 carats were issued; Challis 'Mint Contracts' (n6 above) 720–58.

75 See Joyce Youings *The Dissolution of the Monasteries* Historical Problems series no 14 (London 1971); Mackie *Earlier Tudors* (n138 above) 370–401 . For the costs of war with France and Scotland, see Dietz *English Government Finance* (n1 above) 137–59, 178–84; Mackie *Earlier Tudors* 405–11.

76 Challis 'Debasement' (n1 above) 452–3 Tables 3 and 5, and 457–66 Appendix

The singular importance of these mint profits can be better appreciated by comparing them with Challis's estimates of total revenues from taxation for the period 1544–51 (excluding clerical 'first fruits and tenths'): £976,000, to which may be added another £1,048,255 from rents and sales of crown lands (1544–54). But even that total, of all revenues, did not match estimated military expenditures for this period – about £3.5 million sterling – so that Henry VIII was forced to engage in extensive foreign borrowing, principally in the Low Countries.[77]

Even though the Great Debasement began after Erasmus' death, a correct understanding of its major features provides us with the proper perspective on the earlier monetary changes of Henry VIII in 1526 and also those of Edward IV in 1464–5. By comparing both sets of Henry VIII's monetary changes with those of Edward IV (see 431, 445, 447–9, 453 above), we can see that the Great Debasement was not the only 'aggressive' debasement

* * * * *

Table 6 (detailed accounts for each mint, and each minting period). These figures are vastly greater than Feavearyear's total estimate of the profits: just £227,378.5875, in *Pound Sterling* (n1 above) 62. But these statistics cover only the years 1542–7 and (according to Challis) are based on only a small sample of the accounts. Dietz *English Government Finance* (n1 above) 177, 180, 191 had offered a far higher total estimate of the debasement profits than did Feavearyear, but nevertheless a lower estimate than that supplied by Challis. According to Dietz, the sum of £363,000 was acquired under Henry VIII (1544–7); another £537,000 under Edward VI (1547–January 1551), 'more than the revenues from the court of Augmentation for the same period'; and finally, another £114,500 in mint profits, from 1 Jan to 31 July 1551 – for a total net profit of £1,014,500 sterling. For Dietz's estimates of total revenues and expenditures in this period, see 215–28 Appendix Tables I–VII. See Challis 'Debasement' 454 for a critique of Dietz' statistics on the debasement profits. Gould *The Great Debasement* (n1 above) 187 states that his book 'has eschewed comment on the fiscal aspect of the debasement of the coinage,' since he accepts Challis's statistics, differing only on those concerning the conversion of testoons in 1548 (see 187–98 Appendix E). For Challis's convincing reply and defence of his calculations, see 'The Conversion of Testoons: a Restatement' *British Numismatic Journal* 50 (1980) 67–80; and Challis *Tudor Coinage* (n1 above) 96–100. For another perspective on total mint outputs and profits, but surprisingly only for the period of 1544–51, see Challis 'Lord Hastings to the Great Silver Recoinage' (n1 above) 232–44. For this period, Challis estimates that the Great Debasement produced a silver coinage output of 1,091,666.375 Troy pounds, with a face value of £3,015,895.125, and a gold coinage output of 44,015.656 Troy pounds, with a face value of £1,323,281. See also Challis and Harrison 'Estimate of the Production of Gold and Silver Coinage' (n1 above) 821–35.

77 Challis 'Debasement' (n1 above) 454–5 (without explaining why the comparison periods are not identical); Mackie *Earlier Tudors* (n38 above) 412–13

in English monetary history, as is so often contended. Furthermore, we can gain a far better understanding of Henry VIII's two earlier debasements of 1526, so neglected by historians, but so important in this period of Erasmus' life and career, as purely defensive monetary changes, to be properly compared with the English debasements of 1351 and 1411, though not those of 1464–5.[78]

* * * * *

78 For the earlier English debasements of 1351 and 1411, see John Munro 'Mint Policies, Ratios, and Outputs in England and the Low Countries, 1335–1420: Some Reflections on New Data' *The Numismatic Chronicle* 141 (1981) 71–116, reprinted in John Munro *Bullion Flows and Monetary Policies in England and the Low Countries, 1350–1500* Variorum Collected Studies series cs 355 (Aldershot, Hampshire and Brookfield, Vt 1992) essay no v; Munro *Wool, Cloth, and Gold* (n17 above) 11–41, 58–63, 160–73; Munro 'Maze of Medieval Monetary Metrology' (n3 above) 173–9.

TABLE 1

ENGLISH SILVER COINAGES: FROM 1464 (EDWARD IV) TO 1560 (ELIZABETH I)
Composition of the silver penny, with mint charges and mint prices based on the Troy pound

PART 1: FINENESS AND WEIGHT

date of penny	fineness of silver coin			weight of silver penny		
	ounces (out of 12 oz)	penny-weight (out of 20 dwt)	per cent fine	number per Troy pound[a]	weight in Troy grains[b]	weight in grams
1464 Aug 13	11	2	92.50	480.00	12.000	0.778
1465 Mar 6	11	2	92.50	480.00	12.000	0.778
1466 Sep 29	11	2	92.50	480.00	12.000	0.778
1467 Sep 29	11	2	92.50	480.00	12.000	0.778
1470 Oct 23	11	2	92.50	480.00	12.000	0.778
1471 Apr 14	11	2	92.50	480.00	12.000	0.778
1492 Nov 20	11	2	92.50	480.00	12.000	0.778
1526 Nov 5	11	2	92.50	540.00	10.667	0.691
1542 May 16[c]						
(Gould)	10	0	83.33	576.00	10.000	0.648
(Challis)	9	2	75.83	576.00	10.000	0.648
(Munro)	9	5	77.08	576.00	10.000	0.648
1544 May 28	9	0	75.00	576.00	10.000	0.648
1545 Mar 27	6	0	50.00	576.00	10.000	0.648
1546 Apr 1	4	0	33.33	576.00	10.000	0.648
1547 Apr 5	4	0	33.33	576.00	10.000	0.648
	4	0	33.33	576.00	10.000	0.648
1548 Feb 16	4	0	33.33	576.00	10.000	0.648
1549 Jan 24	8	0	66.67	1152.00	5.000	0.324
1549 Apr 12	6	0	50.00	864.00	6.667	0.432
	6	0	50.00	864.00	6.667	0.432

TABLE 1 (continued)

ENGLISH SILVER COINAGES: FROM 1464 (EDWARD IV) TO 1560 (ELIZABETH I)
Composition of the silver penny, with mint charges and mint prices based on the Troy pound

PART 1: FINENESS AND WEIGHT (continued)

date of penny	fineness of silver coin			weight of silver penny		
	ounces (out of 12 oz)	penny-weight (out of 20 dwt)	per cent fine	number per Troy pound[a]	weight in Troy grains[b]	weight in grams
1550 Feb 1	4	0	33.33	576.00	10.000	0.648
1550 July	6	0	50.00	864.00	6.667	0.432
	6	0	50.00	864.00	6.667	0.432
1551 Apr 14	3	0	25.00	864.00	6.667	0.432
1551 Oct 5	11	1	92.08	720.00	8.000	0.518
1551 Dec 17	4	0	33.33	576.00	10.000	0.648
1553 June 11	4	0	33.33	480.00	12.000	0.778
	3	0	25.00	480.00	12.000	0.778
1553 Aug 20	11	0	91.67	720.00	8.000	0.518
1557 June 28	11	0	91.67	720.00	8.000	0.518
1558 Dec 31	11	0	91.67	720.00	8.000	0.518
1560 Nov 8	11	2	92.50	720.00	8.000	0.518

NOTES

   a Troy pound cut to 5760 Troy grains = 373.242 grams
   b Troy grain = 0.648 grams
   c The fineness of the silver penny, as debased and struck in May 1542, is given according to the estimates of Gould *The Great Debasement*, Challis 'Mint Contracts' (see the list of sources 476 below), and my own best estimate.

TABLE 1 (continued)

PART 2:   PURE SILVER CONTENTS AND VALUES

date of penny	grams pure silver in d	per cent change in silver contents	grams pure silver in £	silver index (1526 = 100)	traite value of Troy lb silver[a]		
					given alloy in £ sterling	given alloy in shillings	0.925 fine in £ sterling
1464 Aug 13	0.719	−20.00	172.624	112.50	2.000	40.000	2.000
1465 Mar 6	0.719	0.00	172.624	112.50	2.000	40.000	2.000
1466 Sep 29	0.719	0.00	172.624	112.50	2.000	40.000	2.000
1467 Sep 29	0.719	0.00	172.624	112.50	2.000	40.000	2.000
1470 Oct 23	0.719	0.00	172.624	112.50	2.000	40.000	2.000
1471 Apr 14	0.719	0.00	172.624	112.50	2.000	40.000	2.000
1492 Nov 20	0.719	0.00	172.624	112.50	2.000	40.000	2.000
1526 Nov 5	0.639	−11.11	153.444	100.00	2.250	45.000	2.250
1542 May 16[b]							
(Gould)	0.540	−15.54	129.598	84.46	2.400	48.000	2.880
(Challis)	0.491	−23.14	117.934	76.86	2.400	48.000	2.880
(Munro)	0.499	−21.88	119.878	78.13	2.400	48.000	2.880
1544 May 28	0.486	−2.70	116.638	76.01	2.400	48.000	2.960
1545 Mar 27	0.324	−33.33	77.759	50.68	2.400	48.000	4.440
1546 Apr 1	0.216	−33.33	51.839	33.78	2.400	48.000	6.660
1547 Apr 5	0.216	0.00	51.839	33.78	2.400	48.000	6.660
	0.216	0.00	51.839	33.78	2.400	48.000	6.660
1548 Feb 16	0.216	0.00	51.839	33.78	2.400	48.000	6.660
1549 Jan 24	0.216	0.00	51.839	33.78	4.800	96.000	6.660
1549 Apr 12	0.216	0.00	51.839	33.78	3.600	72.000	6.660
	0.216	0.00	51.839	33.78	3.600	72.000	6.660
1550 Feb 1	0.216	0.00	51.839	33.78	2.400	48.000	6.660
1550 July	0.216	0.00	51.839	33.78	3.600	72.000	6.660
	0.216	0.00	51.839	33.78	3.600	72.000	6.660

TABLE 1 (continued)

ENGLISH SILVER COINAGES: FROM 1464 (EDWARD IV) TO 1560 (ELIZABETH I)
Composition of the silver penny, with mint charges and mint prices based on the Troy pound

PART 2: PURE SILVER CONTENTS AND VALUES (continued)

| date of penny | grams pure silver in d | per cent change in silver contents | grams pure silver in £ | silver index (1526 = 100) | traite value of Troy lb silver | | |
					given alloy in £ sterling	given alloy in shillings	0.925 fine in £ sterling
1551 Apr 14	0.108	−50.00	25.920	16.89	3.600	72.000	13.320
1551 Oct 5	0.477	342.00	114.565	74.66	3.000	60.000	3.013
1551 Dec 17	0.216	−54.75	51.839	33.78	2.400	48.000	6.660
1553 June 11	0.259	20.00	62.207	40.54	2.000	40.000	5.550
	0.259	20.00	62.207	40.54	2.000	40.000	5.550
1553 Aug 20	0.475	83.33	114.046	74.32	3.000	60.000	3.027
1557 June 28	0.475	0.00	114.046	74.32	3.000	60.000	3.027
1558 Dec 31	0.475	0.00	114.046	74.32	3.000	60.000	3.027
1560 Nov 8	0.480	0.91	115.083	75.00	3.000	60.000	3.000

NOTES

    a See 433 n21 above.
    b See Table 1 part 1 note c.

TABLE 1 (continued)

ENGLISH SILVER COINAGES: FROM 1464 (EDWARD IV) TO 1560 (ELIZABETH I)
Composition of the silver penny, with mint charges and mint prices based on the Troy pound

PART 3: MINT CHARGES AND MINT PRICES FOR SILVER

date of penny	specified silver alloy					pure silver				
	traite value of Troy lb in £ sterling	total mint charges in £ sterling	per cent of total struck	mint price for bullion in £ sterling	per cent of total struck	traite value of Troy lb in £ sterling	total mint charges in £ sterling	per cent of total struck	mint price for bullion in £ sterling	per cent of traite value
1464 Aug 13	2.000	0.240	12.00	1.760	88.00	2.162	0.259	12.00	1.903	88.00
1466 Sep 29	2.000	0.231	11.56	1.769	88.44	2.162	0.250	11.56	1.912	88.44
1467 Sep 29	2.000	0.142	7.11	1.858	92.89	2.162	0.154	7.11	2.008	92.89
1470 Oct 23	2.000	0.107	5.33	1.893	94.67	2.162	0.115	5.33	2.047	94.67
1471 Apr 14	2.000	0.080	4.00	1.920	96.00	2.162	0.086	4.00	2.076	96.00
1492 Nov 20	2.000	0.053	2.67	1.947	97.33	2.162	0.058	2.67	2.105	97.33
1526 Nov 5	2.250	0.050	2.22	2.200	97.78	2.432	0.054	2.22	2.378	97.78
1542 May 16[a]										
(Gould)	2.400	0.400	16.67	2.000	83.33	2.880	0.480	16.67	2.400	83.33
(Challis)	2.400	0.400	16.67	2.000	83.33	3.165	0.527	16.67	2.637	83.33
(Munro)	2.400	0.400	16.67	2.000	83.33	3.114	0.519	16.67	2.595	83.33
1544 May 28	2.400	0.435	18.14	1.965	81.86	3.200	0.581	18.14	2.619	81.86

TABLE 1 (continued)

ENGLISH SILVER COINAGES: FROM 1464 (EDWARD IV) TO 1560 (ELIZABETH I)
Composition of the silver penny, with mint charges and mint prices based on the Troy pound

PART 3: MINT CHARGES AND MINT PRICES FOR SILVER (continued)

date of penny	specified silver alloy					pure silver				
	traite value of Troy lb in £ sterling	total mint charges in £ sterling	per cent of total struck	mint price for bullion in £ sterling	per cent of total struck	traite value of Troy lb in £ sterling	total mint charges in £ sterling	per cent of total struck	mint price for bullion in £ sterling	per cent of traite value
1545 Mar 27	2.400	1.000	41.67	1.400	58.33	4.800	2.000	41.67	2.800	58.33
1546 Apr 1	2.400	1.467	61.11	0.933	38.89	7.200	4.400	61.11	2.800	38.89
1547 Apr 5	2.400	1.333	55.56	1.067	44.44	7.200	4.000	55.56	3.200	44.44
	2.400	1.267	52.78	1.133	47.22	7.200	3.800	52.78	3.400	47.22
1548 Feb 16	2.400	n/a	n/a	n/a	n/a	7.200	n/a	n/a	n/a	n/a
1549 Jan 24	4.800	n/a	n/a	n/a	n/a	7.200	n/a	n/a	n/a	n/a
1549 Apr 12	3.600	1.900	52.78	1.700	47.22	7.200	3.800	52.78	3.400	47.22
	3.600	1.800	50.00	1.800	50.00	7.200	3.600	50.00	3.600	50.00
1550 Feb 1	2.400	n/a	n/a	n/a	n/a	7.200	n/a	n/a	n/a	n/a
1550 July	3.600	1.600	44.44	2.000	55.56	7.200	3.200	44.44	4.000	55.56
	3.600	1.650	45.83	1.950	54.17	7.200	3.300	45.83	3.900	54.17
1551 Apr 14	3.600	2.100	58.33	1.500	41.67	14.400	8.400	58.33	6.000	41.67
1551 Oct 5	3.000	0.050	1.67	2.950	98.33	3.258	0.054	1.67	3.204	98.33
1551 Dec 17	2.400	n/a	n/a	n/a	n/a	7.200	n/a	n/a	n/a	n/a

TABLE 1 (continued)

PART 3: MINT CHARGES AND MINT PRICES FOR SILVER (continued)

date of penny	specified silver alloy					pure silver				
	traite value of Troy lb in £ sterling	total mint charges in £ sterling	per cent of total struck	mint price for bullion in £ sterling	per cent of total struck	traite value of Troy lb in £ sterling	total mint charges in £ sterling	per cent of total struck	mint price for bullion in £ sterling	per cent of traite value
1553 June 11	2.000	n/a	n/a	n/a	n/a	7.200	n/a	n/a	n/a	n/a
	2.0000	n/a	n/a	n/a	n/a	7.200	n/a	n/a	n/a	n/a
1553 Aug 20	3.000	0.073	2.43	2.927	97.57	3.273	0.080	2.43	3.193	97.57
1557 June 28	3.000	0.075	2.50	2.925	97.50	3.273	0.082	2.50	3.191	97.50
1558 Dec 31	3.000	n/a	n/a	n/a	n/a	3.243				
1560 Nov 8	3.000	0.075	2.50	2.925	97.50	3.243	0.081	2.50	3.162	97.50

NOTES

Data not available in mint ordinances and mint accounts are marked 'n/a.'

a See Table 1 part 1 note c.

TABLE 2

ENGLISH GOLD COINAGES: FROM 1464 (EDWARD IV) TO 1560 (ELIZABETH I)
Composition of gold coins, with mint charges and mint prices based on the Troy pound

PART 1: FINENESS AND WEIGHT

date name of coin	fineness of gold coin			weight of gold coin		
	carats (out of 24)	grains (out of 4)	per cent fine	number per Troy pound[a]	weight in Troy grains[b]	weight in grams
1464 Aug 13						
noble	23	3.50	99.48	53.33	108.000	6.998
1465 Mar 6						
ryal, rose noble	23	3.50	99.48	48.00	120.000	7.776
angel-noble	23	3.50	99.48	72.00	80.000	5.184
1469 Mar 2						
ryal, rose noble	23	3.50	99.48	48.00	120.000	7.776
angel-noble	23	3.50	99.48	72.00	80.000	5.184
1471 Mar 6						
ryal, rose noble	23	3.50	99.48	48.00	120.000	7.776
angel-noble	23	3.50	99.48	72.00	80.000	5.184
1477 Feb 3						
ryal, rose noble	23	3.50	99.48	48.00	120.000	7.776
angel-noble	23	3.50	99.48	72.00	80.000	5.184
1489 Oct 28						
sovereign	23	3.50	99.48	24.00	240.000	15.552
1492 Nov 20						
ryal, rose noble	23	3.50	99.48	48.00	120.000	7.776
angel-noble	23	3.50	99.48	72.00	80.000	5.184
sovereign	23	3.50	99.48	24.00	240.000	15.552
1526 Aug 22						
sovereign	23	3.50	99.48	24.00	240.000	15.552
ryal, rose noble	23	3.50	99.48	48.00	120.000	7.776
angel-noble	23	3.50	99.48	72.00	80.000	5.184
crown: rose	22	0.00	91.67	106.67	54.000	3.499
1526 Nov 5						
sovereign	23	3.50	99.48	24.00	240.000	15.552
ryal, rose noble	23	3.50	99.48	48.00	120.000	7.776
angel-noble	23	3.50	99.48	72.00	80.000	5.184
St George noble	23	3.50	99.48	81.00	71.111	4.608
double-rose crown	22	0.00	91.67	100.50	57.313	3.714
half-crown	22	0.00	91.67	201.00	28.657	1.857
1542 May 16						
sovereign	23	0.00	95.83	28.80	200.000	12.960
ryal, rose noble	23	0.00	95.83	57.60	100.000	6.480
angel-noble	23	0.00	95.83	72.00	80.000	5.184
1544 May 28						
sovereign	23	0.00	95.83	28.80	200.000	12.960
ryal, rose noble	23	0.00	95.83	57.60	100.000	6.480

TABLE 2 (continued)

PART 1: FINENESS AND WEIGHT (continued)

date name of coin	fineness of gold coin			weight of gold coin		
	carats (out of 24)	grains (out of 4)	per cent fine	number per Troy pound[a]	weight in Troy grains[b]	weight in grams
1544 May 28 (continued)						
angel-noble	23	0.00	95.83	72.00	80.000	5.184
1545 Mar 27						
sovereign	22	0.00	91.67	30.00	192.000	12.441
ryal, rose noble	22	0.00	91.67	60.00	96.000	6.221
angel-noble	22	0.00	91.67	75.00	76.800	4.977
1545 April						
sovereign	22	0.00	91.67	30.00	192.000	12.441
ryal, rose noble	22	0.00	91.67	60.00	96.000	6.221
angel-noble	22	0.00	91.67	75.00	76.800	4.977
1546 Apr 1						
sovereign	20	0.00	83.33	30.00	192.000	12.441
ryal, rose noble	20	0.00	83.33	60.00	96.000	6.221
angel-noble	20	0.00	83.33	75.00	76.800	4.977
crown	20	0.00	83.33	120.00	48.000	3.110
half-crown	20	0.00	83.33	240.00	24.000	1.555
1546 Apr 1						
sovereign	20	0.00	83.33	30.00	192.000	12.441
ryal, rose noble	20	0.00	83.33	60.00	96.000	6.221
angel-noble	20	0.00	83.33	75.00	76.800	4.977
crown	20	0.00	83.33	120.00	48.000	3.110
half-crown	20	0.00	83.33	240.00	24.000	1.555
1547 April						
sovereign	20	0.00	83.33	30.00	192.000	12.441
ryal, rose noble	20	0.00	83.33	60.00	96.000	6.221
angel-noble	20	0.00	83.33	75.00	76.800	4.977
crown	20	0.00	83.33	120.00	48.000	3.110
half-crown	20	0.00	83.33	240.00	24.000	1.555
1548 Feb 16						
sovereign	20	0.00	83.33	30.00	192.000	12.441
1549 Jan 24						
sovereign	22	0.00	91.67	34.00	169.412	10.978
ryal, rose noble	22	0.00	91.67	68.00	84.706	5.489
crown	22	0.00	91.67	136.00	42.353	2.744
half-crown	22	0.00	91.67	272.00	21.176	1.372
1550 Dec 18						
sovereign	23	3.50	99.48	24.00	240.000	15.552
ryal, rose noble	23	3.50	99.48	48.00	120.000	7.776
angel-noble	23	3.50	99.48	72.00	80.000	5.184

TABLE 2 (continued)

ENGLISH GOLD COINAGES: FROM 1464 (EDWARD IV) TO 1560 (ELIZABETH I)
Composition of gold coins, with mint charges and mint prices based on the Troy pound

PART 1: FINENESS AND WEIGHT (continued)

date name of coin	fineness of gold coin			weight of gold coin		
	carats (out of 24)	grains (out of 4)	per cent fine	number per Troy pound[a]	weight in Troy grains[b]	weight in grams
1551 Oct 5						
sovereign	23	3.50	99.48	24.00	240.000	15.552
angel-noble	23	3.50	99.48	72.00	80.000	5.184
sovereign	22	0.00	91.67	33.00	174.545	11.310
ryal, rose noble	22	0.00	91.67	66.00	87.273	5.655
crown	22	0.00	91.67	132.00	43.636	2.828
1553 Aug 20						
sovereign	23	3.50	99.48	24.00	240.000	15.552
ryal, rose noble	23	3.50	99.48	48.00	120.000	7.776
angel-noble	23	3.50	99.48	72.00	80.000	5.184
1557 Aug 5						
angel-noble	23	3.50	99.48	72.00	80.000	5.184
1558 Apr 30						
sovereign	23	3.50	99.48	24.00	240.000	15.552
angel-noble	23	3.50	99.48	72.00	80.000	5.184
sovereign	22	0.00	91.67	33.00	174.545	11.310
ryal, rose noble	22	0.00	91.67	66.00	87.273	5.655
crown	22	0.00	91.67	132.00	43.636	2.828
1559 Jan						
sovereign	23	3.50	99.48	24.00	240.000	15.552
ryal, rose noble	23	3.50	99.48	48.00	120.000	7.776
angel-noble	23	3.50	99.48	72.00	80.000	5.184
sovereign	22	0.00	91.67	33.00	174.545	11.310
angel-noble	22	0.00	91.67	66.00	87.273	5.655
crown	22	0.00	91.67	132.00	43.636	2.828
1560 Nov 8						
sovereign	23	3.50	99.48	24.00	240.000	15.552
ryal, rose noble	23	3.50	99.48	48.00	120.000	7.776
angel-noble	23	3.50	99.48	72.00	80.000	5.184
sovereign	22	0.00	91.67	33.00	174.545	11.310
angel-noble	22	0.00	91.67	66.00	87.273	5.655
crown	22	0.00	91.67	132.00	43.636	2.828

NOTES

a Troy pound cut to 5760 Troy grains = 373.242 grams
b Troy grain = 0.648 grams

TABLE 2 (continued)

PART 2: PURE GOLD CONTENTS AND VALUES

date name of coin	grams of pure gold		per cent change in gold contents	gold index (1526 = 100)	official value of coin		traite value of Troy lb in £ sterling
	in coin	in £ sterling			shillings & pence	in £ sterling	
1464 Aug 13							
noble	6.962	16.708	−20.00	118.800	8s 4d	0.417	22.222
1465 Mar 6							
ryal, rose noble	7.735	15.471	−7.41	110.000	10s 0d	0.500	24.000
angel-noble	5.157	15.471	−7.41	110.000	6s 8d	0.333	24.000
1469 Mar 2							
ryal, rose noble	7.735	15.471	0.00	110.000	10s 0d	0.500	24.000
angel-noble	5.157	15.471	0.00	110.000	6s 8d	0.333	24.000
1471 Mar 6							
ryal, rose noble	7.735	15.471	0.00	110.000	10s 0d	0.500	24.000
angel-noble	5.157	15.471	0.00	110.000	6s 8d	0.333	24.000
1477 Feb 3							
ryal, rose noble	7.735	15.471	0.00	110.000	10s 0d	0.500	24.000
angel-noble	5.157	15.471	0.00	110.000	6s 8d	0.333	24.000
1489 Oct 28							
sovereign	15.471	15.471	0.00	110.000	20s 0d	1.000	24.000
1492 Nov 20							
ryal, rose noble	7.735	15.471	0.00	110.000	10s 0d	0.500	24.000
angel-noble	5.157	15.471	0.00	110.000	6s 8d	0.333	24.000
sovereign	15.471	15.471	0.00	110.000	20s 0d	1.000	24.000
1526 Aug 22							
sovereign	15.471	14.064	−9.09	100.000	22s 0d	1.100	26.400
ryal, rose noble	7.735	14.064	−9.09	100.000	11s 0d	0.550	26.400
angel-noble	5.157	14.064	−9.09	100.000	7s 4d	0.367	26.400
crown: rose	3.208	14.256	−7.85	101.361	4s 6d	0.225	24.000
1526 Nov 5							
sovereign	15.471	13.752	−2.22	97.778	22s 6d	1.125	27.000
ryal, rose noble	7.735	13.752	−2.22	97.778	11s 3d	0.563	27.000
angel-noble	5.157	13.752	−2.22	97.778	7s 6d	0.375	27.000
St George noble	4.584	13.752	−2.22	97.778	6s 8d	0.333	27.000
double-rose crown	3.404	13.617	−4.48	96.823	5s 0d	0.250	25.125
half-crown	1.702	13.617	−4.48	96.823	2s 6d	0.125	25.125
1542 May 16							
sovereign	12.420	12.420	−9.69	88.307	20s 0d	1.000	28.800
ryal, rose noble	6.210	12.420	−9.69	88.307	10s 0d	0.500	28.800
angel-noble	4.968	12.420	−9.69	88.307	8s 0d	0.400	28.800
1544 May 28							
sovereign	12.420	12.420	0.00	88.307	20s 0d	1.000	28.800
ryal, rose noble	6.210	12.420	0.00	88.307	10s 0d	0.500	28.800

TABLE 2 (continued)

ENGLISH GOLD COINAGES: FROM 1464 (EDWARD IV) TO 1560 (ELIZABETH I)
Composition of gold coins, with mint charges and mint prices based on the Troy pound

PART 2: PURE GOLD CONTENTS AND VALUES (continued)

date / name of coin	grams of pure gold in coin	grams of pure gold in £ sterling	per cent change in gold contents	gold index (1526 = 100)	official value of coin shillings & pence	official value of coin in £ sterling	traite value of Troy lb in £ sterling
1544 May 28 (continued)							
angel-noble	4.968	12.420	0.00	88.307	8s 0d	0.400	28.800
1545 Mar 27							
sovereign	11.405	11.405	−8.17	81.089	20s 0d	1.000	30.000
ryal, rose noble	5.702	11.405	−8.17	81.089	10s 0d	0.500	30.000
angel-noble	4.562	11.405	−8.17	81.089	8s 0d	0.400	30.000
1545 April							
sovereign	11.405	11.405	0.00	81.089	20s 0d	1.000	30.000
ryal, rose noble	5.702	11.405	0.00	81.089	10s 0d	0.500	30.000
angel-noble	4.562	11.405	0.00	81.089	8s 0d	0.400	30.000
1546 Apr 1							
sovereign	10.368	10.368	−9.09	73.717	20s 0d	1.000	30.000
ryal, rose noble	5.184	10.368	−9.09	73.717	10s 0d	0.500	30.000
angel-noble	4.147	10.368	−9.09	73.717	8s 0d	0.400	30.000
crown	2.592	10.368	−9.09	73.717	5s 0d	0.250	30.000
half-crown	1.296	10.368	−9.09	73.717	2s 6d	0.125	30.000
1546 Apr 1							
sovereign	10.368	10.368	0.00	73.717	20s 0d	1.000	30.000
ryal, rose noble	5.184	10.368	0.00	73.717	10s 0d	0.500	30.000
angel-noble	4.147	10.368	0.00	73.717	8s 0d	0.400	30.000
crown	2.592	10.368	0.00	73.717	5s 0d	0.250	30.000
half-crown	1.296	10.368	0.00	73.717	2s 6d	0.125	30.000
1547 April							
sovereign	10.368	10.368	0.00	73.717	20s 0d	1.000	30.000
ryal, rose noble	5.184	10.368	0.00	73.717	10s 0d	0.500	30.000
angel-noble	4.147	10.368	0.00	73.717	8s 0d	0.400	30.000
crown	2.592	10.368	0.00	73.717	5s 0d	0.250	30.000
half-crown	1.296	10.368	0.00	73.717	2s 6d	0.125	30.000
1548 Feb 16							
sovereign	10.368	10.368	0.00	73.717	20s 0d	1.000	30.000
1549 Jan 24							
sovereign	10.063	10.063	−2.94	71.549	20s 0d	1.000	34.000
ryal, rose noble	5.031	10.063	−2.94	71.549	10s 0d	0.500	34.000
crown	2.516	10.063	−2.94	71.549	5s 0d	0.250	34.000
half-crown	1.258	10.063	−2.94	71.549	2s 6d	0.125	34.000
1550 Dec 18							
sovereign	15.471	12.892	28.12	91.667	24s 0d	1.200	28.800
ryal, rose noble	7.735	12.892	28.12	91.667	12s 0d	0.600	28.800
angel-noble	5.157	12.892	28.12	91.667	8s 0d	0.400	28.800

TABLE 2 (continued)

PART 2: PURE GOLD CONTENTS AND VALUES (continued)

date name of coin	grams of pure gold		per cent change in gold contents	gold index (1526 = 100)	official value of coin		traite value of Troy lb in £ sterling
	in coin	in £ sterling			shillings & pence	in £ sterling	
1551 Oct 5							
sovereign	15.471	10.314	−20.00	73.333	30s 0d	1.500	36.000
angel-noble	5.157	10.314	−20.00	73.333	10s 0d	0.500	36.000
sovereign	10.368	10.368	−19.58	73.717	20s 0d	1.000	33.000
ryal, rose noble	5.184	10.368	−19.58	73.717	10s 0d	0.500	33.000
crown	2.592	10.368	−19.58	73.717	5s 0d	0.250	33.000
1553 Aug 20							
sovereign	15.471	10.314	0.00	73.333	30s 0d	1.500	36.000
ryal, rose noble	7.735	10.314	0.00	73.333	15s 0d	0.750	36.000
angel-noble	5.157	10.314	0.00	73.333	10s 0d	0.500	36.000
1557 Aug 5							
angel-noble	5.157	10.314	0.00	73.333	10s 0d	0.500	36.000
1558 Apr 30							
sovereign	15.471	10.314	0.00	73.333	30s 0d	1.500	36.000
angel-noble	5.157	10.314	0.00	73.333	10s 0d	0.500	36.000
sovereign	10.368	10.368	0.52	73.717	20s 0d	1.000	33.000
ryal, rose noble	5.184	10.368	0.52	73.717	10s 0d	0.500	33.000
crown	2.592	10.368	0.52	73.717	5s 0d	0.250	33.000
1559 Jan							
sovereign	15.471	10.314	0.00	73.333	30s 0d	1.500	36.000
ryal, rose noble	7.735	10.314	0.00	73.333	15s 0d	0.750	36.000
angel-noble	5.157	10.368	0.00	73.717	10s 0d	0.500	36.000
sovereign	10.368	10.368	0.00	73.717	20s 0d	1.000	33.000
angel-noble	5.184	10.368	0.00	73.717	10s 0d	0.500	33.000
crown	2.592	10.368	0.00	73.717	5s 0d	0.250	33.000
1560 Nov 8							
sovereign	15.471	10.314	0.00	73.333	30s 0d	1.500	36.000
ryal, rose noble	7.735	10.314	0.00	73.333	15s 0d	0.750	36.000
angel-noble	5.157	10.314	0.00	73.333	10s 0d	0.500	36.000
sovereign	10.368	10.368	0.00	73.717	20s 0d	1.000	33.000
angel-noble	5.184	10.368	0.00	73.717	10s 0d	0.500	33.000
crown	2.592	10.368	0.00	73.717	5s 0d	0.250	33.000

TABLE 2 (continued)

ENGLISH GOLD COINAGES: FROM 1464 (EDWARD IV) TO 1560 (ELIZABETH I)
Composition of gold coins, with mint charges and mint prices based on the Troy pound

PART 3: MINT CHARGES AND MINT PRICES FOR GOLD

date / name of coin	current gold alloy					24 carat gold (fine)				
	traite value of Troy lb in £ sterling	total mint charges in £ sterling	per cent of total struck	mint price for bullion in £ sterling	per cent of total struck	traite value of Troy lb in £ sterling	total mint charges in £ sterling	per cent of total struck	mint price for bullion in £ sterling	per cent of traite value
1464 Aug 13										
sovereign	22.222	2.667	12.00	19.556	88.00	22.339	2.681	12.00	19.658	88.00
1465 Mar 6										
ryal, rose noble	24.000	1.111	4.63	22.889	95.37	24.126	1.117	4.63	23.009	95.37
angel-noble	24.000	1.111	4.63	22.889	95.37	24.126	1.117	4.63	23.009	95.37
1469 Mar 2										
ryal, rose noble	24.000	0.773	3.22	23.227	96.78	24.126	0.777	3.22	23.348	96.78
angel-noble	24.000	0.773	3.22	23.227	96.78	24.126	0.777	3.22	23.348	96.78
1471 Mar 6										
ryal, rose noble	24.000	0.560	2.33	23.440	97.67	24.126	0.563	2.33	23.563	97.67
angel-noble	24.000	0.560	2.33	23.440	97.67	24.126	0.563	2.33	23.563	97.67
1477 Feb 3										
ryal, rose noble	24.000	0.400	1.67	23.600	98.33	24.126	0.402	1.67	23.724	98.33
angel-noble	24.000	0.400	1.67	23.600	98.33	24.126	0.402	1.67	23.724	98.33
1489 Oct 28										
sovereign	24.000	n/a	n/a	n/a	n/a	24.126	n/a	n/a	n/a	n/a
1492 Nov 20										
ryal, rose noble	24.000	0.133	0.56	23.867	99.44	24.126	0.134	0.56	23.992	99.44
angel-noble	24.000	0.133	0.56	23.867	99.44	24.126	0.134	0.56	23.992	99.44
sovereign	24.000	0.133	0.56	23.867	99.44	24.126	0.134	0.56	23.992	99.44

TABLE 2 (continued)

PART 3: MINT CHARGES AND MINT PRICES FOR GOLD (continued)

date / name of coin	current gold alloy					24 carat gold (fine)				
	traite value of Troy lb in £ sterling	total mint charges in £ sterling	per cent of total struck	mint price for bullion in £ sterling	per cent of total struck	traite value of Troy lb in £ sterling	total mint charges in £ sterling	per cent of total struck	mint price for bullion in £ sterling	per cent of traite value
1526 Aug 22										
sovereign	26.400	n/a	n/a	n/a	n/a	26.538	n/a	n/a	n/a	n/a
ryal, rose noble	26.400	n/a	n/a	n/a	n/a	26.538	n/a	n/a	n/a	n/a
angel-noble	26.400	n/a	n/a	n/a	n/a	26.538	n/a	n/a	n/a	n/a
crown: rose	24.000	n/a	n/a	n/a	n/a	26.182	n/a	n/a	n/a	n/a
1526 Nov 5										
sovereign	27.000	0.138	0.51	26.863	99.49	27.141	0.138	0.51	27.003	99.49
ryal, rose noble	27.000	0.138	0.51	26.863	99.49	27.141	0.138	0.51	27.003	99.49
angel-noble	27.000	0.138	0.51	26.863	99.49	27.141	0.138	0.51	27.003	99.49
St George noble	27.000	0.138	0.51	26.863	99.49	27.141	0.138	0.51	27.003	99.49
double-rose crown	25.125	0.150	0.60	24.975	99.40	27.409	0.164	0.60	27.245	99.40
half-crown	25.125	0.150	0.60	24.975	99.40	27.409	0.164	0.60	27.245	99.40
1542 May 16										
sovereign	28.800	1.200	4.17	27.600	95.83	30.052	1.252	4.17	28.800	95.83
ryal, rose noble	28.800	1.200	4.17	27.600	95.83	30.052	1.252	4.17	28.800	95.83
angel-noble	28.800	1.200	4.17	27.600	95.83	30.052	1.252	4.17	28.800	95.83
1544 May 28										
sovereign	28.800	1.200	4.17	27.600	95.83	30.052	1.252	4.17	28.800	95.83
ryal, rose noble	28.800	1.200	4.17	27.600	95.83	30.052	1.252	4.17	28.800	95.83
angel-noble	28.800	1.200	4.17	27.600	95.83	30.052	1.252	4.17	28.800	95.83

TABLE 2 (continued)

ENGLISH GOLD COINAGES: FROM 1464 (EDWARD IV) TO 1560 (ELIZABETH I)
Composition of gold coins, with mint charges and mint prices based on the Troy pound

PART 3: MINT CHARGES AND MINT PRICES FOR GOLD (continued)

date / name of coin	current gold alloy					24 carat gold (fine)				
	traite value of Troy lb in £ sterling	total mint charges in £ sterling	per cent of total struck	mint price for bullion in £ sterling	per cent of total struck	traite value of Troy lb in £ sterling	total mint charges in £ sterling	per cent of total struck	mint price for bullion in £ sterling	per cent of traite value
1545 Mar 27										
sovereign	30.000	2.500	8.33	27.500	91.67	32.727	2.727	8.33	30.000	91.67
ryal, rose noble	30.000	2.500	8.33	27.500	91.67	32.727	2.727	8.33	30.000	91.67
angel-noble	30.000	2.500	8.33	27.500	91.67	32.727	2.727	8.33	30.000	91.67
1545 April										
sovereign	30.000	1.950	6.50	28.050	93.50	32.727	2.127	6.50	30.600	93.50
ryal, rose noble	30.000	1.950	6.50	28.050	93.50	32.727	2.127	6.50	30.600	93.50
angel-noble	30.000	1.950	6.50	28.050	93.50	32.727	2.127	6.50	30.600	93.50
1546 Apr 1										
sovereign	30.000	4.500	15.00	25.500	85.00	36.000	5.400	15.00	30.600	85.00
ryal, rose noble	30.000	4.500	15.00	25.500	85.00	36.000	5.400	15.00	30.600	85.00
angel-noble	30.000	4.500	15.00	25.500	85.00	36.000	5.400	15.00	30.600	85.00
crown	30.000	4.500	15.00	25.500	85.00	36.000	5.400	15.00	30.600	85.00
half-crown	30.000	4.500	15.00	25.500	85.00	36.000	5.400	15.00	30.600	85.00
1546 Apr 1										
sovereign	30.000	4.000	13.33	26.000	86.67	36.000	4.800	13.33	31.200	86.67
ryal, rose noble	30.000	4.000	13.33	26.000	86.67	36.000	4.800	13.33	31.200	86.67
angel-noble	30.000	4.000	13.33	26.000	86.67	36.000	4.800	13.33	31.200	86.67
crown	30.000	4.000	13.33	26.000	86.67	36.000	4.800	13.33	31.200	86.67
half-crown	30.000	4.000	13.33	26.000	86.67	36.000	4.800	13.33	31.200	86.67

TABLE 2 (continued)

PART 3: MINT CHARGES AND MINT PRICES FOR GOLD (continued)

date / name of coin	current gold alloy					24 carat gold (fine)				
	traite value of Troy lb in £ sterling	total mint charges in £ sterling	per cent of total struck	mint price for bullion in £ sterling	per cent of total struck	traite value of Troy lb in £ sterling	total mint charges in £ sterling	per cent of total struck	mint price for bullion in £ sterling	per cent of traite value
1547 April										
sovereign	30.000	1.000	3.33	29.000	96.67	36.000	1.200	3.33	34.800	96.67
ryal, rose noble	30.000	1.000	3.33	29.000	96.67	36.000	1.200	3.33	34.800	96.67
angel-noble	30.000	1.000	3.33	29.000	96.67	36.000	1.200	3.33	34.800	96.67
crown	30.000	1.000	3.33	29.000	96.67	36.000	1.200	3.33	34.800	96.67
half-crown	30.000	1.000	3.33	29.000	96.67	36.000	1.200	3.33	34.800	96.67
1548 Feb 16										
sovereign	30.000	1.000	3.33	29.000	96.67	36.000	1.200	3.33	34.800	96.67
1549 Jan 24										
sovereign	34.000	1.000	2.94	33.000	97.06	37.091	1.091	2.94	36.000	97.06
ryal, rose noble	34.000	1.000	2.94	33.000	97.06	37.091	1.091	2.94	36.000	97.06
crown	34.000	1.000	2.94	33.000	97.06	37.091	1.091	2.94	36.000	97.06
half-crown	34.000	1.000	2.94	33.000	97.06	37.091	1.091	2.94	36.000	97.06
1550 Dec 18										
sovereign	28.800	1.650	5.73	27.150	94.27	28.951	1.659	5.73	27.292	94.27
ryal, rose noble	28.800	1.650	5.73	27.150	94.27	28.951	1.659	5.73	27.292	94.27
angel-noble	28.800	1.650	5.73	27.150	94.27	28.951	1.659	5.73	27.292	94.27

TABLE 2 (continued)

ENGLISH GOLD COINAGES: FROM 1464 (EDWARD IV) TO 1560 (ELIZABETH I)
Composition of gold coins, with mint charges and mint prices based on the Troy pound

PART 3: MINT CHARGES AND MINT PRICES FOR GOLD (continued)

date	name of coin	current gold alloy					24 carat gold (fine)				
		traite value of Troy lb in £ sterling	total mint charges in £ sterling	per cent of total struck	mint price for bullion in £ sterling	per cent of total struck	traite value of Troy lb in £ sterling	total mint charges in £ sterling	per cent of total struck	mint price for bullion in £ sterling	per cent of traite value
1551 Oct 5											
	sovereign	36.000	0.138	0.38	35.863	99.62	36.188	0.138	0.38	36.050	99.62
	angel-noble	36.000	0.138	0.38	35.863	99.62	36.188	0.138	0.38	36.050	99.62
	sovereign	33.000	0.150	0.45	32.850	99.55	36.000	0.164	0.45	35.836	99.55
	ryal, rose noble	33.000	0.150	0.45	32.850	99.55	36.000	0.164	0.45	35.836	99.55
	crown	33.000	0.150	0.45	32.850	99.55	36.000	0.164	0.45	35.836	99.55
1553 Aug 20											
	sovereign	36.000	0.200	0.56	35.800	99.44	36.188	0.201	0.56	35.987	99.44
	ryal, rose noble	36.000	0.200	0.56	35.800	99.44	36.188	0.201	0.56	35.987	99.44
	angel-noble	36.000	0.200	0.56	35.800	99.44	36.188	0.201	0.56	35.987	99.44
1557 Aug 5											
	angel-noble	36.000	0.200	0.56	35.800	99.44	36.188	0.201	0.56	35.987	99.44
1558 Apr 30											
	sovereign	36.000	0.200	0.56	35.800	99.44	36.188	0.201	0.56	35.987	99.44
	angel-noble	36.000	0.200	0.56	35.800	99.44	36.188	0.201	0.56	35.987	99.44
	sovereign	33.000	0.200	0.61	32.800	99.39	36.000	0.218	0.61	35.782	99.39
	ryal, rose noble	33.000	0.200	0.61	32.800	99.39	36.000	0.218	0.61	35.782	99.39
	crown	33.000	0.200	0.61	32.800	99.39	36.000	0.218	0.61	35.782	99.39

PART 3: MINT CHARGES AND MINT PRICES FOR GOLD (continued)

date / name of coin	current gold alloy					24 carat gold (fine)				
	traite value of Troy lb in £ sterling	total mint charges in £ sterling	per cent of total struck	mint price for bullion in £ sterling	per cent of total struck	traite value of Troy lb in £ sterling	total mint charges in £ sterling	per cent of total struck	mint price for bullion in £ sterling	per cent of traite value
1559 Jan										
sovereign	36.000	0.200	0.56	35.800	99.44	36.188	0.201	0.56	35.987	99.44
ryal, rose noble	36.000	0.200	0.56	35.800	99.44	36.188	0.201	0.56	35.987	99.44
angel-noble	36.000	0.200	0.56	35.800	99.44	36.188	0.201	0.56	35.987	99.44
sovereign	33.000	0.200	0.61	32.800	99.39	36.000	0.218	0.61	35.782	99.39
angel-noble	33.000	0.200	0.61	32.800	99.39	36.000	0.218	0.61	35.782	99.39
crown	33.000	0.200	0.61	32.800	99.39	36.000	0.218	0.61	35.782	99.39
1560 Nov 8										
sovereign	36.000	0.200	0.56	35.800	99.44	36.188	0.201	0.56	35.987	99.44
ryal, rose noble	36.000	0.200	0.56	35.800	99.44	36.188	0.201	0.56	35.987	99.44
angel-noble	36.000	0.200	0.56	35.800	99.44	36.188	0.201	0.56	35.987	99.44
sovereign	33.000	0.200	0.61	32.800	99.39	36.000	0.218	0.61	35.782	99.39
angel-noble	33.000	0.200	0.61	32.800	99.39	36.000	0.218	0.61	35.782	99.39
crown	33.000	0.200	0.61	32.800	99.39	36.000	0.218	0.61	35.782	99.39

NOTES

Data not available in mint ordinances and mint accounts are marked 'n/a.'

TABLE 3

OFFICIAL ENGLISH COINAGE RATES FOR GOLD COINS IN THE 1520S

name of coin	22 May 1522		24 Nov 1522		6 July 1525	
	grams fine gold	value in shillings & pence = total pence	grams fine gold	value in shillings & pence = total pence	grams fine gold	value in shillings & pence = total pence
FOREIGN COINS						
ducat and florin	3.559	4s 6d = 54d	3.559	4s 6d = 54d	3.559	4s 6d = 54d
écu au soleil	3.296	4s 4d = 52d	3.296	4s 4d = 52d	3.296	4s 4d = 52d
écu à la couronne	3.275	4s 0d = 48d	3.275	4s 0d = 48d	3.275	4s 0d = 48d
réal d'or	5.275		5.275	6s 10d = 82d	5.275	6s 10d = 82d
Carolus florin	1.700		1.700	2s 1d = 25d	1.700	2s 1d = 25d
Rhenish florin	2.527		2.527	3s 3d = 39d	2.527	3s 3d = 39d
ENGLISH COINS						
sovereign	15.471	20s 0d = 240d	15.471	20s 0d = 240d	15.471	20s 0d = 260d
ryal, or rose noble	7.735	10s 0d = 120d	7.735	10s 0d = 120d	7.735	
angel-noble	5.157	6s 8d = 80d	5.157	6s 8d = 80d	5.157	6s 8d = 80d
crown						
St George noble						

name of coin	22 Aug 1526			5 Nov 1526		
	grams fine gold	value in shillings & pence = total pence	per cent change	grams fine gold	value in shillings & pence = total pence	per cent change
FOREIGN COINS						
ducat and florin	3.559	4s 8d = 56d	3.70	3.559		
écu au soleil	3.296	4s 6d = 54d	3.85	3.296		
écu à la couronne	3.275			3.275		
réal d'or	5.275			5.275		
Carolus florin	1.700			1.700		
Rhenish florin	2.527			2.527		
ENGLISH COINS						
sovereign	15.471	22s 0d = 264d	10.00	15.471	22s 6d = 270d	2.27
ryal, or rose noble	7.735	11s 0d = 132d	10.00	7.735	11s 3d = 135d	2.27
angel-noble	5.157	7s 4d = 88d	10.00	5.157	7s 6d = 90d	2.27
crown	3.208	4s 6d = 54d		3.404	5s 0d = 60d	11.11
St George noble				4.584	6s 8d = 80d	

SOURCES FOR TABLES 1–3

Christopher E. Challis 'Appendix 2: Mint contracts, 1279–1817' in *A New History of the Royal Mint* ed C.E. Challis (Cambridge and New York 1992) 699–758

J.D. Gould *The Great Debasement: Currency and the Economy in Mid-Tudor England* (Oxford 1970) 11–12, Tables I and II

Tudor Royal Proclamations ed Paul L. Hughes and James F. Larkin 2 vols (New Haven and London 1964 I *The Early Tudors (1485–1553*

TABLE OF CORRESPONDENTS

WORKS FREQUENTLY CITED

SHORT-TITLE FORMS
FOR ERASMUS' WORKS

INDEX

TABLE OF CORRESPONDENTS

WORKS FREQUENTLY CITED

This list provides bibliographical information for works referred to in short-title form in this volume. For Erasmus' writings see the short-title list following. Editions of his letters are included in the list below.

AK   *Die Amerbachkorrespondenz* ed Alfred Hartmann and B.R. Jenny (Basel 1942–)

Allen   *Opus epistolarum Des. Erasmi Roterodami* ed P.S. Allen, H.M. Allen, and H.W. Garrod (Oxford 1906–58) 11 vols and index

ASD   *Opera omnia Desiderii Erasmi Roterodami* (Amsterdam 1969–)

Bataillon   Marcel Bataillon *Erasme et l'Espagne* rev ed, text by Daniel Devoto, ed Charles Amiel (Geneva 1991) 3 vols. This posthumous edition replaces the original French edition (Paris 1937) and two editions of the Spanish translation, *Erasmo y España* (Mexico City 1950 and 1966).

BRE   *Briefwechsel des Beatus Rhenanus* ed Adalbert Horawitz and Karl Hartfelder (Leipzig 1886; repr Hildesheim 1966)

CEBR   *Contemporaries of Erasmus: A Biographical Register of the Renaissance and Reformation* ed Peter G. Bietenholz and Thomas B. Deutscher (Toronto 1985–7) 3 vols

CR   *Philippi Melanchthonis opera quae supersunt omnia* ed C.G. Bretschneider et al *Corpus reformatorum* 1–28 (Halle 1834–60; repr 1963)

CWE   *Collected Works of Erasmus* (Toronto 1974–)

Enthoven   *Briefe an Desiderius Erasmus von Rotterdam* ed L.K. Enthoven (Strasbourg 1906)

Epistolae ad diversos   *Epistolae D. Erasmi Roterodami ad diversos et aliquot aliorum ad illum* (Basel: Froben, 31 August 1521)

Epistolae familiares   *Epistolae familiares Des. Erasmi Roterodami ad Bonif. Amerbachium* (Basel: C.A. Serin 1779)

Epistolae floridae   *Des. Erasmi Roterodami epistolarum floridarum liber unus antehac nunquam excusus* (Basel: J. Herwagen, September 1531)

Farge 'Berquin'   James K. Farge 'Les procès de Louis de Berquin: Épisodes
                   dan· la lutte du Parlement de Paris contra l'absolutisme
                   royal,' *Histoire et Archives* 18 (2005) 49–77

Farge *Orthodoxy*   James K. Farge *Orthodoxy and Reform in Early Reformation
                   France: The Faculty of Theology of Paris 1500–1543* Studies in
                   Medieval and Reformation Thought 32 (Leiden 1985)

Farge *Registre*   *Registre des procès-verbaux de la Faculté de théologie de
                   l'Université de Paris de janvier 1524 à novembre 1533* ed James
                   K. Farge (Paris 1990)

Förstemann/Günther *Briefe an Desiderius Erasmus von Rotterdam* ed J. Förstemann
                   and O. Günther, xxvii. Beiheft zum *Zentralblatt für Biblio-
                   thekswesen* (Leipzig 1904; repr Wiesbaden 1968)

Horawitz   *Erasmiana* ed Adalbert Horawitz, Sitzungsberichte der phil.-
                   hist. Classe der kaiserlichen Akademie der Wissenschaften
                   (Vienna 1878, 1880, 1883, 1885) 4 vols. An additional
                   volume, cited by Allen and CWE as 'Horawitz v,' was
                   published in the Sitzungsberichte der Akademie under the
                   title *Erasmus von Rotterdam und Martinus Lipsius* (Vienna
                   1882)

LB   *Desiderii Erasmi Roterodami opera omnia* ed J. Leclerc (Leiden
                   1703–6; repr 1961–2) 10 vols

Locher   Gottfried W. Locher *Die Zwinglische Reformation im Rahmen
                   der europäischen Kirchengeschichte* (Göttingen and Zürich
                   1979)

LP   *Letters and Papers, Foreign and Domestic, of the Reign of Henry
                   VIII* ed J.S. Brewer, J. Gairdner, and R.H. Brodie (London
                   1862–1932) 36 vols

LW   *Luther's Works* ed Jaroslav Pelikan, Helmut T. Lehmann et
                   al (St Louis and Philadelphia 1955–86) 55 vols

Matricule de Montpel- *Matricule de l'Université de médecine de Montpellier (1503–1599)*
lier   ed Marcel Gouron (Geneva 1957)

MBW   *Melanchthons Briefwechsel, kritische und kommentierte Gesam-
                   tausgabe* ed Heinz Scheible et al (Stuttgart-Bad Canstatt
                   1977–   ). The edition comprises two series: *Regesten* (9 vols)
                   and *Texte* (9 vols to date). The numbers of the letters are
                   the same in both series, but only the text volumes (cited as
                   'T 1' etc) have line numbers.

Opus epistolarum	*Opus epistolarum Des. Erasmi Roterodami per autorem diligenter recognitum et adiectis innumeris novis fere ad trientem auctum* (Basel: Froben, Herwagen, and Episcopius 1529)
Pastor	Ludwig von Pastor *The History of the Popes from the Close of the Middle Ages* ed and trans R.F. Kerr et al, 6th ed (London 1938–53) 40 vols
Potter	G. R. Potter *Zwingli* (Cambridge 1976)
Pirckheimeri opera	*Bilibaldi Pirckheimeri ... opera politica, historica, philologica, et epistolica* ed Melchior Goldast (Frankfurt 1610; repr Hildesheim and New York 1969)
Selectae epistolae	*Selectae aliquot epistolae nunquam antehac evulgatae* (Basel: J. Herwagen and H. Froben, c September 1528)
Sieber	Ludwig Sieber *Das Mobiliar des Erasmus: Verzeichnis vom 10. April 1534* (Basel 1891)
WA	*D. Martin Luthers Werke, Kritische Gesamtausgabe* (Weimar 1883–1980) 60 vols
Wengert	Timothy J. Wengert *Law and Gospel: Philip Melanchthon's Debate with John Agricola of Eisleben over 'Poenitentia'* (Grand Rapids 1997)
WPB	*Willibald Pirckheimer Briefwechsel* ed Emil Reicke, Helga Scheible et al (Munich 1940–2009) 7 vols

Titles following colons are longer versions of the same, or are alternative titles. Items entirely enclosed in square brackets are of doubtful authorship. For abbreviations, see Works Frequently Cited.

Acta: Acta Academiae Lovaniensis contra Lutherum *Opuscula* / CWE 71

Adagia: Adagiorum chiliades 1508, etc (Adagiorum collectanea for the primitive form, when required) LB II / ASD II-1–8 / CWE 30–6

Admonitio adversus mendacium: Admonitio adversus mendacium et obtrectationem LB X / CWE 78

Annotationes in Novum Testamentum LB VI / ASD VI-5, 6, 8, 9 / CWE 51–60

Antibarbari LB X / ASD I-1 / CWE 23

Apologia ad annotationes Stunicae: Apologia respondens ad ea quae Iacobus Lopis Stunica taxaverat in prima duntaxat Novi Testamenti aeditione LB IX / ASD IX-2

Apologia ad Caranzam: Apologia ad Sanctium Caranzam, or Apologia de tribus locis, or Responsio ad annotationem Stunicae ... a Sanctio Caranza defensam LB IX

Apologia ad Fabrum: Apologia ad Iacobum Fabrum Stapulensem LB IX / ASD IX-3 / CWE 83

Apologia ad prodromon Stunicae LB IX

Apologia ad Stunicae conclusiones LB IX

Apologia adversus monachos: Apologia adversus monachos quosdam Hispanos LB IX

Apologia adversus Petrum Sutorem: Apologia adversus debacchationes Petri Sutoris LB IX

Apologia adversus rhapsodias Alberti Pii: Apologia ad viginti et quattuor libros A. Pii LB IX / CWE 84

Apologia adversus Stunicae Blasphemiae: Apologia adversus libellum Stunicae cui titulum fecit Blasphemiae et impietates Erasmi LB IX

Apologia contra Latomi dialogum: Apologia contra Iacobi Latomi dialogum de tribus linguis LB IX / CWE 71

Apologia de 'In principio erat sermo' LB IX

Apologia de laude matrimonii: Apologia pro declamatione de laude matrimonii LB IX / CWE 71

Apologia de loco 'Omnes quidem': Apologia de loco 'Omnes quidem resurgemus' LB IX

Apologia qua respondet invectivis Lei: Apologia qua respondet duabus invectivis Eduardi Lei *Opuscula* / ASD IX-4 / CWE 72

Apophthegmata LB IV

Appendix de scriptis Clithovei LB IX / CWE 83

Appendix respondens ad Sutorem: Appendix respondens ad quaedam Antapologiae Petri Sutoris LB IX

Argumenta: Argumenta in omnes epistolas apostolicas nova (with Paraphrases)

Axiomata pro causa Lutheri: Axiomata pro causa Martini Lutheri *Opuscula* CWE 71

Brevissima scholia: In Elenchum Alberti Pii brevissima scholia per eundem Erasmum Roterodamum CWE 84

Carmina LB I, IV, V, VIII / ASD I-7 / CWE 85–6

Catalogus lucubrationum LB I / CWE 9 (Ep 1341A)

Ciceronianus: Dialogus Ciceronianus LB I / ASD I-2 / CWE 28

Colloquia LB I / ASD I-3 / CWE 39–40

Compendium vitae Allen I / CWE 4

Conflictus: Conflictus Thaliae et Barbariei LB I

[Consilium: Consilium cuiusdam ex animo cupientis esse consultum] *Opuscula* / CWE 71

De bello Turcico: Utilissima consultatio de bello Turcis inferendo, et obiter enarratus
   psalmus 28 LB V / ASD V-3 / CWE 64

De civilitate: De civilitate morum puerilium LB I / CWE 25

Declamatio de morte LB IV

Declamatiuncula LB IV

Declarationes ad censuras Lutetiae vulgatas: Declarationes ad censuras Lutetiae vulgatas
   sub nomine facultatis theologiae Parisiensis LB IX

De concordia: De sarcienda ecclesiae concordia, or De amabili ecclesiae concordia [on
   Psalm 83] LB V / ASD V-3 / CWE 65

De conscribendis epistolis LB I / ASD I-2 / CWE 25

De constructione: De constructione octo partium orationis, or Syntaxis LB I /
   ASD I-4

De contemptu mundi: Epistola de contemptu mundi LB V / ASD V-1 / CWE 66

De copia: De duplici copia verborum ac rerum LB I / ASD I-6 / CWE 24

De esu carnium: Epistola apologetica ad Christophorum episcopum Basiliensem de
   interdicto esu carnium LB IX / ASD IX-1

De immensa Dei misericordia: Concio de immensa Dei misericordia LB V /
   CWE 70

De libero arbitrio: De libero arbitrio diatribe LB IX / CWE 76

De praeparatione: De praeparatione ad mortem LB V / ASD V-1 / CWE 70

De pueris instituendis: De pueris statim ac liberaliter instituendis LB I / ASD I-2 /
   CWE 26

De puero Iesu: Concio de puero Iesu LB V / CWE 29

De puritate tabernaculi: Enarratio psalmi 14 qui est de puritate tabernaculi sive ecclesiae
   christianae LB V / ASD V-2 / CWE 65

De ratione studii LB I / ASD I-2 / CWE 24

De recta pronuntiatione: De recta latini graecique sermonis pronuntiatione LB I /
   ASD I-4 / CWE 26

De taedio Iesu: Disputatiuncula de taedio, pavore, tristicia Iesu LB V
   CWE 70

Detectio praestigiarum: Detectio praestigiarum cuiusdam libelli Germanice scripti
   LB X / ASD IX-1 / CWE 78

De vidua christiana LB V / CWE 66

De virtute amplectenda: Oratio de virtute amplectenda LB V / CWE 29

[Dialogus bilinguium ac trilinguium: Chonradi Nastadiensis dialogus bilinguium ac
   trilinguium] *Opuscula* / CWE 7

Dilutio: Dilutio eorum quae Iodocus Clithoveus scripsit adversus declamationem
   suasoriam matrimonii / *Dilutio eorum quae Iodocus Clithoveus scripsit* ed Émile V. Telle
   (Paris 1968) / CWE 83

Divinationes ad notata Bedae: Divinationes ad notata per Bedam de Paraphrasi Erasmi in Matthaeum, et primo de duabus praemissis epistolis LB IX

Ecclesiastes: Ecclesiastes sive de ratione concionandi LB V / ASD V-4, 5
Elenchus in censuras Bedae: In N. Bedae censuras erroneas elenchus LB IX
Enchiridion: Enchiridion militis christiani LB V / CWE 66
Encomium matrimonii (in De conscribendis epistolis)
Encomium medicinae: Declamatio in laudem artis medicae LB I / ASD I-4 / CWE 29
Epistola ad Dorpium LB IX / CWE 3 (Ep 337) / CWE 71
Epistola ad fratres Inferioris Germaniae: Responsio ad fratres Germaniae Inferioris ad epistolam apologeticam incerto autore proditam LB X / ASD IX-1 / CWE 78
Epistola ad gracculos: Epistola ad quosdam impudentissimos gracculos LB X / Ep 2275
Epistola apologetica adversus Stunicam LB IX / Ep 2172
Epistola apologetica de Termino LB X / Ep 2018
Epistola consolatoria: Epistola consolatoria virginibus sacris, or Epistola consolatoria in adversis LB V / CWE 69
Epistola contra pseudevangelicos: Epistola contra quosdam qui se falso iactant evangelicos LB X / ASD IX-1 / CWE 78
Euripidis Hecuba LB I / ASD I-1
Euripidis Iphigenia in Aulide LB I / ASD I-1
Exomologesis: Exomologesis sive modus confitendi LB V
Explanatio symboli: Explanatio symboli apostolorum sive catechismus LB V / ASD V-1 / CWE 70
Ex Plutarcho versa LB IV / ASD IV-2

Formula: Conficiendarum epistolarum formula (see De conscribendis epistolis)

Hyperaspistes LB X / CWE 76–7

In Nucem Ovidii commentarius LB I / ASD I-1 / CWE 29
In Prudentium: Commentarius in duos hymnos Prudentii LB V / CWE 29
In psalmum 1: Enarratio primi psalmi, 'Beatus vir,' iuxta tropologiam potissimum LB V / ASD V-2 / CWE 63
In psalmum 2: Commentarius in psalmum 2, 'Quare fremuerunt gentes?' LB V / ASD V-2 / CWE 63
In psalmum 3: Paraphrasis in tertium psalmum, 'Domine quid multiplicate' LB V / ASD V-2 / CWE 63
In psalmum 4: In psalmum quartum concio LB V / ASD V-2 / CWE 63
In psalmum 22: In psalmum 22 enarratio triplex LB V / ASD V-2 / CWE 64
In psalmum 33: Enarratio psalmi 33 LB V / ASD V-3 / CWE 64
In psalmum 38: Enarratio psalmi 38 LB V / ASD V-3 / CWE 65
In psalmum 85: Concionalis interpretatio, plena pietatis, in psalmum 85 LB V / ASD V-3 / CWE 64
Institutio christiani matrimonii LB V / CWE 69
Institutio principis christiani LB IV / ASD IV-1 / CWE 27

[Julius exclusus: Dialogus Julius exclusus e coelis] *Opuscula* / CWE 27

Lingua LB IV / ASD IV-1A / CWE 29
Liturgia Virginis Matris: Virginis Matris apud Lauretum cultae liturgia LB V / ASD V-1 / CWE 69
Luciani dialogi LB I / ASD I-1

Manifesta mendacia ASD IX-4 / CWE 71
Methodus (see Ratio)
Modus orandi Deum LB V / ASD V-1 / CWE 70
Moria: Moriae encomium LB IV / ASD IV-3 / CWE 27

Notatiunculae: Notatiunculae quaedam extemporales ad naenias Bedaicas, or Responsio ad notulas Bedaicas / LB IX
Novum Testamentum: Novum Testamentum 1519 and later (Novum instrumentum for the first edition, 1516, when required) LB VI / ASD VI-2, 3

Obsecratio ad Virginem Mariam: Obsecratio sive oratio ad Virginem Mariam in rebus adversis, or Obsecratio ad Virginem Matrem Mariam in rebus adversis LB V / CWE 69
Oratio de pace: Oratio de pace et discordia LB VIII
Oratio funebris: Oratio funebris in funere Bertae de Heyen LB VIII / CWE 29

Paean Virgini Matri: Paean Virgini Matri dicendus LB V / CWE 69
Panegyricus: Panegyricus ad Philippum Austriae ducem LB IV / ASD IV-1 / CWE 27
Parabolae: Parabolae sive similia LB I / ASD I-5 / CWE 23
Paraclesis LB V, VI
Paraphrasis in Elegantias Vallae: Paraphrasis in Elegantias Laurentii Vallae LB I / ASD I-4
Paraphrasis in Matthaeum, etc LB VII / ASD VII-6 / CWE 42–50
Peregrinatio apostolorum: Peregrinatio apostolorum Petri et Pauli LB VI, VII
Precatio ad Virginis filium Iesum LB V / CWE 69
Precatio dominica LB V / CWE 69
Precationes: Precationes aliquot novae LB V / CWE 69
Precatio pro pace ecclesiae: Precatio ad Dominum Iesum pro pace ecclesiae LB IV, V / CWE 69
Prologus supputationis: Prologus in supputationem calumniarum Natalis Bedae (1527), or Prologus supputationis errorum in censuris Bedae (1527) LB IX
Purgatio adversus epistolam Lutheri: Purgatio adversus epistolam non sobriam Lutheri LB X / ASD IX-1 / CWE 78

Querela pacis LB IV / ASD IV-2 / CWE 27

Ratio: Ratio seu Methodus compendio perveniendi ad veram theologiam (Methodus for the shorter version originally published in the Novum instrumentum of 1516) LB V, VI

Responsio ad annotationes Lei: Responsio ad annotationes Eduardi Lei LB IX / ASD IX-4 / CWE 72

Responsio ad collationes: Responsio ad collationes cuiusdam iuvenis geronto-didascali LB IX

Responsio ad disputationem de divortio: Responsio ad disputationem cuiusdam Phimostomi de divortio LB IX / ASD IX-4 / CWE 83

Responsio ad epistolam Alberti Pii: Responsio ad epistolam paraeneticam Alberti Pii, or Responsio ad exhortationem Pii LB IX / CWE 84

Responsio ad notulas Bedaicas (*see* Notatiunculae)

Responsio ad Petri Cursii defensionem: Epistola de apologia Cursii LB X / Ep 3032

Responsio adversus febricitantis libellum: Apologia monasticae religionis LB X

Spongia: Spongia adversus aspergines Hutteni LB X / ASD IX-1 / CWE 78

Supputatio: Supputatio errorum in censuris Bedae LB IX

Supputationes: Supputationes errorum in censuris Natalis Bedae: contains Supputatio and reprints of Prologus supputationis; Divinationes ad notata Bedae; Elenchus in censuras Bedae; Appendix respondens ad Sutorem; Appendix de scriptis Clithovei LB IX

Tyrannicida: Tyrannicida, declamatio Lucianicae respondens LB I / ASD I-1 / CWE 29

Virginis et martyris comparatio LB V / CWE 69

Vita Hieronymi: Vita divi Hieronymi Stridonensis *Opuscula* / CWE 61

Index

The design of
THE COLLECTED WORKS
OF ERASMUS
was created
by
ALLAN FLEMING
1929–1977
for
the University
of Toronto
Press